Handbook of Research on Knowledge Management for Contemporary Business Environments

Armando Malheiro
University of Porto, Portugal

Fernanda Ribeiro
University of Porto, Portugal

George Leal Jamil
Fumec University, Brazil

Jose Pocas Rascao
Polytechnic of Setubal, Portugal

Oscar Mealha
University of Aveiro, Portugal

A volume in the Advances in Human Resources Management and Organizational Development (AHRMOD) Book Series

IGI Global
DISSEMINATOR OF KNOWLEDGE

Published in the United States of America by
IGI Global
Business Science Reference (an imprint of IGI Global)
701 E. Chocolate Avenue
Hershey PA, USA 17033
Tel: 717-533-8845
Fax: 717-533-8661
E-mail: cust@igi-global.com
Web site: http://www.igi-global.com

Library of Congress Cataloging-in-Publication Data

Names: Malheiro, Armando, 1957- editor.
Title: Handbook of research on knowledge management for contemporary business environments / Armando Malheiro, [and four other], editors.
Description: Hershey, PA : Business Science Reference, [2018]
Identifiers: LCCN 2017020972| ISBN 9781522537250 (hardcover) | ISBN 9781522537267 (ebook)
Subjects: LCSH: Knowledge management. | Organizational learning. | Information technology.
Classification: LCC HD30.2 .H3642954 2018 | DDC 658.4/038--dc23 LC record available at https://lccn.loc.gov/2017020972

This book is published in the IGI Global book series Advances in Human Resources Management and Organizational Development (AHRMOD) (ISSN: 2327-3372; eISSN: 2327-3380)

British Cataloguing in Publication Data
A Cataloguing in Publication record for this book is available from the British Library.

All work contributed to this book is new, previously-unpublished material. The views expressed in this book are those of the authors, but not necessarily of the publisher.

For electronic access to this publication, please contact: eresources@igi-global.com.

Advances in Human Resources Management and Organizational Development (AHRMOD) Book Series

Patricia Ordóñez de Pablos
Universidad de Oviedo, Spain

ISSN:2327-3372
EISSN:2327-3380

Mission

A solid foundation is essential to the development and success of any organization and can be accomplished through the effective and careful management of an organization's human capital. Research in human resources management and organizational development is necessary in providing business leaders with the tools and methodologies which will assist in the development and maintenance of their organizational structure.

The **Advances in Human Resources Management and Organizational Development (AHRMOD) Book Series** aims to publish the latest research on all aspects of human resources as well as the latest methodologies, tools, and theories regarding organizational development and sustainability. The **AHRMOD Book Series** intends to provide business professionals, managers, researchers, and students with the necessary resources to effectively develop and implement organizational strategies.

Coverage

- Personnel Retention
- Workplace Discrimination
- E-Human Resources Management
- Personnel Policies
- Process Improvement
- Training and Development
- Recruitment Process
- Organizational Learning
- Change Management
- Human Resources Development

IGI Global is currently accepting manuscripts for publication within this series. To submit a proposal for a volume in this series, please contact our Acquisition Editors at Acquisitions@igi-global.com or visit: http://www.igi-global.com/publish/.

The Advances in Human Resources Management and Organizational Development (AHRMOD) Book Series (ISSN 2327-3372) is published by IGI Global, 701 E. Chocolate Avenue, Hershey, PA 17033-1240, USA, www.igi-global.com. This series is composed of titles available for purchase individually; each title is edited to be contextually exclusive from any other title within the series. For pricing and ordering information please visit http://www.igi-global.com/book-series/advances-human-resources-management-organizational/73670. Postmaster: Send all address changes to above address.

Titles in this Series

For a list of additional titles in this series, please visit: www.igi-global.com/book-series

Statistical Tools and Analysis in Human Resources Management
Dipak Kumar Bhattacharyya (Xavier University, India)
Business Science Reference • copyright 2018 • 295pp • H/C (ISBN: 9781522549475) • US $175.00 (our price)

Management Strategies and Technology Fluidity in the Asian Business Sector
Patricia Ordóñez de Pablos (University of Oviedo, Spain)
Business Science Reference • copyright 2018 • 338pp • H/C (ISBN: 9781522540564) • US $225.00 (our price)

Arab Women and Their Evolving Roles in the Global Business Landscape
Ebtihaj Al-A'ali (University of Bahrain, Bahrain) Minwir M. Al-Shammari (University of Bahrain, Bahrain) and Hatem Masri (University of Bahrain, Bahrain)
Business Science Reference • copyright 2018 • 321pp • H/C (ISBN: 9781522537106) • US $200.00 (our price)

Creativity in Workforce Development and Innovation Emerging Research and Opportunities
Sally Blake (Flagler College, USA) and Candice M. Burkett (University of Illinois at Chicago, USA)
Business Science Reference • copyright 2018 • 152pp • H/C (ISBN: 9781522549529) • US $145.00 (our price)

Evaluating Media Richness in Organizational Learning
Albert Gyamfi (Aalborg University Copenhagen, Denmark) and Idongesit Williams (Aalborg University Copenhagen, Denmark)
Business Science Reference • copyright 2018 • 328pp • H/C (ISBN: 9781522529569) • US $185.00 (our price)

Teaching Human Resources and Organizational Behavior at the College Level
John Mendy (University of Lincoln, UK)
Business Science Reference • copyright 2018 • 305pp • H/C (ISBN: 9781522528203) • US $195.00 (our price)

Handbook of Research on Organizational Culture and Diversity in the Modern Workforce
Bryan Christiansen (PryMarke LLC, USA) and Harish C. Chandan (Argosy University, USA)
Business Science Reference • copyright 2017 • 506pp • H/C (ISBN: 9781522522508) • US $255.00 (our price)

Handbook of Research on Human Factors in Contemporary Workforce Development
Bryan Christiansen (PryMarke LLC, USA) and Harish C. Chandan (Argosy University, USA)
Business Science Reference • copyright 2017 • 563pp • H/C (ISBN: 9781522525684) • US $255.00 (our price)

IGI Global
DISSEMINATOR OF KNOWLEDGE

701 East Chocolate Avenue, Hershey, PA 17033, USA
Tel: 717-533-8845 x100 • Fax: 717-533-8661
E-Mail: cust@igi-global.com • www.igi-global.com

Editorial Advisory Board

List of Contributors

Table of Contents

Detailed Table of Contents

A brand is one of the most exciting assets of a company. It has the obvious purposes of identification, recognition, and differentiation, which are mostly directed to the external environment. But it is also responsible for transmitting intangible value, and for that reason, in the last decades, research has been demonstrating that the brand is also a fundamental resource for building commitment and citizenship behaviors among organizational internal audiences. There is also academic evidence that highly committed members of staff are more open to take part of collaborative multidisciplinary activities and more predisposed to share their knowledge. Moreover, commitment tends to increase as a result of brand-related participatory experiences. This chapter suggests that participatory and technology-mediated internal branding activities build on brand knowledge conversion and transfer, hence preparing, holistically, the organization and its members of staff for a generic sense on the benefits of knowledge sharing.

This chapter's mission is to reflect on the steps taken by knowledge (creation, management, and dissemination) in an impact community (IC). Also, it aims to analyze how this knowledge can be capitalized by the IC itself, as well as other ICs, through the replication of good practices. To this end, importance is attached to several stages of the existence of knowledge in an IC: 1) individual knowledge, which each single person carries and integrates into an IC when he/she becomes a member; 2) the combination of all the individual knowledge, which forces one to think in a knowledge management; 3) the moments of knowledge sharing; and 4) the internal and external dissemination of this knowledge. These last two dynamics—sharing and dissemination—result in a replication and multiplication of existing knowledge in an IC.

Environmental turbulence in today's business landscape has elicited deep concerns in contemporary business organizations. As a result, organizations seek to achieve competitive advantage through organizational learning. This chapter presents organizational learning as a key source of competitive advantage in contemporary business organizations. It examines the concept of organizational learning by definition and delves in the four constituents that form the concept of organizational learning, namely knowledge acquisition, knowledge distribution, information interpretation, and organizational memory. Further, the chapter focuses on the factors affecting organizational learning together with competitive advantage as an outcome of organizational learning.

This chapter presents a knowledge management perspective to propose a pair of structural models to determine the relationship between burnout syndrome (BS) and body mass index (BMI) among high and middle managers of Mexican maquiladoras. In developing countries like Mexico there are opportunities to expand burnout study on diversity of contexts and occupations. The Maslach burnout general inventory questionnaire (MB-GI) was used, and sociodemographic data were collected as well as the weight and size of respondents. Instrument shows an acceptable reliability index. Structural equation models are used to determine relationship among variables. From a sample of 361 people, using segmentations of BMI, two segments are distinguished: normal weight and overweight. Model using normal weight participants shows more explanatory qualities about the relationship among burnout dimensions than the one using overweight participants. One can conclude that more factors and variables are needed to explain overweight Mexican managers.

This chapter presents the advanced issues of knowledge management (KM), the advanced issues of knowledge discovery, and the advanced issues of organizational communication. KM with the support of knowledge discovery can improve the ability of organizations to effectively solve problems, adapt, and evolve to meet the changing business requirements. Knowledge discovery enlists the power of computers to assist in the recognizing patterns in data, a task that exceeds human ability as the size of data warehouses significantly increase. The revolution in organizational communication allows people to

students, providing better placements, course excellence, etc. The use of modern information technologies helps in storing huge data but requires the use of data mining technologies to extract useful information and knowledge from this data. Some of the knowledge achievable for higher education institutes through implementing several data mining techniques (classification, association learning, clustering, etc.) is the correlation between specialization and the chosen employment path, determining the subjects, courses, labs with high degree of difficulty, interesting subjects, courses, labs, facilities that might attract new students, etc. This chapter explores efficient clustering algorithms in educational data mining.

This chapter investigates the main concepts and activities of information in strategic decision-making systems. Since information became the global economy value source for organizations, information assumes a key role in contributing to the development of the performance of organizations through the selection of relevant information for businesses. The relationship of the strategic management of information with business activities contributes to the process of strategic decision making for more effective and efficient decisions. The understanding of the importance of information as a strategic resource in the management of organizations is becoming more important to strategists than the formulation of strategy models of industrial society. In the twenty-first century, no manager will be able to set and implement the strategy successfully without a basic understanding of information for strategic decision making.

In recent years we have witnessed a major transformation in society. We went from a society based on industry and transport to another based on information and knowledge. A major challenge for managers is to understand what the information is for formulation, definition, implementation, and control the strategy. The strategy for any organization can be set from the outside in. According to the schools of positioning, the offer of products will have to adapt to changes in the environment. Or from the inside out. According to the movement's schools, the organization influences the middle engaging with your innovative product offerings, since it has skills and capabilities that competitors don't have and that are difficult to imitate or buy. This chapter explores information and business strategies.

Preface

A few years ago, it was usually commented that knowledge, a significant and attractive word, but a difficult concept to define, could become one of the most relevant assets for several activities, such as academic research, business decisions, innovation positioning, market tactics and strategic, internationalization, among others. Time has evolved and, every day, it is possible to understand how these affirmations became true.

Business people, researchers, teachers, academic management professionals, training and educational planners are increasingly dedicating their efforts to the difficult task of knowledge management. Several questions continue to arise, regarding, mainly, to knowledge domain, knowledge contexts, creation, sharing and valuation. These are not theoretical, distant questions, but practical issues that pressure everyday decisions, implementations, investments and execution plans.

Some usual scenarios can detail knowledge issues and potentialities, such as:

- How can we value the production and skills of a worker in the working place, as he or she does not indeed produce, but contribute for the working environment, sponsoring and acting decisively to improve communication?
- What is the real knowledge contribution for one patent – licensing process, where our company is aiming to improve its financial results not essentially from the material, tangible production, but, alternatively, to sell the knowledge generated in our laboratories?
- How can we deal with new demands for customer and market segmentation, as customer behavior seems erratic and fast, bringing confusion for our marketing planning, increasing the risks of mistakes for product and services positioning?
- Are social media contexts useful for the comprehension on how a product, service or company action is really satisfying our final customers?
- How a public, governmental planner can combine different contents of knowledge, such as Demography, Economy, Innovation, Social and several other contents are available and changing all the time, motivated by rapid societal changes?

These, we reinforce, are real problems, simply announced, that could take expressive amount of time to decide, to produce real plans that must address critical implementations, which will respond for risk level in decision-making, dynamic proposition of plans – in both strategic, tactical and operational levels – that can result in market gain or losses and, eventually, in public plans and decisions which could take our citizens to a higher level of living, eliminating risks and problems that impact their routinely lives. These decisions, answers for questions like these, are strictly related to how we can understand knowledge in these contexts, and how we can manage knowledge.

When thinking about a project that will address critical decision-making and dynamics like these, regarding a topic – knowledge – so essential, editors and authors face tough problems, considering that one text which would offer the reader the comfortable situation of a "complete" approach is almost impossible. To produce a reasonable understanding on knowledge tasks, processes, application and valuation, one writer has to research in a wide range of unsolved theoretical issues, propose an objective question, which may take a significant time just to achieve and, finally, pursue its research, methodologically travelling around debates which are composed of practical, emerging and conceptual evidences that are not so immediate to coalesce, sometimes resulting even in conflicting perspectives, which may also be solved by the author. For book editors, to guarantee an independent, balanced and non-biased view of those problems and its proposed solutions is also a problem, as their background pressure for more attention in one point in terms of another too.

The book presented by the team of editors and authors, led by our top-level, senior researcher, author and businessman Dr. José Poças Rascão, is a remarkable work which will allow to address this challenging scenario, enabling its readers to a higher level of understanding these problems, answers propositions and decisions implementation. With a deep and wide coverage, this book encompasses themes ranging from theoretical propositions and definitions, to its application in public and private management arenas, resulting in a useful collection of reviews, ideas, experiences and conclusions around knowledge and several of its "building blocks" for management.

Themes such as innovation, human resources management, strategic decisions, information systems, information technology management and implementation, among others, constitute a platform, where a remarkable contribution results for knowledge management comprehension and practice, completing a desirable context for any interested reader. It's always important to understand that knowledge and its associated managerial processes are necessary element or component of this base that will allow scholars and practitioners to first understand what is really questioned or proposed, then aiming to produce answers for these questions. Frequently, the proposed problem, when we observe knowledge and knowledge management concepts, is not over when an answer is reached indeed. It produces a level of comprehension and planning that will invite us to another panorama that may be addressed and solved. So, it is a dynamic, fast-moving, challenging context that was remarkably considered and dealt in this book.

BOOK ORGANIZATION

Through its 17 chapters, our book *Handbook of Research on Knowledge Management for Contemporary Business Environments* brings you the approach for knowledge issues, questions, plans and practices discussed above, constituting in a well-prepared situation for learning and continuous study perspectives regarding knowledge management.

In the first chapter, a relationship between organizational brands, taken as a decisive, competitive factor, is related to knowledge management principles and processes. Its authors describe, from both theoretical and practical points of view, how branding can be considered more expressive than other factors when applying knowledge in organizational decisions, as it encompasses, through an efficient management, sector and corporative culture, social interactions and relationships.

Chapter 2 results in a complete study on how several aspects of knowledge management produce impacts on the context of Communities of Practices. CoP were regarded, for many years, as a valid and useful concept, that help us to understand how people relate to each other with organizational, systemic or market purposes. This chapter approaches this interesting context from knowledge management perspectives, calling special attention to some of KM critical sub-processes.

Undoubtfully, in the last decades, since its first announcement as a complete process, knowledge management was observed through the appreciation of some of its elements, sub-processes, as definition of required and coherent tasks to be conducted in relationship to each other. Studying knowledge management as a composition of these important and essential conceptions, two sub-processes can be regarded as the most discussed by researchers and practitioners: knowledge creation and sharing. Supported by technologies, business models and other innovative structures, these two critical tasks – creation and sharing – were analyzed in the Chapter 3, together with other needed factors, organizational definitions and actions, such as coordination structures, communication principles and technology. Its conclusion leads to an interesting observation regarding organizational learning and people interactions.

One of the most debated issues around knowledge management and its associated conceptual and practical contexts is the dynamics of tacit and explicit knowledge. Along many years of discussions, researches and productions, these two significant concepts must be observed, as they define knowledge management perspectives, processes and essentials. Chapter 4 helps us to understand how tacit knowledge, as valuable creations which are treated by related methods that support businesses and public management decisions, must be studied in the same level as that traditionally dedicated to explicit knowledge. Inserting this discussion in the modern organizations competitive environment, tacit knowledge is observed by chapter authors from its creation, production to its repercussion for practical applications and organizational plans and actions. Approaching this topic, this text reaches the conception of recommendations for methods for tacit knowledge sharing in modern organizations.

Knowledge and its associated management can become a competitive element, becoming even a factor of competitive advantage for some organizations. In the fifth chapter, authors show the results of this important reflection, regarding these decisive concepts that can base several decisions regarding on how to valuate and understand knowledge management sub-processes and the complete KM process itself. Considering this way, this chapter also prepares the reader to understand organizational issues, competitive pressures – as strategic decision-making, organizational structure changes – and corporative network demands.

Chapter 6 approaches knowledge transfer, resulting in a better comprehension of its perspectives and practices. It discusses, theoretically and practically, knowledge transfer issues, extending from the usual, simple view of a basic communication process, enabling to understand how knowledge transfer is an active part of management that connects creation, capture and application factors and aspects when treating knowledge from organizational perspectives. As approaching this important study, these chapters focus on the importance of educational, training and motivational tools and methods that will help knowledge transfer to be effective, both for explicit and tacit knowledge.

As knowledge management becomes a topic which is a study focus, when question always succeed: How organizations learn? Developing situations, processes, methods and goal planning, organizations try to manage knowledge to understand not only static, temporary lessons, but also can provoke changes on how they learn, turning possible to develop and analyze knowledge for forthcoming competitive scenarios. Chapter 7 helps us recognize the basics of organizational learning, its relationship to cultural, technological and social factors, reaching the rationale on how individuals contribute for this learning systematic process in a potential cycle. In this interesting, multidisciplinary analysis, authors also explore the fundamental relationship with information analysis, storage and distribution, as an associated context.

Chapter 8 aims to produce understanding on knowledge management capabilities and organizational performance, exposing a thorough study conducted with more than two hundred middle level managers, supported by a strong statistical methodology. Knowledge management processes capabilities, composed after a review which treated the usually fragmented approach in the area literature, are then related to organizational performances, allowing the reader to a complete comprehension on how KM infrastructure and organization relate to those capabilities, resulting in a positive which can be considered as an update motivation to invest in better KM procedures, actions and process definition and infrastructure.

A challenging context for working environments, which study psychological disorders Burnout Syndrome, with focus for Body Mass index, is approached by the authors of Chapter 9, observing the case of Mexican maquiladora industry. A detailed descriptive study was conducted, adopting Maslach Burnout General Inventory Questionnaire, from the sociodemographic point of view, over a sample of more than 350 people, producing a scenario to understand how these effects can relate to knowledge management in the working place. As an initial approach for this problem, this chapter produces also a base to be adopted by researchers when conducting researches like this one, in working environments, aiming to understand professional activities and its relation to knowledge management.

Chapter 10 approaches the basics of knowledge management itself, studying the relationship between organizational norms and factors of success and failures for KM adoption. Several characteristics and conceptual fundamentals of KM processes are reinforced, serving for both to build a wide theoretical platform, and to describe what factors will then be studied regarding organizational norms. As "Red Tape" is defined as counterproductive norms, they are selected for this correlation, along with Organizational anomie, considered as the lack of perception of norms by employees. Studied in Brazilian public and private organizations, this work approaches various opportune management themes, strongly relating KM and Business.

Chapter 11 analyzes the context of cognitive heuristics, understood as an opportune knowledge management function, in Healtcare sector, observing especially decision-making in the critical, essential services of emergency departments. One of the main conceptual contributions of this study is to adapt those industry-oriented methods from the classical operations management background, considering some peculiar characteristics in these definitions, which reach the analysis of level of service, regarding knowledge management in a practical, real case. As it may be seen from the chapter, several economic indicators show strong need to manage it.

Relating knowledge management, knowledge discovery and application for organizational communication, chapter twelve aims to answer several questions that emerge in this dynamic, where communication processes, as the final application in the context analyzed, is studied from the strategic point of view, aiming to understand its eventual impact on corporative performance indexes.

Information science is a native multidisciplinary research field, which has been useful to promote improved recognition and domain of several areas of science. It happens with themes such as information technology, information systems, and analytics, among others. Along with some other emerging topics, knowledge management is one of the most challenging themes approached by information science researchers, enabling its development per se and with relation to other fields. Chapter 13 promotes the study of this relationship, enriching the perception of this collaborative relationship, through a descriptive study considering different sources and contributions. It is a chapter that, typically, gives the reader complete condition to develop his / her domain around the based application of knowledge management.

Reading Chapter 14, our reader can develop an understanding of the role of information in all matters that are connected to knowledge management. Information, as an indispensable conceptual paradigm, both as a "thing" and a "process", is an active element in knowledge creation, storage, sharing and communication, integrating actively the process defined as knowledge management. With a scientific point of view, this chapter produces also a fair perspective for further studies development, as it presents a consistent promise on elementary conceptual basis.

In the Chapter 15, authors addressed the important factor of quality, applied to analyze information in its fundamental aspects, as an indispensable element of knowledge management. Originated in the industrial paradigm, quality is a strategic factor, observed from various points, allowing managers, designers and analysts to evaluate issues such as performance, acceptance and user satisfaction. With a discussion of information aspects for information quality, this chapter decisively will help the reader to understand and promote quality evaluation for informational contexts, when knowledge management is the final organizational goal.

Chapter 16 discusses a modern critical issue regarding information: governance. As privacy, property and responsibility for any corporative action gain more evidence, both due to a series of criminal incidents and attacks, which affected even major company's business, Governance is entitled to be a formative criteria and conceptual topic to be exerted in modern organizational arrangements, as an essential parameter. In this chapter, the reader will understand the relationship of corporative information governance in the modern turbulent context, where massive amounts of information are produced every day.

Applying K-Means algorithm for data mining analysis, production and generation is the central topic for Chapter 17. Authors show why this methodological support is becoming quite popular among researchers and practitioners, to approach data mining, which is a powerful arena for knowledge generation in a context where data is generated massively not only by growing human interactions, but also from machines that equips our homes, offices, companies and eventually, places for living. This chapter still advances the observation, applying the K-Means methodology to analyze a corpus of datasets of educational performance of students in one institution.

Concluding this preface, we strongly believe in this book's success, because of its perspective, approach and objectives regarding the essentials of knowledge management. Topics such data, information and knowledge integration, information technology, information systems, multidisciplinary studies, methodological analysis, data mining, data governance, strategy, among many others were efficiently and diligently integrated by our leading editor, Professor José Rascão.

This book contribution can be perceived also for several aspects, as for systems designers, programmers, analysts, scholars and information analysis specialists. As information and knowledge are, nowadays, perceived as a top-level essence for decision-making in corporative contexts, this *Handbook of Research on Knowledge Management for Contemporary Business Environment* faced the challenge on discussing this complex and fast-changing prospects, producing a wide panorama that enables the reader to a higher level of organization and comprehension of various aspects of these processes in the modern scenario.

Good reading! Good perspectives with knowledge management!

George Leal Jamil

Chapter 1
Framing Organisational Knowledge Through the Brand

Catarina Lelis
University of West London, UK

ABSTRACT

A brand is one of the most exciting assets of a company. It has the obvious purposes of identification, recognition, and differentiation, which are mostly directed to the external environment. But it is also responsible for transmitting intangible value, and for that reason, in the last decades, research has been demonstrating that the brand is also a fundamental resource for building commitment and citizenship behaviors among organizational internal audiences. There is also academic evidence that highly committed members of staff are more open to take part of collaborative multidisciplinary activities and more predisposed to share their knowledge. Moreover, commitment tends to increase as a result of brand-related participatory experiences. This chapter suggests that participatory and technology-mediated internal branding activities build on brand knowledge conversion and transfer, hence preparing, holistically, the organization and its members of staff for a generic sense on the benefits of knowledge sharing.

INTRODUCTION

The ideal decision-making process is currently characterised not only by the complexity of specialist knowledge that it incorporates, which in many cases includes several knowledge domains, but also by the increasing speed of responsiveness that has been transforming decision-making into quick moves with reduced processing time. This knowledge-led context brought up the need of guaranteeing multidisciplinary teams when it comes to make a decision, leading to the inclusion in decision-making boards of members of staff, from diverse backgrounds (not only business management or strategy), and many increasingly well educated, trained and informed individuals. However, in some economies (usually both low- and hi-income ones), employee turnover can be vertiginous, meaning that some organisations lose important knowledge and decision-making influencers, in some cases to their competition. These are justifiable reasons for the organisational promotion of knowledge sharing and, in more depth, for the exploration on the factors that will lead people to share their knowledge. Several studies show that organisational

DOI: 10.4018/978-1-5225-3725-0.ch001

commitment is one of them (Oltra, 2005; Scarbrough, 2003; Willem, Scarbrough & Buelens, 2008) and that it depends heavily on the level of involvement employees have with the organisation's culture and values and, consequently, with the brand.

It is mundane that a brand must sustain the differentiation of an organisation (or its products/services) from its competition. Throughout the 20th century the focus on the external impact a brand would have, via the most diverse communication strategies, was monumental. More recently, the role of internal communication and training of staff members for brand awareness has been increasing and gaining support, both from academia and some acknowledged top managers. In fact, in order to successfully represent the identity and define the image of an organisation, a brand must accomplish an essential condition: to become known. This happens when a certain level of brand equity is achieved, being brand equity a measurement tool of a brand's success, deeply connected to the brand's image residing in its external audiences' minds. However, in order to get this, organisations need to develop an intense internal branding work, providing their employees with access to the relevant information concerning their brand(s). Hence, regardless of their role and position, all staff must, first and foremost, understand the brand so then they can appropriate and use it properly — because, more often than not, the organisational brand is an element of constant presence in the professional life of those representing it (Lelis & Mealha, 2014, 2015).

Today, defining, designing, developing and nurturing a brand is a collaborative activity sustained in value creation, both by the organisation and all its stakeholders. The brand is, therefore, a cultural living manifestation, a symbolic construction based on a dynamic process of social interactions, which are grounded on knowledge.

Therefore, this position chapter is focused on one of the most significant assets in which organisational knowledge management should be heavily grounded — the brand. This is due to its value creation potential, centred on meanings exploration, learning and discovery, and their experimentation, appropriation, transformation, combination, re-representation using any universal, recognisable and transferable code, potentially harvesting unimaginable analogies and scenarios that can become rather relevant for organisational decision-making moments. A model that reinforces the assumption that knowledge management can benefit from a strong internal branding process will be presented and discussed, disregarding any organisational context in particular, but providing generic guidance at content and artefact level. Hence, the underpinning thesis is that managing brand knowledge is a way of managing organisational knowledge.

BACKGROUND

A brand has always been the representation of a promise. When an organisation is designated by its name, an identity is being conferred to it, through a fixed, objective and functional element that makes up its brand. Traditionally, for most organisations, there is a tendency (and necessity) to maintain the organisational brand over a certain period of time, guaranteeing its identification and recognition among audiences. A brand must also lead to the differentiation of an organisation from its competition, in some cases in extremely saturated markets. The American Marketing Association defines brand as

...a name, term, sign, symbol or design, or a combination of them, intended to identify the goods and services of one seller or group of sellers and to differentiate them from those of competition (Keller, 2003).

This is considered the classic definition of brand.

The literature on brand history shows that, gradually, the logic of branding has evolved. On a post-modern perspective, the brand becomes much more than a form of commercial differentiation, but rather as something that is intrinsically identitary and capable of conveying a complexity of meanings. During the last years of the 20th century, brands have risen to a level of strategic relevance in the world of business and institutional relations. They have become one of the main tools for the creation and orchestration of organisational/corporate identity; they are now considered crucial factors in the definition of a company's strategy, and important resources in the generation of wealth (Moore, 2007). Currently, the brand is treated as a dynamic and social process, in which all audiences are operational resources in the co-creation of brand value (Merz, He & Vargo, 2009; Neumeier, 2006; Lelis & Mealha, 2015). It is, according to Schultz, Hatch and Ciccolella (2006), a symbolic representation of an identity, a promise, which is expressed through a diversity of artefacts. These authors divide organisational artefacts into four main categories, from which three are particularly relevant within this chapter's context:

- **Cultural Artefacts:** Which purpose is to make explicit the organisational culture. Some examples of cultural artefacts are found in practices that stimulate the sense of affiliation (such as sending out birthday messages), the type of leadership, etc..
- **Strategic Vision Artefacts:** Serving to express, communicate, and guide the organisational vision through vision and mission statements, lists of beliefs and values, and the various communication resources used to make them tangible and operational, such as institutional posters, enchanted or charismatic stories filled with metaphors that allow the recreation of goals. Moreover, the logo, signage systems, slogans and colour palettes are used as artefacts that deliberately convey what the company promises and aspires (Balmer & Greyser, 2002).
- **Image Artefacts:** Are resources that express individuality through the transfer of meanings. Merchandising objects are probably the best example of this (branded t-shirts, pens, caps, mugs, notebooks, etc.).

Being a cherished marketing resource, the brand's focus and efforts have been considerably directed towards the use of these artefacts in external communication, aiming the final consumer. Its roles and relevance on internal communication and on the training of employees for brand awareness and for the conversion of brand knowledge have been, by comparison, inexpressive. It is thought that the use of the aforementioned artefacts as efficient brand promise symbols is only possible when they are associated with certain meanings and when members of staff recognise this association.

KNOWING WHAT TO PROMISE

The brand is, therefore, a living manifestation of a given culture, a symbolic construction, based on a dynamic process of social interactions, and no longer a predetermined, impermeable and static asset (Burmann & Zeplin, 2005; Neumeier, 2006; Schultz & Hatch, 2006; Harris, 2007; Ind & Bjerke, 2007; Merz, He & Vargo, 2009; Arnhold, 2010). Neumeier states, blatantly, in his book "The Brand Gap":

Unlike the old corporate identity paradigm that prized uniformity and consistency, the new brand paradigm sacrifices those qualities in favor of being alive and dynamic. Perfection? It never existed. Control?

Fuhgetaboudit (...) Let the brand live, breathe, make mistakes, be human. (...) Brands can afford to be inconsistent — as long as they don't abandon their defining attributes. They're like people (2006).

Then, he completes his thought with this enlightening definition: *A living brand is a collaborative performance, and every person in the company is an actor* (2006).

If a brand is a promise, every possible interface with the audiences must deliver that promise consistently. Interfaces come in many different shapes and colours: they may be the packaging of a product, the price or the distribution channels, the way employees (actors) behave (act) when crystallising the brand to customers. Whilst the former examples are objectively controlled, employees' interpretations and behaviours reside on a much more subjective quadrant. For that reason, several authors argue on the absolute relevance of elucidating the brand to employees, as they are frequently required to project it and deliver it to customers (Miles & Mangold, 2004; King & Grace, 2010), being staff one of the most relevant brand interfaces.

COMMITMENT TOWARDS BRANDING

Ind (2007) states that, regardless of the role and position assumed, all employees must, first of all, understand and know the brand, so that they can use it properly. Internal branding is an instiller of brand knowledge among internal audiences (Aurand, Gorchels & Bishop, 2005). As today the brand is an element that is present in all the transactions in which organisations are involved, it must be consistently incorporated into internal activities. According to Punjaisri and Wilson (2007) and Wise and Zednickova (2009), internal branding ensures the alignment of employees' behaviour with the brand vision, mission and promise, aligning the brand values with the employees' values by defining an employee brand, which is grounded on the desired brand. Mangold and Miles (2007) define *employee brand* as the brand image that the employees are expected to internalise and that will support them on delivering the brand promise.

Following Neumeier's perspective, Natarajan, Balasubramaniam and Srinivasan (2017) state that for employees to live the brand, a strong and healthy relationship between the organisation and the employees must be guaranteed:

To deliver the desired brand, employees must possess adequate knowledge about it and understand the importance of their role in delivering the brand promise in tune with the brand image (2017).

However, they must also develop a minimum level of commitment. In fact, for Mangold and Miles (2007), internal branding efforts are influenced by two dimensions: the psychological contract employees maintain with the organisation (commitment) and the brand knowledge they hold, which they are expected to be, intrinsically, predisposed to share.

There is a vast amount of literature looking into the organisational factors affecting employees' willingness to share knowledge — inter-group and inter-personal conflicts (De Long & Fahey, 2000; Empson, 2001; Storey & Barnett, 2000; Ward, 2000), perceived sense of fairness (Kim & Mauborgne, 1993), interpersonal trust (Andrews & Delahaye, 2000; Morris & Empson, 1998), organisational commitment (Oltra, 2005; Scarbrough, 2003; Willem, A., Scarbrough, H., & Buelens, M., 2008), rewarding/recognition practices (Abdullah, Hassim, & Chik, 2009; Jarvenpaa & Staples, 2001; Jarvenpaa & Staples, 2000), visibility of knowledge (Hayes & Walsham, 1999). Within the brand-oriented spectrum that defines this chapter, from the above listed factors, organisational commitment — affective attachment that an individual feels to the organisation he/she works for (Mowday, Steers & Porter, 1979) — is the one that seems to have a higher connection to intrinsic motivations, mostly because it is more individual centred, depending on his/her performance, values and goals, and less on the others' (or on the way he/she perceives the others).

On a recent research focused in the higher education sector, Natarajan, Balasubramaniam and Srinivasan (2017) found that internal branding activities have a direct and positive effect on employees' sense of commitment towards the brand, brand knowledge and employee brand image. Although there is no solid empirical evidence that a highly committed member of staff has an increased willingness to share his/her knowledge, there are a number of authors suggesting that the level of employee's organisational commitment may affect knowledge sharing predisposition (Kelloway & Barling, 2000; Bartol & Srivastava, 2002; Hooff & Ridder, 2004). Brand knowledge is, in turn, essential for an active participation in internal branding activities (Mangold & Miles, 2007), which may, *per se*, incorporate socialisation and exchange practices, and also for organisational affective commitment to develop (King & Grace, 2008; King & Grace, 2010). The diagram in Figure 1 depicts this complex ecosystem of inter-related components, which are, on one hand, being nurtured by internal branding and, on the other, informing and supporting its activities.

CREATING AN INTERNAL SENSE OF BRAND KNOWLEDGE

Ind argues that organisations can and should become more human-centred, fully using the intellectual capacity of their employees, creating brand evangelists: *people who believe and will preach for the organisation* (2007). However, brand evangelists can only become so when they know the brand deeply. Ackerman (2000) argues that all employees must know the identity of the organisation in which they work, so that they can play a convincing role in the way they communicate it and expose it to the others. For that reason, academics with thorough and consistent research in this domain agree that effective

Figure 1. Internal Branding components for a brand knowledge-sharing environment

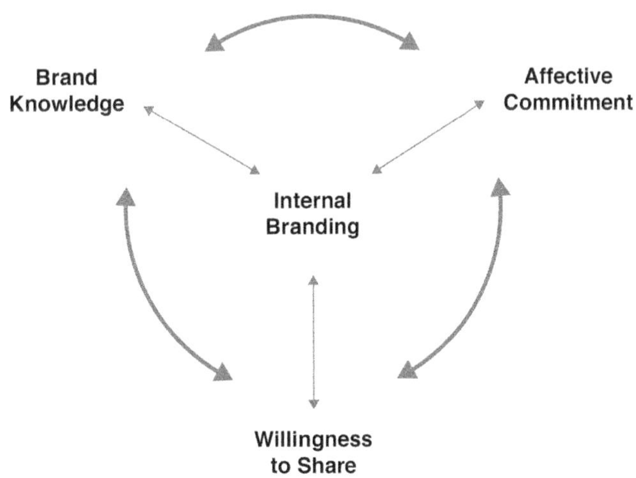

internal branding requires that all employees know and adhere to the organisational brand values (de Chernatony & Riley, 1998; Harris & de Chernatony, 2001). Nevertheless, learning the brand values (which are, more often than not, quite intangible) and incorporating them into the daily work tasks are not simple processes for most employees, especially if there is no objective support for these actions (Aurand, Gorchels & Bishop, 2005). The involvement in activities that explore this theme and that lead the members to participate, with joint decision-making power, allows them to consolidate the information received and transform it into knowledge — that will certainly be useful to them in aligning the brand identity and values with their own. Hence, a properly managed brand identity system is the first step in the transformation of the tacit knowledge that characterises the human capital and culture of an organisation into explicit knowledge, embodied by artefacts of greater tangibility. These brand vehicles are capable of transmitting the brand and communicating it to internal audiences very effectively, allowing them to get a better appreciation of their role and commit to the brand promise (Chong, 2007; McEnally & de Chernatony, 1999).

Based on the terms *tacit knowledge* and *explicit knowledge* largely popularised by Nonaka and Takeuchi (1995), Tress, Tress and Fry (2005) brought them into a more specific research-oriented sense, which fits the brand knowledge context of this chapter:

(…) tacit knowledge is implicit and personal. This means that the knowledge is not directly accessible to others and that it is impossible to assess its significance in relation to existing knowledge. In contrast, explicit knowledge is accessible to others (…) mostly tangible; it is fixed on some kind of medium such as a book, scientific journal, CD, video or a web site. As a consequence, it is brought into the wider context of the public domain. This process allows us to judge results in relation to existing beliefs and commonly held attitudes (Tress, Tress & Fry, 2005).

Hence, while explicit knowledge is codifiable and transmissible in a formal language (Bartol & Srivastava, 2002), tacit or implicit knowledge is hard to articulate and varies immensely from individual to individual.

In a marketing customer-led perspective, Keller (2003) states that brand knowledge consists of brand awareness and brand image, hence, it is mostly tacit. Brand awareness is related to

the strength of the brand in the individuals' memory and can be measured by their ability to identify it under different conditions (Keller, 2003).

Brand image refers to the constructed meaning and perceptions about a brand, grounded on the brand associations held in memory; brand associations usually reflect tangible characteristics of the organisation, of its products, of the brand's visual identity system, or other aspects of greater intangibility, accumulated by experience and interactions with the brand (Keller, 2003).

Richards, Foster and Morgan define brand knowledge as:

… especially (…) the tacit knowledge about a brand that is tucked away and usually not shared, because it is so hard to communicate. Knowledge, then, is the essence of what a brand represents, how it can achieve competitive advantage and ultimately significant value to a business. Brands are, quintessentially, knowledge (1998).

This perspective falls within the objective epistemological position of knowledge, considering brand knowledge as, above all, tacit knowledge, difficult to share and independent from explicit knowledge. For that reason, designer Marty Neumeier (2006) introduces the need to make explicit and collective all the brand knowledge that exists within an organisation: it must be *protected against evaporation*, avoiding its disappearance as people leave the organisation (Neumeier, 2006). This author proposes brand education programs to be distributed throughout the organisation, considering though a multidirectional approach, open to feedback from the brand community.

The knowledge and understanding that members of staff have about the brand is reinforced and driven by the impact and frequency of messages on what the organisation wants for its brand; the more frequent and consistent the messages emanating from the organisation's various communication systems, the greater the knowledge about what the brand should communicate and promise (Mangold & Miles, 2007). Miles, Mangold, Asree and Revell (2011) explain that these messages can be formal or informal, positive or negative and/or can be received inside or outside the organisation, and it is this entire constellation of messages that builds on staff's brand knowledge. It does not necessarily mean their brand awareness and brand associations are aligned with the desired brand image — hence the need of internal branding mechanisms. Brand knowledge and commitment are, in turn, of great relevance for the active participation in internal branding activities (Miles, Mangold, Asree & Revell, 2011).

Managing Brand Knowledge

Since the society began to be described as being knowledge-intensive, it became clear, for many organisations, that their available knowledge would be an increasingly precious resource that would have to be managed. Although knowledge management is a complex activity that, according to Becerra-Fernandez and Sabherwal (2015) includes four main processes – knowledge discovery, knowledge capture, knowledge sharing and knowledge application – within this chapter's scope, the main focus will be on knowledge sharing. These authors define it as a process through which explicit or tacit knowledge is communicated to the others, who will have to understand the message and, expectedly, act upon it. They add that face-to-face meetings or *in situ* observational situations facilitate the sharing of tacit knowledge, whereas exchanges of tangible resources facilitate the sharing of explicit knowledge (this could be illustrated by an employee sending the brand guidelines file to another, by email).

Hoof and Rider (2004) define knowledge sharing as the active process in which individuals either communicate to others what they know, or consult the others in order to learn from them. The authors consider knowledge sharing to be, on one hand, a form of communication, but they also found that a communication climate has a positive influence, not only in knowledge sharing, but also in (affective) commitment. Moreover, it is considered essential the provision of mechanisms that best allow these interactions and the overall management of brand knowledge; Hoof and Rider's (2004) research also provides evidence that the implementation and use of computer-mediated communication (CMC) systems influence commitment (which has a positive influence in knowledge sharing). Among other mechanisms, Bartol and Srivastava (2002) suggest the establishment of communities of practice, in which employees communicate internally, but in an informal and not necessarily systematised manner. Currently, many communities of practice rely on the Internet and are supported by CMC. According to Preece (2000), an online community consists in a group of individuals socially interacting, in an attempt to satisfy a shared purpose (interests, needs, information) or to perform special roles (leadership or moderation).

These communities are supported by computer systems to mediate social interaction and facilitate the sense of unity.

Brand Education Programs

As discussed before, the more frequent the interactions organisations establish with their employees, the greater the brand knowledge that individuals can potentially create, develop and, ultimately, share. Naturally, employees alone cannot achieve this objective, which means that, in addition to being minimally familiarised with the concepts of the brand they represent, they must also understand that their participation in the organic structure that the brand is, represents the creation and conversion of existing knowledge and can, potentially, represent new forms of added value.

Berthon, Pitt and Campbell (2009) argue that the creation of brand communities or moments for individuals to share and interact, help generate the common ground in regard to brand meanings, through the preservation of the same brand-related information. Nonaka and Akutsu (2004) would name it *ba*s for brand experience: *ba* is a Japanese term that can be translated into the English word "place"; in this context, it means the infrastructure (a location, a system, an artefact, or a set of artefacts) for the internal brand experience to happen.

This way, the creation of "Brand Schools" (Schultz & Hatch, 2006) or "Corporate Universities" (Ind, 2007) are tactics to consider because 1) they allow the involvement of unusual groups of individuals, internal members, who are expected to be engaged with the brand, and 2) they potentiate the understanding of what the brand is and represents. By way of example, a few cases may be mentioned:

- **Lego:** The strategy supporting the LEGO Brand School is to invite employees to engage in playful and creative learning activities in which, using material and tangible artefacts deeply embedded in the organisational culture (such as LEGO bricks), individuals should be able to interpret the brand values, combining them and giving rise to tangible artefacts (Schultz, Hatch & Ciccolella, 2006), potentially new LEGO products. This Brand School also includes the *gallery of values*, a game in which staff members are led to articulate their own associations with the organisational/brand values, resorting only to imagery and visual elements (Schultz & Hatch, 2003).
- **UNICEF UK:** According to Ind and Bjerke (2007), UNICEF UK involved all its members of staff in the process of brand definition; 18 months after launch, 89% of employees knew how to incorporate the brand into their tasks and their work in a generic way.
- **Hallmark:** This company maintains a group of internal managers responsible for *brand learning* among employees; regular branding sessions are provided, a brand-based intranet is constantly available, and daily reminders containing the brand promise were implemented into the start up interfaces of the computers' operating system (Aurand, Gorchels & Bishop, 2005).
- **Museum Victoria:** A paradigmatic case of participatory internal branding is that of the Victoria Museum in Melbourne, where all staff members were involved in the process of redesigning the museum's brand, allowing them direct contact with the nature of the practices and research in design (Streader & Whitehouse, 2008).

Each one of these cases demonstrates that the active and loyal involvement of employees in branding processes is considered essential for the success of a brand that is meaningful to them. Moreover, each one of them indicates that participatory internal branding approaches rely heavily on knowledge sharing. Additionally, for employees to be able to experience the brand and engage in internal branding activities, sharing their brand related interpretations and, possibly, the approaches they consider relevant and about which no one has yet reflected, the companies need to develop brand management efforts that focus on the internal context and not only on the external one (Schultz & Hatch, 2006; Harris, 2007).

Momentum, however, is created by communicating the gist of an idea and afterwards, encouraging individuals to interpret it, apply it to their unique situation and then use their individual skills to address it. Momentum taps into the collective wisdom of the staff and invites their participation. Here identity is still in use, but it is not an induced corporate identity communicated from the upper echelons of the company. Instead, individual identity is developed by regularly encouraging employees to interact with the company position. This allows them to reach a greater appreciation of its meaning to them personally, or as smaller teams of people. This is how it should be (Harris, 2007).

Ind and Bjerke (2007) state that employees have the skills, motivations and potential to contribute new and innovative ideas to the organisations in which they work. These ideas can be given in the form of more or less tangible brand artefacts and, in this context, employees can contribute with resources that can be converted into innovation. This is a way for them to share knowledge and for the organisation to strategically convert it into value. However, Burmann and Zeplin (2005) emphasise that, as long as employees consider the brand as irrelevant to their official duties, they will have no interest in understanding its identity or acquiring knowledge about it. The authors add that brand commitment only results in citizenship behaviour if the staff members are given sufficient know-how and resources to enable them a consistent brand experience.

Identity, used as a tool, allows individuals to increase their overall understanding of the organisation and to personally ingest its meaning. Workshops, training programmes and promotion of good dialogue are good methods to achieve this aim (Harris, 2007).

This chapter's objective is to propose a brand knowledge management model, based on participatory repositories-ecologies that can transparently represent the processes of conversion of brand knowledge, while supporting the collaboration of highly heterogeneous people, with many diverse backgrounds and different motivations/expectations. Information and Communication Technologies (ICT), supporting online communities and grounded on popular social web interaction paradigms, are considered appropriate enhancing mechanisms for inclusion, participation and sharing of brand knowledge, and in which recognition practices can easily be implemented.

SOLUTIONS AND RECOMMENDATIONS

Grounded on the previously discussed concepts and interrelations, the processing of brand information that participation implies – such as research, the evaluation of alternatives, the generation of sets of possible choices – leads to the development of individuals who become better informed and more knowledgeable about the organisational brand. The success of the brand experience encourages the individual to become increasingly involved in participatory processes and to contribute to innovation.

Hence, firstly, the brand's tacit features (such as assumptions and cultural artefacts) need to be made explicit and codified (through strategic vision and image artefacts). Once the brand is codified, at the very least, it is necessary to promote internally a basic commitment in order to safeguard the brand's importance to the organisation; communication plays here an essential role, in order to bring knowledge into a sufficiently explicit level.

Tangible artefacts are often used, in the context of internal branding activities, as communication tools, with the purpose of ensuring, as much as possible, the coherence and recognition of the brand by members of staff. Schultz, Hatch and Ciccolella (2006) argue on the importance of providing employees with the opportunity to explore and use these artefacts, associating them with the brand. This can be done using identification processes (generally responding to "Who we are" and "What we do" or even "What we want to do"), and through design activities in which the original meanings, symbolism, function and even aesthetics of artefacts can be transformed, leading to the reinforcement of the previously existing meaning, or to new artefacts with completely different meanings but still grounded on the brand and its promise. This way, organisations would not only be developing engagement, but should also be encouraging their staff to produce and share their own brand representations (verbally, visually or using any other language), making explicit their brand-related knowledge.

In this type of "home-brewed" design environment it is necessary to provide methods of including employees in the creation processes, guiding and educating them, through demonstrations of the thinking that supports the underlying brand strategies. Streader and Whitehouse (2008) point out that, thanks to this type of involvement, employees from the most diverse organisational levels can actually perceive that the design process underlying the brand is not a random form of creative expression, necessarily limited or held by an individual or external agency, but which can be governed by method, discipline and sharing, in an environment open to new possibilities, which includes forms of creative expression held by several individuals. The credibility of the brand's promise will expectedly increase among those representing it. Masino and Zamarian argue that:

As outcomes, artefacts can be seen as vessels carrying the rules influencing users' behavior. As inputs, artefacts can be seen as the devices through which different sources of rationality generate new rules or change the existing ones through interactions and negotiations (Masino & Zamarian, 2003).

Converting Tacit Brand Knowledge Into Explicit Brand Knowledge

Silveira and Silva (2008) propose that it is possible to apply Nonaka and Takeuchi's SECI model to brand knowledge. As its operationalisation is not part of these authors' contribution, it is thereby one of the theoretical suggestions of this chapter, illustrated in Figure 2.

Hence, through Socialisation (converting tacit knowledge to tacit knowledge), employees share organisational and individual experiences, learning and accumulating knowledge about the organisational identity and brand. This sharing process happens when employees are granted access to resources and cultural artefacts, which are of greater intangibility (behaviours, procedures, values), through their contact with older or more experienced colleagues, mostly through observational exchanges that allow them to transfer tacit knowledge into their own mental models.

The Externalisation of brand knowledge (the conversion of tacit knowledge into explicit knowledge) happens when this is expressed mostly through its strategic vision and image artefacts. These are defined by official predetermined artefacts, which must be communicated and explained, but without

Figure 2. The process of brand knowledge conversion. Adapted from Nonaka and Takeuchi (1995)

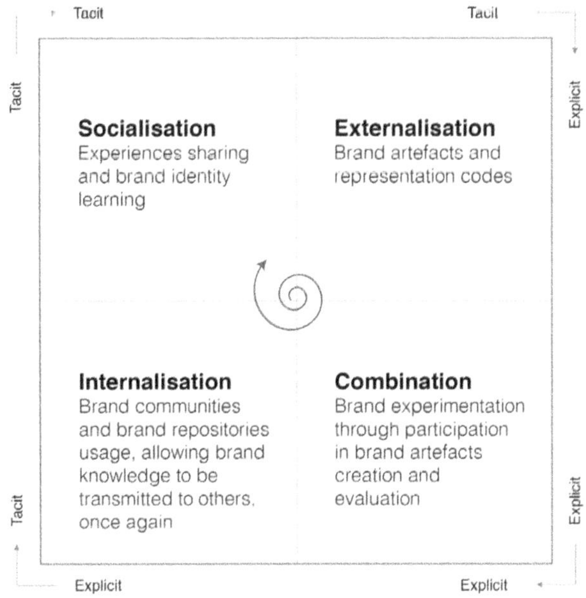

leaving informal artefacts out of the equation, since employees are constantly challenged to take ownership of the brand, to interpret it, and to use their own metaphors, models, diagrams, mnemonics, that will allow their own articulation of tacit brand-related concepts. Such artefacts can draw upon diverse codifications (written identity declarations, logos, imagery, way-finding systems, jingles, dress code, interior design, brand positioning guidelines, tone of voice and also education programs covering the organisational symbolic repertoire, etc.). It is a process that can be easily mediated by technological systems if employees are provided with a consistent context, mostly for the support and orientation of emergent informal artefacts.

The Combination process (conversion of explicit to explicit knowledge) is informed by the direct and overall brand experience. Staff members will be able to act as decision-makers and evaluators, on a brand awareness peer-based process, through which they must also make explicit their brand knowledge, assessing and delivering feedback on their peers' contributions or by manifesting their opinion in regard to formal and informal brand artefacts. This process can also be technologically mediated.

The Internalisation of knowledge (converting explicit into tacit knowledge) takes place when brand artefacts (formal and informal), brand know-how (such as how to assess your peers' ideas) and brand-related experiences are incorporated into brand repertoires such as knowledge management portals. All this knowledge can, at any time, be modified, refuted, added, transmitted to others (new employees, for example), thus initiating a new cycle of knowledge conversion.

Brand Design Activities in Participatory Ecologies

Once the affective conditions of commitment and willingness to share have been met, which are essential for the involvement of employees in brand-related activities, certain requirements must be guaranteed, in order to convert the inaccessible tacit brand knowledge into explicit brand knowledge:

- **Human (Cognitive) Requirements:**
    - Access to organisational identity-related information,
    - Access to the Visual Identity System and to the Brand Guidelines.
- **Technological/Communicational Requirements:**
    - Development of a dedicated *ba*, such as an online brand community.

A crucial challenge, supporting the assumption that brand knowledge is shareable and not exclusive to someone, is the development of structures of participation and interaction that represent the conversion of brand knowledge and facilitate the intervention of various fields of knowledge. According to Tress, Tress and Fry (2005), stakeholder participation can be structured in three different levels: the lowest level is defined by participants getting informed and making sense about a specific topic; the second level refers to the involvement of participants in consultation activities, providing inputs for the topic and transferring knowledge; finally, at the third level, participants can influence the course of activity and become part of the decision-making structure. In the case of brand design activities taking place in participatory ecologies, participation should be conceived acknowledging these three levels, which, from the lowest to the highest would be labelled as follows:

1. Brand Awareness Mentoring
2. Brand Knowledge Sharing
3. Brand Artefacts Decision-Making

Even though it is reasonable that the four different processes of knowledge conversion may happen within each one of these levels, it is also very likely that some of them will be more prominent than others, depending on the level of participation. Accordingly, as explained ahead and illustrated in Figure 3, the first level will be strongly defined by Socialisation and Externalisation, whereas the level of Brand Knowledge Sharing will be characterised by Externalisation and Combination processes and, finally, level three will be supported by both Combination and Internalisation.

Brand Awareness Mentoring

It is essential that all participants have access to the basic information on the strategy underlying the brand, understand the visual identity system and brand guidelines, and are endowed with a minimum of visual literacy that will enable them to represent their brand associations without damaging it. This is, therefore, a process of brand awareness mentoring, which involves the observation and retention of information (Socialisation), but also, and above all, the experimentation, visualisation and confrontation of ideas (Externalisation). In short, it is a learning process, since *(…) learning is a participatory process that involves doing, becoming, and belonging, not simply acquiring* (Barab, MaKinster, Moore & Cunningham, 2001).

The perspective that learning is a participatory process, contrasts sharply with the traditional teaching paradigm, based on the assumption that learners are mere consumers of information. Fischer (2002) proposes that both teaching and work environments should be reconceptualised, fulfilling criteria that would lead them to become spaces in which communities develop, in which individuals are both learners and contributors, and in which individuals who would take the role of mentors/facilitators would support peer-to-peer learning.

Figure 3. The three levels of participation in computer-mediated internal branding

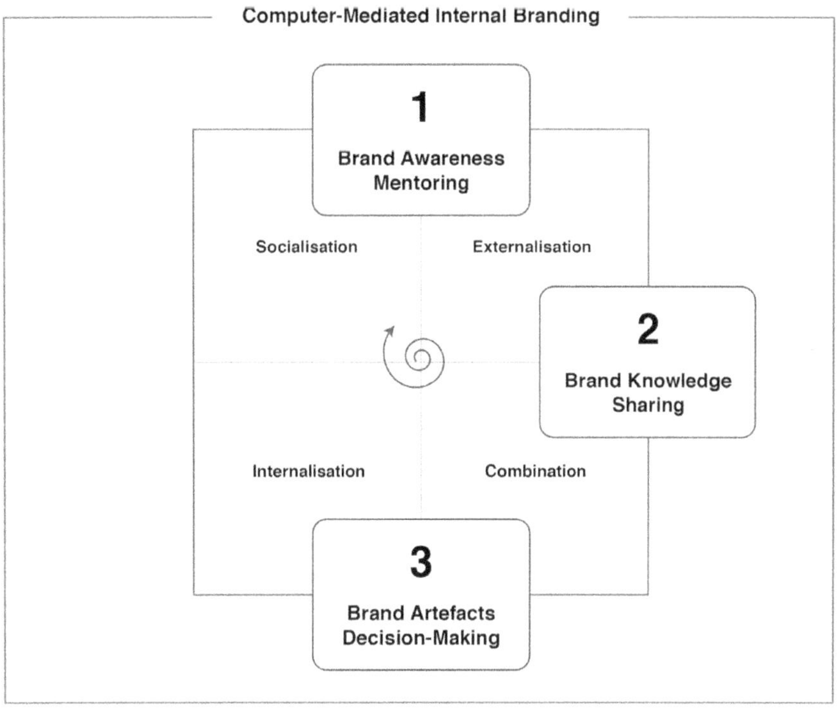

This new learning model is strongly associated with the use of ICT, which minimise learning efforts and ensure easier access to resources and a greater number of interactions (McLoughlin & Lee, 2007). And, within this chapter's position, interactions have a fundamental and determinant role in the brand learning process. However, although learning is much more a process of connection than of acquisition, it needs to be guided. This orientation can be provided by other individuals (the peers, such as other members of staff or individuals assigned to the role of mentors) or by CMC systems with adequate algorithmic abilities. Following the perspective that face-to-face learning programs and CMC environments are the main mechanisms used in internal branding activities (Punjaisri and Wilson, 2007), Brand Awareness Mentoring should be provided by these two agents combined: peers with the support of CMC systems.

By integrating working and learning, people learn within the context of their work on real-world problems. Learning does not take place in a separate phase and in a separate place, but is integrated into the work process. People construct solutions to their own problems, and the sociotechnical environment advises them when they are getting into trouble and provides directly relevant information (Fischer, 2007).

This model follows the position that when technology mediate internal branding processes, individuals cultivate an understanding of the online community in which they participate, an understanding that is influenced by the interactions that they experience and the interpretation they make of these interactions. Therefore, it is considered as essential the availability of technological tools that best allow these interactions and, thereafter, the discovery (and also management) of brand knowledge, through the adaptation, combination, manipulation and creative experimentation of brand artefacts.

Brand Knowledge Sharing

Structures such as the aforementioned "brand schools" and "corporate universities" allow not only Brand Awareness Mentorship programs, but also the share of brand knowledge, with the advantage of promoting not only the transmission of content but, above all, the experimentation associated with the use of existing content and the creation of new one. Semiotics takes on a preponderant role here: the meaning of a brand is produced by those who intellectually, emotionally, and aesthetically engage with brand artefacts, brand discourse or brand-related events; all these points of contact with the brand are symbols that, in the individual's mind, represent ideas, feelings or experiences (Hatch, 2007), *i.e.* brand associations.

It is argued, therefore, that the use of symbolism, functionalities and aesthetics – dimensions that define the artefacts used to convey a brand – help employees to identify themselves with the organisational values. These are pivotal resources for the creation and perception of a community, especially in larger, globalised companies, in which employees are distributed through several offices and have no means to physically interact with each other. When computers mediate these communities, knowledge sharing, sense making, and peer interactions may, potentially, increase.

The formal opportunity to create and share brand artefacts occurs when an organisation launches an open call to everyone's participation, with a view to solving a challenge, more or less defined and more or less extensive in time – which, presumably and traditionally would be assigned to design experts or brand strategy specialists. These participatory activities have the main objective of creating innovation in a shared way, both in relation to processes and in relation to products. Reichwald, Möslein and Piller (2008) argue that value creation (which they refer to as "interactive value creation") includes self-selection and self-management of tasks by participants, and based on the use of and collaboration in artefacts created by the collective. Self-selection refers to the answer to "Who participates?" or, in this case, "Shall I participate or not?", *i.e.* all potential participants decide individually whether to participate. Self-management will allow participants to define their degree of involvement in the activity and what to create, being sure that they are autonomous, free to contribute what they do or know best, if they wish to do so.

Hence, it is possible to conceptualise the creation and sharing of brand artefacts considering a model in which the brand becomes accessible to all employees. Pitt, Watson, Berthon, Wynn and Zinkhan (2006) proposed a framework that takes branding away from the traditional and highly monitored/controlled perspective, through which *the corporation produces a brand's physical embodiment, exclusively narrates the brand's text, unilaterally directs the brand experience, and broadcasts the brand's meaning*, to a diametrically opposed open perspective, in which employees become, themselves, designers and strategists. These, based on the access they already had to organisational and brand identity information, and the mentorship they were previously offered, should now be able to crystallise their brand associations, create a diversity of brand artefacts (Externalisation), generate and live themselves, individually and collectively, brand experiences, and make the meanings of the brand evolve, transferring their brand knowledge through brand artefacts, sharing these in the CMC-led brand community (Combination). Some of them certainly more valid than others, but all these contributions that emerge will reveal the levels of employees' commitment and willingness to share.

Brand Artefacts Decision-Making

This way, instead of presenting the brand repeatedly through more or less standard unidirectional messages, organisations should encourage their employees to produce and share brand associations, and should also consider the most creative ones as potentially new official artefacts. Employees would then become brand actors and brand authors. Aurand, Gorchels and Bishop (2005) refer that *Compensation systems that motivate and reward behaviours that support the brand must be designed and implemented.* Bartol and Srivastava (2002) state that rewards can range from financial offers to non-monetary incentives, such as certificates, praise and visibility.

Collaboration and participation are increasingly recognised as important cultural manifestations of contemporary creative processes. The digital production processes, greatly improved in the late 20th century, have not only facilitated file sharing, but also encouraged the dilution of the boundaries of professional specialisation, minimising the *Not Invented Here* syndrome — the tendency of a group of experts to believe that they hold all the knowledge in their domain, unconditionally rejecting new ideas coming from others who are not specialists in that particular field. It is therefore argued that the ideas of those others, particularly those who are heavily involved with the organisational brand, should be considered, *a priori,* as potentially valid, possibly interesting and eventually able to add value and promote the brand.

Hence, in a joint decision-making manner, another rewarding tactic would be the opportunity for employees to assess their peers' contributions and provide, again, evidence of brand knowledge and of commitment towards the organisation they represent (Combination).

Not really concerned with employees, but rather with a strong focus on external audiences, Prahalad and Ramaswamy (2004) suggest that organisations should adopt a value creation perspective centred on experimentation and knowledge sharing, and in which the brand is the main experiential resource. A few years later, Ind is to reiterate this idea, motivated by the potential of employees' participation, about whom he says it is possible to attribute the title of "brand champions" (2007). This author points out that one of the benefits of involving employees in the brand and its artefacts definition is the high likelihood of this experiential process to become cathartic, by encouraging them to reflect on the brand nature, to know its attributes, and to evaluate the diversity of meanings that emerge with the contributions of all. Hence, it is possible to transpose this framework into the internal context, in which the participants, creators of value, are the employees. However, this transposition is only possible if the creation and conversion of brand knowledge and associated experiences become part of the job and of the entire ecosystem (Internalisation), rather than being isolated, becoming additional activities, competing with priority work obligations.

FUTURE RESEARCH DIRECTIONS

The proposed brand knowledge management model is essentially focused on a company's members of staff (their knowledge, their commitment, their learning capacities, their willingness to share and to be part of a community). The major implementation issue is that the term "members of staff" usually excludes managers, directors, and all those that hold top positions, supposedly expected to oversee these processes, but without any sort of active participation. In fact, these members (of staff) are not always properly engaged and involved with the brand, nor with the related internal branding initiatives and investments, when many employees act upon the examples they get from those in higher levels in the hierarchy. The presented model does not cover an engagement strategy to involve senior management and leadership positions, something that might be addressed in future work.

The technological development and the successful implementation of such a participatory ecology represents, *per se*, an enormous challenge. On one hand, and from a technical point of view, due to the necessity of a consistent system with a strong narrative that would have to accompany and cover all the expected and generic internal branding particularities, but also the unforeseen ones that depend on each organisational context. Software engineering would represent a complementary research area. On the other hand, one must not forget that, currently, organisations are overloaded with digital platforms, intranets, and a myriad of different applications for countless disparate purposes. An additional one might represent an unnecessary burden, for which reason its integration into existing systems would be advisable.

Other possible avenues for future research would be: 1) to investigate the cathartic effects of internal branding, exploring the extensive possibilities of gamification tactics; 2) an in-depth description of the discovery, capture and application phases of brand knowledge, and 3) the definition and proposal of clear learning outcomes for each one of the three levels of participation in computer-mediated internal branding activities.

CONCLUSION

In order to adopt successful brand-building strategies that involve all employees, organisations must ensure a climate of creativity and transfer/combination of knowledge, clear and evident to all. Of course, rewarding systems must be designed and enlightened among those who can give their input and share their knowledge to the organisational collective. Employees should be encouraged to maximise their human capital by developing or optimising their competencies; the best way to do this is not by imposition or through control schemes, but by providing them with participatory activities, resources and infrastructures, involving them in meaningful experiences, through which they can get cognitive, affective, and communicational benefits.

In addition to continue to play a key role in the external audiences' minds (such as existing and potential customers, existing and potential suppliers and partnerships), mostly dressed up as a marketing tool, it seems appropriate that brands should now devote some time and effort to the practices of knowledge management within organisations, through the setup of collaborative multidisciplinary cultures, developing new areas for HR management to intervene, and supporting the highly complex and speedy decision-making moments.

A greater focus on internal branding activities would be the major managerial recommendation: being mostly concerned with brand knowledge creation and conversion, it positions the brand promise and the desired brand image in the employees' minds through interactive learning; it builds their bond with the brand and strengthens their commitment towards the organisation by providing them with opportunities to contribute to the brand and to perform as influencers of the future of the organisation; hopefully, it increases their willingness to share their knowledge, providing the company with a richer framework in which creativity and innovation can genuinely happen.

REFERENCES

Abdullah, H. S., Hassim, A. A., & Chik, R. (2009). Knowledge Sharing in a Knowledge Intensive Organisation: Identifying the Enablers. *International Journal of Business and Management*, *4*(4), 115–123. doi:10.5539/ijbm.v4n4p115

Ackerman, L. D. (2000). *Identity is Destiny: Leadership and the Roots of Value Creation*. San Francisco: Berrett-Koehler Publishers, Inc.

Andrews, K. M., & Delahaye, B. L. (2000). Influences On Knowledge processes In Organizational Learning: The Psychosocial Filter. *Journal of Management Studies*, *37*(6), 797–810. doi:10.1111/1467-6486.00204

Arnhold, U. (2010). *User Generated Branding: Integrating User Generated Content into Brand Management*. Wiesbaden, Germany: GWV Fachverlage GmbH. doi:10.1007/978-3-8349-8857-7

Aurand, T. W., Gorchels, L., & Bishop, T. R. (2005). Human resource management's role in internal branding: An opportunity for cross-functional brand message synergy. *Journal of Product and Brand Management*, *14*(3), 163–169. doi:10.1108/10610420510601030

Balmer, J. M. T., & Greyser, S. A. (2002). Managing the Multiple Identities of the Corporation. *California Management Review*, *44*(3), 72–86. doi:10.2307/41166133

Barab, S. A., Makinster, J. G., Moore, J. A., & Cunningham, D. J. (2001). Designing and Building an On-line Community: The Struggle to Support Sociability in the Inquiry Learning Forum. *Educational Technology Research and Development*, *49*(4), 71–96. doi:10.1007/BF02504948

Bartol, K. M., & Srivastava, A. (2002). Encouraging Knowledge Sharing: The Role of Organizational Reward Systems. *Journal of Leadership & Organizational Studies Organizational Studies*, *9*(1), 64–76. doi:10.1177/107179190200900105

Becerra-Fernandez, I., & Sabherwal, R. (2015). *Knowledge Management Systems and Processes*. New York: Taylor & Francis.

Berthon, P., Pitt, L. F., & Campbell, C. (2009). Does brand meaning exist in similarity or singularity? *Journal of Business Research*, *62*(3), 356–361. doi:10.1016/j.jbusres.2008.05.015

Burmann, C., & Zeplin, S. (2005). Building brand commitment: A behavioural approach to internal brand management. *Journal of Brand Management*, *12*(4), 279–300. doi:10.1057/palgrave.bm.2540223

Chong, M. (2007). The Role of Internal Communication and Training in Infusing Corporate Values and Delivering Brand Promise: Singapore Airlines' Experience. *Corporate Reputation Review*, *10*(3), 201–212. doi:10.1057/palgrave.crr.1550051

Corporate Branding. (2007). Sage Publications. Retrieved 6 May 2010 from http://www.sage-ereference.com/organization/Article_n97.html

de Chernatony, L., & Riley, F. (1998). Modelling the components of the brand. *European Journal of Marketing*, *32*(11/12), 1074–1090. doi:10.1108/03090569810243721 de Long, D. W., & Fahey, L. (2000). Diagnosing cultural barriers to knowledge management. *The Academy of Management Perspectives*, *14*(4), 113–127. doi:10.5465/AME.2000.3979820

Empson, L. (2001). Fear of exploitation and fear of contamination: Impediments to knowledge transfer in mergers between professional service firms. *Human Relations*, *54*(7), 839–862. doi:10.1177/0018726701547003

Fischer, G. (2002). Beyond 'Couch Potatoes': From Consumers to Designers and Active Contributors. *Firstmonday.* Available at http://firstmonday.org/issu

Fischer, G. (2007). Designing Socio-Technical Environments in Support of Meta-Design and Social Creativity. *Computer Supported Collaborative Learning (CSCL '2007).* Rutgers University. Retrieved 14/03/2011 from http://l3d.cs.colorado.edu/~gerhard/papers/CSCL-2007.pdf

Harris, F., & Chernatony, L. D. (2001). Corporate branding and corporate brand performance. *European Journal of Marketing*, *35*(3/4), 441–456. doi:10.1108/03090560110382101

Harris, P. (2007). We the people: The importance of employees in the process of building customer experience. *Journal of Brand Management*, *15*(2), 102–114. doi:10.1057/palgrave.bm.2550123

Hayes, N., & Walsham, G. (1999). Safe Enclaves, Political Enclaves and Knowledge Working. *First International Critical Management Studies Conference.*

Hooff, B. V. D., & Ridder, J. A. (2004). Knowledge sharing in context: The influence of organizational commitment, communication climate and CMC use on knowledge sharing. *Journal of Knowledge Management*, *8*(6), 117–130. doi:10.1108/13673270410567675

Hsu, C., & Cai, L. (2009). Brand Knowledge, Trust and Loyalty-A Conceptual Model of Destination Branding. *International CHRIE Conference*, 1-8. doi: 10.1111/1468-5884.00177

Ind, N. (2007). *Living the Brand: How to Transform Every Member of Your Organization Into a Brand Champion* (3rd ed.). London: Kogan Page.

Ind, N., & Bjerke, R. (2007). *Branding governance: a participatory approach to the brand building process.* West Sussex, UK: John Wiley & Sons Ltd.

Järvenpää, S., & Staples, D. (2000). The use of collaborative electronic media for information sharing: An exploratory study of determinants. *The Journal of Strategic Information Systems*, *9*(2-3), 129–154. doi:10.1016/S0963-8687(00)00042-1

Keller, K. L. (2003). *Strategic Brand Management: building, measuring and managing brand equity.* Upper Saddle River, NJ: Pearson Education.

Kelloway, E. K., & Barling, J. (2000). Knowledge work as organizational behavior. *International Journal of Management Reviews*, *2*(3), 287–304. doi:10.1111/1468-2370.00042

Kim, W. C., & Mauborgne, R. A. (1993). Procedural Justice, Attitudes, and Subsidiary Top Management Compliance With Multinationals' Corporate Strategic Decisions. *Academy of Management Journal*, *36*(3), 502–526. doi:10.2307/256590

King, C., & Grace, D. (2008). Internal branding: Exploring the employee's perspective. *Journal of Brand Management, 15*(5), 358–372. doi:10.1057/palgrave.bm.2550136

King, C., & Grace, D. (2010). Building and measuring employee-based brand equity. *European Journal of Marketing, 44*(7/8), 938–971. doi:10.1108/03090561011047472

Lelis, C., & Mealha, O. (2014). BEODE—Brand Experience Oriented Design Environments. *BrandTrends: Journal of Strategic Communication and Branding, 6*, 6-18.

Lelis, C., & Mealha, O. (2015). Heuristic for brand artefacts co-design: A computer-mediated proposal. *CoDesign, 11*(2), 83–98. doi:10.1080/15710882.2015.1054840

Mangold, W. G., & Miles, S. J. (2007). The employee brand: Is yours an all-star? *Business Horizons, 50*(5), 423–433. doi:10.1016/j.bushor.2007.06.001

Masino, G., & Zamarian, M. (2003). Information technology artefacts as structuring devices in organizations: Design, appropriation and use issues. *Interacting with Computers, 15*(5), 693–707. doi:10.1016/S0953-5438(03)00059-6

McEnally, M., & de Chernatony, L. (1999). The Evolving Nature of Branding: Consumer and Managerial Considerations. *Academy of Marketing Science Review, 2*. Available http://www.amsreview.org/articles/mcena

McLoughlin, C., & Lee, M. (2007). Social software and participatory learning: Pedagogical choices with technology affordances in the Web 2.0 era. *ASCILITE Singapore 2007*. Retrieved 30/09/2011 from www.ascilite.org.au/conferences/singapore07

Merz, M., He, Y., & Vargo, S. L. (2009). The evolving brand logic: A service-dominant logic perspective. *Journal of the Academy of Marketing Science, 37*(3), 328–344. doi:10.100711747-009-0143-3

Miles, S. J., & Mangold, W. G. (2004). A conceptualization of the employee branding process. *Journal of Relationship Marketing, 3*(2-3), 65–87. doi:10.1300/J366v03n02_05

Miles, S. J., Mangold, W. G., Asree, S., & Revell, J. (2011). Assessing the Employee Brand: A Census of One Company. *Journal of Managerial Issues, 23*(4), 491–507.

Moore, L. (2007). Brands. In *Encyclopedia of Business Ethics and Society*. Thousand Oaks, CA: Sage Publications. Retrieved 6 May 2010 from http://www.sage-ereference.com/ethics/Article_n88.html

Morris, T., & Empson, L. (1998). Organization and Expertise: An Exploration of Knowledge Bases and the Management of Accounting and Consulting Firms. *Accounting, Organizations and Society, 23*(5-6), 609–624. doi:10.1016/S0361-3682(98)00032-4

Mowday, R. T., Steers, R. M., & Porter, L. W. (1979). The measurement of organizational commitment. *Journal of Vocational Behavior, 14*(2), 224–247. doi:10.1016/0001-8791(79)90072-1

Natarajan, T., Balasubramaniam, S. A., & Srinivasan, T. (2017). Relationship between Internal Branding. *Employee Brand and Brand Endorsement., 12*, 95–110. doi:10.5539/ijbm.v12n1p95

Neumeier, M. (2006). *The brand gap*. Berkeley, CA: New Riders.

Nonaka, I., & Takeuchi, H. (1995). *The knowledge-creating company - how japanese companies create the dynamics of innovation*. New York: Oxford University Press.

Oltra, V. (2005). Knowledge management effectiveness factors: The role of HRM. *Journal of Knowledge Management*, *9*(4), 70–86. doi:10.1108/13673270510610341

Pitt, L. F., Watson, R., Berthon, P., Wynn, D., & Zinkhan, G. (2006). The Penguin's Window: Corporate Brands From an Open-Source Perspective. *Journal of the Academy of Marketing Science*, *34*(2), 115–127. doi:10.1177/0092070305284972

Prahalad, C. K., & Ramaswamy, V. (2004). The co-creation experiences: The next practice in value creation. *Journal of Interactive Marketing*, *18*(3), 5–14. doi:10.1002/dir.20015

Preece, J. (2000). *Online Communities: designing usability, supporting sociability*. West Sussex, UK: John Wiley & Sons.

Punjaisri, K., & Wilson, A. (2007). The role of internal branding in the delivery of employee brand promise. *Journal of Brand Management*, *15*(1), 57–70. doi:10.1057/palgrave.bm.2550110

Punjaisri, K., & Wilson, A. (2011). Internal branding process: Key mechanisms, outcomes and moderating factors. *European Journal of Marketing*, *45*(9/10), 1521–1537. doi:10.1108/03090561111151871

Reichwald, R., Möslein, K., & Piller, F. (2008). Creating Value Interactively — Challenges for Company Management. Bloomington, IN: iUniverse, Inc.

Richards, I., Foster, D., & Morgan, R. (1998). Brand Knowledge Management: Growing Brand Equity. *Journal of Knowledge Management*, *2*(1), 47–54. doi:10.1108/13673279810800762

Scarbrough, H. (2003). Knowledge management, HRM and the innovation process. *International Journal of Manpower*, *24*(5), 501–516. doi:10.1108/01437720310491053

Schultz, M., & Hatch, M. J. (2003). The Cycles of Corporate Branding: The case the LEGO company. *California Management Review*, *46*(1), 6–26. doi:10.2307/41166229

Schultz, M., & Hatch, M. J. (2006). *A cultural perspective on corporate branding - The case of LEGO Group*. Oxon, UK: Routledge.

Schultz, M., Hatch, M. J., & Ciccolella, F. (2006). *Brand Life in Symbols and Artifacts: the LEGO Company*. Mahwah, NJ: Lawrence Erlbaum.

Silveira, I., & Silva, G. G. (2008). A capacidade do branding na criação do conhecimento da marca. 1° Seminário de Branding e Design Gráfico.

Storey, J., & Barnett, E. (2000). Knowledge management initiatives: Learning from failure. *Journal of Knowledge Management*, *4*(2), 145–156. doi:10.1108/13673270010372279

Streader, T., & Whitehouse, D. (2008). Not another logo! Designing corporate identity systems that drive change within institutional culture: A case study in participatory design. *International DMI Education Conference*.

Tress, B., Tress, G., & Fry, G. (2005). Defining concepts and the process of knowledge production in integrative research. *From landscape research to landscape planning: Aspects of integration, education and application*, 13-26.

Ward, A. (2000). Getting Strategic Value from Constellations of Communities. *Strategy and Leadership*, *28*(2), 4–9. doi:10.1108/10878570010341537

Willem, A., Scarbrough, H., & Buelens, M. (2008). Impact of coherent versus multiple identities on knowledge integration. *Journal of Information Science*, *34*(3), 370–386. doi:10.1177/0165551507086259

Wise, R., & Zednickova, J. (2009). The rise and rise of the B2B brand. *The Journal of Business Strategy*, *30*(1), 4–13. doi:10.1108/02756660910926911

KEY TERMS AND DEFINITIONS

Artefact: A tangible or intangible human creation, representative of a culture or specific context.

Brand Guidelines: Document(s) that essentially present(s) a set of rules explaining how the brand works; also commonly referred to as "brand standards," "brand manual," "style guide," or "brand book."

Computer-Mediated Communication: Human communication that takes place through the support and use of information and communication technologies and electronic devices.

Employee: Someone who works part-time or full-time, in a fixed-term or permanent position, under an employment contract and is paid for the completion of the contractual duties; a member of staff, regardless of his/her hierarchical level.

Human-Centered: Characterizes approaches that strategically include users at the core of their activities.

Multidisciplinary Team: A group of individuals who have different vocational abilities, each providing specific contributions to the same project or objective.

Participatory Ecology: A technological system of interactions in which the participation of its organisms is considered an essential component.

Visual Identity System: A set of visual elements that help crystallize the brand, such as the name, the logo, the color palette, the selected typography, the extended visual language.

Chapter 2
Knowledge Creation, Management, and Dissemination in Impact Communities

Ana Melro
University of Aveiro, Portugal

Lídia Oliveira
University of Aveiro, Portugal

ABSTRACT

This chapter's mission is to reflect on the steps taken by knowledge (creation, management, and dissemination) in an impact community (IC). Also, it aims to analyze how this knowledge can be capitalized by the IC itself, as well as other ICs, through the replication of good practices. To this end, importance is attached to several stages of the existence of knowledge in an IC: 1) individual knowledge, which each single person carries and integrates into an IC when he/she becomes a member; 2) the combination of all the individual knowledge, which forces one to think in a knowledge management; 3) the moments of knowledge sharing; and 4) the internal and external dissemination of this knowledge. These last two dynamics—sharing and dissemination—result in a replication and multiplication of existing knowledge in an IC.

INTRODUCTION

Communities of Practice (CoPs) are aggregations of people who mobilize their energy to solve common problems through social learning processes. Among other goals, one of the most privileged of belonging to a CoP is the knowledge sharing, which takes place after its creation and is maximized with its internal and external dissemination.

One of the areas that is currently being explored is the creation of CoP by social entrepreneurs, the so-called Impact Communities (IC), that is, groups of people whose goal is to change the territory through

DOI: 10.4018/978-1-5225-3725-0.ch002

social problems' resolution. They are IC because the creation of value for society is their ultimate purpose, as well as the promotion of change, and this takes into account the direct, indirect beneficiaries and other stakeholders, as well as the use of local resources and / or sustainability, innovation and growth.

Nowadays, Social Innovation is an area where more and more academics and practitioners dedicate their studies and interest. The development of the area has been such that it has moved on to a new phase of creation of IC, spaces where local people gather together to contribute to the socio-economic and cultural territory development.

IC are fed by the definition of CoP with respect to its scope and form, but in material terms they present specific contents, also considering the specificities of its members: social entrepreneurs. The IC arise from the spontaneous desire of social entrepreneurs to come together as a group, to jointly discuss and try to solve problems they face in the development of their initiatives and / or present good examples of managing initiatives. What unites these people in an IC is the desire to find solutions to social problems and transform the territory where they operate. This is the particularity of IC in relation to CoP, the interest is not only self-centered (sometimes this doesn't exist at all), but often it is to solve a problem that affects the environment, someone known, a particular group, or other.

What are the strategies for creating, managing and disseminating knowledge in/of IC? What are the strategies of knowledge internal transfer? How do territories benefit from this knowledge, by becoming Smart Territories as a result? What role for Media and Information and Communication Technologies?

These questions are always an issue in an Impact Community, whether in a conscious way, with procedure manuals being prepared and distributed; or in an unconscious way, bringing some chaos to the IC (in)formality.

Considering the specificities of people belonging to an IC, some concerns have emerged that underline the importance of this chapter:

1. The small number of social entrepreneurs in Portugal (2015 numbers of the Global Entrepreneurship Monitor[1], refer to about 2.9% of the total population) may mean that integration into an IC will make social entrepreneurs' scale of action grow larger because together they are more and because the range of action becomes more embracing;
2. The large number of organizations in the third sector, according to the Cooperativa António Sérgio para a Economia Social (António Sérgio Cooperative for Social Economy)[2] are about 55,000, which implies that, in Portugal, organizations of a more caring nature are replicating more problems and needs than solutions;
3. The lack of funding for innovative social initiatives (mostly justified by the non-compliance of Social Security parameters) often means the difficulty in Social Entrepreneurship initiatives to guarantee their continuity;
4. Given the dispersion of Social Entrepreneurship initiatives, it implies that they do not communicate and are not known, so they do not share problems, solutions or good practices;
5. The lack of knowledge of sharing and communication collaborative tools results in working in niches that does not allow to leverage more and better solutions.

Considering the aforementioned concerns, the paper has four main objectives:

1. To reflect on the creation of IC in the Portuguese context, but with a proposal of replication in countries with similar characteristics;

2. To reflect on knowledge creation in the IC, analyzing the cycle, which roles are assumed by the members and what manifestations are perceived throughout this knowledge creation;
3. To evaluate the knowledge management in the IC, if it is and how it is carried out and suggest knowledge management frameworks;
4. To reflect on the knowledge dissemination, to foster the internal and external sharing practices of the crested knowledge in an IC through the suggestion of a specific framework for this purpose, using existing technological tools.

In a period of increasing demands in terms of process flexibility and information sharing, it is important that these two dynamics - flexibility and sharing - are carried out in a thoughtful and articulated way with other dynamics. IC, being informal spaces of collaboration, need more processes' codification, so that the information transfer, when necessary, is carried out without entropy and in such a way that the knowledge creation, management and dissemination are carried out and ensure the extraction of the maximum potential of existing knowledge and allow openness for latent knowledge to be exposed.

For the accomplishment of this chapter several phases will be crossed, the first is the systematic review of literature on IC creation; on knowledge creation, management and dissemination in the specific context of IC; the role of information and communication technologies in the knowledge management and dissemination. The second phase is the analysis of the potential creation of IC in Portugal, using the Portuguese Social Entrepreneurship initiatives and social entrepreneurs' characteristics. The third phase is the analysis of the implementation of an IC pilot, from the moment of its creation, through the motivations of the social entrepreneurs for belonging to the IC, to the strategies of communication and knowledge sharing, realizing which critical success factors are important for the maintenance of an IC.

It is intended with these methodological steps to understand the emergence of an IC and its maintenance, but above all, the knowledge creation, management and dissemination, in order to answer the questions: what is the key element that triggers the creation of an IC? How knowledge sharing occurs within an IC? How are the existing knowledge and the sharing / dissemination of good practices / knowledge in an IC perceived? What importance is given to knowledge management in an IC?

BACKGROUND

Social Innovation and Entrepreneurship

The first reference to the concept of entrepreneurship was done by Jean-Baptiste Say, and defined as the transfer of economic resources from a small area to one of greater productivity and income (Say, 1841). A few years later, in the twentieth century, Schumpeter (1949) dedicated his interests to the same concept, pointing out that entrepreneurs are agents of change who explore new forms (or old, but with the application of some novelty) of production, and organization of the business or industrial sector (1949).

Central to the distinction between traditional / commercial and social entrepreneurship is the mission. In 1998, Gregory Dees explained the concept of social entrepreneurship by referring that it includes the characteristics pointed out by Say, Schumpeter and others (Peter Drucker, 1985; Howard Stevenson, 1991), but also include the adoption of a mission that contributes to the creation of social value. The social mission (and the search for results) is then the engine for the search for innovative processes, sustainable solutions and continuous learning (Dees, 1998).

Mort, Weerawardena and Carnegie (2003) concluded that social entrepreneurship has a multidimensional nature, since it consists of a number of interrelated attributes or dimensions and exists in multidimensional domains. The authors analyzed the concept considering the latent model of Law, Wong and Mobley (1998). Thus, social entrepreneurs are motivated by a social mission (as Dees, 1998 had already stated); have a balanced judgment when faced with moments of complexity; they always look for opportunities to increase the value created for the beneficiaries of their solutions; finally, they make decisions using innovative instruments, in a proactive way and with some degree of risk (Mort, G. S., Weerawardena, J., & Carnegie, K., 2003).

In 2004, Mair and Martí defined social entrepreneurship as:

a process involving the innovative use and combination of resources to pursue opportunities to catalyze social change and / or address social needs (Mair & Martí, 2004).

That is, they include the innovation factor, the existence of an opportunity and the promotion of social change.

A few years later, Martin and Osberg (2007) defined social entrepreneurship as having three essential components: the identification of a group of causes that creates exclusion, marginalization or suffering situations of a segment of humanity; the identification of an opportunity to act in the solution of the problem encountered; and the achievement of a new balance which would eliminate or reduce exclusion, marginalization or suffering situations of the target audience or even of a wider group of society (Martin & Osberg, 2007).

Santos (2012) wrote the definition of social entrepreneurship that IES-Social Business School[3] would use until the present moment and that gives meaning to the way the association develops its work, as well as to the evolution of its training offer. According to the author,

the process of social entrepreneurship enables the second invisible hand of the economic system, this one based on other-regarding rather than self-interest. By pursuing their regard for others and addressing opportunities for value creation in a distributed way, social entrepreneurs drive the economy closer to an efficient outcome by systematically identifying neglected problems with positive externalities and developing mechanisms to incorporate these externalities into the economic system. (Santos, 2012).

As for the concept of social innovation, Phills, Deiglmeier, and Miller (2008) describe it as a more efficient, effective and sustainable solution than existing solutions to solving a social problem, which seeks above all value creation for society (Phills, J. A., Deiglmeier, K., & Miller, D. T., 2008).

At this point, it is understood that social entrepreneurship and social innovation are two concepts easily confused in their similarities and that, for this reason, they are mentioned side by side, considering the way they complement each other, rather than the differences that separates them.

The difference between Social Entrepreneurship and Social Innovation is that the first one is considered as being more stable, lasting and sustainable, with a vision of profit making, even if it has a social mission of reinvesting in the solution to solve social problems.

Social Innovation is more dynamic, related to the constant search for new ideas, products and services. As Mulgan (2006) points out,

Social innovation refers to innovative activities and services that are motivated by the goal of meeting a social need and that are predominantly diffused through organizations whose primary purposes are social. (Mulgan, 2006).

The similarity between the two concepts is the social mission, both have as purpose to solve problems of a specific territory or group of people. In fact, Social Entrepreneurship often seeks Innovation to bring some change to the existing balance (Phillips, Lee, Ghobadian, O'Regan, & James, 2015). And, because of the similarity, which is what most characterizes also the two concepts, they often arise associated, Social Innovation and Entrepreneurship.

IMPACT COMMUNITIES AND KNOWLEDGE

Communities of Practice (CoP) are understood as

a group of people who share a concern or a passion for something they do, and learn how to do it better as they interact regularly (Wenger-Trayner & Wenger-Trayner, 2015).

It is the authors' belief that CoP are a powerful tool for project development, as they give the agents of change the opportunity to learn and improve through the regular interaction and sharing practices.

When a group of social innovators and entrepreneurs come together, informally or formally, Impact Communities (IC) emerge. The purpose is to solve social problems in a given territory, to find answers to some problems encountered when trying to implement initiatives in the field. What Toivonen (2013) defines as Social Innovation Communities (SIC).

SIC are defined by the author as,

a perplexing entity that escapes easy categorization: it is heavily networked but not to definable simply as "a network"; practice-focused but not a community of practice (in Wenger's sense); an ecosystem-builder yet not an ecosystem; and concerned with collective processes but not with centrally coordinated "collective impact" (Toivonen, 2013).

SIC are:

an emergent collaborative organization characterized by entrepreneurial projects, loosely shared changemaking cultures as well as online/offline spaces; it continuously facilitates informal but productive interactions between relatively diverse actors, most of whom share an interest in social innovation (in a broad sense) and in open collaboration beyond the bounds of any single organization or narrowly defined issue. (Toivonen, 2016).

The article focus on the concept of IC, since the interest are SIC, but with the evidence on the impact that these produce in the territory, on the positive change produced. Thus, groups of social entrepreneurs that meet, face-to-face or virtually, with the ultimate goal of developing the territory where their initiatives are implemented. This development happens because the solution found for social problems aims to create a positive impact on people and, consequently, on the territory.

Impact is the direct or indirect change caused by some given action. A time to learn and share those learnings it's also important for social entrepreneurs to achieve their goals.

Moreover, because of what it is the definition of IC used in this research, one understands that the way people gather and share knowledge will help create a bigger positive impact in society, result of social entrepreneurs work.

Knowledge production is the result of established connections between individuals: it makes no sense to analyze these connections - the network - or even knowledge production as if they are isolated elements, but rather as being in permanent interaction since all actors contribute to the same end.

By actors, one consider individuals, objects, institutions, technology, and all that is involved in the knowledge production network (Latour, 2010). Moreover, as Latour states,

that means that whenever you wish to define an entity (an agent, an actant, an actor) you have to deploy its attributes, that is, its network. To try to follow an actor-network is a bit like defining a wave-corpuscle in the 1930s: any entity can be seized either as an actor (a corpuscle) or as a network (a wave). It is in this complete reversibility – an actor is nothing but a network, except that a network is nothing but actors – that resides the main originality of this theory. Here again, network is the concept that helps you redistribute and reallocate action. (Latour, 2010).

The Actor-Network theory proposed by Bruno Latour (2005) and Michel Callon (1986) is, by its scope, applicable to any scientific area, namely, communities' communication processes. In this perspective, what was interesting was precisely to consider that each link is important for communication to be carried out and that the IC has the desired result - the result here being the creation of value for society through the resolution of social problems. Both IC members (internal and external - in this case IES-SBS), as well as the technological tools available, human resources, local organizations and the organizations where IC members work, the environment and the established relationships among the members are important actors in this network that allows communication and, consequently, knowledge production and Smart Territories development.

Knowledge creation, management and dissemination are processes that occur when several factors are combined. One of them, and the most important, is the existence of human critical mass capable of thinking the world and finding ways of changing it for the better, in this specific case, Social Entrepreneurship.

MAIN FOCUS OF THE CHAPTER

Knowledge Creation in Impact Communities

[…] *in a community that exhibits connectivist dynamics, knowledge is not merely distributed from one person to another, but is rather emergent from the communicative behaviour of the whole* (Downes, 2012). This citation lists structural concepts for the article development: community; Learning Theories, namely, connectivism; knowledge and communication, with several points in common and of interrelation between all of them.

The teaching-learning process requires the existence of an emitter and a receiver, since it is performed through a communication dynamic. Those emitter and receiver may not be singular, but a collective of people. Teaching-learning can happen from one to many, one to one or even many to many. Thus, it implies the existence of a community, an IC, where the teaching-learning process occurs, which is the knowledge creation. For this, it is considered that the process must be adaptable, not linear but interactive, with a strong dynamic component of fluid-acquisition and constant transmission.

Education and communication for/of entrepreneurship has a relevant role in established networks, through the various living environments, that promote and allow the emergence of learning collective environments, more or less structured, but always with the purpose of promoting learning, knowledge creation, the connection between people and knowledge. Education for entrepreneurship is at the same time effective in a media ecosystem, in which ICTs induce and promote the immaterial approximation of actors, generating collective learning environments.

Learning generation is the transfer of a set of data and information that gathered in a coherent and consistent way, produce knowledge. This only gains the utility that underlies it (even by the definition that is attributed to it) when transformed into moments of sharing and construction: effective learning with behavior changes.

Allied to what has just been mentioned, and the definition of Social Innovation and Entrepreneurship used in this chapter, if, on the one hand, the learning generation and sharing are important variables to generate change; on the other hand, it is necessary that this learnings generates local dynamism and territorial development.

IC are, therefore, (1) spaces for the knowledge creation, as a result of the interaction of their members and; (2) spaces for sharing such knowledge with members or others with the same interests and contribute to change. The Communities are directed towards the outside, hence their aim is to contribute to (3) revitalizing their members (solving problems that may arise in the development of their initiatives or encouraging action in the community) and the territory and, consequently; (4) territorial development, which should be the objective underlying the constitution of a Community and its action over time.

Knowledge Management in Impact Communities

Learning spaces are being perceived since late 20th century. Although original and interesting ways of learning have always existed, only in that period specialists start to think about the deep changes needed so that learning can be flexible, spreadable and shareable.

Knowledge generation exists because once existed data and information. In fact, every territory is a living space of data and information relevant to the understanding of its evolution. But the action of man is necessary for these contents to be managed and disseminated.

Furthermore, the learning generation is precisely the transformation of a set of data and information without utility in a coherent and consistent knowledge. This, in turn, it only gains utility when transformed into sharing and building moments: the effective learning.

Allied to what was mentioned and to Social Entrepreneurship, there is the felt need for local change, through the resolution of social and/or environmental problems. Thus, if on the one hand, knowledge generation and sharing is an important variable to promote change; it is also necessary that that knowledge creates local dynamics and territorial development.

And when a group of people get together with the same purpose, in this case, to produce social change, then the focus should be on the territory development where they perform their activities. Thus, it is necessary to bear in mind which goals are intended to achieve at the micro level (the IC) and at the macro level (the society), having a deep knowledge about the territory, its existent problems and solutions.

Knowledge Dissemination in Impact Communities

The concept of Network Learning Communities was used to express the relationship created and existing between individuals belonging to a community, as well as the learning processes that are being promoted, extending in time and disseminated in space, especially with the Information and Communication Technologies (Rajagopal, Brinke, Bruggen, & Sloep, 2012).

The role of media in knowledge dissemination produced within the IC and social relations can be seen in a constructivist reading (Cole, 2003; 1996; Vygotski, 2007; 1934), since artifacts are now mediators of most human activities. Technological change supposes changes in habitus (Bourdieu, 2010; 1979), and in turn, technologies and their uses are modified by changes in the same habitus and, consequently, in individuals.

The Internet is responsible for facilitating communication, both internal and external. E-mail is now the privileged medium for exchanging ideas, responding in a labor and training contexts. But it is also with the use of the Internet that true collaborative communities are created. Crumlish and Malone (2009) agree that social experiences that have been unleashed can be a very enriching way of generating content, new products, business models or even productive processes, so companies are starting to accept the creation and use of social networks and incorporating them as another mode of production (Crumlish & Malone, 2009). According to Almeida (2012) there are three essential aspects in the existence of these networks and in the use of electronic mail: communication that exists, the fact that it is an important business tool and because it is an auxiliary of E-learning (Almeida, 2012).

Thus, among the advantages of using Web 2.0 we have the following: computers and smartphones include the emergence of more knowledgeable, critical and demanding citizens; the relevance attached to informal learning and innovation, the blurring of hierarchies and the shift to network-based heads. And among the disadvantages are: the possible weak participation of some individuals who feel less knowledgeable about the technologies, and thus excluded from the communication process, it may even be delivered to some elites, who in a way repress participation and collaboration; the lack of privacy; and the risk of poor participation. (Fernandes, Mozzicafreddo, & Cardoso, 2010).

The emphasis should not be placed on technology, but on culture, facilitating and encouraging the use of technology, but always on a logic of favoring the more flexible and less labor-intensive realization of work and training practices (Fernandes, Mozzicafreddo, & Cardoso., 2010). Collaboration, teamwork, information flows management, speed, efficiency, automation of repetitive tasks, minimization of their duration, innovation, personal and professional enrichment, are some keywords of the network communities of this millennium.

Schaffers, Brodt, Pallot, Prinz, and Instituu (2006) show that there are four types of support guaranteed in what the functions performance is related: what happens in the same time and space; what occurs in a different time and in a distributed space, but both predictable; when time and space are different and unpredictable; and, finally, the workplace in which employees are aware of time and space. The transition from one category to another takes place through a greater or lesser media usage, especially mobile technologies, through which it is possible to attend meetings at a distance, respond to emails, participate in discussions, as well as being part of collaborative work communities (Schaffers, H., Brodt, T., Pallot, M., Prinz, W., & Instituut, T., 2006).

The way in which the relationships between individuals are developed has changed over the years, making close what is distant, allowing those who are distant to participate. This is one of the great advantages of implementing communication processes based on communication technologies and the model of Schaffers et al. (2006) is an example of this. Technologies should be the means to facilitate communication between members, whether in the same space or not, be it synchronous or asynchronous communication, communication with the outside world or between members.

SOLUTIONS AND RECOMMENDATIONS

IC are defined as spaces where learning is generated and disseminated; are open to this dissemination, sharing and interaction; promote the development of people and the territory; are therefore a way of creating value for society. (Putz & Arnold, 2001). Thus, as tools that serve the IC, ICTs are perceived as mediators in these processes of learning and social interaction (Moreira, Costa, & Vieira, 2016); promoters of knowledge sharing; places where knowledge can be accessed, just as the recognition of territories as intelligent and sustainable is made public.

Geographical dispersion of Social Innovation and Entrepreneurship initiatives, as well as the lack of mechanisms that allow the knowledge of these initiatives to be created, has as a consequence the fact that sharing and cooperation is not always a practice among the initiatives or even the entrepreneurs. More than that, and except some cases, working alone, lack of communication and even the lack of similar solutions in close territories are the most common problems when analyzing work practices (Sacchetti & Campbell, 2014).

But how can social entrepreneurs be the creators of their own community, even with the support and knowledge of specific organizations as IES-Social Business School? The goal is to put social entrepreneurs in communication, sharing learning and knowledge disseminating, through a hybrid learning strategy, combining online and offline communication.

The solution considers the ICT tools available to this effect, since it takes into account the geographic dispersion of the Community, the location and the contact points between its members. It also takes into consideration the proficiency in the use of ICT by these same members and the time of existence of the IC itself, including the importance of maintaining face-to-face contacts at frequent intervals.

For communications that seek to bring the elements together and continuously over time, you can turn to Facebook. In fact, this is a tool that is suggested to use since the beginning of the IC existence, since it encourages the sharing of varied information and can be added and withdrawn members at any time.

For scheduling face-to-face meetings, email is an excellent tool, complemented by Facebook and event sharing. In this way, the objectives of the meeting, the location and the hours can be added, as well as sharing some important document for the meeting preparation. To enhance the presence of those who are further away geographically, it is suggested to use skype.

But there is still the issue of the IC dissemination in the territory and the work developed and it is considered that the use of newsletters is a quick way to disseminate what has been done and even to have a perception of that work by IC members.

The strategy involves combining several tools and modes of action in each one of them, being the email, a social network, a synchronous online conversation tool and the newsletters. This combination is what guarantees that the knowledge dissemination exists and sharing and the learning generation occurs.

FUTURE RESEARCH DIRECTIONS

The IC creation are drivers of the learning process of many to many, where communication can occur face-to-face or virtually, by using sharing and online conversation tools (such as skype).

Through the IC, its participants will be able to share challenges, experiences, solutions, knowledge, learning and work together if there are synergies between initiatives. Basically, legitimacy is conferred on all those who are part of the Community, since the goal is not the transmission of knowledge but the sharing, everyone will have something to add and learn (Gilchrist, 2009).

In order to indicate future work, it is considered that the relationship between the Big Data concept, Open Data practices, Social Innovation and the development of Smart Territories would be a very relevant area, understanding how the learning Collective Environments of social entrepreneurs, combining existing information about the territory and citizens, could promote better decisions of the initiatives and, consequently, the resolution of a more sustainable way of the problem.

Engagement is an important part of an IC whether upstream or downstream. As mentioned by Elkjaer (1999), only a full participation in the community activities can guarantee a sense of belonging. And this sense of belonging guarantees the IC sustainability.

ICT support the characterization of IC as open spaces, or open learning networks (Mott, 2010) and consequently as personal learning networks (Rajagopal, K., Brinke, D. J., Bruggen, J. Van, & Sloep, P. B., 2012). ICTs are important to feed the involvement and learning in an IC today, considering the importance they assume in the lives of individuals, but also the importance they have for people who are connected 24/7, increasing the feeling of belonging.

ICTs also allow the transmission of knowledge among SIC members and, as referred by Bradbury and Middlemiss (2015).

If a participant's knowledge has been passed on to other generations, then it re-mains in the shared repertoire of the community when they leave. The passing-on of knowledge, therefore, contributes to the association being able to sustain itself in the long term (Bradbury & Middlemiss, 2015).

It is understood that established networks that promote the emergence of more or less structured IC have a preponderant role, but always with the purpose of promoting learning, knowledge ant its dissemination, and the connection between people. IC guarantee the sense of belonging and concrete and achievable action, through the pursuit of clear goals, stable and permanent in time. To this end, it is desirable that they make use of the existing ICT, which can be important aids to the achievement of all the above conditions, and also to help people who are geographically distant feeling that belong to the IC, and are not inhibited of collaborating, participating and communicating.

CONCLUSION

As said in the beginning, this article intended to:

1. To reflect on the creation of IC in the Portuguese context, but with a proposal of replication in countries with similar characteristics;

2. To reflect on knowledge creation in the IC, analyzing the cycle, which roles are assumed by the members and what manifestations are perceived throughout this knowledge creation;
3. To evaluate the knowledge management in the IC, if it is and how it is carried out and suggest knowledge management frameworks;
4. To reflect on the knowledge dissemination, to foster the internal and external sharing practices of the crested knowledge in an IC through the suggestion of a specific framework for this purpose, using existing technological tools.

Those objectives intended to produce knowledge on how ICs can be an important tool for the development of more sustainable, efficient and effective Social Entrepreneurship initiatives. As a consequence of this and of knowledge sharing, networks and Smart Territories will arise.

Therefore, there are some important final considerations to present at this stage:

- ICs are spaces of learning and knowledge sharing;
- IC empower people to develop more efficient, effective and impactful initiatives;
- Social Entrepreneurship has the potential to create Smart Territories and improve its inhabitants quality of life;
- ICTs are important tools that, when combined, promote the three previous conclusions;
- ICTs contribute to the development of ICs, since it allows them to be spaces of communication, share and learning in a broader sense of time and space (Galbraith, B., Cleland, B., Martin, S., Wallace, J., Mulvenna, M., & McAdam, R., 2013).

There are several transformations that have taken place over the years in society. Two of them have been discussed in the chapter, intersecting each other by the potential they bring to each other: the importance attributed to the way of solving social problems, through Social Innovation and Entrepreneurship and the integration of communication technologies in labor processes.

Joining Social Innovation and Entrepreneurship (SIE) and communication technologies we have all the potential brought to the constitution of IC, with new forms of communication between people who are distant, efficiency in productive processes of social problems solving and, consequently, territorial development. These are the so-called IC.

The great motivation to belong to an IC is to learn. Learning is the engine of the constitution of an IC. But this is also a negative aspect, because being IES-SBS the bridge between the moments that made the entrepreneurs know each other and the constitution of an IC, there is a certain dependence on the search for knowledge and learning. IES-SBS, as being the promoter of the IC, is frequently called to intervene in several training moments, what was intended to be avoided.

ICs are one of the best ways to learn and disseminate knowledge, especially when taking into account its implementation the communication processes, which should be open, flexible and efficient, so that they can also promote ways of working with these three characteristics.

Furthermore, it is understood that ICs, being spaces that reflect and act on the territory through social entrepreneurs, have a preponderant role in the transformation of territories into Smart Territories.

IC promote, as mentioned, reflection and action in very specific aspects, social and / or environmental problems, meaning that they are a point of contact between several central areas: economy; mobility; environment; people; living; governance.

IC mobilize economic agents to solve social problems related to mobility, environment, life, people, acting directly and indirectly on the governance model of all spaces, organizations and entities.

ACKNOWLEDGMENT

This research was supported by the Fundação para a Ciência e Tecnologia [grant number SFRH/BPD/112579/2015].

REFERENCES

Bourdieu, P. (1979). *A distinção: uma crítica social da faculdade do juízo. História e Sociedade* (Vol. 2). Lisboa: Edições 70.

Bradbury, S., & Middlemiss, L. (2015). The role of learning in sustainable communities of practice. *Local Environment, 20*(7), 796–810. doi:10.1080/13549839.2013.872091

Callon, M. (1986). Some elements of a sociology of translation: domestication of the scallops and the fishermen of St Brieuc Bay. In *Power, action and belief: a new sociology of knowledge?* (pp. 196–223). London: Routledge.

Cole, M. (2003). *Cultural psychology: a once and future discipline (6th ed.).* Cambridge, MA: Harvard University Press.

Crumlish, C., & Malone, E. (2009). *Designing Social Interfaces.* O'Reilly Media.

de Almeida, P. P. (2012). *Variações Sobre o Trabalho Moderno. Coleção Questões de Partida.* Lisboa: Editora Mundos Sociais.

Dees, J. G. (1998). The Meaning of 'Social Entrepreneurship'. *Innovation*, 1–5.

Downes, S. (2012). *Connectivism and Connective Knowledge. Essays on meaning and learning networks.* National Research Council Canada.

Drucker, P. (1985). *Innovation and entrepreneurship: practice and principles.* New York: Harper & Row.

Elkjaer, B. (1999). In Search of a Social Learning Theory. In M. Easterby-Smith, J. Burgoyne, & L. Araujo (Eds.), *Organizational learning and the learning organization* (pp. 75–91). London: Sage. Retrieved from http://citeseerx.ist.psu.edu/viewdoc/download?doi=10.1.1.474.1667&rep=rep1&type=pdf

Fernandes, S., Mozzicafreddo, J., & Cardoso, G. (2010). *Contributo da Web 2.0 para a inovação nos processos de trabalho nas organizações públicas - Ambiente de trabalho 2.0. Departamento de Ciência Política e Políticas Públicas.* Lisboa: Instituto Universitário de Lisboa.

Galbraith, B., Cleland, B., Martin, S., Wallace, J., Mulvenna, M., & McAdam, R. (2013). Engaging user communities with eParticipation technology: Findings from a European project. *Technology Analysis and Strategic Management*, *25*(3), 281–294. doi:10.1080/09537325.2013.764986

Gilchrist, A. (2009). *The well-connected community. A networking approach to community development.* Bristol, UK: The Policy Press. doi:10.1332/policypress/9781847420565.001.0001

Latour, B. (2005). *Reassembling the Social – An Introduction to Actor-Network-Theory*. Oxford, UK: Oxford University Press.

Latour, B. (2010). Networks, Societies, Spheres: Reflections of an Actor-network Theorist. In *International Seminar on Network Theory: Network Multidimensionality in the Digital Age* (pp. 1–18). Los Angeles, CA: Annenberg School for Communication and Journalism.

Law, K. S., Wong, C.-S., & Mobley, W. H. (1998). Toward a Taxonomy of Multidimensional Constructs. *Academy of Management Review*, *23*(4), 741–755.

Mair, J., & Martí, I. (2004). *Social Entrepreneurship Research: a Source of Explanation, Prediction, and Delight (No. 546)*. Navarra.

Martin, R. L., & Osberg, S. (2007). Social Entrepreneurship: The Case for Definition. *Stanford Social Innovation Review*, 28–39. Retrieved from https://www.law.berkeley.edu/php-programs/courses/fileDL.php?fID=7288

Moreira, J. A., Costa, P. M., & Vieira, C. P. (2016). Navegar na web: as redes sociais como espaços de comunicação, partilha de conhecimento e de promoção de competências de aprendizagem. In P. Dias, D. Moreira, & A. Quintas-Mendes (Eds.), *Práticas e Cenários de Inovação em Educação Online* (pp. 99–126). Lisbon: Universidade Aberta.

Mort, G. S., Weerawardena, J., & Carnegie, K. (2003). Social entrepreneurship: Towards conceptualization. *International Journal of Nonprofit and Voluntary Sector Marketing*, *8*(1), 76–88. doi:10.1002/nvsm.202

Mott, J. (2010). Envisioning the Post-LMS Era: The Open Learning Network. *EDUCAUSE Quarterly*, *33*(1), 1–8. Retrieved from http://er.educause.edu/articles/2010/3/envisioning-the-postlms-era-the-open-learning-network

Mulgan, G. (2006). The Process of Social Innovation. *Innovations: Technology, Governance, Globalization*, *1*(2), 145–162. doi:10.1162/itgg.2006.1.2.145

Mulgan, G., Tucker, S., Ali, R., & Sanders, B. (2007). Social Innovation: what is it, why it matters and how can be accelerated. London: Academic Press.

Phillips, W., Lee, H., Ghobadian, A., O'Regan, N., & James, P. (2015). Social Innovation and Social Entrepreneurship: A Systematic Review. *Group & Organization Management*, *40*(3), 428–461. doi:10.1177/1059601114560063

Phills, J. A., Deiglmeier, K., & Miller, D. T. (2008). Social Innovation. *Stanford Social Innovation Review*, 34–43.

Putz, P., & Arnold, P. (2001). Communities of Practice: Guidelines for the design of online seminars in higher education. *Education Communication and Information*, *1*(2), 181–195. doi:10.1080/14636310120091922

Rajagopal, K., Brinke, D. J., Van Bruggen, J., & Sloep, P. B. (2012). Understanding personal learning networks: Their structure, content and the networking skills needed to optimally use them. *First Monday*, *17*(1). doi:10.5210/fm.v17i1.3559

Sacchetti, S., & Campbell, C. (2014). Creating Space for Communities: Social Enterprise and the Bright Side of Social Capital. *Journal of Entrepreneurial and Organizational Diversity*, 32–48.

Santos, F. M. (2012). A Positive Theory of Social Entrepreneurship. *Journal of Business Ethics*, *111*(3), 335–351. doi:10.100710551-012-1413-4

Say, J.-B. (1841). *Traité D'Économie Politique ou Simple exposition de la manière dont se forment, se distribuent et se consomment les richesses*. Paris: Institut Coppet.

Schaffers, H., Brodt, T., Pallot, M., Prinz, W., & Instituut, T. (2006). *The Future Workspace. Perspectives on Mobile and Collaborative Working*. Holanda: MOSAIC.

Schumpeter, J. A. (1949). *Theory of Economic Development*. Cambridge, MA: Harvard University Press.

Stevenson, H. H., & Sahlman, W. A. (1991). *Introduction to the Entrepreneurial Venture*. Boston, MA: Harvard Business School Press.

Toivonen, T. (2013). *The Emergence of the Social Innovation Community: Towards Collaborative Changemaking?* Retrieved from https://ssrn.com/abstract=2369540

Toivonen, T. (2016). What is the Social Innovation Community? Conceptualizing an Emergent Collaborative Organization. *Journal of Social Entrepreneurship*, *7*(1), 49–73. doi:10.1080/19420676.2014.997779

Vygotski, L. (2007). *Pensamento e Linguagem*. Lisboa: Relógio d'Água.

Wenger-Trayner, E., & Wenger-Trayner, B. (2015). *Communities of practice a brief introduction*. Retrieved from http://wenger-trayner.com/wp-content/uploads/2015/04/07-Brief-introduction-to-communities-of-practice.pdf

KEY TERMS AND DEFINITIONS

Cooperation: The process through which people are open and put in practice ways of sharing data, information, and knowledge. This can include processes, privileged information regarding a territory, a person or groups of people. The goal is to share and work together, mostly to achieve a common goal.

Impact Communities (IC): Spontaneous groups of people, and what makes them arise is the sharing of common goals, be it the answer to a concrete problem, the finding of solutions, the sharing of experiences, the contribution to the improvement of a territory, the search for personal enrichment, or learning sharing, among many other factors, but always with others in the constructive sense.

Information and Communication Technologies: Information is acquired through the processing of previously created data or the joining together of several different data that, in turn, after the treatment of information, become knowledge. While communication has its essence in communication and not in the content. Technology is what mediates the transmission of information and communication between an artifact and the user.

Information Sharing Practices: Similar to the previous one, however, this practice does not include the necessity of working together. This is understood as a way of developing a framework that allows actors to access information in a more efficient way.

Knowledge: Exists when an amount of data is transformed (after its analysis) into information and this information is again transformed and then related to other information(s) to provide knowledge. The transformation and relation of groups of information provides knowledge. It is the sharing process that provides the knowledge existence.

Social Entrepreneurship: The path a person follows to change their society or community, increasing the positive impact of his/her actions by solving a societal problem. It is important that the initiative has a concrete and sustainable business model be as much extended in time as possible (considering the possibility of replication), but also seeking its own extinction (it means the problem is solved). Furthermore, it should enable its target population to continue that positive path (and this includes being consulted, being part of the solution, and aim to end the problem they are facing) in an innovative way (different from the main alternative solution).

Social Innovation: The process of being constantly looking for new processes, products, and ways of doing. It is different from the previous concept because it is more dynamic and does not consider the need to make money that guarantees the idea sustainability.

ENDNOTES

1 http://www.gemconsortium.org/

2 http://www.cases.pt/

3 IES-SBS stands for Social Entrepreneurship Institute and Social Business School. It is a Portuguese non-profit association, with the mission to inspire and empower for a better world through Social Entrepreneurship. It offers training courses according to the projects' life cycle and knowledge in SE.

Chapter 3
The Importance of Knowledge Creation and Knowledge Sharing

Kijpokin Kasemsap
Suan Sunandha Rajabhat University, Thailand

ABSTRACT

This chapter explains the overview of knowledge creation; the applications of knowledge creation; the overview of knowledge sharing; knowledge sharing and social media; and the advanced issues of knowledge sharing. Knowledge creation and knowledge sharing are the essential components of knowledge management (KM) for achieving sustainable competitive advantage. With the support of advanced technologies, knowledge creation and knowledge sharing can be productively utilized in various organizations. When knowledge is created and shared, executives and management must distribute that knowledge to their employees toward organizational success in a timely and effective manner. To gain the effective organizational learning, creating and sharing knowledge should be added in the organizational policy, and should be executed through workplace communication among organizational employees.

INTRODUCTION

Regarding knowledge creation, knowledge can be established through positive interactions between explicit and tacit knowledge (Kasemsap, 2017a). Tacit knowledge is the core value element for enterprises to obtain the competitive advantages in the knowledge economy era (Jin-Feng, Ming-Yan, Li-Jie, & Jun-Ju, 2017). Engaging in knowledge creation enhances an individual's task knowledge through the practices of sharing and applying knowledge (Muhammed, Doll, & Deng, 2013). Knowledge management (KM) involves the strategies and processes designed to identify, organize, and share both intellectual assets (Kasemsap, 2017b) and organizational resources (Kasemsap, 2018a)

KM becomes popular among modern organizations toward enhancing competitive advantage, innovation, and effectiveness in the knowledge age (Kasemsap, 2018b), is related to the behavior of contemporary organizations (Huang, Davison, Liu, & Gu, 2008), and aims to create an effective environment that

DOI: 10.4018/978-1-5225-3725-0.ch003

facilitates knowledge execution in order to improve knowledge creation and organizational performance (Kaschig, Maier, & Sandow, 2016). Regarding KM, knowledge acquisition and knowledge transfer significantly affect knowledge creation (Seleim & Khalil, 2009). Since KM programs are put in place to monitor workers in the performance of their jobs; knowledge creation is an essential component in the achievement of goals and production of economic benefit of an organization (Jennex, 2013).

In order to improve the level of decision making and competitive advantage, organizations try to learn and develop new KM techniques that are suited in the global economy (Xia & Gupta, 2008). The concept of knowledge sharing is gaining popularity due to both increased awareness and new KM initiatives (Majid & Wey, 2009). Knowledge sharing is an interactive process where organizations must work on hard information resources (e.g., the basic cornerstones of any knowledge sharing) and must make constant investment into soft information resources, learning, intellectual capital, and process design in order to manage their information resources (Widén-Wulff & Suomi, 2007).

The literature considers knowledge sharing as an important factor for driving innovation as well as the organization's business performance, as both explicit and tacit knowledge sharing promotes a novel approach for business-knowledge process (Oyemomi, Liu, Neaga, & Alkhuraiji, 2016). Knowledge strategy affects multinational firms' knowledge sharing in host country networks (Bhatti, Larimo, & Carrasco, 2016). Thus, network interactions are a source of learning and knowledge acquisition for firms to fill their knowledge gaps in the knowledge era (Bhatti et al., 2016).

This chapter is based on a literature review of knowledge creation and knowledge sharing. The extensive literature of knowledge creation and knowledge sharing provides a contribution to practitioners and researchers by explaining their importance in the knowledge age.

BACKGROUND

Knowledge is created in social interactions among individuals and between individuals and their organizations so it is a dynamic human process (Somoza, Prado, & Rivera, 2011), and is considered ecological and organic in a way that it is flexible enough to rapidly affect many shifts in the business environment (Hori & Ohashi, 2007). The increased reliance on KM systems has made certain theorists to suggest that this will enable the development of knowledge creation, thus leading up to more effective knowledge creation by the easy codification and sharing of knowledge (Värlander, 2010).

A diverse set of resources (e.g., experts with different backgrounds and abilities) provides a broad knowledge base at the individual level, thus offering greater potential for knowledge creation (Fong, 2011). The theory of knowledge creation lists various issues (e.g., organization's intention, autonomy, creative chaos, redundancy, and requisite variety) as the enablers of knowledge creation. These issues are necessary when a manager supervises the knowledge-creating process on the level of organization (Matsudaira, 2013). Knowledge creation is not only an important step in most KM initiatives, but also has far reaching implications on the consequent steps in the KM process (Wickramasinghe, 2011).

Knowledge sharing as one of the most important parts of the KM system means that an individual, team, and the organization share the knowledge with other members in the form of activities through various ways (Navimipour & Charband, 2016). Small and Sage (2008) stated that a better understanding of knowledge sharing influences can result in the enhanced decision making of knowledge sharing interventions that can result in the improvements in knowledge sharing behavior (KSB). KSB has received increased attention in the context of business due to its important role in enhancing organizational competitive advantage (Li, Zhang, Zhang, & Zhou, 2017).

Contemporary literature usually views knowledge creation and knowledge sharing as either independent or positively related processes (Andreeva, 2009). There are many studies exploring the relationship between users' knowledge utilization and their innovation-related KSB in the context of online user community and the mediating effects of users' social capital and their perceived behavioral control on this relationship (Hau & Kang, 2016). Social capital can help increase the economic growth, organizational performance, and KM via social media platforms in the digital age (Kasemsap, 2017c). Social networks, high institutional trust, social trust, and a tendency to comply with regulations are the important social characteristics which facilitate the application of social capital initiatives in higher education institutions (Kasemsap, 2014).

ASPECTS OF KNOWLEDGE CREATION AND KNOWLEDGE SHARING

This section provides the overview of knowledge creation; the applications of knowledge creation; the overview of knowledge sharing; knowledge sharing and social media; the advanced issues of knowledge sharing.

Overview of Knowledge Creation

As organizations learn from newly created knowledge, not only do they improve existing processes, but dynamic capabilities also develop to integrate knowledge into creative ideas, novel solutions, and new products (Chung, Liang, Peng, & Chen, 2014). Knowledge-based creativity and competitiveness in the cultural industry is determined by the form of work organization and the knowledge enabling conditions (Maisiri, 2017) concerning knowledge enablers, creation processes, and performance (Nassim, 2011).

Knowledge and the flow of information become the essential organizational drivers of innovative ideas and value (Yusof & Shafiei, 2011). SECI (i.e., socialization, externalization, combination, and internalization) model explains the process of knowledge creation through conversion between tacit and explicit knowledge (Mäkäräinen-Suni & Hong, 2011). Being conscious of the cultural situatedness of the SECI model can lead to a more adequate utilization of the model for organizational knowledge creation (Haag, Duan, & Mathews, 2010).

Applications of Knowledge Creation

The real promise of organizational communication technologies may lie in their potential to facilitate participative discourse among knowledge workers at all levels in distributed locations and time zones (Lichtenstein, Parker, & Cybulski, 2005). Knowledge creation is a primary attraction of virtual community for many of its members (Weeks & Veltri, 2013). The emergence of virtual community has brought a profound impact on the human interaction and methods of information exchange in modern society (Kang & Rosen, 2006).

Knowledge creation positively affects Six Sigma project success, and Six Sigma project success leads to improved organizational performance (Sin, Zailani, Iranmanesh, & Ramayah, 2015). Six Sigma is the initiative focused on increasing profits by eliminating variability, defects, and wastes that weaken customer loyalty (Kasemsap, 2016). Knowledge creation plays an important role in the technology commercialization (TC) performance by partially mediating the relationship between cross-functional collaboration and TC performance (Lin, Wang, & Kung, 2015).

Overview of Knowledge Sharing

Knowledge sharing is one of the most important parts in KM, and is predicted by individual differences, such as gender, collectivist values, mastery goal orientations, and academic self-efficacy (Asterhan & Bouton, 2017). In order to promote KSB, people in business need to understand the mechanism that effectively drives to contribute their valuable knowledge with others (Razak, Pangil, Zin, Yunus, & Asnawi, 2016).

Sharing needed information with employees empowers them and that allows them to show voluntary behaviors in favor of their organizations (Akturan & Çekmecelioğlu, 2016). Individual preference for communication context (IPCC) significantly moderates the effect that knowledge sharing via interactive systems (KSIS) has on the outcome of knowledge sharing in modern organizations (Ou, Davison, & Wong, 2016). Adaptability, openness, and innovation orientation are related to the improvement of a buyer–supplier relationship, which can promote the sharing of tacit and explicit knowledge among business partners in supply chain (Yang, Yu, Liu, & Rui, 2016).

Knowledge sharing is crucial in the enhancement of knowledge resource to contribute toward the strategic development of the firm (Cunningham, Seaman, & McGuire, 2016). Motivation of knowledge sharing are business growth, partnership, and customer satisfaction (Sulistiyani & Harwiki, 2016). Individuals who are highly competent in their work abilities are less likely to share what they know when they perceive that there are few rewards or when knowledge sharing is not recognized by the organization (Yue Wah, Menkhoff, Loh, & Evers, 2007).

Cultural collectivism has a positive impact on attitudes toward effective knowledge sharing (Arpaci & Baloğlu, 2016). While intrinsic motivation, innovative values and job autonomy are the important drivers of knowledge sharing within the business units, extrinsic motivation, result-oriented values, and participation in corporate employee development are more important for knowledge sharing across business units (Dasí, Pedersen, Gooderham, Elter, & Hildrum, 2017).

Knowledge Sharing and Social Media

Social media platforms, through the Internet and other web-based technologies, have become a method of communication and knowledge sharing (Cevik et al., 2016). Social media platforms are only useful for knowledge sharing if some people contribute their knowledge that can leak from them, and other people significantly retrieve knowledge that is leaking (Leonardi, 2017). Knowledge self-efficacy, social interaction ties, and the norm of reciprocity positively affect the knowledge sharing activities in social media (Kwahk & Park, 2016).

Knowledge sharing can be enhanced if team members believe in their collaboration capability to effectively execute their teamwork (Omar, Dahalan, & Yusoff, 2016). Students frequently choose to engage in social media, specifically Facebook, to share knowledge within a specific learning context, which will be useful for educators (Moghavvemi, Sharabati, Paramanathan, & Rahin, 2017). Virtual communities consist of social media users whose relationships are strengthened through information and knowledge transfers toward knowledge sharing, as well as interactions among members (Chen &

Kuo, 2017). Knowledge sharing among virtual alliance members is intended to avoid repetitive investment in knowledge innovation and waste of knowledge resources, so as to get a higher starting point in knowledge innovation, thus improving the efficiency of organizational knowledge innovation (Li, Yang, & Zhang, 2016).

Advanced Issues of Knowledge Sharing

Information technology in today's world considers as the support net for sharing knowledge and information coming more important as well as the promoter of mutual cooperation when it comes to the development of additional education of adults (Jakobsone, Cakula, & Florea, 2017). In modern learning environments, working smarter means using technology platforms for developing trust and knowledge collaboration to deliver both business solutions and innovations (Olaisen & Revang, 2017). Knowledge sharing plays an important role in the domain of information security, due to its positive effect on employees' information security awareness (Safa & Solms, 2016).

Effectively coordinating the collective efforts of organization members and sharing knowledge among them are the interrelated enablers of organizational competitiveness (Wen & Qiang, 2016). Consumer voluntary sharing of electronic service knowledge in an online community is of great value to both business and consumers (Yuan, Lin, & Zhuo, 2016). Knowledge sharing in family firms is bidirectional leading to innovative outcomes and change (Woodfield & Husted, 2017).

FUTURE RESEARCH DIRECTIONS

The classification of the extensive literature in the domains of knowledge creation and knowledge sharing will provide the potential opportunities for future research. Knowledge discovery involves the process of finding the hidden knowledge in the large amounts of data with the support of advanced technologies (Kasemsap, 2017d). Organizational learning is the organization-wide continuous process, and can be applied concerning both internal and external changes in organizations (Kasemsap, 2017e). Investigating the correlations among knowledge creation, knowledge sharing, knowledge discovery, and organizational learning should be further studied.

CONCLUSION

This chapter indicated the overview of knowledge creation; the applications of knowledge creation; the overview of knowledge sharing; knowledge sharing and social media; and the advanced issues of knowledge sharing. Knowledge creation and knowledge sharing are the essential components of KM for achieving sustainable competitive advantage. With the support of advanced technologies, knowledge creation and knowledge sharing can be productively utilized in various organizations. When knowledge is created and shared, executives and management must distribute that knowledge to their employees toward organizational success in a timely and effective manner. To gain the effective organizational learning, creating and sharing knowledge should be added in the organizational policy, and should be executed through workplace communication among organizational employees.

REFERENCES

Akturan, A., & Çekmecelioğlu, H. G. (2016). The effects of knowledge sharing and organizational citizenship behaviors on creative behaviors in educational institutions. *Procedia: Social and Behavioral Sciences*, *235*, 342–350. doi:10.1016/j.sbspro.2016.11.042

Andreeva, T. (2009). Tensions between knowledge creation and knowledge sharing: Individual preferences of employees in knowledge-intensive organizations. In D. Jemielniak & J. Kociatkiewicz (Eds.), *Handbook of research on knowledge-intensive organizations* (pp. 459–477). Hershey, PA: IGI Global. doi:10.4018/978-1-60566-176-6.ch028

Arpaci, I., & Baloğlu, M. (2016). The impact of cultural collectivism on knowledge sharing among information technology majoring undergraduates. *Computers in Human Behavior*, *56*, 65–71. doi:10.1016/j.chb.2015.11.031

Asterhan, C. S. C., & Bouton, E. (2017). Teenage peer-to-peer knowledge sharing through social network sites in secondary schools. *Computers & Education*, *110*, 16–34. doi:10.1016/j.compedu.2017.03.007

Bhatti, W. A., Larimo, J., & Carrasco, I. (2016). Strategy's effect on knowledge sharing in host country networks. *Journal of Business Research*, *69*(11), 4769–4774. doi:10.1016/j.jbusres.2016.04.028

Cevik, A. A., Aksel, G., Akoglu, H., Eroglu, S. E., Dogan, N. O., & Altunci, Y. A. (2016). Social media, FOAMed in medical education and knowledge sharing: Local experiences with international perspective. *Turkish Journal of Emergency Medicine*, *16*(3), 112–117. doi:10.1016/j.tjem.2016.07.001 PMID:27857988

Chen, P. T., & Kuo, S. C. (2017). Innovation resistance and strategic implications of enterprise social media websites in Taiwan through knowledge sharing perspective. *Technological Forecasting and Social Change*, *118*, 55–69. doi:10.1016/j.techfore.2017.02.002

Chung, T. R., Liang, T., Peng, C., & Chen, D. (2014). How knowledge creation capabilities lead to competitive advantage. In M. Chilton & J. Bloodgood (Eds.), *Knowledge management and competitive advantage: Issues and potential solutions* (pp. 36–52). Hershey, PA: IGI Global. doi:10.4018/978-1-4666-4679-7.ch003

Cunningham, J., Seaman, C., & McGuire, D. (2016). Knowledge sharing in small family firms: A leadership perspective. *Journal of Family Business Strategy*, *7*(1), 34–46. doi:10.1016/j.jfbs.2015.10.002

Dasí, A., Pedersen, T., Gooderham, P. N., Elter, F., & Hildrum, J. (2017). The effect of organizational separation on individuals' knowledge sharing in MNCs. *Journal of World Business*, *52*(3), 431–446. doi:10.1016/j.jwb.2017.01.008

Fong, P. S. (2011). Multidisciplinary project teams. In D. Schwartz & D. Te'eni (Eds.), Encyclopedia of knowledge management (2nd ed.; pp. 1183–1191). Hershey, PA: IGI Global. doi:10.4018/978-1-59904-931-1.ch113

Haag, M., Duan, Y., & Mathews, B. (2010). The impact of culture on the application of the SECI model. In D. Harorimana (Ed.), *Cultural implications of knowledge sharing, management and transfer: Identifying competitive advantage* (pp. 26–47). Hershey, PA: IGI Global. doi:10.4018/978-1-60566-790-4.ch002

Hau, Y. S., & Kang, M. (2016). Extending lead user theory to users' innovation-related knowledge sharing in the online user community: The mediating roles of social capital and perceived behavioral control. *International Journal of Information Management*, *36*(4), 520–530. doi:10.1016/j.ijinfomgt.2016.02.008

Hori, M., & Ohashi, M. (2007). Knowledge creation and adaptive collaboration based on XML web services. In G. Putnik & M. Cruz-Cunha (Eds.), *Knowledge and technology management in virtual organizations: Issues, trends, opportunities and solutions* (pp. 292–305). Hershey, PA: IGI Global. doi:10.4018/978-1-59904-165-0.ch014

Huang, Q., Davison, R. M., Liu, H., & Gu, J. (2008). The impact of leadership style on knowledge-sharing intentions in China. *Journal of Global Information Management*, *16*(4), 67–91. doi:10.4018/jgim.2008100104

Jakobsone, A., Cakula, S., & Florea, M. (2017). Modelling of knowledge sharing for the provision of sustainable cooperation between adult educational institutions and enterprises. *Procedia Computer Science*, *104*, 160–165. doi:10.1016/j.procs.2017.01.095

Jennex, M. E. (2013). *Dynamic models for knowledge-driven organizations*. Hershey, PA: IGI Global. doi:10.4018/978-1-4666-2485-6

Jin-Feng, W., Ming-Yan, C., Li-Jie, F., & Jun-Ju, Y. (2017). The construction of enterprise tacit knowledge sharing stimulation system oriented to employee individual. *Procedia Engineering*, *174*, 289–300. doi:10.1016/j.proeng.2017.01.139

Kang, K. W., & Rosen, D. E. (2006). Knowledge creation in online communities. In M. Khosrow-Pour (Ed.), *Encyclopedia of e-commerce, e-government, and mobile commerce* (pp. 691–697). Hershey, PA: IGI Global. doi:10.4018/978-1-59140-799-7.ch111

Kaschig, A., Maier, R., & Sandow, A. (2016). The effects of collecting and connecting activities on knowledge creation in organizations. *The Journal of Strategic Information Systems*, *25*(4), 243–258. doi:10.1016/j.jsis.2016.08.002

Kasemsap, K. (2014). The role of social capital in higher education institutions. In N. Baporikar (Ed.), *Handbook of research on higher education in the MENA region: Policy and practice* (pp. 119–147). Hershey, PA: IGI Global. doi:10.4018/978-1-4666-6198-1.ch007

Kasemsap, K. (2016). Applying Lean Production and Six Sigma in global operations. In U. Akkucuk (Ed.), *Handbook of research on waste management techniques for sustainability* (pp. 44–74). Hershey, PA: IGI Global. doi:10.4018/978-1-4666-9723-2.ch003

Kasemsap, K. (2017a). Investigating the roles of neuroscience and knowledge management in higher education. In S. Mukerji & P. Tripathi (Eds.), *Handbook of research on administration, policy, and leadership in higher education* (pp. 112–140). Hershey, PA: IGI Global. doi:10.4018/978-1-5225-0672-0.ch006

Kasemsap, K. (2017b). Mastering knowledge management in academic libraries. In B. Gunjal (Ed.), *Managing knowledge and scholarly assets in academic libraries* (pp. 27–55). Hershey, PA: IGI Global. doi:10.4018/978-1-5225-1741-2.ch002

Kasemsap, K. (2017c). The fundamentals of social capital. In G. Koç, M. Claes, & B. Christiansen (Eds.), *Cultural influences on architecture* (pp. 259–292). Hershey, PA: IGI Global. doi:10.4018/978-1-5225-1744-3.ch010

Kasemsap, K. (2017d). Knowledge discovery and data visualization: Theories and perspectives. *International Journal of Organizational and Collective Intelligence*, *7*(3), 56–69. doi:10.4018/IJOCI.2017070105

Kasemsap, K. (2017e). Organizational learning: Advanced issues and trends. In A. Bencsik (Ed.), *Knowledge management initiatives and strategies in small and medium enterprises* (pp. 42–66). Hershey, PA: IGI Global. doi:10.4018/978-1-5225-1642-2.ch003

Kasemsap, K. (2018a). Knowledge management: Applications and implications. In A. Gyamfi & I. Williams (Eds.), *Evaluating media richness in organizational learning* (pp. 232–261). Hershey, PA: IGI Global. doi:10.4018/978-1-5225-2956-9.ch012

Kasemsap, K. (2018b). Promoting strategic human resource management, organizational learning, and knowledge management in modern organizations. In M. Khosrow-Pour (Ed.), *Encyclopedia of information science and technology* (4th ed.; pp. 4347–4357). Hershey, PA: IGI Global. doi:10.4018/978-1-5225-2255-3.ch377

Kwahk, K. Y., & Park, D. H. (2016). The effects of network sharing on knowledge-sharing activities and job performance in enterprise social media environments. *Computers in Human Behavior*, *55*, 826–839. doi:10.1016/j.chb.2015.09.044

Leonardi, P. M. (2017). The social media revolution: Sharing and learning in the age of leaky knowledge. *Information and Organization*, *27*(1), 47–59. doi:10.1016/j.infoandorg.2017.01.004

Li, X., Zhang, J., Zhang, S., & Zhou, M. (2017). A multilevel analysis of the role of interactional justice in promoting knowledge-sharing behavior: The mediated role of organizational commitment. *Industrial Marketing Management*, *62*, 226–233. doi:10.1016/j.indmarman.2016.09.006

Li, Z., Yang, F., & Zhang, D. (2016). The virtual alliance knowledge sharing model and selection strategy. *Procedia Computer Science*, *91*, 276–283. doi:10.1016/j.procs.2016.07.075

Lichtenstein, S., Parker, C. M., & Cybulski, M. (2005). Email and knowledge creation: Supporting inquiring systems. In J. Courtney, J. Haynes, & D. Paradice (Eds.), *Inquiring organizations: Moving from knowledge management to wisdom* (pp. 89–108). Hershey, PA: IGI Global. doi:10.4018/978-1-59140-309-8.ch005

Lin, Y., Wang, Y., & Kung, L. A. (2015). Influences of cross-functional collaboration and knowledge creation on technology commercialization: Evidence from high-tech industries. *Industrial Marketing Management*, *49*, 128–138. doi:10.1016/j.indmarman.2015.04.002

Maisiri, E. (2017). Utilization of indigenous knowledge for competitiveness among curio makers of Matobo National Park, Zimbabwe. In P. Ngulube (Ed.), *Handbook of research on social, cultural, and educational considerations of indigenous knowledge in developing countries* (pp. 202–225). Hershey, PA: IGI Global. doi:10.4018/978-1-5225-0838-0.ch011

Majid, S., & Wey, S. M. (2009). Perceptions and knowledge sharing practices of graduate students in Singapore. *International Journal of Knowledge Management*, *5*(2), 21–32. doi:10.4018/jkm.2009040102

Mäkäräinen-Suni, I., & Hong, J. (2011). Ba and communities of practice in research and strategic communities as a way forward. In O. Hernáez & E. Bueno Campos (Eds.), *Handbook of research on communities of practice for organizational management and networking: Methodologies for competitive advantage* (pp. 46–69). Hershey, PA: IGI Global. doi:10.4018/978-1-60566-802-4.ch004

Matsudaira, Y. (2013). Ethos as enablers of organisational knowledge creation. In I. Management Association (Ed.), Industrial engineering: Concepts, methodologies, tools, and applications (pp. 1749–1765). Hershey, PA: IGI Global. doi:10.4018/978-1-4666-1945-6.ch093

Moghavvemi, S., Sharabati, M., Paramanathan, T., & Rahin, N. M. (2017). The impact of perceived enjoyment, perceived reciprocal benefits and knowledge power on students' knowledge sharing through Facebook. *International Journal of Management Education*, *15*(1), 1–12. doi:10.1016/j.ijme.2016.11.002

Muhammed, S., Doll, W. J., & Deng, X. (2013). Impact of knowledge management practices on task knowledge: An individual level study. In M. Jennex (Ed.), *Dynamic models for knowledge-driven organizations* (pp. 282–301). Hershey, PA: IGI Global. doi:10.4018/978-1-4666-2485-6.ch017

Nassim, B. (2011). Investigating the impact of knowledge management factors on new product development performance. In M. Jennex (Ed.), *Global aspects and cultural perspectives on knowledge management: Emerging dimensions* (pp. 210–226). Hershey, PA: IGI Global. doi:10.4018/978-1-60960-555-1.ch014

Navimipour, N. J., & Charband, Y. (2016). Knowledge sharing mechanisms and techniques in project teams: Literature review, classification, and current trends. *Computers in Human Behavior*, *62*, 730–742. doi:10.1016/j.chb.2016.05.003

Olaisen, J., & Revang, O. (2017). Working smarter and greener: Collaborative knowledge sharing in virtual global project teams. *International Journal of Information Management*, *37*(1), 1441–1448. doi:10.1016/j.ijinfomgt.2016.10.002

Omar, M. K., Dahalan, N. A., & Yusoff, Y. H. M. (2016). Social media usage, perceived team-efficacy and knowledge sharing behaviour among employees of an oil and gas organisation in Malaysia. *Procedia Economics and Finance*, *37*, 309–316. doi:10.1016/S2212-5671(16)30130-7

Ou, C. X. J., Davison, R. M., & Wong, L. H. M. (2016). Using interactive systems for knowledge sharing: The impact of individual contextual preferences in China. *Information & Management*, *53*(2), 145–156. doi:10.1016/j.im.2015.09.007

Oyemomi, O., Liu, S., Neaga, I., & Alkhuraiji, A. (2016). How knowledge sharing and business process contribute to organizational performance: Using the fsQCA approach. *Journal of Business Research*, *69*(11), 5222–5227. doi:10.1016/j.jbusres.2016.04.116

Razak, N. A., Pangil, F., Zin, M. L. M., Yunus, N. A. M., & Asnawi, N. H. (2016). Theories of knowledge sharing behavior in business strategy. *Procedia Economics and Finance*, *37*, 545–553. doi:10.1016/S2212-5671(16)30163-0

Safa, N. S., & Solms, R. V. (2016). An information security knowledge sharing model in organizations. *Computers in Human Behavior*, *57*, 442–451. doi:10.1016/j.chb.2015.12.037

Seleim, A., & Khalil, O. (2009). Knowledge management and organizational performance in the Egyptian software firms. In P. Tiako (Ed.), *Software applications: Concepts, methodologies, tools, and applications* (pp. 2614–2644). Hershey, PA: IGI Global. doi:10.4018/978-1-60566-060-8.ch153

Sin, A. B., Zailani, S., Iranmanesh, M., & Ramayah, T. (2015). Structural equation modelling on knowledge creation in Six Sigma DMAIC project and its impact on organizational performance. *International Journal of Production Economics*, *168*, 105–117. doi:10.1016/j.ijpe.2015.06.007

Small, C. T., & Sage, A. P. (2008). A complex adaptive systems-based enterprise knowledge sharing model. *International Journal of Information Technologies and Systems Approach*, *1*(2), 38–56. doi:10.4018/jitsa.2008070103

Somoza, M. L., Prado, J. A., & Rivera, C. M. (2011). Knowledge creation, Ba and CoP: The experience at IADE-UAM. In O. Hernáez & E. Bueno Campos (Eds.), *Handbook of research on communities of practice for organizational management and networking: Methodologies for competitive advantage* (pp. 145–161). Hershey, PA: IGI Global. doi:10.4018/978-1-60566-802-4.ch009

Sulistiyani, R., & Harwiki, W. (2016). How SMEs build innovation capability based on knowledge sharing behavior? Phenomenological approach. *Procedia: Social and Behavioral Sciences*, *219*, 741–747. doi:10.1016/j.sbspro.2016.05.070

Värlander, S. (2010). The role of situated embodied interaction in the banking customer knowledge creation process. In M. Jennex (Ed.), *Ubiquitous developments in knowledge management: Integrations and trends* (pp. 236–251). Hershey, PA: IGI Global. doi:10.4018/978-1-60566-954-0.ch015

Weeks, M. R., & Veltri, N. F. (2013). Virtual communities as narrative networks: Developing a model of knowledge creation for crowdsourced environments. *International Journal of Knowledge Management*, *9*(1), 21–41. doi:10.4018/jkm.2013010102

Wen, Q., & Qiang, M. (2016). Coordination and knowledge sharing in construction project-based organization: A longitudinal structural equation model analysis. *Automation in Construction*, *72*, 309–320. doi:10.1016/j.autcon.2016.06.002

Wickramasinghe, N. (2011). Knowledge creation. In D. Schwartz & D. Te'eni (Eds.), Encyclopedia of knowledge management (2nd ed.; pp. 527–538). Hershey, PA: IGI Global. doi:10.4018/978-1-59904-931-1.ch051

Widén-Wulff, G., & Suomi, R. (2007). Utilization of information resources for business success: The knowledge sharing model. *Information Resources Management Journal*, *20*(1), 46–67. doi:10.4018/irmj.2007010104

Woodfield, P., & Husted, K. (2017). Intergenerational knowledge sharing in family firms: Case-based evidence from the New Zealand wine industry. *Journal of Family Business Strategy*, *8*(1), 57–69. doi:10.1016/j.jfbs.2017.01.001

Xia, H., & Gupta, A. (2008). Common knowledge sharing model of 24-hour knowledge factory of grid computing based on case based reasoning. *International Journal of Knowledge Management*, *4*(3), 1–18. doi:10.4018/jkm.2008070101

Yang, J., Yu, G., Liu, M., & Rui, M. (2016). Improving learning alliance performance for manufacturers: Does knowledge sharing matter? *International Journal of Production Economics*, *171*, 301–308. doi:10.1016/j.ijpe.2015.09.022

Yuan, D., Lin, Z., & Zhuo, R. (2016). What drives consumer knowledge sharing in online travel communities?: Personal attributes or e-service factors? *Computers in Human Behavior*, *63*, 68–74. doi:10.1016/j.chb.2016.05.019

Yue Wah, C., Menkhoff, T., Loh, B., & Evers, H. (2007). Social capital and knowledge sharing in knowledge-based organizations: An empirical study. *International Journal of Knowledge Management*, *3*(1), 29–48. doi:10.4018/jkm.2007010103

Yusof, N., & Shafiei, M. W. (2011). Knowledge creation and sharing in the Malaysian housebuilding industry: Improving the housing delivery system. In M. Al-Shammari (Ed.), *Knowledge management in emerging economies: Social, organizational and cultural implementation* (pp. 141–156). Hershey, PA: IGI Global. doi:10.4018/978-1-61692-886-5.ch008

ADDITIONAL READING

Ambos, T. C., Ambos, B., Eich, K. J., & Puck, J. (2016). Imbalance and isolation: How team configurations affect global knowledge sharing. *Journal of International Management*, *22*(4), 316–332. doi:10.1016/j.intman.2016.03.005

Bouncken, R. B., Pesch, R., & Reuschl, A. (2016). Copoiesis: Mutual knowledge creation in alliances. *Journal of Innovation & Knowledge*, *1*(1), 44–50. doi:10.1016/j.jik.2016.01.008

Burton, B. G., & Martin, B. (2017). Knowledge creation and student engagement within 3D virtual worlds. *International Journal of Virtual and Augmented Reality*, *1*(1), 43–59. doi:10.4018/IJVAR.2017010104

Chumg, H. F., Seaton, J., Cooke, L., & Ding, W. Y. (2016). Factors affecting employees' knowledge-sharing behaviour in the virtual organisation from the perspectives of well-being and organisational behaviour. *Computers in Human Behavior*, *64*, 432–448. doi:10.1016/j.chb.2016.07.011

Dufva, M., & Ahlqvist, T. (2015). Knowledge creation dynamics in foresight: A knowledge typology and exploratory method to analyse foresight workshops. *Technological Forecasting and Social Change*, *94*, 251–268. doi:10.1016/j.techfore.2014.10.007

Hautala, J. (2015). Interaction in the artistic knowledge creation process: The case of artists in Finnish Lapland. *Geoforum*, *65*, 351–362. doi:10.1016/j.geoforum.2015.01.002

Hejduk, I., & Tomczyk, P. (2015). Young workers' occupational safety knowledge creation and habits. *Procedia Manufacturing*, *3*, 395–401. doi:10.1016/j.promfg.2015.07.184

Hernández-González, Y., & Corral, S. (2017). An extended peer communities' knowledge sharing approach for environmental governance. *Land Use Policy*, *63*, 140–148. doi:10.1016/j.landusepol.2016.12.023

Hussain, K., Konar, R., & Ali, F. (2016). Measuring service innovation performance through team culture and knowledge sharing behaviour in hotel services: A PLS approach. *Procedia: Social and Behavioral Sciences*, *224*, 35–43. doi:10.1016/j.sbspro.2016.05.397

Kang, H. D., & Lee, J. J. (2016). Scientific celebrity, competition, and knowledge creation: The case of stem cell research in South Korea. *Journal of Engineering and Technology Management*, *39*, 26–44. doi:10.1016/j.jengtecman.2016.01.001

Kao, S. C., & Wu, C. H. (2016). The role of creation mode and social networking mode in knowledge creation performance: Mediation effect of creation process. *Information & Management*, *53*(6), 803–816. doi:10.1016/j.im.2016.03.002

Kazadi, K., Lievens, A., & Mahr, D. (2016). Stakeholder co-creation during the innovation process: Identifying capabilities for knowledge creation among multiple stakeholders. *Journal of Business Research*, *69*(2), 525–540. doi:10.1016/j.jbusres.2015.05.009

Lederer, J., Ogwang, F., & Karungi, J. (2017). Knowledge identification and creation among local stakeholders in CDM waste composting projects: A case study from Uganda. *Resources, Conservation and Recycling*, *122*, 339–352. doi:10.1016/j.resconrec.2017.03.005

Lee, J. C., Shiue, Y. C., & Chen, C. Y. (2016). Examining the impacts of organizational culture and top management support of knowledge sharing on the success of software process improvement. *Computers in Human Behavior*, *54*, 462–474. doi:10.1016/j.chb.2015.08.030

Loebbecke, C., van Fenema, P. C., & Powell, P. (2016). Managing inter-organizational knowledge sharing. *The Journal of Strategic Information Systems*, *25*(1), 4–14. doi:10.1016/j.jsis.2015.12.002

Marsina, S., Hamranova, A., Okruhlica, F., & Bolek, V. (2015). Knowledge creation and learning within the building project orientation of organizations. *Procedia Manufacturing*, *3*, 723–730. doi:10.1016/j.promfg.2015.07.315

Martini, L. (2016). Knowledge sharing in a creative city. *Procedia Computer Science*, *99*, 79–90. doi:10.1016/j.procs.2016.09.102

Maruta, R. (2014). The creation and management of organizational knowledge. *Knowledge-Based Systems*, *67*, 26–34. doi:10.1016/j.knosys.2014.06.012

Othman, S. H., & Beydoun, G. (2016). A metamodel-based knowledge sharing system for disaster management. *Expert Systems with Applications*, *63*, 49–65. doi:10.1016/j.eswa.2016.06.018

Pee, L. G., & Lee, J. (2015). Intrinsically motivating employees' online knowledge sharing: Understanding the effects of job design. *International Journal of Information Management*, *35*(6), 679–690. doi:10.1016/j.ijinfomgt.2015.08.002

Rice, R. G., & Spence, P. R. (2016). Thor visits Lexington: Exploration of the knowledge-sharing gap and risk management learning in social media during multiple winter storms. *Computers in Human Behavior*, *65*, 612–618. doi:10.1016/j.chb.2016.05.088

Stephens, J. P., & Carmeli, A. (2016). The positive effect of expressing negative emotions on knowledge creation capability and performance of project teams. *International Journal of Project Management*, *34*(5), 862–873. doi:10.1016/j.ijproman.2016.03.003

Vick, T. E., Nagano, M. S., & Popadiuk, S. (2015). Information culture and its influences in knowledge creation: Evidence from university teams engaged in collaborative innovation projects. *International Journal of Information Management*, *35*(3), 292–298. doi:10.1016/j.ijinfomgt.2015.01.010

Wang, H., & Wang, S. (2016). Application of ontology modularization to human-web interface design for knowledge sharing. *Expert Systems with Applications*, *46*, 122–128. doi:10.1016/j.eswa.2015.10.027

Wang, J. (2016). Knowledge creation in collaboration networks: Effects of tie configuration. *Research Policy*, *45*(1), 68–80. doi:10.1016/j.respol.2015.09.003

Wang, Z., Sharma, P. N., & Cao, J. (2016). From knowledge sharing to firm performance: A predictive model comparison. *Journal of Business Research*, *69*(10), 4650–4658. doi:10.1016/j.jbusres.2016.03.055

Yan, Z., Wang, T., Chen, Y., & Zhang, H. (2016). Knowledge sharing in online health communities: A social exchange theory perspective. *Information & Management*, *53*(5), 643–653. doi:10.1016/j.im.2016.02.001

Yilmaz, R. (2016). Knowledge sharing behaviors in e-learning community: Exploring the role of academic self-efficacy and sense of community. *Computers in Human Behavior*, *63*, 373–382. doi:10.1016/j.chb.2016.05.055

Zahedi, M., Shahin, M., & Babar, M. A. (2016). A systematic review of knowledge sharing challenges and practices in global software development. *International Journal of Information Management*, *36*(6), 995–1019. doi:10.1016/j.ijinfomgt.2016.06.007

KEY TERMS AND DEFINITIONS

Innovation: The establishment of new matters and processes.

Knowledge: The information that can be gained through study and learning.

Knowledge Creation: The generation of new information through proactive interactions among organizational employees.

Knowledge Management: The sophisticated method that can enhance the creation and sharing of knowledge.

Knowledge Sharing: The procedure through which explicit or tacit knowledge can be shared among organizational employees.

Knowledge Sharing Behavior: The action that individuals aim to share their knowledge.

Social Media: The online communication tool that allows individuals to share and distribute information among users.

Technology: The advanced tool and system that can make users feel comfortable.

Chapter 4
Sharing Tacit Knowledge:
The Essence of Knowledge Management

Ayesha Khatun
Assam University, India

ABSTRACT

Twenty-first century markets are unstable: technologies rapidly proliferate, competitors multiply, products and services become obsolete almost overnight. It is knowledge that can help the organizations to remain competitive. But as knowledge is the source of competitive advantage for the organization, it is also the source of competitive advantage for individuals. People think that knowledge is power, so sharing the same may lead to losing the power. Moreover, the very nature of tacit knowledge poses many difficulties in sharing the same. But sharing tacit knowledge is a vital part of the knowledge management process because it is tacit knowledge that is inimitable and is unique for the firm and hence provides competitive advantage. Studies found that personal interaction and informal networks work as the most successful means of sharing tacit knowledge. This chapter discusses the concept of tacit knowledge and attempts to discuss and suggest some effective methods of sharing tacit knowledge in organizations.

INTRODUCTION

Knowledge Management (KM) is one of the most discussed topics of 21st century in the context of business excellence and sustainable competitive advantage. Knowledge Management is in high demand in service sectors like defense, education, consultancy firms, health service, IT etc. It is found that the world economy has had shifted from agrarian era to industrial to banking and finance to IT and now to knowledge. Multiple factors have led to this current "knowledge boom".

The increased focus on knowledge economy and knowledge society has definitely led to the emergence of Knowledge Management, irrespective of the nature of business operation. In fact, in knowledge economy, Knowledge Management is believed to be the path to sustainable competitive advantage (Dunford, 2000).

In a knowledge driven economy, organization's intangible assets are increasingly becoming a differentiating competitive factor, particularly in service industries. Indeed, intangible assets such as trade

DOI: 10.4018/978-1-5225-3725-0.ch004

marks and company's repuation and skills pertaining to employee's know-how and the corporate culture are both recognised as quintessence of competitive advantage.

Companies are spending huge amount of money on KM. For example Ernst & Young spends about 6% of its revenue on KM, McKinsey and Co. spends about 10% of its revenue on KM, Buckman Laboratories, a specialty chemicals firm spends around 2.5% of its revenues on KM and an author, Duane Sharp finds that where KM practices have been successful, the returns generated by these practices (ROI) have often exceeded 10 times the original investment (Sharp, 2003). Moreover, firm like Rank Xerox (the European arm of Xerox Corporation), has saved more than $1.5 billion over the past several years by identifying and replicating internal best practices.

Many world class corporations have adopted highly dedicated KM practices. To name a few Ernst & Young –Knowledge Process Landscape, Hewlett & Packard-Knowledge Links and KPMG Peat Marwick US has developed an intranet called Knowledge Web (K-Web) as the basis of their KM practices. Studies found that sharing knowledge is the crucial part of knowledge management and hence the success of knowledge management depends on effective sharing of knowledge. It is said that knowledge economy is the economy of sharing.

Let us systematically discuss about knowledge, tacit knowledge and how tacit knowledge could be shared and why the same is so important in the context of knowledge management.

Knowledge

There is no universal definition of knowledge. The question of what the conditions are, that must be met for something to qualify as "knowledge" is as old as the philosophy itself. Different authors have defined knowledge in different ways.

Philosopher like Plato defined knowledge as "Justified true belief" but this definition was strongly criticized by Edmund Gettier saying that the term belief is very much individualistic and there are many such examples where justified belief does not lead to knowledge.

According to Bertrand Russell, renowned philosopher "knowledge" is something to which there is no definite and unambiguous answer. It is a very vague concept for two reasons-first, because the meaning of a word is always more or less vague except in logic and pure mathematics; and second, because all that we count as knowledge is in a greater or less degree uncertainty and there is no way of deciding how much uncertainty makes a belief unworthy to be called "knowledge", e.g., how much loss of hair makes a man bald. He also opines that defining knowledge as a "true belief" is too wide and individualistic as it is based on one's own belief. The author also defines knowledge as a matter of degree. The highest degree is found in facts of perception, and in the cogency of very simple arguments. The next highest degree is in vivid memories (Russell, 2012). Again, Noam Chomsky defines knowledge as a manufactured consent. He says, knowledge is not constant rather it is manufactured by media for their own benefits.

Knowledge as defined by the Oxford Dictionary of English is, "Facts, information, and skills acquired through experience or education; the theoretical and practical understanding of a subject".

Knowledge is defined as what we know. It involves the mental processes of comprehension, understanding and learning that go on in the mind and only in the mind, and however much they involve interaction with the world outside the mind, and interaction with others much they can transfer the knowledge.

David Gurteen defines knowledge as knowledge is about know-how and know-why. He emphasized the know-how part because it allows us to be creative-to fall back on principles –to reinvent your know-how (Gurteen, 1999).

Wilson says whenever, we wish to express what we know, we can only do so by uttering messages of one kind or another –oral, written, graphic, gestural or even through body language. Such messages do not carry knowledge, they constitute information, which a knowing mind may assimilate, understand, comprehend and incorporate into its own knowledge structures. These structures are not identical as these are biographically determined. Therefore, the knowledge built from the messages can never be exactly the same as the knowledge base from which the messages were uttered (Wilson, 2002).

In another word, we can define knowledge as the ability to encode information and/or understand a message. It is the encoded information or a message understood.

Thus, knowledge refers to the ideas or understandings that an entity creates and/or possesses (Ram Shukla, 2012) through the mental process of thinking, reasoning, abstraction and comprehension that are used to take effective action to achieve the entity's goal. Unlike information, knowledge is deeply influenced by the beliefs and values of the entity.

However, as the focus of this paper is on tacit knowledge in the context of knowledge management in organizations we would look forward to some definitions of knowledge given in the context of management of organization. So, knowledge has been primarily defined with respect to its utilization within a given scheme, platform or functional framework.

Knowledge is acquired by learning and experience. It is created from thinking, reasoning and abstraction. It is stored within brain and shared mind servers. And it is shared through the internet, intranet, the ICT/communication/media etc. (Sidharta Chatterjee, 2014).

Knowledge could be described as seed knowledge. Nature of seed knowledge keeps varying depending on the context for its use and the context of management. The seed knowledge could be totally intangible without reference to any tangible object or could refer to some data or information about a tangible product or a service. Generally, Universities and other academic research institutes provide this seed knowledge (Mruthyunjaya, 2011).

Knowledge is directly defined as capital. It is said that there are two types of capital in an organization viz., social and human capital. Social capital refers to knowledge that is embedded within the organizational relationships and routines. Whereas, human capital includes individual tacit and explicit knowledge brought into the organization through its knowledge workers (Juani Swart, 2003).

T. H. Davenport (1998) a profound knowledge consultant and one of the most cited authors of knowledge management defines knowledge as "information combined with experience, context, interpretation, and reflection. It is a high value form of information that is ready to apply to decisions and actions". Again, Peter Senge defines knowledge as the ability to make effective decisions and take effective actions.

Davenport and Prusak (2000) define knowledge as, "knowledge is a fluid mix of framed experiences, values, contextual information, and expert insight that provides a framework for evaluating and incorporating new experiences and information. It originates and is applied in the mind of knower. In organizations, it often becomes embedded not only in documents or repositories but also in organizational routines, processes, practices and norms".

Spender in 1996, combined the tacit and explicit dimension of knowledge as discussed by Nonaka with individual and social knowledge by creating a matrix highlighting four types of organization's knowledge. They are-

1. Individual explicit knowledge; Spender calls this as conscious knowledge which is storable and retrievable from personal records and memory.

2. Individual tacit knowledge; this is called as automatic knowledge. This knowledge is based on people's theoretical and practical experience and learning. It resides in human brain and is difficult to express and document.
3. Social explicit knowledge; Spender terms this as objectified knowledge which embodies registered patents and designs or information stored on databases.
4. Social tacit knowledge; Spender calls this as collective knowledge, this represents all knowledge embedded in social and institutional practices, systems, workflows, and culture.

Tacit Knowledge

The term "tacit knowledge" is attributed to Michael Polanyi. He coined the term in his book "Personal Knowledge: Towards a Post Critical Philosophy" in 1958. Later on in his book "The Tacit Dimension" he asserted that "we can know more than we can tell". He for the first time distinguished knowledge between tacit and explicit. Polanyi also mentioned that all knowledge rooted to tacit knowledge.

In simple terms, knowledge which resides in human head is known as tacit knowledge. Tacit knowledge entails information that is difficult to express, formalize or share. It stands in contrast to explicit knowledge, which is conscious and can be put in words. Tacit knowledge is unconsciously acquired from the experiences one has while immersed in an environment. Tacit knowledge is "knowing how" and "knowing-why" while explicit knowledge is "knowing what".

It collects all those things that we know how to do but perhaps we do not know how to explain. According to Polanyi, tacit knowledge is knowledge that the actor knows he has but which he cannot describe in terms other than its own performance, e.g., the knowledge of driving.

Tacit knowledge is the personal and context specific knowledge of a person that resides in the human mind, behaviour and perception (Duffy, 2000). Tacit knowledge is higly personal, subjective, difficult to formalise, articulate and communicate fully, experienced based, contextualised, job specific, transferred through conversation or narrative, not captured by formal education or trainning and may even be sub-conscious but capable of becoming explicit though its not easy (Nonaka and Takeuchi, 1995 ; Hislop, 2013).

Tacit knowledge is special knowledge engrained in personal experience and concerning personal acceptance, views and standards(Brelade and Harman, 2000). In conventional observations of the role of knowledge in business organizations, tacit knowledge is sometimes observed as the actual key to getting things completed and producing fresh value (Ailar Rahimli, 2012).

People can never document the skill that they possess they can only document the outcome of the skill they possess. They cannot explain in document "why they do something the way they do". This could be learned only from personal interaction and observation.

The possessor of tacit knowledge himself/herself do not know that they possess the same and even when they come to know they do not know how to share the same because tacit knowledge is not separable from the performance. So unless and until a person observes closely and performs on his or her own can never gather tacit knowledge completely e.g., cooking, driving, the art of sculpture, carpenter etc. However, frequent personal interaction can help transferring the same to some extent.

Tacit knowledge is that knowledge which resides in human brain. It is the experience, intelligence and know-how skills of the people in the organization. Unlike explicit knowledge, tacit knowledge cannot be documented easily or expressed in explicit form and hence it's tough to share tacit knowledge with others. Tacit knowledge could be gathered from observation and experience.

Tacit knowledge constitutes the major part of the body of knowledge. Tacit knowledge is that knowledge which cannot be easily articulated and thus only exists in people's hands and minds and manifest itself through their actions(Stenmark, 2000).

Tacit knowledge develops when unconscious, inductive mental processes create a representation of the structure of the environment showing the relationship between important variables.

Tacit knowledge often allows us to perform at a higher level than that which our explicit knowledge does. There are four categories of tacit knowledge according to Lubit (2001), they are-

1. Hard to pin down skills-know how
2. Mental models; these show us how the world is constructed, which elements are central and how the parts are related.
3. Ways of approaching problems; this concerns how people approach problems. This underlies the decision trees people use.
4. Organizational routines; much of the tacit knowledge of a firm is stored in its routine. The term routine refers to regular and predictable behavior patterns. Routines include ways of producing things, ways of hiring and firing personnel, ways of handling inventory, decision making procedures, advertising policy, R & D procedures etc.

Apart from this, Nonaka and Tekuchi's (1995) model of knowledge conversion plays a vital role in the literature of knowledge management as well as knowledge transfer.

SECI process of Knowledge Creation (Figure 1).

Thus, it is socialization which leads to creation and sharing of tacit knowledge. In socialization we gather tacit knowledge and hold it back as tacit only where as in externalization tacit knowledge is converted to explicit form and in internalization explicit knowledge is converted to tacit. And last but of course, not the least, combination leads conversion of explicit knowledge to explicit knowledge again.

Organizational knowledge is divided into organizational static substance knowledge and organizational dynamic process knowledge. Static substance knowledge refers to explicit knowledge or the bodies of knowledge in terms of mission, vision, science, technology, management theory as well as

Figure 1. Knowledge conversion model borrowed from Nonaka & Takeuchi, 1995

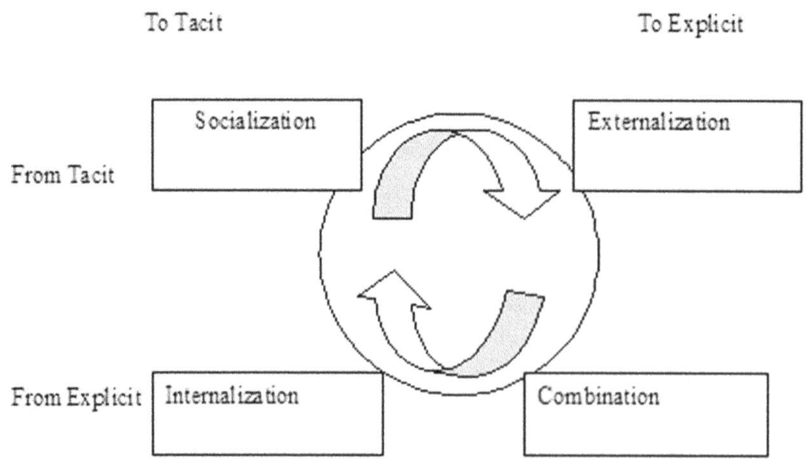

the information and Data upon which knowledge is based. Organizational dynamic process knowledge relates to human actions or the activities of organizational operations, called the organizational human activity system. Example of static substance knowledge and dynamic process knowledge is cookbook and cooking (Fei Gao, 2008).

Again knowledge is mainly divided into two categories, viz., tangible knowledge and intangible knowledge. Both the types are used in formulating organizational strategies. Tangible knowledge are those which are codified, documented and can be easily shared whereas intangible knowledge resides in human brain. It is the experience, intelligence and know-how skill of the people in the organization (Madan, 2010). This intangible knowledge is the tacit knowledge.

Knowledge Management

Knowledge Management, as discussed and defined by the world class authors like T. H. Davenport, L. Prusak, Karl Eric Sveiby, Nonaka, Takeuchi and many more, is an art of creating value from intangible assets in the organization (Sveiby, 1996; Leibowtiz, 1999; Sinha, 2014; Pankaj Madan, 2010; Svetlana Sajeva, 2010; Neumann & Eduardo, 2011; Nonaka & Takuchi, 1995). However, Sveiby dislikes calling this as knowledge management as he feels knowledge is a human faculty, not something which can be managed except by the individual himself/herself. He prefers to call this as "knowledge focused" or "knowledge creating" (as used by Nonaka, 1995).

Knowledge management is a process that transforms individual knowledge into organizational knowledge (Jelena Rasula, 2012; Linda Argote, 2000). Argote, however, adds that knowledge gets manifested through the transformation process from group to department to division to organization based on the encoding, decoding and performance of the recipients units. Knowledge transfer, thus, can be measured by measuring changes in knowledge or changes in performance of the recipients units. Internal knowledge transfer through interactions involving people is a basis of competitive advantage in firms.

Leidner (1999) defines knowledge management as "a systematic and organizationally specified process for acquiring, organizing and communicating both tacit and explicit knowledge of employees so that other employees may make use of it to be more effective and productive in their work". KM is also defined as a process that encompasses the knowledge identification, acquisition, creation, storage, dissemination, and application of knowledge within an organization. The process of KM however, does not exist "in vacuum". It should be integrated into other organizational processes that create value (Svetlana Sajeva, 2010).

Knowledge sharing is significant in that knowledge held by individuals cannot become organizational knowledge until it is shared throughout the organization. According to Sung Jung Jo, organizational culture is significantly associated with organizational commitment and commitment is associated with knowledge sharing intension (Sung Jung Jo, 2011).

Dunford emphasizes that knowledge sharing though is very crucial but simply sharing knowledge is not enough, sharing quality information and relevant knowledge matters (Dunford, 2000).

Sharing habit is strongly related to cultural background as mentioned above because both knowledge and culture are related to human mind. And due to globalization of the economy, organizations experience multi-cultured people which again affect the organizational culture and thus KM too (Irina Bogdana Pugna, 2014).

As most of the authors say that a major problem in KM is how to convince people within organization to share their information Babita Gupta has identified the following four processes of knowledge conversion, to ease the process of knowledge share:

1. **Socialization:** Sharing of experiences gained through observation, practice and imitation. It generally occurs through workshops, seminars, apprenticeships, conferences as well as water cooler.
2. **Capture:** The conversion of tacit knowledge into explicit knowledge.
3. **Dissemination:** Copying and distribution of explicit knowledge.
4. **Internalization:** Process of experiencing knowledge through an explicit source. i.e., one can combine the experience of reading the workshop report with previous experiences (Babita Gupta, 2000).

The definition and process of knowledge management itself states that knowledge management is mainly about leveraging and sharing individual knowledge for better use by the organization. However, let us now discuss why sharing knowledge and tacit knowledge in particular is important in knowledge management.

Sharing Tacit Knowledge: The Essence of Knowledge Management

Knowledge sharing is the corner stone of many organizations' knowledge management strategy. Moreover, tacit knowledge is very much significant in the context of knowledge management because it is inimitable. The main aim of knowledge management is to attain sustainable competitive advantage and managing tacit knowledge leads to achieve this.

Knowledge generation and transfer is an essential source of firm's sustainable competitive advantage (Margit Osterloh, 2002) because it is difficult for competitors to imitate. In the words of Spender also, competitive advantages grow from firm specific knowledge (Spender, 1993) and firm specific knowledge here means knowledge which is not common in different firms and hence lies in tacit knowledge.

Knowledge is perishable. When it's not used it soon loses its value. So it should be used and shared. Moreover, people do not take job for life. Thus, when they leave the organization their knowledge also leave, particularly tacit knowledge. Hence, sharing knowledge is the essence of success as success is the result of collaborative task of the team in the organization. Thus, creating a knowledge sharing culture in the organization is the need of the hour in 21st century. Organizational culture is the only factor which can create a sharing culture in the organization. Organizational culture can be thought of as relatively rigid tacit infrastructure of ideas that shape not only our thinking but also our behavior and perception of our business environment. It effectively establishes a set of guidelines by which members of an organization work and how those organizations are structured (Gurteen, 1999).

When knowledge becomes explicit it becomes information for others and information can be easily shared intra-organization as well as inter-organizations. Tacit knowledge is the only thing which cannot be shared and explicated totally and thus this provides competitive advantage to the organization and when the same is managed properly it leads to sustainable competitive advantage.

However, tacit knowledge should be shared among the employees internally so that the same should be used more and more to carry out the day to day works and achieve excellences. Knowledge management by its nature manages explicit knowledge with great ease but unless and until it emphasizes on gathering tacit knowledge and managing the same with care organization wide, organization cannot reap full benefits of knowledge management. In other words, knowledge management without full focus on tacit knowledge will become information management.

Challenges of Sharing Tacit Knowledge

The ability of the organization to transfer knowledge is a critical factor in Knowledge Management. Despite the growing significance of knowledge sharing practices for organization's competitiveness and market performance, several barriers make it difficult for knowledge management to achieve the goals and deliver a positive return on investment. In general, barriers could be categorized into three categories, viz.,

1. **Individual:** Distribution of the right knowledge from the right person to the right person at the right time is one of the biggest challenges of knowledge sharing. Barriers at individual level are manifold. Some of the barriers of this level are-
    a. Lack of motivation to share. Moreover, the contribution of a particular employee's tacit knowledge to a team output cannot be measured and paid accordingly. This requires motivation to some other level ((Margit Osterloh, 2002).
    b. General lack of time to share knowledge, and time to identify colleagues in the need of specific knowledge.
    c. Apprehension of fear that sharing may reduce or jeopardize people's job security.
    d. Low awareness and realization of the value and benefit of the possessed knowledge to others.
    e. Dominance in sharing explicit over tacit knowledge such as know-how and experience that requires hands on learning, observation, dialogue and interactive problem solving.
    f. Use of strong hierarchy, position based status and formal power.
    g. Age differences as well as gender differences.
    h. Lack of trust in people because they may misuse knowledge or take unjust credit.
    i. Poor communication and interpersonal skills.
    j. Lack of trust in the accuracy and credibility of knowledge due to the source.
2. **Organizational:** One of the key issues of sharing knowledge in an organizational context is related to the right corporate environment and conditions. Barriers related to organizations are as follows-
    a. Integration of Knowledge Management strategy and sharing initiatives into the company's goals and strategic approach is missing or unclear.
    b. Lack of leadership or managerial direction in terms of clearly communicating the benefits and values of knowledge sharing practices.
    c. Shortage of formal and informal spaces to share, reflect and generate knowledge.
    d. Lack of transparent rewards and recognition system that would motivate people to share more of their knowledge.
    e. Existing corporate culture does not provide sufficient support for sharing practices.
    f. Knowledge retention of highly skilled and experienced staff is not a high priority.
3. **Technological:** Knowledge sharing is as much a people and organizational issue as it is a technology challenge. There is little doubt that technology can act as a facilitator to encourage and support knowledge sharing processes by making knowledge sharing easier and more effective. The key

issue is however, to choose and implement a suitable technology that provides a close fit between people and organization. Some potential technology barriers are as mentioned below-

a. Lack of integration of IT system and processes .i.e., the way people do things.
b. Lack of technical support.
c. Reluctance to use IT systems due to lack of familiarity and experience with them.
d. Lack of communication and demonstration of all advantages of any new systems over existing ones.

Thus, Cos wishing to make their Knowledge Management strategy and integrated knowledge sharing a success, need to pay attention to a large number of potential knowledge sharing barriers like-barriers related to culture, infrastructure, IS/IT system etc. (Reige, 2005).

Stenmark (2000), says that the elusiveness of tacit knowledge can be derived from at least two reasons-first, Davenport and Prusak (2000) observe that tacit knowledge-"incorporates so much accrued and embedded learning that its rules may be impossible to separate from how an individual acts".

Second, tacit knowledge is something that resides within us and manifests itself through our actions, we therefore, do not need to document it for our own sake. We just use it.

Strategies and Techniques to Overcome the Challenges of Sharing Tacit Knowledge

Few organizations involve the entire organization in knowledge sharing activities like Buckman Labs, Dow Chemical, Ernst & Young, Hewlett & Packard, Monsanto, and Xerox. But this seems useful only if all employees need to work with and apply at least most of the knowledge they receive. Some companies however, protect specific parts of their knowledge and information, restricting access to selected people and groups only such as BMW, Microsoft etc. Thus, which information to be shared with whom should be very carefully determined as information overload leads to chaos and many others issues.

Moreover, simply sharing is not enough. Better and purposeful sharing of relevant knowledge translates into accelerated individual and organizational learning and innovation.

Knowledge transfer is a continuing problem in organizations and thus, how it works needs to be understood. There is no universal solution to this problem of knowledge sharing barriers. Thus, needs to be organization specific. However, there are some common factors according to Swee C. Goh, 2002; Lubit, 2001; Stenmark, 2000 which affect knowledge sharing in organizations and thus, need to be paid attention to are-

1. Creating an environment of mutual trust among individuals in the organization can go a long way in the success of knowledge transfer. The behavior of leaders should also be consistent with a philosophy of openness.
2. Positive organizational culture can be an enabler of knowledge transfer. A culture of continuous improvements and learning linked to problem solving and focused on specific values such as customer satisfaction is desired.
3. Existence of strong cooperative and collaborative culture is the pre-requisite of knowledge transfer between individuals and groups. Knowledge transfer also depends on the knowledge recipients. Recipients' motivation, absorptive capacity and retentive capacity should be taken care of.

4. More inter-personal communication, mentoring, team work, chat rooms, personal intranets and opportunities for face to face communication such as group dialogues and personal reflections on experiences and lessons learned should be encouraged for transfer of tacit knowledge.
5. Working with experts and coaches.
6. Encouraging the formation of informal networks and new groups in the organizations.
7. An organizational design that encourages horizontal communication.
8. Where bouts of the knowledge should be identified and explicated. When the risk of being tapped of their knowledge and being replaced by a database is gone, the user's reluctance to contribute is reduced.
9. Recording tacit knowledge i.e., writing and studying the learning histories can be a very efficient way to transmit tacit knowledge.
10. The reward system must not be focused purely on monetary rewards. Intrinsic rewards like recognition and appreciation leads to sharing of more tacit knowledge (Goh, 2002).

Figure 2. An integrated framework of tacit knowledge in organizations created for this study

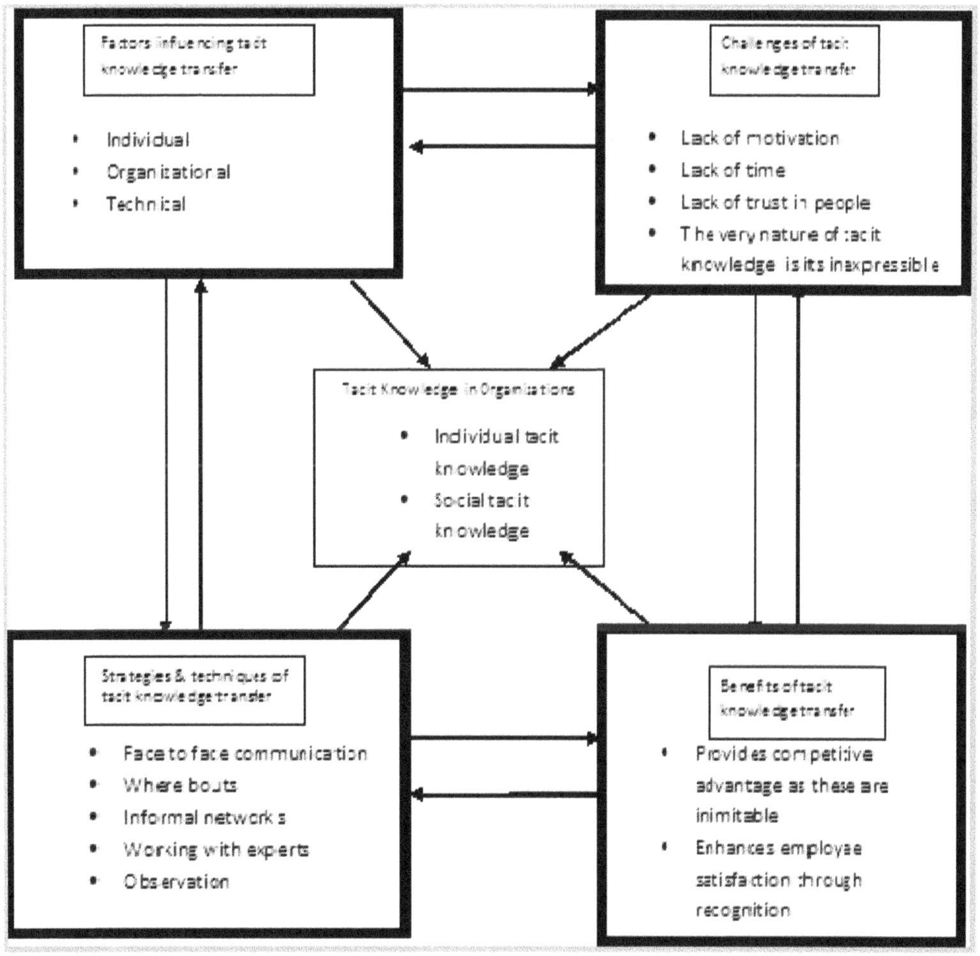

In the context of sharing knowledge, a study was conducted by Chiang in 2011 on sharing knowledge through Social Networking Sites (SNS) and the study found that SNS can capture more tacit knowledge than formal repository in terms of moods, hunches, insights, experiences, relationships and cultural swings. SNS like LinkedIn.com, Facebook.com, Bebo.com, Myspace.com, Ning.com, Orkut.com etc. could be used for the said purpose. However, the success of a virtual community depends on the motivation of its members to actively participate in knowledge generation and sharing activities, but this should not be used at work time else it may lead to loss of productivity (Chiang, 2011).

The whole concept of tacit knowledge is represented in Figure 2.

Figure 2 shows that all the dimensions of tacit knowledge in organizations are interrelated to each other, and in fact all the elements of an organization are related to each other and hence one leads to the other.

CONCLUSION

Knowledge management is a process of creating, storing, sharing and applying knowledge for achieving excellence in work and attaining sustainable competitive advantage. Most of the steps of knowledge management and in fact the whole concept of knowledge management is dependent on effective knowledge sharing because without sharing knowledge, creation of new knowledge, having sufficient knowledge organization wide and applying the same would not be possible. However, sharing knowledge is associated with many challenges especially in the case of sharing tacit knowledge which is the essence of knowledge management. The very nature of tacit knowledge leads to all the challenges and at the same time leads all the unique benefits which are not present in the case of explicit knowledge.

It is because of the challenges of the tacit knowledge that it provides the unique benefits to the firm and leads to the creation of sustainable competitive advantage. As tacit knowledge resides in human brain so unless and until the same workforce is hired by the competitors it is not possible to imitate the same knowledge. Hiring the same total workforce is though not impossible but very challenging and time taking so by the time the competitor hires the same the firm can enjoy its competitive advantage for a reasonable period of time.

REFERENCES

Babita Gupta, L. S. (2000). Knowledge Management Practices and Challenges. *Industrial Management & Data Systems*, *100*(1), 17–21. doi:10.1108/02635570010273018

Brelade & Harman. (2000). Using Human Resource Management to put Knowledge to Work. *Knowledge Management Review*, *3*(1), 26–29.

Chatterjee. (2014). Managing Constraints and Removing obstacles to Knowledge Management. *The IUP Journal of Knowledge Management*, *12*(4), 24–39.

Chiang, H. H., Han, T.-S., & Chuang, J.-S. (2011). The Rellationship between High Commitment HRM and Knowledge Sharing Behaviour and its Mediators. *International Journal Of Manpower(Emerald)*, *32*(5/6), 604–622. doi:10.1108/01437721111158224

Davenport, D. W. (1998). Successful Knowledge Management Projects. *Sloan Management Review, 39*(2), 43–57.

Dhamdhere, S. N. (2015). Knowledge Management Model for Higher Educational Institutes. *Journal of Commerce and Management Thought*, *6*(1), 130–161. doi:10.5958/0976-478x.2015.00010.5

Duffy, J. (2000). Knowledge Management: To be or not to be? *Information Management Journal*, *34*(1), 64–67.

Dunford, R. (2000). Key Challenges in the search for the effective management of knowledge in management consulting firms. *Journal of Knowledge Management, 4*(4), 295-302.

Fei Gao, M. L. (2008). Knowledge, Management, and Knowledge Management in Business Operations. *Journal of Knowledge Management (Emerald)*, *12*(2), 3–17. doi:10.1108/13673270810859479

Goh, S. C. (2002). Managing Effective Knowledge Transfer: An Integrative Framework and Some Practice Implications. *Journal of Knowledge Management, 6*(1), 23-30.

Gurteen, D. (1999). Creating a Knowledge Sharing Culture. Knowledge Management Magazine, 2(5).

Hislop D. (2013). *Knowledge Management in Organization: A Critical Introduction* (3rd ed.). Oxford University Press.

Ikujiro Nonaka, H. T. (1995). *The Knowledge Creating Company: How Japanese Companies Create the Dynamics of Innovation*. New York: Oxford University Press.

Juani Swart, N. K. (2003). Sharing Knowledge in Knowledge Intensive Firms. *Human Resource Management Journal*, *13*(2), 60–75. doi:10.1111/j.1748-8583.2003.tb00091.x

Leibowitz, J. (1999). Key Ingredients to the Success of an Organization's Knowledge Management Strategy. *Knowledge and Process Management*, *6*(1), 37–40. doi:

Leidner, M. A. (1999). *KMS-Emerging views and practices from the field.* Academic Press.

Linda Argote, P. I. (2000). Knowledge Transfer: A basis for competitive advantage in firms. *Organizational Behavior and Human Decision Processes*, *82*(1), 150–169. doi:10.1006/obhd.2000.2893

Lubit, R. (2001). Tacit Knowledge and Knowledge Management: The keys to Sustainable Competitive Advantage". *Organizational Dynamics*, *29*(4), 164–178. doi:10.1016/S0090-2616(01)00026-2

Margit Osterloh, B. S. (2002). Motivation Knowledge Transfer and Organizatinal Forms. *Organization Science*, *11*(5), 538–550. doi:10.1287/orsc.11.5.538.15204

Mruthyunjaya, H. C. (2011). *Knowledge Management.* New Delhi: PHI.

Neumann, G. (2011). The Changing Role of Knowledge in Companies: How to Improve Business Performance Through Knowledge. *The Electronic Journal of Knowledge Management, 9(1)*, 73–84.

Pankaj Madan, S. K. (2010). Contribution of Knowledge Management Practices in Creating Sustainable Competitive Advantage for Business Schools in India. *Journal of Information and Knowledge Management*, *9*(4), 387–397. doi:10.1142/S0219649210002760

Rahimli. (2012). Knowledge Management and Competitive advantage. Information and Knowledge Management, 2(7).

Rasula, J., Vuksic, B. V., & Stemberger, I. M. (2012). The Impact of Knowledge Management on Organizational *Performance. Economic and Business Review*, *14*(2), 147–168.

Reige, A. (2005). Three-dozen knowledge -sharing barriers managers must consider. *Journal of Knowledge Management, 9*(3), 18-35.

Russel, B. (2012). *Human Knowledge- Its scope and limits*. London: George Allen & Unwin Ltd.

Sharp, D. (2003). Knowledge Management Today: Challenges and Opportunities. *Information Systems*, 32–37.

Shukla, R. (2012). Knowledge Management in Higher Education. *International Journal of Reviews, Surveys and Research, 1*(1).

Sinha, A. (2014). KM in Academic Libraries. *Journal of Indian Research*, *2*(1), 123–125.

Spender, J. (1993). Competitive Advantage from Tacit Knowledge? Unpacking the Concept and Its Strategic Implications. *ACAD Manage Proc*, 37-41.

Stenmark, D. (2000). Turning Tacit Knowledge Tangible. *33rd Hawaii International Conference on System Sciences*.

Sung Jung Jo, B.-K. J. (2011). Knowledge Sharing: The nflurnces of learning organization culture, organizational commitment and organizational citizenship behaviour. *Journal of Leadership & Organizational Studies*, *18*(3), 353–364. doi:10.1177/1548051811405208

Sveiby, K. E. (1996, March 1). Retrieved March 28, 2016, from www.seviby.com: http://www.sveiby.com/articles/KnowledgeManagement.html

Svetlana Sajeva, R. J. (2010). Determination of essential knowledge Management System Componeents and their Parameters. *Social Sciences*, *1*(67), 80–90.

Thomas, H., & Davenport, L. P. (2000). *Working Knowledge-How Organizations Manage What they Know*. Boston: Harvard Business School Press.

Wilson, T. D. (2002). The Nonsense of Knowledge Management. Information Research, 8(1).

KEY TERMS AND DEFINITIONS

Knowledge: Knowledge refers to the ideas, information, understandings, skills, and insights possessed by an entity acquired from learning and/or experience through the mental process of thinking, reasoning, abstraction, and comprehension. Unlike information, knowledge is deeply influenced by the beliefs and values of the entity.

Knowledge Management: Knowledge management is a management philosophy that aims to make visible the knowledge available in the organization and entails a process of knowledge creation, storage, sharing, and application, and integrates the same with business processes in the organization. In short, knowledge management leads to knowledge-focused activities in the organization to make the processes prompt and competitive.

Tacit Knowledge: Tacit knowledge is that knowledge that resides in the human brain. It is the experience, intelligence, and know-how of the people in the organization. Unlike explicit knowledge, tacit knowledge cannot be documented easily or expressed in explicit form, and hence, it is tough to share tacit knowledge with others. Tacit knowledge could be gathered from observation and experience.

Chapter 5
Knowledge Management and the Competitiveness of Learning Organizations

Faten Louati
Manouba University, Tunisia

ABSTRACT

Knowledge management is becoming a source of discriminative value in the competitive positioning of companies and is becoming a lever for the development and emergence of new forms of organization. In fact, knowledge is the result of a cooperative process in collective action. The next step is to promote the creation of this knowledge and its sharing by managing the cooperative work of a community of people: we no longer manage the knowledge itself, but the collective that creates it, where the notion of "cooperative management of knowledge" applies. The author reflects on the organizational factor: Can it influence the practice of knowledge management within the companies willing to improve their innovation processes in order to achieve competitiveness? This reflection falls within the field of management sciences through studying the organizational solutions to ensure a better capitalization, sharing and new knowledge creation, and a better comprehension of the success conditions of the knowledge management approach, which consists of adaptation to the environment.

INTRODUCTION

Information and communication technologies have involved changes, as major as they have been irreversible, reflecting the passage from a material economy based on goods and services to an intangible economy based on knowledge. These changes lead companies to adapt and integrate a technology which has involved an evolution in business management and an evolution in the ways they face off against competition especially with the phenomenon of globalization resulting from a globally systemic transition and of a process of economic reorganization, propelled by the search for competitiveness of the firms and the states.

DOI: 10.4018/978-1-5225-3725-0.ch005

Today's company may find it very beneficial to be conceived of as being a learning organization, it must be able to analyze its own operation and to improve itself as a company through training, because knowledge has become, even more a company's capital and physical resources, the essential ingredient of value creation (Mack, 1995). Additionally, knowledge is has become a favorable factor for skills acquisition, which must be managed to ensure a better competitiveness (Nonaka, 1994; Ermine, 2003; Harvey, 2011; Barbaroux, 2012). Hence, the author focuses on knowledge management which has a significant impact on company competitiveness. The combination of competitiveness and knowledge management practice leads companies to follow an approach designed to guarantee:

- A durable competitive advantage,
- Increasingly conclusive results,
- Performance successes achievements that are qualitatively and definitively better than successes which definitely exceed those of its competitors,
- Distinctive competences,
- Sufficiently developed innovation processes, and
- A better adaptation to the environment.

Being competitive, nowadays, implies a great capacity to face its competitors, to satisfy its customers in a personalized way, to present know-how with regards to the products and the services offered on the market and to cooperate, with other companies, in intensive knowledge-based activities while (equally) equitably exploiting opportunities presented by new information and communication technologies in order to sustainably guarantee the effectiveness and the efficiency of the company (Wang, Zhongfeng, & Yang, 2011, Schiuma, 2012).

Certainly, this powerful manner of maintaining knowledge is not easy and it differs from one company to another and from one sector to another (Ribald, 2002)—especially, facing the environmental changes which became a constant determining this knowledge-based research on the market. This environment evolution affects the management process, the business relations, and the means of communication (Dube & Pare, 1999; Bergeron, Poulin, & Ellouz, 2000). Then, the question is to know whether the traditional methods of management are always valid and whether the companies have to put forms of mechanistic organization – rather, forms of organic organization – in place to improve their innovation processes? The theoretical framework of this research focuses on the need for the implementation of learning organizations with structure networks which weave fabrics of information exchange, defining the same values and seeking to solve common problems. These organizations must be built like a training system—i.e., they must develop a structure of operation in which two-way communication constitutes the link facilitating development and learning.

Today, the central role of knowledge management within the companies makes it imperative to apprehend the conditions for success. From this, the lack interest in assessing the effects of the environment's moderation of the direct relationship between knowledge management and the competitiveness of the company is an often-ignored problematic.

This research falls under a theoretical prospect and seeks to explore an approach of knowledge management (an approach found within those organizations with a structure network in place) as being a source of competitiveness. The general problematic of this research may be expressed thus:

To which extent can the organizational factor influence the practice of knowledge management, being regarded as a source of competitiveness?

To answer this question, the author has carried out a quantitative study based on the technique of investigation containing an elaborate questionnaire and managed within a sample of Tunisian companies belonging to the services sector.

The structure of the paper is as follows:

- The first section presents the conceptual framework of the research. The author has based it on a specialized literature review in order to define and operationalize the various concepts.
- The second section presents the methodology of the quantitative research.
- In the third section, the author strives to provide the principal research results and to discuss them in parallel while referring back and forth to the empirical and the theoretical observations (Charreire & Durieux, 2003).

The objective of this paper is to propose:

- A model of knowledge management accompanied by learning organizational structures.
- This model will provide enterprise managers with practical responses relative to the tangible and the intangible benefits of knowledge management adoption.
- The conditions facilitating its implementation.

THE THEORETICAL FRAMEWORK: KNOWLEDGE MANAGEMENT

In the present section, the author exhibits a literature review which will enable us to well define the concept of knowledge management and to present its three main objectives.

Definition of Knowledge Management

A vast research area tends to define knowledge as being a resource and a cognitive asset likely to be codified, stored, and diffused in the organization (Bruneau & Pujos, 1992; Langdon, 1998; Epingard, 1999; Foray, 2000; Knauf, 2010; Habib, 2010). In fact, this knowledge – whether individual or collective – must be managed (Bruneau & Pujos, 1992; Antoine & Blum, 2014). The authors of numerous research studies relate to knowledge management (Tisseyere, 1999; Jacob & Pariat, 2002; Michel, 2001; Dupuich-Rabasse, 2008; Sandhawalia & Dalcher, 2011; Barbaroux, 2012; Schiuma, 2012). As being a set of methods of organizations and technologies used with the aim of creating, collecting, organizing, storing, diffusing, using, and transferring knowledge within the company: knowledge materialized through internal and external documents, but similarly materialized in the form of intellectual capital and of experiments detained by collaborators or field experts (Reix, 1995).

In order to increase and accelerate knowledge valorization, Ballay (1999) proposes a knowledge management system composed of four steps—namely:

- **Interaction:** Group work; discussion; sharing;
- **Integration:** Tests; business processes;
- **Capitalization:** To protect, codify, record, standardize, preserve, and reactivate; and
- **Transmission:** Training; tutoring.

In this research, knowledge management is considered an approach, a new organization, a new approach for defining the actors' roles in this organization, a new leverage effect for the development of these organizations and, finally, a new use for information technologies (Tisseyere, 1999), at the same time. It is a set of concepts, methods, and technologies allowing for the collective development and use of shared knowledge. This management emerged from the need for managing the intellectual capital of the companies as well as possible, for maintaining an important competitive advantage.

The Objectives of Knowledge Management

In order to adequately address the subject of knowledge management and the chapter's objectives, the author will distinguish, first of all, its tacit and codifiable aspects. This distinction is said of Polany who can be understood as being the founder of a new approach of knowledge production within the organization and with regards to among its management. This approach was then expanded in 1987 by winter.

The explicit or the codified knowledge is a formalized knowledge, transmissible by means of a formal language with a systematic language, through a code. Consideration of the codified knowledge as being more important leads to forms of mechanistic and office automation organization (Reix, 1995).

Tacit or embodied knowledge is knowledge fixed in the action, and the use of knowledge in specific contexts. It can take very diverse forms like expertise, skills, and know-how. It is difficult to measure. Consideration of the embodied knowledge as being more important leads to forms of organic organization (Reix, 1995).

The primary goal of knowledge management is to create, consolidate, store, transfer, and share knowledge within the organization—doing so in line with the strategy of an intensive innovation regime or in order to improve competitiveness (Antoine & Blum, 2014).

In fact, the distinction between the embodied or the codified nature must be definitely managed. Three objectives can be, therefore, presented:

- **Knowledge Capitalization:** A question of analyzing, developing, maintaining and safely storing knowledge and making sure that it does not depreciate (Ballay, 1999; Ermine, 2003).
- **Knowledge Sharing:** A fundamental expectation of knowledge management, with which it is often confused (Deltour & Roussel, 2010; Knauf, 2010; Harvey, 2011).
- **Knowledge Creation:** Strongly related to permanent innovation. (Nonaka, 1994; Wang, D., Zhongfeng, S.U., & Yang, D., 2011; Barbaroux, 2012).

Building on this literature, the author has retained that knowledge management is a process designed to capitalize, share and create new knowledge. Consequently, we are aware of the difficulty of measuring intangible stock management. The theories advance, within this framework, that this management can be measured by the degree of the managers' perception towards this practice, as well as its various aspects. This management exists when the organization implements measurements to create and capitalize knowledge in order to achieve its goals; to then share this knowledge between the members of the organization and to (finally) then apply it to create value (Ramirez, 1999; Gold, Malhotra, & Segars, 2001; Ermine, 2003; Ferraresi, Quandt, dos Santos, & Frega, 2012; Arduin, Grundstein, & Rosenthal-Sabroux, 2015).

The Contributions of Knowledge Management to the Objectives of the Company

The contributions of knowledge management to the company objectives constitute the analytical grid of success of such a program. These expected contributions can be summarized as follows (Tisseyere, 1999):

- **The Dissemination of Excellence or the "Best Practices" Within the Company:** Knowledge management is the best possible aid to achieve the dissemination of excellence. It is, thus, necessary to implement a "body of knowledge" which makes it possible to capitalize these best practices and to position the company in terms of the know-how of its managers.
- **The Capacity to Select the Best Decisions:** During information overload (in terms of the data being unstructured and there being a lack of tools to finely analyze these data), knowledge management – through its capacity to disseminate information regarding (and knowledge of) that which is in direct contact with an observed phenomenon – makes it possible to restore a proper "signal to-noise ratio" for a relevant analysis of these data. The elements used are therefore the body of knowledge and the sharing tools which contribute towards transforming peace-building actors into knowledge workers. These tools make it possible to have the necessary information and knowledge and, similarly, the means of drawing, filtering and analyzing it all.
- **The Reduction of the Decision Cycles:** The decision cycles are reduced by the instantaneity of the availability of the company's "best practices" and knowledge thanks to the sharing tools and, particularly, the work flows implemented to "trace" the decisions and the decision making.
- **Subjectivity Reduction:** The availability of structured information – resulting from the availability of classical computer resources and of unstructured information resulting from a body of knowledge accessed through tools of dissemination – allows "tracing" all the reasons for a decision.
- **The Development of the Innovation Capacity:** The availability of knowledge about an organization through a body of knowledge and contact with the company's best experts via a culture of conducted sharing, inevitably, has a new innovation capacity, if the management knowledge system is a part of the integral life of the company.
- **The Development of the Learning Capacity:** It is the indirect effect of the implementation of a body of knowledge; the training of the new arrivals in an organization is facilitated and accelerated: *It is a network and a transversal dissemination of information.*

DEVELOPMENT OF A NEW MODEL OF KNOWLEDGE ORGANIZATION AND SHARING

The implementation of organizations with a structure network presupposes the creation of a high degree of knowledge.

The Development of Learning Organizations

Following the presence of multiple changes which have marked the life of the company – particularly, the changes in consumers' tastes; the reduction of the lifetime of the strategic activities and the products; and the proliferation of information and communication technologies – there was an emergence of the flexible organization—one which is able to perceive the changes in time to consolidate its competitive position in the market. This flexible organization is a qualifying learning organization which falls under a dynamic prospect, the objective of which is to create value starting from the knowledge acquired (Bounfour, 1998, Arduin, P.E., Grundstein, M., & Rosenthal-Sabroux, C., 2015). It is open, communicative, creative, inclusive, and integrated; and it is characterized by an elevated level of improved staff versatility, weak rules and weak formalization of procedures, and the recourse to lateral communications for solving the problems encountered (Tarondeau, 1998).

By studying the relationship of dependence between the organization and its creation, even knowledge management research – for instance, Kalika (2006) – advances the idea that the organization has a strong impact on knowledge management:

[It] is particularly through opening possibilities of cross-sharing that the organization can become more learning (…) The question arises, then, whether the structure and its management support sharing and whether the information system is used to this end (Kalika 2006).

Advantages of the Implementation of a Structure Network

Today, each company must implement a structure which supports learning—i.e. a structure network. The advantages of such structure depend on the will of its members to work together, to innovate, to create new knowledge, to solve problems of shared interests and to achieve the same objectives.

The networks weave fabrics of information exchange and mutual obligations—likely to be used as a basis for closer relations, which must be managed (Powell, 1990). The network organizations offer "tailor-made" products (Dube & Pare, 1999) while setting up infrastructures answering specific expectations, which enables them to reduce overall costs and to increase effectiveness and profitability—which consequently helps to maintain competition (Hatch, 2000).

The network company is accompanied by a flattening of the structures encouraging the adoption of a light hierarchical structure to support information sharing:

The increased use of information technologies seems to be accompanied by a flattening of the structures, i.e., a reduction in the hierarchical levels of management (Reix, 1990).

Apart from the flattening of the structures, the companies with a structure network adopt a less formalized communication style; a decentralization of decision-making powers; and an implementation of a horizontal organization of the activities. In the same direction, any company which aspires to become a learning organization must start with creating a favorable environment for exchange (Racheline, 1999). It must be able to analyze data which it receives in order to extract significant information. It is, therefore, necessary for the organization to define and share its values, its vision of what it is (its *raison d'être*), and its vision of what it wants to achieve. These learning organizations must find a culture which calls for change and for the adaptation of the existing and also future structures to support exchange and information sharing. Indeed, any company which wants to make its knowledge management succeed well must initially go through a culture of capitalization and mutual enrichment which is supposed to serve the individual interest of the employee at the level of her or his position and serve the collective interest of the company as whole (Kalika, 2006).

Knowledge Management and Company Competitiveness: Complex Links

To ensure the success of a knowledge management process, it is necessary to analyze the chain of integration of knowledge in the firm—doing so in order to identify and manage the different stages of enrichment of this cognitive resource and its incorporation into the activity of the firm. This is the value chain of knowledge (VCK), according to Ermine (2012).

The link between knowledge management and companies' competitiveness is problematic and complex. The objective of this section is to study how the approach of knowledge management can be a source of competitiveness for companies. The author wonders about its contribution and its impact on organizations. It's very important to enrich and deepen the debate on this topic.

Contributions of Cognitive Stock Management to Companies' Competitiveness

A company should define its knowledge base—in other words, it should take steps to evaluate its strengths and its weaknesses; and should define the points to be reinforced. Starting from its previously formed knowledge base – in other words, its knowledge measurement – the company can deploy its messages internally and externally, particularly towards its customers and its partners (Bonfour, 1998). This common knowledge base is an essential lever in the development of competitive advantages where the methods of access must be organized to constitute a living memory accessible to everyone (Boblin & Brenner, 1996).

In accordance with the approach developed by Grant (1996), the company's competitiveness fundamentally depends on the diversity and the strategic value of its specific knowledge and on its capacity to integrate short-terms insights of individuals into the company's long-term institutional memory. The competitiveness of the companies is thus based on the capacity to combine and coordinate their practices around a heritage of knowledge which must be carefully managed. This practice of knowledge management is determining factor who succeeds in competitors' race for market share (Knauf, 2010; Wang, D., Zhongfeng, S.U., & Yang, D., 2011; Schiuma, 2012), it enables the company to maintain a durable competitive advantage (Barney, 1991).

Indeed, knowledge on which competitiveness is based depends, partly, on external resources and on the capacity of companies to manage them and to articulate them by means of institutional strategic resources. More and more, companies seek to specialize in terms of 'knowledge blocks' and 'fields of competence' which they control and on which they base their competitive positions. This evolution goes through various forms of cooperation *vis-à-vis* the multiplicity of the public or private partners who have many advantages (particularly in terms of flexibility and reactivity). We consider, in this chapter, cooperation as being an

operational or structural implementation of the strategies aiming at obtaining competitive advantages in terms of quality and innovation in complex and turbulent environments where [the] capacities of rapid adaptation or anticipation are essential [ways] to confront the competitors (Tarondeau & Wright, 1995).

The theories of knowledge management have focused on the direct relationship between knowledge management and innovation (Hatchuel, Le Masson, & Benoit, 2001; Denervaud & Chatin, 2009; Attour & Ayerbe, 2012; Sandhawalia & Dalcher, 2011). This management aims at combining the individuals' knowledge in order to create and to apply new knowledge with the objective of improving the innovation process (Harkema & Browayes, 2003). At this level, Yann De Kermadec (2001) suggests that knowledge management is, at once, at the core of innovation and that simultaneously, it is nourished by innovation. This innovation is an endogenous and cumulative technological creative process (Ermine, 2003); it is a new major criterion of competitiveness.

According to Scarbrought, Swan, Newell, & Hislop (2000), the embodied knowledge is a source of innovation—since *knowledge management which concentrates on the creation of structure networks for knowledge transfer will [be severely] limited in terms of contribution to innovation.* Thus, any company which wants to improve its competitiveness in term of innovation, must bet on its embodied knowledge rather than its codified knowledge, since they are not easily transferable through networks. Similarly (and in a the same vein), Spender and Grant (1996) affirm that the embodied knowledge plays a more important part in the innovation process than the codified knowledge – except that knowledge transfer, generally, takes time—since they are difficult to imitate.

According to Miller and Morris (published in 1998 in New York, NY by Wiley), innovation depends on the ability of firms to combine various internal and external sources of tacit and explicit knowledge with business processes that are based on a balance between market forces and technological dynamics. This calls for the emergence of new forms of organization that rely on collaboration and knowledge sharing among stakeholders (Barbaroux, 2014a).

The implemented processes for knowledge creation (whether embodied or codified) are based on techniques known as creativity:

These techniques are organized around working groups, with the goal of providing new ideas, which are then evaluated and integrated in an activity of innovative design, which validates and executes the idea (demonstration, model, prototype, etc.) until obtaining an appropriate innovative concept, [and] then, capitalizing and identifying the knowledge heritage (Ermine, 2003).

Suggestion of Knowledge Management Through the Implementation of Learning Organizations

In this part, we present the dimensions of the knowledge management model (Figure 1).

To begin, it must be remembered that a model is a simplified representation of an object intended to be clarified. The relationship between the model and the object is subjective (Moigne, 1991). Indeed, the model does not seek to realize the totality of the object, but rather to realize some of the dimensions relevant to the desired objective. It makes it possible to order the activities which are, and the management system which is, practiced by the managers and which can be used in a given situation.

The suggested model reflects the existence of a direct and an indirect relationship between the model dimensions. It is based on the following assumptions:

- First, the organization has an effect on knowledge management (Reix, 1995; Ermine, 2003; Kalika, 2006, Ferray & Presque, 2011, Dudezert, A., Dugage, M.R., Chauvin, F., Martin, F., Lemieux, E., Boisserpe, P.…& Bruillon, E., 2012).

- Second, knowledge management is based on a knowledge valorization process. It is a question of identifying, capitalizing, and sharing the "knowledge capital" through involving the whole staff.
- Third, the various strategic organizations and the needs for improvement of the company's competitiveness must be organized around the process of knowledge management. This management is, therefore, a source of competitiveness (Penrose, 1959; Tarondeau & Wright, 1995; Reix, 1995; Bontis, Dragonetti, Jacobsen, & Roos, 1999; Le Boterf, 2002; Ferraresi, A.A., Quandt, C.O., dos Santos, S.A., & Frega, J.R., 2012; Prax, 2012). Rare are the research studies approaching knowledge management as a mediating variable (Dube & Pare, 1999; Hatch, 2000). The innovation of our research consists in studying the contribution of the organizational factor in the competitiveness of the Tunisian companies through the indirect effects of knowledge management (Foray & Lundvall, 1996).
- Fourth dimension of the model is a moderating variable which facilitates and reinforces the relationship between knowledge management and competitiveness. The company must adopt a culture which plays a role in the adoption of the company's "knowledge management" approach (Tisseyere, 1999), which will lead to differences in terms of value creation and competitive advantage.

RESEARCH METHODOLOGY

The author discusses, in what follows, the methodology employed in the empirical research in the present study. The objectives are to become better familiar with the practice of knowledge management within the prototypical Tunisian companies and to better understand how the "organizational" factor can, at the same time, influence it and can determine its behavior in the pursuit of competitiveness.

Figure 1. Model of knowledge management through the implementation of organizational structures, as a source of competitiveness

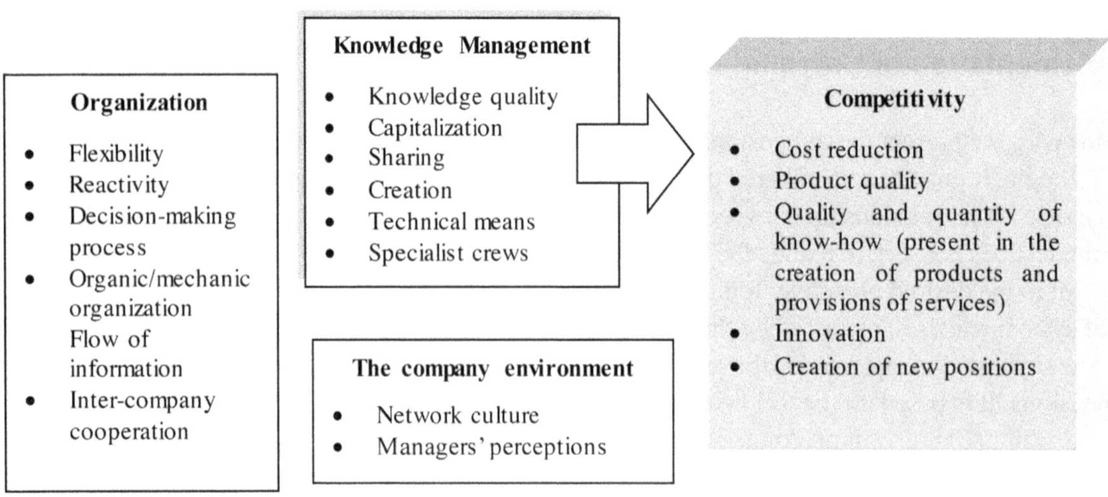

Data Collection

The adopted empirical methodology is an exploratory methodology which is characterized by the flexibility of the methods used to go deeper into the subject and to acquire a more comprehensive vision of it (Evrad, Pras, & Roux, 2003). The objective of this study is to become familiar with the practice of knowledge management within Tunisian companies.

Hence, the most appropriate empirical technique of survey to this study is that of the survey by questionnaire. The choice of this technique is due to the significant number of companies which the author has sought (and currently seeks) to survey and to the number of the items measuring the variables of our conceptual model. Indeed, in order to test and to validate the model, a questionnaire formed by specific questions and variables drawn from the literature review is built. Thereby, the author has used a nominal scale to measure the nominal variables (qualitative). The respondents had to choose between several alternatives for some questions, and between binary variables of a yes/no type for other questions.

Initially, a pre-test was launched near 20 companies operating in a 'transforming' sector to purify the items proposed in our questionnaire and to test the degree of influence of the variables on each other to be carried out. Secondly, a principal survey to analyze the practice of knowledge management aims to capitalize on, share, and create new knowledge and to study its impact on the competitiveness with regards to Tunisian companies.

Methods and Techniques of Data Analysis

Within the framework of this empirical research, we resorted to:

- **A Bivariate Analysis:** To measure the combination, we have used the chi-square test, which consists in testing the dependence or the independence of the variables;
- **A Multivariate Analysis:** To analyze the relationships of direct and indirect dependence between the variables of the conceptual model, through a mediating variable. In the same way, this analysis was used to check the company environment's moderating effect on the direct relationship which exists between knowledge management and competitiveness.

The Reasons Behind the Choice of the Branch of Industry

The author has chosen the companies belonging to the branch of services which based on knowledge and which are more affected by the technological changes than other branches are.

[The] [m]ore the activity integrates a significant part of the services, [the] more the strategic nature of the ICT is perceived in the companies. Three sectors are, particularly, well equipped in terms of knowledge management: Informatics Services and Telecommunications, financial and real estate activities, and business services. Knowledge management becomes increasingly current near the companies where the service dimension is an integral part of the core business (Kalika, 2006).

Data collection made it possible to collect a sample of 99 companies; they are small and medium-sized private companies established on only one site in Tunisia. The surveyed companies belong to the services branch of industry—that is to say, 91.9% of the total number of companies.

The Degree of Formalization of the Surveyed Company

The study of the degree of formalization of the surveyed Tunisian companies leads one to classify them into organic or mechanistic companies. The indicators selected to classify the companies into organic organizations are:

- An ambiguous definition of roles (6.1% of the surveyed companies);
- A communication based on mutual adjustment (20.2% of the surveyed companies);
- The existence of informal working groups (15.2% of the surveyed companies); and
- A significant role having been assigned to the culture of the company (13.1% of the surveyed companies).

These surveyed companies are based on the embodied knowledge.

The indicators selected to classify the companies implementing forms of mechanistic organization are:

- A strict and depersonalized definition of the roles (14.1% of the surveyed companies);
- A form of communication based on formal messages (12.1% of the surveyed companies);
- A process codified in written procedures (16.2%of the surveyed companies); and
- A monitoring system based on codified elements (3% of the surveyed companies).

These surveyed companies are based on the company's formalized knowledge.

The innovation should not only cover the design and the development of the new products and services but it must, similarly, cover the production system and its organization in order to develop a competing base likely to help the company to be more profitable and more efficient in the market. The innovation practiced by the surveyed companies comes from multiple sources:

- The conceptualization of a new service (66.7% of the surveyed companies);
- The introduction of a new production process (5.1% of the surveyed companies);
- The opening of a new market opportunity (11.1% of the surveyed companies);
- The conquest of a new source of raw materials (0% of the surveyed companies); and
- The implementation of a new form of flexible organization—adopting a short management chain (12.1% of the sample).

RESEARCH RESULTS AND RECOMMENDATIONS

In this section, the author introduces the principal results of the explanatory research analyses while discussing these results in order to make comparisons between the obtained results and the former research studies.

The Organizational Dimension and the Knowledge Management Approach

The effect of the organizational dimension on the approach of knowledge management shows that:

- The new business organization models (based on knowledge) on which the Tunisian companies are based require the improvement of their creative knowledge processes. For it, an approach of knowledge management seems to be essential to capitalize, share, and create other new knowledge.
- At the organizational level, the companies seek:
  - A better information flow among the services;
  - Adoption of "customer-oriented" strategies in order to manage the relationship with the latter—who must, henceforth, contribute to the design of the product which he buys. This strategy requires the construction of a team and an inspiring series of communications (internal and external) to create specific and advanced knowledge (Appendix 1).

These results contribute to validate the works of Sandhawalia and Dalcher (2011), Ferray and Presque (2011), and Dudezert et al. (2012) which insist on the implementation of flexible and learning organizations to encourage knowledge sharing.

Knowledge Management: A Challenge to a New Competitiveness

The analysis of the results makes it possible to draw three conclusions as to the effect of knowledge management on competitiveness:

Efficiency Related to the Practice of Knowledge Management

The objective of knowledge management approach is to contribute to tangible and numerical results which are reflected in cost reduction. It should be noted that:

- 56.6% of the sample seek to reduce the design costs,
- 17.2% seek to reduce the manufacturing costs,
- 22.2% seek to reduce the distribution costs, and
- 4% of the sample seeks to reduce the costs of the maintenance and the optimization of the time factor.

Thus, knowledge management as a strategic resource helps the companies to be more competitive in keeping their costs down.

Cooperation between the companies (Appendix 2) has a competitive advantage which results in cost reduction (the chi-square test is significant = 0.000)—knowing that

- 56.6% of the Tunisian companies choose vertical cooperation (subcontracting; partnerships) and that
- 43.4% of the sample choose horizontal cooperation (joint ventures; multi-nationalization; strategic alliances).

These results contribute towards validating the works of Tarondeau (1998), Durand (2000), and Ermine (2003) according to which knowledge is a strategic resource; and contribute towards validating the works of Erceau (1997) and Djeflat (2004) with regards to the importance of knowledge management practice in order to reduce the costs of the companies.

Knowledge Management: A Source of Innovation

In order to fulfil the requirements of the market in terms of innovation, the surveyed companies set up a practice of knowledge management – and this, through two actions: knowledge capitalization (in order to save collective memory and knowledge to integrate them, later, into the system of production what makes it possible to maintain significant competitive advantages) and new knowledge creation (the improvement of the creative action in the actors by their becoming committed in the improvement of the innovation process).

If innovation is conditioned by capitalization and by knowledge creation within the companies, these two actions depend on the implementation of qualifying staff who devote time and who specialize in knowledge management (Appendix 3). These results contribute towards validating the works of Schiuma (2012) and Barbaroux (2012), according to which knowledge management is an approach at the core of innovation which helps the companies to remain competitive in the market.

The retention of a competitive advantage in terms of innovation is conditioned by a high degree of formalization of the organization. In other words, the retention of formalized knowledge, by the Tunisian companies, has the most important effect on the improvement of their innovation processes (Appendix 4). If these companies seek, for example, a new design of their products and services or the opening of new markets, they must set up mechanistic organizations based on formal messages and a monitoring system based on the codified elements.

The results of the analysis carried out within the framework of the Tunisian companies do not converge with the former works of Spender and Grant (1996), Scarbrough et al. (2000), and Djeflat (2004), according to whom the embodied knowledge plays a more important role than knowledge formalized in the innovation process. Neither do they converge with the most recent works of Bettiol, Di Maria, and Grandinetti (2012) which advance that, in such companies, the codified knowledge makes it possible to improve the product quality, the production capacity, and the innovation—which ensures the continuity and the good market positioning of the company.

The Lack of Integration of Knowledge Management in Company Strategy

Certain Tunisian companies (12%) do not integrate knowledge management in their strategies. It is considered, for these companies, as being a secondary activity which can entail additional expenditures. These managerial and individual difficulties can be a barrier to the sharing of knowledge.

Within this framework, a clear communication of the direction of the vision regarding the importance of knowledge sharing in the organization strategy is beneficial (Harvey, 2011). This appeal to for leader-

Table 1. Distribution according to the restrictive constraints of knowledge management practice

	Frequency	Percentage	Valid	Cumulative Percentage
Valid				
Lack of means and Technical difficulties	14	14.1	14.1	14.1
Lack of time to manage knowledge	29	29.3	29.3	43.4
Lack of specialists and managerial difficulties	41	41.4	41.4	84.8
Cultural difficulties	15	15.2	15.2	100.0
Total	99	100.0	100.0	

ship development in order to manage and communicate the advantages of information sharing and for an organizational structure which is supportive of knowledge circulation. The organizational factor is not a solely unique factor in determining better knowledge management.

ADAPTATION TO THE COMPANY ENVIRONMENT

A Tunisian company which seeks to manufacture new products and/or to conceptualize new services must construct a motivating team working in order to lead the process of capitalization, sharing, and the creation of specific and innovating knowledge while seeking to satisfy the needs of the organization at the internal and the external levels:

- **At the Internal Level:** The company must establish communication based on the mutual adjustment through direct interaction; facilitate its decision-making process; form abstract working groups; and circulate information among the services for greater transparency.
- **At the External Level:** The company must circulate information with its customers and its partners and implement forms of cooperation with based on knowledge in order to benefit from the experiments of the other companies.

This adaptation to the company's environment requires certain reactivity from the company in order to take hold of circumstances and to detect the threats and the opportunities in time, in a context where the company is supposed to implement flexible organizations, the reliability of which is linked to creating value starting from the cumulated knowledge through presenting innovative products (services). This challenge of the competitors' differentiation encourages the companies to train teams of specialists in order to manage the knowledge coming from the new models in the organizations with a structure network. This, in turn, which opens capitalization possibilities and satisfactory transverse sharing (among other things)—the objectives of knowledge management.

The Tunisian company must adapt to its cultural environment, which refers to the degree of development of the Net culture (ICT use, Internet, computer-based technologies, e-commerce…) and to the managers' perception towards knowledge management. This adaptation enables the company to improve the knowledge quality and, thereafter, to improve its market position. It similarly enables the company to develop (according to the basic, advanced, or innovating retained knowledge) knowledge localization strategies (9.1% of the sample), specialization strategies (45.5% of the sample) or differentiation strategies (44.4% of the sample).

Thus, the developed culture within the companies calls for change and for the adaption of structures to support information exchange and sharing. Consequently, the cultural context is dynamic (since it is produced and reproduced by the companies' actions, and since it is continuously in transformation). The company must permanently ensure the maintenance (whether proactively or reactively) of its adaptation to the changing conditions of its cultural environment—a process which requires the implementation of the organizational structures, which develops the spirit of transverse sharing; it is where knowledge management is more likely to succeed.

Considering the obtained tangible results following the use of knowledge, a good management practice is essential in order to develop this reproducible knowledge. Indeed, the results show that the incarnation of knowledge management practice in the culture of the Tunisian companies is a regulating variable initially supporting the improvement of the innovation and the creativity process. Second, information transfer and knowledge sharing among the various company members, finally, result in the drawing of significant competitive advantages in terms of the appearance of the new highly-qualified positions based on advanced knowledge.

These results contribute to validating the works of Manfred (1995), Tisseyere (1999), Schware (2005), Kalika (2006), and Wang et al. (2011) as to the need to adapt the company to its cultural environment in order to moderate the direct connection between knowledge management and company competitiveness. They also validate the most recent works of Ferraresi et al. (2012) which show that knowledge management contributes to the development of new strategies and to the improvement of the innovation process. It must be part of the daily life of all aspects of the company and must be based on an organizational culture, which makes it possible to align with the strategic objectives of the organization and to create considerable, tangible results.

CONCLUSION

The present research has, firstly, tried to initially perform a state-of-the-art analysis of the concept of knowledge management. Secondly, the author has tried to analyze the organizational dimension of this practice within those companies which are implementing structure networks. The author has considered, in this paper, a company organized within a network in which each company in that network is accompanied by a flatness of organizational structure—encouraging the adoption of a shorter hierarchical line in order to interweave the fabric of information exchanges via a culture of mutual enrichment, to promote the spirit of transverse sharing.

The management of this knowledge is an essential practice for protecting and developing the knowledge retained by the Tunisian companies and, similarly, to reduce the costs (particularly the design costs) and to create new highly qualified positions based on the advancements in knowledge.

The Tunisian companies which use codified knowledge based on formal messages, written procedures, and standardization of procedures manage to quickly improve their innovation process. In other words, those companies which have an important degree of formalization have a greater effect on innovation than do companies without a comparative level of formalization.

The majority of the Tunisian companies surveyed, rather, opt for vertical cooperation such as partnership and subcontracting. These cooperative liaisons contribute to the development of new strategies, indirectly, supported by the process of knowledge management (capitalization, sharing, and creation of new knowledge). Thus, such cooperation seems to be the best solution—since it can link several strategic resources coming from two or several companies whose knowledge constitutes their principal resource.

The research analysis demonstrates that competitiveness is a multidimensional result and that knowledge management is a mediating variable which plays an indirect role in reinforcing the direct relationship which exists between the organizational dimension and company competitiveness.

Similarly, the results show that 88% of the Tunisian companies surveyed adopt a knowledge management approach as a way to systematically manage a cognitive process which itself is a mean of capitalizing, sharing, and creating new knowledge. Nevertheless, the lack of leadership in the communication of the benefits associated with the sharing of practices – i.e., the lack of qualified and qualifying specialists to manage knowledge – constitutes an organizational barrier to the sharing of knowledge. The second barrier is individual in nature: It is the lack of time to manage knowledge; this practice is perceived as being an additional expenditure.

The practical contribution of this research summarizes, in its presentation to company managers, certain important conditions for the success of knowledge management practice. Taking into consideration this learning, the organizational structures play a main function in the improvement of companies' competitiveness. The author has presented a knowledge management model which highlights the need for adopting a long-term vision, especially towards a changing environmental context—since it is very difficult to establish, with certainty, a causal model of competitiveness.

FUTURE RESEARCH DIRECTIONS

This research is bounded within limits comprised, primarily, of the choices in – and the difficulty of – measuring the cognitive process management variables. The effects of the measurability of knowledge management nowadays were not studied. Consequently, other measurements could have been taken into account to study the manner of capitalizing, sharing, and creating knowledge. The obtained results should not necessarily be generalized, since our study relates to a unique branch of industry.

In order to address these limitations, other studies can be conducted in order to enrich our research, which may relate to a large number of variables, using other factors such as the technological and/or human factors which can influence knowledge management practice and which play a role in company competitiveness. It could also be interesting to carry out a comparative study with other countries similar to, or different from, Tunisia – and to recommend other studies covering the same issue but embracing all sectors: a multi-sector study enabling researchers to generalize the results and to compare knowledge management practice in various industrial sectors.

REFERENCES

Antoine, A., & Blum, G. (2014). La gestion des connaissances ou le Knowledge Management (KM). *Revue Internationale de Psychosociologie et de Gestion des Comportements Organisationnels. ESKA, 49*, 23–31. doi:10.3917/rips.049.0021

Arduin, P. E., Grundstein, M., & Rosenthal-Sabroux, C. (2015). *Système d'information et de connaissance*. London, UK: ISTE Editions.

Attour, A., & Ayerbe, C. (2012). Connaissances et innovation au sein des écosystèmes d'affaires, le cas des services mobiles. *Revue Française de Gestion, 221*, 78–94. doi:10.3166/rfg.221.77-94

Ballay, J. F. (1999). Les processus clés de la gestion des savoirs. *L'Expansion Management Review, 95*, 111–119.

Barbarroux, P. (2012). Identifying collaborative innovation capabilities within knowledge-intensive environments: Insights from the ARPANET project. *European Journal of Innovation Management, 15*(2), 232–258. doi:10.1108/14601061211220995

Barbarroux, P. (2014a). Innovation disruptive et naissance d'un écosystème: Voyage aux origines de l'internet? *Revue d'Économie Industrielle, Ecosystèmes et Modèles d'Affaires, 146*(2), 27-59. Retrieved from www.cairn.info/article_p.php?ID_ARTICLE=REI_146_0027

Barney, J. (1991). Firm resources and sustained competitive advantage. *Journal of Management, 17*(1), 99–120. doi:10.1177/014920639101700108

Bergeron, F., Poulin, D., & Ellouz, S. (2000). Les technologies de l'information: Un synonyme d'alliance réussie. *Proceedings of the 9th Conférence de Management Stratégique*. Montpellier: AIMS. Retrieved from http://jepelet.free.fr/studies/MBA/strategie/doc/chap5/bergeron.pdf

Bettiol, M., Di Maria, E., & Grandinetti, R. (2012). Codification and creativity: Knowledge management strategies in KIBS. *Journal of Knowledge Management, 16*(4), 550–562. doi:10.1108/13673271211246130

Boblin, N., & Brenner, P. (1996). L'art de mesurer l'apprentissage organisationnel. *L'Expansion Management Review*, 17-23.

Bontis, N., Dragonetti, N. C., Jacobsen, K., & Roos, G. (1999). Les indicateurs de l'immatériel. *L'Expansion Management Review, 95*, 37–46.

Bounfour, A. (1998). *Le management des ressources immatérielles. Maîtriser les Nouveaux Leviers de l'Avantage Compétitif*. Paris, France: Dunod.

Bruneau, J. M., & Pujos, J. F. (1992). *Le management des connaissances dans l'entreprise*. Paris, France: Les Éditions d'Organisation.

Charreire, S., & Durieux, F. (2003). Explorer et tester: Deux voies pour la recherche. In *Méthodes de Recherche en Management*. Paris, France: Dunod.

De Kermadec, Y. (2001). *Innover grâce au brevet: Une révolution déclenchée par internet*. Paris, France: INSEP Consulting Éditions.

Deltour, F., & Roussel, C. S. (2010). L'intégration des connaissances par les équipes projets ERP: deux études de cas en PME. *Système d'information et management, 15*(1), 98-34.

Denervaud, I., & Chatin, O. (2009). *L'ADN de l'entreprise innovante, comment accroître les capacités créatives des entreprises*. Paris, France: Pearson Education.

Djeflat, A. (2007). Les nouvelles exigences de la PME dans une économie fondée sur la connaissance, cas des entreprises maghrébines, TIC & développement. *La Revue Électronique*. Retrieved from http://www.tic.ird.fr

Dube, L., & Pare, G. (1999). Les technologies de l'information et l'organisation à l'ère du virtuel. *Gestion, 24*(2), 14–22.

Dudezert, A., Dugage, M. R., Chauvin, F., Martin, F., Lemieux, E., Boisserpe, P., ... Bruillon, E. (2012). Le knowledge management au cœur de la stratégie d'entreprise. *Documentaliste - Sciences de l'Information, 49*(2), 26–43. doi:10.3917/docsi.492.0026

Dupuich-Rabasse, F. (2008). *Management et gestion des compétences*. Paris, France: L'Harmattan.

Durand, T. (2000). L'alchimie de la compétence. *Revue Française de Gestion, 127*(1), 84–102.

Epinard, P. (1999). *L'investissement immatériel, cœur d'une économie fondée sur le savoir*. Paris, France: CNRS Éditions.

Erceau, J. (1997). Subir l'information ou partager la connaissance. *L'Expansion Management Review*, 104-110.

Ermine, J. L. (2003). *La gestion des connaissances*. Paris, France: Lavoisier.

Ermine, J. L., Moradi, M., & Brunel, S. (2012). Une chaîne de valeur de la connaissance. International Management, 16, 29-40. doi:10.7202/1012391ar

Evrad, Y., Pras, B., & Roux, E. (2003). *Market, études et recherches en marketing* (3rd ed.). Paris, France: Dunod.

Ferraresi, A. A., Quandt, C. O., dos Santos, S. A., & Frega, J. R. (2012). Knowledge management and strategic orientation: Leveraging innovativeness and performance. *Journal of Knowledge Management, 16*(5), 688–701. doi:10.1108/13673271211262754

Ferray, M., & Presque, Y. V. A. (2011). *Management de la connaissance, knowledge management, apprentissage organisationnel et la société de la connaissance* (2nd ed.). Paris, France: Economica.

Foray, D. (2000). *L'économie de la connaissance (Collection Repères)*. Paris, France: La Découverte.

Foray, D., & Lundvall, B. A. (1996). The knowledge-based economy: From the economics of knowledge to the learning economy. In *Employment and growth in the knowledge-based economy*. Paris, France: The Organisation for Economic Co-operation and Development.

Gold, A., Malhotra, A., & Segars, A. (2001). Knowledge management: An organizational capabilities perspective. *Journal of Management Information Systems, 18*(1), 185–214. doi:10.1080/07421222.2001.11045669

Grant, R. M. (1996). Prospering in dynamically-competitive environments: Organizational capability as knowledge integration. *Organization Science, 7*(4), 375–387. doi:10.1287/orsc.7.4.375

Habib, J. (2010). La dynamique de création de connaissances dans le processus d'innovation: Analyse comparée de quatre études de cas dans le secteur de la santé electronique. *Système d'Information et Management, 15*(4), 93-133. Retrieved from http://aisel.aisnet.org/sim/vol15/iss4/4

Harkema, S. J., & Browayes, M. J. (2003). Managing innovation successfully: A complex process, *Proceedings of the European Academy of Management (EURAM)*.

Harvey, J. F. (2011). Comment favoriser le partage des connaissances? Le cas des communautés de pratique pilotées. *Revue Internationale de Gestion, 35*(4), 73–80. doi:10.3917/riges.354.0073

Hatch, M. J. (2000). *Théories des organisations, de l'intérêt des perspectives multiples*. Paris, France: De Boeck Université.

Hatchuel, A., Le Masson, P., & Benoit, W. (2002). De la gestion des connaissances aux organisation orientées conception. *Revue Internationale des Sciences Sociales, 171*(1), 29–42. doi:10.3917/riss.171.0029

Jacob, R., & Pariat, R. (2002). Savez-vous vraiment ce que vous savez. *Réseau CEFRIO, 3*(2), 3-7. Retrieved from http://www.cefrio.qc.ca/media/uploader/Reseau_Cefrio-final_2002.pdf

Kalika, M. (2006). *Management et TIC*. Éditions Liaisons.

Knauf, A. (2010). *Les dispositifs d'intelligence économique, compétences et fonctions utiles à leur pilotage*. Paris, France: L'Harmattan.

Langdon, M. (1998). La chaîne de la connaissance, stratégie d'entreprise pour Internet (Village ed.). Paris, France: Mondial.

Le Boterf, G. (2002). Mise en place d'une démarche compétence. *Revue de l'Entreprise, 60*, 41–50.

Mack, M. (1995, September-October). L'organisation apprenante comme système de transformation de la connaissance en valeur. *Revue Française de Gestion, 105*, 43–48.

Michel, J. (2001). Le knowledge management, entre effet de mode et (ré) invention de la roue. *Documentaliste - Sciences de l'Information, 38*(3-4), 176–186. doi:10.3917/docsi.383.0176

Miller, W., & Morris, L. (1999). Fourth generation R&D: Managing knowledge. *Technology and Innovation*. Innovation Labs. Accessed from https:// journals.sagepub.com/doi/abs/10.1177/2394964315627259

Nonaka, I. (1994, February). A dynamic theory of organizational knowledge creation. Organization Science, 5(1), 14-37. doi:1047-7039/94/0501/0014

Paillard, S. (Ed.). (2002). Les indicateurs de l'économie de la connaissance. Commissariat général du plan: Service du Developpement Technologique et Industrie. La documentation française.

Penrose, E. (1959). Les principes du management des ressources fondées sur le savoir. *Revue Française de Gestion, 105*, 70–75.

Powell, W. W. (1990). Neither markets nor hierarchy: Network forms of organisation. *Research in Organizational Behavior, 12*, 295–336.

Prax, J. Y. (2012). *Manuel du knowledge management, mettre en réseau les hommes et les savoirs pour créer de la valeur* (3rd ed.). Paris, France: Dunod.

Racheline, P. (1999). Les hébreux et l'entreprise apprenante. *L'Expansion Management Review*, 120-126.

Ramirez, R. (1999). *Pour une nouvelle conception de la création de valeur: L'art de l'entreprise globale. In Guide de la mondialisation* (pp. 108–113). Paris, France: Les Echos.

Reix, R. (1990). L'impact organisationnel des nouvelles technologies de l'information. *Revue Française de Gestion, 77*, 100–106.

Reix, R. (1995). Savoir tacite et savoir formalisé dans l'entreprise. *Revue Française de Gestion, 105*, 17–28.

Sandhawalia, B. S., & Dalcher, D. (2011). Developing knowledge management capabilities: A structured approach. *Journal of Knowledge Management, 2*(15), 313–328. doi:10.1108/13673271111119718

Scarbrought, H., Swan, J., Newell, S., & Hislop, D. (2000). *Innovation processes and the management of knowledge, knowledge management: Concepts and controversies*. Coventry, UK: University of Warwick.

Schiuma, G. (2012). Managing knowledge for business performance improvement. *Journal of Knowledge Management, 4*(16), 515–522. doi:10.1108/13673271211246103

Schware, R. (2005). *E-Development: From excitement to effectiveness*. Washington, DC: Banque Mondiale. doi:10.1596/0-8213-6442-1

Spender, J. C., & Grant, R. M. (1996). Knowledge and the firm: Overview. *Strategic Management Journal, 17*(SI). doi:10.1002mj.4250171103

Tarondeau, J. C. (1998). *Le management des savoirs*. Paris, France: Presses Universitaires de France.

Tarondeau, J. C., & Wright, R. W. (1995). La transversalité dans les organisations ou le contrôle par les processus. *Revue Française de Gestion, 104*, 112–121.

Tisseyre, R. C. (1999). *Knowledge management: Théorie et pratique de la gestion des connaissances*. Paris, France: Hermes Sciences Publications.

Wang, D., Zhongfeng, S. U., & Yang, D. (2011). Organizational culture and knowledge creation capability. *Journal of Knowledge Management, 15*(3), 363–373. doi:10.1108/13673271111137385

KEY TERMS AND DEFINITIONS

Competitiveness: The ability of a firm to offer, in relation to its competitors, products of higher value at equal or lower-cost and to build competitive positions that enable superior economic performance.

Environment: Complex set of internal and external factors that affect the company's decisions and the evolution of its business. The more dynamic the environment, the more dynamic the organizational structure becomes.

Innovation: The mechanism by which organizations produce new products, processes, and systems necessary to adapt to the changing markets, technologies, and modes of competition.

Knowledge Management: A set of methods of organizations and technologies used with the aim of creating, collecting, organizing, storing, diffusing, using, and transferring knowledge within the company.

Learning Organization: The learning organization is a professional organization that learns from its own professional practices, but beyond that, it adapts, evolves, creates, and recombines knowledge. It develops its own skills through its professional experience, rich in its successes and defeats.

Structure Network: A form of organization that connects different players of different qualifications and status: employees, suppliers, customers, banks, and even competitors.

Tunisian Companies: Companies operating in the Tunisian market.

APPENDIX 1

Table 2. List of dependencies between customer relationship management and knowledge management

Variable 1	*	Variable 2	X2	ddl	Asymptotic Significance
Customer relationship management	*	Team building and effective communication	8.390	1	0.04
Customer relationship management	*	Advanced knowledge	6.016	1	0.014
Customer relationship management	*	Knowledge management approach	3.841	1	0.05
Customer relationship management	*	Objectives of knowledge management	7.331	2	0.026
Customer relationship management	*	Specialists to manage knowledge	5.734	1	0.017

APPENDIX 2

Table 3. Listing of dependency between the forms of inter-companies cooperation and costs reduction

Variable 1	*	Variable 2	X2	ddl	Asymptotic Significance
Inter-company cooperation	*	Reduction of costs	25.191	6	0.000

APPENDIX 3

Table 4. List of dependencies between knowledge management and innovation

Variable 1	*	Variable 2	X2	ddl	Asymptotic Significance
Knowledge quality	*	Differentiation through innovation	7.704	2	0.021
Basic knowledge	*	Differentiation through innovation	4.440	1	0.035
Basic knowledge	*	Manufacture of a new product	8.250	1	0.004
Basic knowledge	*	Manufacture of a new product	4.474	1	0.034
Knowledge capitalization	*	Manufacture of a new product	9.438	1	0.002
Knowledge capitalization	*	Sorts of innovation	9.848	4	0.043
New knowledge creation	*	Sorts of innovation	9.742	4	0.045
Specialists to manage knowledge	*	New product development	4.123	1	0.042
Dedication of time to manage knowledge	*	Sorts of innovation	9.620	4	0.047
Dedication of time to manage knowledge	*	Differentiation through innovation	8.334	1	0.004

APPENDIX 4

Table 5. List of dependencies between the degree of formalization of the organization and its innovation

Variable 1	*	Variable 2	X2	ddl	Asymptotic Significance
Communication based on mutual adjustment	*	Opening of a new market	5.581	1	0.018
Communication based on formal messages	*	Sorts of innovation	10.944	4	0.027
Communication based on formal messages	*	Conceptualization of a new service	6.425	1	0.011
Control system based on codified elements	*	Opening of a new market	5.295	1	0.021
Control system based on codified elements	*	Development of a new product	8.250	1	0.004
Control system based on codified elements	*	Differentiation through innovation	4.919	1	0.027
Important role assigned to the enterprise culture	*	Opening of a new market	3.862	1	0.049

Chapter 6
Organizational Learning and Competitive Advantage

Juliana Mulaa Namada
United States International University – Africa, Kenya

ABSTRACT

Environmental turbulence in today's business landscape has elicited deep concerns in contemporary business organizations. As a result, organizations seek to achieve competitive advantage through organizational learning. This chapter presents organizational learning as a key source of competitive advantage in contemporary business organizations. It examines the concept of organizational learning by definition and delves in the four constituents that form the concept of organizational learning, namely knowledge acquisition, knowledge distribution, information interpretation, and organizational memory. Further, the chapter focuses on the factors affecting organizational learning together with competitive advantage as an outcome of organizational learning.

INTRODUCTION

In today's knowledge economy, learning has become a fundamental competency required by organizations that desire to survive and thrive in their respective industries. Market leaders are often asking learning questions, always seeking for opportunities to learn how internal processes can be managed and how best the acquired knowledge throughout the entire organization. With a focus on organizational learning and competitive advantage, many organizations achieve prosperity and sustainability within the current competitive business environment. Organizational learning enables firms to respond quickly and adapt to the turbulent business environment. Similarly competitive advantage through innovation, focus, cost leadership or differentiation strategies enables firms in various sectors to sustain supper profits.

The Concept of Organizational Learning

Organizational learning is portrayed differently by different scholars. It means new insights according to Argyris and Schon (1978), new structures (Chandler, 1962), new systems (Miles, 1982) or a combination

DOI: 10.4018/978-1-5225-3725-0.ch006

of all of the above. Fiol & Lyles (1985) defined organizational learning as the development of insights, knowledge, associations between past actions and the effectiveness of those actions and future actions. Further, Cummings and Whorley (2009) defined organizational learning as a change process which enhances the ability of an organization to acquire and develop new knowledge. Organizational learning results from; assimilating information; translating information into knowledge; applying knowledge to real words; and receiving feedback. In a nutshell, organizational learning is a composition of individual learning, development of culture, continuous improvement, innovation, and applying systems which learn.

There are two orientations to learning; adaptive learning and generative learning. Adaptive learning involves an unintentionalphenomenon that brings about a relatively definite change in behavior and ispowered by an individual's reaction towards different stimuli in their immediate environment. Generative learning on the other hand, revolves around the concept of an individual adding on new behaviors, knowledge, and skills to what they already have and applying these to their various situations. McKenna (1992) established that in team learning, it is essential for people to move beyond themselves and permit a collective learning to occur.

Learning happens at three levels within an organization. This includes individual, group and institutional learning. The levels of learning interact to make up organizational learning.Individual learning occurs when employees acquire knowledge, development skills and adopt new attitudes and beliefs which enable the organization to succeed. Individuals are important in organizational learning process. At its basic level, the individuals within an organization are involved in perceiving similarities, differences, patterns and possibilities. Through intuition, some individuals focus on the expert view translated into tacit knowledge while the others focus on the entrepreneurial view which enables them to generate new knowledge. Individual learning is transformed into group learning through shared understanding.

For team learning to occur, it requires insights to be thought through, actions to be innovative and coordinated, and each team member to understand the role they're required to play. Group learning occurs as members of a group discover how to contribute to performance. Team members learn from each other, share goals and place value on member interaction. Organizational learning refers to ongoing processes which facilitate individuals and groups to learn. It occurs where there is a shared understanding in the whole organization. According to Starbucks and Whalen (2008), organizational learning is information, insights, knowledge and mental models of members. Further a study by Bryson, Crosby, and Stone, (2006) discovered that the organization's provision of capability development opportunities as well as an individual's proactive behavior had an impact on employees' motivation to engage in learning at their workplace. Institutionalization is the process of embedding learning that has occurred by the individuals and group into the organization through knowledge acquisition, information distribution, information interpretation and organizational memory.

Knowledge Acquisition

This is the process by which knowledge is obtained. Organizational activities intended to acquire knowledge are customer surveys, research, development activities, performance reviews and analyses of competitor products. Huber (1991) presupposes that an organization acquires knowledge through five main processes; congenital learning, experiential learning, vicarious learning, grafting and searching. He observed that there exist a time interval between when the organization is first conceived and the arbitrary "birth" event when the organization is incorporated. During this interval, the founders employ vicarious learning, grafting or learning on behalf of the organization to be.

Congenital knowledge base is the knowledge that a firm's founders bring from previous international experiences. It is a combination of knowledge inherited at conception and knowledge acquired both locally and internationally. The nature of an organization is greatly influenced by its founders and the argument that an organization is a reflection of its top management holds true (Hambrick& Mason. 1984; Huber, 1991). What an organization has at inception influences what it searches for, what it experiences and how it interprets what it encounters.

Experiential learning as a way of knowledge acquisition is varied and includes experiments to test the acceptability of new products; self-appraisal, unsystematic learning and experience based learning curves. Organizations acquire knowledge through direct experiences, unintentional ways and other times through systematic efforts. When there is lack of fit between the organization and its environment, the organization either fails to survive (atrophies and dies) or undergoes costly transformations (Mintzberg, 1990; Huber, 1991, Grant, 2003). This necessitates the need for environmental scanning for knowledge acquisition.Organizations scan their environment for information about changes, new technologies and changing customer preferences. Environmental scanning varies in intensity from high vigilance to active scanning, routine scanning or mere maintenance of state of alertness for non-routine but relevant information.

Vicarious learning is learning that is derived from indirect sources such as hearing or observation, rather than direct, hands-on or through instruction. It could be obtained from expert exposure through apprenticeship and tacit knowledge. Performance monitoring is yet another way of acquiring information. Learning happens through exposure to the learning experiences of others. Processes such as reinforcement, explanation, correction are effective for the observer as well as for the original participant. The mediums of knowledge transmission are dialogue and other forms of indirect communication. Through performance monitoring, organizations assess how well they meet their own standards. Aspects measured include inventory levels, quality standards, customer demands and stake holder expectations. Crozier (1965) maintained a pessimistic position that organizations can not correct their behavior by learning from their past mistakes. Huber (1991) counters this argument and categorically states that performance monitoring improves firm performance through use of feedback from key stakeholders.

Information Distribution

Information distribution refers to the processes through which individuals, groups, or different units of the organization share data and information among themselves. It is a determinant of both the occurrence and breath of organizational learning. Occurrence relates to where an organizational system integrates information gathered from different departments for use by the whole organization. Information breath on the other hand defines the quantity and the type of information available to the organization through different departments. The whole process becomes a learning experience for the organization because information from different departments is sharedby other members of the organization, thereby facilitating common understanding. When information is widely distributed in an organization such that it has multiple sources of origin and its retrieval is easy, then individuals and units are likely to be able to learn. Huber (1991) posits that one of the organizational processes that facilitate the coupling of those who need non routine information and those who have it is internal employee transfer, whether employee initiated or employer initiated. Extant literature on organizational communications has revealed a great deal about information distribution in organizations, through numerous reviews. Drawing on these reviews, a number of propositions emerge which explain in detail organizational information distribution as presented below;

Propositions Concerning Information Distribution in Organizations

1. The probability that unit A will route information to unit B is:
   a. Positively related to A's view of the information's relevance to B,
   b. Positively related to B's power and status,
   c. Negatively related to A's view of A's costs of routing the information to B
   d. Negatively related to A's workload,
   e. Positively related to the rewards but negatively related to the penalties that A expects
   f. Positively related to the frequency A has routed information to B in the recent past.
2. The probability of delay in the routing of information by A to B is:
   a. Positively related to the workload of A,
   b. Positively related to links in the communication chain connecting A to B,
   c. Negatively related to A's view of the timeliness of the information for B
3. The probability or extent of information distortion by A when communicating to B is:
   a. Positively related to A's goal attainment that will result from the distortion,
   b. Negatively related to the penalty that A expects to incur as a result of the distortion,
   c. Positively related to the amount of discretion allowed in the presentation format,
   d. Positively related to the difference between the actual and expected information,
   e. Positively related to A's work overload,
   f. Positively related to the number of sequential links connecting A with B.

From Huber (1982) and Huber and Daft (1987)

Combining information from different subunits leads not only to new information but also to new understanding. Information distribution makes the retrieval process easier within the organization due to the many sources of the same information. Combining information from several departments lead to new understanding by members of the organization and so facilitates the development of new information. In this way, information distribution is a precursor and an important component of organizational learning.

Information Interpretation

Interpretation pertains to the process by which managers translate data into knowledge and understanding about the environment. Weick (1984) defined interpretation as "a process of translating events, developing shared understanding and conceptual schemes" (p. 286). However, the question that rises from the definition is whether learning occurs when units develop a common interpretation or when they develop different interpretations of the same information. In response to Weicks' definition, Huber (1991) contents that more learning occur when varied interpretations are developed because such variations change the range of organization's potential behavior, which is congruent with the definition of learning.

Dutton, Fahey and Narayanan (1983) provide a rich conceptual description of interpretation in the context of development of corporate strategy. It seems likely that the extent of shared interpretation of new information is affected by the uniformity of prior cognitive maps possessed by organization units.

This is normally exemplified by the uniformity of framing the organization as it is communicated and the richness of the media used to convey the information. Again, information load on the units and the amount of unlearning that may be necessary before new information granted is also affected by learning capability. Unlearning is a process through which learners discard knowledge which is obsolete and misleading. Huber (1991) gives an example of unlearning by an organization as the discharge of managers who are unable to move from outdated ways of doing things and those who belong to the old school of thought that has become irrelevant and dysfunctional. Interpretation is the process of translating events, developing models for understanding, bringing out meaning and assembling conceptual schemes amongst employees.

Organizations could use either passive or active modes in interpreation. The interpretation could be done through undirected viewing or conditional viewing. Organizations vary on environmental beliefs and their instruments into the environment. These varieties are at either the internal industry environment or external environment. The process of interpretation varies according to equivocality reduction and assembly rules (Starbuck & Whalen, 2008). Equivocality is the extent to which data is unclear and yields multiple interpretations and it is more in organizations characterized by undirected viewing. Assembly rules are the procedures that organization uses to process data into collective interpretation.The content and extent of enforcement depend on each organization. Weick (1979) noted that the greater the equivocality, the lesser the rules used to arrive at an interpretation.The smaller the equivocalitythe greater the number of rules in the organization and the greater the equivocality, the more times the information or data is cycled among members before common interpretation is reached.

In a turbulent business environment, organizations adopt enacting mode which reflects active and intrusive strategy. Organizations in this mode construct their own environments like the case of blue ocean strategy. They gather information by experimenting and seeing what happens within the competitive environment before taking action. They experiment, test, stimulate while ignoring traditional expectation.These organizations tend to construct markets rather than waiting for an assessment of demand to know what to produce. In such organizations emphasis is on detecting the right answers in an analyzed environment rather than shaping the answer. Thoseorganizations use market research, trend analysis and forecasting to predict problem and opportunities.Interpretation focuses on the environment, characteristics and expectations of the competing organizations. They assure an analyzable environment, relying on established data collection procedures.

Organizational Memory

Organizational memory refers to the accumulated body of data, information, and knowledge created in the course of an organization's existence. It is largely undocumented experiences, insights, knowledge

Figure 1. Relationship between scanning interpretation and learning
Starbuck, W. H. &Whalen,P.S. (2008). Learning by Organizations: Organizational Learning and Knowledge Management, Vol, II, Northamptone, USA, Edward and Elgar Publishing Inc. p 286.

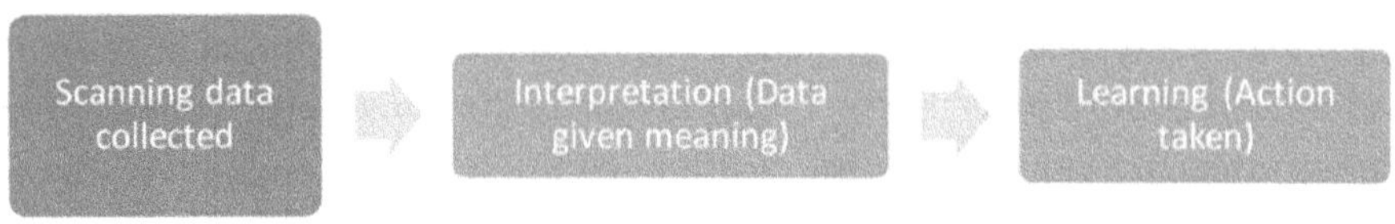

Table 1. Model of organization interpretation

	Undirected Viewing	Enacting
Unanalyzable	-Constrained interpretation -Non-routine -Interpret data -Rumor -Chance -Opportunities	-Expectation -Testing -Conversion -Invention -Learn by doing
Analyzable	-Conditioned viewing -Interprets with traditional boundaries -Passive detection -Routine -Formal data	-Discovering -Formal search -Questioning -Surveys -Data gathering -Active detection
	Passive	Active
	Organizational Intrusiveness	

Starbuck, W. H. & Whalen,P.S. (2008). Learning by Organizations: Organizational Learning and Knowledge Management, Vol, II, Northamptone, USA, Edward & Elgar Publishing Inc. p 289.

and skills acquired over the years by individuals within an organization. It can be transferred to new employees through formal and informal mentoring and training but could easily be lost and destroyed through attrition and organizational change. Organizational memory is a function of both human components exemplified in the mind and computer based programs. Most of the soft information is stored in the minds of the members of the organization. These members have organizational experience which makes them experts in organizational experience through some exposure to specific routine operations. This expertise according to Nonoka (1991) is tacit knowledge which is undocumented but engrained in the mind of the expert. Transmission of this information from one member to another may be difficult but could be facilitated through apprenticeship. Other key stakeholders, like the customers, suppliers, competitors and the distributors hold in their mind, valuable information through continuous interaction with organizational departments.

Human components of organizational memory are rich in information because they include all the stakeholders both internal and external to the organization. However, it is worth noting that the human components are adversely affected by the human limitation and the organization could end up losing substantial amount of such type of information. Employee turnover, for example leads to a great loss of organizational memory. Unprecedented illness affecting the employees may also abruptly lead to loss of information. An employee with a wealth of knowledge could die from an abrupt accident, or suffer stroke or body shock which may all lead to memory loss, thus leading to loss of information. Business intelligence conducted by other organizations also makes information regarded as business secretes to be shared illegally with other competing organizations in the same industry thus exposing the competitive advantage of one organization to the other organization.

Environmental turbulence presents a variety of challenges to organizational learning. For example, inability of forecasting with precision causes great loss of some information due to ignorance. Some crucial information is simply lost because the holding component is oblivious of use in the future. Further, the human component is also affected by the internal environment within the organization including the set standards, norms and culture. Mintzberg's (1975) work indicates that managers and supervisors routinely acquire and mentally store "soft" information for business purposes. Organizations information is used on routine basis both for operations and reporting.

Due to human limitations, organizations have come up with computer based organizational memory. This is a technique where organizations information is stored in computers. Some organizations use a computer expert system known as fuzzy neural networks as a backup of their memory.Using computer based systems; organizations use expert systems through softwareprograms. Such expert systems have properties, such as accessibility, reliability, and "own-ability," that are are useful components of organizational memories. Computer based memory are stored in form of electronic mails transmitted, electronic bulletins, reports and storage backups. Organizations store a great deal of "hard" information on a routine basis, some-times for operating reasons and sometimes to satisfy the reporting requirements of other units or organizations.

The ability to learn depends on organization memory. In manufacturing industries, information related to the time necessary to complete fabrication of certain products, to receive shipment of ordered material and to recruit employees are all created, transmitted and stored using electronic mail, electronic bulletins or electronic blackboard system. A great deal of organizational knowledge about how to do things is stored in the form of standard operating procedures, routines, and scripts (Feldman, 1989). Huber (1991) emphasizes the critical role of organizational memory by stating that to be able to learn that which has been learned must be stored in memory and then brought forth from memory.

Factors Affecting Organizational Learning

The environment in which an organization is operating has a profound influence on the learning processes. Organizational learning is largely affected by both micro and macro factors within the business environment. External factors such as the wider societal and the institutional context may impact in specific ways upon the learning process and hence affect the organizational ability to mobilize knowledge. For example, regulatory policies and financial incentives influence the forms of learning and the ultimate potential for learning. Industry conditions, such as aggressive international competition can influence the viability and imperatives of knowledge exchange in international joint ventures and strategic partners.

Organizational learning is affected by several factors which are internal and external to the business environment. They include structure, culture, knowledge sharing organizational leadership, internal work environment, external networks and the experience of the organizational members. In terms of organizational structure different categories of structure like formalized structure, centralized structures affect organization learning differently provided by the organization. The public sector on the other hand faces a number of particular pressures influencing the need for and processes of organizational learning. These pressures include: local, national and international competition from the private sectors for service delivery and increasing public expectations of services.

Organizational Structure

Structure is a pattern of relationships which define responsibilities and roles within an organization. Mintzberg (1991) defined structure as the set of all the ways in which the work is divided into different tasks achieving coordination within the organization. Organizational structure indicates to what degree organizations approve decision-making power, standardize the rules and regulations and integrate members and employees to establish their association and formal interactions (Chen, Huang, & Hsiao, 2010).

The design and structure of organizations regulates the relations and interactions between people. An appropriate structure can facilitate the information processing cycle, a process that requires significant human interactions. Organizational structure usually determines organizational learning itself (Fiol & Lyles, 1985). It therefore plays a crucial role in determining the learning processes within the organization.

Organizational learning is depended on the nature of the structure in place. Formalization is one key type of structural orientation which facilitates organizational learning. It refers to the standardization of jobs in the organization and directing behavioral limit of employees based on rules and regulations. In organizations with high levels of formalization, job descriptions are explicitly explained. The importance of formalization is underscored in organizational learning through the espoused theory. Highly formalized organizations practice written procedures and structured information flows widely which reduces discussions of alternatives to creative solutions (Pugh, Hickson & Turner, 1968). With low levels of formalization, jobs are less structured and there is more flexibility and freedom when dealing with organizational activities (Sivadas and Dwyer, 2000). It allows employees to take initiative and willingness to take alternatives into account when executing their duties. The social interplay and association is witnessed more when executing activities.

A less formalized structure can encourage social interactions, creativity and learning processes (Martínez-León & Martínez-García, 2011). While formalization reduces ambiguity and provides direction to employees, it is not without disadvantages including the reduction of innovativeness because employees are used to behaving in a certain manner (Carpenter, Bauer, & Erdogan, 2016). The greater the uncertainty in an environment the greater the organization needs to learn. Firms purposefully adopt structures and strategies to encourage learning. The structures of an organization define the way the processes interact (Chandler, 1990). It gives rise to organizational learning. Information structures and communication flows facilitate integrative learning. Development structures provide a vehicle for learning about new technological developments within the industry.

Complexity is the degree to which activities, processes and routines within the organization are differentiated. Differentiation may be horizontal, vertical or spatial and may affect the effectiveness of communication (FAO, 2016). Knowledge is the result of the learning process and is an intangible asset that is found in the minds of individuals, processes, routines, and organizational capacities, as well as, in relationships that companies maintain with their environments (Martı´nez-Leo´n &Martı´nez-Garcı´a, 2011). It is argued that organizational learning, hence knowledge transfer, takes place in the individual, group, and organizational levels and the extent or nature of an organization's structural complexity may have an effect on the aspect of organizational learning (Crossan, Lane, & White, 1999). Less differentiated structures encourage learning because it provides room for discussions, interpretations and the development of consensus about shared understanding.

Centralization is the degree to which decision-making takes place at upper levels of the organization. If the degree of decentralization is high, there is delegation of authority, and employees can execute their activities with minimum need of approval from an upper level manager. Decentralization promotes communication in organizations which creates a workplace with a faster response to change. Dicle and Okan (2015) posited that decentralization facilitates interpersonal exchange and social interaction, essential for transferring strategic knowledge.The number of levels that a company structure has is also important. In tall structures, the number of employees reporting to each manager tends to be smaller, resulting in greater opportunities for managers to supervise and monitor employee activities. In contrast, flat structures involve a larger number of employees reporting to each manager. With a flatter organizational structure, job behaviors are less structured and there is tendency for employees to have more freedom when dealing with organizational activities. This brings willingness to take alternatives into account thus facilitating learning. This flexible social interaction and collaboration is observed when implementing tasks and may encourage organizational learning (Robbins & Decenzo, 2001).

Corporate structures may also differ in terms of departmentalization, which is broadly categorized as either functional or divisional. Woods (2004) define the functional structure as one whereby jobs are grouped based on similarity in functions and that such structures may have departments such as marketing, manufacturing, finance, accounting, human resources, and information technology. The primary forms of departmentalization are by function, process, product, market, customer, geographic area, and sometimes matrix. In many organizations, combinations of these forms are used. Structure shapes the effectiveness of an organization in terms of inter-departmental working relationships, product and service development lead times, quality, efficiency, and responsiveness to customer demands. Montana and Charnov (1993) posited that it also influences sharing of mental models (learning and "un-learning") of individual employees and working team morale, motivation, commitment, and satisfaction.

An organic structure is one that is very flexible and is able to adapt well to changes. Normally it exhibits little job specialization, few layers of management, decentralized decision-making, and not much direct supervision. Organic structures are flexible and encourage individual thought process. This type of structure is presumed to encourage learning in an organization as the adopted organization philosophy promotes the encouragement of creativity of individuals. It is based on the hypothesis that productivity and adaptability to rapid change is increased when employees are placed at the center of their environment and they are allowed to manage themselves and their resources learning is likely to take place. When creativity is accounted for and rewarded and where their continuous development is encouraged through provision of opportunities and resources (Montana & Charnov, 1993). In an organic structure, members discuss more openly and information flows freely enhancing possibilities of arriving at solutions to problems. Members' insights are valued and are evaluated to without any form of reprimand. Such initiatives encourage individual initiatives hence facilitating learning.

Organizational Culture

Organizational culture is a system of shared assumptions, values, and beliefs, which informs and governs how people behave in organizations. These shared values have an influence on the people in the organization and dictate how they dress, act, and perform their jobs. A culture is formed or created when an organization is established, and it evolves over time. It exists in the form of artifacts, language, behavior patterns, norms, values, heroes, symbols, beliefs, attitudes, ethical codes, basic assumptions and the organization's history. A learning culture is a community of workers who are continuously and collectively seeking improvement through new knowledge, new skills, and new applications of knowledge and skills to achieve the goals of the organization. It is a culture of inquiry where employees feel safe asking tough questions about the purpose and quality of what they are doing for customers, themselves, and other stakeholders.

There are three important cultures of management that influence learning in the organization are the culture of engineering, leadership and operations. Sharing of knowledge in an organization is a vital component of organizational learning and it is influenced by the organization's culture. Pillania (2006) in her study of the impact of organization culture on knowledge management found that cultural mindsets and misconceptions about knowledge sharing in organizations prevented them from adopting learning practices that could promote an organization's performance. Leidner, Alavi and Kayworth (2006) studied the effects of organization culture on knowledge management practices. Their findings indicated that values at the organization level influence the ways in which business values were formed and that these values varied from group to group. They also noted that the value system created different outcomes for the organization.

Cultural evolvements of factors affect different organizations in terms of leadership history, technology, industry and the organization. Culture also shapes clients and customer's attitudes, the organization's expectations, the organization's information and control systems. It also impacts on the legislation and the environment of the organization, procedures and policies, reward systems and value systems. Hence to create a learning environment, it is important to promote inquiry and trust with confrontational attitudes. To achieve this, Mchugh, Groves and Alker (1998) explained that an organization needs mechanisms for discarding unwanted values through a process of 'unlearning' and also mechanisms for finding and evaluating organizational theories of action.

The importance of organizational culture is such that the culture of a workplace makes the organization what it is since it is the sum of attitudes, customs and beliefs that distinguish one group of people from another. According to Sponaugle (2016) culture serves as a unifier of people and allows them to learn from one another. The pursuit of learning is woven into the fabric of organizational life. Tharpe (2009) observed that the key to using culture to improve learning and performance in an organization lies in matching culture or attributes to organizational goals. Some cultures might be appropriate in certain contexts than others.Every organization develops and maintains a unique culture, which provides guidelines and boundaries for the behavior of the members of the organization (McLaughlin, 2016). Organizations have subcultures as groups made up of members from different cultures or subcultures within the same organization may have difficulty communicating with each other, even if they speak the same native language.

There are different types of organizational culture including the control type, market type, collaborative type and adhocracy culture. The control culture values institutionalization, management, and an all-around characterized structure for power and basic leadership. According to Tharpe (2009), the control culture is characterized or portrayed by solidness. This culture is not deemed to be supportive to organizational learning as it is backward looking and does not embrace change. It is heavily led by systems and procedures. On the other hand, market culture is said to have a positive correlation with organizational learning due to the fact that it transforms the organization into an aggressive competing and customer focused entity seeking to learn from the competitive environment (OCAI, 2016).Collaborative type of learning focuses on the many stakeholders to search for information, find meaning and strategies to a common problem. It benefits from the concerted effort to find a solution to an organizational problem.

Adhocracy oriented cultures are dynamic and entrepreneurial in nature. They have a focus on risk taking, innovation, and being action oriented. Quinn and Cameron (2005) established that adhocracy organizations value flexibility, adaptability, and thrive in what would have earlier been viewed as unmanageable chaos. High-tech companies like Google, Microsoft and IBM are prototypical adhocracy culture. Tharpe (2009) noted that this culture allows individuals to improve their chances of introducing new ideas and knowledge in a way that may not be planned but is more innovative and efficient, working in coherence with the strategy and without generating duplication of effort. It may be concluded that a high level of autonomy at work produces more effective organizational learning outcomes as it facilitates new knowledge creation (Martı´nez-Leo´n & Martı´nez-Garcı´a, 2011).

Adhocracy cultures help individuals to share knowledge and engage in learning-related activities effectively and reduce barriers to shared learning. Cummings and Whorley (2009) observed that learning organizations have flat managerial hierarchies and empower individuals. Another observation they made was that a learning organization's culture needs to greatly influence how individuals gather, process, and share information in the organization. They purported that this type of culture needs to be based on openness, creativity, and experimentation. Mistakes or errors are considered a normal part of the learning process and individuals are able to learn from their failures and develop themselves as well as their organizations. Organizations with this culture create a set of norms, symbols, and behaviors which encourage learning in organizations. This type of culture facilitates continuous improvement and adaptation at all levels in an organization.

Internal Work Environment and External Networks

The work environment facilitates learning and creative behavior in an organization. Project teams may set ideal environment for developing inquiry skills to enable the employees better understand the assumptions and the consequences of different project actions. Project based learning sets stage for reflective practice to benefit both the individual and the organization. Organizations develop internal linking mechanisms which act as the bridges that connect different functions in an organization. Cross team linkages interdepartmental cooperation and internal collaborations enhance internal learning. It is through this mechanisms that business collaborations and problem solving is done. These mechanisms include project teams, committees and taskforces and formal meetings. When members from different departments form different teams work on a specified project, they end up sharing knowledge for the common good. Therefore the nature of teams and the freedom accorded to these members throughout the working period contribute to learning in an organization. Investigative taskforces within an organization impact on learning. Taskforces are normally appointed to establish root causes of different problems in an organization. Through this mechanisms learning and innovation is created through combining different knowledge and skills of the individuals from different disciplines and departments.

The social networks affect organizations ability to learn in a number of ways. Ferreira, Santos and Serra (2010) noted that networks enable investing firms intending to establish multinational corporations (MNCs) to obtain valuable host country information through their social ties to either local partner firms or other firms operating in those markets . Through such networks they establish contacts with industry stakeholders including suppliers, customers, distributors, financial organizations, industry associations and the regulators. Similarly, Hansen (1999) noted that organizations may benefit from the transfer of explicit and tacit knowledge within a network. Networks make it easier to identify new relevant knowledge and transfer itat a lower transaction cost. Network contacts improve innovation capabilities. For example, small firms connected to large firms perform better in innovations than otherwise due to technological and skill transfer. By connecting with other organizations, companies gain access to the physical informational resources which enable them to select foreign markets and create entry initiatives through the network contacts. This suggests that networks have the ability to convey information from one organization to the other. Further, the networks act as a buffering mechanism against environmental uncertainties by providing access to the physical, financial and social resources needed by the organizations.

External links with other organizations are drivers of learning. These external linkages could be achieved through joint ventures, licensing, acquisitions strategic alliances and even mergers with different organizations. Lei et al. (1997) studied the relationship between strategic alliance and organizational learning and found that organizations could build cooperative advantage by learning from partnerships with other organizations. He explains that alliance-based learning is influenced by the contextual factors that surrounded organizations in partnership. These factors take the form of the business activity of the organization, the type of knowledge that is shared between organizations, and the organization's reward systems. Learning is not associated with an organization's performance alone but also with the organization's partnership with other organizations through their network interpretations, structures, and practices.

Knowledge Sharing

Knowledge sharing is fundamentally the act of making knowledge available to others inside the organization. According to Ngah and Ibrahim (2016) knowledge sharing enables managers to keep the individual learning flowing throughout the company and integrate it for practical application. Knowledge sharing is believed to be the most vital procedure of information administration (Bok & Kim, 2002). Information sharing is a proportional procedure of learning trade and analyses variables that clarify why people take part in this procedure.Jackson, Chuang, Harden, Jiang and Joseph (2006) concluded that knowledge sharing is the means through which representatives can add to learning application and development of an organization.

Learning through sharing is the operational core of knowledge management. An organizations that manifests important characteristics of a learning organization places emphasis on learning through sharing (Hong &Kuo, 1999). How knowledge sharing may be connected with organizational learning and competitive advantage is of fundamental significance to organizations. If an organization share its knowledge and enhances its learning, it becomes more effective and competitive (Skinnarland, Itera, Oslo, & Sharp, 2016). The retrieval processes is affected by task certainty (or uncertainty), communication strength and communication diversity (structural dimension and content dimension).

Knowledge sharing affects the nature of organizational culture. In their study of the relationships of organizational culture toward knowledge sharing in organizations,Gwo-Guang and Lee (2007) found out that a culture that values flexibility and has an external focus was more likely to successfully promote and manage knowledge sharing in the organization. Conversely, defensive cultural norms impacted performance negatively both at the individual and organization level. Chang and Lee (2007) in studying the relationship between organization culture and its impact on the operation of learning within the organization discovered that culture did influence learning behaviors of individuals in the organization. They also found that transformational leadership had a much more positive relationship with organizational learning than transactional leadership.

Members' Previous Experience

Members' experience determines the rate of learning and unlearning in an organization. Actions and activities of members are key impetus in determining organizational learning. Huber (1991) identified a sample of obstacles to organizational learning from experience. He contends that the organization's members are sensors of experience who function to align information in an organization. Some of these shortcomings are pervasive and others depend on the member's position, background, and style. An organization's members generate feed forward information as well as receiving feedback information in an organization. Feedback of the results of organizational action is often distorted or suppressed or arrives after the need for learning as a basis for changing the action has passed. This is because positive feedback is effectively communicated and appropriate action taken while negative feedback is shunned and not shared widely depending on the perception of the unit managers. Units capable of learning from the experience of other units may not have access to this experience as a consequence of either message routine rules or organizational politics.

How Organizational Learning Affect Competitive Advantage

Competitive advantage is the *panacea* of business survival. According to Porter (1985) competitive advantage is a function of either providing comparable buyer value more efficiently than competitors or performing activities at comparable cost but in unique ways that create more buyer value than competitors. Further, Shah, Mansouri, Esfahan, and Niki (2013) defined competitive advantage as a collection of organization's unique features that allows it to perform better than competitors and competitors are not able to easily replicate such features. Organizational learning theorists have recognized the strategic importance of organizational learning as a means of providing a sustainable competitive advantage and achieving strategic renewal. Bustinza, Molina and Aranda (2010) observed that organizational learning enables firms to create new products, processes and deliver customer value. Through learning organizations are also able to respond quickly and timely to changing environment.

Organizations engage in the pursuit of new knowledge (exploration) and development of things already known (exploitation). Levinthal and March (1993) argued that an organization that engages exclusively in exploration suffers from the fact that it never gains the returns of its knowledge while an organization that engages exclusively in exploitation suffers from obsolescence. According to the two scholars the answer lies in engaging in sufficient exploitation to ensure current viability while devoting enough energy to exploration to ensure future viability. Survival requires a balance and the precise mix of exploitation and exploration. Learning leads organizations into dynamics of exploration and exploitation as well as positive contribution to competitive position.

There are two characteristic features of learning that are important to competitive advantage. First, learning generally increases performance in the form of increased profitability, return on investment and growth in market share. Secondly, learning increases reliability by enabling firms to develop sustainable business models hence providing superior products and services. More experienced and extensively trained individuals generally do better than less experienced ones. They produce fewer surprises and wastage of production material and time. Competitive advantage is clearly enhanced by average performance that learning ordinarily offers. Indeed this feature of learning makes it a prime contributor to competitive advantage as observed by Crossan & Bedrow 2003. By increasing the reliability of individuals and groups, learning tends to reduce exploratory deviations. Senge (1990) postulated that as researchers have considered the stability of differences in firm performance in the face of the changing business environments many have come to view the ability to learn as an important and unique source of sustainable competitive advantage. This is reflected in the attention to learning in management circles.

Different types of learning contribute to competitive advantage differently. According to Senge (1990), there are two types of learning in organizations namely adaptive learning and generative learning. He notes that adaptive learning is about copying and increasing adaptiveness of the organization to the environment. This also allows them to use their creativity in their environment (Stewart, 2001).This characteristic is summarized as having the ability to develop both individual and collective knowledge in the organization. The second one is that those who work for the organization are enlightened and are engaged in their work, striving to reach their potential, by sharing the vision of a worthy goal with collective goal. They also have mental models to guide them in pursuit of personal mastery and their personal goals are in alignment with the mission of the organization. In essence, organizational learning is a way ofimproving performance and boosting competitive advantage and it continuously enhances an organization's capacity to adapt to its external environment through reflective praxis (Lyles, 2012).

Organizational learning results into change which is beneficial to organizations. Senge (1994) also notes that learning in organizations is identified as continuous change of procedures, processes, behaviors patterns and evolving culture. Learning organizations have figured out how to tap people's commitment and capacity to learn at all levels in an organization and therefore he sees this as a sustainable source of competitive advantage, whereby an organization is able to learn faster than its competition. Quoting the Chinese philosopher, Confucius, "without learning the wise become foolish, by learning the foolish became wise", Learn as if you could never have enough of learning.This fits well with the actual need for organizations to continuously learn to cope with the dynamic challenges in their environment and also of the globalized world.

The rate of learning by the employees of an organization also account positively to competitive advantage. Employees who learn quickly through staff training, refresher courses and other continuous improvement initiatives are able to respond timely to the needs of the organization both internally and externally. When teams learn through meetings, brain storming or training sessions that use Strengths, Weaknesses, Opportunities and Threats (SWOT) they end up improving the adaptation capabilities of the organization. They also explore the opportunities they could exploit to become better. From these discussions and sharing, members of the team are able to share knowledge, identify warning signs and take advantage of the opportunities in the environment. This leads to a highly innovative team which is able to be collaborative and enhances the ability to use the combined intellectual team power to solve problems and also tap opportunities. This makes the learning organization to have a sustained competitive advantage within the industries where they operate.

Organizational learning is seen as a continuous improvement not only for individuals within the organization but also for partners and stakeholders affiliated to organizations. Benchmarking is seen as a tool for organizational learning. Another benefit of organizational learning is the ability of organizations to develop entrepreneurial capacity which is important to the innovation processes taken up to act on opportunities that help build and grow the organization. Through learning, organizations are able to bring together the necessary resources that are vital to the implementation of new concepts they create. Learning also means effective implementation of programs, better strategies, policies, actions, decisions, resource allocations, and many more benefits that will all lead to the organization's ability to grow, develop and adapt efficiently to the changes around them.

Organizations with the ability to learn are always abreast with current affairs in their environment in terms of business, industry, and operational environment. Different studies have come up with different theories that can help an organization understand its environment. For instance, an organization can use the SWOT analysis where the company evaluates its internal environment in terms of its strengths and weaknesses as well as its external environment in terms of available opportunities and threats. An organization that is able to capitalize on its strengths and improve on its weaknesses is in a better position than one that is not aware of its strengths and weaknesses. An organization identifies the different opportunities in the environment and find out how it could capitalize on them for its benefit as compared to its competitors. At the same time, the organization must be aware of any threats so that it can prevent their impact on business or better still avoid them at all costs. Continuous scanning of the environment gives an organization an advantage over its competitors.

The process of organizational learning facilitates strategic leadership. Through learning, organizations produce leaders who are able to identify the right leadership style to adopt in order to work in harmony and motivate their employees in different circumstances. Such leaders are able to develop talent and with foresight employ high performing employees who act as game changers in the competitive business environment. Organizational learning enables leaders to remain flexible in all situations of business operations. Leaders who are willing to learn from their employees start to gain. Leaders who listen and accommodate the views of others before making a final decision become a source of motivation to employees. In this case, employees work in support of the decision and hence achieve organizational objectives. Experiential learning is enhanced by analysis of feedback, cause and effect relationships and organizational outcomes. Huber (1991) observed that organizational experience enhances performance. Britain (1998) found that experience predicted organizational survival. Therefore, experience enhances organization effectiveness and hence an important variable in strategic planning of the organization.

Organizational learning affects systems thinking and enables members of the business team to adapt business purpose as their own leading to an increase in personal and organizational growth. Systems thinking allow followers of organizations to accept the cruel realities of competition and learn to adapt with the changes happening in their environment. Stakeholders with high levels of private mastery are able to commit into their lives and see themselves as a part of the complete system. Thus employees with high level of private mastery once combined with the members of the cluster or an organization influence others to own an equivalent thought. Being grounded in reality from insights acquired through learning, such employees objectively establishes the areas where enhancements are required in the organization. They become a vicinity of the system and see themselves as a part of the holistic development of the organization (Martins, 2015).

Mental models facilitate organizational learning processes. A good analogy facilitates easy understanding of the planet. Mental models aid managers in finding drawbacks, as well as the advanced issues inthe company. Mental models developed from learning insights help investors and managers to perceive the globe, since they modify an incomprehensibly difficult world. The necessity to modify arises from our restricted psychological capabilities. The human mind's resolution to the overwhelming complexness of today's world is to create mental models.

Strategic analysis of mental models enhances development of organizations competitive setting. Hodgkinson (2003) noted that data structures impactedon perception, processing data, problem resolution, reasoning, and higher cognitive process. However, finding advanced strategic issues demands that managers come up with choices concerning expectations and the potential outcomes ensuing from their choices. These problem-solving processes have a positive influence on competitive setting (Rehder, 2003). Therefore, it's crucial to grasp managers' inferences concerning chains of cause-effect relationships linking specific call choices to outcomes.

The process of organizational learning creates an environment which facilitates competitive advantage. Oyateru (2011) argues that organizational learning creates an environment for employees to synergize at a group level and come up with better ideas while questioning obsolete ideas. A good organizational culture fostered by a learning organization facilitates synergy of employees that work towards better performance of the organization. Pedlar et al. (1991) highlighted that team based organizational learning promotes a participative environment that encourages employees to contribute their insight to policy making. In such a team there is sharing of information that can be valuable to an organization and synergy of ideas. Balu (2008) emphasizes that market champions keep asking learning questions, keep learning how to do things better and keep sharing knowledge throughout the organization. Therefore learning provides the catalyst and the intellectual resource to create a sustainable competitive advantage.

CONCLUSION

Organizational learning leads to competitive advantage and it is an antecedent of sustainability within the business environment. This chapter introduced the concept of organizational learning by providing several definitions from different scholars and showed how organizations learn. Extant literature has shown that organizations learn through four distinct processes including organizational of knowledge acquisition, information distribution, interpretation and organizational memory. Factors influencing organizational learning are both internal and external to the business environment. In today's complex and competitive business environment, organizational learning presents a key tool to the achievement of competitive advantage through exploitation and exploration. Huber (1991) observed that variables likely to influence the effectiveness of organizational memory include membership attrition, information distribution and interpretation of the information, norms and methods of storing the information and the methods for locating and retrieving stored information.

REFERENCES

Brown, A. (1998). *Organizational Culture.* London: Financial Times Pitman.

Bryson, J. M., Crosby, B. C., & Stone, M. M. (2006). The Design and Implementation of Cross-Sector Collaborations: Propositions from the Literature. *Public Administration Review*, *66*(1), 44–55. doi:10.1111/j.1540-6210.2006.00665.x

Carpenter, M., Bauer, T., & Erdogan, B. (2016, March 11). *Organizational Structure.* Retrieved from http://catalog.flatworldknowledge.com/bookhub/5?e=carpenter-ch07_s01

Chen, C.-J., Huang, J.-W., & Hsiao, Y.-C. (2010). Knowledge management and Innovativeness: The Role of Organizational Climate and Structure. *International Journal of Manpower*, *31*(8), 848–870. doi:10.1108/01437721011088548

Crossan, M. M., Lane, R. E., & White, R. E. (1999). An Organizational Learning Framework: From Intuition to Institution. *Academy of Management Review*, *24*(3), 522–537.

Cummings, T. G., & Whorley, C. G. (2009). *Organizational Development and change. Cengage learning.*

Daft, R. L., & Huber, G. P. (1987). How Organizations Learn: A Communication Framework. *Research in the Sociology of Organizations*, *5*, 1–36.

Dicle, Ü., & Okan, R. Y. (2015). The Relationship between Organizational Structure and Organizational Learning in Turkish Automotive R&D Companies. *International Journal of Managerial Studies and Research*, 62-71.

Dutton, J. E., Fahey, L., & Narayana, V. K. (1983). Toward understanding strategic Issue Diagnosis. *Strategic Management Journal*, *4*(4), 307–323. doi:10.1002mj.4250040403

Feldman, M. (1989). *Order without Design: Information Production and Policy Making*. Stanford, CA: Stanford University Press.

Ferreira, M. P., Santos, J. C., & Serra, F. A. R. (2010). *The International Entrepreneurial Firms Social Networks. Cadernos Abape, 8*(1), 134–145.

Fiol, C. M., & Lyles, M. A. (1985). Organizational Learning. *Academy of Management Review, 10*(4), 803–813.

Gill, J. S. (2003). *The Managers Organizational Learning*. Mumbai: Jaico Publishing Hse.

Grant, R. M. (2003). Strategic Planning in a Turbulent Environment: Evidence from the Oil Majors. *Strategic Management Journal, 24*(6), 49–517. doi:10.1002mj.314

Hambrick, D. C., & Mason, P. A. (1984). Upper Echelons: The Organization as a Reflection of its Top Managers. *Academy of Management Review, 9*(2), 193–206.

Hansen, M. T. (1999). The search-transfer problem: The role of weak ties in sharing knowledge across organization subunits. *Administrative Science Quarterly, 44*(1), 82–111. doi:10.2307/2667032

Hodgkinson, G. P. (2003). The interface of cognitive and industrial, work and organizational psychology. *Journal of Occupational and Organizational Psychology, 76*(1), 1–25. doi:10.1348/096317903321208862

Hong, J. (1999). Structuring for Organizational Learning. *The Learning Organization, 6*(4), 173–186. doi:10.1108/09696479910280631

Hong, J.-C., & Kuo, C.-L. (1999). Knowledge Management in the Learning Organization. *Leadership and Organization Development Journal, 20*(4), 207–215. doi:10.1108/01437739910277019

Huber, G. P. (1982). Organizational Information Systems: Determinants of their Performance and Behavior. *Management Science, 28*(2), 135–155. doi:10.1287/mnsc.28.2.138

Huber, G. P. (1991). Organizational learning: The contributing processes and the literatures. *Organization Science, 2*(1), 88–115. doi:10.1287/orsc.2.1.88

Ipe, M. (2003). Knowledge Sharing on Organizations: A Conceptual Framework. *Human Resource Development Review, 2*(4), 3370358. doi:10.1177/1534484303257985

Jackson, S., Chuang, C.-H., Harden, E. E., Jiang, Y., & Joseph, J. M. (2006). Toward Developing Human Resource Management Systems for Knowledge Intensive Teamwork. *Research in Personnel and Human Management, 25*(6), 27–70.

Leidner, D. L., Alavi, M., & Kayworth, T. (2006). The Role of Culture in Knowledge Management: A Case Study of Two Global Firms. *International Journal of e-Collaboration, 2*(1), 17–40. doi:10.4018/jec.2006010102

Lyle, E. R. (2012). Learning organization. *International Journal of Business and Social Science, 3*(6).

March, J. G., & Simon, H. A. (1958). *Organizations*. New York, NY: Wiley.

Mariano, S., & Casey, A. (2016, March 11). *The process of knowledge retrieval: A case study of an American High-Technology Research, Engineering and Consulting Company*. Retrieved from http://www2.warwick.ac.uk/fac/soc/wbs/conf/olkc/archive/olkc1/papers/298_mariano.pdf

Martínez-León, M., & Martínez-García, J. A. (2011). The Influence of Organizational Structure on Organizational Learning. *International Journal of Manpower*, *32*(5), 537–566. doi:10.1108/01437721111158198

Martins, A. T. (2015). *How Personal Mastery can increase Organizational Performance*. Retrieved on 19th march 2017, from http://www.strategicbusinessteam.com/self-improvement-advice/how-personal-mastery-can-increase-organizational-performance/

Mc Kenna, S. D. (1992). A Culture Instrument: Driving Organisational Learning. *Leadership and Organization Development Journal*, *13*(6), 24–29. doi:10.1108/EUM0000000001174

McHugh, D., Groves, D., & Alker, A. (1998). Managing learning: What do we learn from a learning organization? *The Learning Organization*, *5*(5), 209–220. doi:10.1108/09696479810238215

McLaughlin, J. (2016). *Understanding Organizational Culture*. Retrieved from study.com: http://study.com/academy/lesson/what-is-organizational-culture-definition-characteristics.html

Mintzberg, H. (1975). The Manager's Job: Folklore and Fact. *Harvard Business Review*, *53*, 49–61.

Mintzberg, H. (1990). The design school: Reconsidering the basic premises of strategic management. *Strategic Management Journal*, *11*(3), 171–195. doi:10.1002mj.4250110302

Mintzberg, H. (1991). Learning 1, planning 0 reply to Igor Ansoff. Research notes and communications. *Strategic Management Journal*, *12*(6), 463–466. doi:10.1002mj.4250120606

Newman, M. (1985). Managerial Access to Information: Strategies for Prevention and Promotion. *Journal of Management Studies*, *22*(2), 193–212. doi:10.1111/j.1467-6486.1985.tb00072.x

Ngah, R., & Ibrahim, A. R. (2016, March 11). *The Effect of Knowledge Sharing on Organizational Performance in Small and Medium Enterprises*. Retrieved from kmice.cms: http://www.kmice.cms.net.my/ProcKMICe/KMICe2010/Paper/PG467_472.pdf

Nonaka, I., & Takeuchi, H. (1995). *The Knowledge Creating Company*. Oxford, UK: Oxford University Press.

Oyateru, D. (2011). *The Learning Organization and Competitive Advantage: A study of The service sector*. Retrieved from http://trap.ncirl.ie/567/1/Dupe's_ThesisEditied_version_

Pedler, M., Burgoyne, J., & Boydell, T. (1991). The Learning Company. A Strategy for Sustainable Development. McGraw-Hill.

Pugh, D. S., Hickson, D. J., & Turner, C. (1968). Dimensions of Organization Structure. *Administrative Science Quarterly*, *13*(1), 65–105. doi:10.2307/2391262

Quinn, R. E., & Cameron, K. S. (2005). *Diagnosing and Changing Organizational Culture: Based on the Competing Values Framework*. John Wiley and Sons.

Rehder, B. (2003). Categorization as causal reasoning. *Cognitive Science*, *27*(5), 709–748. doi:10.120715516709cog2705_2

Robins, S. P. (1989). *Organization Behaviour, Concepts, Controversies and Applications*. New Delhi: Prentice-Hall.

Shahmansouri, S., Esfahan, M. D., & Niki, N. (2013). Explain the Theory of Competitive Advantage and Comparison with Industries based on Advanced Technology. *International Journal of Economy. Management and Social Sciences*, *2*, 841–848.

Skinnarland, K. I., Asa, I., Oslo, & Sharp, P. (2016, March 11). *Knowledge Sharing (KS), Organizational Learning and Competitive Advantage in a Scandinavian Hotel Company*. Retrieved from http://www2.warwick.ac.uk/fac/soc/wbs/conf/olkc/archive/olkc6/papers/id_110_sharp_p_skinnarland_k.pdf

Sponaugle, B. (2016, March 11). *Types of Organizational Culture: Which One Are You*. Retrieved from udemy.com: https://blog.udemy.com/types-of-organizational-culture/

Starbucks, W. H., & Whalen, P. S. (2008). *Learning by Organizations: Organizational Learning and Knowledge Management* (Vol. 2). Northamptone: Edward and Elgar Publishing Inc. doi:10.4337/9781785366970

Tharpe, B. M. (2009). *Organizational Culture White Paper*. Haworth.

KEY TERMS AND DEFINITIONS

Business Environment: A combination of all external and internal factors that influence the operations of a business.

Competitive Advantage: An advantage a firm gets over competitors in the same industry by offering consumers greater value, either by means of lower prices, greater benefits, or service.

Information Distribution: The process by which an organization identifies and distributes the right information to its stakeholders.

Information Interpretation: The process through which organizations make sense of new information that they have acquired both directly and indirectly.

Knowledge Acquisition: The process of sourcing, extracting, structuring, and organizing information for use by an organization.

Organizational Learning: Organizational learning is the process of creating, retaining, and transferring knowledge within an organization through employees and systems.

Organization Memory: It is the accumulated body of data, information, collective recollection of experiences, inferences of meaning, and knowledge created in the course of an organization's existence.

Chapter 7
Knowledge Management of Work Stress in Mexican Manufacturing Environments:
Models of the Relationships Between Burnout and the Body Mass Index Among Middle and Senior Managers

Oziely Daniela Armenta-Hernández
Autonomous University of Ciudad Juárez, Mexico

Jorge Luis García-Alcaraz
Autonomous University of Ciudad Juárez, Mexico

Aide Aracely Maldonado-Macías
Autonomous University of Ciudad Juarez, Mexico

Miguel Angel Serrano-Rosa
Universidad de Valencia, Spain

Liliana Avelar-Sosa
Autonomous University of Ciudad Juarez, Mexico

ABSTRACT

This chapter presents a knowledge management perspective to propose a pair of structural models to determine the relationship between burnout syndrome (BS) and body mass index (BMI) among high and middle managers of Mexican maquiladoras. In developing countries like Mexico there are opportunities to expand burnout study on diversity of contexts and occupations. The Maslach burnout general inventory questionnaire (MB-GI) was used, and sociodemographic data were collected as well as the weight and size of respondents. Instrument shows an acceptable reliability index. Structural equation models are used to determine relationship among variables. From a sample of 361 people, using segmentations of BMI, two segments are distinguished: normal weight and overweight. Model using normal weight participants shows more explanatory qualities about the relationship among burnout dimensions than the one using overweight participants. One can conclude that more factors and variables are needed to explain overweight Mexican managers.

DOI: 10.4018/978-1-5225-3725-0.ch007

INTRODUCTION

The concept of Burnout Syndrome (BS), was first introduced by Bradley 1969. BS directly affects individuals and is characterized by excessive and progressive fatigue, energy depletion, and motivation loss. Also, according to Freudenberger (1998), BS affects attitudes, modals, and behaviors in general, which is why it is important to study it. Likewise, as Gonzales and Guillermo (2009) argue, research on BS first appeared in 2000. Since then, many studies have been conducted across industrial sectors. For instance, Medellin (2008) reported a study of BS in the automotive industry, whereas Aguirre, Medellín, Vázquez, Gutiérrez, and Fernández (2014) reported the effects of this syndrome in the assembling industry. Likewise, Aranda and Ibarra (2014) discuss BS in the electronics industry.

According to Llaneza (2002), it has been demonstrated that the prevalence of work-related diseases or multi-causal diseases – especially those related to stress – increases exponentially in developing countries. In their model, Serrano, Moya-Albiol & Salvador (2009) prove that occupational stress is at the adaptive stage in human beings. When the adaptive response is not positive, chronic stress appears, along with BS. Both stress and BS are considered to be pathological conditions. In Mexico, BS has been studied only among helping professions, such as nurses, physicians, and teachers (Juárez-García, A., Idrovo, A. J., Camacho-Ávila, A., & Placencia-Reyes, O., 2014), whereas other occupations have been neglected. Although BS research in the industrial context is scarce, it has been demonstrated that BS is present in industrial workers (Camacho-Alamilla, Maldonado-Macías, García-Alcaraz, Hernández-Arellano, 2014; Maldonado-Macías, Camacho-Alamilla, Torres, Alcaraz, Limón, 2015; Armenta-Hernández, Maldonado-Macías, García- Alcaraz, 2015).

The few works studying occupational stress along with BS have found that both conditions are interrelated. Also, Ahola et al. (2012) found that professional efficacy directly reduces overweight, although authors did not find any other relationship between the remaining BS dimensions and stress at work. Similarly, both BS and stress do not seem to be studied together in relation to obesity and overweight, especially in the manufacturing industry. To overcome this limitation, authors (Camacho, Maldonado, García, Palacios & Valenzuela, 2015) proposed a structural equation model associating BS and obesity among middle and senior managers of manufacturing companies in Ciudad Juárez.

PROBLEM STATEMENT

Two mayor aspects were consider in this research, first, the incidence of stress-related disorders in Mexico is increasing; second, available studies on BS have not provided clear results as regards the relationship between BS and the different BMI levels.

According to a study conducted by the International Labour Organization (ILO, 2016), 40% of Mexican workers – that is, 18.4 million people – suffer from stress, and 75% of such people associate their condition to work-related situations. In this sense, stress can represent between 0.5% and 3.5% of losses in a country's (Gross Domestic Product) GDP. Additionally, on a world scale, the WHO stated that while cardiovascular diseases were the first cause of death globally, overweight and obesity were two other major causes.

Health disorders affect an individual's capacity to perform their daily activities, thereby causing low productivity and quality losses, among other repercussions (Forbes, 2011; Marrau, 2009). At the company level, the consequences of health disorders have a negative impact on production costs (Arenas & Cantú, 2013; Gestal, 2003; Juno & Noriega, 2004; Valecillo, M., Quevedo, A.L., Lubo, A., Dos Santos, A., Montiel, M., Camejo, & Sánchez, M., 2009; Kim & Han, 2014).

Relationships between BS and overweight or obesity have not been clarified in literature. Authors (Ahola, K., Pulkki-Råback, L., Kouvonen, A., Rossi, H., Aromaa, A., & Lönnqvist, J., 2012) found out that professional efficacy is related to decreasing obesity and overweight, whereas (Nevanpera, N. J., Hopsu, L., Kuosma, E., Ukkola, O., Uitti, J., & Laitinen, J. H., 2012; Proper, Koppes, Meijer & Bemelmans 2013) linked emotional exhaustion to eating disorders and uncontrolled emotions. Similarly, consequences of BS and workplace stress increase the occurrence of cardiovascular, respiratory, and gastrointestinal diseases, among other physical and mental disorders. In addition, the fatality rate among industrial employees increases every year (Ahola, Vaananen, Koskinen, Kouvonen, & Shirom, 2010) and so does the risks of suffering from diabetes, some types of cancers (Dávila-Torres, J., González-Izquierdo, J. d. J., & Barrera-Cruz, A., 2015), and cardiovascular diseases, being the latter the main cause of death globally in 2012 (WHO, 2015). Other studies have related BS with some work related variables; Borda et al (2007) argue that BS can be associated with variables such as the job position and parenthood, other studies claim that such variables are not related to either BS or stress at work (Acosta y Burguillos 2014; Carlotto 2006; De Pablo 2007). In this manner, additional factors can contribute to explaining these conditions and syndromes (Calvo, Sánchez, Rosado & García, 2011). In this sense, the main contribution of this research is to analyze those relationships between Burnout and Body Mass Index to explain in a better way the occurrence of overweight and obesity among senior and middle managers. The dissemination of the knowledge of these relationships among organizations may be helpful to develop organizational strategies for their management and prevention.

Senior and middle managers make important and transcendent decisions. They are responsible for the organizational strategy of the company, have a group of people under supervision, and are directly responsible for what these people do, as well as the impact of their actions on the organization's performance.

OBJECTIVES

General Objective

The objective of this research is to determine the relationship between BS and the Body Mass Index (BMI) for middle and senior managers of the manufacturing industry in Ciudad Juárez.

Specific Objectives

1. To perform a descriptive analysis of the sample.
2. To describe BS prevalence using three forms (average scores, degrees, and levels).
3. To determine the relationships between the BS dimensions and the BMI for senior and middle managers having a normal weight.
4. To determine the relationships between the BS dimensions and the BMI for senior and middle managers having overweight.

JUSTIFICATION

This research contributes to the body of knowledge on the effects of stress, overweight, and obesity. According to Benevides and Pereira (2006), it is important to have a better understanding of these conditions to improve the quality of life and health of individuals. Determination of the relationships that exist among these variables will offer valuable data on the characteristics of sufferers, and this will support companies in their efforts to implement preventive measures and strategies for the most vulnerable.

To prevent BS, the relationship between BS dimensions and the BMI for both normal-weight and obese participants must be better understood. These findings will help companies involved in this research to improve their knowledge about the prevalence of BS among their employees and not only company performance, but also staff performance, since many authors have described the consequences of BS and overweight at a personal level (Aguayo, C. Vargas, E. De la Fuente, & L.M. Lozano, 2011).

SCOOP AND DELIMITATION

In this research, BS is studied in its three dimensions (emotional exhaustion, depersonalization and low professional efficacy) and the BMI is studied normal weight (18.5-24.9 kg/m^2) and overweight (25-29.9 kg/m^2). Similarly, the sample includes middle and senior managers of manufacturing enterprises, including executives, supervisors, group leaders, manufacturing administrative staff, and office administrators. For such reasons, results found in this research may be valid only for manufacturing companies that have similar organizational structure to the one here discussed.

Sociodemographic variables such as weight, height, gender, age, marital status, number of children, job position, seniority, work schedule, and company name were considered. In addition, as previously mentioned, study was conducted in the manufacturing sector of Ciudad Juárez. According to the association of manufacturers of this city (Asociación de Maquiladoras de Ciudad Juárez-Index Ciudad Juárez, AMAC), in November 2013, Mexico catered for 5,087 manufacturing companies, 326 of which were located in Ciudad Juárez, Chihuahua. Moreover, the region employs about 230,373 industrial workers. These facts were important for conducting a study of BS among middle and senior managers of the manufacturing industry of Ciudad Juárez.

THEORETICAL FRAMEWORK

Occupational Stress

Stress has been defined as a physiological response to specific situations, stimuli, or threats, known as stressors. Melgosa (1999) explains the three stages of stress: alarm, resistance, and exhaustion. The alarm stage is key to recognizing a stressor, whereas the resistance stage occurs when people do not get any relief from the first stage; in other words, it is the response to continuous stress. Finally, the exhaustion stage is when sufferers experience partial or total collapse of the organs. Exhaustion symptoms include tiredness, tension, depression, and stress-related diseases.

Rivera (2013) defines occupational stress as a set of emotional, cognitive, physiological, and behavioral reactions to potentially harmful work-related situations, such as the organization, the content, or the environment. Work-related stress is also characterized by high levels of excitement and anxiety as responses to the inability to cope with a given situation. Also, stressed workers are usually not satisfied with their work performance. Finally, as regards its impact on health, work-related stress produces chronic and permanent wear and tear of the biological system, thereby contributing to the incidence of physical, psycho-emotional, and behavior disorders (Calabrese, 2010).

Burnout Syndrome

BS comprises three-dimensional condition characterized by exhaustion, depersonalization, and reduced professional accomplishment among professions directly dealing with clients or patients. From a different perspective, Edelwich and Brodsky (1980) defined Burnout as the gradual loss of idealism, energy, and motivation among helping professions as a result of work-related conditions.

The Body Mass Index (BMI)

Obesity and overweight are two global problems that affect both, developed and developing countries. The World Health Organization (WHO, 2010) considers obesity as an epidemic of a multicausal, chronic, non-communicable disease that starts at an early age. Experts projected in 2015 an amount of 2.3 billion adults with overweight and more than 700 million obese; however, latest data of 2016 have shown that 7 out of 10 adults continue to be overweight with a prevalence of 72.5% percent exceeding experts' projections.

Overweight is an abnormal accumulation of fat, generally from 10% to 20% over an individual's body weight, considering their height. Also, according to the World Health Organization, overweight is a BMI ranging from 25kg/m^2 to 29,9kg/m^2, whereas obesity is a BMI greater than or equal to 30 (Jensen & Ryan, 2013). The leading causes of overweight and obesity are unhealthy eating habits or an imbalance between calories consumed and calories expended. Similarly, the World Health Organization claims that the common health consequences of overweight and obesity include cardiovascular diseases and musculoskeletal disorders; however, there are many ways to prevent and counteract these diseases and disorders. For instance, Klein (2011) proposes to improve the life style by doing exercise and modifying the eating habits.

Dimensions of Burnout Syndrome

According to Maslach (2001), BS is a three-dimensional syndrome characterized by:

- **Emotional Exhaustion:** A state of depletion of energy and resources resulting from working directly with patients and/or customers. It has physical and psychological manifestations and is mainly characterized by fatigue. Emotionally exhausted people feel they have nothing left to give to others.
- **Depersonalization:** The development of a callous attitude, negative feelings, and cynical behavior. It is characterized by increasing irritability, loss of motivation, isolation, and hostile attitudes toward coworkers and customers.
- **Low Professional Efficacy:** Characterized by feelings of inefficacy and incompetence that contribute to a sense of low personal and professional accomplishment. This dimension of BS affects

the ability to do the job and may deteriorate work relationships. Similarly, there is loss of productivity and low self-esteem, and sufferers are incapable of tolerating occupational pressures. Low professional efficacy is also considered as the inability of a person to properly adapt to their reality (Maslach 2001).

Conceptualization of Overweight and Obesity

Overweight is a main public health concern affecting both developed and developing countries. The World Health Organization considers obesity as an epidemic of a multicausal, chronic, non-communicable disease that starts at an early age. Experts project that by 2015, 2.3 billion adults will be overweight and more than 700 million will be obese. Also, overweight is an abnormal accumulation of fat, generally from 10% to 20% over an individual's body weight, considering their height. According to the World Health Organization, overweight is a BMI ranging from 25kg/m^2 to 29,9kg/m^2 (Jensen & Ryan, 2013).

The leading causes of overweight are wrong eating habits or an imbalance between calories consumed and calories expended. Similarly, the World Health Organization claims that the common health consequences of overweight include cardiovascular diseases and musculoskeletal disorders. However, there are many ways to prevent and counteract these diseases and disorders. Klein (2011), for instance, proposes to improve the life style by doing exercise and modifying the eating habits.

Knowledge Management in Healthcare

The definition of knowledge management is that knowledge must involve an agent, who uses knowledge to perform the actions necessary to reach a goal. Knowledge management is an emerging field that has commanded attention and support from the industrial community. Many organizations currently engage in knowledge management in order to leverage knowledge both within their organization and externally to their shareholders and customers. Knowledge management involves the creation of value from organizations intangible assets (Arroyo & Castillo, 2017; Mazita, Amlus, Kamsidi, & Zaniel, 2016). In this manner, knowledge management about the effects of BS on BMI that could impact overweight and obesity of employees may be an area for growing opportunities for both, the company as well as personnel.

Another potential area, could be found in the development of decision support systems and knowledge management systems regarding psychosocial risks at work and healthcare. Healthcare is a knowledge intensive industry, the importance of medical knowledge has been highlighted in the ongoing initiatives to promote evidence-based medicine and clinical quality. The Agency for Healthcare Research and Quality 2012 cited strong evidence that clinical decision support systems and knowledge management systems can be effective in improving health care process measures across diverse settings using both commercially and locally developed systems. It is likely that these systems will become a key part of the infrastructure of all healthcare organizations over the next few years (Lobach D, Sanders GD, Bright TJ, 2012).

The Manufacturing Industry of Ciudad Juárez

Ciudad Juárez is one of the Mexican major manufacturing regions. Worldwide, it is recognized as a key industrial center thanks to its status as border city. According to the Association of Manufacturers

(AMAC, 2013), Ciudad Juárez caters for 329 of the 5,111 manufacturing companies located in Mexico, 29% of these industries are automotive manufacturers, 7% are electrical manufacturers, 18 are electronics manufacturers, 9% produce plastic or metal goods, 9% are packaging manufacturing companies, and 3% provide customer services.

MATERIALS

This section describes and explains the materials employed to conduct the study.

The Survey

The Maslach Burnout Inventory–General Survey (Moreno, B., Rodríguez, R., & Escobar, E., 2001) was administrated as an instrument for data acquisition; further analyses were made using these data to determine the relationships among work content variables and BS using structural modelling. In addition, a sociodemographic questionnaire was designed to gather information such as age, gender, number of children, marital status, and academic background.

The Maslach Burnout Inventory-General Survey (MBI-GS)

The Maslach Burnout Inventory–General Survey (Schaufeli, W.B., Leiter, M.P., Maslach, C., & Jackson, S.E., 1996) was administered to measure BS dimensions. Unlike the Maslach Burnout Inventory Survey (MBI), the MBI-GS is not exclusive to human service professions. The Spanish version of the MBI-GS by Moreno et al. (2001) was used, which includes 16 items to analyze the three BS dimensions: emotional exhaustion (5 items), cynicism (5 items), and professional efficacy (6 items). The survey had to be answered using a seven-point Likert scale (never, rarely in a year, sometimes in a year, on many occasions in a year, frequently in a year, almost every day, always). In this sense, low scores in *professional efficacy* and high scores in *emotional exhaustion* and *cynicism* indicated existence of *BS*. Two examples of items found in the MBI-GS are the following: *I am able to effectively solve problems at work* (item 5) and *I feel fulfilled when I do something good at work* (item 11). Previous studies confirm the structure of the three factors (Gil-Monte, 2002). Internal consistency indices of the MBI-GS, obtained through the Cronbach alpha, are 0.89 for Emotional Exhaustion, 0.84 for Cynicism, and 0.85 for Professional Efficacy.

To determine BS levels, the methodology proposed by Guerrero and Vicente (2001), previously adopted by Maldonado, et al. (2015).

Software WarpPLS

This software uses Partial Least Squares algorithms (PLS) for structural equations modeling (SEM). It provides users with a broad range of features, several of which are not available in other SEM software (Kock, 2013). Moreover, WarpPLS is the first and only to offer classic PLS algorithms together with factor-based PLS algorithms (Kock, 2014).

METHODOLOGY

This section thoroughly describes each step followed to meet the research goal.

Survey Administration

To measure BS, it was used the Spanish version of the Maslach Burnout Inventory General Survey (MBI-GS), validated by Moreno et al. (2001). Some of the advantages of using this questionnaire are that the MBI-GS is not exclusive to human service professions; moreover, previous studies have demonstrated its reliability in the three dimensions (Gil-Monte, 2002) using the Cronbach's alpha index, which showed values higher than 0.7 in all dimensions. According to (George & Mallery, 2003), values above 0.7 are acceptable indicators of reliability. Written consent from participants was collected individually using a proper format and according to the University requirements.

Sample Definition

The sample was non-probabilistic, it was obtained using the snowball sampling technique to select individuals with the desired characteristics. Meetings were scheduled with six manufacturing companies in Ciudad Juárez to present the research among company's doctors and managers.

Fieldwork and Survey Administration

Surveys were administered to manufacturing companies during sessions previously scheduled by their Human Resources departments. As previously mentioned, the sample comprised middle and senior managers.

Figure 1. Methodology

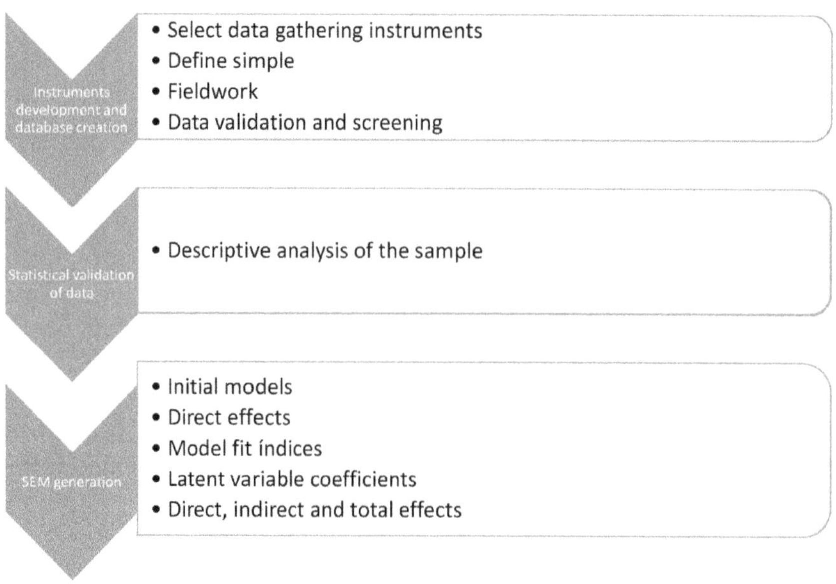

Database Creation and Screening

An electronic database was created with data collected using SPSS software. The database included information from 361 participants. This sample finally it was classified according to each participant's BMI. For the visualization of data, a descriptive analysis of the sample it was performed to detect missing values and atypical values. In the MBI-GS, missing values and atypical values were replaced by the median value of the items, since the questionnaire collected ordinal data. On the other hand, since the IMC values were ordinal data, missing values and atypical values were replaced by the mean.

Statistical Validation of Data

The descriptive analysis of the sample was performed using SPSS® v.20 software. At this stage, sociodemographic information was analyzed and frequency percentages were provided for the characteristics studied (gender, academic background, marital status, type of employment contract, seniority, work schedule, job position, etc.). Similarly, the analysis provided quartile values for each characteristic and frequency percentages for BS levels: none, low, medium, high and extreme.

Latent Variables Validation

The Cronbach alpha index was calculated to validate the data collected. Cronbach's alpha measures the reliability of the data on a scale. The denomination "alpha" was proposed by Cronbach (1951) and the index represents the average covariance between pairs of articles. It can be calculated using the variations or the correlation between the items. In this investigation, the Cronbach's alpha was calculated taking into account the correlation of the items and using the formula presented below:

$$1.\ \alpha est = \frac{kp}{1+p\left(k-1\right)}$$

k= number of itemsp=average of correlation of items

In this formula, the validation ranges from 0 to 1 on a scale that considers 0.7 as an acceptable value, although values greater than 0.90 are more satisfying.

After the data capture process, data were detected by means of the substitution of median and atypical values for the median and mean values (García, 2014). Median ordinal data and mean continuous data.

Occurrence of Burnout Syndrome in Average Scores

Following the suggestions of Vicente (2001), SPSS software was used to calculate the occurrence of BS in average scores. First, each observed variable was analyzed; then, each dimension is examined to obtain the median, as well as the maximum and minimum score of each dimension. Finally, these scores are compared with findings reported in previous studies, such as that of Guerrero, Vicente (2001).

Occurrence of Burnout Syndrome in Degrees

BS levels were defined (high, medium and low) by analyzing whether the mean scores fit the first, second or third tertile. For this, BS was divided into its three grades: low, medium and high with cut points in the 33rd and 66th percentiles (Vicente, 2001).

Occurrence of Burnout Syndrome in Levels

In this part, the level of BS suffered in five categories is presented. To obtain the occurrence of BS in the levels, the data on the occurrence BS in grades were used and the 27 combinations were made to obtain the categories. Readers can consult the section of the appendix to consult the table of combinations.

Structural Equation Models

At this stage, the two models of structural equations were created and validated. These models include the latent variables under study. The first model seeks to study the relationships between BS and normal weight, while the second model analyzes the relationships between BS and overweight. The relationships between latent variables refer to the research hypotheses. These hypotheses were analyzed using WarpPLS 4.0 software, using the P-value as inclusion criterion.

Hypothetical Models

The research hypotheses were proposed by considering findings of previous studies. Such studies have demonstrated significant relationships between the BS dimensions and the BMI. For instance, (Dallman, 2010) found a rapport between emotional exhaustion and anxiety, eating disorders, and emotional dissatisfaction. Likewise, Ahola (2012) found no relationship between cynicism and the BMI, although professional efficacy did seem to be related to the BMI. In other words, the author found that professional efficacy grows as workers increase their physical activity. Figure 2 and Figure 3 depict the two models to be analyzed.

Direct Effects

In SEM, direct effects are represented as arrows directly connecting two latent variables. Direct effects help validate research hypotheses.

Model Fit Indices

To validate the models, nine indexes proposed by Knock (2013) were calculated: Average path coefficient (APC), average R-square (ARS), average adjusted R-square (AARS), average block variation Inflation factor AVIF) Full Collinearity VIF (AFVIF), Tenenhaus Adjustment Quality (GoF), Simpson Paradox Relationship (SPR), R-Square Contribution Coefficient (RSCR) and Statistical Suppression Coefficient (SSR).

Figure 2. Proposed Model: Burnout Syndrome - Normal Weight Relationship

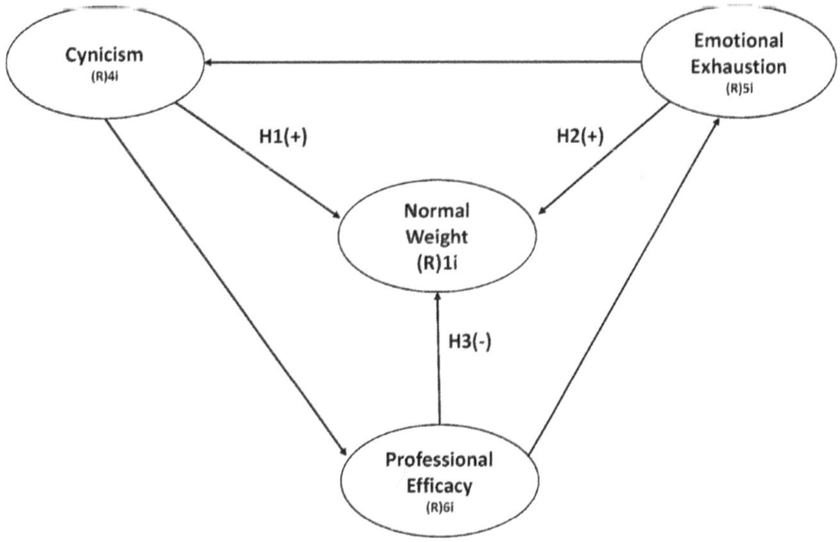

Figure 3. Proposed Model: Burnout Syndrome - Overweight Relationship

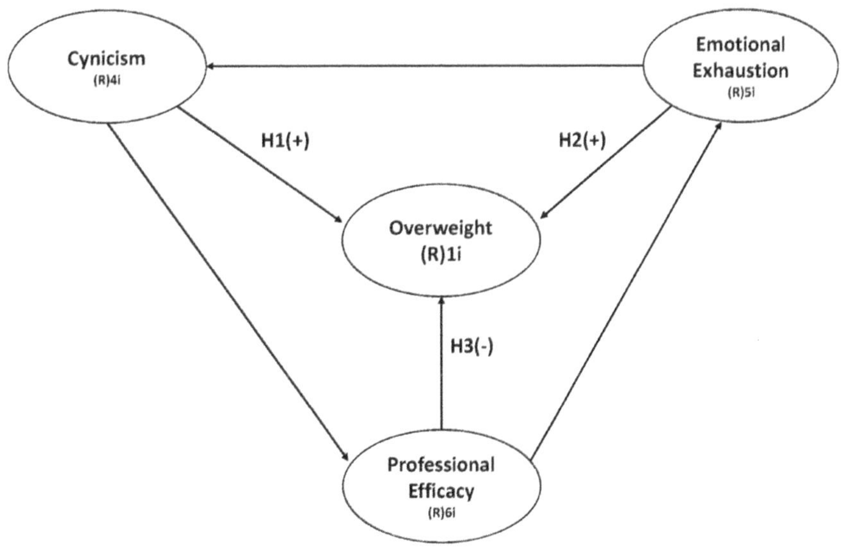

Coefficient of Latent Variables

Seven indexes were used to validate the surveys: R-square (R2), adjusted R-squared, Q-square (Q2), composite reliability index, Cronbach's alpha, variance inflation factors (VIF), and average full collinearity FIV (AFVIF)

Sum of Effects

To estimate direct, indirect and total effects we rely on WarpPLS 5.0 software. For the direct effects, the R2 value of each dependent latent variable was analyzed to determine the percentage of the explained variance. As for the indirect effects, they were produced through the mediation of the variables using two or more model paths. The total effects of each relationship were obtained by adding direct and indirect effects.

RESULTS

Survey Administration and Validation

This section discusses how the survey was administered and validated. The study was conducted in manufacturing companies located in Ciudad Juarez, Chihuahua, Mexico. A non-probabilistic sample was selected and the questionnaires were administered during the sessions previously scheduled by the human resources department of each company. Three of the companies studied manufacture automotive parts, two manufacture electric products and produce various products.

Descriptive Analysis of the Sample

The descriptive analysis of the overweight sample revealed that men suffer more from obesity than women (72.94% versus 27.06%, respectively). As regards age, it seems that 31-40-year old employees are more prone to overweight (38.24%), followed by 41-50 year-old (27.65%), whereas employees under 30 (22.94%) or those older than 50 (11.18%) are less commonly affected. Also, the minimum age reported was 18, whereas 60 years old was the maximum age, 37.65 the mean, and 9.24 the standard deviation. Such results indicate that overweight is more prevalent among young working adults.

As regards the relationship between academic background and overweight, it was found that 66.67% of employees holding a bachelor degree were obese, but only 9.52% of workers with a master's degree suffer from this condition. These results may suggest that employees academically more educated have more tools to cope with stress and reduce the presence of obesity. Likewise, the descriptive analysis demonstrated that 87.5% of the sample holds a contract of indefinite duration, while 9.52% of the surveyed employees works under a temporary contract.

Table 1. Surveyed Companies

Company	Frequency	Percentage
Company 1	41	11.4
Company 2	42	11.6
Company 3	53	14.7
Company 4	100	27.7
Company 5	103	28.5
Company 6	22	6.1
Total	361	100.0

As far as seniority is concerned, the minimum length reported was 1 month, 360 months was the maximum, 102.41 months was the mean, and 83.58 months was the standard deviation. Similarly, it was found that overweight is more prevalent among employees with longer seniority, namely with over 73 months (52.69%). Such results may suggest that for senior workers the fear of job loss makes them more susceptible to the effects of stress and overweight.

Results also indicate that married employees (38.08%) are more vulnerable to obesity than unmarried workers (28.24%) or those living in free union (11.38%). Similarly, it was found that only 1.8% of employees have lost a spouse. As for working hours, it seems that overweight affects more employees with long working hours. In this case, 30.3% of the sample works 48 hours per week, 29.76% work more than 56 hours, 25.45% work 45 hours and only 14.55% of the sample works 42 hours weekly.

Regarding the anthropometric information, it was found a 1.49 meters (m) as minimum height, 1.90 m as maximum, 1.71m as average height and 0.085m as standard deviation. Regarding the variable of weight, the descriptive analysis reported 49 kilograms (kgs) as minimum weight, 100 kgs maximum, an average weight of 80.54 kgs and 8.69 kgs as standard deviation. Finally, when analyzing the departments of the company, overweight is more frequent in the engineering department (34.71%), followed by the production and maintenance department (31.76%), administrative offices (17.06%), and finally the Department of Environment and Security (5.29%).

Results by Average Scores

Table 2 shows the average scores of the three dimensions of BS. Note that emotional exhaustion shows an average value of 10.29, while cynicism or depersonalization shows an average value of 6.0970, and 28.5540 was the average value for professional effectiveness

Results by Degrees

Table 3 shows the degrees of BS obtained from the sample. The mean scores, more specifically the mean values that were used from the above table to categorize the BS grade for each dimension. According to mean scores, the sample provided a Medium degree of BS in all three dimensions.

Results by Levels of Burnout

Table 4 presents the obtained results for the five levels of BS. According to these results, 93 participants do not suffer from any level of BS, whereas the remaining 268 suffer from this condition in any of the four remaining levels: low, medium, high, and extreme.

Table 2. Occurrence of Burnout Syndrome: Average Score

Average Scores					
Dimension	**N**	**Minimum**	**Maximum**	**Mean**	**Standard Deviation**
Emotional Exhaustion	361	.00	30.00	10.2909	6.31719
Cynicism/ Depersonalization	361	.00	30.00	6.0970	5.51604
Professional Efficacy	361	11.00	36.00	28.5540	5.85121

Table 3. Degrees of Burnout

Degrees of Burnout	Emotional Exhaustion	Cynicism/ Depersonalization	Professional Efficacy
LOW	< 7	< 3	> 33
MEDIUM	8 – 12 (10.29)	4 – 7 (6.09)	28 – 32 (28.55)
HIGH	> 13	> 8	< 27

Table 4. Levels of Burnout

	Frequency	Percentage	Valid Percentage	Cumulative Percentage
None	93	25.8	25.8	25.8
Low	45	12.5	12.5	38.2
Medium	56	15.5	15.5	53.7
High	84	23.3	23.3	77.0
Extreme	83	23.0	23.0	100.0
Total	361	100.0	100.0	

Figure 4 introduces the prevalence of BS expressed in percentages. More specifically, the graph presents the percentage of participants that suffer from BS in any of its five levels.

As can be observed, 98 participants do not suffer from BS representing 25.76% of the sample, whereas 45 participants, or 12.47% of the sample, suffer from a low level of BS. Similarly, 15.51% or 56 participants present a medium level of BS. On the other hand, 23.27% of the sample (84 participants) presents high levels of BS, whereas the remaining 22.99% (83 participants) suffers from extreme levels.

Figure 4. Graph of Levels of Burnout in Percentages

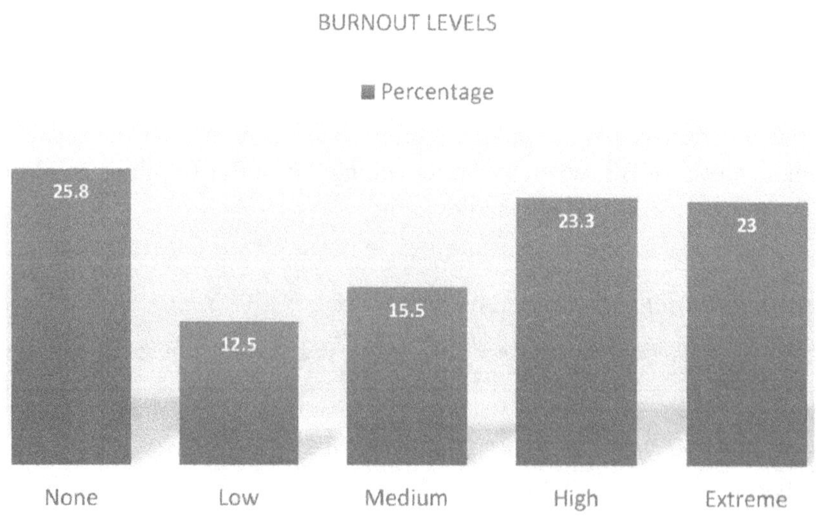

Two Structural Equation Models

The models presented in the following sections take as basis the results discussed above to find any possible relationships among the three BS dimensions and the BMI, namely normal weight and overweight. Such relationships can explain better what causes BS, overweight, and obesity. The models interpret the rapports between BS and normal weight and between BS and overweight as direct/indirect or positive/negative relationships.

Model of the Relationships Between BS Dimensions and Normal Weight

In this model, the three BS dimensions was associate with the BMI of participants with normal weight.

Every path in the model is associated with a β value and a P value; the former represents a measure of dependency between the involved variables, while the latter indicates whether a relationship is statistically significant at a 95% confidence level.

Validation of Latent Variables and Model Efficiency Indices

Table 5 presents the quality indices of every variable forming the latent variables. Note that the Cronbach's alpha and composite reliability values were above 0.7. Only variables with a good reliability index were maintained.

As for latent variables, AVE confirmed the survey's discriminant validity, since all its values were higher than 0.5. Similarly, because VIFs values were lower than 3.3, the existence of no multicollinearity was confirmed (Kock, 2013). Finally, all the values of the Q-Squared were higher than 0 and very

Figure 5. Model of the relationships between BS dimensions and normal weight

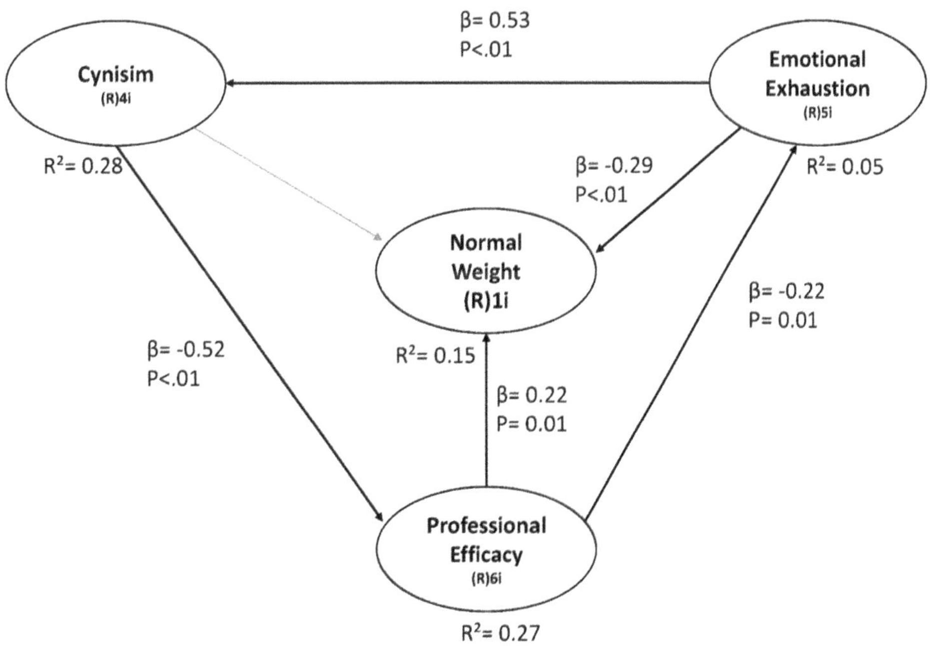

Figure 6. Model of BS dimensions and Normal Weight

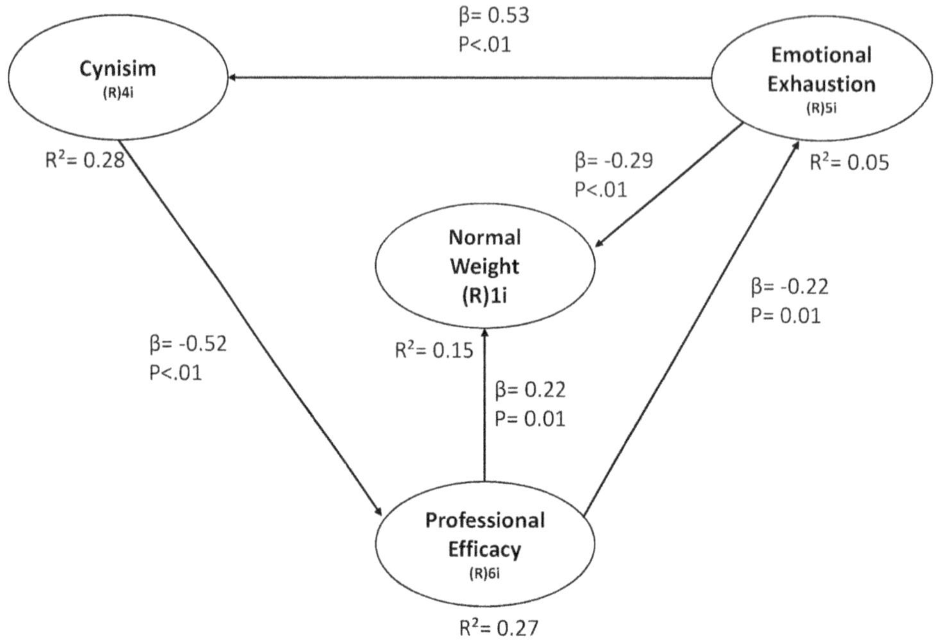

Table 5. Validation of Latent Variables

	Cynicism	Emotional Exhaustion	Professional Efficacy	NORMAL
R-Squared	0.284	0.05	0.27	0.146
Adjusted R-Squared	0.276	0.04	0.262	0.127
Composite Reliability	0.939	0.941	0.919	1
Cronbach's Alpha	0.913	0.922	0.893	1
Average Variance Extracted	0.794	0.762	0.654	1
Full collinearity VIFs	1.657	1.342	1.344	1.09
Q-Squared	0.288	0.056	0.27	0.153

similar to their corresponding R-Squared values. Such results demonstrated that all latent variables had enough validity from a parametric perspective. Table 6 introduces the loadings and cross-loadings of the latent variables. Such results proved that the P value of every element was statistically significant at a 95% confidence level.

Model Fit Indices

Table 7 presents the model fit indices obtained for this model. Considering the P values of APC, ARS, and AARS, it was concluded that the model was efficient and all the parameters had medium explanatory

Table 6. Validity of Cross-Loadings

	Cynicism	Emotional Exhaustion	Professional Efficacy	Normal	P Value
Cynicism	-0.885	0.047	0.067	-0.02	<0.001
Cynicism	-0.921	0.115	-0.073	-0.07	<0.001
Cynicism	-0.852	-0.103	-0.051	0.03	<0.001
Cynicism	-0.904	-0.065	0.057	0.062	<0.001
Emotional Exhaustion	0.105	-0.896	0.011	0.069	<0.001
Emotional Exhaustion	-0.139	-0.885	-0.039	-0.036	<0.001
Emotional Exhaustion	0.064	-0.849	0.023	-0.071	<0.001
Emotional Exhaustion	-0.057	-0.855	-0.003	-0.03	<0.001
Emotional Exhaustion	0.027	-0.878	0.008	0.065	<0.001
Professional Efficacy	0.296	-0.019	-0.733	-0.067	<0.001
Professional Efficacy	-0.211	-0.012	-0.772	-0.132	<0.001
Professional Efficacy	0.223	0.147	-0.822	0.129	<0.001
Professional Efficacy	-0.1	0.015	-0.866	0.066	<0.001
Professional Efficacy	-0.167	-0.047	-0.867	0.08	<0.001
Professional Efficacy	-0.008	-0.09	-0.783	-0.104	<0.001
BMI	0	0	0	-1	<0.001

Table 7. Model fit indices

	Value	Decision Criteria
Average Path Coefficient (APC)	0.358	P<0.001
Average R-Squared (ARS)	0.188	P=0.014
Average Adjusted R-Squared (AARS)	0.176	P=0.019
Average block Variance Inflation Factor (AVIF)	1.009	acceptable <= 5, ideally <= 3.3
Average Full collinearity VIF (AFVIF)	1.358	acceptable <= 5, ideally <= 3.3
Tenenhaus GoF (GoF)	0.388	small >= 0.1, medium >= 0.25, large >= 0.36
Simpson's Paradox Ratio (SPR)	1.00	acceptable if >= 0.7, ideally= 1
R-Squared Contribution Ratio (RSCR)	1.00	acceptable >= 0.9, ideally <= 1.00
Statistical Suppression Ratio (SSR)	1.00	acceptable >= 0.7

capacity. Similarly, the Tenenhaus GoF demonstrated that the model had medium explanatory capacity. In conclusion, the model proposed in this section to explain the relationship between BS dimensions and normal weight is efficient.

Direct Effects

Figure 7 presents the effects between latent variables. The ß and P values helped us interpret and explain these direct effects. As previously mentioned, ß values represent the dependency measure between two

Figure 7. Direct Effects of the Initial Model

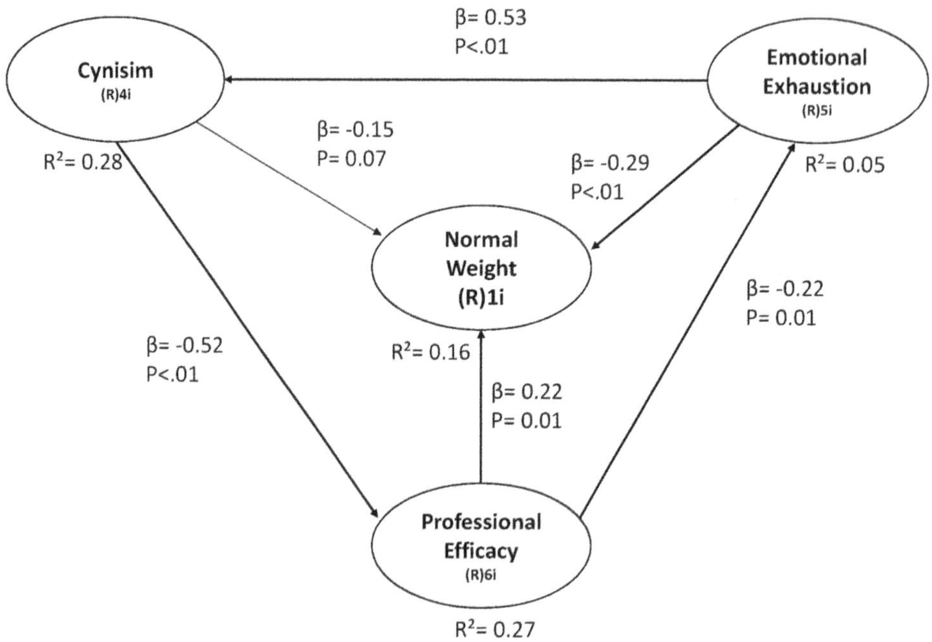

latent variables, while P values define whether a relationship is statistically significant at a 95% confidence level. For a relationship to be statistically significant, its P value had to be lower than 0.5. As can be observed, latent variables Emotional Exhaustion and Professional Efficacy are directly significant, whereas Cynicism is rather indirectly significant.

Figure 8 shows the effects between latent variables for the final model. In this figure, the relationships that were statistically not significant were eliminated.

Table 8 presents the conclusions regarding the R^2 values. The table indicates that latent variable Emotional Exhaustion is 5% explained by latent variable Professional Efficacy. As for Cynicism, it is 26% explained by Emotional Exhaustion, whereas Professional Efficacy depends on Cynicism in 27%. Also, the model shows that latent variable Normal Weight can be 15% explained by both Emotional Exhaustion and Professional Efficacy. In conclusion, Professional Efficacy can significantly reduce both Emotional Exhaustion and Cynicism. If a company does not pay attention to the Professional Efficacy of its employees, this may have a negative impact on its productivity.

Sum of Indirect Effects

In structural equation models, relationships are not always direct. Table 9 presents the sum of indirect effects for every relationship in the final model. P values higher than 0.5 refer to indirect relationships that are statistically not significant.

Three indirect relationships are worth being highlighted. First, it was found that when Normal Weight increased by one standard deviation, Cynicism decreased by 0.147 units and had a variability of 7%. As for the relationship between Professional Efficacy and Emotional Exhaustion, it was found that when the

Figure 8. Direct Effects for the Final Model

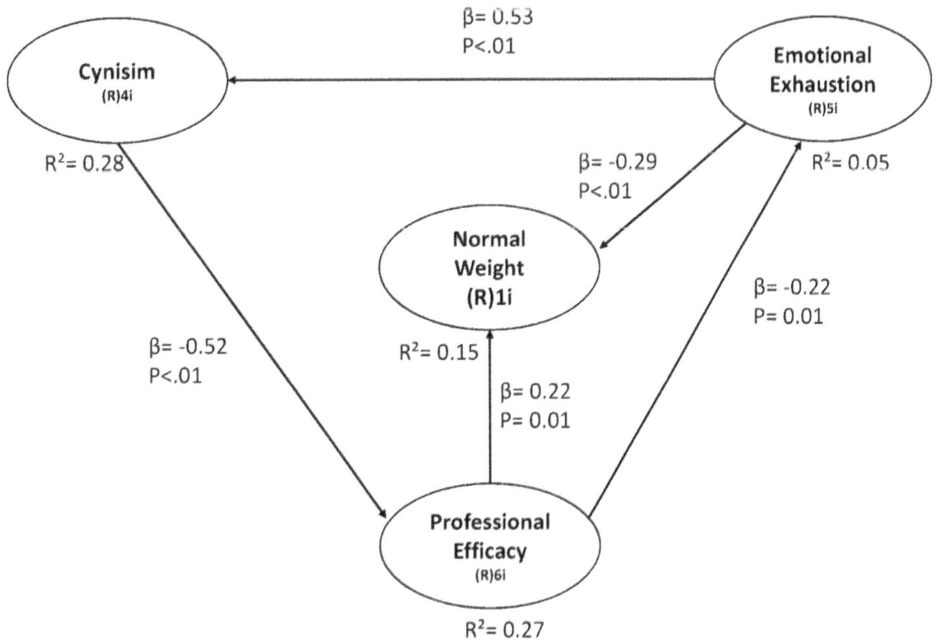

Table 8. Effect Sizes

	Cynicism	Emotional Exhaustion	Professional Efficacy
Cynicism		0.258	
Emotional Exhaustion			0.05
Professional Efficacy	0.27		
Normal Weight		0.093	0.053

former increased by one standard deviation, the latter decreased by 0.277 units and had a variability of 5%. Finally, with respect to Cynicism and Professional Efficacy, the results revealed that when Cynicism increased by one standard deviation, Professional Efficacy decreased by 0.119 units and had a variability of 7%. All the remaining relationships can be similarly interpreted.

Total Effects

Table 10 presents the total effects for every relationship of the model. Total effects are the sum of direct and indirect effects. As in the previous section, P values higher than 0.5 belong to relationships that are statistically not significant at a 95% confidence level.

The two largest total effects involve latent variables Emotional Exhaustion, Professional Efficacy and Normal Weight. In the relationship between Emotional Exhaustion and Professional Efficacy, when Emotional Exhaustion increased by one standard deviation, Professional Efficacy decreased by 0.224

Table 9. Sum of Indirect Effects

	Cynicism	Emotional Exhaustion	Professional Efficacy
Cynicism	β.062 p=.145 ES=.062		β=-.119 p=.046 ES=.07
Emotional Exhaustion	β=.116 p=.05 ES=.070	β=.062 p=.145 ES=.058	
Professional Efficacy		β=-.277 p˂.001 ES=.067	β=.062 p=.145 ES=.058
Normal Weight	β=-.147 p=.019 ES=.07	β=-.06 p=.153 ES=.058	β=.066 p=.178 ES=.071

Table 10. Total Effects

	Cynicism	Emotional Exhaustion	Professional Efficacy
Cynicism	β=.62 p=.145 ES=.058	β=.533 p˂.001 ES=.088	β=-.119 p=.046 ES=.07
Emotional Exhaustion	β=.116 p=.05 ES=.070	β=.062 p=.145 ES=.058	β=-.224 p=.011 ES=.096
Professional Efficacy	β=-.519 p˂.001 ES=.089	β=-.277 p˂.001 ES=.067	β=.062 p=.145 ES=.058
Normal Weight	β=-.147 p=.019 ES=.07	β=-.355 p˂.001 ES=.093	β=.283 p=.002 ES=.095

units with 9.6% of variability. As for the relationship between Normal Weight and Professional Efficacy, it was found that when Normal Weight increased by one standard deviation, Professional Efficacy increased by 0.283 units. The remaining relationships can be similarly interpreted.

Model of the Relationships Between BS Dimensions and Overweight

In this second model, the three BS dimensions are associated with overweight (Figure 9).

Figure 9. Relationships between BS dimensions and Overweight: Initial Model

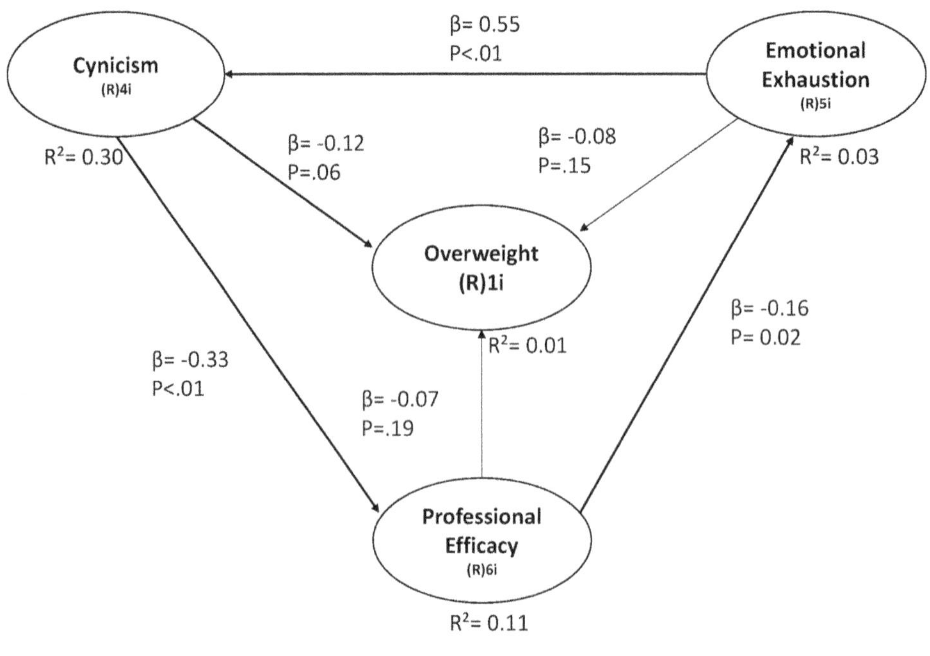

Results and Model Efficiency

Table 10 presents the quality indicators of the observed variables contained in the four latent variables. As can be observed, values of the Cronbach's alpha and the composite reliability index are higher than 0.7, the threshold. Only variables that showed acceptable reliability were maintained.

As for the latent variables, it was proved that all of them had enough convergent validity, since all AVE values were higher than 0.5. Likewise, VIFs values, which were lower than 3.3 in all cases, confirmed the existence of no collinearity (Kock, 2013). Finally, since Q-Squared values were obtained above 0 and similar to their corresponding R-Squared values, it was concluded that the four latent variables had enough parametric validity.

Estimates presented in the table demonstrated the model's efficiency, since all P values were lower than 0.5. Likewise, the values of these indices confirmed medium explanatory capacity of all the model's parameters, whereas the Tenenhaus GoF confirmed the model's medium explanatory capacity. In summary, the model that it was propose to explain the relationships between the three BS dimensions and overweight is efficient.

Validation of Latent Variables and Model Efficiency

Table 11 presents the quality indicators of variables contained in the four latent variables. As can be observed, values of the Cronbach's alpha and the composite reliability index are higher than 0.7, the threshold. Only variables that showed acceptable reliability were maintained.

As for latent variables, it was proved that all of them had enough convergent validity, since all AVE values were higher than 0.5. Likewise, VIFs values, which were lower than 3.3 in all cases, confirmed

Figure 10. Relationships between Burnout dimensions and Overweight: Final Model

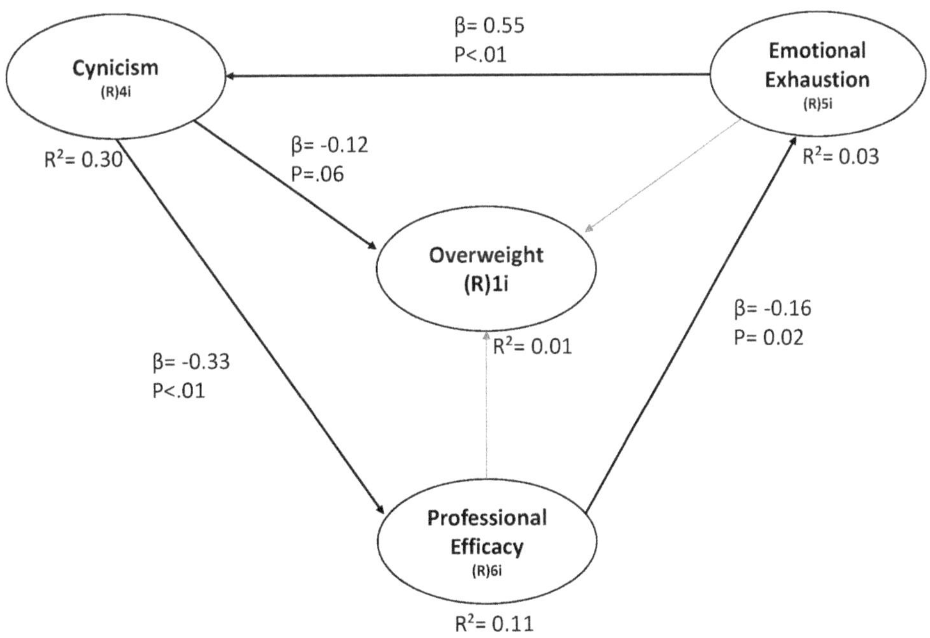

Table 11. Validation of Latent Variables

	Cynicism	Emotional Exhaustion	Professional Efficacy	Normal Weight
R-Squared	0.284	0.05	0.27	0.146
Adjusted R-Squared	0.276	0.04	0.262	0.127
Composite Reliability Index	0.939	0.941	0.919	1
Cronbach's Alpha	0.913	0.922	0.893	1
Average Variance Extracted	0.794	0.762	0.654	1
Full collinearity VIFs	1.657	1.342	1.344	1.09
Q-Squared	0.288	0.056	0.27	0.153

the existence of no collinearity (Kock, 2013) among latent variables. In addition, since Q-square values above 0 and similar to their corresponding R-squares were obtained, it was concluded that the four latent variables had enough parametric validity. Finally, Table 12 introduces the loadings and cross-loadings of latent variables. As observed, all P values are lower than 0.05, which implies that both loadings and cross-loadings are statistically significant.

Because the P values of APC, ARS, and AARS were lower than 0.5, it was concluded that the model was efficient and all the model parameters had medium explanatory capacity. Similarly, the Tenenhaus GoF demonstrated that this model had medium explanatory capacity. In conclusion, the model that it was propose in this section is efficient.

Table 12. Loadings and Cross-Loadings

	Cynicism	Emotional Exhaustion	Professional Efficacy	Overweight	P Value
Cynicism	0.846	-0.098	0.009	-0.034	<0.001
Cynicism	0.832	0.031	-0.001	-0.022	<0.001
Cynicism	0.861	0.052	-0.043	-0.011	<0.001
Cynicism	0.923	0.014	0.033	0.062	<0.001
Emotional Exhaustion	-0.038	0.876	-0.022	-0.043	<0.001
Emotional Exhaustion	-0.056	0.902	0.073	-0.058	<0.001
Emotional Exhaustion	0.104	0.877	-0.006	0.034	<0.001
Emotional Exhaustion	0.013	0.828	-0.092	0.079	<0.001
Emotional Exhaustion	-0.021	0.853	0.04	-0.007	<0.001
Professional Efficacy	-0.11	0.064	0.687	0.012	<0.001
Professional Efficacy	-0.126	0.018	0.792	0.023	<0.001
Professional Efficacy	0.128	0.028	0.806	-0.066	<0.001
Professional Efficacy	-0.039	0.038	0.839	0.026	<0.001
Professional Efficacy	-0.046	0.114	0.864	0.02	<0.001
Professional Efficacy	0.2	-0.29	0.731	-0.018	<0.001
BMI	0	0	0	1	<0.001

Table 13. General Results of the Burnout - Overweight Model

	Value	Decision Criteria
Average Path Coefficient (APC)	0.29	P<0.001
Average R-Squared (ARS)	0.112	P=0.034
Average Adjusted R-Squared (AARS)	0.107	P=0.039
Average block VIF (AVIF)	1.214	acceptable <= 5, ideal <= 3.3
Average Full collinearity VIF (AFVIF)	1.232	acceptable <= 5, ideal <= 3.3
Tenenhaus GoF (GoF)	0.296	small >= 0.1, medium>= 0.25, large >= 0.36
Simpson's Paradox Ratio (SPR)	1.00	acceptable >= 0.7, ideally: 1
R-Squared Contribution Ratio (RSCR)	1	acceptable >= 0.9, ideally: 1
Statistical Suppression Ratio	1	acceptable >= 0.7

Direct Effects

Figure 11 illustrates the effects between latent variables. Every effect was associated with a ß value and a P value. The former represents a dependency measure between two latent variables, and the latter indicates whether a relationship is statistically significant at a 95% confidence level. For a relationship to be statistically significant, its corresponding P value had to be lower than 0.5. As can be observed, Cynicism is the only BS dimension that is directly significant, whereas Emotional Exhaustion is indirectly significant.

Figure 11. Relationships Burnout - Overweight: Final Model

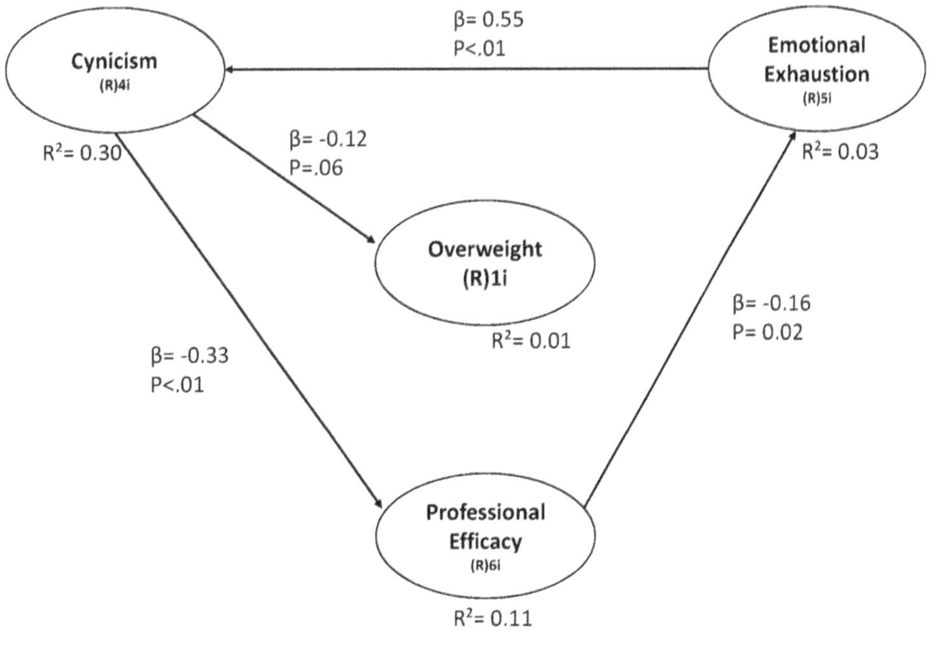

Conclusions regarding R^2 values are presented in Table 14. In this analysis, it was found that latent variable Emotional Exhaustion was 2.6% explained by latent variable Professional Efficacy. As for Cynicism, it seemed to be 29.8% explained by Emotional Exhaustion, whereas Professional Efficacy was 11.1% explained by Cynicism. Finally, Normal Weight is 1.4% explained by Cynicism. Such results demonstrated that Professional Efficacy can significantly reduce Emotional Exhaustion and Cynicism. Therefore, companies are advised to provide employees with suitable opportunities to maintain or increase their efficiency at work, otherwise it may affect the overall organization's productivity.

Sum of Indirect Effects

In structural equation models, relationships are not always direct. Table 15 presents the sum of indirect effects for every relationship in the final model. P values higher than 0.5 indicate that such relationships are not statistically significant. In this table, the relationship between Overweight and Cynicism is worth being emphasized, since the results demonstrated that when Overweight increased by one standard deviation, Cynicism decreased 0.147 units with 7% of variability.

Total Effects

Table 16 presents the total effects for every relationship in the final model. Some relationships are statistically not significant since their corresponding P-values were higher than 0.05. On the other hand, the relationship between Cynicism and Emotional Exhaustion showed the largest total effects. In fact, results revealed that when Cynicism increased by one standard deviation, Emotional Exhaustion increased by 0.546 units, with 29.8% of variability. In addition, it was found that when Professional Efficacy increased by one standard deviation, Cynicism decreased by 0.333 units, with 11.1% of variability.

Table 14. Effect Sizes

	Cynicism	Emotional Exhaustion	Professional Efficacy	Normal Weight
Cynicism		0.298		
Emotional Exhaustion			0.026	
Professional Efficacy	0.111			
Normal Weight	0.014			

Table 15. Sum of indirect effects

	Cynicism	Emotional Exhaustion	Professional Efficacy
Cynicism	β.029 p=.253 ES=.029	β=-.088 p=.05 ES=.017	
Emotional Exhaustion	β=.054 p=.158 ES=.029	β=.029 p=.253 ES=.029	
Professional Efficacy	β=-.182 p=<.001 ES=.023	β=.029 p=.253 ES=.029	
Overweight	β=-.065 p=.114 ES=.007	β=.010 p=.406 ES=.000	

Table 16. Total effects

	Cynicism	Emotional Exhaustion	Professional Efficacy
Cynicism	β=.029 p=.253 ES=.029	β=.546 p<.001 ES=.298	β=-.088 p=.050 ES=.017
Emotional Exhaustion	β=.054 p=.158 ES=.029	β=.029 p=.253 ES=.029	β=-.162 p=.015 ES=.026
Professional Efficacy	β=-.333 p<.001 ES=.111	β=-.182 p<.001 ES=.023	β=.029 p=.253 ES=.029
Overweight	β=-.119 p=.057 ES=.014	β=-.065 p=.114 ES=.007	β=.010 p=.406 ES=.000

CONCLUSION AND RECOMMENDATIONS

The objective of this research was to associate the three BS dimensions with the BMI among individuals with normal and overweight. To achieve this, a sample of middle and senior managers of the manufacturing industry in Ciudad Juarez, Mexico was studied. The model showing the relationships between BS and normal weight showed a significant explanatory power of 15%. Meanwhile, the model that seeks to explain the relationships between BS and overweight reported only 1% of significant explanatory power. Tables 17 and 18 present the conclusions concerning the hypothetical relations between BS and normal weight and between BS and overweight, respectively.

The results can be compared with previous studies conducted under a similar focus. For instance, according to Koppes, Meijer, and Bemelmans (2013), Emotional Exhaustion as a dimension of BS can be associated with eating disorders and stress, which in turn have an impact on the presence of both overweight and obesity. Also, Montiel (2014) and Barattuci (2011) reported that industrial workers and managerial positions in general tend to skip meals often or replace them by caffeinated, soft drinks, and/or unhealthy foods. Unfortunately, such foods have a strong impact on anxiety and stress. Finally, authors such as Ahola (2012) and Camacho et al. (2015) point out that Professional Efficacy can be directly related to weight loss because individuals are more active. However, Emotional Exhaustion increases the likelihood of suffering from overweight or obesity, since eating habits are usually altered. In other

Table 17. Conclusions regarding the relationships between Burnout and Normal Weight

	NORMAL WEIGHT		
	Explained Variance= 15%		
Hypothesis	**P and β values**	**Conclusions**	**Decision**
H1: There is a relationship between Professional Efficacy and Normal Weight for middle and senior managers of the manufacturing industry in Ciudad Juárez, Chihuahua, Mexico.	P=.01 β=.22	There is enough statistical evidence to prove that this relationship is positive, since when Professional Efficacy increases by one standard deviation, Normal Weight increases by 0.22 units.	ACCEPTED
H2: There is a relationship between Emotional Exhaustion and Normal Weight for middle and senior managers of the manufacturing industry in Ciudad Juárez, Chihuahua, Mexico.	P<.01 β=-.29	There is enough statistical evidence to prove that this relationship is positive, since when Emotional Exhaustion increases by one standard deviation, Normal Weight decreases by 0.29 units.	ACCEPTED
H3: There is a relationship between Cynicism and Normal Weight for middle and senior managers of the manufacturing industry in Ciudad Juárez, Chihuahua, Mexico.	P=.07 β=.15	No statistically significant relationships were found between Cynicism and Normal Weight.	REJECTED

Table 18. Conclusions regarding the relationships between Burnout and Overweight

	OVERWEIGHT		
	Explained Variance= 1%		
Hypothesis	P and β values	Conclusions	Decision
H1: There is a relationship between Professional Efficacy and Overweight for middle and senior managers of the manufacturing industry in Ciudad Juárez, Chihuahua, Mexico.	P=.19 β=-.07	No statistically significant relationships were found between Professional Efficacy and Overweight.	REJECTED
H2: There is a negative relationship between Emotional Exhaustion and Overweight for middle and senior managers of the manufacturing industry in Ciudad Juárez, Chihuahua, Mexico.	P=.15 β=.08	No statistically significant relationships were found between Emotional Exhaustion and Overweight.	REJECTED
H3: There is a relationship between Cynicism and Overweight for middle and senior managers of the manufacturing industry in Ciudad Juárez, Chihuahua, Mexico.	P=.056 β=-.12	There is enough statistical evidence to prove that this this relationship is negative, because when Cynicism increases by one standard deviation, Overweight decreases by 0.12 units.	ACCEPTED

words, as a result of being tired, it is common to skip meals, eat at wrong times, or make poor choices regarding the quality of meals (fast foods, greasy foods…).

According to the results, it seems that BS barely explains or does not explain at all the variability of overweight. Is believed that is due to the fact that other aspects, such as a lack of physical activity and/or sleep, unhealthy eating habits, and genetic factors, can have a deeper impact on overweight than psychosocial factors, and therefore, they have a stronger explanatory power. On the other hand, it seems that burnout does have a strong impact on individuals with normal weight. This may happen because such people still have an ordinary life style, especially in terms of eating habits and physical activity, since their weight is not a major concern.

As for Emotional Exhaustion, the negative relationship between this latent variable and Normal Weight seems to be congruent, since the more emotionally exhausted people feel, the less healthy they eat. Also, the positive relationship between Professional Efficacy and Normal Weight implies that efficient people are more active, and even motivated. Fortunately, both efficacy and motivation contribute a positive attitude at work.

The model that associates BS and overweight is more challenging to explain, since as previously mentioned, in addition to BS-related factors, other variables can explain the prevalence of overweight. Still, the model revealed that Cynicism has an impact on overweight, since cynicism usually entails negative attitudes, which in turn may lead to risk behaviors that can affect the BMI. Such risk behaviors include wrong eating habits, lack of physical activity, and/or unconcern about one's health.

Definitely, such results infer whether BS loses explanatory power as the BMI increases from normal weight to overweight. Indeed, psychosocial factors such as BS affect the physical health but only to a certain extent; then, when we exceed the limits, physiological variables and factors related to the life-style (lack of physical activity and/or sleep, wrong eating habits, genetic factors, etc.) may have a more prominent role when explaining the causes of overweight and obesity. However, it is important to mention that, from a preventive perspective, psychosocial factors and the perception of reality may be the ones which trigger behaviors that can eventually become unhealthy habits.

From Normal Weight to Overweight and Obesity, the line may be too blurred to go back so easily. Therefore, it is important that knowledge management contribution in this research help develop organizational strategies to promote among their employees maintain a normal weight to avoid unhealthy weight gain that compromises the individual's health and organization performance. Also, middle and senior managers must bear in mind that overweight and obesity are chronic diseases that persist, become more serious, and are difficult to eradicate if they are not properly treated and monitored. Fortunately, both conditions can be easily prevented by neutralizing those psychosocial factors that stop us from maintaining a healthy lifestyle.

As recommendations for future research, it is suggested the incorporation of other measuring instruments that can explain more in depth the occurrence of BS. Such instruments should be able to collect information regarding eating habits, physical activity, and stress coping strategies. It is also recommended to include measures of abdominal circumference. Finally, companies are advised to provide employees with personal, social and psychological support to detect indicators of stress and burnout and take the necessary preventive measures. Such strategies would contribute to a healthier lifestyle and work environment.

REFERENCES

Acosta, H. (2014). *Burnout y su relación con variables sociodemográficas, socio laborales y organizacionales en profesores universitarios chilenos*. Universitat Jaume I Departamento de Psicología Evolutiva, Educativa, Social y Metodología Castellón de la Plana, España.

Acosta, M., & Burguillos, A. I. (2014). Stress and burnout in teachers of primary and secondary education of Huelva: Coping like protection factor. *International Journal of Developmental and Educational Psychology*, *1*(4), 303–331.

Aguayo, C. V., la Fuente, E. D., & Lozano, L. M. (2011). A meta-analytic reliability generalization study of the Maslach Burnout Inventory. *International Journal of Clinical and Health Psychology*, *11*, 343–361.

Aguirre, N. H., Medellín, J., Vázquez, L., Gutiérrez, G., & Fernández, M. C. (2014). Síndrome de quemarse por el trabajo y su relación con el puesto de trabajo en empleados de la industria maquiladora. *Revista PsicologiaCientifica.com, 16*(1). Retrieved from http://www.psicologiacientifica.com/sindromequemarse-trabajo-relacion-puesto-trabajo-empleados

Ahola, K., Honkonen, T., Isometsä, E., Kalimo, R., Nykyri, E., Aromaa, A., & Lönnqvist, J. (2005). The relationship between job-related burnout and depressive disorders — results from the Finnish Health 2000 Study. *Journal of Affective Disorders*, *88*(1), 55–62. doi:10.1016/j.jad.2005.06.004 PMID:16038984

Ahola, K., Pulkki-Råback, L., Kouvonen, A., Rossi, H., Aromaa, A., & Lönnqvist, J. (2012). Burnout and Behavior-Related Health Risk Factors: Results From the PopulationBased Finnish Health 2000 Study. *Journal of Occupational and Environmental Medicine*, *54*(1), 17–22. doi:10.1097/JOM.0b013e31823ea9d9 PMID:22157806

Ahola, K., Vaananen, A., Koskinen, A., Kouvonen, A., & Shirom, A. (2010). Burnout as a predictor of all-cause mortality among industrial employees: A 10-year prospective register-linkage study. *Journal of Psychosomatic Research*, *69*(1), 51–57. doi:10.1016/j.jpsychores.2010.01.002 PMID:20630263

Aranda, I. (2014). Factores psicosociales y trastornos psíquicos en trabajadores de una empresa maquiladora de electrónica, Guadalajara, México. Revista Costarricense de Salud Pública, 23(1).

Arenas, L., & Cantú, O. (2013). Factores de riesgo de trastornos musculo-esqueléticos crónicos laborales. *Medicina Interna de México*, *29*(4), 370–379.

Armenta. (2015). *Determinación de la presencia de Burnout y el índice de estrés del trabajo en mandos medios y superiores de la industria maquiladora de ciudad Juárez*. Tesis.

Arroyo, S., & Castillo, V. M. (2017). Innovacion y Gestion del conocimiento en las organizaciones. Inceptum, 7(12).

Asociación-de-Maquiladoras-A, C. (2013). *Panorama general 2013*. Retrieved from http://www.indexjuarez.org/INICIO/2013/Maquila%20Overview%202013/MAQUIL A%20OVERVIEW%202013.pdf

Barattucci, Y. (2011). *Estrés y Alimentación. (Licenciatura en Nutrición)*. Universidad Fasta.

Benevides-Pereira, A., Moreno-Jiménez, B., Garrosa Hernández, E., & González, J.L. (2006). *Un estudio transcultural acerca de los procesos de estrés y burnout en profesores*. Interpsiquis.

Borda, N., & Aun, B. (2007). Síndrome de Burnout en estudiantes de internado del Hospital Universidad del Norte. *Salud Uninorte. Barranquilla (Col.)*, *23*(1), 43–51.

Calabrese, G. (2006). Impacto del estrés laboral en el anestesiólogo. *Revista Colombiana de Anestesiología*, *34*(4), 233–240.

Calabrese, G. (2010). Impacto del estrés laboral crónico en la salud del anestesiólogo. *Revista mexicana de anestesiología, 33*(1), S183-S185.

Calvo-Porral, C., Martínez-Fernández, V. A., & Juanatey-Boga, O. (2011). Análisis de dos modelos de ecuaciones estructurales alternativos para medir la intencion de compra. *Revista Investigación Operacional*, *34*(3), 230–243.

Camacho-Alamilla, R., Maldonado-Macias, A., García-Alcaraz, J. L., & Hernández-Arellano, J. L. (2014). Determination of Burnout Syndrome among Middle and Senior Managment Personnel in Autootive Industry in Juarez City México. In C. EspejoGuasco, E. De la Vega Bustillos, & E. Chacón Martínez (Eds.), Ergonomía Ocupacional. Investigaciones y aplicaciones (Vol. 7, pp. 306-317). Sociedad de Ergonomistas de México, A.C.

Camacho, R., Maldonado, A., García, J.L., Palacios, J. & Valenzuela, J. Camacho, Maldonado, García, Palacios, & Valenzuela. (2015). Modelo estructural del síndrome de Burnout y obesidad en mandos medios y superiores de la industria maquiladora en Ciudad Juárez. *Culcyt, 55*, 78-85.

Carlotto, M., & De Santos Palazzo, L. (2006). Síndrome de burnout factores asociados: un estodo epidemiológico com profesores. *Cadernos Saude Pública, 22*(5).

Carlson, R. (2014). *Fisiología de la conducta (8th ed.)*. Pearson-Educación.

Cronbach, L. (1951). Coefficient alpha and the internal structure of tests. *Psychometrika*, *16*(3), 297–334. doi:10.1007/BF02310555

Dallman, M. F. (2010). Stress-induced obesity and the emotional nervous system. *Trends in Endocrinology and Metabolism, 21*(3), 159–165. doi:10.1016/j.tem.2009.10.004 PMID:19926299

Dávila-Torres, J., González-Izquierdo, J. J., & Barrera-Cruz, A. (2015). Panorama de la obesidad en México. *Obesity in Mexico, 53*(2), 240. Retrieved from http://search.ebscohost.com/login.aspx?direct=true&db=edb&AN=101483297&lang=es&site=eds-live

De Pablo, C. (2007). *Estrés y hostigamiento laboral* (2nd ed.). Jaén: Formación Alcalá.

Edelwich, J., & Brodsky, A. (1980). *Burnout: Stages of disillusionment in the helping professions. Nueva York.* Human Sciences Press.

Forbes, R. (2011). El síndrome de burnout: síntomas, causas y medidas de atención en la empresa. *Éxito empresarial, 160.*

Freudenberger. (1998). *Desgaste profesional: burnout personalidad y salud percibida.* Empleo, estrés y salud.

George, D., & Mallery, P. (2003). SPSS for Windows step by step: A Simple Guide and Reference. 11.0 Update (4th ed.). Boston: Allyn & Bacon.

Gestal, J. (2003). *Riesgos laborales del personal sanitario (3rd ed.).* Madrid: McGraw Hill Interamericana.

Gil-Monte, P. (2008). El síndrome de quemarse por el trabajo (*burnout*) como fenómeno transcultural. *Información psicológica*, 91-92. Retrieved from http://www.uv.es/unipsico/pdf/Publicaciones/Articulos/01_SQT/2007_08_Gil_Monte.pdf

Gil-Monte, P. R. (2002). Validez Factorial de la adaptación al español de Maslach Burnout Inventory Genereal Survey. *Salud Pública de México*, *44*(1), 33–40. doi:10.1590/S0036-36342002000100005 PMID:11910717

Gil Monte, P. R., & Peiro, J. M. (1997). *Desgaste psíquico en el trabajo: El síndrome de Quemarse.* Madrid: Síntesis Psicológica.

Guerrero, E., & Vicente, F. (2001). *Síndrome de "Burnout" o desgaste profesional y afrontamiento del estrés en el profesorado.* Cáceres: Universidad de Extremadura.

Hair, J. F., Black, W. C., Babin, B., Anderson, R. E., & Tatham, R. L. (2006). *Multivariate data analysis* (Vol. 6). Pearson Prentice Hall.

International Labour Organization (ILO). (2016). *Mental Health in the workplace.* Retrieved from http://www.newunionism.net/library/working%20life/ILO%20%20Mental%20Health%20in%20the%20Workplace%20-%202000.pdf

Jensen, M. D., Ryan, D. H., & Apvian, C. M. (2014). 2013 AHA/ACC/TOS guideline for the management of overweight and obesity in adults: A report of the American College of Cardiology/American Heart Association Task Force on Practice Guidelines and The Obesity Society. *Circulation, 129*(25), S102–S138. doi:10.1161/01.cir.0000437739.71477.ee PMID:24222017

Juárez-García, A., Idrovo, A. J., Camacho-Ávila, A., & Placencia-Reyes, O. (2014). Síndorme de burnout en población mexicana: Una revisión sistemática. *Salud Mental, 37*(2), 159–176. doi:10.17711/SM.0185-3325.2014.020

Juno, J., & Noriega, M. (2004). Los Trastornos Musculoesqueléticos y la Fatiga como Indicadores de Deficiencias Ergonómicas y en la Organización del Trabajo. *Salud de los Trabajadores, 12*(2), 27-41

Kim, H. (2014). Job conditions, unmet expectations, and burnout in public child welfare workers: How different from other social workers? *Children and Youth Services Review, 33*(2), 358–367. doi:10.1016/j.childyouth.2010.10.001

Klein, S., Fabbrini, E., & Romijn, J. A. (2011). Obesity. In Williams Textbook of Endocrinology (12th ed.). Philadelphia, PA: Saunders Elsevier.

Kock, N. (2013). *WarpPLS©4.0 User Manual.* Laredo, TX: ScriptWarp Systems.

Kock, N. (2014). *A note on how to conduct a factor-based PLS-SEM analysis.* Laredo, TX: ScriptWarp Systems.

Llaneza, J. (2002). *Ergonomía y psicología aplicada: Manual para la formación del especialista.* España: Lex Nova.

Lobach, D., Sanders, G. D., & Bright, T. J. (2012). *Enabling Health Care Decisionmaking Through Clinical Decision Support and Knowledge Management.* Rockville, MD: Agency for Healthcare Research and Quality (US). Available from: https://www.ncbi.nlm.nih.gov/books/NBK97318/

Maldonado-Macías, A., Camacho-Alamilla, R., Torres, S. G. V., Alcaraz, J. L. G., & Limón, J. (2015). Determination of Burnout Syndrome among Middle and Senior Managers in Manufacturing Industry in Ciudad Juarez. *Procedia Manufacturing, 3*, 6459–6466. doi:10.1016/j.promfg.2015.07.927

Marrau, M. (2009). El síndrome de quemarse por el trabajo (burnout), en el marco contextualizador del estrés laboral. *Fundamentos en humanidades, 19*(1), 167-177.

Maslach, C., & Jackson, S. E. (1981). *MBI: Maslach Burnout Inventory. Manual.* Palo Alto, CA: University of California, Consulting Psychologist Press.

Maslach, C., & Leiter, M. P. (2008). Early predictors of job burnout and engagement. *The Journal of Applied Psychology, 93*(3), 498–512. doi:10.1037/0021-9010.93.3.498 PMID:18457483

Mazita, A., & Kamsidi, Z. (2016). A critical review on the effect of knowledge management on the organization performance. Journal of Technical and Vocational Education, 1(2), 20-25.

Melgosa, J. (1999). Sin Estrés. Editorial Safeliz, S.L.

Montiel, O., Ramírez, A., Esparza, V. M., & Guerrero, A. (2014). Relatos de vida de gerentes de producción en la industria maquiladora de Cd. Juárez, México. *Global Conference on Business & Finance Proceedings, 9*(1), 1700-1709. Retrieved from http://ezproxy.uacj.mx/login?url=http://search.ebscohost.com/login.aspx?direct=true&db=bth&AN=94260555&lang=es&site=eds-live Moreno

Moreno, B., Rodríguez, R., & Escobar, E. (2001). La evaluación del burnout profesional factorialización del MBI-GS. Un análisis preliminar. *Ansiedad y Estrés, 7*, 69–78.

Nevanpera, N. J., Hopsu, L., Kuosma, E., Ukkola, O., Uitti, J., & Laitinen, J. H. (2012). Occupational burnout, eating behavior, and weight among working women. *The American Journal of Clinical Nutrition, 95*(4), 934–943. doi:10.3945/ajcn.111.014191 PMID:22378728

Organización Mundial de la Salud – OMS. (2010). *Health impact of psychosocial, hazards at work: an overview*. Retrieved from http://whqlibdoc.who.int/publications/2010/9789241500272_eng.pdf

Organización Mundial de la Salud – OMS Europa. (2015). *Mental health and well-being at the workplace- protection and inclusion in challenging times*. Retrieved from http://www.euro.who.int/__data/assets/pdf_file/0018/124047/e94345.pdf

Proper, K. I., Koppes, L. J., Meijer, S., & Bemelmans, J. E. (2013). The Association Between Body Mass Index Status and Sick Leave and the Role of Emotional Exhaustion—A Mediation Analysis Among a Representative Sample of Dutch Employees. *Journal of Occupational and Environmental Medicine, 55*(10), 1213–1218. doi:10.1097/JOM.0b013e31829f2f5c PMID:24064779

Rivera, J. (2013). Estrés laboral y sus repercusiones. *Revista Mexicana de Anestesiología, 36*(3), 173–175.

Schaufeli, W. B., & Enzmann, D. (1998). *The burnout companion to study and practice: A critical analisys*. Padstow, UK: Taylor & Francis.

Schaufeli, W. B., Leiter, M. P., Maslach, C., & Jackson, S. E. (1996). The Maslach Burnout Inventory-General Survey. In C. Maslach, S. E. Jackson, & M. P. Leiter (Eds.), *Maslach Burnout Inventory*. Palo Alto, CA: Consulting Psychologis Press.

Serrano, M. A., Moya, L., & Salvador, A. ((2009). Estrés laboral y salud: Indicadores cardiovasculares y endocrinos. *Anales de Psicología, 25*, 150-159.

SPSS. (2007). *Manual del Usuario de SPSS Statistics Base 17.0*. Chicago, IL: SPSS Inc.

Valecillo, M., Quevedo, A.L., Lubo, A., Dos Santos, A., Montiel, M., Camejo, & Sánchez, M. (2009). Síntomas musculoesqueléticos y estrés laboral en el personal de enfermería de un hospital militar. *Salud trab, 17*(2), 85-95.

Vicente, A., Diaz, C., Zimmermann, M., & Galiana, L. (2012). *El trastorno musculoesquelético en el ámbito laboral en cifras. Departamento de información e investigación del Instituto Nacional de Seguridad e Higiene en el Trabajo. MEISS*. Gobierno de España.

Chapter 8
Advanced Issues of Knowledge Management, Knowledge Discovery, and Organizational Communication

Kijpokin Kasemsap
Suan Sunandha Rajabhat University, Thailand

ABSTRACT

This chapter presents the advanced issues of knowledge management (KM), the advanced issues of knowledge discovery, and the advanced issues of organizational communication. KM with the support of knowledge discovery can improve the ability of organizations to effectively solve problems, adapt, and evolve to meet the changing business requirements. Knowledge discovery enlists the power of computers to assist in the recognizing patterns in data, a task that exceeds human ability as the size of data warehouses significantly increase. The revolution in organizational communication allows people to directly talk to each other without the use of managers. Effective organizational communication allows organizations to be more efficient by bringing needed expertise and knowledge on demand. The chapter argues that encouraging KM, knowledge discovery, and organizational communication has the potential to enhance organizational performance and reach strategic goals in the digital age.

INTRODUCTION

Knowledge is recognized as one of the most critical resources for achieving both innovation (Valentim, Lisboa, & Franco, 2016) and competitive advantage (Filieri & Willison, 2016). As companies become more international in their reach, developing mechanisms and practices that facilitate knowledge management (KM) and the development of common mind-sets across diverse cultural boundaries becomes more crucial (Mabey & Zhao, 2017). Regarding KM methods, knowledge discovery can assist in investigating various patterns toward providing the practical insight into the stored data (Kasemsap, 2017a).

DOI: 10.4018/978-1-5225-3725-0.ch008

When faced with a new technological paradigm, incumbent firms can opt for both internal development and external sourcing to obtain the necessary new knowledge (Grigoriou & Rothaermel, 2017). KM is used to achieve business process improvement by embedding KM within problem processes (Massingham & Al Holaibi, 2017). The process of KM-related knowledge utilization to create new products can occur internally, through research and development (R&D) activities, as well as externally, by making investments in creating links with suppliers, universities, customers, and a wide range of actors in the innovation system (Wang & Libaers, 2016).

All organizations depend on communication (Te'eni, 2008). Communication is recognized to affect the interpersonal relationships (Chen, Gable, & Hu, 2013). Effective communication between employers and employees would not only enhance employees' morale and job performance, but also demonstrate employers' successful leadership (Shen & Austin, 2017). Internal communication approaches must be tailored to the organizational culture, size, industry, managerial system, financial resources, employees, and nature of the business environment (Richet, 2016).

Top and middle managers can play a significant role in supporting KM and organizational communication (Al Saifi, Dillon, & McQueen, 2016) toward enhancing organizational innovation performance (Caridi-Zahavi, Carmeli, & Arazy, 2016). Organizational communication leads to the major changes in the way in which social care services are managed (Andrioni & Popp, 2012). The efficient organizational communication gains increased importance in the success or failure of an organization, regardless of the specifics of the conducted activities (Mitrofan & Bulborea, 2013).

This chapter is based on a literature review of KM, knowledge discovery, and organizational communication. The extensive literatures of KM, knowledge discovery, and organizational communication provide a contribution to practitioners and researchers by presenting their applications and approaches in modern organizations.

BACKGROUND

Understanding relative statures of channels for disseminating knowledge is of practical interest to both generators and consumers of knowledge flows in the knowledge era (Chen et al., 2017). KM-related absorptive capacity allows modern businesses and SMEs to access knowledge, and plays an important role in their ability to explore and exploit opportunities in their competitive business environment (Valentim et al., 2016) toward effective decision making (Alvarez, Cilleruelo, & Zamanillo, 2016).

KM practitioners should facilitate a knowledge sharing environment, where new ideas and solutions can be developed, and consequently innovation outcomes are likely to occur (Costa & Monteiro, 2016). Companies should pay more attention to the KM practices to support the strategy formulation capabilities (Aktürk & Kurt, 2016). Firms should develop and leverage internal and external knowledge-based resource capabilities to respond to both opportunities and threats created by technological innovation (Gaimon, Hora, & Ramachandran, 2017).

The information society brings challenges and opportunities to the employee communication process (Capriotti, 2009). Technological achievements that significantly influence communication management are social media platforms in virtual environment (Lalic, Marjanovic, & Lalic, 2012). Social media is the beneficial method for people to communicate and share their interests (Cruz-Cunha, Gonçalves, Lopes, Miranda, & Putnik, 2012). Organizational communication received great attention from scholars and the business community more than 40 years ago due to the changes in global business environments (Mohamad, Bakar, Halim, & Ismail, 2014).

Companies need to develop new approaches in organizational communication, while social media becomes the significant tool for organizing effective communication (Badea, 2014). Organizational communication must be included in the concept of the General Theory of Systems (GTS), a method that explains the elements and the functions of the respective process (Cecan & Marian, 2015). Communication is necessary for preventing coordination failure in the newly formed group (Fehr, 2017). Organizational communication network is a personal or professional set of relationships among individuals or organizations (Hossain, Murshed, & Uddin, 2013).

ASPECTS OF KNOWLEDGE MANAGEMENT, KNOWLEDGE DISCOVERY, AND ORGANIZATIONAL COMMUNICATION

This section provides the advanced issues of KM, the advanced issues of knowledge discovery, and the advanced issues of organizational communication.

Advanced Issues of Knowledge Management

Knowledge is an important company resource, particularly when the organization is striving to create new products and services and to be more innovative (Alexander, Neyer, & Huizingh, 2016). Regarding KM, knowledge-based approach and collaborative process management involve a combination of structured and non-structured processes (Ferreira, Faria, Azevedo, & Marques, 2017). Structured process management can be reduced to a set of fully-defined rules leading to high efficiency and low flexibility, whereas the management of non-structured process is not prone to a full formalization (Ferreira, Faria, Azevedo, & Marques, 2017).

One of the key challenges for innovation and technology-mediated knowledge collaboration within organizational settings is motivating contributors to share their knowledge (Arazy, Gellatly, Brainin, & Nov, 2016). The mixture of different types of external knowledge partners in combination with internal R&D capabilities is crucial in understanding the roles of open innovation and KM in emerging economies (Chen, Vanhaverbeke, & Du, 2016). Learning organization is the organization that obtains knowledge in order to survive in a rapidly changing environment (Kasemsap, 2016). Learning organization fully mediates the relationship between KM capabilities and organizational performance (Ngah, Tai, & Bontis, 2016).

Strategic alliances offer powerful tools for firms to explore business opportunities, and alliances can explore in technology and organization dimensions toward effective KM (Zhang, 2016). Organizational innovation with the support of strategic alliances (Vlaisavljevic, Cabello-Medina, & Pérez-Luño, 2016) can play an important role in determining how effectively knowledge can be utilized by employees to identify various business opportunities (Ma & Huang, 2016).

Advanced Issues of Knowledge Discovery

Knowledge discovery-related process model was first discussed in 1989 (Alnoukari & El Sheikh, 2012). Knowledge discovery is the overall process of converting raw data into useful information (Yu, 2009), and is a wide area of research where machine learning, data mining, and data warehousing techniques converge to the common goal of describing and understanding the world (Rodrigues, Gama, & Lopes, 2010). Knowledge discovery and data mining aim at finding useful information from the massive collections of data, and then extracting useful knowledge from the information (Wu, McGinnity, Prasad, & Bell, 2009). Interoperability and data quality must be addressed in any framework for knowledge discovery on the Internet (Hu & Peyton, 2012).

Knowledge discovery involves the developments of strategies and procedures for making sense out of massive data (Narang, Kumar, & Verma, 2017). Knowledge discovery methods often discover a large number of patterns (Kontonasios, Spyropoulou, & De Bie, 2012). Efficient knowledge discovery can be achieved by introducing the domain knowledge of experts to the creation of business action (Yada, 2004). A key issue in any discovery system is to ensure the consistency, accuracy, and completeness of the discovered knowledge (Owrang O, 2009). E-mail exchange, content consulting, forum participation, and chats can be processed with the support of knowledge discovery approach (Salazar & Vergara, 2008).

The Grid can be effectively exploited for deploying knowledge discovery applications because of the high-performance it can offer and its distributed infrastructure (Congiusta, Talia, & Trunfio, 2008). For the effective use of Grids in knowledge discovery, the development of middleware is critical to support data management, data transfer, data mining, and knowledge representation (Congiusta et al., 2008). Data mining tasks are often distributed because they involve data and tools located over geographically distributed environments (Cesario, Lackovic, Talia, & Trunfio, 2013).

Advanced Issues of Organizational Communication

Communication is the exchange of information between two or more people with the intent that the sender's message be understood and considered by the receivers in their cognition, affect, and behavior (Te'eni, 2008). At the international level, communication in the management of human resources is more important because attraction, selection, and training is not only for the regional level, and needs to be adapted to international standards (Vasilcovschi, 2013).

Communication satisfaction is a mediator between perceived justice and organizational citizenship behaviors (OCB) (Chan & La, 2017). OCB is the extent to which an employee's voluntary support and behavior contributes to the organization's success (Kasemsap, 2017b). Organizational communication has a significant effect on job satisfaction and job performance of the employees (Giri & Kumar, 2010). Job satisfaction is the sense of inner fulfillment and pride achieved when performing a particular job (Kasemsap, 2017c).

Job satisfaction leads to a positive ambience at the workplace and is essential to ensure the higher revenues for the organization (Kasemsap, 2017d). Job satisfaction, leader-member exchange (LMX), and organizational justice have mediated positive effect on OCB (Kasemsap, 2013a). Improving the quality of job satisfaction increases the employee's senses of organizational commitment, OCB, and organizational performance (Kasemsap, 2013b). Organizational commitment positively mediates the relationships between leadership behavior and job performance and between job satisfaction and job performance (Kasemsap, 2013c).

The understanding of communication-related technological application is significant in determining the usefulness of virtual groups in organizations, and in the designing of electronic collaborative activities

(Nikoi & Boateng, 2014). Different communication technologies, such as mobile phone and computer mediated communication (CMC), have become a powerful force in the ongoing globalization process and have strong effects on the development of multinational companies by helping them to achieve efficiency, coordination, and communication (Xia & Mao, 2016).

Today, most business communications and transactions are conducted via CMC, and e-mail is the most familiar type of CMC (Madanchian & Taherdoost, 2016). E-mail, social media, and other types of computer-mediated workplace communication tools can enhance flexibility in how employees perform their jobs, expand networking opportunities, increase profits, cut costs, and enable collaboration among diverse groups across the globe (Chory, Vela, & Avtgis, 2016).

Effective leadership inspires and empowers employees to realize their fullest potential and manage their potentials to achieve common goals (Kasemsap, 2017e). Authentic organizational leadership and transparent organizational communication are the effective drivers for a favorable reputation in the eyes of corporate insiders (Men, 2014).

FUTURE RESEARCH DIRECTIONS

The classification of the extensive literature in the domains of KM, knowledge discovery, and organizational communication will provide the potential opportunities for future research. Effective information system can encourage the processes of information integration and information sharing toward enhancing entrepreneurial success, increasing business growth and gaining customer satisfaction in global supply chain (Kasemsap, 2017f). Considering the relationships among KM, knowledge discovery, organizational communication, information integration, and information sharing should be further studied.

CONCLUSION

This chapter indicated the advanced issues of KM, the advanced issues of knowledge discovery, and the advanced issues of organizational communication. KM improves the ability of organizations to effectively solve problems, adapt, and evolve to meet the changing business requirements. KM recognizes that organizations are a complex system made up of both the people that work for the organization, and the processes, procedures, and information systems that drive business growth in modern organizations. Knowledge discovery enlists the power of computers to assist in the recognizing patterns in data, a task that is exceeds human ability as the size of data warehouses significantly increase.

The revolution in organizational communication allows people to directly talk to each other without the use of managers. Effective organizational communication allows organizations to be more efficient by bringing needed expertise and knowledge on demand. Modern organizations need to build a new culture that promotes knowledge sharing and constant learning while preserving and recording appropriate information. This is essential in order for corporate knowledge to be effectively retained and enhanced through organizational communication. Encouraging KM, knowledge discovery, and organizational communication has the potential to enhance organizational performance and reach strategic goals in the digital age.

REFERENCES

Aktürk, B. K., & Kurt, M. (2016). An empirical study of the relationship between knowledge management practices and strategy formulation capabilities. *Procedia: Social and Behavioral Sciences, 235*, 739–745. doi:10.1016/j.sbspro.2016.11.075

Al Saifi, S., Dillon, S., & McQueen, R. (2016). The relationship between management support and knowledge sharing: An exploratory study of manufacturing firms. *Knowledge and Process Management, 23*(2), 124–135. doi:10.1002/kpm.1506

Alexander, A. T., Neyer, A. K., & Huizingh, K. R. E. (2016). Introduction to the special issue: Transferring knowledge for innovation. *R & D Management, 46*(2), 305–311. doi:10.1111/radm.12195

Alvarez, I., Cilleruelo, E., & Zamanillo, I. (2016). Is formality in knowledge management practices related to the size of organizations? The Basque case. *Human Factors and Ergonomics in Manufacturing & Service Industries, 26*(1), 127–144. doi:10.1002/hfm.20618

Andrioni, F., & Popp, L. E. (2012). Organizational communication in social care organizations from Hunedoara county, Romania. *Procedia: Social and Behavioral Sciences, 62*, 590–594. doi:10.1016/j.sbspro.2012.09.099

Arazy, O., Gellatly, I., Brainin, E., & Nov, O. (2016). Motivation to share knowledge using wiki technology and the moderating effect of role perceptions. *Journal of the Association for Information Science and Technology, 67*(10), 2362–2378. doi:10.1002/asi.23579

Badea, M. (2014). Social media and organizational communication. *Procedia: Social and Behavioral Sciences, 149*, 70–75. doi:10.1016/j.sbspro.2014.08.192

Capriotti, P. (2009). E-communication in the information society and the impact of new technologies on employee communication. In T. Torres-Coronas & M. Arias-Oliva (Eds.), *Encyclopedia of human resources information systems: Challenges in e-HRM* (pp. 248–255). Hershey, PA: IGI Global. doi:10.4018/978-1-59904-883-3.ch038

Caridi-Zahavi, O., Carmeli, A., & Arazy, O. (2016). The influence of CEOs' visionary innovation leadership on the performance of high-technology ventures: The mediating roles of connectivity and knowledge integration. *Journal of Product Innovation Management, 33*(3), 356–376. doi:10.1111/jpim.12275

Cecan, S., & Marian, L. (2015). Theoretical and practical considerations regarding the risk factors in organizational communication. *Procedia Technology, 19*, 1053–1058. doi:10.1016/j.protcy.2015.02.150

Cesario, E., Lackovic, M., Talia, D., & Trunfio, P. (2013). Programming knowledge discovery workflows in service-oriented distributed systems. *Concurrency and Computation, 25*(10), 1482–1504. doi:10.1002/cpe.2936

Chan, S. H. J., & Lai, H. Y. I. (2017). Understanding the link between communication satisfaction, perceived justice and organizational citizenship behavior. *Journal of Business Research, 70*, 214–223. doi:10.1016/j.jbusres.2016.08.017

Chen, L., Gable, G. G., & Hu, H. (2013). Communication and organizational social networks: A simulation model. *Computational & Mathematical Organization Theory*, *19*(4), 460–479. doi:10.100710588-012-9131-0

Chen, L., Holsapple, C. W., Hsiao, S. H., Ke, Z., Oh, J. Y., & Yang, Z. (2017). Knowledge-dissemination channels: Analytics of stature evaluation. *Journal of the Association for Information Science and Technology*, *68*(4), 911–930. doi:10.1002/asi.23725

Chen, Y., Vanhaverbeke, W., & Du, J. (2016). The interaction between internal R&D and different types of external knowledge sourcing: An empirical study of Chinese innovative firms. *R & D Management*, *46*(S3), 1006–1023. doi:10.1111/radm.12162

Chory, R. M., Vela, L. E., & Avtgis, T. A. (2016). Organizational surveillance of computer-mediated workplace communication: Employee privacy concerns and responses. *Employee Responsibilities and Rights Journal*, *28*(1), 23–43. doi:10.100710672-015-9267-4

Congiusta, A., Talia, D., & Trunfio, P. (2008). Using grids for distributed knowledge discovery. In G. Felici & C. Vercellis (Eds.), *Mathematical methods for knowledge discovery and data mining* (pp. 284–298). Hershey, PA: IGI Global. doi:10.4018/978-1-59904-528-3.ch017

Costa, V., & Monteiro, S. (2016). Knowledge processes, absorptive capacity and innovation: A mediation analysis. *Knowledge and Process Management*, *23*(3), 207–218. doi:10.1002/kpm.1507

Cruz-Cunha, M. M., Gonçalves, P., Lopes, N., Miranda, E. M., & Putnik, G. D. (2012). *Handbook of research on business social networking: Organizational, managerial, and technological dimensions* (Vols. 1–2). Hershey, PA: IGI Global. doi:10.4018/978-1-61350-168-9

Fehr, D. (2017). Costly communication and learning from failure in organizational coordination. *European Economic Review*, *93*, 106–122. doi:10.1016/j.euroecorev.2017.01.006

Ferreira, F., Faria, J., Azevedo, A., & Marques, A. L. (2017). Product lifecycle management in knowledge intensive collaborative environments: An application to automotive industry. *International Journal of Information Management*, *37*(1), 1474–1487. doi:10.1016/j.ijinfomgt.2016.05.006

Filieri, R., & Willison, R. (2016). Antecedents of knowledge sourcing and reuse from a knowledge repository in the virtual product prototyping: The role of knowledge and system quality dimensions. *Knowledge and Process Management*, *23*(2), 147–160. doi:10.1002/kpm.1512

Gaimon, C., Hora, M., & Ramachandran, K. (2017). Towards building multidisciplinary knowledge on management of technology: An introduction to the special issue. *Production and Operations Management*, *26*(4), 567–578. doi:10.1111/poms.12668

Giri, V. N., & Kumar, B. P. (2010). Assessing the impact of organizational communication on job satisfaction and job performance. *Psychological Studies*, *55*(2), 137–143. doi:10.100712646-010-0013-6

Grigoriou, K., & Rothaermel, F. T. (2017). Organizing for knowledge generation: Internal knowledge networks and the contingent effect of external knowledge sourcing. *Strategic Management Journal*, *38*(2), 395–414. doi:10.1002mj.2489

Hossain, L., Murshed, S. T., & Uddin, S. (2013). Communication network dynamics during organizational crisis. *Journal of Informetrics*, *7*(1), 16–35. doi:10.1016/j.joi.2012.07.006

Hu, J., & Peyton, L. (2012). A framework for privacy assurance and ubiquitous knowledge discovery in health 2.0 data mashups. In I. Management Association (Ed.), Cyber crime: Concepts, methodologies, tools and applications (pp. 263–283). Hershey, PA: IGI Global. doi:10.4018/978-1-61350-323-2.ch204

Kasemsap, K. (2013a). Innovative human resource practice: A synthesized framework and causal model of leader-member exchange, organizational justice, job satisfaction, and organizational citizenship behavior. *International Journal of e-Education, e-Business, e-Management and e-Learning, 3*(1), 13–18. doi:10.7763/IJEEEE.2013.V3.185

Kasemsap, K. (2013b). Conceptual framework: Factors affecting performance of pulp and paper mill employees in Thailand. *International Proceedings of Economics Development and Research*, *57*, 133–137. doi:10.7763/IPEDR. 2012. V57. 25

Kasemsap, K. (2013c). Strategic human resource practice: A functional framework and causal model of leadership behavior, job satisfaction, organizational commitment, and job performance. *Journal of Social and Development Sciences*, *4*(5), 198–204.

Kasemsap, K. (2016). The roles of e-learning, organizational learning, and knowledge management in the learning organizations. In E. Railean, G. Walker, A. Elçi, & L. Jackson (Eds.), *Handbook of research on applied learning theory and design in modern education* (pp. 786–816). Hershey, PA: IGI Global. doi:10.4018/978-1-4666-9634-1.ch039

Kasemsap, K. (2017a). Knowledge discovery and data visualization: Theories and perspectives. *International Journal of Organizational and Collective Intelligence*, *7*(3), 56–69. doi:10.4018/IJOCI.2017070105

Kasemsap, K. (2017b). The fundamentals of organizational citizenship behavior. In B. Christiansen & H. Chandan (Eds.), *Handbook of research on human factors in contemporary workforce development* (pp. 1–23). Hershey, PA: IGI Global. doi:10.4018/978-1-5225-2568-4.ch001

Kasemsap, K. (2017c). The significance of job satisfaction in modern organizations. In B. Christiansen & H. Chandan (Eds.), *Handbook of research on human factors in contemporary workforce development* (pp. 181–200). Hershey, PA: IGI Global. doi:10.4018/978-1-5225-2568-4.ch008

Kasemsap, K. (2017d). Examining the roles of job satisfaction and organizational commitment in the global workplace. In P. Ordoñez de Pablos & R. Tennyson (Eds.), *Handbook of research on human resources strategies for the new millennial workforce* (pp. 148–176). Hershey, PA: IGI Global. doi:10.4018/978-1-5225-0948-6.ch008

Kasemsap, K. (2017e). Management education and leadership styles: Current issues and approaches. In N. Baporikar (Ed.), *Innovation and shifting perspectives in management education* (pp. 166–193). Hershey, PA: IGI Global. doi:10.4018/978-1-5225-1019-2.ch008

Kasemsap, K. (2017f). Advocating information system, information integration, and information sharing in global supply chain. In G. Jamil, A. Soares, & C. Pessoa (Eds.), *Handbook of research on information management for effective logistics and supply chains* (pp. 107–130). Hershey, PA: IGI Global. doi:10.4018/978-1-5225-0973-8.ch006

Kontonasios, K. N., Spyropoulou, E., & De Bie, T. (2012). Knowledge discovery interestingness measures based on unexpectedness. *Wiley Interdisciplinary Reviews: Data Mining and Knowledge Discovery*, *2*(5), 386–399. doi:10.1002/widm.1063

Lalic, D., Marjanovic, U., & Lalic, B. (2012). The influence of social networks on communication satisfaction within the organizations. In M. Cruz-Cunha, P. Gonçalves, N. Lopes, E. Miranda, & G. Putnik (Eds.), *Handbook of research on business social networking: Organizational, managerial, and technological dimensions* (pp. 545–566). Hershey, PA: IGI Global. doi:10.4018/978-1-61350-168-9.ch029

Ma, R., & Huang, Y. C. (2016). Opportunity-based strategic orientation, knowledge acquisition, and entrepreneurial alertness: The perspective of the global sourcing suppliers in China. *Journal of Small Business Management*, *54*(3), 953–972. doi:10.1111/jsbm.12222

Mabey, C., & Zhao, S. (2017). Managing five paradoxes of knowledge exchange in networked organizations: New priorities for HRM? *Human Resource Management Journal*, *27*(1), 39–57. doi:10.1111/1748-8583.12106

Madanchian, M., & Taherdoost, H. (2016). Perusing of organizational culture effects on e-mail communication. *Procedia Technology*, *22*, 1076–1083. doi:10.1016/j.protcy.2016.01.152

Martinsons, M. G., Davison, R. M., & Huang, Q. (2017). Strategic knowledge management failures in small professional service firms in China. *International Journal of Information Management*, *37*(4), 327–338. doi:10.1016/j.ijinfomgt.2017.04.003

Massingham, O., & Al Holaibi, M. (2017). Embedding knowledge management into business processes. *Knowledge and Process Management*, *24*(1), 53–71. doi:10.1002/kpm.1534

Men, L. R. (2014). Internal reputation management: The impact of authentic leadership and transparent communication. *Corporate Reputation Review*, *17*(4), 254–272. doi:10.1057/crr.2014.14

Mitrofan, N., & Bulborea, A. (2013). The role of organizational communication in structuring interpersonal relationships. *Procedia: Social and Behavioral Sciences*, *76*, 511–515. doi:10.1016/j.sbspro.2013.04.155

Mohamad, B., Bakar, H. A., Halim, H., & Ismail, A. R. (2014). Corporate communication management (CCM) and organisational performance: A review of the current literature, conceptual model and research propositions. *Procedia: Social and Behavioral Sciences*, *155*, 115–122. doi:10.1016/j.sbspro.2014.10.266

Narang, S. K., Kumar, S., & Verma, V. (2017). Knowledge discovery from massive data streams. In A. Singh, N. Dey, A. Ashour, & V. Santhi (Eds.), *Web semantics for textual and visual information retrieval* (pp. 109–143). Hershey, PA: IGI Global. doi:10.4018/978-1-5225-2483-0.ch006

Ngah, R., Tai, T., & Bontis, N. (2016). Knowledge management capabilities and organizational performance in roads and transport authority of Dubai: The mediating role of learning organization. *Knowledge and Process Management*, *23*(3), 184–193. doi:10.1002/kpm.1504

Nikoi, E., & Boateng, K. (2014). *Collaborative communication processes and decision making in organizations.* Hershey, PA: IGI Global. doi:10.4018/978-1-4666-4478-6

Owrang, O. M. M. (2009). Discovering quality knowledge from relational databases. In J. Erickson (Ed.), *Database technologies: Concepts, methodologies, tools, and applications* (pp. 238–256). Hershey, PA: IGI Global. doi:10.4018/978-1-60566-058-5.ch018

Richet, J. (2016). Internal communication failure in times of change. In A. Goksoy (Ed.), *Organizational change management strategies in modern business* (pp. 289–300). Hershey, PA: IGI Global. doi:10.4018/978-1-4666-9533-7.ch014

Rodrigues, P. P., Gama, J., & Lopes, L. (2010). Knowledge discovery for sensor network comprehension. In A. Cuzzocrea (Ed.), *Intelligent techniques for warehousing and mining sensor network data* (pp. 118–135). Hershey, PA: IGI Global. doi:10.4018/978-1-60566-328-9.ch006

Salazar, A., & Vergara, L. (2008). Knowledge discovery from e-learning activities. In F. García-Peñalvo (Ed.), *Advances in e-learning: Experiences and methodologies* (pp. 173–198). Hershey, PA: IGI Global. doi:10.4018/978-1-59904-756-0.ch010

Shen, L., & Austin, L. (2017). Communication and job satisfaction. In B. Christiansen & H. Chandan (Eds.), *Handbook of research on human factors in contemporary workforce development* (pp. 201–225). Hershey, PA: IGI Global. doi:10.4018/978-1-5225-2568-4.ch009

Te'eni, D. (2008). Organizational communication. In M. Jennex (Ed.), *Knowledge management: Concepts, methodologies, tools, and applications* (pp. 3004–3012). Hershey, PA: IGI Global. doi:10.4018/978-1-59904-933-5.ch245

Valentim, L., Lisboa, J. V., & Franco, M. (2016). Knowledge management practices and absorptive capacity in small and medium-sized enterprises: Is there really a linkage? *R & D Management*, *46*(4), 711–725. doi:10.1111/radm.12108

Vasilcovschi, N. (2013). Organizational communication-strategies at international level. *Transition Studies Review*, *19*(4), 493–502. doi:10.100711300-013-0259-5

Vlaisavljevic, V., Cabello-Medina, C., & Pérez-Luño, A. (2016). Coping with diversity in alliances for innovation: The role of relational social capital and knowledge codifiability. *British Journal of Management*, *27*(2), 304–322. doi:10.1111/1467-8551.12155

Wang, T., & Libaers, D. (2016). Nonmimetic knowledge and innovation performance: Empirical evidence from developing countries. *Journal of Product Innovation Management*, *33*(5), 570–588. doi:10.1111/jpim.12306

Wu, Q., McGinnity, M., Prasad, G., & Bell, D. (2009). Knowledge discovery in databases with diversity of data types. In J. Wang (Ed.), *Encyclopedia of data warehousing and mining* (2nd ed.; pp. 1117–1123). Hershey, PA: IGI Global. doi:10.4018/978-1-60566-010-3.ch173

Xia, Y., & Mao, Y. (2016). Mobile phone usage in organizational communication and decision-making: Experience of employees in a multinational company's China branch. In I. Management Association (Ed.), Leadership and personnel management: Concepts, methodologies, tools, and applications (pp. 1673–1689). Hershey, PA: IGI Global. doi:10.4018/978-1-4666-9624-2.ch074

Yada, K. (2004). Knowledge discovery process and introduction of domain knowledge. In B. Montano (Ed.), *Innovations of knowledge management* (pp. 86–98). Hershey, PA: IGI Global. doi:10.4018/978-1-59140-281-7.ch005

Yu, L. (2009). Knowledge discovery from genomics microarrays. In M. Khosrow-Pour (Ed.), *Encyclopedia of information science and technology* (2nd ed.; pp. 2332–2336). Hershey, PA: IGI Global. doi:10.4018/978-1-60566-026-4.ch369

Zhang, J. (2016). Facilitating exploration alliances in multiple dimensions: The influences of firm technological knowledge breadth. *R & D Management*, *46*(S1), 159–173. doi:10.1111/radm.12127

ADDITIONAL READING

Ali, N., Tretiakov, A., Whiddett, D., & Hunter, I. (2017). Knowledge management systems success in healthcare: Leadership matters. *International Journal of Medical Informatics*, *97*, 331–340. doi:10.1016/j.ijmedinf.2016.11.004 PMID:27919392

Andreeva, T., Vanhala, M., Sergeeva, A., Ritala, P., & Kianto, A. (2017). When the fit between HR practices backfires: Exploring the interaction effects between rewards for and appraisal of knowledge behaviours on innovation. *Human Resource Management Journal*, *27*(2), 209–227. doi:10.1111/1748-8583.12133

Borca, C., & Baesu, V. (2014). A possible managerial approach for internal organizational communication characterization. *Procedia: Social and Behavioral Sciences*, *124*, 496–503. doi:10.1016/j.sbspro.2014.02.512

Brummel, R. F., Nelson, K. C., & Jakes, P. J. (2012). Burning through organizational boundaries? Examining inter-organizational communication networks in policy-mandated collaborative bushfire planning groups. *Global Environmental Change*, *22*(2), 516–528. doi:10.1016/j.gloenvcha.2011.12.004

Cepeda-Carrion, I., Martelo-Landroguez, S., Leal-Rodríguez, A. L., & Leal-Millán, A. (2017). Critical processes of knowledge management: An approach toward the creation of customer value. *European Research on Management and Business Economics*, *23*(1), 1–7. doi:10.1016/j.iedeen.2016.03.001

Cerchione, R., & Esposito, E. (2017). Using knowledge management systems: A taxonomy of SME strategies. *International Journal of Information Management*, *37*(1), 1551–1562. doi:10.1016/j.ijinfomgt.2016.10.007

Chirico, F., & Salvato, C. (2016). Knowledge internalization and product development in family firms: When relational and affective factors matter. *Entrepreneurship Theory and Practice*, *40*(1), 201–229. doi:10.1111/etap.12114

Král, P., & Králová, V. (2016). Approaches to changing organizational structure: The effect of drivers and communication. *Journal of Business Research*, *69*(11), 5169–5174. doi:10.1016/j.jbusres.2016.04.099

Lee, V. H., Foo, A. T. L., Leong, L. Y., & Ooi, K. B. (2016). Can competitive advantage be achieved through knowledge management? A case study on SMEs. *Expert Systems with Applications*, *65*, 136–151. doi:10.1016/j.eswa.2016.08.042

Li, J., Liu, M., & Liu, X. (2016). Why do employees resist knowledge management systems? An empirical study from the status quo bias and inertia perspectives. *Computers in Human Behavior*, *65*, 189–200. doi:10.1016/j.chb.2016.08.028

Lin, H. E., McDonough, E. F. III, Yang, J., & Wang, C. (2017). Aligning knowledge assets for exploitation, exploration, and ambidexterity: A study of companies in high-tech parks in China. *Journal of Product Innovation Management*, *34*(2), 122–140. doi:10.1111/jpim.12337

Liu, Y., Wang, L., Yuan, C., & Li, Y. (2012). Information communication, organizational capability and new product development: An empirical study of Chinese firms. *The Journal of Technology Transfer*, *37*(4), 416–432. doi:10.100710961-010-9188-1

Mao, H., Liu, S., Zhang, J., & Deng, Z. (2016). Information technology resource, knowledge management capability, and competitive advantage: The moderating role of resource commitment. *International Journal of Information Management*, *36*(6), 1062–1074. doi:10.1016/j.ijinfomgt.2016.07.001

Nordin, S. M., Sivapalan, S., Bhattacharyya, E., Ahmad, H. H. W. F. W., & Abdullah, A. (2014). Organizational communication climate and conflict management: Communications management in an oil and gas company. *Procedia: Social and Behavioral Sciences*, *109*, 1046–1058. doi:10.1016/j.sbspro.2013.12.587

Pogutz, S., & Winn, M. I. (2016). Cultivating ecological knowledge for corporate sustainability: Barilla's innovative approach to sustainable farming. *Business Strategy and the Environment*, *25*(6), 435–448. doi:10.1002/bse.1916

Preston, D. S., Chen, D. Q., Swink, M., & Meade, L. (2017). Generating supplier benefits through buyer-enabled knowledge enrichment: A social capital perspective. *Decision Sciences*, *48*(2), 248–287. doi:10.1111/deci.12220

Rodgers, W., Mubako, G. N., & Hall, L. (2017). Knowledge management: The effect of knowledge transfer on professional skepticism in audit engagement planning. *Computers in Human Behavior*, *70*, 564–574. doi:10.1016/j.chb.2016.12.069

Rubinstein, S., Martin-Rios, C., Erhardt, N., Gittell, J. H., & George, V. P. (2016). Organizational responses to uncertainty in the airline industry: Changes in patterns of communication networks. *Journal of Air Transport Management*, *57*, 217–227. doi:10.1016/j.jairtraman.2016.07.021

Sapir, A., Drori, I., & Ellis, S. (2016). The practices of knowledge creation: Collaboration between peripheral and core occupational communities. *European Management Review*, *13*(1), 19–36. doi:10.1111/emre.12064

Shamim, S., Cang, S., & Yu, H. (2017). Supervisory orientation, employee goal orientation, and knowledge management among front line hotel employees. *International Journal of Hospitality Management*, *62*, 21–32. doi:10.1016/j.ijhm.2016.11.013

Silla, I., Navajas, J., & Koves, G. K. (2017). Organizational culture and a safety-conscious work environment: The mediating role of employee communication satisfaction. *Journal of Safety Research*, *61*, 121–127. doi:10.1016/j.jsr.2017.02.005 PMID:28454857

Stewart, S. A., & Abidi, S. S. R. (2017). Leveraging medical taxonomies to improve knowledge management within online communities of practice: The knowledge maps system. *Computer Methods and Programs in Biomedicine*, *143*, 121–127. doi:10.1016/j.cmpb.2017.03.003 PMID:28391809

Su, Z., Peng, M. W., & Xie, E. (2016). A strategy tripod perspective on knowledge creation capability. *British Journal of Management*, *27*(1), 58–76. doi:10.1111/1467-8551.12097

Tang, C. (2016). Accessed external knowledge, centrality of intra-team knowledge networks, and R&D employee creativity. *R & D Management*, *46*(S3), 992–1005. doi:10.1111/radm.12160

Tregidga, H., Milne, M., & Lehman, G. (2012). Analyzing the quality, meaning and accountability of organizational reporting and communication: Directions for future research. *Accounting Forum*, *36*(3), 223–230. doi:10.1016/j.accfor.2012.07.001

Uddin, S., Hamra, J., & Hossain, L. (2013). Exploring communication networks to understand organizational crisis using exponential random graph models. *Computational & Mathematical Organization Theory*, *19*(1), 25–41. doi:10.100710588-011-9104-8

Valentine, S., & Hollingworth, D. (2015). Communication of organizational strategy and coordinated decision making as catalysts for enhanced perceptions of corporate ethical values in a financial services company. *Employee Responsibilities and Rights Journal*, *27*(3), 213–229. doi:10.100710672-014-9253-2

Vasantha, G. V. A., Chakrabarti, A., & Corney, J. (2016). A knowledge flow model to capture unstructured product development processes. *Knowledge and Process Management*, *23*(2), 91–109. doi:10.1002/kpm.1501

Wan, S., Li, D., Gao, J., Roy, R., & Tong, Y. (2017). Process and knowledge management in a collaborative maintenance planning system for high value machine tools. *Computers in Industry*, *84*, 14–24. doi:10.1016/j.compind.2016.11.002

Weinreich, R., & Groher, I. (2016). Software architecture knowledge management approaches and their support for knowledge management activities: A systematic literature review. *Information and Software Technology*, *80*, 265–286. doi:10.1016/j.infsof.2016.09.007

Yildirim, O. (2014). The impact of organizational communication on organizational citizenship behavior: Research findings. *Procedia: Social and Behavioral Sciences*, *150*, 1095–1100. doi:10.1016/j.sbspro.2014.09.124

KEY TERMS AND DEFINITIONS

Communication: The two-way exchange of opinions, news, and information by writing, speech, or gestures including body language and facial reactions.

Data Mining: The process used by companies to turn raw data into useful information.

Information: Knowledge acquired in any manner.

Innovation: The act of introducing something new.

Knowledge: The range of information, awareness, or understanding.

Knowledge Discovery: The process of discovering useful knowledge from a collection of data.

Knowledge Management: The efficient handling of knowledge or information and related resources within an organization.

Organizational Communication: The process by which activities of a society are collected and coordinated to reach the goals of both individuals and the collective group.

Chapter 9
Healthcare Professionals' Decision Making in Emergency Units:
An Operation Impact Analysis Considering Their Cognitive Heuristics

Ana Carolina Pereira de Vasconcelos Silva
Rio de Janeiro State University, Brazil

Thais Spiegel
Rio de Janeiro State University, Brazil

Daniel Bouzon Nagem Assad
Rio de Janeiro State University, Brazil

ABSTRACT

Cognitive theories on decision making show that individuals often do not decide in a full and rational way; they instead use cognitive strategies that allow them to overcome the limitations imposed by their limited rationality and the difficulties derived from uncertainty. In this context, this chapter aims to analyze the impact on operations caused by decisions taken by healthcare professionals in an emergency department when influenced by heuristics. Therefore, a systematic review of the literature for extracting the heuristics of healthcare professionals and a non-systematic review for constructing the theoretical framework about operations management, health operations management, hospital organizations, and heuristics were performed. Thus, having also described the object of study, the analytical model could be built. Then, three approaches were proposed for the synthesis, and deployment proposals were exposed for each.

DOI: 10.4018/978-1-5225-3725-0.ch009

INTRODUCTION

The operations management consists of planning, managing and controlling operational necessary activities to obtain products and services to the consumer market. This idea can be extended to health systems, transportation systems, municipal systems, all essential to the functioning of society (Spiegel, 2013). When applied to the health sector, the methods and approaches of operations management, originally developed in an industrial environment, have peculiar characteristics. By not following a commercial logic, there is a paradox between the level of service that must be offered and the costs associated with this offer, since it is conditioned to human needs (Osmo, 2012). For Hopp & Lovejoy (2013), there is an "operation science" in hospital management, just as there is a "medical science" that guides the patients treatment.

For instance, in emergency department (ED), the human resources has several agents involved in decision making, such as medical directors, trauma surgeons, residents, nurses, nursing technicians, pharmacists, secretaries / receptionists, assistants Social, on-call specialists, among others (Hopp & Lovejoy, 2013). Marewsky and Gigerenzer (2012) mention that doctor's decisions, for example, are made under uncertain conditions as without knowing precisely whether a diagnosis is correct or whether a treatment will actually cure a patient, and often under time constraints. Therefore, heuristics emerge as cognitive strategies that can provide good solutions to complex problems under time and cognitive ability constraints (Kattan, 2009) where decision making unconsciously use constraints to simplify the information as a "trigger " or "shortcut" to certain information that follows some pattern for the decision maker, thus exerting influence in the judgment of the information and in the decision making.

The perspective adopted in this chapter, when considering the human being as a key element in organizational decision making, is to investigate how decisions, when influenced by heuristics, can impact health operations. It is intended, therefore, to show impacts on the operations of the organization in light of the influence of heuristics in the decision-making of health professionals, thus taking into consideration the "person-dependent" model, a relevant characteristic in health organizations.

Regarding its nature, the research is applied, since it aims to generate knowledge to solve specific and practical problems. It addresses the problem in a qualitative way, because methods are used to discover the properties, phenomena, situations, people, meanings. A centrally exploratory methodology is adopted, which main objective is to make the problem explicit or to construct hypotheses, usually with a bibliographical survey, interviews with people with practical experience and case analysis. Respecting the technical procedures adopted, the survey of the elements that constitute the model are constructed based on a review of the literature. Regarding the analytical model, the health professionals' decisions will be taken throughout the patient care process and for each decision made, the following is analyzed: if the heuristic (h_n) influences the decision (d_n), which and how category (c_n) will be impacted and in what way. To do this, 10 decisions, 8 heuristics and 12 categories of operations are combined in order to allow for synthesis and unfolding resulting from the model.

BACKGROUND

The public health system is characterized in Brazil by the SUS (Unic Health System), which is based on the 1988 Constitution and the Organic Health Law (8,080 / 1990). According to article 197, *health actions and services are of public relevance, and it is a Government responsibility to provide, under the terms of the law, its regulation, supervision and control.* In this way, the SUS is based on the health context as a right of everyone and the duty of the State,

ensuring political and economic measures aimed at reducing the risk of disease and other diseases and universal and equal access to actions and services for its promotion, protection and recovery(article 196 of the 1988 Constitution).

As a challenge to this system, in many regions of the world, the healthcare industry is facing a dilemma because of the poor-quality standards of the services offered and, at the same time, a strong pressure to increase efficiency and productivity and reduce costs (Vahatalo & Kallio, 2015). Researches such as those of Zucchi et al. (2000) point to the need to contain spending on health that, from the macroeconomic point of view, is insoluble in the long term. Reinforcing this perspective, a recent study by the OECD (2015) shows that this problem is common to many countries.

The singularities of hospital organizations (demand fluctuations, different needs for treatment, asymmetry of professional knowledge, among others) hinder an optimized decision-making by health professionals, rendering inopportune or inadequate methods of analysis faced with time pressures and need for quick problem solving (Motta, 2011). According to Osmo (2011), one of the fundamental characteristics of hospital organizations is their psychosocial importance, since it is not a mere administrative and technological arrangement in which people work in accordance with the requirements of the service plan, but above all else, a social human system. Pitta (1994) identifies several groups that make up such organizations, such as patients, medical staff, nursing staff, nutritionists, and so many other teams involved in combating disease and lengthening the life span and even accompanying death. Thus, for Osmo (2011),

although the technological and scientific advance in this type of organization is remarkable and necessary, it is the work of the people that determines the quality and effectiveness of the treatment (Osmo, 2011).

In that way, the ability to make choices is seen as an essential element of human action. The decision maker is initially considered a rational agent who always behaves according to the expected rule, maximizing the usefulness or value of the result of a decision (Spiege, 2014). In this context, several theoretical models are constructed to mark decision-making, directed by a simplification strategy, but they are not very efficient. This apparent negligence on the part of the decision makers in front of the models was a first stimulus to associate other factors that influence in the decision-making. Organizations are seen as psychic phenomena, in the sense that they are conscious and unconscious processes that create and maintain them (Morgan, 2010). Thus, in human decisions, the cognitive limitations that lead the decision-maker to construct simplified models to deal with the world have been considered in human decisions. One of the most notorious formulations of these limitations is that of Simon (1957), who calls them limited rationality. These cognitive limitations are thus influenced by several factors, such as heuristics (Spiegel, 2017). It means that the knowledge and tools available are not always adequate to address existing health problems and there is a constant and endless need to generate new information and develop better and more effective ways of protecting and promoting health and reducing disease (Brazil, 2007).

From a review of the literature, Li and Fawcett (2014) have identified that intuition and heuristics are the main decision-making strategies related to, for example, the use of physical immobilization of patients in intensive care units, since the rapid and reflexive nature intuition and heuristics allow nurses to respond quickly to urgent and emerging cases. However, for them, it is problematic when nurses simply base their decisions on experience rather than also use results from clinical practice studies. In addition, such a rapid response can lead nurses to make decisions without proper evaluation, which can lead to biases and errors. Thus, he highlights the two possibilities of impacts of heuristics in this decision, that of faster results and therefore, positive for the patient and errors, for not incorporating research evidence into their experience to make decisions and make an appropriate evaluation.

In order to question and challenge the theory that optimization always leads to more sensible decisions and that heuristics are always the second best option, Gaissmaier, Wegwarth and Gigerenzer (2009) developed two decision support tools, one based on optimization and one based on heuristics and applied to two specific situations and concluded that heuristics are neither good nor bad in themselves but, if applied in situations for which they have been adapted, can be good tools for physicians and residents. This, however, requires that heuristics be discussed openly in medicine, criticized, refined, and then taught to residents rather than simply dismissed as harmful or irrelevant, so that a more uniform and explicit use of well-accepted heuristics has the potential to reduce variations in diagnoses and improve the overall picture of health care (Gaissmaier, Wegwarth & Gigerenzer, 2009).

ANALYTICAL MODEL: A FIRST FORMULATION OF THE POTENTIAL IMPACTS OF HEURISTICS IN THE DECISIONS OF HEALTH PROFESSIONALS AND ITS REFLECTIONS IN THE OPERATION OF BRAZILIAN EMERGENCY CARE UNIT

Emergency Care Unit: Process and Operations Category

In Brazil, Emergency Care Units aim to solve most of the emergencies, such as high blood pressure and high fever, fractures, cuts, heart attack and stroke. They help to reduce queues in the hospital's emergency department. These units offer simplified structure, with X-ray, electrocardiography, laboratory examination and observation beds. Brazilian government estimate that 97% of the cases are solved in this kind of unit. When the patient arrive, the doctors provide relief, control the problem and detail the diagnosis. They analyze whether it is necessary to refer the patient to a hospital or keep him on observation for 24 hours (Spiegel & Assad, 2017).

According to Ordinance No. 2648 of the Ministry of Health, which redefines the guidelines for the implementation of the Emergency Unit (UPA 24h) and the emergency services 24 hours of the Emergency Care Network, the UPA 24h is the intermediary complexity health establishment located between Basic Health Care and the Hospital Network. Therefore, an organized emergency care network should be set up in strategic locations for the configuration of the emergency care network, to operate uninterruptedly in the 24 (twenty-four) hours of the day and on all days of the week, including holidays and optional points; and have an interdisciplinary multi-professional team compatible with its size.

The processes of care that patients undergo in an Emergency Unit follow 3 main stages. The first stage of care, the reception, consists of a technical reception with qualified listening by professionals of the nursing team, to attend the spontaneous demand, with the aim of identifying risk in becoming ill and, thus, orienting, prioritizing and deciding on the necessary referrals for solving the user problem.

Thus, the patient can be directed directly to the stabilization / observation rooms, can be directed to the reception to perform the registration or can be redirected to the basic care network. The registration stage consists of collecting information from the patient so that accountability purposes about their stay and procedures in the unit. In this way, personal and residence data are recorded.

The second stage is the risk classification that aims to organize the flow of patients, so that the most serious conditions are prioritized, assuming, therefore, that the system has less capacity than demand. The nurse who acts in the risk classification, besides classifying the patient according to its severity, thus avoiding possible damages to their health, has the role of directing the patient to the reference service when this is necessary (Marques & Lima, 2007). The role of health care providers in the health services sector is not always in line with an emergency situation and can be influenced by several factors, such as access conditions, agility in care and users' relationship with health professionals, services and systems. The process of risk classification is done through protocols established in each service unit (Brasil, 2004). According to the SUS Risk Classification Protocol, the criteria for assigning color associated with priority are shown in Table 1.

At the medical assignment, the patient is evaluated by the physician/doctor, who decides to refer the patient so that his / her state of health is reestablished. The patient directed to the observation room receives care from the medical, nursing, physiotherapy and nutrition staff so that his / her condition is stabilized and his / her state of health reestablished. The patient who needs immediate medication is then referred to the medication room, where he receives the care of the nursing team and has his prescription administered. In case of need for exams, the patient is directed to the examination area (blood, urine, feces or x-ray, tomography, electrocardiogram), so that it is later reassessed by the Return, to complete the diagnosis. When the patient needs medium / long-term medication, the doctor prescribes the medication and directs the patient to the unit's pharmacy so that the medication can be withdrawn.

Table 1. Criteria for patient care priority assignment

Priority	Clinical settings
Red priority Extremely severe cases requiring immediate medical care. Priority on yellow, green and blue patients. The patient will not be submitted to the risk classification and cardiorespiratory cases will be taken to the Resuscitation Room (stabilization).	1- Emergency 2- Immediate medical care or less than 15 minutes 3- Re-evaluation every 15 minutes 4- Nursing Care Continuous
Yellow priority Cases that present warning signs and need priority service, but without immediate risk. Priority about green and blue patients. Patient will wait for care in chair, bed or bed according to need.	1- Urgency 2- Medical care < 30 minutes 3- Re-evaluation every 30 minutes
Green priority Cases that require medical attention, but without gravity. Priority about blue patients. Patient will wait for medical care in a chair (waiting room), will be informed that the time for care will be higher and that more serious patients will be attended to earlier.	1- Lower urgency 2- Medical care < 1 hour 3- Re-evaluation every 1 hour
Blue priority Cases that do not have complaints that justify immediate medical care, your case will be resolved by the nurse (reference to another unit), or will have a waiting time superior to all other colors.	1- Not urgency 2- Same-day or referral for other services

Source: The authors, adapted by Protocol with Risk Classification of SUS (Protocolo de Acolhimento com Classificação de Risco do SUS).

Patients who will not be treated in the unit because they have blue priority or those who need specialist follow-up will be redirected to the basic unit or hospital care network for their treatment.

Known the patient's flow, it is necessary to see that the operations categories are a cut of the operation to facilitate, among others, their understanding. Thus, for the analysis in question, the categories used by Hayes et al. (2008) were adjusted from the context of the analysis (Table 2).

Health Care Professionals Heuristics

This section aims to list the heuristics extracted from the literature, which will be taken into account in the analytical model. Thus, Table 3 shows the selected heuristics and their respective definitions.

Decisions in Emergency Care Unit

This section brings the decisions made by health professionals in the processes of reception, risk classification and medical consultation. It should be noted that the explicit decisions are not taken isolated, nor in the order in which they are placed on the board, but Table 4 disposal is justified only in order to facilitate the analysis of impacts on the operation in a linear manner.

Table 2. Operations category adapted to analysis context

Operations categories	Description
O1: Care network (basic and hospital)	Intermediate complexity health establishment, in an organized network of attention to the urgencies, with the Basic Attention and with the Hospital Network.
O2: Patient process / flow in unit	Variety of path patterns that result in patient care.
O3: Organizational Performance Indicators	Performance evaluation of the organization from the level of service established by the contracts / management agreements.
O4: Human resources systems	Dimensioning and skills of health professionals in the unit for patient care at established levels of service.
O5: Quality Systems	Adherence to protocols and indicators associated with these.
O6: Planning and control	Planning of acquisition and availability of equipment, medicines and materials, supplies of support services (pharmacy, x-ray, nutrition).
O7: Product and process development systems	Development of equipment / tests / medicines / protocols
O8: Capacity	Availability by resource for patient care.
O9: Facilities / infrastructure	Area, fixed equipment, furniture associated with the capacity of patient care.
O10: Work organization	Specification of the content, methods and interrelationships between the positions, in order to satisfy the organizational and technological requirements, as well as the social and individual requirements of the occupant of the position. Semi-autonomous groups: self-regulation (FLEURY, 1980). Workload: relationship between the demands of work and the worker's biological and psychological capacity (FRUTUOSO, 2005).
O11: Allocation of financial resources to the unit	Availability and allocation of financial resources to the unit to guarantee service at the established level of service.
O12: Plant maintenance (clinical engineering)	Need for building maintenance and equipment associated with patient care.

Source: The authors, adapted by Hayes et al. (2008).

Table 3. Health care professionals heuristics retrieved from literature

Heuristics	Definitions
H1: *Anchoring*	Anchoring happens when a physician remains anchored to salient features in the patient's initial presentation too early in the diagnostic process without adjusting the outcome when further information are available.
H2: *Framing effect*	The way in which problems are framed strongly influence the way in which physicians evaluate the situation and make their diagnoses.
H3: *Fundamental attribution error*	It is a typical error occurring with psychiatric patients or marginalized groups and consists in the tendency to be judgmental and blame patients for their illness instead of examining the situational circumstances that might have been responsible.
H4: *Gambler's fallacy*	The gambler's fallacy is defined as a cognitive error that leads physicians to believe that independent events are related. It happens when physicians consider that the probability that a patient has a particular diagnosis might be influenced by preceding but independent events (i.e. the diagnosis of the previous patients).
H5: *Posterior probability error*	It is the opposite of the Gambler's fallacy in the sense that physicians tend to persist on the same diagnosis if they have already done it in several previous occasions. Common things for most patients continue to be common (i.e. headache) and the probability of the diagnosis of a nonbenign headache remains underestimated.
H6: *Representativeness*	In medicine, it is a cognitive distortion that makes people judge the probability or frequency of a diagnostic hypothesis by considering how much the hypothesis resembles available clinical data.
H7: Unpacking principle	The failure to elicit all relevant information (unpacking) in establishing a differential diagnosis may result in significant possibilities being missed.
H8: Avoiding a rare diagnosis	The reasons of this behavior are various: fear of seeming unrealistic, under confidence in his own clinical judgment, etc.

Source: Adapted from Gorini & Pravettoni (2011).

Analysis of Decisions Impacts on Categories of Operations

The model was constructed by the following analyses: if the the decision (d_n) were influenced/conformed by the heuristic (h_n), which and how category (c_n) will be impacted and in what way. For this purpose, 10 decisions, 8 heuristics and 12 categories of operations are combined in order to allow for synthesis and unfolding resulting from the model.

A path of these will be detailed in the chapter as an illustration of the process and later the analyzes, already considering the set of paths covered, will be realized. The path chosen was the reception process, in the pre-classification decision for the anchorage heuristic.

SOLUTIONS AND RECOMMENDATIONS

The synthesis consists in consolidating the results of the analysis by processes, in order to verify the general picture of the impacts on the decisions. It was decided to synthesize by processes rather than decisions, since decision-making was an option to facilitate the organization and exposition of the analytical model. These decisions in each case can be taken simultaneously. In this way, a summation of the types of impacts that the decisions associated to the process can generate when conformed by each heuristic is performed in Table 6.

Table 4. Health professional decisions in the reception processes, risk classification and medical consultation

Process	Decision	Health care professional	Decision description
P1: Reception	D1: Pre-classification	Nurse	The nurse is responsible for receptioning and evaluating whether the patient will be cared in the unit or will be redirected to other unit.
	D2: Directing to the observation / stabilization room	Nurse	The nurse decides whether or not the patient is going to the observation / stabilization room.
P2: Risk classification	D1: Priority assignment (risk associated with protocol color)	Nurse	The nurse decides which vital signs need to be checked for patient evaluation and classifies the patient to be prioritized in the medical appointment queue according to their life risk.
	D2: Redirecting to other units	Nurse	The nurse decides whether or not the patient should be redirected to other units based on their severity.
	D3: Directing the observation room	Nurse	The nurse decides whether or not the patient is going to the observation room.
P3: Registration	-	-	Not applicable.
P4: Medical appointment (closed diagnosis is embedded in doctor's decisions)	D1: Request for exams	Doctor	The doctor decides if there is a need to request complementary tests to make the diagnosis.
	D2: Medication request	Doctor	The doctor decides if it is necessary to prescribe medication to the patient, either for administration in the place, or for withdrawal at the pharmacy.
	D3: Directing to the observation room	Doctor	The doctor decides whether or not the patient is going to the observation room.
	D4: Redirecting to other units	Doctor	The doctor decides whether or not the patient should be referred to other units to continue the health treatment.
	D5: Discharge	Doctor	The doctor decides whether the patient can be discharged or discharged from the unit.

Source: The authors.

Table 5. Categories negatively and positively impacted by the anchorage heuristic of the pre-classification decision

Priority	Clinical settings
Red priority Extremely severe cases requiring immediate medical care. Priority on yellow, green and blue patients. The patient will not be submitted to the risk classification and cardiorespiratory cases will be taken to the Resuscitation Room (stabilization).	1- Emergency 2- Immediate medical care or less than 15 minutes 3- Re-evaluation every 15 minutes 4- Nursing Care Continuous
Yellow priority Cases that present warning signs and need priority service, but without immediate risk. Priority about green and blue patients. Patient will wait for care in chair, bed or bed according to need.	1- Urgency 2- Medical care < 30 minutes 3- Re-evaluation every 30 minutes
Green priority Cases that require medical attention, but without gravity. Priority about blue patients. Patient will wait for medical care in a chair (waiting room), will be informed that the time for care will be higher and that more serious patients will be attended to earlier.	1- Lower urgency 2- Medical care < 1 hour 3- Re-evaluation every 1 hour
Blue priority Cases that do not have complaints that justify immediate medical care, your case will be resolved by the nurse (reference to another unit), or will have a waiting time superior to all other colors.	1- Not urgency 2- Same-day or referral for other services

Source: The authors.

Figure 1. Analytical model structure
Source: The authors.

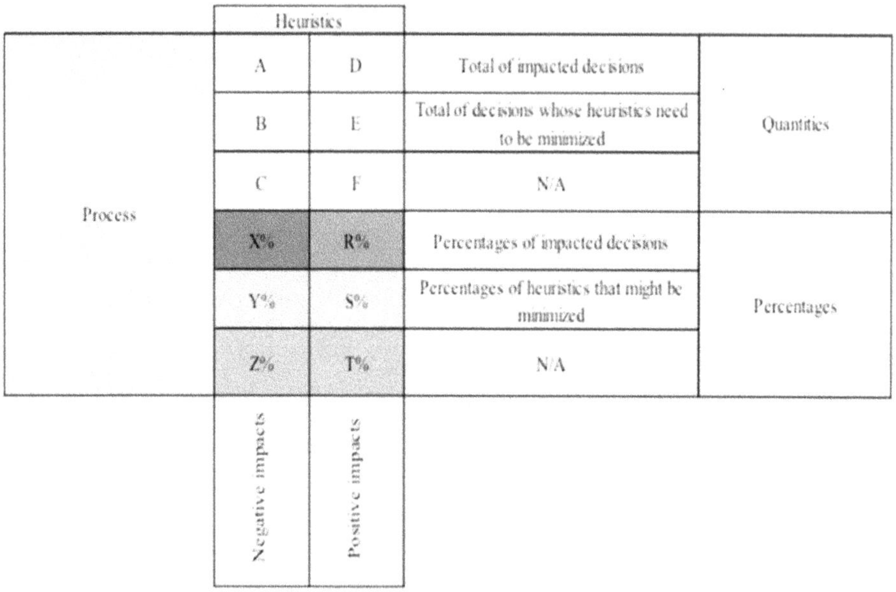

Figure 2. Generic structure of the synthesis by processes
Source: The authors.

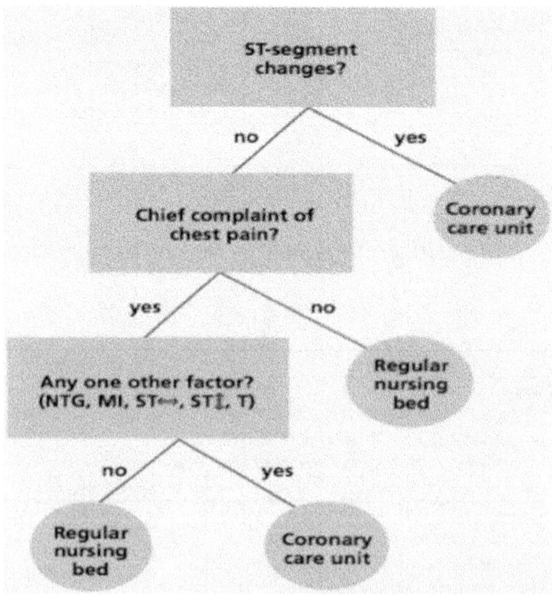

Thus, for example, the first set of values related to the reception process and the anchorage heuristic, means that, in the analysis of negative impacts, 20 categories of this process are negatively impacted and 4 are not impacted, which means in percentage values 83% and 17%, respectively. For the analysis of positive impacts, 14 categories are positively impacted, for 6 of them the influence of the heuristic in question needs to be minimized and 4 are not impacted, representing, therefore, 58%, 25% and 17%, respectively.

It can be observed that the order of magnitude of the percentage of categories impacted by process is very similar, does not vary much from process to process. Thus, the main heuristics that need to have their effect minimized and those that have the greatest potential for positive impact are the same for all processes.

Thus, in view of the intrinsic paradox to the nature of heuristics in the case analyzed, reliability of diagnosis and treatment vs. speed of decision and service, it is up to the technical staff to explain the factors that can influence their decisions and to highlight the types of impact on the operation that these factors can cause. Wegwart, Gaissmaier and Gigerenzer (2009) stress that a more uniform and explicit use of well-accepted heuristics has the potential to reduce variations in diagnoses and improve the overall picture of health care.

For the heuristics H1: Anchoring and H6: Representativeness that need to have their potential positive impacts reinforced (associated with shorter service times) and their negative impacts mitigated (associated with greater probability of error in diagnosis), systems are proposed that trace diagnostic possibilities from key words extracted from the patient's complaint, by systems, for example ("forcing" the heuristic of the anchorage to reduce the time of service) and from this, the professional could resort to his experience to judge which diagnosis is most likely.

A second option would be to expose the possible tracks through explanatory leaflets.

In this line, Gaissmaier, Wegwart and Gigerenzer (2009) propose as alternative to complex tools or decisions totally based on intuition, a tool that they call a fast and frugal decision tree, which they consider to be an intelligent heuristic. This takes into account the important variables for decision making. For the authors, the tool tested proved to be accurate, allowed quick decisions and was frugal. Figure 3 represents an example of this tool proposed by Gaissmaier, Wegwart and Gigerenzer (2009).

Figure 3. Example of a fast and frugal decision tree for decision support in a coronary care unit
Source: Gaissmaier, Wegwarth & Gigernzer, G, 2009.

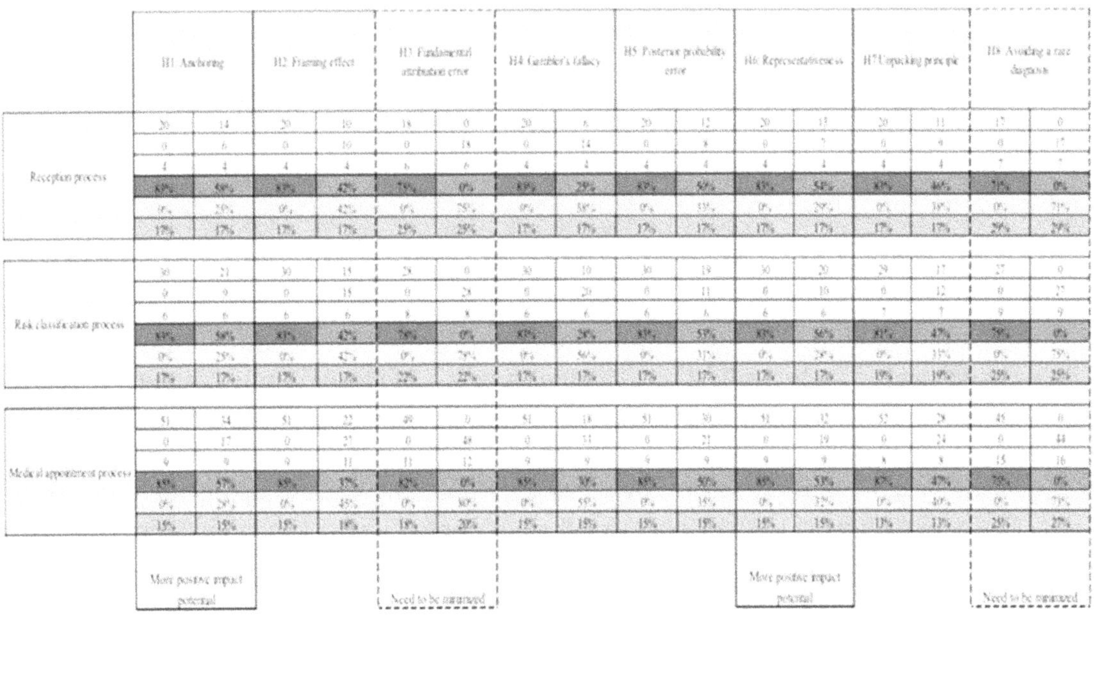

Table 6. Process synthesis

Impacted category	Negative impacts	Positive impacts
O1: Care network (basic and hospital)	The nurse, influenced by the anchorage heuristic, can distort the demand. For example, by redirecting a patient that would need to be taken care of in the unit, it overloads the network, impacting a need for capacity readjustment by the network (other units). On the other hand, if a nurse receives a patient that does not need care in the unit, because she is influenced by this heuristic, it ends up paying off a demand from the basic care network.	N / A - This heuristic needs to be minimized.
O2: Patient process / flow in unit	If anchored by a striking feature of the patient's speech, the nurse may decide to attend a patient who would not need care or not attend a patient who would need it. Thus, patient referrals along the flows can occur in the wrong way, resulting in intensification of the flow of a certain type of patient unnecessarily.	If she anchors herself in a relevant feature of speech, it can perform screening more quickly. If it goes faster, more patients can be taken care of.
O3: Organizational Performance Indicators	The nurse, if conformed by the heuristic of the anchorage, allows the entry of patients who would not need care in the unit, end up impacting the leadtime, average length of stay, mortality rate, patient satisfaction, which are performance indicators of organization.	Rapidly identify patients who need care impact indicators such as leadtime, mortality rates, and patient satisfaction.
O4: Human resources systems	The distortions of demand could imply rescaling of human resources, since these may have been dimensioned from an expected demand, to guarantee a stipulated level of service.	Identifying whether or not the patient needs care faster may mean having fewer human resources allocated to perform the activity in question.
O5: Quality Systems	While the nurse, conformed by the anchorage heuristic, does not investigate other symptoms to adjust her initial decision, she may redirect to the primary care a patient who would require urgent care, impairing their treatment, or allows a patient to enter who would not need urgent care, hampering the care of other patients. There is no adherence to the protocol and indicators can be impacted as a percentage of patients with Sepsis, CVA or Stroke adhering to the protocol, for example.	Being conformed by the anchorage heuristic can be a good guideline for faster pre-classification. Using a striking feature of the patient's speech can ensure a timely pre-diagnosis.
O6: Planning and control	The planning of equipment acquisition and purchase of drugs and materials can be hampered by a distortion of demand.	N / A - this heuristic needs to be minimized.

Source: The authors.

One proposal applied to the medical consultation process could be the implementation of fast-track. Yoon (2003) points out that this is an organizational approach in which, from a screening system that gives priority to those considered to be more severely ill or injured, the average waiting time in a single service queuing system can be minimized by serving, The customer whose service waiting time is the shortest. This approach would simultaneously allow to reinforce H1: Anchoring heuristics and H6: Representativeness and minimize H8: Refusal of a rare diagnosis (Avoiding a rare diagnosis), since the stratification process proposed by fast-track predicts the " Grouping "of demand so that, by reducing the possibilities of possible diagnoses, it can condition the doctor to conceive them more quickly. It is worth emphasizing that if this grouping allows less dispersed service times around a mean, the possibility of defining "cycle times" increases to more accurately estimate the capacity of the clinic's attendance, thus enabling a better dimensioning of resources for the Maintaining the level of service established in management contracts. Such a proposition, however, has as its key element the effectiveness of the screening service, especially with respect to minimizing H3: Fundamental attribution error, since this activity potentiates the impacts on the medical consultation within the organizational approach of fast -track.

About the heuristics H3: Fundamental attribution error and H8: Refusal of a rare diagnosis, it is argued that they must have their potential negative impacts minimized, since they were not identified in the analytical model Positive impacts. Both are heuristics associated with the negligence of the use of protocols / rules of service, directly impacting the patient's due care. Thus, proposals related to systems that "force" the use of minimal protocols, possibly linked to Information Technology (IT), are pertinent so that the professional must follow pre-established steps that minimize the possibility of underestimating a diagnosis.

FUTURE RESEARCH DIRECTIONS

The research addresses the subject in a generic way, so that to make feasible an application in the field it would be necessary to construct a method to identify the heuristics that influence a given decision maker, and it is therefore necessary a discussion with professionals with knowledge in psychology and neuroscience, for example. In addition, a proposal deriving from this is how these other heuristics (derived from biological, social, cultural, religious, etc. characteristics) that can be identified coexist with those that were discussed in the research for a specific case. It is necessary to evaluate, for example, whether they converge or diverge to a certain pattern of behavior. In addition, it is also worth identifying the patients' heuristics, since the object consists of a service delivery, and in what way they impact the organization and the decisions of the health professionals. One discussion that emerges from this is whether professionals should then be empowered to figure out and "circumvent" them.

In addition to the questions about the heuristics survey, future work could also move towards proposing and testing ways to minimize or reinforce the effects of certain heuristics. The unfolding essay brings discussions in this direction, but it does not aim to be exhaustive, nor, for being generic, was able to evaluate the general picture in the organization that each proposition could generate, that would make feasible organizational projects.

CONCLUSION

The research proposed in this chapter has allowed us to understand how heuristics, extracted from the literature, influence the decisions of health professionals in an emergency unit and what are the potential impacts resulting from this influence in the categories of operations. The extraction of the health professional's heuristics from the literature and the compilation of the categories of operations, as well as the description of the type of health operation and the identification of the main decisions taken by health professionals in this type of operation enabled the construction of the analysis. It was possible, then, from the constructed analysis model, to understand the impacts of the decisions in the categories of operations when influenced by the heuristics. The syntheses made possible the development of the essay about the potential unfolding results of the analytical model.

Therefore, this research elucidates a potential application of knowledge of the influence of heuristics on human judgment in specific situations and also contributes to the body of knowledge on the subject by developing an analytical model that establishes a baseline map on the potential effects on health operations if heuristics are present in decision makers. Thus, it consists of a first step, creating a starting platform that can guide empirical research, in a possible direct observation to confirm certain influences in the decisions of health professionals applied to a real situation, and can, in this sense of empirical application, Help to understand the potential impacts of these influences on the studied object. It can also be understood as an effort in the direction of increasing the degree of comprehension about health units, from a better understanding about a method to approach them.

The approach is not a single possibility and is therefore only a way to better understand the object studied. In addition, the method of analysis was linear, not encompassing all the complexity of the judgment of the decision maker. In addition, the object of study is a particular type of health unit, and cannot therefore be generalized directly to any health unit. As there was no empirical adherence to the model on the application and validation in the field, it is also considered for the object studied in the first moment, a set of hypotheses, which can be tested in future works.

REFERENCES

Abbês, C., & Massaro, A. (2004). Acolhimento com avaliação e classificação de risco: um paradigma ético estético no fazer em saúde. *Ministério da Saúde. Núcleo Técnico da Política Nacional de Humanização. Brasília-dF. Série B. Textos Básicos em Saúde*. Retrived from: http://bvsms.saude.gov.br/bvs/publicacoes/acolhimento.pdf

Alberta Heritage Foundation for Medical Research. (2003). *Emergency department fast-track system*. Alberta Heritage Foundation for Medical Research.

Brasil, C. C. (1990). Lei nº 8.080, de 19 de setembro de 1990: Dispõe sobre as condições para a promoção, proteção e recuperação da saúde, a organização eo funcionamento dos serviços correspondentes e dá outras providências. *Diário Oficial da união, 128*(182). Retrived from: http://www.planalto.gov.br/ccivil_03/leis/l8080.htm

Gorini, A., & Pravettoni, G. (2011). An overview on cognitive aspects implicated in medical decisions. *European Journal of Internal Medicine, 22*(6), 547–553. doi:10.1016/j.ejim.2011.06.008 PMID:22075278

Hayes, R. H., Upton, D., & Pisano, G. (2008). Produção, estratégia e tecnologia: Em busca da vantagem competitiva. *The Bookman*.

Hopp, W. J., & Lovejoy, W. S. (2013). *Hospital operations: Principles of high efficiency health care*. FT Press.

Kattan, M. W. (2009). *Encyclopedia of medical decision making* (Vol. 1). Sage. doi:10.4135/9781412971980

Li, X., & Fawcett, T. N. (2014). Clinical decision making on the use of physical restraint in intensive care units. *International Journal of Nursing Sciences*, *1*(4), 446–450. doi:10.1016/j.ijnss.2014.09.003

Marewski, J. N., & Gigerenzer, G. (2012). Heuristic decision making in medicine. *Dialogues in Clinical Neuroscience*, *14*(1), 77–89. PMID:22577307

Marques, G. Q., & Da Silva Lima, M. A. D. (2007). Demandas de usuários a um serviço de pronto atendimento e seu acolhimento ao sistema de saúde. *Revista Latino-americana de enfermagem*, *15*(1), 13-19. Retrived from: http://www.scielo.br/pdf/rlae/v15n1/pt_v15n1a03.pdf

Ministério Da Saúde. (2007). *Pesquisa para Saúde Por que pesquisa em Saúde? Textos para tomada de decisão*. Council on Health Research for Development and Global Forum for Health Research. Secretaria de Ciência, Tecnologia e Insumos Estratégicos Departamento de Ciência e Tecnologia, Brasília.

Morgan, G., Bergamini, C. W., & Coda, R. (2010). *Imagens da organização*. São Paulo: Atlas.

Motta, P. (2012). *Formulação de políticas e definição de objetivos: Imposições do contexto administrativo. In Gestão em Saúde*. Rio de Janeiro: Guanabara Koogan.

OECD. (2015). *Fiscal Sustainability of Health Systems: Bridging Health and Finance Perspectives*. Paris: OECD Publishing.

Osmo, A. A. (2012). *Processo gerencial. In Gestão em saúde* (pp. 127–137). Rio de Janeiro: Guanabara Koogan.

Pitta, A. (1994). *Hospital: dor e morte como ofício*. Hucitec.

Simon, H. A. (1957). *Models of man: Social and rational; mathematical essays on rational human behavior in society setting*. Wiley.

Spiegel, T. (2013). *Cognitive sciences contributions to operations management: analysis of experience impact in operations manager*. Federal University of Rio de Janeiro.

Spiegel, T. (2014) An Overview of Cognition Roles in Decision-Making. In Encyclopedia of Business Analytics and Optimization. IGI Global. doi:10.4018/978-1-4666-5202-6.ch008

Spiegel, T. (2017). Influences of Personal Experience in Decision-Making. In Exploring the Influence of Personal Values and Cultures in the Workplace. IGI Global. doi:10.4018/978-1-5225-2480-9.ch005

Spiegel, T., & Assad, D. B. N. (2016). Operations Project and Management in Trauma Centers: The Case of Brazilian Units. In Handbook of Research on Healthcare Administration and Management. IGI Global. doi:10.4018/978-1-5225-0920-2.ch007

Vähätalo, M., & Kallio, T. J. (2015). Organising health services through modularity. *International Journal of Operations & Production Management*, *35*(6), 925–945. doi:10.1108/IJOPM-12-2013-0523

Wegwarth, O., Gaissmaier, W., & Gigerenzer, G. (2009). Smart strategies for doctors and doctors-in-training: Heuristics in medicine. *Medical Education*, *43*(8), 721–728. doi:10.1111/j.1365-2923.2009.03359.x PMID:19573016

Zucchi, P., Del Nero, C., & Malik, A. M. (2000). Gastos em saúde: Os fatores que agem na demanda e na oferta dos serviços de saúde. *Saúde e Sociedade*, *9*(1-2), 127–150. doi:10.1590/S0104-12902000000100010

KEY TERMS AND DEFINITIONS

Cognitive Heuristics: Cognitive strategies that can provide good solutions to complex problems under time and cognitive ability constraints.

Emergency Unit: The structure that aims to solve most of the emergencies (intermediate severity injuries), such as high blood pressure and fever, fractures, cuts, heart attack, and stroke. They help to reduce queues in the hospital's emergency department.

Healthcare Operations Management: The decisions and actions that occur within the limits defined by the operating system design. These include activities such as the implementation of policies, procedures and strategies, contingent decision making, process coordination, problem identification and resolution, response to uncertainty and unforeseen problems, and rewarding people.

Healthcare Professionals: Professionals responsible for healthcare and whose decisions impact all of the organization. We can cite medical directors, trauma surgeons, residents, nurses, nursing technicians, pharmacists, social assistants, among others.

Operations Management: A multidisciplinary field that investigates the design, management, and improvement of processes aimed at the development, production, distribution, and delivery of products and services.

Patient Process/Flow: Variety of path patterns that result in patient care.

Red Priority: Extremely severe cases; patients requiring immediate medical care.

Chapter 10
Information Science and Its Relation to Other Areas of Knowledge

José Poças Rascão
Polytechnic Institute of Setúbal, Portugal

ABSTRACT

The purpose of this chapter is to contribute to a better understanding of the relationship between information science and other areas of knowledge based on the aggregation of existing literature. It is a descriptive study, with the goal of identifying and characterizing the relationship among different areas of expertise. The structure of the chapter summarizes the existing academic work, seeking to generate new knowledge. The results can be used to integrate the relationship of the different areas of knowledge. The chapter seeks to first identify apparent relationships and then focuses in more detail on some of them. It concludes with the implications for future research.

INTRODUCTION

The proposed work intents to provide a reflection on the emergence and evolution of information science, taking into account the context in which it operates. To understand an area or topic is necessary at first, the knowledge of its origins and its history. Thus, we present firstly a short history of the evolution of information science and its development over the past decades.

The consolidation of a particular field of knowledge gives, among other things, the existence of a scientific community. This in turn consists of a number of researchers and scientists concerned to discuss and solve problems that arise in the area. A shared by members of a community paradigm results in the consolidation of the scientific community.

Origin of Information Science

It is difficult to determine when a new science emerges even in the case of a recent scientific discipline such as Information Science. However Foskett (1969) and Ingwersen (1992) indicate the date of 1958 as

DOI: 10.4018/978-1-5225-3725-0.ch010

one of the milestones in the formalization of the new discipline when was founded in the UK the Institute of Information Scientists (IIS). Meadows (1990) describe the origin 78 of the new discipline from specialized libraries (in industries and other organizations).

According to the same author the discipline has undergone a marked development after World War II due to the emergence of the Mathematical Theory of Information described by Shannon and Weaver in the late 40s. This theory was adopted by many other areas of knowledge, because it explains the problems of transmitting messages through mechanical communication channels. The industrialization of the trade press promoted the literature explosion, no less important than the advent of the Gutenberg press occurred around 1450, whose effects were more evident after the 2ed world war phenomenon. Their contribution to the development of information science was small but important to the history of the area, which drew attention to two necessities.

The first theory which defined clearly the nature of the information of which the professionals were concerned and, secondly, to define the conceptual framework to be applied in the organization of that type of information. According to Pinheiro and Loureiro (1995) Norbert Wiener in 1948 in his book Cybernetics or Control and Communication in the Animal and Machine, and Claude Shannon and Warren Weaver in 1949 in the book The Mathematical Theory of Communication, marked the beginning of what would become the information science. Yet according to the authors, is in the 60's are drafted early concepts and definitions and begins the debate about the origins and theoretical foundations of the new field of knowledge (Pine & Loureiro, 1995).

The authors point to several events that occurred in the 60s which meant the true landmarks of the formation of a new field. A conference held at the Georgia Institute of Technology in 1962, The Weinberg Report 1963, Computer Work, Mikhailov, in 1966, the study by Rees and Saracevic in 1967, and the definition of Borko, in Information Science: what is it in 1968? Borko (1968) defined information science as a discipline that investigates the properties and behavior of information, the forces governing the flow and the processing means to optimize its accessibility and use. It relates to the body of knowledge related to the production, collection, organization, storage, retrieval, interpretation, transmission, transformation and utilization of information.

This includes the investigation of the representation of information in natural and artificial systems [...]. Have a component of pure science that investigates the essence of the matter without considering its application and another component of applied science that develops services and products [...]. For Goffman (1970) the purpose of information science is to establish a unified scientific approach to studying the various phenomena involving the notion of information, if such phenomena are found in biological processes in human existence or machines created by humans. Consequently, it must be related to the establishment of a set of fundamental principles that govern the behavior of the entire communication process and its associated information systems.

Griffith (1980) proposed a similar definition that provides information science as a discipline that seeks the creation and structuring of a scientific, technological and systemic corpus related to the transference of information knowledge. Saracevic (1991) studied the evolution of Information Science and defined it as, *a dedicated scientific issues and problems facing the effective communication of knowledge and records of knowledge among human beings, the social context professional practice field institutional or individual use and information needs.*

In treating these issues are considered of particular interest the advantages of information and communication (ICT) technologies.

Information Science was born after the second world war, to solve a big problem, which was also the major concern or Documentation or the Information Retrieval which is to gather, organize and make accessible the cultural, scientific and technological knowledge produced worldwide.

Information science is a new science which was born from the exact sciences, i.e., striving to achieve precise knowledge from the inspiration of mathematical and quantitative models.

(Bronowsk, 1977), based on the objective sought to formulate universal laws of "behavioral" information. Strongly influenced by the empirical sciences sought to establish universal laws that represent the informational phenomenon and hence the need to resort to mathematical models (information theory), physical (entropy) or biological (epidemiological theory). In the seventies, there appears a character that redirects the focus of information science: *the man (DM) and as such the humanities and social sciences also start to contribute with their methods and practices for the composition of this emerging science* (Cardoso, 1996).

Initially much tied to computing and automatic information retrieval, according to (Gonzalez Gomez, 2000), from the 1970s, makes its actual enrollment in the social sciences as a *symptom of ongoing changes that affect the production and management of knowledge in the West* (Gonzalez Gomez, 2000). It is from that decade that we can refer to the *social foundations of information*. However, some important issues face us right now, which is the branch of information science that is closest to sciences? Which are the theories, concepts and methods that feed information science? Early studies in information science as a social science intend in a study the social reality in statistical perspective, i.e. quantitative.

Berger and Luckmann (1985) presented the reality as something that is socially constructed and not an existence in itself and pave the way for understanding information not as something given that would have meaning and importance per se, but as a process. This is something that will be perceived and understood in various ways by people, which, according to the definition of Borko (1968) on the behavior and information flows, is something that is out of the people and the definition of Buckland (1991) who sees the information as "something" outside people. The subjectivity of information is fundamental to understanding the different levels of reality and the distinction between different forms of knowledge and the mechanisms of its setting and legitimating. People need to be included in studies of information and in their daily interactions, forms of expression and language, rites and social processes.

Several studies can be presented as an example of the incorporation of these concepts in the context of information science studies, such as the approach done and inaugurated by Dervin, Atwood and Palmour, studies of MacMullin and Taylor on the values of the people, nature studies inspired by the theory of Maturana and Varela, the hermeneutic approach of cognitive information science, studies of Capurro (2003) on information networks based on the theoretical framework of Bourdieu (1983), as well as bibliometric studies and scientific communication and the contributions of Foucault's Archaeology of Knowledge and the Sociology of Science (Latour, Knorr - Cetina, among others). Information Science is a discipline that has a very wide field of practice but does not have a defined theoretical field as is the case of other areas, as linguistics, anthropology and so on.

The information science yet has not been reached a theoretical construct that integrates all concepts and practices. Therefore operates based on more or less fragmented theoretical constructions, for example, the representation of the information would be a construct, among others. The most important feature of information science is its interdisciplinary nature in which the magnitude of the problems (ecological, ethnic and demographic) is demanding innovative solutions. Information science has been consolidated from elements "borrowed" among others, by mathematics, physics, biology, psychology, sociology, anthropology, semiotics, communication theory and other sciences that have contributed to its rationality and applicability (Cardoso 1996). *Information science is not to be looked at as a classical discipline, but as a prototype of the new kind of science (Wersig, 1993).*

Information science evolves to new levels of dialogue and inclusion in the social sciences. the reflection on the evolution of information science, its relationship with the social sciences and as science model as a whole, is essential for the continued research that incorporates all of the accumulated knowledge in this process. Scientific research being one of the main ways to formulate theories of an area, as the Information science research, has over the past decades, being consolidated and opened new horizons of discussions. A big contribution has been given by teachers and researchers in the various international universities.

It may be noted that some important steps were taken towards theoretically strengthen the area of Information Science and researches are booming and have a scientific community that over the years has been consolidated internationally. Many challenges face today the Information science. As an applied science, must meet the demand for information by the company and, as an object of research, the needs of key concepts in the field. Conducting research and sociability are the safest paths for the creation and sharing of new paradigms. Thus, it becomes increasingly important to seek the theoretical, philosophical and social reasons in the field of Information Science and especially strengthen further its scientific community.

Relationship With Other Sciences

Interdisciplinary

Interdisciplinary can be understood as *dialogue between the fields of knowledge* by the words of Japiassu (1976), or *mutual appropriation of methodologies, principles, theories, concepts and constructs between two or more knowledge areas* (Pine, 2004). To Klein (2004) the concept of interdisciplinary is connected with the complexity. The convergence between these two ideas has significant implications for understanding the nature of knowledge, the solution of scientific problems and the dialogue between the sciences and the humanities. According to Klein (2004) the nature of complex systems provides a comprehensive rationality for interdisciplinary studies unifies seemingly divergent approaches and serves as a criterion to direct the integration process.

The ultimate goal of interdisciplinary research understands the portion of the world shaped by a complex system. Interdisciplinary is characterized by the exchange of knowledge, by transforming the areas of knowledge and the sharing of objectives. Interdisciplinary is not a simple appropriation of concepts, theories and methods from one area of knowledge to another, only materializes from the concrete dialogue between different areas of knowledge. The effective interdisciplinary is one that is updated in the field of theoretical abstractions, establishing methodologies, but also interventions that promote different areas of knowledge in the social (Gomes, 2001). According to Klein (2004) interdisciplinary approach stems from the need to understand complex objects, which a single area of expertise and would be unable to deal with the proper coverage. Among these we mention the phenomena of the explosion of information and cultural diversity, social and technological problems multifaceted concepts such as "body," "mind" and "life." One sees the development of a significant number of areas of multi or interdisciplinary knowledge since the mid- twentieth century and among them is the science of information.

Information Science and Knowledge

Although the terms information and knowledge are used very often are not the same thing. Information is not the same as data, although the two words are often confused, so you must understand that the subtle distinction between these concepts is essential. The data do not carry meaning or significance of the facts, images or sounds, since it lacks the essential to establishing a complete relational meaning element, lacking an internal relational structure to a cognitive purpose. This structure is one of the attributes of the information. The data is transformed into information when its creator joins its meaning (Davenport & Prusak, 1998).

Zikmund (2000, p.19) defines knowledge as *the mix of information, experience and understanding provide a structure that can be applied in the evaluation of new information or new situations*. The information "feeds" knowledge. Knowledge can thus be defined as the ability of a person to deal with information structures related to a new context. New contexts involving change - dynamic actions. Knowledge cannot be shared, though the technique and the components of the information can be shared. When a person internalizes the information to the point he can use it, we call it knowledge (Zikmund, 2000).

This is a fluid mix of experience, values, contextual information, and expert insight; we provide a structured framework for evaluating and incorporating new experiences and information, in organizations and not only in documents and reports, but also in organizational routines, processes, practices and norms. Knowledge originates and is applied in the minds of knower's (Davenport & Prusak, 1998; Zikmund, 2000). Knowledge is the valid and accepted information, integrating data, documents, information and sometimes hypotheses. The need to know that someone filters combines and interprets the information. The information can be considered as a "substance" may be acquired, stored and possessed by a person or by a group and transmitted from person to person or from group to group. Information has certain stability and perhaps faces you better as occurring at the company (Davenport & Prusak, 1998).

Although we can store it employing various physical media, the information itself is not physical, but rather abstract and very little purely mental. The knowledge is stored in people's memories, but the information is out there in the world. Whatever is there somewhere between the physical world around people and mental human thoughts. Knowledge = Internalized information + ability to use it in new situations. Knowledge is fundamentally and intrinsically within people. These is more complex and unpredictable at the individual level than in the entire society sago, so it is not surprising that knowledge results more difficult to obtain than information. The knowledge exists primarily within people, is an integral part of human complexity and unpredictability (Davenport & Prusak, 1998).

Knowledge presents a fundamental duality: it is something storable (at least sometimes we want to do it) and something flowing (something that communicates from person to person). It is possibly the duality of knowledge (something that flows and has a storage process) which complicates their treatment and management. According to Dahlberg (2006) knowledge is organized into units of knowledge (concepts) according with their characteristics (objects / subjects / topics). The organization of knowledge is related to a process of conceptual analysis of a domain of knowledge and from there it is structured / architected generating a representation of knowledge about this field that will be used for the organization of information on this area of knowledge.

Information Science and Education

According to Davenport and Prusak (2002) the only sustainable advantage of organizations is what they collectively know how effectively use what they know and the readiness with which they acquire and use new knowledge. Learning organizations represent an ideal that has been pursued in the age of intellectual capital appreciation. A learning organization is an organization that facilitates the learning of all its members. According to the authors ' organizations may rely on intuition and be lucky for some years, but the most successful are those who remain in tune with the factual information - from the inside out and outside-in and use in the process decision-making (2001).

The knowledge produced or collected by information science, about the processes of the organization and the use of information can make a significant contribution to the managers of organizations as well as for managers of education systems. The term "jurisdiction" is used as a way to establish the educational and curricular objectives. The concept of "competence" sheds light on the use and the ability to apply the knowledge learned in the various disciplines in concrete situations. According to the informational pyramid of Barreto (2002a) about human needs, the individual moves from bottom to top, from one stage to another only when all the requirements at that stage are met. At the base of the pyramid would be people who primarily seek information useful for the needs of security, order, and freedom from fear and threat.

In the following stage people seek information that guarantees the safe stay in the different contexts in which they live and want to stay. Seeking information for they own benefit and the institution in which they work. At the top people are linked to information with commitments of reflection, creativity and realize their potential. The search for information can be deduced and adds quality from the base to the top of the pyramid. According to the same author the provision of information is inverted in quantitative and qualitative terms seeking information pyramid, setting up situations of rationing and surplus information in extremes.

By analogy, it is understood that the educational information is at the top of the pyramid of the offer. At the base, the utilitarian information: statutes, regulations, school records, internal communications etc. These, in addition to diversity, are by nature its transience, which may even justify the imbalance between demands and supply Barreto (2002c). The author considers the existence of three types of information sought:

- **Basic:** Responsible for basic information needs of the individual in the exercise of his citizenship, such as the need for housing, food, clothing, health and education;
- **Contextual:** Responsible for current account information so that the individual can stay and keep his fields of professional, social, economic and political life, and the reflective information that guides the thinking, research,

- **Innovation:** Is the search for information that leads to creative thinking of reformatting and re-working information on new information, enabling innovation in all its aspects.

Whereas the pedagogical information abound, it is possible to assume that the problems related to information in schools lie in obtaining, organizing and use of that which constitutes the base of the pyramid of supply, i.e., despite the offer, no reflexive demand. The demands that are imposed, it seems, are the basic and contextual. All these arguments lead us to information science, as the area of knowledge with the potential to contribute to education in understanding and overcoming their problems.

The Model McGee and Prusak (1994) involves the recognition of strategic information (one that makes a difference and allows a return above average in economic terms), supplies, filter, collection, classification and storage, processing and presentation development products and services, distribution, dissemination, analysis and use of information. Davenport (2001) proposes an ecological approach to information, with emphasis on the environment: teams, culture, behavior, work process, informational politics, technology - allows some inferences and analogies regarding assumptions and critical components.

Nonaka and Takeuchi (1997), with the Theory of Knowledge Creation in Business, contradictory to launch an absolute, static and nonhuman nature of knowledge, established by traditional epistemology, presented knowledge as a dynamic human process for justifying personal belief with the truth. And establish the conditions for the creation of new knowledge, analyzing the possibilities of converting tacit knowledge into explicit. Chun Wei Choo (2003) reveals and analyzes the interdependence between three modes of use of information in an organization - creating meanings, knowledge building and decision making - demonstrating their complementarily. Furthermore, proposes *an approach to analyze and compare the behaviors of the use of information in organizations.* Information science, as we have seen, has much to offer so that they can increase the "knowledge" and develop appropriate "skills".

Information Science and Human Cognition

According to Saracevic (1996), the 60 information science concerned with the properties of the information and the *"forces" that made the management of their flows and means to facilitate their use, i.e., tried to be formalized.* According to Lima (2008) studies of information science focused on the process of information communication. From the 80s the management was included in the 90 studies focused on the use / information needs for people and managers of organizations. For understand the informational phenomenon for multiple perspectives and operating with language.

According to Saracevic (1996) information science is "a field devoted to the scientific questions and focused or individual professional practice to problems of effective communication of knowledge and its records between human beings in the social, institutional, and use information needs. Among the various functions is to describe the information intellectually. Capurro (1991) states that,

human beings are biological information processing. The information is encoded doubly true. The information science aims to study the information itself, i.e., contributing to its construction and analysis, proposing to establish a consistent scientific approach to the study of various phenomena that surround the notion of information, they are found in biological processes in human existence, or the machines.

The Understanding of the Human Mind

Cognitive science is an interdisciplinary area of study that among other relates to cognitive psychology to computer science with neuroscience and linguistics (Lima, 2003). According to the same author's research the human cognition have sought to grasp how people think, perceive and interpret the world. Studies on the nature and cognitive development of human beings are facing four major theories of cognitive development: Piaget's theory:

human cognition is a form of biological adaptation in which knowledge is built gradually from the development of cognitive structures that are organized according to the stages of development of intelligence.

Thus, the cognitive development is linked to accommodation and assimilation processes that promote balance which varies with age (Flavell, Miller, PH, & Miller SA, 1999; Sternberg, 2000); Piagetian theories:

emphasize the cognitive skills such as process and coordinate elements enabling the differentiation of information in determining a subjective to achieve a goal. Also, include the concept of mediation and interaction in problem solving;

Vygotsky's theory (1998): Knowledge is constructed in interactions between individuals in society, triggering learning. Thus, the mediation process is established when two or more people work together in an activity. (Flavell, 1979; Miller, PH, & Miller, SA, 1999) a survey of information processing encompasses the understanding of the text, i.e. the cognitive activity that involves perception, memory, inference and deduction Understanding text occurs from the knowledge of the world and various types of text, requiring semantic awareness.

According to (Sternberg, 2000) processing of the text in memory is as follows and sequence: 1st perception of graphical representation occurs, then the translation of letters into sounds and chaining these sounds in a word, it is necessary to master the lexical processes that are used to identify letters and words and activate the relevant information in memory on these words. According to (Sternberg, 2000; Koch; Travaglia, 2001) the process of understanding involves semantic coding, acquisition of new vocabulary, creation of mental models and understanding of text ideas. Semantic coding is the process by which sensory information is translated into words. The vocabulary acquisition adds to the existing significant new vocabulary terms. Mental models are a set of propositions that can lead to more than one mental model and simulate the reality that surrounds us (Johnson - Laird, 1983).

According to Eysenck and Keane (1994) and Seternberg (2000), among others, the mental models most commonly used are: schemas - cognitive structures are related to a set of knowledge stored in temporal or causal sequence, in which are kept the sets of features objects and beings around us. For example, procedures for operating equipment; plans - are a body of knowledge about how to act to achieve certain goals. For example: how to win a game of chess, or script Scripts - are stereotyped and predetermined actions applied to defined situations. For example, the script applied we are going to the movies or a restaurant; Superstructures or textual layouts - set of knowledge acquired in proportion as we read different types of texts and we perform correlation between them. When we read a text we strive to maintain the highest number of information in our memory for text comprehension. We do not try to store the exact words, but try to extract the ideas of word groups, store them to try to retrieve them later.

Authors such as Kintsch and Van Dijl (1983) about the information processing model also included the production model through analysis and synthesis called situational model., I.e., a common model for all readers. They argue that the key thematic propositions linger longer in the memory, those that are considered less important. According to Jacob and Shaw (1998) the cognitive point of view of information science implies that each measure (perceptual or symbolic) information processing is mediated by a system of categories and concepts which, for the mechanism of information processing constitute a model of the world, i.e., all activities involving cognitive activities.

Information Science and Linguistics

Linguistic after the 60s, with the revolution developed by Noam Chomsky, gained the status of transformational science and has since constantly being requested for the construction of concepts in various fields of human knowledge, and information science, which were originated after World War II, received a commission to handle the processing and transmission of the knowledge produced and with the responsibility of ensuring the social role of information. This interface also opened in the 60s, has been enriched with new approaches. According to Moles (1974) language via language and social function of science information, via communication, provided one of the key issues in the documentary medium in the late twentieth century. Foucault (1999) says that *the existence of language is paramount, since the words were tasked and empowered to represent the thought.*

Thought represented by the vocabulary and the fertility of its elements in which two operative modes were included: fixed, in which the word is the basis of limited, restricted, and flexible construction, in which the words have multiple definitions and are endowed with associative combinations. Information Science investigates the properties and behavior of information, the forces that manage the flow of information and media technology (pencil and paper or information technology and communication) to process information, with the aim of your organization, storage, retrieval and dissemination, has debut connection with the mediation of linguistic analysis that uses documentary techniques, methods and processes to describe the content of the documents.

According to Foucault (1999) what distinguishes language from all other signs and allows you to play a decisive role in the representation is not the fact that it is individual or collective, natural or artificial, but the fact she analyzes the representation according to a necessarily successive order

(...), language cannot represent the thought immediately, in its entirety, must dispose of it by following a linear order. (...) It is this narrow sense that the analysis is language of thought: Not a simple representation, but profound establishment of order in the space.

The area of documents, in general, involves threads that are inserted into the parts forming the whole of their content. The linguistics and information science are embedded in the area of knowledge organization and representation of the formation, characterized by theoretical foundations, classification and indexing methods; knowledge representation for language and terminology, classification and indexing classification, structure and building systems applied; universal classification systems; organizational knowledge environment.

According to Ercília Mendonça (2000) Information science, as a broad area of research, has the bibliometrics field of librarianship, their area of quantitative studies because bibliometrics indicates the quantitative treatment of written communication through several applications, with the frequency of words in the text which is the most used method. According to the same author the linguistic, semantic and grammatical rules are considered cornerstones in the treatment, standardization, translation, construction and dissemination of information through the process descriptors. The translation of the term descriptor and the issue of linguistic borrowing are two of the major challenges of the documentary was because if press by a term that represents a clear and objective manner, the information through standardization and standardization of loanwords that currently plague Brazilian terminology.

Nakayama (2000) is used in the area of language descriptors in the construction process, which describes grammatical classes that serve as the basis for forming the terms. This problematic use of language in the formation of descriptors covering several areas of human knowledge, specifically through the informational area, such as terminology, the translation studies and, more recently, the socio- terminology - a hyper -specialization of terminology. According to Correia (1995), discusses the linguistic structures the lexicon, the vocabulary, the word, the sign, the language and the whole range of terms involving relationships. In the formation of concepts and the adoption of documentary languages, it is essential to build vocabulary as a means of standardization and information retrieval.

On the other hand, also discusses the polysemy of words, since *the same word can denote completely different entities*. There is no unambiguous relationship between a significant form and concept; this likewise is related to various concepts. This refers to the concept of metaphor derived from the meanings proposed by dictionaries. Within these extensions of meanings, also discusses the importance of the area as lexicographic factor enhancement of knowledge, because it acknowledges the need for a scientific technical vocabulary, as an important research tool. According to Figueiredo (1995), the concept of relevance in communication analysis is intrinsically linked to the laws of bibliometrics, it appeared within the context of measurement of a source of information and presents a probabilistic connotation and is studied by information scientists and semanticists According to the latter,

the information with meaningful content is equivalent to the relevant information. The concept of relevance cannot be studied as an isolated phenomenon; it depends on many factors in this communication process.

According to Noam Chomsky (1995), the semantics is housed in studies of psychology, sociology and logic, which generated three categories of semantics. Semantic oriented psychology comes to solving problems of cognitive communication between humans. The studies focused on the logic deals with the issue of the sign and the object, with the application of the correct meaning. In sociology, attempts to clarify the relationship between form and meaning of a word (term) that interacts in communication between individuals and society. We can talk about various forms of language, such as the documentary language, the language of knowledge, language indexing, language technology, language systems, language curriculum, bibliometric language, normative language, artificial language, natural language, the theoretical language, cognitive language, the language of thought, terminological language, intellectual language.

The essence of all these languages is not the parts but the whole, which is the language that makes the dependent parts of a principle of analysis, because language is the object of knowledge itself. The fact that process and transmit knowledge puts in information science, and only there, the responsibility of deepening in the humanities and social sciences, and this process is not without its own linguistic approach because information today, acquired strategic nature becoming an element of influence and power in the whole sphere of human knowledge. According to the same author is the act of knowing (language) and presentation (content) information science define its object of study - information - and this information cannot be issued without a proper language. Information science should not expect turnkey solutions from linguistics, since this is resize your theoretical field, select universes of more limited research and developing new prospects in order to explain your phenomenon.

Information Science and Journalism

Journalism is strongly influenced by the focus in the daily press. So when it comes to journalism, it is believed than when someone prints a page (paper or electronic), i.e., that which circulates through society and turns to cover the everyday, whose gaze focuses on news and journalistic products whose focus lies in the presentation of what happens in the world. According to Buitoni (1990) journalism seeks to show and tell the world everything about an event, and talk about everything. The information is linked to the notion of news and that has its origin and explanation. The concept of information is always present in journalistic products. In fact, expressions such as informative journalism or informational content are linked to news. When it comes a new automatically talking about information for journalism.

Which is the content of journalism? The news information, i.e. news topic is described as the subject of information. For example: news - economic crisis in Europe - the information is all that characterizes / describes the economic crisis from its origins to its aftermath. Capurro and Hjørland (2007) argue that the semantic of the information associated with various scientific areas. In journalism, the periodic information in the media is often singled out as the sole source to obtain knowledge on certain topics. However, the information that is beyond the contents? Did the information itself may be the subject of study? What is the relationship of "science journalism" with the more established epistemological aspects from information?

Starting from the news as the subject of study, such as concept, knowledge, journalistic information and textual genres allow you to build a panorama in which they think the information one this context and beyond. According to Landowski (1992) the media (printed or electronic) are intended to inform us of how we live and how we design this around us. In this sense the everyday is the great representative of the media reading done on social life. Even experiencing strong competition from other media, the newspaper / newsletter continues to assert its vocation to tell us everything and all dimensions of our presence in the world. The newspaper is an exceptionally powerful tool in the integration of multiple universes which it takes as a reference object.

The same author states that a newspaper as a semiotic subject whose brands is a social figure leads people to engage a conduct of acceptance or rejection. The different perspectives to look at a newspaper as a global point of view, lead us to question its ideological content, its narrative structures and forms of discourse in terms of time, space and subject, thus emanating its own identity (tone, style and effect). The journalistic discourse can be seen by the same author as a whole whose parts are complementary in the way it is written its everyday speech and the way it is described normatively. The integration of thematic universes puts the newspaper in the center of the social universe and its dynamics, revealing the point of view of the meanings a social function through its printed material (paper or electronic).

Sociological perspective in the newspaper also has a social function for Berganza Conde (2008). Park sees the newspaper less as an institution (as a social structure) and more like a living organism that adapts itself to the social needs of individuals and groups in an increasingly urbanized society (Park, 2008a). Throughout its history, from the seventeenth to the twentieth century, the newspaper news just reached its way in the first decades of the twentieth century. At that time people were more interested in news than in political and abstract doctrines. The growth of urban life and its dynamics required a press release that said what was happening and what was needed to know. The news for the journalist were the material on which would write the editorial. The journalist refused to take responsibility for allowing his readers to know that he knew of things that should not have happened (Park, 2008a). So, the news has become the product of the daily production of newspapers, or came into existence a journalism that not only defines what would be newsworthy, but also valued the significance of this selection.

Any newspaper lives with two concerns: 1) public opinion - to form there must be a free press and independent and that values democracy, 2) promote the integration of people in social and political life, by reading the newspaper. To Park (2008) the transparent journalism and press freedom are crucial in the production of knowledge (the news content) factors. Social integration of individuals indicates not only the news (something that causes people to speak) as integrative fashion, but also as a means of social control. The purpose of news is to guide people and society in general in the real world. According to the author the news and newspapers are seen as normative mechanisms that tend to maintain individuals dominated by a particular state of mind common to them and determinant to the behavior and attitudes. According to Park *new strives to capture the public's mind and direct your attention to certain events related to the unusual and the unexpected* (Marocco; Berger, 2006). The idea of objective journalism is directly related to other expensive empirical and theoretical concepts to the reality of journalism, for example, the concept of truth. Tambosi (2005) approaches the notion of truth to the information in journalism, to talk about the production of knowledge in society.

The final product of journalistic activities - news - consists of several steps and processes involved in its production (contexts and environments), who produces and what are the "raw materials" for their existence. The news is the result of events that erupt into everyday society (local, regional, global). Assuming that the reputation of a number of forces, such as social personal actions, ideological, technological, cultural, (Sousa, 2002). The news are not limited only in its production - phase comprising the (reliable) sources, collection, selection (filtering), treatment and ranking (information architecture) and which are the less visible steps (Sousa, 2002). Without wishing to discuss this topic because I have no skills to do so, it can be said that journalism over time went through the following phases: informative journalism (the journalist was a passive actor) - evangelist / communicator of events in society that had its peak in the nineteenth century and objective journalism (1920; 1940) which marked the first relationship with society and constructivism or "absolute objectivity" journalism, in which journalists are active in the construction of reality (Teasing process 1993).

After the Second World War appears a new type of journalism: the explanation. This intends to be a new type of information space in which already coexist other media that tell more quickly [...]. Journalism explanation covers the facts in depth and uses the basic genres in a balanced way (narrative and commentary), contextualizing them in a new perspective through which the reader finds value judgments situated immediately next to the narration of the facts (Fontcuberta, 1993, p.103). As pointed out by Pérez Quesada (1998, p.25), the birth

of explanatory journalism, which incorporates the evaluative data to news, documentary, interpretive and also a good deal of elements opinion, causes, in turn, the disappearance of classical boundary between story (description) and comment (comment) [...],

in: Information & Soc: Est, João Pessoa, v.20, n.1, p.25-37, Jan. / April 2010.

Alsina (2005) defines news as a traditional concept that translates the narration and the conversion of a fact or event in a text. For the author the conversion of a fact or event in news is basically a linguistic operation that allows you to print in a certain meaning a sequence of verbal signs (oral or written) and nonverbal, that is, the news is a representation of everyday social reality produced institutionally. To Lager (2005) the word news (news) in English can be replaced by journalistic information that is not only a structuring conveniently processed and stored data such as computer science or opposes military intelligence and information (reporting and analysis) to inform (episodic story). Information as a whole differ understandable and comprehensive news because this is a regular occurrence or change of facts or events and assumes a more concise presentation (Lager, 2005).

Torres Muñoz (1997) refers to "content" condition information and states that the quality of journalistic information, as something that should be thought about as a result of the evaluative process in the construction of news which is of some value added by the journalist. Park (2008) part of the two conceptions of the philosopher and American psychologist William James to formulate his thoughts, that is, states that there are two basic forms of knowledge: familiarity with things (with acquaintance) or "knowledge" and knowledge of things (knowledge about) or "knowledge about". From these two conceptions, the author situates the news as a kind of intermediate knowledge among the first to know, more tacit, common sense or practice, and the second, more systematic, formal and scientific. According to Capurro and Hjorlan (2007) the idea of informing as an act of selection and evaluation - that perspective shared by Scientific Advisor for Communication and Information Science, is something that feeds the knowledge and is communicated by the news.

Information Science and Economics

The world situation is evolving faster than the ability of scientific demonstration is able to systematize its understanding. At the heart of globalization is the technological development. With all respect for Weber (1864-1920) and the strength of certain ideologies, we must acknowledge that when Adam Smith (1968) (division of labor) and Marx (productive forces) put the technical improvements as the engine of social change were strictly certain. Today we live in a profound technological revolution. Over the last twenty years has been accumulated more technological knowledge than in the entire history of mankind.

This has a positive side to the significant level of increased productivity that has been achieved by advances in health, information and many other progresses. Technological advancement has not had a corresponding advance in institutional terms, so, it becomes explosive for society. Industrial fishing is done with massive boats that clean seas without worrying about tomorrow, modern transport led to the establishment of a worldwide network of production and distribution of drugs that destroy thousands of lives. Laboratories rehearse genetic manipulations without any control or regulation, and so on (Murteira, 2001). Improve management capacity has become a matter of survival for organizations. Technologies redefine the concepts of time and space. The planet has become a global village. Communications today allow easier and faster performing an operation in New York or Tokyo handbag to travel a short distance.

International financial markets daily transfer over a trillion dollars without any control of the central banks. Chinese textile factories closed in Europe or any other country in the world. The economy has become global as regulatory instruments continue to be of national or regional level (Murteira, 2001). International regulatory institutions such as the UN, the GATT, the IMF and the World Bank articulated nations and not the supra- national space. Capitalism nations today strike a precarious balance between business efficiency and social justice. Global capitalism is not accountable to anyone (Murteira, 2001). This lack of regulatory instruments of the global economy worsens global polarization between rich and poor. Companies have to assume its social and environmental responsibility. The reality is that while the planet "shrinks", it becomes closer to the people who are shelved increasingly in urban areas, the economic and social precipice between populations increases rapidly, there is a close proximity between wealth and poverty, luxury and deprivation and it is to be an explosive mixture and unsustainable in the medium term.

The balance of terror is no longer the country level, but at the door of our homes (Murteira, 2001). Another aspect of institutional transformation is given us by the urbanization process that is radically changing the way of life of populations worldwide, within a few generations. Urbanization just-in-time when government decisions could be taken by the central government. Today with the widespread urbanization, large, medium and small cities have to respond to simple daily problems (school, health, small production, etc.) and become increasingly absurd to expect endless times in different State agencies. Another aspect of transformation is structural transformation of work. Unemployment did not already appear from the absence of economic growth, but economic growth itself. Anyone waiting for the situation to improve probably misses the train. Is a little importance to the division of activities into primary, secondary or tertiary sector, since this technique division hampers the hierarchical understanding of the economic and social system in different subsystems (Murteira, 2001). No more jobs for life.

Big companies started to work with multiple spaces. Russian researchers can hire cheaper in India, transfer the software programming to India, outsource production in Indonesia or Thailand, but retain the services of general system organization, coordination of marketing and similar services, in Europe or the United USA. With this is reduced the space of formal employment and increases informal employment and the informal economy. While on one hand it develops the democratization of global management and the world advances in apparent modernization process, otherwise the company will be broken down by the base. In terms of completion may present five key trends in globalization: technological development, economic polarization, urbanization and the transformation of work. The company urgently needs to pull the reins on its development and to acquire the institutional instruments to capitalize scientific advances in human development.

The Globalization of Information

In an era of communications to the world scale, information is the bond that unites us. It is be able to transmit it in large quantities quickly from continent to continent, have turned a widely separated and diverse world into a single global megalopolis. The messenger walk gave way to highways of information worldwide. Whatever it may be a valuable asset to be compiled, stored, duplicated, sold, stolen and sometimes source murder. Many people around the world spend their workday to gather study and process information. Industries were developed to produce equipment (hardware and software) to store and process information. Organizations have many physical goods that have to be managed, such as products, and other financial assets. Information on the surrounding environment in terms of strategic management today requires constant attention and can be considered as the most valuable asset and therefore calls on the knowledge-based economy, information is assuming an ever-greater share of the cost of doing business successfully.

In industrial society petroleum (crude) was an important source of energy used to move the engines and feed factories. But before the chemical energy of oil could be triggered, the crude had to be refined, i.e. transformed into usable forms, such as gasoline and heating oil. Similarly the information is the source of energy that propels the "engines" of information and knowledge society, but we need to be able to use, to convert it into usable form: knowledge. But when we refine the information to become knowledge quality outweighs quantity. When we convert information into knowledge we add value and so, it became more expensive. During the past years, in most Western countries has been seen that the industrial sector is largely responsible for the wealth they have accumulated since the nineteenth century, is losing weight in the Gross Domestic Product (GDP) compared to the services sector, resulting from the transformation of industrial society, the informational society (Moore, 1997) for three reasons: organizations increasingly depend on the intelligent use of information and will be turning in information intensive organizations; people in their daily acts consume large amounts of information, both in terms of leisure, both in terms of business, is emerging of covert information industry within the diversity of the service sector, as a sector enough to be a (perhaps the best) of the major sectors of the economy entity (primary, secondary and tertiary).

The industry may consist of three sectors: the information content, the distribution of information (access centers and distribution channels, such as telecommunications operators and Internet) and information processing (information technologies). The transformation of informational intensive organizations is perhaps the clearest detonating change for the informational society. The analysis of the most successful organizations in the world seems to indicate that it originated in better management of information and knowledge about global and immediate surroundings, i.e., those who were better able to detect the needs of the market and better adapted in configuration terms, methods, processes and cultural shapes that allow to combine with the external information generated internally to generate distinctive competitive advantages (Porter, 1998). The globalization concept often used for business organizations, has to be seen beyond the opening but not the borders of countries, markets and the organizations themselves.

The information regardless of its geographical origin or the time point is within reach through the phone keypad, computer or television screen. The world is seen, increasingly, as a field of opportunities, business and markets, as with the evolution of Information Technology and Communication (ICT), is revolutionizing the concepts of management, the attitude of managers, the performance of organizations, and especially the position of the markets. It is necessary to rethink concepts such as strategy or Organization or even the structure of, and new concepts such as the Organizational Planning, Informational, etc. The information, enhanced by the Information Technology and Communication, assumes the role and importance due by creating value in a market where customer knowledge, competitors, suppliers and other economic managers, becomes vital to the design and implementation of business strategies.

The Information in the Context of Globalization

The information revolution is an advanced stage of development. Started in business, but it certainly will affect all organizations and society. The meaning of information will radically change both for companies and for people. This is not a revolution in technology (hardware, software or speed) and is not happening in information and communication technologies, but in the concepts and will be led by experts of information science. Until now and for about fifty years the technologies of information and communication technologies (ICT) have focused on data - collection, storage, transmission and presentation and focused on the "T" of "IT". The new information revolution focuses on the "I" (Drucker, 1999).

There are around 50 years the general opinion was that the computer would find applications in organizations which have a significant impact and would revolutionize the work of top managers. So far the impact occurred where nobody predicted - in operations (Drucker, 1999).

Information Science and Management

In the last twenty years have been seen a major transformation in society, i.e., we move from a society based on industry and transport, to one based on information and knowledge. A major challenge for managers is to understand where the information is, how to manage, interpret and decision (s) allows you to take in an era of communications to the scale of the globe, since information is the bond that unites us. By being able to transmit it in large quantities quickly from continent to continent, we transform the world into a global metropolis, so the global economy, information and knowledge can be a major competitive advantage of organizations (Davenport & Laurence Prusak Thomas, 1998).

Another of the challenges facing managers is plenty of information in today's society, whose most obvious sign of the emergence of this kind of society, it is the combination of the production of large amounts of information, the intensive use of information technologies and communication and continuous learning process. Linking these three aspects suggests that from the information society we have passed quickly to the knowledge society. The symbolic culture of this society implies new ways of learning, organization and management and therefore the management of information. In the information and knowledge society there are several hierarchical levels or progressive stages directly related to the learning process of this knowledge, so we can consider three stages: data, information and knowledge.

Many people in organizations spend their day-to-day work to gather, analyze and process information; some industries were developed based on the resource information to produce technologies (process technology – the computer; technology product - the software and technology of communication - communications equipment + software), i.e., to store, process, transmit and access information easily. Managers cannot open a newspaper without reading the term information. Many books have the term information. Many people in organizations have activity as the term information. That will be easy to tell which is will tell it. However, when we begin to think of the term information have some difficulty in the set.

Part of the difficulty in understanding the information managers is that they are so used to dealing with it on a day- to-day who are not aware of the complexities involved. Managers only realize the difficulties they face a new language. The potential for misunderstandings is always present. Given the importance of communication in organizations who are involved in decision making, whether or operational manager, need to find ways to reduce the possibility of error. To do this one need to understand how communication unfolds - how information is transmitted from person to person, from computer to computer and between the person and the computer. The need to understand the information - what it is and how it flows - not just limited to large organizations. Whenever a person communicates with another, there is a flow of information, because communication is a means to provide information from one person to another.

The information that top managers need is of two types: information to identify new opportunities (internal on the skills and capabilities of the organization and external information about global and immediate surroundings) business. This is not structured and continues to merely consist of data to have the meaning that needs to be structured, since not all information makes sense and is important. The external data is one that is increasingly important to support the strategic decision making, but needs to be monitored and organized for the work of strategic managers.

Information Science and ICT

The concept of the technology is immediately understood by those who make use of it and refer to it constantly. There is unanimity on an implicit concept, but it is essential to explain, i.e. technology is a complex body of knowledge, resources and know-how, organized with a view to production. Thus, one can speak of the production of high density integrated circuits and customized technologies, supported by a global network of design and manufacturing linked by satellites (Ribaut Jean -Michel; Bruno & Daniel Lebidois Martinet, 1991). Any technology encompasses three components: The Knowledge - which by itself does not constitute a technology;

- **Means:** Featuring the technology, but that is not reducible to them, in unskilled hands any technology represents a wasted investment,
- **The Know- How:** With no means is a specialization, but cannot get any result and quickly falls into disuse for lack of implementation.

Organizations to improve their competitive position proceed in two ways, i.e. firstly observe and analyze customer needs to be satisfied and this can cause technological innovations or analyze the advantages of replacing one technology with another that will improve their performance. Any technology always appeals to various scientific disciplines, such as laser technology gathers knowledge of optics, electronics, fluid mechanics and thermodynamics. Scientific research aims at the acquisition or enhancement of knowledge (provisional certainties), while the creation of technologies aimed at the production under industrial conditions. The technology only makes sense in terms of a guaranteed result: a technology exists only when it is validated and when it allows a production under specific conditions, i.e. the technology solves a problem. Information Technologies and Communication can be defined as the set of knowledge, material resources (infrastructure) and know -how required for the production, marketing and use of goods and or services related to the temporary or permanent storage of data as well as processing and communication thereof.

The emergence and evolution of technologies represent a decisive impetus for the emergence of new perspectives and ways of looking at issues with how to compete. The use of information and communication technologies have been expanding gradually, so that the English expression "Information Systems" is that which in Portuguese can be translated as "Systems" that do not represent a systematic, complete and organized the collecting, sorting, processing, analysis, interpretation and dissemination of information in organizations. Information technology and communication allow for the storage, processing, access and transmission of data streams (information), so, one if you cannot confuse the technology process (hardware) and the technology product (software) with the product (information). Understanding the difference between what is information for the management of the business and information technology and communication is vital for managers because of the simple reason that the information helps managers making decisions, whatever the technology support.

But managers also cannot forget that the technologies of information and communication, as support, allow for competitive advantage regardless of the market share and size of business. In reflection on this topic, Should be distinguished support the collection, processing and transmission of data (technological infrastructure - hardware software and communications) and the information resulting from the collection, sorting, processing and analysis of information, i.e. the information embodied in flow system (that is between the action information, i.e. data and product information).

The Age of the Post- Shannon's Theory of Communication

The research work of Claude Shannon (1916-2001) led to the definition of information theory and classical communication, whose first publication in 1948 was seen as a cornerstone of twentieth century science, Shannon having been compared to Einstein and Darwin In terms of their intellectual impact on a significant number of problems and the digital transmission and encryption of information on the theory of investment applications. The theoretical concepts of information are today also penetrating very quickly in the field of genetic biology, transmission of cellular signals and neuroscience.

Shannon's theory was seen as a perfect theory, this is full, proper settings for all appropriate or interesting problems of communication - that is mathematically rigorous produces results that are "heavy" in various ways and provides a working definition of what is possible in particular with respect to the signal power of communication channels sufficiently mixed. Shannon's theory was the "shelf" for thirty to forty years and was forgotten by the actual practice of engineering (to be discussed elsewhere). But in the last ten to fifteen years the scientific method engineering abruptly broke with theory and even more surprisingly that has excelled in some fields of research. The impulse method for many of these fields has emerged in the field of engineering and wireless communications, where the only characteristic of wireless channel has created a number of interesting changes in classical information theory.

The readjustment to the practical problems of engineering method was clarified, when the theory of Shannon stopped on certain key assumptions, since not all been fully explored or defined (or perhaps more properly understood) in the original development of the field research. While we could understand these assumptions, it also becomes possible to see beyond them and what we are witnessing is the emergence of the various concepts of architecture Signal Post-Shannon where standard theoretical work of Shannon has been enlarged or even replaced by latest methods of engineering (many examples can be discussed).

The Information Science and Policy

The word describes power exerting influence beyond the purely economic, the political approaches, a term we use broadly that is, a process of negotiation and compromise between individuals and groups. Bolman and Deal (1997) formulated the following propositions about the world of organizational politics: organizations are made up of various individuals and interest groups sometimes antagonistic; there are enduring differences among groups and individuals in values, beliefs, information and perceptions of reality. Most important decisions involve the allocation of scarce resources; Scarce resources and enduring differences give conflict a central role in organizational dynamics and make power the most important resource; Goals and decisions emerge from "wars" negotiations and maneuvers in search of positions among different stakeholders.

Exist in almost every organization three systems whose means can be described as legitimate: formal authority, the established culture and know-how. We can however find a fourth system, the policy whose means are not formally legitimate (Guth & Macmillan, 1985). The political system as influences can act to ensure that the most "strong" members of an organization are placed in leadership positions; policy can ensure that all sides of an issue are fully discussed, while other systems influence can promote only one; policy may be required to stimulate the necessary changes that are blocked by more legitimate influence systems; According to Dowbor Ladislaus (2010) the information must be relevant to what citizens do, but the main problem arises is that of architecture (organization) of the information according to the needs of the "actors" for the needs of political intervention in the social and human development, whose challenge is not easy to overcome, given the volume of relevant and irrelevant information that surrounds, the result of technological development. Democratic politics that have objectives for social inclusion need to create channels of communication through which relevant information can flow in a transparent and organized manner. The purpose of democracy is to recognize the right to inform and be informed, to speak and be heard, it which is imperative to participation (Martin - Barbero, 2009).

A challenge for public policy is to promote new forms of citizenship based on dialogue with civil society by engaging all individuals, through dialogue as a fundamental concept in the relationship between the state and civil society to consolidate democracy. According to Nestor Canclini (2008) is necessary to recognize the differences and inequalities in the context of globalization and technological development, in order to propose/ build alternative political power on the one hand, and on the other to understand that globalization and technology create inequalities and lead to policy failure. Well, this necessarily entails the legitimacy of indigenous knowledge and information, coming from different human groups, as well as the globalized technological social networks. The recognition of diversity is the basis for the consolidation of democracy. It is necessary to understand how information is crucial in participatory political processes to human development to the fullest from the daily life of citizens. Public information plays a decisive role in the consolidation of democracy, and the construction of collective memory, in which the flow of information feeds both the government and civil society.

The Information Science and Ethics

The concern with the ethical principles and moral values diffuses with globalization and makes us reflect on a society with social responsibilities. According to Sá (2007), the word ethics is sometimes understood to mean moral, but not always properly. It has also been understood as a science of human conduct toward the being and the like, to study the action of men and their value considerations. For Du Mont (1991), ethics establishes the principles of behavior that help people choose alternative forms of action. These considerations lead us to the definitions of ethics and morals, inviting us to refer to ethics as the study of codes and ethics of the profession. Targino (2006) tells us that the definitions of ethics originate from the Greek word ethos, as the etymology suggests, that is, the part of philosophy that deals with the reflection on the habits and actions."While moral" from the Latin word mores respects to acts and practices per se, i.e., the set of objective standards of conduct, mutable in time and space.

According to Targino (2006) ethics comes from the Greek denotes is duty; logos, discourse or treatise, etymologically equivalent to treaty or science of duty, and designating the doctrinal precepts relating to various professions, highlighting the ethical conduct in the context of society, and especially with regard to their social responsibility. Confirmation of right or wrong is usually determined by legislation, although not all situations can be included in such codes, since the laws are made for the welfare of society and will change over time, social groups and locations where these groups live. Therefore, the ethical or unethical actions social are being down. From its birth, the human being begins to live in social groups, which engage and undergo a process of exchanging knowledge, habits and customs, allowing its oral growth.

Thus, Du Mont (1991) says that the basic components of an ethical system are retained by the individual, group or society values. Ethical or unethical procedures start from the human society and raise issues and ethical discussions, bring paradigm shifts and make us rethink the actions of our daily live. People, groups or independent of social origins, live in accordance with the ethical aspects disseminated in society. Among the groups that disseminate these concepts, we cite the family, the school, the church, the preferred club, college, friends, and other political party. The interaction with these institutions is important because it is through them that individuals accumulate unique experiences, enriching their knowledge (Targino, 2006). Ethics is related to the incorporation of moral standards in the conduct of persons involved in the dissemination of information in order to guide the performance of the same.

According to Campbell (1999), *professional ethics is the application of general ethics in professional activities*, since the professional incorporates principles and values themselves, to experience them in their professional activities. It is through the profession that people can fulfill themselves, exercising their: capabilities, skills, wisdom and intelligence, affirming their personality, raising their morale and may be useful to the community and to elevate and highlight it. The concern with ethics and social values lead us to reflect on the social responsibilities in institutions, businesses and the social group. For Du Mont (1991), social responsibility is an ethical concept that involves notions of change, how human needs must be met. Furthermore, the author emphasizes the interest in the social dimensions of information service, which has to do with improving the quality of life. Social responsibility has gained greater prominence from the 90s, experiencing a major influence in society, the media in the organizational world.

According Cajazeiras (2006) Social responsibility was often confused with "welfare" (donations) and therefore proposed *another conception of social responsibility* that follows the industrial advances, globalization and the intense flow of information and technology with immediate prestige, causing degradation of the quality of life, intensifying environmental problems and precariousness of labor relations. According to Peter Annunciation (2012) the relationship of ethics to information is closely linked to its utility value and usufruct. The information is only economically and socially relevant if it is useful, or if there is capacity to interpret, understand and use it. This means that whenever the conditions are created for the changing patterns of interpretation or whether or recovery may be influencing the conduct or behavior of the receiver and thus to enter the field of information ethics.

According the same author the information convey to people who do something involving the receipt and communication of intelligence and knowledge. Is the information recognized as valid, accepted and related to certain contexts should provide support for knowledge generation, decision and consequent action. The screening ability, combination and interpretation allow the development of skills related to the use, the responsibility in the use and innovation.

CONCLUSION

Information science is often presented as a new area of knowledge, which is still in development and does not yet have its own identity. As it draws on concepts and theories from other related fields to solve its problems, has been labeled as an interdisciplinary area. The 1960s were the first years in which were proposed the concepts of information science. One of the first definitions was given during a conference at the Institute of Technology of Georgia in October 1961 and April 1962: The Science of Information is the science that investigates the properties and behavior of information, the forces governing the flow of information and means of processing the information for better accessibility and usability.

The processes include the source, dissemination, collection, organization, storage, retrieval, interpretation and use. Is related to or is derived from mathematics, logic, linguistics, psychology, computer technology, operational research, graphic arts, communications, library science, management and other fields of knowledge (Shera & Cleveland, 1977). Due to its complex nature, there has been research and debate on its origins and founders, about their theories. Pinheiro and Loureiro (1995) claim that this science promoted [...] *discussions and debates and continuing its scientific status and autonomy, passing through the object of study, information, terminology problems, to reach the interdisciplinary connections.* Borko (1968) presents information science as an interdisciplinary science derived from and related to various scientific fields. This feature has been reaffirmed as an element of the definition of information science in different geographic locations, by different authors.

In Germany, Wersig and Neveling (1975) defended the interdisciplinary nature of information science, as part of its social responsibility and, years later, as a feature of their nature of postmodern science (Wersig, 1993). Le Coadic (2004) was one of the defenders of the identification of information science, as an "interdisciplinary" science. McGarry (1999) identifies various interfaces of information science based on different aspects of the phenomenon of information component. The discussion also appeared in other contexts, such as the Chinese, as can be seen in the work of Yuexião (1988) on the coordination of different levels of problems studied by several researchers of information science. There is a general consensus among researchers on various interdisciplinary areas and the way it manifests itself.

A group of researchers argues that interdisciplinary of information science is of its own nature. Silva (1999) and justifies the interdisciplinary of information science, taking into account two factors: the first and most important is that [...] *the problems addressed by information science cannot be solved with approaches and constructions of any single discipline - so interdisciplinary is predetermined, as in many modern fields.* Rees and Smith (an unpublished article in 1967 quoted by Shera, 1980) argue that information science is a branch of research that uses the content, methods and techniques of various sciences to arrive at an understanding of information, behavior and movement properties and the second factor is that [...] *interdisciplinary of information science has been introduced and is being perpetuated by differences by many researchers addressing the problems described* (Silva, 1999). Furthermore, he notes that in information science are changing relations with the various sciences that interdisciplinary evolution is far from complete. Rubin (2010) argues that [...] *the boundaries of librarianship and information science continue to expand, the issues proliferate and grow in complexity and the challenges we face are serious and relentless.*

According to Foskett (1980) information science is a discipline: [...] *that arises from a "cross-fertilization*" of ideas that include the ancient art of librarianship, the new art of computing, the arts of new media and sciences such as psychology and linguistics, which in its modern forms, are directly related to all communication problems - the transfer of organized thought. Bates (2007) considers the science of specified a meta-discipline, since all academic science research can be found somewhere in a spectrum ranging from the arts, through the human social sciences, business, behavioral sciences and natural sciences and mathematics. According to Bates, the three Meta disciplines are education, communication / journalism and information. The first is related to aspects of learning all the sciences.

The second is with the transmission of knowledge and the third with the collection, organization, retrieval and presentation of information in all fields. Rubin (2010 reiterates this thought by saying that the information science does not belong to any of the fields of arts, humanities social sciences, business, computing, behavioral sciences, natural sciences or mathematics, *information science can be orthogonal to the conventional sciences.* Interdisciplinary the terms and relationship were used as general terms to indicate the interaction / relationship with other areas of knowledge without trying to indicate the degree of complexity of interaction / relationship's concept of interdisciplinary involves the notion of interaction between the sciences and or knowledge area that can occur at different levels of complexity. The following figure summarizes the interactions between information science and other sciences.

Table 1.

Areas of Knowledge	Interaction / Relationship / Objective	Areas of Knowledge	Interaction / Relationship / Objective
Business	Reduction of uncertainty / risk economic value Control and Decision Support in Product of Food Science	Education Knowledge	Storage knowledge transfer learning
Cognitive Sciences	Feeds knowledge Knowledge Organization Accumulation of knowledge Transfer of knowledge	Communication Sciences	News Description of the news Message disclosure
Political Science	Sources power Public information Communication / Disséмination	Exact Sciences	Data simulation forecast models
Health Sciences	Element diagnostic support Support in decision making Therapeutic monitoring	Sciences Law	Law Rights and Duties decision communication
Sciences: Linguistics, Literature and Art	Supplies (objects, events) Knowledge representation disclosure	Science Communication Ethics	Well evil correct wrong
Computer Science	Collection (data) Storage (data) Transmission (data) Recovery (access)		

Information Science has imported different knowledge from other sciences and so was considered by some authors as an interdisciplinary science. The interdisciplinary approach is valuable for innovation and for the theoretical development. Information Science is a social science inters multi and trans disciplinary who cares about the principles and practices of creation, organization and dissemination / distribution of information and its flows, using multiple forms of spread and multiple channels to solve the information problems. This reflection seeks to contribute to demonstrate the interdisciplinary of information science, as its own object of study points to the importance of a character able to see which areas of knowledge that actually interact with it and justify the inclusion of these areas knowledge of the composition of the main core of information science.

REFERENCES

Alsina, M. R. (1992). La construcción de la noticia. In Ed. Rev. Ampl. Barcelona: Paidós.

Barreto, A. A. (1997). As tecnologias intensivas de informação e comunicação e o reposicionamento dos atores do setor. *Info*, 97.

Bateson, G. (1987). Steps to Ecology of Mind. London: Ballantine.

Berger, P., & Luckmann, T. (1985). *A construção social da realidade: tratado de sociologia do conhecimento*. Petrópolis: Vozes.

Boisot, M. H. (1998). *Knowledge Assets: Securing Competitive Advantage in the Information Economy*. Oxford University Press.

Boland, R. J. (1987). The In-formation of Information Systems. Academic Press.

Borko, H. (1968). Information science: What is this? *American Documentation*, *19*(1), 3–5. doi:10.1002/asi.5090190103

Bourdieu, P. (1983). Esboço de uma teoria da prática. In R. Ortiz (Ed.), *Pierre Bourdieu: sociologia* (pp. 46–81). São Paulo: Ática.

Bronowski, J. (1977). O senso comum da ciência. In *Belo Horizonte*. São Paulo: Editora da USP.

Buckland, M. (1991). Information as a thing. *JASIS*, *42*(5), 351–360. doi:

Capurro, R. (1996). *On the genealogy of information. First published in: Information. New questions to a multidisciplinary concept*. Akademie V. Retrieved from http://www.capurro.de/cottinf.htm

Capurro, R., & Hjorland, B. (2003). The concept of information. In B. Cronin (Ed.), Annual Review of Information Science and Technology (Vol. 37, pp. 343–411). Academic Press.

Capurro, R., & Hjorland, B. (2007). O conceito de informação, Perspectivas em Ciência da Informação. *Belo Horizonte, 12*(1). Retrieved from http://www. eci.ufmg.br/pcionline/index.php/pci/article/ viewFile/54/47

Cardoso, A. M. P. (1996). Pós-Modernidade e informação: Conceitos complementares? *Perspectivas em Ciência da Informação, Belo Horizonte*, *1*(1), 63–79.

Choo, C. W. (2003). *A organização do conhecimento: como as organizações usam a informação para criar conhecimento, construir conhecimento e tomar decisões*. São Paulo: SENAC.

Classificação Decimal Universal. (1997). Edição padrão internacional em língua portuguesa. Brasília: IBICT.

Correia, M. (1995). O léxico na economia da língua. *Ciência da Informação, Brasília*, *24*(3), 299–307.

Dahlberg, I. (1978). Teoria do conceito. *Ciência da Informação, 7*(2), 101-107.

Davenport, T. H., & Prusak, L. (1998). *Working Knowledge*. Boston: Harvard Business School Press.

Davenport, T. H., & Prusak, L. (2001). *Ecologia da informação*. São Paulo: Futura.

Dias, E. J. W. (2002). O específico da ciência da informação. In *O campo da ciência da informação: gênese, conexões e especificidades* (pp. 87–99). João Pessoa: Editora Universitária.

Douglas, M. (1986). *How Institutions Think*. London: Routledge.

Dowbor, L. (2010). *Informação para a cidadania e o desenvolvimento sustentável*. Retrieved from http://dowbor.org/09propriedadeintelectual7out.doc

Drucker, P. (1969). The Pratice of Management. Pan Books, Ltd.

Drucker, P. (2000). Management Challenges for the 21 st Century. Edição Portuguesa da Livraria Civilização Editora.

Dubois, J. (1973). *Dicionário de lingüistica*. São Paulo: Cultrix.

Ercilia, S.M. (2000). Artigo aceito para publicação em 24-10-2000. *Ci. Inf., 29*(3), 50-70.

Figueiredo, L.M. (1977). O conceito de relevância e suas implicações. *Ciência da Informação, 6*(2), 75-78.

Figueiredo, N. M. (1994). *Estudos de uso e usuários da informação*. Brasília: IBICT.

Fonseca, E. N. (1987). Ciência da Informação e prática bibliotecária. *Ciência da Informação, Brasília, 16*(2), 25–127.

Fontcuberta, M. (1993). *La noticia*. Barcelona: Paidós.

Foucault, M. (1997). *As palavras e as coisas*. São Paulo: Martins Fontes.

Foucault, M. (1997). *A arqueologia do saber*. Rio de Janeiro: Forense.

Gómez, M. N. G. (2000). Metodología de pesquisa no campo da Ciencia da informação. *DataGrama-Zero, 1*(6).

Hjelmslev, L. (1961). *Prolegômenos a uma teoria da linguagem*. São Paulo: Perspectiva.

Ingwersen, P. (1992). Information and information science in context. *Libri, 42*(2), 99–135. doi:10.1515/libr.1992.42.2.99

Jamil, G., & Armando Malheiro. (2013). *Rethinking the Conceptual Base for New Practical Applications in Information Value and Quality*. IGI Global.

Lage, N. (1999). *Linguagem Jornalística*. São Paulo: Ática.

Lage, N. (2005). *A Reportagem: teoria e técnica de entrevista e pesquisa jornalística*. Rio de Janeiro: Record.

Landowski, E. (1992). *A sociedade refl etida*. São Paulo: EDUC/Pontes.

Le Coadic, Y.-F. (1997), La science de l'information (2nd ed.). Paris: Universitaires de France.

Le Coadic, Y. F. (1998). *Le besoin d'information*. Paris: ADBS Editions.

Martín-Barbero, J. (2009). La educación desde la comunicación. *Eduteka*. Retrieved from http://www.eduteka.org/pdfdir/SaberNarrar.pdf

Meadows, J. (1990). Science de l'information. *Brises, l6*.

Meadows, J. (1991). Science de l'information. *Brises, 16*(1), 9-13.

Mikhailov, A. I. (1980). Estrutura e principais propriedades da informação científica. In Ciência da informação ou informática? Rio de Janeiro: Calunga.

Moles, A. A. (1974). *Sociodinâmica da cultura*. São Paulo: Perspectiva.

Mostafa, S.P. (1996). Ciência da informação: uma ciência, uma revista. *Ciência da Informação, 25*(3).

Müeller, S. P. M. (1985). O ensino de biblioteconomia no Brasil. *Ciência da Informação, 14*(1), 3–15.

Muñoz Torres, J. R. (1997). Aproximación al concepto de Información Periodística Especializada. In *Estudios sobre información periodística especializada*. Valencia: Fundación Universitaria San Pablo C.E.U.

Murteira, Mendes, & Martins. (2001). *Serviços Informacionais e transição para a economia do conhecimento em Portugal*. IDEG/ISCTE, estudo realizado para o GEPE do Ministério da Economia.

Nakayama, H. (1986). Tradução e adaptação de tesauros. *Ciência daInformação, 15*(1), 5-25.

Nonaka, I., & Takeuchi, H. (1997). *Criação de conhecimento na empresa: como as empresas japonesas geram a dinâmica da inovação*. Rio de Janeiro: Campus.

Park, R. E. (2008a). A história natural do jornal. In A era glacial do jornalismo: teorias sociais da imprensa (vol. 2). Porto Alegre: Sulina.

Park, R. E. (2008b). A notícia como forma de conhecimento: um capítulo dentro da sociologia do conhecimento. In *A era glacial do jornalismo: teorias sociais da imprensa* (Vol. 2, pp. 51–70). Porto Alegre: Sulina.

Pinheiro, L., & Loureiro, J. (1995). Traçados e limites da ciência da informação. *Ciência da informação, 24*(1).

Porter, M. (1985). *Competitive Advantage: Creating and Sustaining Superior Performance*. New York: The Free Press.

Prusak, L., & McGee, J. (1994). *Gerenciamento estratégico da informação*. Rio de Janeiro: Campus.

Quesada Pérez, M. (1998). *Periodismo Especializado*. Madrid: Ediciones Internacionales Universitárias.

Rascão, J. (2012). Novas Realidades na Gestão e na Gestão da Informação. Sílabo, Lda.

Saracevic, T. (1992). Information Science: origin, evolution and relations. In *Conceptions of library and information science. Proceedings of the international conference for the celebration of 20th anniversary of the Departament os Information Studies*. University of Tampere.

Schumpeter, J. A. (1934). *The Theory of Economic Development*. Cambridge, MA: Harvard University Press.

Shannon, C.E. (1948). A mathematical theory of communication. *Bell System Technical Journal, 27*, 379-423, 623-656.

Shannon, C. E., & Weaver, W. (1949). *A mathematical theory of communication*. Chicago: University of Illinois Press.

Shera, J. (1997). Epistemologia social, semântica geral e biblioteconomia. *Ciência da Informação, 6*(1), 9-12.

Sousa, J. P. (2002). Teorias da notícia e do jornalismo. Chapecó. *Argos*.

Stewart, T. A. (1988). *Intellectual Capital: The New Wealth of Organizations, Currency. Stigler, Memoirs of an Unregulated Economist*. New York: Basic Books.

Traquina, N. (1993). As Notícias. Jornalismo: Questões, Teorias e "Estórias", 167-176.

Wersig, G. (1993). Information science: The study of postmodern knowledge usage. *Information Processing & Management, 29*(2), 229–239. doi:10.1016/0306-4573(93)90006-Y

Zikmund, W. G. (2000). *"Bussiness" Research Methods* (6th ed.). Dryden Press Harcourt College Publishers.

Zorrinho. (2004). *Aula aberta*. Escola Superior de Ciências Empresariais do Instituto Politécnico de Setúbal.

Chapter 11
The Information: A Science, an Industry

José Poças Rascão
Polytechnic Institute of Setúbal, Portugal

ABSTRACT

The purpose of this chapter is to contribute to a reflection on the emergence and evolution of information science, taking into consideration the context in which it is inserted. The information and knowledge society requires a science that studies the properties of information and the processes of its construction, communication, and use, based on the aggregation of existing literature. This chapter is a descriptive research, with the goal of identifying and characterizing the properties of information as an object of study of information sciences and the processes of its use as an industry. The structure of the chapter synthesizes the existing academic work, seeking to generate new knowledge. The results can be used to integrate the properties of the information in the different properties and/or areas of knowledge. The chapter seeks to firstly identify the properties and the apparent processes and then focuses in greater detail on some of them.

INTRODUCTION

The current society is living a time in which the stage of development can be described as modern, but it took a character so large, unexpected and complex enough to the point of distinguishing itself from modernity, overtaking it, for what we could call postmodern.

According to Santos (1986) and Harvey (1992), featuring the current society is, *roughly speaking*, the narcissism of the people, the superficiality, recovery of appearances at the expense of the essences, the high technological sophistication, the instantaneous and integrated communication (sound, image, text), usually transmitted via internet and captured on screens (lowercase or, on the contrary, enormous) of liquid crystal, the hyper-realism, i.e., data transformation and processing of the artistic achievements up to then and many others.

DOI: 10.4018/978-1-5225-3725-0.ch011

However, the great mark of this strange and stunning time is the fragmentation of everything and everyone. If modern man *"stresses"* faced with multiple activities in which unfolds almost to infinity, the post modernity disrupts the human being by means of an internal Division, often schizophrenic, in multiple subjectivities and identities.

Man has forgotten history, he eventually denies it, and his main concern is centered solely on the material aspects of existence attachment to the pleasures of the senses, extolling the present moment in a way almost infantile and pressurizing everything and dispersing him by a thousand possibilities and expending the best human energies.

It is in human, political and socio-cultural environment, in everything *"hyper and Hypo"*, confused and indefinite, that Information Science, endowed for the meantime with scarce theoretical resources and conceptualizations about its own identity and affirmation, is called to intervene and to forward the issues that are not a glitch, such as production, storage, organization and circulation of knowledge (the information feeds the knowledge).

The proposed work is to provide a reflection on the emergence and evolution of information science, taking into consideration the context in which it is inserted. To understand an area or topic is necessary at first, knowledge of its origins and its history. So, it presented first a little history of the evolution of science information and its development over the past decades.

The consolidation of a particular field of knowledge is, among other things, the existence of a scientific community. This in turn is composed of a number of researchers and scientists concerned to discuss and solve the problems that arise in the area. Thus the existence of a shared paradigm by members of a community will result in consolidation of the scientific community.

THE ORIGIN OF INFORMATION SCIENCE

It is difficult to point the emergence of a new science even in the case of a recent scientific discipline such as information science. However, Foskett (1969) and Ingwersen (1992) indicate the date of 1958 as one of the landmarks in the formalization of the new discipline when it was founded in the United Kingdom the *Institute of Information Scientists* (IIS). To Meadows (1990) describes the origin of the new discipline from the specialized libraries (in industrial and other organizations).

According to Meadows (1990) discipline has undergone a sharp development after World War II due to the emergence of the mathematical theory of Information described by Shannon and Weaver in the late 40. This theory was adopted by many other areas, because it explains the problems of transmission of messages through mechanical communication channels. The industrialization of commercial press promoted literature phenomenon explosion not less important than the advent of the Gutenberg press occurred about1450, whose effects were more evident after the Second World War.

Its contribution to the development of information science was small but important to the history of the area, since they attracted attention for two needs. First to clearly define the nature of the information with which the professionals of the area concerned and, second, to set the framework to be applied in the Organization of that type of information. According to (Days, 2002), that is the consensus of the authors of the area that the information science emerged in the mid-20th century.

According to Pinheiro & Lena (1995) Norbert Wiener in 1948, in its book "*Cybernetics or control and communication in the animal and machine*", and Claude Shannon and Warren Weaver in 1949, in the book "*The mathematical theory of communication*", marked the beginning of what would become the information science. According to the authors, is in the 60 that are drawn the first concepts and definitions and, if starts the debate on the origin and the theoretical foundations of the new field of knowledge (Pinheiro & Loureiro, 1995, p. 42). The authors point out several facts in the 60s which meant the true mark of the formation of a new disciplinary field:

- The Conference held at the *Georgia Institute of Technology* in 1962,
- The *Weinberg* Report in 1963,
- The Computer work, Mikhailov, in 1966,
- The study of Rees and Saracevic in 1967 and,
- The definition of Borko, *in Information Science: what is it?,* in 1968.

Borko (1968) defined the information science as a discipline that investigates the properties and behavior of the information, the forces that govern the flow and it's processing to optimize its accessibility and use. It relates to the body of knowledge pertaining to production, collection, compilation, storage, retrieval, interpretation, transmission, processing and use of the information. This includes the investigation of information representation in natural and artificial systems (...). It has a component of pure science that investigates the essence of the subject without regard to your application and another component of applied science that develops services and products (...).

For Goffman (1970) the objective of information science is to establish a unified scientific approach to study the various phenomena that involve the notion of information, if such features are found in biological processes in human existence or on machines created by humans. Consequently, the subject must be related to the establishment of a set of fundamental principles that govern the behavior of the whole process of communication and their associated information systems.

Griffith (1980) proposed similar definition that establishes the information science as a discipline that aims the creation and structuring of a body of scientific, technological and systemic knowledge related to the transfer of information.

Saracevic (1991) studied the evolution of the information science and defined it as "a field dedicated to scientific and professional practice issues, focused on the problems of effective knowledge communication and record-keeping of knowledge among human beings, the social context, institutional or individual use and information needs. The treatment of these issues is considered of particular interest the advantages of modern information and communication technologies (ICT's)".

The information science was born after World War II, to solve a big problem, which was also the major concern of both the Documentation and the Information Retrieval which is to gather, organize and make accessible the cultural, scientific and technological knowledge produced in the world.

The science of information is a recent science and was born from the exact sciences that are looking to achieve an exact knowledge from the inspiration of mathematical and quantitative models. (Bronowski, 1977, p. 47), based on objectivity sought to formulate universal laws of the "behavior" of information. Strongly influenced by the empirical Sciences intended to establish universal laws that represent the informational phenomenon and hence the need for resorting to mathematical models (information theory), physical (Entropy) or biological (epidemiological theory).

According to Cardoso, (1996, pp. 73-74), in the Decade of 70, comes into play a character that redirects the focus of information science: "the man (decision-makers) and as such the humanities and Social Sciences also contributing with their methods and practices, to the composition of this emerging science". Initially they were close to computation and automatic recovery of information, according to González de Gomez, (2000, pp. 2-6), from the years 1970, makes your effective inscription in the social sciences, as a "symptom of the ongoing changes that would affect the production and direction of knowledge in the West".

It is from this decade that we can refer to the "social foundations of information". However, there are some important issues we face now, to which branch of science the information science is closest? What are the theories, concepts and methods that feed the information science?

The first studies in information science as a social science were to study the social reality in Statistics perspectives, i.e. quantitative. Berger & Luckmann (1985) presented the reality as something that is socially constructed rather than as an existence in itself and open the way to the understanding of information not as a given, something that would have meaning and importance in *itself*, but as a process.

That is, something that will be perceived and understood in various ways by people, that according to the definition of Borko (1968) about the behavior and information flows, is something that is out of the people and with the definition of Buckland (1991) who sees the information as a "thing" outside people.

The subjectivity of the information becomes critical to the understanding of the different planes of reality and of the distinction between the different forms of knowledge and the mechanisms of your configuration and legitimating. People need to be included in information studies and in their day-to-day interactions, forms of expression and language, rites and social processes.

Several studies can be presented as an example of the incorporation of these concepts in the context of the study of information science, such as, the *dosensemaking* approach inaugurated by Durbin, Atwood & Palmour, MacMullin studies & Taylor on the values of the people, the studies of cognitive theory-inspired nature of Maturana & Varela of the hermeneutic approach of information science, studies of Capurro (2003) on the information networks based on the theoretical framework of Bourdieu (1983. p. 46-81) as well as the Bibliometric studies and scientific communication and contributions of Archeology of knowledge of Foucault and the Sociology of Science (Latour, Knorr-Cetina, among others).

The information science is a discipline that has a fairly broad field of practices but not yet a theoretical field defined as is the case with other areas of knowledge such as linguistics, anthropology and other. Not here yet to a theoretical construction that integrates all your concepts and practices.

It therefore operates on the basis of theoretical constructions more or less fragmented, for example, the representation of the information would be a construct, among others etc. The most important feature of information science is the interdisciplinary nature in your that the magnitude of the problems faced (ecological, demographic and ethnic) is demanding innovative solutions.

The science of information comes from consolidating elements "borrowed" among others, in mathematics, physics, biology, psychology, sociology, anthropology, the semi logy and by the communication theory and other sciences that contributed to its rationality and applicability (Cardoso, 1996, p. 74). *"Information science is not to be looked at as a classical discipline, but as the prototype of the new kind of science" (Wersig, 1993, p. 235).*

The information science evolves to new stages of dialogue and inclusion in the social sciences. Reflection on the development of information science, its relations with the social sciences and as a model of science as a whole, it is essential to continue research and incorporating all the knowledge accumulated in this process.

Being scientific research one of the main ways to formulate theories of an area, what is realized is that research in information science comes over the past few decades, consolidating and opening new horizons of discussions. Great contribution has been given by teachers and researchers in the various international universities.

Can be seen that some important steps have been taken in order to strengthen the theory of information science area and that research in information science are expanding and have a scientific community that over the years has been consolidating internationally. Are many and different challenges that present themselves today, for information science.

As applied science, needs to respond to the demand for information and society, while research object, conceptual fundamental needs of the area. The realization and sociability are the safest paths for creating and sharing new paradigms. Thus, it becomes increasingly important to look for the theoretical foundation, social and philosophical in the field of information science and in particular further strengthen its scientific community.

THE SCIENCE OF INFORMATION

The science of information has become a rigorous social science that relies on rigorous techniques and aims to study the general properties of information (nature, Genesis and effects), namely:

- The analysis of production processes, communication and use of information;
- The design of products and systems that enable your production, communications, storage and use;

Production of Information

It is form the scientific and technical activities that arise from scientific and technical knowledge that will become, after registered, on scientific and technical information. But in reverse these activities there and come true, by this information. The information is "the blood" of science. Without information, science develops and lives. No research information would be useless and there would be no knowledge.

Information is a precious fluid, continuously produced and renovated and only matter if it circulates, and above all, if it circulates freely. The research activity consists in applying reasoning to the body of knowledge accumulated over time and stored in libraries (paper or electronic/digital) and documentation centers. The processing of that knowledge becomes possible after entering into circulation, which is at the origin of scientific discoveries and technological innovations.

The Growth of Information

Research activities have never had neither the accuracy nor the extension they have nowadays. At the beginning the investigation was purely speculative; science had no vocation to serve some technical development. To become its experimental vocation became produce knowledge to satisfy economic needs and practices. Likewise it interests rulers and, the managers of the organizations that for half a century have appropriated the researchers ' profession of faith: "what's good for science is good for society."

The world reality is evolving faster than the ability of scientific demonstration is able to systematize your understanding. In the center of the globalization's technological development with respect for Weber (1864-1920) and by force of certain ideologies, it must be recognized that when Adam Smith (1968) (Division of labor) or Marx (productive forces) put the evolution of the techniques as the engine of social change, were strictly certain.

The system of production of knowledge integrated in economic and social development with the production system. Industrialization goes through science and science goes through industrialization.

Quantitative Models of Growth

In industrial society the *crude* oil constituted an important source of energy used to move the engines and feed factories. But before the chemical energy of the oil could be triggered, the *oil* had to be refined, i.e. in usable forms, such as gasoline and heating fuel. Similarly, the information is the source of energy that propels the "*engines*" of the information and knowledge society, but so we can use we need to convert into a usable form: the knowledge.

But when we refine the information to turn it into knowledge quality weighs more than the quantity. When we convert information into knowledge we add value and make it more expensive.

During the last years, in most Western countries it has been seen that the industrial sector, responsible in large measure for the wealth they have accumulated since the 19th century, is losing weight in gross domestic product (GDP) compared to the services sector, a result of the transformation of industrial society, in informational society (Moore, 1997) for reasons:

- Organizations increasingly depend on the intelligent use of information and turning in information-intensive organizations;
- People in their everyday actions consume large quantities of information in terms of leisure activities both in terms of business;
- Is emerging to covert information industry within the diversity of the service sector, as an entity to be a sector (maybe the best) of major economic sectors (primary, secondary and tertiary sector). The industry may consist of three sectors:
    - The information content,
    - The information distribution (access centers and distribution channels, such as telecommunications operators and the Internet);
    - The information processing (information technologies)

The transformation of organizations in intensive informational is perhaps the clearest change detonating to informational society. The analysis of the most successful organizations in the world seems to indicate that this originated in the better management of information and knowledge about the global and immediate surroundings, that is, those who were able to detect better the needs of the market and where better adapted in terms of setting, methods, processes and cultural forms that have made it possible to combine the information with the generated internally to generate distinctive competitive advantages (Porter, 1998).

Quality Characteristics of Growth

The quantitative feature gives us a picture of the progress of the sciences and techniques. This growth differs according to the disciplines, regions of the world and time. It is not because two countries or two disciplines produce the same number of articles that have the same State of "health". The discontinuity in growth is a result of the objectives of the decision makers, since sometimes there is more emphasis on one or another discipline: now to theory, now to experimentation.

The high growth of knowledge and information allows to understand which the place science and technology occupy in the hierarchy of social factors:

- Technological development-which overtook the domains accessible to our organs of the senses and that no one would have thought the overtaking arrived to that point;
- The map of science and scientific subjects underwent deep changes. Ancient disciplines broadened and widened the scope of their activity; mergers between disciplines giving rise to new inter-disciplines.
- Emergence of new products, production processes, activities and businesses that are based on scientific and technical progress.

Actors in the Production

The scientific community is a social group formed by people whose profession to scientific and technological research of your social condition and unbound material, related to each other by concern for the truth and is abstract to exchange ideas.

There are real scientific communities, segmented according to subjects, languages, Nations and even political ideologies, motivated by a strong spirit of competition, where the investigator who wins is the one who first publishes the information.

The scientific communities work as primitive communities, through the donation system. The investigator transfers free of charge for his scientific community the information he holds, not expecting in return any economic contribution. But that donation can only exist if the scientific communities provide for him the consideration which is the confirmation of the individual as a scientist. First there is recognition by the community, interpersonal after institutional confirmation which is recognized by the volume of original publications.

The Institutions

The members of the scientific communities work in social and economic institutions, such as, academies, scientific societies, associations of researchers, laboratories and universities. Five stages surveyed this institutionalization:

- **The Isolated Scientist:** Development of scientific activities without institutional support;
- **The Scientific Amateur:** Attempts to collective work by peers and disciples;
- **The Academic Science**: The academies have enabled experts from natural sciences, devote themselves fully to their work (universities provide it specialists of social sciences);
- **Organized Science:** Provides the Foundation for a program of research development and research training. Is the current model best known;
- The big science is characterized by the dimensions of the laboratories, size of budgets for research, the complexity of the equipment and the importance of national or international professional community that works.

THE COMMUNICATION OF INFORMATION

The scientific communities are essentially networks of organizations and formal and informal social relations which perform several functions, among them; one is dominant that is communication. It allows communication to ensure the exchange of information on work in progress, putting scientists in touch with each other.

The motivations of researchers are of two types:

- Scientific-if science progresses is thanks to the work carried out by scientists about related problems; researchers need to stay in touch with colleagues to inform and inform them about the work in progress or completed;
- Of a personal nature which is related to the professional career of the persons concerned.

Communication Practices

According to Yves-François Le Coadic (1994) the practice of communication is an important part of the time taken by the investigator. For example, in some Sciences, such as the physical sciences are assessed in 40% of the time of work of researchers is spent in communication activity: reading, writing, contacts.

Communication Processes

In terms of communication processes the researchers use two processes: a written, formal and other oral, informal.

- The written communication (formal) comprises the primary publications, where they occur for the first time to the public, in the form of the product information, the results of research and the secondary and tertiary publications, primary dependent once they summarize and index them;

According to Yves-François Le Coadic (1994) the written communication was born more than 300 years ago, due to the need for communication of research results between researchers, whose number grew. Communication is the main characteristic of scientific production, since it will allow the recognition of peer and investigator will ensure success in the scientific community to which it belongs.

Oral communication (informal) consists of public forms, such as congresses, conferences, symposiums, seminars, etc. and private ways, as for example, conversations, letters, etc., of distribution of information. This means of communication of information, do not have the same stability of formal means of communication.

The exchange of information between two investigators during a conversation consists of a survey of something, with the risk of be modified immediately, while in the notification the investigator is bound by a code of ethics to publish the information only once in a single article.

The difference between the processes of formal communication (written) and informal (oral) the information relates to the audience, to storage, to actuality and authenticity, orientation, redundancy and interactivity.

Table 1. Differences of communication of information

Formal (Written)	Informal Process (Oral)
Public (audience attendance important)	Private (audience restricted)
Information stored on a permanent basis and recoverable	Information not stored and non-recoverable
Information passed (historic)	Recent information
Proven information	Unproven information
Uniform dissemination	Flow direction chosen by the producer
Moderate redundancy	Redundancy sometimes very important
Absence of direct interaction	Direct interaction

Source: adapted from Yves-François Le Coadic (1994), La Science de l'information, Presses Universitaires de France, Paris

The two serve different purposes regarding to the work of researchers and the functioning of the information system, both being essential, but used in different times, whose chronology of events can be seen in Figure 1.

INFORMATION TECHNIQUES

Before 1948

It can be said that until the 1950 technical system deployed in the information sector was supported in the paper and in the book. The production, communication and oral use of information appealed to an

Figure 1. Chronology of communication processes
Garvey, W. D., (1979), Communication: the essence of science, Oxford, Pergamon Press

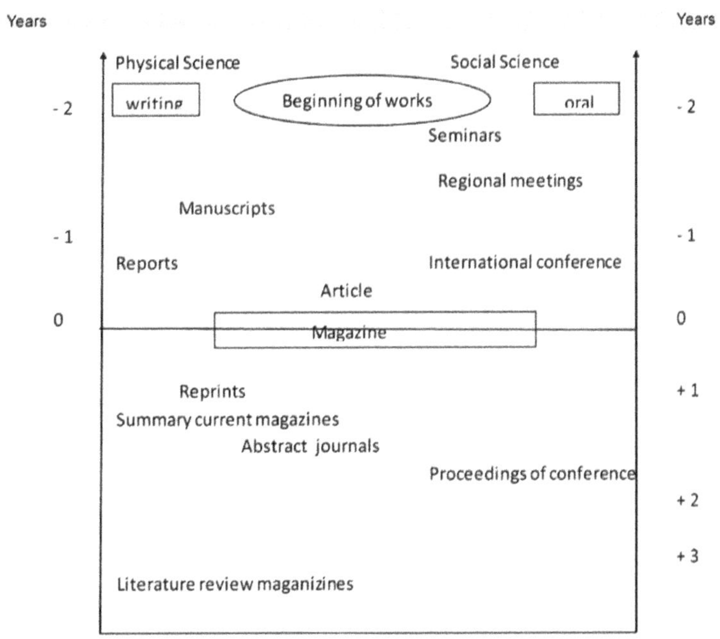

instrument, the writing, with the materialization of a support material, of which the most widespread is the paper. Books and collections of books are print volumes that contain a number of fairly large pages and that do not appear on a regular basis like magazines. They are objects of study in a perspective not informational. It was through the bibliopoly that tried to establish a connection with the content.

After 1948

The year 1948 was the year of the discovery of the transistor and the development of the first immaterial information holders, which caused a big change in Western civilization, which tends to replace the techniques of information production techniques: "the major technical changes that marked the second half of the 20th century due to the advances of information and communication technologies, techniques that indicate a step further, towards dematerialization "(Yves-François Le Coadic, 1994),

Traditional Techniques of Information

The book and the journal, made of paper, deserve to be studied, because they were the preferred means of communication of information. It presents a summary of the main techniques:

- Writing technique-scientific magazine from your creation remained virtually unchanged. According to John Ziman (1974), "the General form of a scientific paper has changed least in almost 300 years than all other forms of literature, with the exception of the light comedy". However, Bernal (1967), related to the development of new methods of communication of information.

According to Garvey, w. d., (1979), a revised paper is an ordered set, formalized and made public. The ordered set of articles is a basic unit of information process that is selected according to your scientific merit: what does it mean that the works presented were conducted and their results correspond to a breakthrough, i.e. enhance previous results and open new perspectives. The selection is made by editorial committees or drafting, that are not only cognitive but also social filters.

The magazine only publishes the formalized set of articles that have been reviewed and that can be found and cited without ambiguity. Hence the impressive unity of form and aspect used that feature articles, resorting increasingly to the language (English) which implies a clear advantage and the minimization of the cultural difficulties of communication. The target audience is the entire scientific community that submits an article with a view to your publication.

- Oral technique-the Conference, conferences, meetings, symposia, etc., are infrequent meetings, on average once a year, and of a limited duration (two to three days) of researchers in a particular field of knowledge, in order to discuss a theme set by the organizers (Tapia, c., 1980).

These events are summoned by a scientific community and develop in a simple way, switching communications with informal exchanges in committees and in the hallways. It is an opportunity for researchers will be able to exchange information with peers, but is also an opportunity to present a communication that will be made later in the annals of publishing event.

Electronic and Digital Techniques

Since the input-output devices (transmitter-receiver) that are the terminals, the transmission devices are physical lines or radio waves, through storage and processing devices that are computers, electronic techniques have in common the fact of sending, receiving, transmitting and storing or processing electrical signals (physical components), that is, streams of electrons or optical signals (streams of photons). Are the main techniques:

- Evolution since 1948:
  - **The Electronics Electricity:** From the emergence of the transistor electronics had a remarkable development of your performance;
  - Copper wire to fiber optics-jump accompanied by the evolution of the capabilities of cable networks and microwave;
  - **The Analog to Digital:** Increasing scanning techniques. All formal information can be coded, stored, processed and transmitted by the same processes and the same networks (Mercier, p. a., Plassard, v. Scardigli, (1984).
  - **Of the Electromagnetic Optoelectronic:** Until recently the magnetic support of information/data provided solutions for storage and processing. Optoelectronics technology today allows a higher density of data/information at least 10 times higher than the best performances of magnetic techniques.

Electronic techniques are the result of a merger of three technical pillars-information technology, communications and electronic media.

A sign is an electrical or optical magnitude that varies the pace of data transmitted and is connected to the sign (language element that associates a significant a meaning) by means of a code. The signs (set of data) are converted to signals by a transducer that can be a microphone, keyboard, camera or sensor.

The signal initially was analog and its variations were in function of time, being continuous and reproducing the form of a physical quantity, such as the sound. If your frequency is measured in cycles per second, in hertz. More and more digital and vary discontinuously in function of time and can only have a finite number of values. The sign used can only have two values (bit-on or off), each representing an alternative or all or nothing.

In text encoding, the characters transmitted correspond to the various symbols of the alphabet (uppercase and lowercase), the decimal numbers, signs of arithmetic and logical operations and the score. The encoding corresponds to assign to each of these characters a binary number given, whose number of bits depends on the code used. The signal transmission speed is expressed in bits per second.

Generic Techniques

The input-output devices (terminals) are electronic and optical equipment that allow the exchange of electrical or optical signals with the computer. These terminals are connected to the computer through transmission devices. The entry of the signals is usually done through a keyboard like the traditional typewriters – can also be done by voice recognition or written text. Output devices – reception of signals is done by means of paper and printing or displaying a monochrome cathode-ray screen or color.

The different devices mentioned above are controlled by a centralized management protocol, implemented in the microprocessor and controls proper development of operations at the time, ensures the transfer of signals between the different terminal devices and coordinates transmissions between the terminal and the server computer.

The transmission devices are networks – set of communications media, true multiple infrastructure purposes identify the characteristics of transmission:

- **Mode of Transmission:** Direction of transmission (serial or parallel, synchronous or asynchronous);
- **Electronic Network Architecture:** Layers and protocols;
- **Physical Configuration:** (Topology Star, tree, ring, mesh).

The means of transmission are the rows (pairs of wires, coaxial cables, microwave, and optical fibers) which are a mixture of physical lines and airwaves.

Switching devices enable routing and control your transmissions through network nodes. Interconnection devices (modem-modulator-demodulator) interconnection devices are used to connect the terminal to the networks of transmission of signals that converts the digital signals sent by terminal keyboard or digital and analog signals.

Today there are numerous local networks (LAN) and (WAN) to packet-switched interconnect, forming a giant international network called the INTERNET (1983) that allows many computers to "talk" to each other. This connection allows access to many informational resources stored in them (computerized catalogues of libraries, bibliographic information, genetic numerical oceanographic, image, etc.), which will not stop to proliferate. To identify them and locate them using the information recovery programs, such as the World Wide Web (WWW).

Electronic Information Techniques of Today and Tomorrow

Nowadays, for example a documentation centre, library or Museum that are pro-step electronics coexist some of the following techniques:

- Analog-video, audio
- Prints-computer, terminals, network, scanner

Tomorrow in this center of documentation and or in this electronic library, digital techniques will supersede the analogue. At the end of this decade from our terminal (e.g. tablet) we can access the distance, to collections of a library or documentation centre electronic Museum that will offer consultation services and electronic information supply.

Storing selected information from various sources, users/customers will form "manuals". It may also have access to pieces of music and videos to capture and storage or immediate hearing. Has grow the practice of payment for the use of the information. These institutions will become hypermarkets.

Processing devices and storage of data (computer) are the essential technical components-microprocessor (chip) (small-scale integrated circuit that allows the storage, fast recovery and processing a huge amount of data), magnetic and optical discs and programs (software – set of instructions that control the computer tasks).

The interconnection of computers is made by means of networks that it allows building what some called the essential infrastructure of the information and knowledge society: the electronic auto information highways which transmit quickly large volume of texts, sounds and images from one location to another. From a technical point of view, this forecast is close to fruition, the same cannot be said with regard to the widespread and easy access to information, since until now gave more emphasis to technology than to information.

INFORMATION: A SCIENCE, AN INDUSTRY

A Science

All science is a social activity determined by historical and socio-economic conditions. So, it was with the science of nature, physics, with the development of industrial society. Physics was born with the advent of the commercial system. Some of its branches formed independent sciences, such as chemistry and biology. The industrial society had need of a production system that will allow increased use of nature. The development of this industrial production needed "a science that studies the physical properties of natural objects and forms of action of forces of nature" (Engels, 1820-1895).

Similarly, to the information and knowledge society requires a science that study the properties of information and the processes of your construction, communication and use under the triple influence of:

- Production and development of scientific and technical information needs, such as the development of scientific activities of a scientific and technical culture and demands for scientific information;
- Creation of an information industry (producers, electronic and digital storage, large museums and libraries, cultural tourism).
- Emergence of the industry of information and communication technologies that are becoming knowledge-based deposits.

The effect of these changes – cultural, economic and technological – has allowed information industry a high growth rate, compared with the other sectors/industries. Such changes have provoked an epistemological change simultaneously. This makes us see that the object of the science of information is not the same of librarianship and its revered sister disciplines. It is no longer a library, book, document, documentation centre, the Museum and the object, but rather the information.

The science of information putting its concern in solving a social problem and social oriented looking for information, in the field of the social sciences — Sciences of man and society, which are the primary means for access to an understanding of the social and cultural.

The research of information science has been developed based on social needs and was directed and financed by it. With the development of information and communication technologies the dominant concern of researchers has been the usefulness of technologies, the effectiveness in the decision-making process, the practical and the practice and very little theoretical, the theory.

This is late compared to the empirical and there is above all a lack of connection between the two. The science of information becomes a rigorous social science, under the effect of both a growing social demand as new social objectives and important economic advances. The scientific studies carried out in other areas of knowledge, such as psychology, sociology, economics, information and communication technologies, etc., have contributed to these scientific theories.

AN INDUSTRY

Resource

A resource is anything that can be thought of as strength or a weakness of an organization, so this gets a competitive advantage if it acquires or develops superior resources or a combination of superior resources "(Wernerfelt, 1985, in: Nelson António, 2003).

To Teece, Pisano and Shuen (1997) define how resources ' specific assets of a company that are difficult if not impossible to imitate ' (in: Nelson António, 2003). For your time Prahalad and Hamel (1990) define resource as a "nuclear powers".

A resource incorporates several strategic management skills as a way to explain how some organizations have performance superior to their competitors. This vision means organizations as a set of features and capabilities where the first task of management is to maximize the value of existing resources and capacities, while developing the resource base of the future (Grant 1991, p. 110).

The distinction between features and services, it's not your life, but the fact that the resources consist of a set of services and potential that can be set regardless of your usage, while the services cannot therefore be defined (Penrose, 1959 p. 25). The resources of an organization at any given time are those that are tangible or intangible assets and that are connected to the Organization as the capital, equipment, skills and knowledge of employees, the marks and the technological systems (Wernerfelt 1984, p. 172).

However, few resources are productive, but require cooperation and coordination together. This capacity of the set of features to perform some tasks or activities is referred to as a capacity. In order to make productive use of this set of resources, organizations acquire resources that are called market factors, such as the labor market or capital.

Strategic market factors are defined as those markets in which organizations acquire the resources needed to market its strategic products (Barney 1986, p. 1231). Organizations acquire resources such as market factors, work and develop capabilities that make use of these resources, in order to complete the products and services that are sold in one or more markets.

Economic Profitability

For the economy the need does it feel a certain lack the desire to be eliminated. The need is so the desire to have a means to prevent or to end an unpleasant feeling or to provoke, conserve or enhance a nice feeling (Sabaté, f. Tarragó, 1989).

The media that serve people to meet their needs are designated by economists like goods. A *well* is because, all that we recognize as able to satisfy a need, regardless of any other judgment (for example moral judgment). The goods can be classified in several ways. The first interest is that distinguishes the so-called free goods (ex: the air we breathe, the water) of economic goods. A *well* is economic one that is characterized by scarcity, i.e. you are one that exists in quantities less than those required, given the need felt (Sabaté, f. Tarragó, 1989).

The usefulness of a *good* refers to the quality and capacity of that good in satisfying the needs that are proper to that good. The usefulness of an asset is the ability of this *well* to meet the needs that are subjective sensations, it follows that the same *well* can have different use for different people, depending on the intensity with which these may experience or feel the needs that can be satisfied with this *well* (Sabaté, f. Tarragó, 1989).

Closely associated with the concept of utility is the concept of "*economic value*" of which we can say that it is the quality of everything that gives importance, because it is considered that deserves esteem. So, the value of a given well also depends on each person, since each can feel distinct appreciation for a really good (Sabaté, f. Tarragó, 1989).

The organizations are seeking the economic return through the sale of their products or services. In a competitive environment, an organization can achieve better performance than their competitors, because it has better features or because the Organization makes better use of their distinctive skills (Penrose, 1959 p. 54). A distinctive competency is defined as a distinguished qualification, complementary assets and routines of the organization which together allow the company to coordinate a specific set of activities that provide the basis for competitive advantage (Dosi and Teece, in: Williamson 1999, p. 1094).

Competitive advantage is referred to as economic profitability (Porter 1980). Subsequently the resource base sees the strategy as a continuous research of profitability. Profitability is then defined as the excess return of a resource that you are the owner of an opportunity cost (Mahoney and Pandian 1992). In other words, profitability can be measured as a normal financial return.

To differentiate the possible sources of profitability, some types are distinguished. For example, the return can be performed by ((Mahoney and Pandian 1992):

- Superior ability to manage to coordinate the resources (Penrose 1959);
- Possession of a valuable resource which is rare;
- Government protection when barriers to entry of new competitors are high;
- Take risks and business acumen in uncertain and complex immersive media;
- Make better use of the resources of the Organization, of any of the physical assets and human capital.

The resource base is an attempt to explain why the organizations differ in terms of features and capabilities and how these differences can lead to positions of sustained profitability, producing superior financial return. Base resources therefore serve the purpose of focusing explicitly the function of resources and the capacity of organizations, such as the origin of strategy and organizational performance. This exploration of the relationship between resources, competition and profit includes, among other issues, the role of imperfect information in the creation of differences in profitability between competitors (Grant 1991, p. 3, Barney 1986, Itami 1987).

Profitability of Information

The information is a complex concept, ubiquitous since the emergence of life and inherent in any evolutionary process and thus served and continues to serve as a framework for reflection so much in biology, physics, psychology, in management, in Linguistics, as in many other branches of science.

The power of information resulted from the development of information and communication technologies during the twentieth century, such as occurred two centuries ago with the concept of energy, key factor of the industrial revolution.

The imperfections of information are some of the imperfections that competitive clash the ideal perfect market economic (Yao 1988). The market is characterized by numerous customers and suppliers of homogeneous products and whose price engine determines the most efficient organization of the market. Looking for the information, all customers and suppliers are complete and perfectly informed about all relevant aspects of the trade.

While the ideal market serves as the most important neoclassical economic theory, appropriation of the contemporary economic theories tends to allow this unlike the appropriation of unrealistic theories. Therefore, we assume that the perfect market and perfectly informed customers and vendors is a myth. For this reason it is proposed that the markets are characterized by imperfect competition and that the imperfections of information are an important trend. (Yao 1988).

The amount of return that the organization can perform depends on the cost of resources, of the cost of acquisition of new resources and your economic value when sold the products. In the case of being perfectly competitive markets, customers and vendors both will have the same thrilling expectations about the value and the cost of resources and products.

Consequently, suppliers never sell the resource or your product, if the total value is not reflected in the price, or customers will pay a higher price than the cost. Under these circumstances the perfect market, the strategy can only produce the normal return, as opposed to the above referenced return, i.e. profitability.

Imperfections of Information

To understand how the economic profitability can be identified and suitable for strategic intelligence is through knowledge of the origin of imperfections of information. The costs of economic transactions (CTE) describe these origins and three types of imperfections of information result of them (Williamson, 1975).

The transaction costs theory assigns two behavioral appropriations to the man: the limits of rationality and opportunism. We assume that men are intentionally rational, but are limited by this. The limits of rationality are out of the inability of the human brain. This involves neuron-psychological boundaries of a skill on the one hand, and on the other, the limits of language. Physical limits take the form of value and the storage limits of the power of individuals to receive, store and process the information without errors (Williamson 1975, p. 21).

Human cognitive abilities are as a rule insufficient to understand particularly complex tasks, to recognize the need for relevant information and to render completely all relevant information (Wigand, Picot et al. 1997, p. 75). It explains the limited rationality of rational information behavior (Simon 1955). Instead of a full search of relevant information, the only decision maker attempts to get a subjective satisfaction, the incomplete information level (Wigand, Picot et al. 1997, p. 75). This type of behavior is known as "satisfactory": looking for a solution which meets the aspirations of the decider level and therefore the acceptable.

Humans are not only rational; they also assume some opportunistic behavior. Williamson (1975) describes how opportunism "for own interests shrewdly" involving "disbelief of the threats and opportunities", in order to perform the individual advantages (Williamson, 1975 p. 26). These advantages are also suitable for "select and distort the information discovery or discredit the opportunities that lead to future" (Williamson, 1975, p. 26). The claim is that, although not all humans to behave opportunistically, is difficult to predict in advance whether they will behave or not, as such.

These two types of behaviors reflect the relationship between suppliers and customers. The combination of opportunistic and rational behavior is the main cause for the three types of information imperfections in the market of transactions:

- **Asymmetric Information:** An asymmetric distribution of information from the parties involved in a transaction causes a strategic opportunity. The critical impact of information on optimal allocation of risk is not merely your presence or absence, but your inappropriateness between economic agents (Arrow 1969, p. 55). Williamson (1975) joins two conditions under which the asymmetry of information provides a strategic opportunity for transactions:
  - High costs to obtain equality of information;
  - Propensity to opportunistic behavior (Williamson, 1975, p. 31). In other words, the asymmetric information occurs when one of the parties has information that is unknown by the other and difficult to obtain by the other party and an opportunity to exploit this information advantage through strategic alternatives.

The asymmetric information may result in a favorable situation for suppliers or customers depending on the one that has that information. The opportunity is caused by hidden information for the current transaction. One of the parties in a commercial transaction is better informed about a relevant variable than the other. Is the invisibility of this private information which constitutes the essence of the imperfections of information and introduces the risk to another party (Douma and Schreuder 1992, p. 54).

Considering the possibility of opportunistic behavior, the part that has the hidden information, has no incentive to reveal the information, if it is detrimental to her. As a result, any vendor who enters the market with a product or service that is particularly suitable for a specific market segment, with the major benefits of competitors who benefit from this hidden information. The imperfections of information are known as enemies of the selection (Arrow 1984).

- **Ambiguity of the Information:** The ambiguity of information in a business transaction may cause a strategic opportunity. Although in the case of complete information, different interpretations on the same information may occur. As a result of opportunism, these representations can be opportunistic in the sense that they can lead to a single advantage to any supplier or customer.

The strategic opportunity for one of them discovers when such an interpretation is not recognized by other and results in:

- Customer will pay a high price for a product;
- Will the supplier to offer a product at a low price.

As a result of this behavior, the opportunistic part with the opportunistic interpretation has no incentives to share this information, if she becomes a disadvantage for him.

- **Incomplete Information:** The strategic opportunity of incomplete information is tightly related to the assumption of rationality. The limits of rationality are interested certainly in the extension of the limits of rationality are achieved-I mean under conditions of uncertainty and complexity. In the absence of any of these terms of ownership of the shares can be quite specific quotas of this principle. (Williamson, 1975, p. 22).

In an environment characterized by a high degree of complexity and uncertainty, the possibility of certain events occurs, quickly become numerous. Under these circumstances, it is impossible for humans to acquire and analyze complete information relevant to the strategic decision-making. As explained before, this inability leads to behavior "satisfactory". The opportunity of incomplete information occurs when a client is not fully informed about the range of possibilities of the transaction and the products offered and vice versa.

Therefore, a client that allows an incomplete comparison of suppliers and their mutual differences can start a transaction with the worst supplier. For the supplier this opportunity could be exploited by the establishment of a brand and advertising, in order to become part of the subset of suppliers in incomplete comparison of clients.

Use of the Information on Organizational Management

Managers manage men in addition to other resources-including information that is subject to the filter of the cognitive capacities and to the "game" of influences and alliances. The definition of the strategy tends to take the form of a perspective rooted in the collective intentions and reflecting the patterns of use of resources and capacities as a *competitive advantage.* Managers tend to regard the information as a *"substance"* which can be acquired, stored and possessed.

The *information* gives stability and comfort and managers to internalize it in turn it into knowledge about the sector and on the surroundings. There is however limitations in forward-looking models used, since they do not take into account the *non-quantifiable information* (the signs of the changes).

When strategy is driven by supply and demand tends to not be set for a period of x years with annual reviews. Managers actively exploit the imperfections of information through product and market factors, as a way to achieve *competitive advantages.*

The sources of information that the "analysts" and "strategists" use are usually especially strategic predictions made by macroeconomic credible institutions in global terms, favoring the quantitative information to the detriment of qualitative information.

The *Information* provides them with wealth creation and value for customers and shareholders; The *Information* allows them to increase the time available for strategic decision-making;

CONCLUSION

The information science is a science with precise origins, an object and a well-defined content (the information) and experts easily identified. Has about a quarter-century of existence, time of a generation and an adulthood that has a definition of the object of study, your methods, some basic concepts and fundamental laws and increasingly refers to your own history which is a sign of your maturity.

The object is a field, the information that permeates the space. Is a vital resource which is still not sufficiently measured the extent of your or non-use, for lack of attention to their users.

The content is characterized by inter-disciplinarily between the different Sciences, such as the social sciences and Humanities, mathematics and physics. It uses techniques and bold technologies that pose the paper universe to irreversibly the electronic universe, which allows the storage and transmission of digital form. Once scanned information can be conveyed by different means, through communication networks.

The different stages of technical and economic maturity of the components provided (voice, text, image), the centre of gravity of informational practices shifts from a pole made up of paper to an electronic pole where the oral and visual take the place that the textual left them with the emergence of a new informational culture.

Future generations will be more demanding in relation to these means, particularly the audiovisual, less formal than textual media: will have less time and probably will be less interested in obtaining the information through constant reading and the text may be presented orally.

This science is at the origin of an industry, a market and trade information and which will grow very quickly. The information market diversifies and customers change rapidly. The information trade is struggling with the problem of copyright and intellectual property rights stands out for the sale of informational products of significant added value.

Information science specialists and professionals in the sector, such as publishers, booksellers, documentalists, librarians, archivists, museologists concerned with the creation, storage, communication and use of information are closer and further away from the book, the document and the object.

REFERENCES

Bartholy & Grandpierre. (1978). *La Science*. Epistemologie general.

Berger, P., & Luckmann, T. (1985). *A construção social da realidade: tratado de sociologia do conhecimento*. Petrópolis: Vozes.

Bernal, J. D. (1967). *The Social function of science*. Cambridge, MA: MIT Press.

Borko, H. (1968). Information science: What is this? *American Documentation*, *19*(1), 3–5. doi:10.1002/asi.5090190103

Bourdieu, P. (1983). Esboço de uma teoria da prática. In R. Ortiz (Ed.), *Pierre Bourdieu: sociologia* (pp. 46–81). São Paulo: Ática.

Bronowski, J. (1977). O senso comum da ciência. In *Belo Horizonte*. Editora da USP.

Buckland, M. (1991). Information as a thing. *JASIS*, *42*(5), 351–360. doi:

Capurro, R., & Hjorland, B. (2003). The concept of information. *Annual Review of Information Science and Technology*, 37, 343–411.

Cardoso, A. M. P. (1996). Pós-Modernidade e informação: Conceitos complementares? *Perspectivas em Ciência da Informação, Belo Horizonte*, *1*(1), 63–79.

Coadic, L. (1994). *La Science de l'Information*. Paris: Presses Universitaires de France.

Dias, E. J. W. (2002). O específico da ciência da informação. In *O campo da ciência da informação: gênese, conexões e especificidades* (pp. 87–99). João Pessoa: Editora Universitária.

Garvey, W. D. (1979). *Communication: the essence of science*. Oxford, UK: Pergamon Press.

Gómez, M. N. G. (2000). Metodología de pesquisa no campo da Ciencia da informação. *DataGrama-Zero, 1*(6).

Illich, L. (1982). *Le genre vernaculaire*. Editions du Seuil.

Ingwersen, P. (1992). Information and information science in context. *Libri, 42*(2), 99–135. doi:10.1515/libr.1992.42.2.99

Jamil & Armando Malheiro. (2013). *Rethinking the Conceptual Base for New Practical Applications in Information Value and Quality*. IGI Global.

Le Coadic, Y.-F. (1997), La science de l'information (2nd ed.). Paris: Universitaires de France.

Le Coadic, Y. F. (1998). *Le besoin d'information*. Paris: ADBS Editions.

Meadows, J. (1990). Science de l'information. *Brises, l6.*

Mercier, P. A., & Plassard, V. S. (1984). Société digital les nouvelles technologies au future quotidien. Editions du Seuil.

Mikhailov, A. I. (1980). Estrutura e principais propriedades da informação científica. In Ciência da informação ou informática? Rio de Janeiro: Calunga.

Pinheiro, L., & Loureiro, J. (1995). Traçados e limites da ciência da informação. *Ciência da informação, 24*(1).

Porter, M. (1985). *Competitive Advantage: Creating and Sustaining Superior Performance*. New York: The Free Press.

Rascão, J. (2012). Novas Realidades na Gestão e na Gestão da Informação. Editora, Sílabo, Lda.

Sabaté, F. T. (1989). *Fundamentos de Economia de la Empresa (2nd ed.)*. Barcelona: Librería Hispano Americana.

Saracevic, T. (1992). Information Science: origin, evolution and relations. In *Conceptions of library and information science. Proceedings of the international conference for the celebration of 20th anniversary of the Department of Information Studies*. University of Tampere.

Sève, L. (1969). *Marxisme et théorie de la personalité*. Paris: Editions Sociales.

Shannon, C.E. (1948). A mathematical theory of communication. *Bell System Technical Journal, 27*, 379-423, 623-656.

Shannon, C. E., & Weaver, W. (1949). *A mathematical theory of communication*. Chicago: University of Illinois Press.

Tapia, C. (1980). *Colloques et sociétés*. Paris: Publications de la Sorbonne.

Taton, R. (1981). *Histoire general des Sciences*. Paris: PUF.

Wersig, G. (1993). Information science: The study of postmodern knowledge usage [mar]. *Information Processing & Management*, *29*(2), 229–239. doi:10.1016/0306-4573(93)90006-Y

Ziman, J. (1974). *Public Knowledge*. Cambridge University Press.

KEY TERMS AND DEFINITIONS

Profitability of Information: Information is a complex concept, ubiquitous since the emergence of life and inherent in any evolutionary process, and thus served and continues to serve as a framework for reflection so much in biology, physics, psychology, management, linguistics, and in many other branches of science. The power of information resulted from the development of information and communication technologies during the twentieth century, such as occurred two centuries ago with the concept of energy, a key factor of the industrial revolution.

Chapter 12
Subjectivism of Information

Antonio Juan Briones Penalver
Polytechnic University of Cartagena, Spain

ABSTRACT

Objectivism has given the domain, rationality, definition, and purpose that are commonly attributed to information and knowledge management, as well as the definitions of the concepts of information, knowledge, communication, and learning. Objectivism does not provide a theoretical foundation to information management; the question that arises is whether subjectivism may or may not offer a compelling alternative. Finally, the answer is no because the subjectivist rarely pays attention to what the fundamental lines of private organizations are and pays attention increasingly to the public sector, in the realization of economic value. Thus, there is no other way but to combine objectivism with subjectivism in a comprehensive approach of integrated information management. However, this chapter illustrates the differences between the philosophical principles of thought.

OBJECTIVES

This chapter has as its main objective to know if subjectivism may or may not offer a compelling alternative to objectivism, in the theoretical foundation and practice for the information management.

WHAT IS SUBJECTIVISM?

Subjectivism is a philosophical tradition which opposes itself to objectivism. Subjectivism means *provide an alternative to human experience and understanding, instead of objective truth* (Lakoff & Johnson, 1980). In objectivism, human behavior is the result of forces that act in the world, that people cannot control, and are difficult to comprehend. The interest and motivation of objectivism is therefore providing people as law, the rational knowledge that will help them work successfully in the outside world.

Since the objectivism is directed to the external aspects of the understanding, the internal aspects are the primary domain of subjectivism. What motivates the subjectivism is the awareness; understanding, truth, and meaning that are relative to the physical and cultural context, people's way of life, as well as

DOI: 10.4018/978-1-5225-3725-0.ch012

the mental structures of how the world works (Putnam, 1983). When the contexts and mental conceptions of people are seriously opposed to each other, there can be no valid objective, understanding, truth, and universal meaning. On the other hand, understanding, truth and meaning are not strictly personal. When the meaning is entirely personal, each individual understanding may be called a truth.

In this extreme case of subjectivism, the human sense would be totally spontaneous. The imaginative sky would be the limit. The story mentioned of the Trobiand Papuas illustrates how objectivism and subjectivism extreme visions are both inadequate, at least for those aspects of reality that are related to human intervention, such as the information management. The meaning the Papua gave to the game of cricket is neither objective nor personal, but subjective. The meaning the Papua gave to the game of cricket is neither objective nor personal, but subjective. They gave a common sense to the game, which is now common knowledge. The location of this fact prevents them from participating in the World Championship, but presumably they do not care. Subjectivity is relevant to many forms of organization, because it allows the collective action of the organizational units – a Department, a management team, a network of professionals – based on experience and locally sharing understandings (Weick, 1995).

The example of the Papuas illustrates also the truth and the true knowledge are always dependent on how people understand experimentally their worlds and where people find meaning and significant in their lives. For time, what people give importance is not only relevant in the objectivism of their rational knowledge, but also of their imagination, intuition, emotions, values, beliefs, experiences and aspirations.

All Papua could explain, we are not only objective and rational, because the economists would have said it, but also *imaginatively rational* (Lakoff & Johnson, 1980). Sometimes we want something more and we go around. We have a dream and spend enormous amounts of time, energy and money chasing it. Sometimes we do not share information simply because we do not like the others, even if it damages our reputation. This imaginative rationality is elaborated in the literature of subjectivism, for example, linking ICT to hospitality (Ciborra, 2004), learning the identity (Wenger, 1998), information to power (Introna, 1997), and the technological objects to sociability (Knorr-Cetina, 1997). In objectivism, all human aspects are ignored.

In the research of objectivism, economic rationality and the disembodied truths of human beings are separated from objects in their environment. The fundamental interest of subjectivism is to restore the ' bridge ' between the world of objects and of the subject. We are part of the environment and as such, we change it and we are changed by it. Here, in the subjectivism, understanding, truth and meaning come from interaction with the physical environment and with the people. When developing relevant knowledge of the practice, we must not focus so much on the inherent properties of the objects, but more in their interaction characteristics (Lakoff & Johnson, 1980). The properties of the interaction are subjective meanings given to objects that are out of people and make sense of their world in the process of human communication and negotiation, reflecting what they believe is important to their private lives and organizations.

Returning to the example of the roses, the objectivism of knowledge represents its inherent properties, the characteristics of rose that are independent of any human observer, such as the thorns. However, nobody gives roses to their girlfriend because they have thorns, but because they are understood as the symbol of love. When the donor and the receiver unite this symbolic meaning of the rose, the message is transverse. The Objectivists are right when they claim that the objects exist in an objective reality independent of the will and the thought of the human being. We do not build the objects-a rose is a rose, but we build our interactions with them (Tsoukas, 2005).

Understanding, truth and meaning are not always fixed or even lie on objects waiting to be ' driven ' and ' extracted ', but are dynamically negotiated and socially constructed. Be the symbol of love is not an inherent property of the roses, but an interactive property that emerges from the imagination of the person. We learn to understand such meanings interacting with the world. We learn by doing.

BUILDING INTERACTIONS IN SOCIAL SOCIOLOGY

Sociology is another science that has been plagued by the challenge of objectivism and subjectivism, both fighting for what should be done about the basic study of the domain: the object or the subject, the structure or the action, the social system or human conduct, the person in a broad sense or the individual skill of that person, if that is the group, the organization or the technological infrastructure. In the sociological theories of objectivism such as functionalism and structuralism, people determine the human behavior, however in the subjectivism, the action and the meaning are adapted with precedence, for example, in the interpretative sociology of subjectivism.

Both live in parallel Empires, seeing the other as an enemy. In the last two decades, the dualism between objectivism and subjectivism was a prime theme of Sociology (Bourdieu, 1972; Giddens, 1984), having resulted in new social theories, such as the theory of activity (Engeström, Y., Engeström, R., & Vähääho, 1999) and actor-network theory (Latour, 2005). A duality is,

a single conceptual unit which is formed by two inseparable and mutually constitutive elements whose tension and inherent complementarily gives wealth and dynamism to the concept (Wenger, 1998).

As a result, the person, organization or an information system for example-are no longer seen as simply posing embarrassment to individual freedom and creativity, but also because they provide the harmony and coherence that give meaning to the potential fragmentation of human action and discord.

Each organization or information system confines and allows the behavior of its members and is continuously recreated simultaneously by the actions of the same. In short, the object and the subject are fixed in each other and made it possible. Given that the object and the subject are fixated on each other, we need to understand better how they interact with each other. As they do in the Intranet (object) as interacts with its users (subjects)? The virtual world, how does it motivate its millions of users to participate? The subjectivist suggests a vision of objects as tools in context to give them meaning, understanding and learning. Try to explain what makes sense and meaning to people, when they are building their social practices around the objects. Objects become *affiliated objects* (Suchman, 2005), when they help people, for example, build the cohesion of the configuration as a group and help them to create, sustain and evaluate identity; when they shake the person's imagination, creativity and enthusiasm; when they allow people to subjectively learn and develop knowledge by telling other stories about their experiences; when they allow people to "decree" a part of the world, just as the Papuans appropriated the game of cricket.

All these processes of affiliation turn cold, the lifeless objects within the social objects that are captured by the notion of sociability: why do people give shape to their lives and how the form is influenced to find sense and meaning? Because I share information with others and what makes it impossible for me to do it? Knorr-Cetina (1997) invented the term *object-centered sociality* to indicate that people's lives increasingly occur around objects, such as the Website, games and social networking tools. The notion of sociality is useful to explain why they choose to do so and because some objects are more attractive than others.

Otherwise, the subjectivist does not understand ICT and technology in General as the neutral means that transfer simply objects of producers to consumers, as the Objectivists claim. On the one hand, technology is providing and sometimes imposing a context that implicitly structure social practices by the encoding of how the context must be interpreted, as, for example, in the ERP management software. On the other hand, the adoption of technology always involves negotiation between the various groups involved-managers, computer users – where in the process they all imagine the technology with their own meanings, purposes and functionalities (Bijker, W. E., Hughes, T. P., & Pinch, T., 1987). Once in a while, the constitutive nature of objects (in this case the technology) and sub-objects (all interested parties in negotiation) are emphasized.

The subjectivism of information management means understanding the sociability and social practices centered on the objects. Create an identity for the information management upon such understanding requires more than knowing the inherent properties of the objects, because the Objectivists. Apart, for example, to know what are the possibilities and impossibilities of technologies, that is, what technologies can and cannot do information managers should be aware of its interactive features, that is, its features and amenities to learn, because the subjectivity of the people determines the meaning of the objects and how these objects are used actually. In contemporary sociology and the theory based on social practice, the focus in social practices is the way to revive the traditional division between objectivism and subjectivism. Social practices are structured spaces where individuals interact subjectively with the facilitators and the greatest social constraints (Giddens, 1984). Each organization or department uses a lot of such practices. All professionals involved in such organizational practices decide subjectively their own truths, understandings and meanings in relation to the entire organization, as well as the constituent structure.

CONCEPTUAL IMPLICATIONS: COMMUNICATION, INFORMATION, KNOWLEDGE AND LEARNING

After this brief introduction to subjectivism as a philosophical tradition and theory based on social practice with growing influence in the implementation of this tradition, the question that arises is: what are the implications of subjectivism in information management. What is and what might be the subjectivism of information management? In the following paragraphs, is presented firstly the definition of subjectivism in respect to the concepts of communication, information, knowledge and learning, related to information management. Illustrating the fundamental differences with the objectivism then were extracted some implications for the management (of information) and to the organization, before continuing with the interpretations of the subjectivism on their domains, rationality, and goal setting.

Reflecting the ambition for the dynamic theorization of individual and social processes, subjectivists prefer verbs rather than nouns. Favor words to help understanding, such as making sense, inform, know and learn. In this way, they differ simultaneously from objectivism and its static concepts, as well as avoid the frequent mechanistic discussions about the nature and content of the data, information and knowledge, as well as of its sequence. There are some attempts to define these notions, once the perspectives of objectivism and subjectivism are accommodated (Bates, 2005). Likewise, the notions of information and knowledge management are rarely used, because the subjectivist often protest against the views of information and knowledge as objects, and against the implications of how information and knowledge may or may not be managed.

We are certain that the notions of information and knowledge management originated in the mind of the objectivists. In addition, the thousands of years of philosophical debate resulted in no clear and indisputable definition of knowledge. On the contrary, the epistemology or the science of how people do to know are and have always been a respected branch of philosophy. With all these contradictions in mind, nevertheless presents definitions of fundamental concepts of information management, not alluding to a definitive conclusion, but to illustrate what it is or what might be the subjectivism of information management.

The Communication

In objectivism, the communication consists of natural exchanges of information between people who maintain anonymous relationships. The interaction and human communication are deepened what is regarded in its essence – the transaction of objects. In this informational approach to communication, discrete objects are transferred from a sender to a receiver, the metaphor of the passive channel is relevant only when the meaning of words exchanged is fixed and is not responsible for any human interpretation. Subjectivists underline that truth, understanding and meaning are anything fixed in real life, and are dependent on the processes of human interaction and negotiation.

People populate their mental structures, the disarticulation of the common knowledge and the context determine what is considered to be true, as they understand their contexts and which are the meanings related to the world in which they live. So, the words and the language became an intrinsic part of human sense, implies That occur differences of interpretation between people; a more or less linear and more or less broad perspective in communication and in interaction is required. Subjectivism accepts the possibility of divergent direction in terms of behavior; sees the differences as unavoidable facts of life. The subjectivist definition of communication and interaction that admits this possibility is explicitly: *a symbolic process, through which reality is produced, maintained, repaired and transformed* (Carey, 1989).

Communication and interaction are busy giving subjective meanings, mutual understandings and relationships not anonymous to social relationships. The meanings are not exchanged, but built the subjectivity in the interaction with the world, as Papuans built the game of cricket. The game was adapted to what they believed to be more important to their lives, in their context, space time and expressing their group identity. This broader vision of communication denies the objectivist and economic slope of artificial division of the communication process of supply and demand. Moreover, it would be a disappointment to see the supply side of information as the natural realm of objectivism and the demand side or its use as the domain of subjectivism.

In a communication, people are constantly between the question asked and the answer, do and make sense, verbal and non-verbal. Human communication mediated by ICT in whole or in part disconnects us, giving the impression that the supply and demand of information can be divided into domains, and can be managed separately. Neither the object nor the subject can be isolated from reality and both are limited by the interactivity of the continuous and dynamic processes that give them life. In addition, the vision of subjectivism in communication and interaction brings into focus all the properties of the interaction that binds people and objects that are far removed from the purposes of objectivism in terms of rationality and economic quantification.

The Information

The emphasis of the subjectivist lies in making sense and in the interpretation of the relations with the largest number of entities that affect the vision of information. The information is typically defined as *the difference that makes the difference* (Bateson, 1972), which always implies a difference to an auditor or to a reader. Many signs-data — reach us daily and those who pass our perceptual filters must be interpreted to make sense. What surprises us in this process of making sense is called information; is the built difference that informs us. Then, the subjectivist emphasize that these same signals or data can be interpreted in many ways. People differ in their goals and ambitions, have different mental structures lack, make sense and evaluation, and live in cultural, social and institutional contexts. Would the Papuans also see the rose as a symbol of love?

For all these reasons, the divergent understandings may result of the same data. The same person can reach other meanings in other contexts. This definition of information differentiates the subjectivism of objectivism once more. Universally aimed at the objective truths, the objectivist excludes divergent direction of human behavior of their repertoire. Consequently, cannot make the distinction between data, information and knowledge. From this perspective, on the supply side a newspaper can be called a data, information or knowledge system. Journalists are skillful in writing their articles, why can we not call a journal a system of knowledge? The view on the demand side, the name makes no difference and, hence, is not informative. The paper is a paper and if does or does not the difference can be left only to the description of the reader.

Hence, it is impossible to set the default which is the right information to the right person, at what time and in what format, as is assumed in the Objectivist definition of information management. We can supply people the structured data (Boland, 1987); what they can do with it can only be partly suggested by others. For the same reason, information economists call the information – anything that can be digitized (Shapiro & Varian, 1999) – the subjectivist describes it as data. Another difference between objectivism and subjectivism is related to the economic theory of uncertainty. Some latest developments in the economy, information and data are defined as the reduction of uncertainty (Babe, 1994). Here, the information is assigned the function of increasing rationality in human decision making. If all the information were available, there would be no more uncertainty. However, people are not generally able to process all the information required for rational decision making and are required to be rational in most cases (Simon, 1976).

In addition, people are tending to be opportunistic (Williamson, 1975); appropriate information of the ways that serve their social practices (Putnam, 1983); are always asking for more information, and do not always use it (Feldman & March, 1981); to justify certain decisions collect the information after the decision (Weick, 1995); the medium can affect the form and content of a message (Trevino, L. K., R. L. Daft & R. H. Lengel, 1990); the way people dress can be important as how they use information (Fiske, 1991). The information is a much more complex phenomenon than economists can handle.

Regardless of the subjectivist definition of information it can be said that the data are poorly problematized in the social sciences. There is an insurmountable body of literature in the sociology of knowledge (Berger & Luckmann, 1966) which is not very uniform by the similar interest in data or information. As in the economy, the data is apparently assumed to be there, mysteriously fallen from heaven. Consequently, not only the collection, search, refinement, storage, preservation and dissemination of the data is to be considered part of the work of the management of information, but should also pay attention to the generation of the data.

Knowledge and Learning

In objectivism, knowledge consists of the abstracted representations of the practice that are stored cognitively in the human mind; while learning is perceived as how objective information is absorbed. The experimental knowledge manifested in social practices that emerge from the interaction and social negotiation is critical, unlike knowledge of representation that we have of the objects in the world. Telling the truth, understanding and meaning are constructed subjectively; which implies that knowledge resides not only in the individual mind, but also in people's relations. There is a reality beyond the individual, constructed subjectively.

So, the knowledge can not only be defined in terms of its individual and cognitive dimension. The methodological individualism of economists needs to be extended to a social, interactive dimension, as a basis to subjectivism, the need to use the word knows instead of knowledge (Choo, 2006). In academic jargon, the epistemology of pluralism is required so that it can be identified as the individual knowledge is related to social practices that are created and sustained in the communities, and networks in organizations. Individual knowledge gets its meaning only by knowing the habits, norms, values and dynamics of the context in which they stand. A typical definition of knowledge or expertise that fits these requirements is: *distinctive assessment*, which is

a tool of distinctions (...) among the actors who have to facilitate and shape to their rational practice in business, while building and reconstructing the context (Spender & Scherer, 2007).

As a prerequisite for action, allows us to distinguish the good from the bad taste and all the other distinctions that inform our senses and decision-making. It emerges from the interaction of learning. A definition of learning is the construction of new truths, understandings and meanings to guide actions (Berger & Luckmann, 1966). These are actively derived from participation in social practices (Wenger, 1998). Communication, interaction, knowledge and learning in action are dynamic processes that generate and are generated by the social practices in which they occur. These visions of knowledge and learning question the popular separation between explicit and tacit knowledge (Nonaka & Takeuchi, 1995). At times, the artificial division between supply and demand of information and knowledge generates confusion. Calling data to a database, groupware system or the explicit knowledge of Intranet more than suggests that the tacit and explicit knowledge dimensions can be isolated and converted in others.

The objectivist assumes that knowledge can be acquired through the objects and these objects have meaning for them. These assumptions can only lead to disappointment about what we can realistically expect from the technologies. The technologies do not build the meaning; distribute the data to wait patiently to make human sense, neither more nor less. As intended by Polanyi (1962), the inventor of these notions of tacit and explicit knowledge constitute each other. It can be conceptually distinct, but never separated, neither in theory nor in practice. In summary, information and knowledge are human and social phenomena in the subjectivism which cannot be separated from the ' producers ' and ' consumers '. However, economists are right when they claim that coding and objectification are required to determine the economic value of information and knowledge. Information and knowledge are sometimes seen as objects, the best to be traded on the market.

ORGANIZATIONAL IMPLICATIONS: A PRACTICE-BASED ORGANIZATION AND MANAGEMENT

Subjectivism settings discussed above leads to very different answers on how communication, information, knowledge and learning can or should be arranged and managed. Although the subjectivist is much less specific and United in this regard, we see four fundamental principles: first, compared with the objectivism, subjectivism leads our attention to social practices of organizations and individual ' soaked in practice (Tsoukas, 2005). Scholars call this ontological shift movement. In objectivism, people are separated from the world, because the environment is considered to be made up of different objects that exist independently of the human person.

As a result, the Objectivist would rather talk about the Organization, business processes or information architecture, and tend to underestimate the active role of people in working with these objects. On subjectivism, people are part of the world and are dipped in their social practices. The objects and people interact dynamically, and that makes other things possible. Transcending the division between objects and people, the *individual committed to practice* must therefore be our focal point of attention. Information management can help support the processes of communication and interaction with these individuals generate their social practices and thus in their organizations and society. The second implication of subjectivism in theory and in practice is the methodology.

What is the basis of knowledge on which we have based our interventions on organizational practice? The illusion of the simple message of social theory based on practice is that we must build, the Organization of our knowledge about what people actually do when carrying out social practices, rather than on the theories abstracted from practice, as the market model perfect discussed earlier. Without independent knowledge of social practices, we are unable to effectively control such practices or to build up the theory. The subjectivist invites information managers to focus their behavior on the information that people need for decision making. To study the current behavior of the information, we need different methodologies from those applied in the theoretical model approaches of objectivism or top-down organizational policies that are based on such approaches.

The ethnographic and participant observer methodologies are the main candidates, because they allow themselves to gain rich understanding of ' learning organization ' (Schatzki, 2006) and use the knowledge gained to improve social practices. Virtual Ethnography is a recent development in the methodology of research that extends the traditional notion of context as being physically and the site with the idea of connectivity between people and distributed systems (Hine, 2000). The third implication of subjectivism to manage and organize is that it should focus on the behavior of information in social practices because it opens the door to many other forms of interaction that people increase more and use it to shape the behavior of the information, or exceeding the limits of inside Organization for which they work.

The market as the Exchange is not denied in the subjectivism, but is supplemented with other forms of organization, such as, *intentional networks* (Nardi, B. A., Whittaker, S., & Schwarz, H., 2002), ' actors ' network (Latour, 1996), ' strong and weak ties (Granovetter, 1973), and us (Engeström, Y., Engeström, R., & Vähääho, 1999), to mention a few of the titles referenced in the literature. Examples are people who gather around many social networking tools. The implication for the management of information is that the new balances have to be found in the management information systems to support decision-making to managers. When it raises the behavior of communication, interaction, knowledge and learning, the boundaries of organizations become increasingly artificial.

The last implication of social theory based on practice deals with the finer distinction between objectivism and subjectivism: we see and pursue only a ' objective truth ' or we recognize and organize multiple realities? For the management of information: we only offer the right information for every situation or we are (too) much more refined in support social practices? What do the Papuas in our Organization (and we're not all Papuans sometimes?). Arrange for a truth and go hand in hand as, for example, the aspiration to apply ICT in standardization and control of business processes. The main motivation is the control of management. However, we started talking about the construction of information to make sense, learn and make decisions (Choo, 2006). The aim of subjectivism is to support better than control multiple realities, we all need to build subjective truths in the negotiation with the structures in which we live and work. That is what the subjectivism of information management is about to do-support decision-making.

CONCLUSION

Conceptual Implications: Domain of Information Management, Rationality and Objective

Synthesizing these aspects are the following perspectives that differentiate the objectivism from subjectivism: from transaction to interaction; of the properties inherent in interactive properties; of the information objects to information that makes a difference; the exchange of information to communication; of knowledge to learn; learning how the absorption learning as knowledge construction; the person social practices; the theoretical model approaches to practice-based approaches; the market to all the forms of organization; of an objective truth multiple realities; the control to support in decision-making. All these perspectives show the need to revamp the information management domain, rationality, and goal setting.

In the field of subjectivism, information management based on practice, it is proposed, be focused on information related to the social objects. However, the social objects can be documents, databases, intranets, Websites, virtual games, archives, libraries, information technology infrastructure or any other information related to the objects. Its identity is built through knowledge of the inherent properties of the objects – which may or may not do with these social objects and their properties of interaction, that is, the meaning that people give to these objects. The rationality of information management subjectivism is what we need to understand what people in general, managers, customers, suppliers, and so on. find significance and significant to make them more than mere objects.

Such lights are required for information managers aspire to achieve the objectives supporting better communication processes, interaction, knowledge and learning through that people create in their social practices surrounding information objects using or not the features of technological objects. Choo (2007) demonstrates how information management can help the organizational groups to increase the use of subjectivity of information in decision-making processes, making these processes less dependent on individual subjectivity. Finally, while the management involves exercise of influence on the chosen objectives, information management can be defined as the theory and practice of forming the object-centered sociality as informational guide people in their interactions with the organizational or social objectives. With this function the information management can best be organized, be relevant in practice.

Thus, the subjectivism of information management goes beyond rationality of objectivist management of information about the objects, despite being called products, resources or assets. Means that the processes of communication, interaction, knowledge and learning, related people in a subjective construction of truth, understanding and the meaning of these objects, relate these in turn to what people find crucial in their organizational and private lives. As systems of interpretation of what people should or should not do, organizations are organizers of information (Douglas, 1986) that guide the human sense, if this is intentional or not (Moran & Ghoshal, 1999).

Organizations are formative contexts (Ciborra & Lanzara, 1994) that not only make sense, but also give sense (Weick, 1995). However, the human sense invalidates the constraints to management and organization. On the question of identity (Wenger, 1988) and in Economics (Boisot, 1998), the person participates in all kinds of social practices, both formal and informal, and creates the meanings to them, mediated or not by his employer. In addition, on all topics, many different meanings are produced dynamically globally and compete their acceptance. For both reasons, organizations can indirectly influence the generation of meanings through the facilities of the processes of communication, interaction, knowledge and learning and promote a formative context in which the potential value of these processes can be carried out.

In this sense, information management cannot manage meaning; can only help build the subjectivity of truth, understanding and meaning in relation to organizational objectives. Finally, if the subjectivism of information management is set as described, then what is the subjectivism of knowledge management? As in the example of objectivism, we don't see much difference, but for a different reason. Economists cannot easily distinguish between information and knowledge, because sooner or later, they will worry about this wealth of separate concepts of objects in search of economic value. Subjectivism distinguishes knowledge information in a meaningful way, but sees further info as a meaning in knowledge management and social skills. This distinction, however, makes no difference to the nature and content of the information management or knowledge.

From the pragmatic point of view, the managers of information or knowledge are engaged in the same line of investigation. It presents what relates to the management of information and the separation between objectivism and subjectivism. Compared with the objectivism, subjectivism offers additional insights and often superior to information managers. Illustrates how humans understand the reality, including all its limitations, and gives insights into depth with the organizational dynamics involved. In addition, does not reduce the objects themselves, but see them as tools in context to the meaning, understanding and learning. To return to the title of this article: the rose is the object, its economic value is the price, but for one person may not have price.

The actual value of a rose is in the interaction of the person, not itself or its price. It is in the symbolic meaning of the people and their imagination about the objects. The economy cannot *take ownership* of the interval between the symbolic value and economic value of the objects, although the range is precisely the marketing of making sense of one to one. Subjectivism includes a higher truth (Lakoff & Johnson, 1980). The self-examination of the higher truth, in the imagination of the rationalism of the person can help information managers improve its use and describe the informative objects. However, subjectivism also has its downsides. Lack a coherent structure and a paradigm for example, perfect market model in the economy that could help organizations to organize its information and its knowledge. Instead, there are many heterogeneous and isolated approaches, which are hindering the credibility of value added.

In addition, the theories of subjectivism are often accused of lack of theoretical rigor, are more descriptive than prescriptive, are poor in the practical implications, and are therefore more difficult to ' sell ' the managers and politicians (Bonifacio, M., Camussone, P., & Zini, C., 2004). However, the subjectivist rarely focusses their attention in private organizations and increasingly focus on public organizations in the realization of economic value. As a result, download the game and state that the information and knowledge must be encoded and lemmatized as result of economic value. Our conclusion is that the subjectivism also does not provide a sufficiently reasoned basis for information managers, because the economy is part of the life of organizations.

Although the subjectivism has recently given a giant leap transcending the Cartesianism between the object and the person emphasizing social practices and the object-centered sociality, the inglorious Division still exists. How can we make it grow? Superficially, the objectivism and subjectivism are in opposition. They look at themselves as rivals in a duel. The objectivism is oriented to the external aspects of human understanding and aims to support people with the objective knowledge to operate successfully in the outside world. Subjectivism is more oriented towards the internal aspects of understanding and aspirations of human beings to illuminate the complexity and irreducibility of social processes in which it is involved.

As a result, both perspectives miss the interest and motivation with respect to each other. Both refer to as humans can understand each other (Lakoff & Johnson, 1980), so we will benefit if we could combine the two lines of development in each other's way. Given that information management is guided by the objectivism, have that information management to add economic value to organizations, paradoxically should incorporate this line of thought is widely ignored by the economy: subjectivism.

In order for information management to become a discipline that combines the ability to compromise the objectivism and subjectivism, as well as the dualism between these two philosophical traditions, needs to be re-conceptualized, meaning that both traditions require, allow the enrichment of one another. Figure 1 demonstrates what means the objectivism and subjectivism as a duality. We see first a white vase with black background or two guys with white background?

This example illustrates the concept of a ' figure ' and ' plan ', because it was developed in gestures of Psychology (King, 2005). This concept implies that we are inclined to the foreground of the dominant form (Figure 1) and our other interests concern the plan, when faced with ambiguity. Use this concept for the foreground and background as a metaphor emphasizing that tends to favor an interpretation to the detriment of another. Some prefer the objectivism and subjectivism, and others use this preference because the interpretive lens through which the world is selectively determined. The concept of figure-plan also stresses that the world is not objectively ' out of it ', but built as makes sense in ambiguous situations.

Finally, this concept indicates that the whole is more than the sum of its parts. Regardless of our preferences, the first plans cannot exist without second thoughts (bottom), and vice versa. Are mutually essential and therefore should never be separated. Seeing the objectivism and subjectivism in this dualism

Figure 1. The ambiguity of the image

can be concluded that the value of both can be enhanced by the combination of the two. It implies that the information manager must know the foreground while the other, as a background. In management meetings, for example, objectivism can be in first place, however observing the actual information practices social behavior can be an opportunity to view the subjectivism as foreground. Whatever the occasion, however, the integrated management of the information implies that one must always inform the other.

ACKNOWLEDGMENT

The Objectivism is the dominant culture of the Western world. The Objectivism as an "umbrella" for all schools of thought and theories that are based on the idea that for knowledge development, should see the world as consisting of distinct objects that can and should be separated from its inventors and users. Built over time by the traditional rationalist and empiricist theory, this idea is deeply entrenched in the sciences, such as economics, computer science, mathematics and sociology, as well as, in the disciplines of business, such as accounting and financial management. Also includes a large part of the management of information and the adjacent fields of knowledge and learning, in theory and in practice. Information management is default Objectivist. The Objectivism is associated with the ' scientific truth, rationality, precision, clarity, and impartiality "(Lakoff & Johnson, 1980:189). The Objectivists claim that human behavior is determined by the forces of the outside world. People, however, cannot control these outside forces and find it hard to understand them.

The Profº Juan Antonio-Briones Peñalver asked for my help in the study and participation in the drafting of this chapter. The question posed was whether the subjectivism may or may not offer a compelling alternative. Finally, the answer is no because the subjectivist rarely pay attention to what are the fundamental lines of private organizations and pay attention increasingly to the public sector, in the realization of economic value. Thus, there is no other way but to combine the Objectivism with subjectivism in a comprehensive approach and integrated information management. However, as illustrated in this article, the differences between both the philosophical principles of thought are fundamental. In recent years, advocates of subjectivism and the practice based on social theory, in one of its main applications, made a giant leap, transcending the fracture between the object and the subject suggesting that should focus attention on social practices and sociability centered on the object. After this suggestion, demonstrates that the subjectivism, the base information management practice may be to include a new definition for this class.

REFERENCES

Babe, R. E. (1994). The Place of Information in Economics. In R. E. Babe (Ed.), *Information and Communication in Economics* (pp. 41–67). Boston: Kluwer Academic Publishers. doi:10.1007/978-94-011-2204-7_2

Baets, W. (1996). Some Empirical Evidence on IS strategy Alignment in Banking. *Information & Management*, *30*(4), 155–177. doi:10.1016/0378-7206(95)00056-9

Bateson, G. (1972). *Steps to Ecology of Mind: Collected Essays in Anthropology, Psychiatry, Evolution, and Epistemology*. University Of Chicago Press.

Beck, U. (1992). *Risk Society*. London: Sage Publications.

Berger, P. L., & Luckmann, T. (1966). *The Social Construction of Reality: A Treatise in the Sociology of Knowledge*. New York: Anchor Books.

Bijker, W. E., Hughes, T. P., & Pinch, T. (Eds.). (1987). *The Social Construction of Technological Systems: New Directions in the Sociology and History of Technology*. Cambridge, MA: MIT Press.

Boisot, M. H. (1998). *Knowledge Assets – Securing Competitive Advantage in the Information Age*. Oxford, UK: Oxford University Press.

Boland, R. J. (1987). The In-Formation of Information Systems. In *Critical Issues in Information Systems Research*. Boland.

Bonifacio, M., Camussone, P., & Zini, C. (2004). Managing the KM Trade-Off: Knowledge Centralization versus Distribution. *Journal of Universal Computer Science, 10*(3), 162–175.

Bourdieu, P. (1977). *Outline of a Theory of Practice*. Cambridge, UK: Cambridge University Press. doi:10.1017/CBO9780511812507

Capurro, R., & Hjorland, B. (2003). The concept of information. In B. Cronin (Ed.), Annual Review of Information Science and Technology (Vol. 37, pp. 343–411). Academic Press.

Carey, J. W. (1989). *Communication As Culture: Essays on Media and Society*. Winchester, MA: Unwind Hyman.

Chaiklin, S., Hedegaard, M., & Jensen, U. (Eds.), *Activity Theory and Social Practice: Cultural-Historical Approaches*. Aarhus, Denmark: Aarhus University Press.

Choo, C. W. (2006). *The knowing organization; how organizations use information to construct meaning, create knowledge, and make decisions*. Oxford, UK: Oxford University Press.

Choo, C. W. (2007). Social Use of Information. In *Information Management: Setting the Scene*. Oxford, UK: Elsevier.

Ciborra, C. U. (2004). *The Labyrinths of Information: Challenging the Wisdom of Systems*. Oxford, UK: Oxford University Press. doi:10.1093/acprof:oso/9780199275267.001.0001

Davenport, T. H., & Prusak, L. (1997). *Information Ecology: Mastering the Information and Knowledge Environment*. Oxford University Press.

Davenport, T. H., & Prusak, L. (1997). *Information Ecology*. Oxford University Press.

Davenport, T. H., & Prusak, L. (1998). *Working Knowledge*. Boston: Harvard Business School Press.

Davenport, T. H., & Markus, M. L. (1999). Rigor versus Relevance Revisited: Response to Benbasat and Zmud. *MIS Quarterly, 23*(1), 19-23.

Douglas, M. (1986). *How Institutions Think*. London: Routledge.

Engeström, Y. (1999). Activity theory and individual and social transformation. In Y. Engeström, R. Miettinen, & R. L. Punamaki (Eds.), *Perspectives on Activity Theory* (pp. 19–38). Cambridge, UK: Cambridge University Press. doi:10.1017/CBO9780511812774.003

Feldman, M. S., & March, J. G. (1981). Information in Organizations as Signal and Symbol. *Administrative Science Quarterly*, *26*(2), 171–186. doi:10.2307/2392467

Fiske, J. (1991). *Introduction to Communication Studies* (2nd ed.). London: Rutledge.

Giddens, A. (1984). *The Constitution of Society*. Cambridge, UK: Polity Press.

Granovetter, M. (1973). The strength of weak ties. *American Journal of Sociology*, *78*(6), 1360–1380. doi:10.1086/225469

Gurbaxani, V., & Whang, S. (1991). The Impact of Information Systems on Organizations and Markets. *Communications of the ACM*, *34*(1), 59–73. doi:10.1145/99977.99990

Hayek, F. A. (1945). The Use of Knowledge in Society. *The American Economic Review*, *35*, 519–530.

Introna, L. D. (1997). *Management, Information and Power*. MacMillan Press Ltd.

Kakihara, M., & Sørensen, C. (2002). Exploring Knowledge Emergence: From Chaos to Organizational Knowledge. *Journal of Global Information Technology Management*, *5*(33), 48–66. doi:10.1080/1097198X.2002.10856331

King, D. B. (2005). *Max Wertheimer & Gestalt Theory*. New Brunswick, NJ: Transaction Publisher.

Knorr-cetina, K. (1997). Sociality with objects: Social relations in postsocial knowledge societies. *Theory, Culture & Society*, *14*(4), 1–30. doi:10.1177/026327697014004001

Lakoff, G., & Johnson, M. (1980). *Metaphors We Live By*. Chicago: The University of Chicago Press.

Latour, B. (2005). *Reassembling the Social: An Introduction to Actor-Network Theory*. Oxford, UK: Oxford University Press.

Maes, R. (2007). Information management: an integrative perspective. In A. Huizing & E. de Vries (Eds.), *Information Management: Setting the Scene*. London: Elsevier.

Moran, P., & Ghoshal, S. (1999). Markets, Firms, and the Process of Economic Development. *Academy of Management Review*, *24*(3), 390–412.

Nardi, B. A., Whittaker, S., & Schwarz, H. (2002). Networkers and their activity in intentional networks. *Computer Supported Cooperative Work*, *11*(1/2), 205–242. doi:10.1023/A:1015241914483

Nonaka, I., & Takeuchi, H. (1995). *The Knowledge-creating Company*. New York: Oxford University Press.

Putnam, L. L. (1983). The Interpretative Perspective: An Alternative to Functionalism. In L. L. Putnam & M. E. Pacanowsky (Eds.), Communication and Organizations: An Interpretative Approach. Sage Publications.

Sennett, R. (2007). *The Culture of the New Capitalism*. New Haven, CT: Yale University Press.

Shapiro, C., & Varian, H. R. (1999). *Information Rules – A Strategic Guide to the Network Economy.* Boston: Harvard Business School Press.

Simon, H. A. (1976). *Administrative Behaviour* (3rd ed.). New York: Free Press.

Spender, J. C., & Scherer, A. G. (2007). The Philosophical Foundations of Knowledge Management. *Editor's Introduction. Organization, 14*(1), 5–28.

Stigler. (1988). *Memoirs of an Unregulated Economist*. New York: Basic Books.

Suchman, L. (2005). Affiliative Objects. *Organization, 12*(3), 379–399. doi:10.1177/1350508405051276

Trevino, L. K., Daft, R. L., & Lengel, R. H. (1990). Understanding Managers Media Choices: A Symbolic Interactionist Perspective. In J. Fulk & C. Steinfield (Eds.), *Organizations and Communication Technology*. Newbury Park, CA: Sage. doi:10.4135/9781483325385.n4

Tsoukas, H. (2005). *Complex Knowledge*. Oxford, UK: Oxford University Press.

Van Grembergen, W., & Haes, D. E. S. (2007). Implementing IT governance: Models, practices and cases. Hershey, PA: IGI Global.

Weick, K. E. (1995). *Sensemaking in Organizations*. Thousand Oaks, CA: Sage.

Wenger, E. (1998). *Communicaties of practice: learning, meaning, and identity*. Cambridge, UK: Cambridge University Press. doi:10.1017/CBO9780511803932

Williamson, O. E. (1975). *Markets and Hierarchies: Analysis and Antitrust Implications*. New York: Free Press.

Wilson, T. D. (1997). *Information management: International Encyclopedia of Information and Library Science*. London: Routledge.

Wittel, A. (2001). Toward a Network Sociality. *Theory, Culture & Society, 18*(6), 51–76. doi:10.1177/026327601018006003

Woolsey Biggart, N., & Delbridge, R. (2004). Systems of exchange. *Academy of Management Review, 29*(1), 28–49.

KEY TERMS AND DEFINITIONS

Knowledge and Learning: In objectivism, knowledge consists of the abstracted representations of the practice that are stored cognitively in the human mind, while learning is perceived as how objective information is absorbed. The experimental knowledge manifested in social practices that emerges from the interaction and social negotiation is critical, unlike knowledge of representation that we have of the objects in the world. Telling the truth, understanding, and meaning are constructed subjectively, which implies that knowledge resides not only in the individual mind, but also in people's relations. There is a reality beyond the individual, constructed subjectively.

Chapter 13
Quality Information Concepts, Evolution, and Applications

José Poças Rascão
Polytechnic Institute of Setúbal, Portugal

ABSTRACT

The purpose of this chapter is to contribute to a better understanding of the concept of quality of information in the field of information sciences, as well as in other areas of knowledge, based on the aggregation of existing literature. Is a descriptive research, with the aim of identifying and characterizing the attributes of quality of information as universal among the different areas of knowledge. The structure of the chapter synthesizes the existing academic work, seeking to generate new knowledge. The results can be used for practical application in different areas of knowledge. The chapter seeks to firstly identify the apparent attributes and then focuses in greater detail on some of these attributes.

INTRODUCTION

The quality of information is a recent theme. However there is a widespread consensus among researchers that is essential to the survival of any organization and as such this concept should be defined, measured and evaluated to support decision-makers. In the organizational context is one of the foundations for the survival and increased competitiveness. Some researchers have proposed models and methodologies to measure the quality of the information available.

This chapter aims to provide a reflection on the quality of the information, taking into account the context in which it is inserted and contribute to a better understanding of this concept in information science, based on the aggregation of existing literature. Is a descriptive research with the aim of identifying and characterizing the major attributes of quality information succinct approach the concepts of information, quality and information quality introduce player in the topic, looking to generate new knowledge. The results can be used by different Sciences and or areas of knowledge.

DOI: 10.4018/978-1-5225-3725-0.ch013

INFORMATION

In the last years have seen a major transformation in the civilized world, that is to say, post-industrial age to the information age and knowledge. These days are the knowledge and information that links society and organizations, having become the information itself in an industry.

This dependence on knowledge and information will tend to increase in the coming years, the basic understanding of the importance of the information will be as important as they were before the expertise in the fields, in the age of the farmer or the basic industrial skills, in the industrial age. It is necessary to understand the resource information securely and efficiently. The innocence of the importance of information can be compared with the innocence of Madame Marie Curie when handled the radioactive uranium in his laboratory, unaware of the dangers to which they are exposed, and eventually pay that innocence with scientific life itself.

Objectivism and Subjectivism of Information

Objectivism

In the handling of information is necessary to move from innocence to knowledge, so that the users/decision makers can have an understanding scientifically based on information for decision-making and that can manage. Information and knowledge have been affected by the Objectivist thought. The Objectivism has given the domain, rationality, the definition and purpose that are commonly attributed to information and knowledge, as well as the definitions of the concepts of information, knowledge, communication and learning.

In addition, information and knowledge show a deep appreciation for how the market is organized, as suggested by economists. Be an influential theory means that the underlying theoretical assumptions are internalized in systems where people believe and that can turn into an ideology. The objectivism is the dominant culture of the Western world. The objectivism as an "umbrella" for all schools of thought and theories that are based on the idea that for knowledge development should see the world as consisting of distinct objects that can and should be separated from its inventors and users. Built over time by the traditional rationalist and empiricist theory, this idea is deeply entrenched in the sciences, such as economics, computer science, mathematics and sociology, as well as, in the disciplines of business, such as accounting and financial management. Also includes a large part of the management of information and the adjacent fields of knowledge and learning, in theory and in practice. Information management is default objectivist.

The objectivism is associated with the ' scientific truth, rationality, precision, clarity, and impartiality "(Lakoff & Johnson, 1980:189). The objectivists claim that human behavior is determined by the forces of the outside world. People, however, cannot control these outside forces and find it hard to understand them. The foreign forces and their control must be supported by knowledge, in order to help people master your surroundings, so that can lead to successful performance. Therefore, for the development of knowledge becomes relevant in practice, focus on the external aspects of how to understand the world.

The outside world to humans is thought to be composed of different real objects. These objects have inherent properties implying why they are not affected by the way one thinks about them or how to use. A rose is a rose, regardless of how someone perceives.

The live objects in themselves, immune to the subjectivity of our thoughts, feelings and emotions. They have specific meanings that can be known for research of their properties. Roses have thorns, distinct smells and other fixed properties together define our interactions and understanding of this category. Once the properties are fully understood, the true knowledge is durable. Building a theory based on the properties of information and knowledge is an approach favored by the relevant literature (Shapiro & Varian, 1999 and 1998, Boisot). Generally the reasoning is that traditional theories were developed for the industrial society that help organizations control the physical goods. The information and knowledge, however, have properties and characteristics derived from those assets. The typical example of such idiosyncratic properties implies, for example, that information can be easily copied with minimal cost or that knowledge can enjoy its use. Understand these objective properties and structure them in a cause and structure of abstract relationships of their effect, create the theory that guides organizations in the information and knowledge society.

Can understand our surroundings and abstracting the properties of objects and use the knowledge gained to determine our relationship with the objects. In Objectivism, knowledge consists of ' abstract ' discrete representation of the beads understanding of objective reality and learning is a step-by-step process directed to the constant refinement of these factual representations. Clearly outlining objects with inherent properties and understanding how these properties relate to each other, it is considered to be the gateway to knowledge and mastery over the environment for those who have this knowledge. Since the knowledge on objectivism is factual, objective and is transferable to others the meaning of communication. Through communication, the fixed meanings of objects are transferred from a sender to a receiver, a vision of communication which is known as the channel metaphor (Bryant, 2007). In this view, the main source of miscommunication is subjectivism human. Communication failures can occur when the sender uses an inappropriate language or when the receiver is unaware of the exact meaning of the language used and misinterpret the message.

In objectivism, subjectivity must also be suspect for other reasons. Because successful performance in the surroundings are entirely dependent on him, the creation of knowledge cannot be left to individuals, as they are prone to human error stimulated by personal and cultural biases, prejudices or other subjective limitations. The only real knowledge is considered to be objective and rational knowledge, for which needs the effort of science with regard to the accuracy of the unfortunate truths. Science allows us to abstract the experimental knowledge of practice in such a way that the correct, the General and the final reality might be data that are objective, universal and unconditionally true. People can be objective, but only if they use clear language, consisting of words with fixed meanings, combining reality with what is being described. Science provides us with the language. In addition, scientific methodologies allow you to present the models resulting from rational behavior, as prescriptive theories that tell us how to succeed in the external environment. This view of positivism in science, the methodology and knowledge also prevails in the Literatures of information and knowledge. Finally, the Objectivism to subjectivism is preferred, because it helps to be above personal judgments of illusions and human errors and, accordingly, promotes clarity and impartiality of the human relationships.

Subjectivism

Subjectivism is the philosophical tradition that emerged in the 20th century with discontent with the objectivism which plays a game on elusive scientific theory. The subjectivism as a term of "umbrella"' for all schools of thought and theories that depart from the idea that the development of knowledge, we must focus on the human beings and see them as acting in the world through the make sense and that modify the context in which they live. It's not my ambition to give a complete overview of the theories of subjectivism; since it is a task too daunting to me too. With the intention to introduce a number of basic understandings of subjectivism used the neoclassical model of the perfect market. Considered neoclassical economics and the practice of social theory based on representative applications of objectivism and subjectivism, respectively, as the light of the judgment in both worlds of thought. Developed in hermeneutics, in phenomenology, sociology and interpretative in critical theory, subjectivism won particularly meaning in the sciences, such as sociology, anthropology, psychology, and Semiotics. Subjectivism can also be found in the literature of management and organizations, for example, in cognitive theories of organizations or in the social theories of organizational learning (Boniface et al., 2004).

With this is not to say that the subjectivism became the dominant branch of thought in many sciences. More than that, it is often taken as an alternative to objectivist thought, which is also the case of the literature of information science. There is however a greater awareness that information and knowledge are social phenomena and not just economic objects. No matter, how can they be understood the philosophical differences between objectivism and subjectivism, as have profound implications. Compared with the objectivism, subjectivism involves redefining the fundamental concepts of information management, a new set of underlying assumptions of reformulation of its domain, rationality, purpose and definition, and a different perspective of management and organization. Subjectivism is a different view of the world, certainly.

Subjectivism is a philosophical tradition which opposes to objectivism. Subjectivism means "provide an alternative to human experience and understanding, instead of objective truth" (Lakoff & Johnson, 1980). In Objectivism, human behavior is the result of forces that act in the world and that people cannot control, and are difficult to comprehend. The interest and motivation of objectivism is therefore providing people as law, the rational knowledge that will help you work successfully in the outside world. Since the objectivism is directed to the external aspects of the understanding, the internal aspects are the primary domain of subjectivism. What motivates the subjectivism is the awareness; understanding, truth, and meaning that are relative to the physical and cultural context, the way of life of the people, as well as the mental structures of how the world works (Putnam .1983). When the contexts and the concessions people mental oppose seriously against each other, there can be no objective, understanding, truth and meaning valid universal. On the other hand, understanding, truth and meaning are not strictly personal. When the meaning is entirely personal, each individual understanding may be called a truth.

In this extreme case of subjectivism, the human sense would be totally spontaneous. The sky would be the limit imaginative. The story mentioned the Trobiand Papuas illustrates how objectivism and subjectivism extreme visions are both inadequate, at least for those aspects of reality that are related to human intervention. The meaning of the Papuas gave the game of Cricket is not objective or personal, but subjective. They gave meaning to the game together, which is now common knowledge. In its context and in social practice, this knowledge is true. The location of this fact prevents them from participating in the World Championship, but presumably they don't care. Subjectivity is relevant to many forms of organization, because it allows the collective action of the organizational units – a Department, a management team, a network of professionals – on the basis of experience and locally shared understandings (Weick, 1995). The example of the Papuas illustrates also the truth and the true knowledge are always dependent on how people understand experimentally their worlds and what people find meaning and significant in their lives. In turn, what people give importance is not only relevant in the objectivism of her rational knowledge, but also in your imagination, intuition, emotions, values, beliefs, experiences and aspirations.

QUALITY

The term *quality* comes from the Latin *qualitative*, and is used in different situations. For example, when speaking on the quality of life of the people of a country or region, when speaking of the quality of the water that you drink or the air you breathe, the quality of service provided by a given company or when speaking of the quality of a product. As the term has several uses, their meaning is not always clear and objective definition.

With regard to products and/or services sold on the market, there are several definitions for quality: "compliance with the requirements of customers", "cost/benefit", "fitness for use", " added value which similar products do not have "; "do it right the first time"; "products and/or services with effectiveness". Anyway, the term is generally used to mean "Excellence" of a product or service. The quality of a product or service can be looked at from two of optical producer and customer, even as Deming, (1990), "the quality can only be defined in terms of who evaluates". From the point of view of the producer, the quality associated with the design and production of a product that meets customer needs. From the point of view of the customer, the quality is associated to the value and usefulness of the product, being recognized in some cases linked to the price.

From the point of view of customers, quality is not one-dimensional. I mean, customers do not evaluate a product taking into account just one of its features, but several. For example, the size, color, durability, design, role etc. So, quality is a multidimensional. Quality has many dimensions and is therefore more difficult to define. So, it can be difficult even for the client to express what it considers a quality product. The client does not evaluate whether a product and or service possess quality just by price, or by a particular feature, on the contrary, the quality is determined when the product or service and reach the customer expectation. The definition of quality must always be related to customer satisfaction.

From the point of view of the company, however, if the goal is to offer quality products and services, the concept cannot be left to chance. Must be defined clearly and objectively. This means that the company must determine what the needs of customers are and, in the light of these, set product quality requirements. The requirements are defined in terms of variables such as length, width, height, weight, color, resistance, durability, functions performed, delivery time, sympathy who meets the client, speed of service, effectiveness of service, etc. Each requirement is then quantified so that quality can be interpreted by all (company, workers, managers and customers) in exactly the same way.

The products must display these requirements, advertising makes up around those requirements (and not others), quality control to ensure that these requirements are present in the product, the satisfaction measurement is done to determine the extent to which these requirements are present and to what extent will really meet the needs. The entire operation of the "quality company" revolves around the concept of quality offer that was set. Quality is a property, attribute or condition of people able to distinguish it from other. On a scale of values is a quality property, attribute or condition that allows you to accept or refuse any thing (Almeida, 1994, p. 5; Neihmy, Guimarães (1996, p. 112). The quality indicates, for example, the relative value of the products and or services, the efficiency and effectiveness of the processes in the production of goods and services. Business science the quality of products and or services can be leveraged to achieve competitive advantages (Almeida, 1994, p. 5; Neihmy, Guimarães (1996, p. 111).

EVOLUTION OF THE CONCEPT OF QUALITY OF INFORMATION

The term quality of information is a recent term and was approached for the first time in the Seminary of Nordie *Council for Scientific Information and Research Libraries* in 1989 in Copenhagen, Denmark (Cabral, 2008). According to Marchand (1989) and Cabral (2008), the concept of quality of information can be discussed according to the following criteria:

- **Transcendence:** The value of information is recognized as absolute and universal (synonym of excellence) or is intrinsic quality (e.g. a poem, a mathematical formula, etc.);
- **Product:** The information while thing that can be measured, quantified, sold, copied;
- **Production:** Quality of information as established standards by the customers; any deviation from the standards means quality reduction.
- **Decision Makers/Users:** The types and sources of information that more satisfy the makers/users of the subjectivisms point of view and with weak possibilities of operationalization.
- **Aspect of Value:** The value of information is regarded as more comprehensive category and as one of its attributes.

English (2001) based on the principles of quality of Denning, Ishikawa, Juran and Crosby (1990) and other authors that have implemented quality models in the industrial age. Are identified some attributes of the quality of the information, such as: accuracy, updating, reliability, effectiveness, efficiency, among others. Second Strong; Lee; Wang (1997) there are three roles in the cycle of information: the information producers, the raw material for the information, the Trustees of the information you provide and control the means to store and maintain the information and even consumers of information to perform their duties. According to Li and Chi (2002) there are three approaches to identify the attributes or characteristics of the quality of information:

- **Intuitive:** Identification of attributes based on the experience of *experts* and intuition of the important attributes;
- **Empirical:** Identification of attributes by users/decision-makers;
- **Theoretical:** Attributes of existing theories emphasis (analog, and ontological).

Huang, Lee, Wang (1999) reviewed the three approaches used in the literature and proposed the systemic definition based on Ontology with logical foundations derived from the vision of quality of information under the user's optical/decision maker.

Huang, Lee and Wang (1999) quality of information contexts were defined and proposed a vocabulary of the characteristics and dimensions of the quality of the information in a continuous cycle. Proposed also an information quality program adapted to the concept of total quality management that uses the five principles for the industry, considering the information as a product.

Table 1. Attributes, and dimensions of the quality of information on user/decision maker

Attributes/Categories	Dimensions of the Quality of Information
Intrinsic	• Lens • Accurate • Credible • Trusted
Contextual	• Relevant • Current • Complete • With value (accumulated)
Representational	• Interpretable • Clara • Concise • Need
Accessibility	• Accessible • Easy to handle • Safe

Source: Cabral, a. t. s., (2008), in: Transformation, Campinas, 20 (1): 29-45, Jan/Apr.

Table 2. Attributes, and dimensions of the quality of information on product

Attributes/Categories	Dimensions of the Quality of Information
Intrinsic	• Lens • Accurate • Credible • Trusted
Contextual	• Relevant • Current • Complete • With value (accumulated)
Representational	• Interpretable • Clara • Concise • Need
Accessibility	• Accessible • Safe

Source: Cabral, a. t. s., (2008), in: Transformation, Campinas, 20 (1): 29-45, Jan/Apr.

PERCEPTION OF THE QUALITY OF INFORMATION

The perception is the brain function that allows the individual to organize and interpret sensory impressions, in order to assign meaning to the surroundings, from a history of past experiences. The process consists in the acquisition, interpretation, selection and arrangement of the information obtained, and may or may not rely on any information from the memory. This cognitive activity occurs thanks to the sense organs that convey the information obtained. First, the organs receptors detect and receive the stimulation, a process called sensation. Then, this stimulus is translated into nerve impulses that are sent to the brain, where they are processed. This whole sequence starts with the attention, a process of selective observation in operating various determinants: external factors and internal factors. By external factors we understand that agents arise outside the body, or stimuli that the organs of the senses. As an example, we can consider the movement of the stimulus, its intensity, contrast and incongruity. The internal factors are related to our being and our personality. We can take as an example the motivation for the stimulus, the experiences that we had previously, the greater or lesser knowledge and understanding of the stimulus, the social and the expectation, among others.

As we acquire new information, our perception about a given subject will-if changing. However, it should be noted that even in the absence of stimulus change, your interpretation may vary, by influence of experiences witnessed by the subject. So, after the arrival of the information to the brain, structure and organize the representations of the world. Is it that gives meaning to what we see, hear and feel, given that the information coming from the sensory organs is processed in the brain, nervous system structure in which the stimuli they gain meaning and therefore meaning. However, if the brain or sensory organs are not in balance with the characteristics of the environment, perceptions may not correspond to what actually is observed, look and feel, hence the existence of perceptions, hallucinations or illusions of the senses.

Sometimes, it may not be any perception vis-à-vis the stimulus. This situation occurs when the object perceived has no basis in the reality of the person concerned, so that she may simply not realize, and eventually ignore it. The perception represents a single cognitive process. Is distinct from memory, because, while this is related to past events, the perception is directly related to observable events in the present moment. Also considering the different perception of thought and conscience, as the perception refers to the subjectivity of human being. The perception is born from a stimulus from the outside, contrary to conscience and thought processes are more intimate and there are no stimuli, so you only need to resort to memory. The pain is a response of the brain resulting from the activation of local stimuli, which may result from any kind of perception. Relates to tactile perception, being extremely important for humans, given allow the transmission of information that there is something in the body that is not at its most balanced and healthy. The pain is considered subjective, as the information transmitted by the brain cause of pain is always the same, simply varies in intensity. This is clearly influenced by the psychological state of the individual and by the sensitivity of the site that is being applied.

The presence and condition of the individual are extremely important for the perception of the stimulus, given that the individual has different types of perception that allow you to adapt the information received and thus arrange the representations of the world. Thus, there are several types of perception, visual and auditory perceptions represent the most developed in humans, given that were fundamental to the survival of the human species.

- **Visual Perception:** Perception of light by the visual system. It is characterized by the perception of forms, spatial relationships, colors, light intensity and moves.
- **Auditory Perception:** Perception of sounds by ear. The study of auditory perception is based on the analysis of the perception of timbres, heights and frequencies, the perception of loudness and volume, and also the rhythmic perception, intensely related to temporal perception.
- **Olfactory Perception:** Perception of odors. Despite the smell but a sense in humans, this is extremely important for our palate, particularly during feeding.
- **Gustatory Perception:** Perception of flavors by the tongue usually associated with the pleasure. Such as smell, represents one of the least developed senses in humans.
- **Tactile Perception:** Perception of objects and sensations in the skin. This kind of perception allows you to recognize the presence, shape, size and temperature of objects in contact with the body. In addition, it is extremely important for the human being to allow proper positioning of your body as the physical protection of the same. This kind of perception is not uniform, since your hands, tongue and lips have a greater sensitivity, making it more accessible for the same identification of stimuli.
- **Temporal Perception:** Perception of temporal durations, production of rhythms, temporal order and concurrency. This kind of perception is extraordinarily important in music, hence directly related to auditory perception. The temporal perception is not exclusively identified by any organs, resulting combined identification by the sense organs and brain potential.
- **Spatial Perception:** Perception of distances between objects. There is no specific body to identify the spatial perception, since the perception of distance and the relative size of objects implies the combination of auditory, visual and temporal perception. In this way, we can identify whether a subject is closer or pushing through sound more or less intense by he produced, by observation of its dimensions or by analysis of increase or decrease their sharpness.

- Second (Klein & Hirschleim, 1987), the perception of quality of information influences our view of the facts and/or events but also our perception of communication (Mokros, 1993, Schement, 1993) and the conduct of research (Newman, 2001, Schement 1993). This means that the perception of the quality of information, have a profound influence in the field of information sciences. The concept of quality of information is handled in a pragmatic manner by the people and nothing much reflection. It has been the practice that has led to the construction of the concept of quality of information. The concepts of quality of information not perceived clearly by the people and the quality attributes of the information mix and thin clear distinction is between them.

The practice and use of information give people the understanding of academic concept that he intuitively work without knowing the theory that builds the definitions and concepts. Some of the information quality attributes are not evident to the people. They do not choose the information by the concepts; work on intuitively using common sense and the tune to express his perception of the quality of the information. There is no evidence of explicit knowledge or familiarity with the subject. If a tacit knowledge, disorganized and marked by comparisons and synonyms. The perception of the quality of the information is not clear to people, is closer to the popular knowledge than scientific knowledge. Maybe by the lack of clear concepts that support unambiguous interpretations that qualify the information.

QUALITY OF INFORMATION

For Oleto, r. r., (2006), the quality of information is a difficult concept, since it is an abstract noun and quick understanding through common sense, but understanding complex, when it seeks a more accurate description. According to Ferreira (1975, p. 1165) "quality is one of the fundamental categories of thought: way to be claimed or refuses a thing". It can also be defined as "a sensitive aspect that cannot be measured things." Given the amount of information available, the individuals and organizations live the problem of select/filter, among so much information, those who have quality to support in decision-making.

But what are the criteria to be observed in the process of filtering available information to verify that you have quality information? Can you leave the problem of selection delivered to the good sense of the makers/users, with the assumption that the concept of quality of the information is similar to that of beauty: "I recognize the beauty when I see it"? The output normally used by science is through an operational definition that leads to the level of the quantitative observations. This operation is not always satisfactory, since it depends on the level of knowledge of the concept, theory in which it is involved and the instrumental possibilities of measurement. In addition to the previously mentioned difficulties with the concept of information quality in information science, seems to set deeper difficulties, as can be evidenced in the work of deconstruction of the concept made by Nehmy and Paim (1998) and Nehmy (1996). According to the same authors, under the epistemological point of view, the notion of quality of the information, as defined, is vague, ambiguous, imprecise and subjective and should be rejected as scientific concept. Yet the science of information does studies on the quality of the information, but more conducive to the operationalization of the concept with regard to objectives, product-based aspects.

Approach of the Quality of Information Based on Product

The approach based on the product emphasis of information as thing, according to the concept of Bukland (1991, p. 351-360) and assigns some dimensions or attributes to the quality of the information, such as comprehensiveness, timeliness, objectivity, reliability, accuracy, accessibility and validity. These attributes give multidimensionality to quality of information (Paim, Nehmy and Guimarães, 1996). Nehmy (1996, p. 30) considers the attributes scope and objectivity as intrinsic values of information. Second Buckland (1991) attribute accessibility is important to the area of information, especially for the provision of services, since the major concern is the reduction of the time required for customers/users to have access to the information they need for decision-making to achieve personal goals or institutional work.

For Palm, Nehmy, Guimarâes (1996, p. 116) reliability means credibility on content and source of information and relate it with the idea of cognitive authority – prestige, respect, reputation of the source, author or institution, that is, it resembles a kind of faith. The precision has the meaning of accuracy, correctness, which brings us to how to record true to fact represented. The concept of validity assumes integrity of the source of information. According to Campos (1992, p. 2) States that "a product or service is one that corresponds to reliably, affordably, safely and on time to the customer's needs". The Brazilian Association of technical standards (ABNT, 1994, p. 3-4) defines the quality of the information as an entity that confers the ability to explicit and implicit needs of the customers that is; quality is defined as "fitness for use" or "fitness for purpose" or "customer satisfaction" or "compliance with the requirements".

Approach of the Quality of Information Based on User/Decision Maker

Second Saracevic (1996, p. 46) in 70 years the information recovery paradigm has shifted towards the background, turning to the users/decision-makers and their interactions, reflecting a deeper understanding of the problem. Durbin and Nilan (1986) made a census of the issues that were being discussed and which pointed to multiple paths, but focused on the user/decision maker. The authors have confirmed the existence of a tension existing in the literature between visible research in information science and practice. The different authors appealed to research on the needs and use of information by users/decision-makers with the argument that it was necessary to refocus the research, since the current were not promoting the basis for this reorientation.

Among the topics for which you made more attention of researchers were: the need to give greater attention to users/decision-makers and the centrality of the needs and use of information set from the users/decision-makers. Nehmy and Paim (1998, p. 42) associate the relevance of information quality lens, seen working from assumptions of adequacy of indexing topics and issues documents classification of bibliographic research, where research is defined by the representation of a need for information. In such a perspective the relevance is associated with the match between a source and a receiver. Paim, Nehmy and Guimaraes (1996, p. 116) associate effectiveness the adequacy of information on troubleshooting subject-user. The effectiveness is due to the use of the information, i.e. the information is effective if it contributes to some positive results for the subject of the action, as for example in decision making. The review of the existing literature, it was found that several authors present different attributes/criteria to evaluate the quality of information. According to the literature review, Table 3 shows the attributes/criteria summary of different authors.

Table 3. Attributes and criteria of the quality of information on user/decision maker

Dimension	Attributes/Quality Criteria	Definition
Time	At the right time	The information must be supplied at the right time, when required.
	Update	The information should be updated when it is provided
	Frequency	The information must be provided as many as often as necessary
	Opportunity	The information should be available to the right person at the right time.
	Reduction of uncertainty	Good information reduces uncertainty. Good information involves differences that *makes a difference;*
	Element of surprise	The information can be used to obtain competitive advantages;
	Accessibility	The information is only useful if people have access to it; the *accessibility* is within reach of those who can get the information in time to be used efficiently and in the format that makes it useful. Electronic storage makes the information more easily accessible than pencil and paper technology
	Period	The information should be provided on past, present and future periods
Context	Accuracy/correction	The information must be free from errors
	Relevance	The information must relate to the information needs of a specific receptor for a specific situation. It should be noted what is relevant, the exceptions
	Relevance	The information shall relate to the facts, be available and be important to the person who requires. The information will help people to make decisions
	Integrity	All the information that is required must be provided
	Completeness	Complete information contains all the important facts
	Brevity	Only the information that is required must be provided
	Amplitude/flexibility	Information can have a wide range or narrow or an internal or external focus
	Performance	The information could prove the measure performance of activities completed, of the progress made or accumulated resources. Assessing the impact of information on desired results
	Simplicity	The information should be simple, not overly complex
	Veridicality	The information must be verified and its correctness can be ensured
	Reliability	The information depends on some other factor such as the method of data collection and the source of information. The user needs to believe in information to feel safe when taking decisions.
	Accuracy	The information must be *accurate*, this means that if the information is not accurate, loses interest
	Comparison	The information should reflect a comparison of the plans running (planned vs. real vs. detour) and trends (above, below or within the expectations), as for example the comparison with prior periods (year, month and accumulated, etc.)
Form	Clarity on interpretability	The information should be provided in a way that is easy to understand
	Detail	The information should be provided in detail, summarized or synthesis. The information shall be in a level of proper synthesis at the level of decision-makers/user, without presenting anything irrelevant to the decision maker/user and a degree of excessive synthesis with respect to your interest.
	Order	The information should be arranged in a predetermined sequence
	Presentation	The information should be presented in the form of narrative, numerical, or other graphics
	Media/media	Information can be provided in the form of printed paper documents, video monitors or other media

Source: adapted from Bio (1996); Stair & Reynolds (2011) and O'Brien (2004)

QUALITY EVALUATION MODEL OF INFORMATION

Second Parasuraman et al. (1985), the assessment of the quality of information can be measured by two indicators and moments:

- The expected quality (and) of information-based on the needs of the use of information
- The perceived quality (P) of the information-based on the use of the information in decision making.

Second Parasuraman et al. (1985), the quality of information (Q) results from the difference between the perception (P) and expectations (and) the quality of information, namely (Q = P-E). Thus, if the resulting *gap* is negative, so the quality level is below than expected, resulting in unacceptable quality. These indicators can assist in identifying the *gaps* between expectations and the perception of the quality of the information.

The *Gap* Model (Parasuraman et al., 1985) can be adapted to the context of quality of information:

- **1 Gap:** The difference between the expectations of *users of information* and awareness of decision-makers about these expectations;
- **2 Gap:** The difference between the perception of the decision maker (s) in relation to the expectations of the *user (s) of the information* and the *specifications of the information*;
- **3 Gap:** The difference between the *specifications of the information* and the *information actually offered*;
- **4 Gap:** The difference between the *information provided* and what is communicated to the user (s);
- **5 Gap:** The difference between what the *user (s) of information* (m) receives and the perception that he (s) has (have) the *information provided.*

The *gaps* model was adapted to the quality of information evidencing that the expectation of the users can be a confluence of information needs:

- For performance measurements (*ad hoc* or not; cross-references and indicators);
- To evaluate decision scenarios (simulations), and
- For queries of historical information (reports and graphs).

According to Jiang et al. (2003), issues related to the quality of information in order to identify the *gaps* that exist:

- **The Gap of Expectations:** What are the clients ' expectations about the information provided? What are the expectations of managers of information? Information managers understand the expectations of its customers/users? If not, where are the *gaps*? This measure of *gap* of expectations includes expectations of current customers, perception of managers of information about those expectations, and the ability of managers based on standards of quality of information.

Table 4. Dimensions and attributes of the quality of information expected and perceived

	Expectations (E)	Perceptions (P)
Time	**Readiness** -the information **should** be provided when necessary.	**Readiness** – information **is** provided when required
	Punctuality -the information **should** be close to the fact.	**Punctuality** -the information is close to the fact.
	Update -the information **should** be updated when provided	**Update** -the information is updated when provided.
	Frequency -the information should be provided as many times as are necessary.	**Frequency** – information **is** provided as many times as are necessary.
	Period -the information **should** be provided on past, present and future periods.	**Period** -the information **is** provided on past, present and future periods
Context	**Accuracy/correction** -the information **should** be free of errors.	**Accuracy/correction** -the information **is** error-free.
	Relevance/exception -the information **should** be related to information needs of a specific receptor for a specific situation should be highlighted; what's relevant, the exceptions.	**Relevance/exception** -the information **is** related to the information needs of a specific receptor for a particular situation; is what is relevant, the exceptions
	Integrity -all necessary information **should** be provided.	**Integrity** -all necessary information **is** provided.
	Completeness -complete information **should** contain all the important facts.	**Completeness** -complete information **contains** all the important facts
	Brevity – only the necessary information should be provided.	**Brevity** – only the necessary information **is** provided.
	Amplitude/flexibility – the information **should** have a wide range or narrow, or an internal or external focus.	**Amplitude/flexibility** -the information **has** a wide range or narrow, or an internal or external focus.
	Performance – information **should** reveal performance by measuring completed activities, the progress achieved or accumulated resources.	**Performance** – the information **reveals** the performance measurement activities completed, of the progress made or accumulated resources.
	Simplicity - the information **should** be simple, not overly complex.	**Simplicity** - the information **is** simple, not overly complex.
	Verifiability - **it should** be possible to verify the information and to ensure its correctness.	**Verifiability** - **it is** possible to verify the information and to ensure its correctness.
	Reliability -the information **should** be reliable and can be used without risk to decision-making.	**Reliability** -the information **is** reliable and can be used without risk to decision-making.
	Comparison – the information **should** reflect the comparison of planned with the accomplished, as well as trends.	**Comparison** – the information **reflects** the comparison of planned with the accomplished, as well as trends.
Form	**Clarity** -the information **should** be provided in a way that was easy to understand.	**Clarity** -the information **is** provided in a way that is easy to understand.
	Detail – the information **should** appear in a level of proper synthesis at the level of the user, without presenting anything irrelevant and either a degree of excessive synthesis with respect to your interest.	**Detail** – the information **appear** at a level appropriate to the level of synthesis, without presenting anything irrelevant and either a degree of excessive synthesis with respect to your interest.
	Order -the information **should** be organized in a predetermined sequence presented.	**Order** -the information **is** organized in a predetermined sequence presented.
	Presentation -the information **should** be presented in narrative form, numbers, or other graphics.	**Presentation** -the information **is** presented in narrative form, numbers, or other graphics.
	Media -the information **should** be provided in the form of printed paper documents, video monitors or other media.	**Media** -the information **is** provided in the form of printed paper documents, video monitors or other media.
(1) (2)	(3) (4)	(5) (6) (7)
Strongly disagree		strongly agree

Source: adapted from Bio (1996), Stair & Reynolds (2011), O'Brien (2004) and Salomi et al. (2005)

- **The Gap of Perception:** What are the perceptions of customers about the information given to them? What are the perceptions of managers of information on the performance of information? They accept? If not, customers are very satisfied with the information provided to them?
- **The Gap of Performance:** Represents an inability to meet the expectations. The information and the user of information: what are the perceptions of users about the quality of the information? They are satisfied with the information provided? If not, what information do they need to be improved? What are the perceptions of managers of information about the quality of the information? They are satisfied with their performance? If not, what information do they need to be improved? These measures represent the gap (G) between the perspectives of users and information managers.
- **The Gap of Satisfaction:** There is a gap in the quality of information as between users and managers of information? If yes, what are the dimensions and attributes that contribute to this gap? These are independent for the two groups (users and managers) and the expectations and perceptions of each group are uniquely identified.

According to Jiang et al. (2003), it is believed that the answers to these questions enable a diagnosis Rico about the quality of the information provided and to provide a measure to promote better management of quality of information. Large *gaps* indicate that information managers do not understand the information needs of their customers/users; a misunderstanding can make information of poor quality are offered to customers/users, resulting in dissatisfaction and seriously affecting the decision-making process.

CONCLUSION

Some authors question whether it is possible to measure the quality of information, since the perception of the quality of the information is not clear to many users / decision-makers. Some relevant questions can be put. You can select or work information from certain attributes/concepts? You can set how many and which attributes/concepts that are sufficient to ensure the quality of information?

To answer these and other questions have been presented some models that can be applied in different organizational environments. The quality of information is a new theme and multidimensional with a vast field for experimentation and application. There are many models offered, but few applications. It should be stressed that whatever the model or tool to be used or adapted, will be necessary to take into account the following premises:

- Identify a domain or context of organizational interest to analyze the quality of information, targeting the specific needs of information in this context;
- The need to identify ontologically the concepts and relationships that exist in that domain or context of interest, in order to help users/decision-makers to reach a consensus in the understanding of this area of knowledge, in order to clarify the differences and seek consensus about their meaning and importance;

Table 5. Implementation of the model for evaluating the quality of information according to the expectations of the evaluator

Evaluation of the Quality of Information														
Expectations (E)														
	Information Quality Attributes	**INF 1**	**INF 2**	**INF 3**	**INF 4**	**INF 5**	**INF 6**	**INF 7**	**INF 8**	**INF 9**	**INF 10**	**Media**		
Time	Readiness													
	Punctuality													
	Update													
	Frequency													
	Opportunity													
	Reduction of uncertainty													
	Element of surprise													
	Accessibility													
	Period													
Context	Accuracy/ correction													
	Relevance													
	Integrity													
	Completeness													
	Brevity													
	Amplitude/ flexibility													
	Performance													
	Simplicity													
	Verifiability													
	Reliability													
	Accuracy													
	Comparison													
Form	Clarity on interpretability													
	Detail													
	Order													
	Presentation													
	Media/media													
(1)		(2)		(3)			(4)		(5)			(6)		(7)
Strongly disagree														strongly agree

Source: adapted from Bio (1996), Stair & Reynolds (2011), O'Brien (2004) and Salomi et al. (2005)

Table 6. Implementation of the model for evaluating the quality of information according to the Perceptions of the evaluator

Evaluation of the Quality of Information														
Perceptions (P)														
	Information Quality Attributes	**INF 1**	**INF 2**	**INF 3**	**INF 4**	**INF 5**	**INF 6**	**INF 7**	**INF 8**	**INF 9**	**INF 10**	**Media**		
Team	Readiness													
	Punctuality													
	Update													
	Frequency													
	Opportunity													
	Reduction of uncertainty													
	Element of surprise													
	Accessibility													
	Period													
Context	Accuracy/ correction													
	Relevance													
	Integrity													
	Completeness													
	Brevity													
	Amplitude/ flexibility													
	Performance													
	Simplicity													
	Verifiability													
	Reliability													
	Accuracy													
	Comparison													
Form	Clarity on interpretability													
	Detail													
	Order													
	Presentation													
	Media/media													
(1)		(2)		(3)			(4)		(5)			(6)		(7)
Strongly disagree														strongly agree

Source: adapted from Bio (1996), Stair & Reynolds (2011), O'Brien (2004) and Salomi et al. (2005)

Table 7. Implementation of the model for evaluating the quality of information according to the expectations of the evaluator

Evaluation of the Quality of Information														
GAPS of satisfaction (Q = P-E)														
	Information Quality Attributes	**INF 1**	**INF 2**	**INF 3**	**INF 4**	**INF 5**	**INF 6**	**INF 7**	**INF 8**	**INF 9**	**INF 10**	**Media**	**Detour**	**Trend**
Team	**Readiness**													
	Punctuality													
	Update													
	Frequency													
	Opportunity													
	Reduction of uncertainty													
	Element of surprise													
	Accessibility													
	Period													
Context	**Accuracy/ correction**													
	Relevance													
	Integrity													
	Completeness													
	Brevity													
	Amplitude/ flexibility													
	Performance													
	Simplicity													
	Verifiabilty													
	Reliability													
	Accuracy													
	Comparison													
Form	**Clarity on interpretability**													
	Detail													
	Order													
	Presentation													
	Media/media													
(1)		(2)		(3)			(4)		(5)			(6)		(7)
Strongly disagree														strongly agree

Source: adapted from Bio (1996), Stair & Reynolds (2011), O'Brien (2004) and Salomi et al. (2005)

- Look for aspects that you can complete the survey on the quality of information, not only defining or adapting a model, but applying to the real world, mapping the level of quality of the information and seeking to identify the aspects that influence positively or negatively the informational process of organization, decision-making/use;

Regardless of the approach taken (intuitive, empirical, analog or otherwise) to measure the quality of the information is crucial to understanding the factors that facilitate and impede the learning of the quality of information in organizations. We are aware that the quality evaluation model of the proposed information will add value for both organizations, in terms of efficiency and effectiveness, as well as to users and decision-makers, as well as to the academic world.

REFERENCES

Ballou, D. P., & Pazer, H. L. (1985). Modeling data and process quality in multi-input, multioutput information systems. *Management Science*, *31*(2), 530–545. doi:10.1287/mnsc.31.2.150

Barbosa, R. R. (2007). O uso de fontes de informação por consultores empresariais: Um estudo junto ao mercado de consultoria de Belo Horizonte. *Perspectivas em Ciência da Informação, Belo Horizonte*, *13*(1), 95–101.

Bardin, L. (2002). *Análise de Conteúdo*. Lisboa: Edições 70.

Barreto, A. A. (2011). A eficiência Técnica e Econômica e a viabilidade de produtos e serviços de informação. *Ciência da Informação, 25*(3), 1-18. Retrieved from http://revista.ibict.br/ciinf/index.php

Batista, E. (2004). *O. Sistema de Informação: o uso consciente da tecnologia para o gerenciamento.* São Paulo: Saraiva.

Bio, S. R. (1996). *Sistemas de Informação: um enfoque gerencial.* São Paulo: Atlas.

Bobrowski, M., Marre, M., & Yankelevich, D. (1999). A Homogeneous framework to measure data quality. In *International Conference on Information Quality.* Cambridge, MA: MIT.

Boisot, M. H. (1998). *Knowledge Assets – Securing Competitive Advantage in the Information Age.* Oxford, UK: Oxford University Press.

Bonifacio, M., & Camussone, P., & Zini, C. (2004). Managing the KM Trade-Off: Knowledge Centralization versus Distribution. *Journal of Universal Computer Science*, *10*(3), 162–175.

Bryant, A., & Maes, R. (2005). *The role of the information architect: Conquering cognitive parochialism.* Retrieved from www.imresearch.org

Buckland, M. K. (1991). Information as thing. *Journal of the American Society for Information Science*, *42*(5), 351–360. doi:

Burgess, M. S. E., Gray, W. A., & Fiddian, N. J. (2004). Quality measures and the information consumer. In *International Conference on Information Quality*. Cambridge, MA: MIT.

Caballero, I., Gómez, Ó., & Piattini, M. (2004). Getting better information quality by assessing and improving information quality management. In *International Conference on Information Quality*. Cambridge, MA: MIT.

Calazans, A. T. S. (2006). Conceitos e uso da informação organizacional e informação estratégica. *Pesquisa Brasileira em Ciência da Informação e Biblioteconomia, 1*(2).

Campos, V. F. (1992). TQC: controle de qualidade total (no estilo japonês). Belo Horizonte: Fundação Christiano Ottoni: UFMG.

Casanova, M. B. (1990). Information: the major element for change. In I. Wormell (Ed.), *Information quality: definitions and dimentions* (pp. 42–53). London: Taylor Graham.

Cervo, A. L., & Bervian, P. A. (2002). *Metodologia científica. 5*. São Paulo: Pearson Prentice Hall.

Choo, C. W. (1998). *The Knowing Organization: How Organizations Use Information for Construct Meaning, Create Knowledge and Make Decisions*. Oxford Press.

Chow, W. S., & Lui, K. H. (2003). A Structural Analysis of the Significance of a Set of the Original TQM Measurement Items in Information Systems Function. *Journal of Computer Information Systems*.

Cooney, J. P. (1991). Qual o real valor da informação? *Revista Escola de Biblioteconomia/UFMG, Belo Horizonte, 20*(2), 176-190.

Cronbach, L. J. (1951). Coefficient alpha and the internal structure of tests. *Psychometrika, 16*(3), 297–334. doi:10.1007/BF02310555

Crosby, P. B. (1979). *Quality is free*. New York: McGraw-Hill.

Dai, Y. S., Gao, Q., Fan, Z., & Kang, R. G. (2007). User perceived quality of online social information services: from the perspective of knowledge management. *Proceedings of the 2007 IEEE IEEM*, 482-486. 10.1109/IEEM.2007.4419236

Davenport, T. H. (1998). *Ecologia da Informação: por que só a tecnologia não basta para o sucesso na era da informação. 6*. São Paulo: Futura.

Davenport, T. H., & Prusak, L. (1998). *Conhecimento empresarial: como as organizações gerenciam o seu capital intelectual*. Rio de Janeiro: Campus.

Davidson, B., Lee, Y. W., & Wang, R. (2004). Developing Data Production Maps: Meeting patient discharge data submission requirements. *International Journal of Healthcare Technology and Management, 6*(2), 223–240. doi:10.1504/IJHTM.2004.004978

Delone, W. H., & Mclean, E. R. (1992). Information systems success: The quest for the dependent variable. *Information Systems Research, 3*(1), 60–95. doi:10.1287/isre.3.1.60

Deming, W. E. (1990). Qualidade: a revolução da administração. Marques Saraiva.

Dervin, B., & Nilan, M. (1986). Information needs and uses. *Annual Review of Information Science & Technology, 21*, 3–32.

English, L. P. (2001), Information quality management: The next frontier. *ASQ's Annual Quality Congress Proceedings*, 529-533.

English, L. P. (2005). Information Quality: Critical ingredient for national security. *Journal of Database Management*, *16*(1), 18–32. doi:10.4018/jdm.2005010102

Ferreira. (1975). *Novo dicionário da língua portuguesa*. Rio de Janeiro: Nova Fronteira.

Freitas, A. L. P., Manhães, N. R. C., & Cozendey, M. I. (2006). Emprego do Servqual na avaliação da qualidade de serviços de tecnologia da informação: uma análise experimental. In *ENEGEP, 26., 2006. Fortaleza. Anais...*. Fortaleza: ENEGEP.

Furquim, T. (2004). Fatores motivadores de uso de site web: Um estudo de caso. *Ciência da Informação*, *33*(1), 48–54. doi:10.1590/S0100-19652004000100006

Gackowski, Z. J. (2005), Operations quality of data and information: teleological operations research-bases approach, call for discussion. In *International Conference on Information Quality*. Cambridge, MA: MIT.

Gelle, E., & Karhu, K. (2003). Information Quality for Strategic Technology Planning. *Industrial Management & Data Systems*, *103*(8), 633–643. doi:10.1108/02635570310497675

Gil, A. C. (2002). *Como elaborar projetos de pesquisa. 4*. São Paulo: Atlas.

Ginman, M. (1989), Quality information, and information for quality. In *Information quality definitions and dimensions: Proceedings of a NORDINFO Seminar*. Royal School of Librarianship.

Goodhue, D. L. (1995). Understanding user evaluations of information systems. *Management Science*, *4*(12), 1827–1844. doi:10.1287/mnsc.41.12.1827

Gruber, T.R. (1995). Towards principles for the design of ontologies used for knowledge sharing. *Int. J. Human-Computer Studies*, *43*(5-6).

Guimarães, C. G. (1996). Problematização do conceito "qualidade" da informação. *Perspectivas em Ciência da Informação, Belo Horizonte*, *1*(1), 111–119.

Huang, K. T., Lee, Y.W., & Wang, R.Y. (1999). Quality information and Knowledge. Prentice-Hall.

Jiang, J. J., Klein, G., Tesch, D., & Chen, H. (2003). Closing the user and provider service quality gap: A method for measuring service quality that includes both the user and IS service provider perspectives. *Communications of the ACM*, *46*(2), 72–76. doi:10.1145/606272.606276

Juran, J. M. (1990). *Planejando para a qualidade*. São Paulo: Pioneira.

Khan, B. K., Strong, D. M., & Wang, R. Y. (2002). Information quality benckmarks: Product and service performance. *Communications of the ACM*, *45*(4).

Lakoff, G., & Johnson, M. (1980). *Metaphors We Live By*. Chicago: The University of Chicago Press.

Lau, H. C. W., Choy, K. L., Wong, C. W. Y., & Fung, R. Y. K. (2003). A Generic Management Information System for Small and Medium Enterprises. *International Journal Manufacturing Technology and Management*, *5*(1), 162–176. doi:10.1504/IJMTM.2003.002539

Law, W. K., & Woo, M. T. (2003). Quality Control Information Representation Using Object-oriented Data Models. *International Journal of Computer Integrated Manufacturing*, *16*(3), 192–209. doi:10.1080/0951192021000036849

Le Coadic, Y. (2004). *A Ciência da Informação*. Brasília: Briquet de Lemos.

Le Coadic, Y.-F. (1996). *A ciência da informação*. Brasília: Briquet de Lemos Livros.

Lee, Y. W., Strong, D. M., Kahn, B., & Wang, R. Y. (2002). Aimq: A methodology for information quality assessment. *Information & Management*, *40*(2), 133–146. doi:10.1016/S0378-7206(02)00043-5

Li, S., & Lin, B. (2006). Accessing information sharing and information quality in supply chain management. *Decision Support Systems*, *42*(3), 1641–1656. doi:10.1016/j.dss.2006.02.011

Lillrank, P. (2003). The quality of information. *International Journal of Quality & Reliability Management*, *20*(6), 691–703. doi:10.1108/02656710310482131

Lima, L. F. R., Maçada, A. C. G., & Vargas, L. M. (2006). Research into information Quality: a study of the state of the art in IQ and its consolidation. In *International Conference on Information Quality*. Cambridge, MA: MIT.

Lin, S., Gao, J., & Koronios, A. (2006). The need for a data quality framework in asset management. *Australian Workshop on Information Quality Proceedings*.

Liu, L., & Chi, L. N. (2004). Evolutional data quality: a theory specific view. In *International Conference on Information Quality*. Cambridge, MA: MIT.

Lopes, I. L. A. S. (2004). Novos paradigmas para avaliação da qualidade da informação em saúde recuperada na web. *Ciência da Informação*, *33*(1), 81–90. doi:10.1590/S0100-19652004000100010

Madnick, S., Wang, R., & Xian, X. (2004). The Desing and Implementation of a Corporate Householding Knowledge Processor to Improve Data Quality. *Journal of Management Systems*, *20*(3), 41–69.

Mandke, V. V., & Nayar, M. K. (2004). Quality: The information integrity imperative. *Total Quality Management*, *15*(5), 645–654. doi:10.1080/14783360410001680134

Marchand, D. (1989), Managing information quality. In *Information quality definitions and dimensions proceedings*. Royal School of Librarianship.

Marchand, D. (1990). Managing Information quality. In I. Wormell (Ed.), *Information quality: definitions and dimensions* (pp. 7–17). London: Taylor Graham.

McGee, J., & Prusak, L. (1994). *Gerenciamento estratégico da informação: aumente a competitividade e a eficiência de sua empresa utilizando a informação como uma ferramenta estratégica. 12*. Rio de Janeiro: Campos.

Mick, C. K., Lindsey, G. N., & Callahan, D. (1980). Toward usable user studies. *Journal of the American Society for Information Science*, *31*(5), 347–356. doi:10.1002/asi.4630310506

Miguel, P. A. C. (2007). Estudo de caso na engenharia de produção: Estruturação e recomendações para sua condução. *Revista Produção*, *17*(1), 216–229. doi:10.1590/S0103-65132007000100015

Miller, B., Malloy, M. A., Masek, E., & Wild, C. (2001). Towards a framework for managing the information environment. *Information, Knowledge, Systems Management, 2*(4), 359–384.

Moresi, E. A. D. (2011). Delineando o valor do sistema de informação de uma organização. *Ciência da Informação, 29*(1), 14-24. Retrieved from http://www.scielo.br/pdf/ci/v29n1/v29n1a2.pdf

Morgan, G. (1996). *Imagens da Organização*. São Paulo: Atlas.

Naumann, F., & Rolker, C. (1996). *Assessment methods for information quality criteria*. German Research Society. Retrieved from http://www.hiqiq.com/quality.html

Nbr ISO 8402. (1994). Gestão da qualidade e garantia da qualidade.

Nehmy, R. M. Q. (1996). *Leitura epistemológico-social da qualidade da informação. 1996. Dissertação (Mestrado em Ciências da Informação)*. Belo Horizonte: Escola de Ciência da Informação, Universidade Federal de Minas Gerais.

Nehmy, R. M. Q., & Paim, I. (1998). A desconstrução do conceito de qualidade da informação. *Ciência da Informação, 27*(1), 36–45. doi:10.1590/S0100-19651998000100005

Neto, R. D. C. A. (2002). *Gestão do conhecimento em organizações*. Curitiba: Saraiva.

Neus, A. (2001). Managing information quality in virtual communities of practice. In *International Conference on Information Quality*. Cambridge, MA: MIT.

O'Brien, J. A. (2004). *Sistemas de informação e as decisões gerenciais na era da internet. 2*. São Paulo: Saraiva.

Olaisen, J. (1989). Information quality factors and the cognitive authority of electronic information. In I. Wormell (Ed.), *Information quality definitions and dimensions: Proceedings of a Nordinfo Seminar, Royal School of Librarianship* (pp. 91–121). Copenhagen: Taylor Graham.

Oleto, R. R. (2003). *A qualidade da informação na percepção do usuário em diferentes contextos informacionais. Tese (Doutorado)*. Universidade Federal de Minas Gerais, Escola de Ciência.

Oleto, R. R. (2006). Percepção da qualidade da informação. *Ciência da Informação, 35*(1), 57–62. doi:10.1590/S0100-19652006000100007

Oliveira, D. P. R. (1992). *Sistemas de Informações Gerenciais: Estratégias e táticas operacionais. 8*. São Paulo: Atlas.

Oliveira, D. P. R. (2002). *Sistemas, organização e métodos: uma abordagem gerencial* (13th ed.). São Paulo: Editora Atlas.

Paim, I., & Nehmy, R.M.Q. (1998). Questões sobre a avaliação da informação: Uma abordagem inspirada em Giddens. *Perspectivas em Ciência da Informação, Belo Horizonte, 3*(1), 81–95.

Paim, I. (1998). A desconstrução do conceito de "qualidade da informação". *Ciência da Informação, Brasília, 27*(1), 36–45.

Paim, I., & Nehmy, R. M. Q. (1996). Problematização do conceito "Qualidade" da Informação. *Perspectivas em Ciência da Informação, Belo Horizonte, 1*(1), 111–119.

Parasuraman, A., Zeithaml, V. A., & Berry, L. L. (1985). A conceptual model of services quality and its implication for future research. *Journal of Marketing*, *49*(4), 41–50. doi:10.2307/1251430

Parasuraman, A., Zeithaml, V. A., & Berry, L. L. (1988). Servqual: A multiple-item scale for measuring consumer perceptions of service quality. *Journal of Retailing*, *64*(1), 12–40.

Pipino, L. L., Yang, W., & Wang, R. Y. (2002). Data quality assessment. *Communications of the ACM*, *45*(4), 211–218. doi:10.1145/505248.506010

Pires, M. G., & Marcondes, R. C. (2004). Conhecimento, Inovação e Competência em Organizações Financeiras: Uma análise sob o ponto de vista de Gestores de Bancos. RAC, Edição especial, 61-78.

Prusak, L. (1998). *Conhecimento Empresarial: como as organizações gerenciam o seu capital intelectual.* Rio de Janeiro: Campus.

Putnam, L. L. (1983). The Interpretative Perspective: An Alternative to Functionalism. In L. L. Putnam & M. E. Pacanowsky (Eds.), Communication and Organizations: An Interpretative Approach. Sage Publications.

Salomi, G. G. E., Miguel, P. A. C., & Abackerli, A. J. (2005). Servqual x Servperf: Comparação entre instrumentos de avaliação da qualidade de serviços internos. Gestão & Produção, 12(2), 279-293.

Saracevic, T. (1996). Ciência da informação: Origem, evolução e relações. *Perspectivas em Ciência da Informação, Belo Horizonte*, *1*(1), 41–62.

Shapiro, C., & Varian, H. R. (1999). *Information Rules – A Strategic Guide to the Network Economy.* Boston: Harvard Business School Press.

Silva, A. P., & Favaretto, F. (2007). *Sistemas de Informação: um fator competitivopara empresas de pequeno porte.* XIV SIMPEP.

Stair, R. M., & Reynolds, G. W. (2011). *Princípios de sistemas de informação. 9.* São Paulo: Cengage Learning.

Strong, D. M., Lee, Y. W., & Wang, R. Y. (1997). Data quality in context. *Communications of the ACM*, *40*(5), 103–109. doi:10.1145/253769.253804

Strong, D. M., Lee, Y. W., & Wang, R. Y. (1997). 10 Potholes in the road to information quality. *IEEE Computer*, *18*(162), 38–46. doi:10.1109/2.607057

Suganuma, S. (2005). *Qualidade da Informação uma construção metodológica de definição de conceito. 2005. Dissertação (Mestrado em Ciência da Informação).* Brasília: Faculdade de Economia, Administração, Contabilidade e Ciência da Informação e Documentação, Universidade de Brasília.

Toften, K., & Olsen, S. O. (2004). The Relationships Among Quality, Cost, Value, and Use of Export Market Information: An empirical study. *Journal of International Marketing*, *12*(2), 104–131. doi:10.1509/jimk.12.2.104.32899

Torquato, F. G. (1986). *Comunicação Empresarial/Comunicação Institucional: Conceitos, estratégias, sistemas, estrutura, planejamento e técnicas. 5.* São Paulo: Summus.

Townsend, P., & Gebhardt, J. (2002). Simple Quality for Smaller Organizations. *Quality Progress*, *35*(10), 76–80.

Valls, V. M. V., & Waldomiro, C. S. (1998). A gestão da qualidade em serviços de informação no Brasil: Uma revisão da literatura. *Perspectivas em Ciência da Informação, Belo Horizonte*, *3*(1), 47–59.

Vergara, S. C. (2002). *Projetos e Relatório de Pesquisa em Administração. 3*. São Paulo: Atlas.

Wand, Y., & Wang, R. Y. (1996). Data quality dimensions in ontological foundations. *Communications of the ACM*, *39*(11), 86–95. doi:10.1145/240455.240479

Wang, R. W., Storey, V., & Firth, C. P. (1995). A framework of analysis for data quality research. *IEEE Transactions on Knowledge and Data Engineering*, *7*(4), 623–640. doi:10.1109/69.404034

Wang, R. Y., & Strong, D. M. (1996). Beyond Accuracy: What data quality means to data consumers. *Journal of Management Information Systems*, *12*(4), 5–33. doi:10.1080/07421222.1996.11518099

Wang, R. Y., Ziad, M., & Lee, Y. W. (2000). Data Quality. Kluwer Academic Publishers.

Weick, K. C. (1999). Theory Construction as Disciplined Imagination. *Academy of Management Review*, *14*(4), 516-531.

Wurman, R. S. (1989). Information Anxiety. *The New York Times,* p. 32.

Chapter 14
Re-Imagining Data Governance

Kevin J. Sweeney
Stats NZ, New Zealand

ABSTRACT

Contemporary business environments reflect the growing influence of data as a mission-critical resource of relevance across the enterprise, suggesting a need for robust infrastructures to enable good data management practice. This includes data governance, a particularly foundational infrastructure with a crucial role to play. Data governance models in common use however, reflecting traditional top-down, hierarchical structures, and relying on designated governance roles, are not equipped to effectively embed data accountability within dynamic business environments. In response, this chapter offers a new approach designed to foster accountability by cultivating data knowledge and promoting good data management behavior amongst all relevant staff. Drawing from an operational data governance framework developed for New Zealand government, the new model employs a core set of capabilities and a steady states model to map data flow. It provides a deliberately business-centric view of data accountability and offers a means of maturing data thinking to support improved integration across operating scales.

INTRODUCTION

Almost it seems while we weren't looking, the world around us has changed.

Far reaching developments in technology, transitioning for all intents and purposes from the stuff of lofty ideas to indispensable components of our daily lives, continue to emerge at a profoundly rapid rate, undermining our ability to leverage traditional means of informing our choices and values (Allenby, 2015). And all the while we accept this state of flux as something altogether normal.

Fuelling that accelerated pace of change and shaping our opinions about the possibilities of technological disruption, is a vast network of data, sometimes visible, often unseen. Driven by interactions between producers and consumers, directed by the gravitational forces of sources and sinks, coursing in a myriad of ways through a complex labyrinth of connections, data streams continuously through its channels as the lifeblood of our modern world. And much like the technological tools that we employ for everything from managing an investment portfolio to locating the closest cup of coffee, the underlying data that we leverage for our varied purposes has thoroughly permeated our personal lives.

DOI: 10.4018/978-1-5225-3725-0.ch014

So too in business contexts, the proliferation of data and subsequent dependencies on it have recrafted operating environments, leading to a landscape of playing fields reflecting new sets of rules and novel realities, but also rife with possibility. Success in contemporary business environments is dependent more than ever before on the ability to harness and leverage the vast potential of data, on a willingness to adopt a sufficiently aspirational strategy that is nonetheless founded on solid data management principles and delivered through appropriate organisational infrastructure.

In response, this chapter presents a new approach to a particularly critical infrastructure, data governance, designed to better equip organisations to manage increasingly important data assets in the face of unconventional and rapidly changing operating environments.

Based on a Data Governance Framework developed for New Zealand government, the proposed model turns traditional governance on its head, to mature thinking beyond a longstanding bias that favours hierarchical and decidedly top-down execution. Emphasising instead elements of a bottom-up implementation that cultivates deeper levels of data knowledge and improved principles-based data management behaviours, it accentuates the role and relevance of governance within the operational contexts of line staff. This distinct shift in thinking about the purpose of governance addresses existing capability gaps and serves to embed data management good practice and accountability as an inherent, business-as-usual outcome across all parts of the enterprise.

BACKGROUND

Attitudes, Expectations and Opportunities

Notably, as more efficient and relevant technologies are adopted with increasing frequency, giving rise to a condition where a steady flow of new developments is the norm, the public hardly has time, or the inclination for that matter, to respond in a thoughtful manner. And this can have profound repercussions on how society operates. As Allenby (2015) explains, "The cycle time of technology innovations and the rapidity with which they ripple through society have become far faster than the institutions and mechanisms that we've traditionally relied on to inform and enforce our choices and values."

This shift in the traditional norms associated with technological choice extends to data as well. As the stuff that keeps their apps functioning, data is regarded by many consumers as something of a given, if acknowledged at all. It need not be thoughtfully considered because it is always there, always available and always in a format that is readily interpretable and consumable through familiar user interfaces. This engenders high levels of expectation amongst those consumers for data to deliver, to offer itself as intuitive information in response to any expressed need. And it better not make them wait.

A public that operates in an environment where data is a resource upon which it can unquestionably rely, where it is freed from the burden of choice, is also a user community with the opportunity to expand its thinking around the role of data. The idea of a so-called Age of Data has been around for some time, but based on recent advancements in the technology to collect, store and serve data, such an age may truly be upon us (Lohr, 2012). In a time when the collection of data is nothing if not efficient, where data is streamed continuously from sources across a wide range of contexts, users are increasingly well placed to consider how to glean more and truly meaningful value from that data.

The same opportunities exist within business operating environments, where data, imbued with an expanded sense of legitimacy, has the opportunity to lift itself out of the rather narrow and technical purview of information managers and analysts. Relevant now to a much broader and more diverse audience of interest, it has increasingly become a topic of consideration in the executive board room, amongst business process architects, for strategists and for those developing policy (Clarke, 2017; Kemp, 2013). In these and other ways, data is recognised for the ubiquitous resource it is, permeating essentially all parts of the enterprise with significant implications for productivity, competitiveness, strategic outcomes and ultimately long-term sustainability and success.

Implications

Having achieved an elevated level of consequence, data is in a position to drive change, transitioning from a by-product or characteristic of technology to a disruptive entity on its own merits, influencing the path of technological developments itself (Wessel, 2016).

Noteworthy in this regard is big data, that which is of sufficiently large volume and is collected, processed and made available at a significantly high enough rate and frequency to test the capacity of current data systems (Gandomi & Haider, 2015). As a disruptive phenomenon, big data has amongst other things challenged organisations to develop the means to integrate internal proprietary datasets with external, public and often unstructured data, across different types of systems, applications, and infrastructure. In much the same way, indications are that linked data, and in particular linked open data, may represent the next data disruption, similarly influencing the nature of organisational change (Harper, 2017).

The demands and opportunities stemming from the expanding role of data have translated into an explosive growth in the business of managing its proliferation. Interviewed by *The Economist*, Cukier (2010) noted even several years ago that IBM, Oracle, Microsoft and SAP had together spent more than $15 billion (US) on acquiring firms specialising in data management and analytics. Estimations at that time put the data management industry's worth at more than $100 billion (US), with annual growth at 10%, a rate twice that of the software industry as a whole.

These evolving characteristics of the data environment highlight the need for a shift in thinking about data and correspondingly, a reassessment of management models. The status quo approach, developed in a time when data occupied a position of lesser significance and was characterised by a reduced level of complexity, and when management requirements placed upon it were less stringent and of limited operational relevance, is no longer sufficient.

While the data ecosystem has expanded in scope and developed in numerous ways and with great rapidity, the models and frameworks for participation in it have not. Thinking has remained trapped in place, imprisoned by the constraints of familiarity and history. Far from being innocuous, this misalignment of approach and reality has resulted in actual degradation as obsolete frameworks have, in response to an increasingly complex operating environment, only become more unwieldy. Linked inexorably to highly structured organisational charts, traditional data governance frameworks are ill-equipped to respond to change and therefore pose a risk to agile, customer-oriented operating models.

Rather than continuing to move forward with modified versions of traditional models, this suggests a need to consider new approaches that are designed to treat data as the legitimate and profoundly valuable resource that it is. It speaks to the importance of promoting proper behaviours and a style of management practice that leverages a comprehensive and holistic level of understanding of the data assets so vital to the service of our respective needs.

GOVERNING DATA TRADITIONALLY

Governance is a critical and yet often underappreciated enabler for the promotion and perpetuation of appropriate data management behaviours. While in the general sense it represents a familiar concept that is thoroughly treated in the literature, it is important to characterise what is meant exactly by governance when applied to data.

Put into use across many different contexts, governance broadly refers to the practice established to formally organise operations in a way that encompasses strategic considerations, establishes an authority and provides a set of operating standards and norms (Institute of Directors in New Zealand, n.d.; Bevir, 2012). Data governance draws from many of the same conceptual foundations and delivers many of the same outcomes as governance generally, but as practice linked to an especially salient operating resource, it also offers benefits that are particularly relevant and meaningful. And as an organisation's data and its associated management becomes more integral to successful operations across the enterprise, the implementation of a considered governance approach, targeted to this aspect of the business, becomes correspondingly more important.

When established as a framework, data governance represents an effective means of encouraging and supporting accountability while supplying mechanisms and processes for outcomes like issue resolution. These frameworks serve as a set of established pathways for that which governance is meant to help deliver – namely decisions, conflict resolution and authoritative direction for ensuring good practice.

If an organisation decides to adopt an agile business model, to better respond for instance to a fluid market populated with ever more demanding customers, the need for structure provided by an underlying governance framework is paradoxically even more crucial. This is certainly the case for data governance in environments where data is increasingly open and accessible (Lämmerhirt, 2017).

Data assets in these less familiar operating environments will represent if anything an even more important component of the business strategy, integral to the solutions developed to serve a changing customer base, while helping to shape new types of relationships with key suppliers, stakeholders and competitors. Their contribution to the insights that inform business decisions, even more important in times of uncertainty, affirms the need for an appropriate level of management and governance oversight (Higson & Waltho, 2009).

Political Data Governance

Data governance has arguably been in existence in some form since there has been data, but can be considered a relatively modern manifestation of governance practice, its particular relevance coming to light with the growing influence of data in contemporary contexts. In his blog on the history of data governance, Chen (2010) suggests a series of eras since the 1960s, with data governance practice reflecting changing conditions and transitioning from an applications-based approach to one emphasising the role of enterprise repositories, and most recently one assuming a policy-centric view.

Though a fairly recent expression of governance, data governance has thus far drawn heavily from traditional implementations of governance models and frameworks employed in other contexts. The characteristics of the established approach are referred to in this chapter collectively as *political data governance*. The use of the term political suggests a strongly institutionalised and potentially bureaucratic approach to governing data assets, drawing from existing structures that reflect a decidedly hierarchical and roles-based view of organisation.

Political data governance frameworks are typically established in a top-down fashion as a ranked collection of governing bodies and roles, and are instituted in a way that either draws directly from or is otherwise closely linked to the staff organisational chart. Senior staff therefore are likewise given greater authority within the political data governance model to provide approvals or pass along binding decisions about organisational data assets. It is often a collection of these executive or senior roles that populate the governance bodies positioned at the apex of the hierarchy, leveraging the political governance structure to distribute their experience and insights down though the rest of the organisation.

Current State Challenges

While a data governance framework represents an important organisational infrastructure, it does not currently enjoy widespread acceptance nor exhibit a consistent record of ongoing success in those instances where it is implemented (Morgan, 2017; Sweden, 2008). The reasons for this less than admirable track record may in some cases be linked to organisation-specific factors, but it is argued here that it can be traced in particular to a perpetuation of historic governance models in environments where they are increasingly mismatched.

Retaining a natural bias for the familiar, those responsible for instituting and deploying data governance are inclined to incorporate organisational data assets under the umbrella of those governance frameworks with which they are most comfortable. But in doing so they are also preserving the inherent shortcomings of that style of infrastructure, made even more apparent in modern contexts that are characterised by increasingly agile business models. And they increasingly find themselves in opposition to a broader trend towards flatter organisational structures, instituted to facilitate innovation and support responsive business models (The Wharton School, 2003; Gotkin, 2012).

Top-Down Hierarchies

Because political data governance frameworks often closely reflect the organisation's personnel structure, they typically adopt a corresponding hierarchy. The existing staff-oriented structure provides a logical and familiar means of embedding governance and appears to supply a pre-established pathway for outcomes to move easily into and throughout the organisation.

Due to the highly structured and multi-layered nature of such frameworks, however, the options for communicating outcomes are generally inflexible and it is not unusual for outputs of high-level governance bodies to make their way to operational line staff in an indirect and at times convoluted fashion. Decisions emerging from such groups might be used for instance to inform a new policy, which in turn generates guidance materials that help shape operating models, that then serve as reference for the development and implementation of processes and procedures, which eventually get implemented as part of line staff workflow.

Furthermore, by the time these outcomes navigate the highly structured governance frame, moving from one committee to the next and awaiting a series of required senior staff level approvals to reach line staff, they can emerge as a trickle, a shadow of their former selves. Their relevance to operational staff, if it existed in the first place, is likely lost. The governing value is not what is delivered, but instead has likely been overwhelmed and replaced by something reflecting the layers of bureaucracy experienced along the way. And this failing only fuels opinions that governance and its outcomes are of little practical value, of bearing only occasionally and then for the most part only to that small group of senior leadership atop the org chart.

These challenges inherent to a traditional model of data governance are particularly prevalent in modern business contexts, which are more often as not subject to a steady diet of transformational change (Hutchins 2011; Rick, 2014). As the business model is transformed and the associated organisational structure reconfigured to accommodate adjusted strategic outcomes, the links to a closely aligned political governance model are broken. This necessitates a complete re-build of the political data governance framework to reflect the new organisational structure, a requirement that becomes less palatable as the frequency of re-structures increases.

A Roles-Based Approach

Political data governance models are often organised around the implementation of particular roles, including those of Data Custodian, Data Steward and Data Trustee (Dataversity, 2012). Established either as distinct positions, or more likely, as designations for a set of additional responsibilities assigned to existing staff, these roles are put in place to champion and administer good governance practice across the organisation.

The Data Custodian, Steward and Trustee roles often operate as something of one-stop data shops. Those occupying these positions are expected on some level to provide subject matter expertise for the organisation's data assets, in combination with a level of familiarity with data policies, procedures, compliance requirements and the relevant elements of the organisation's strategic agenda (Sweden, 2009).

If considered across the full range of scales at which data operates and the myriad of environments in which it requires governing, a key challenge associated with a designated roles-based approach is the lack of consistency. The literature on data governance is characterised by a high level of variability in role definitions, to the point where it can be difficult to find a consistent description between any two sources. Data Stewards as defined in one source might very well encapsulate the same responsibilities and perspectives associated with Data Custodians in another source and those linked to Data Trustees in a third.

Indicating more than just variation in position descriptions, this disparity in role responsibilities is important in that those roles reflect the organisation's view on data governance generally. This becomes significant as the lack of consistency manifests itself in many different situations - including interactions between organisations within a country or those between organisations in different countries - and becomes a barrier to data-based engagement across both business and political boundaries. In current business environments where increasingly sophisticated analytical models require integration of data from multiple sources, this level of governance inconsistency amongst data producers and consumers can pose a significant threat to successful outcomes.

Within the enterprise there are several difficulties associated with the use of a roles-based approach. If the responsibilities associated with these designations are layered on top of those in place for existing positions, which is often the case, the result can be a "Custodian's burden." These staff are expected to deliver to essentially two roles, with the obvious risk that when stretched in this manner they are likely to deliver at less than optimal levels for both the governance role and their substantive position.

Additionally, if distinct roles are created to look after data governance, there is the real possibility that other staff will cede the associated data accountability to individuals in those roles. Aware that there is a designated person looking after such matters, line staff, already busy and perhaps perceiving no obvious connection to governance outcomes, are de-motivated to adopt associated good data management practice as part of their own jobs. The result is an organisation where desired data practices are consistently front of mind for a limited set of staff.

Organisations that adopt a roles-based approach are also likely to undermine their capacity to adjust to changes in operating environments, including transitioning when required to an agile and more flexible business model. The use of designated data governance roles, which incorporate expectations like comprehensive oversight for data assets across their lifecycle, tends to anchor organisations in historic and outdated thinking and impairs their ability to respond to changing environments. A continued reliance on these traditional roles, including an expectation that they continue to effectively deliver their responsibilities in new and unfamiliar environments, something they are not designed to do, creates operational and strategic risk.

Consequences of an Outdated Model

Though they might be based often in perceptions, the negative impressions that can arise from the shortcomings of a political data governance framework exert a powerful influence, and are not easily dismissed. As organisations attempt to remain relevant by adjusting business models to improve their responsiveness, these negative views on governance correspondingly take on new levels of significance.

Data governance can become a burden in that context, a barrier to the delivery of desired outcomes. Seen then as bureaucracy in the worst sense of the word, it is something that appears to impede efficient data flow, which itself is recognised as a critical component of responsive delivery. This effectively, if unintentionally, establishes data governance as something antithetical to the strategic direction.

In the end, applying an outdated model to govern the assets of an organisation functioning in a substantially new, highly dynamic and less certain business environment represents the root cause of political data governance failings. There is a corresponding need therefore to mature thinking in regard to governing data and in doing so, improve and future-proof the treatment of these critical assets.

A FRAMEWORK FOR CONTEMPORARY ENVIRONMENTS

The numerous challenges inherent to the use of traditional approaches to data governance, along with a recognition that a viable framework is needed more than ever in light of contemporary operating conditions, suggests the time is right for a reassessment, a re-imagining, of how data assets are best governed. This means that the learnings to be gleaned from testing new thinking in various business contexts have a good chance of generating value and organisations would be well advised to consider moving beyond their norms to explore and consider adopting a data governance framework offering greater potential.

New Zealand's Data Governance Framework

With this in mind, a behavioural capability-based framework for data governance has been developed in New Zealand for use across central government (Sweeney, 2017). Initiated as a recommended framework within Stats NZ, the country's national statistical agency, the new approach to data governance is being tested and refined for implementation as an all of government solution by a collaborative group of central government agencies.

While efforts continue to further validate it as an option that delivers effectively across different operating contexts, the New Zealand framework in its current state is substantially complete and available for consideration and to inform thinking. Its core components have been used to articulate the reconceptualisation of data governance proposed in this chapter.

Underlying Concepts

The proposed approach is predicated on a need to refresh basic thinking about data governance and achieve a level of clarity about what it truly means and how it can deliver genuine and persistent value. This implies a significant realignment, a shift to a new positon on the topic that involves revisiting the existing paradigm. If data governance frameworks are to deliver to their full potential, and continue to do so as operating contexts change, their design thinking needs to move beyond established views, allowing for a re-imagining of what those frameworks can provide. It is important therefore to understand the underlying concepts used to guide that new thinking.

Infrastructure's Infrastructure

As governance occupies a particularly constitutional position within any organisation, much like the foundation of a building, any work on that level requires a clearing away of significant material to reach the critical structural and load-bearing elements. This type of unpacking is necessary to return to a state that precedes the influence of subsequent governance approaches that have for numerous reasons become the norm and resulted in the model that dominates implementations today.

Achieving this requires clarity about what governance is meant to deliver. Though it can be perceived in some circumstances as a manifestation of bureaucracy and therefore an imposition, a properly implemented governance framework offers potential as a particularly powerful mechanism for improving efficiencies, promoting and embedding good practice, growing institutional knowledge, and in all of these ways, facilitating desired outcomes, both operational and strategic. This enabling characteristic suggests that governance frameworks, including those for data, have an important role to play as basic infrastructure.

Governance is infrastructure in its purest form – a powerfully supportive device linked closely with an organisation's very identity, and positioned at this level, offering the potential to permeate and influence all parts of the enterprise. In this role as essential infrastructure, governance frameworks lay the groundwork for the proper establishment of other infrastructures that facilitate things like good practice data management. As the infrastructure for infrastructure therefore, governance has a uniquely significant role to play as an enabler within the enterprise. If a data governance framework is to deliver to its full potential it must be seen in this light, emphasising its enabling potential as a core component of its value proposition for the organisation.

A Basis in Principles

Since governance as infrastructure is situated at such a foundational level, it can exert a profound influence on how well an organisation operates and realises its prospects for success. As such it is important that a data governance framework be grounded in a set of accepted principles that encourage sound data practice. The nature of these principles will vary to some extent, depending on the operating imperatives of a given organisation, but should persist over time. As an example, the data governance principles initially established for New Zealand government (Sweeney, 2017) are included in *Appendix 1*.

Instilling Data Accountability

It is not unreasonable to treat accountability as a synonym for governance. At an elemental level, data governance frameworks can be considered in this way, infrastructure that is implemented for the express purpose of promoting and embedding accountability as a core element in the treatment of organisational data assets (Dataversity, 2012; Callahan, 2006). Data governance accountability is an important means of facilitating good data management behaviours, and supports data stewardship by encouraging a proactive and highly engaged level of responsibility amongst staff in their data-handling roles.

Reflecting the significance of accountability amongst data governance outcomes, the deficiencies of traditional data governance implementations can often be traced to a failure to embed a robust system of data asset accountability throughout an organisation.

There may be a host of reasons behind this failing, but a data governance framework meant to succeed in contemporary business environments should be designed in particular to address two significant and common defects: 1) poor data management behaviours, and 2) a deficient knowledge of data assets. Both shortcomings represent a gap in capability, either people or information, and both indicate an incomplete view of conduct, either that associated with staff in their data stewardship responsibilities or that of the data assets themselves moving within the context of the organisational business process model.

An organisation can confidently defend its claim to having delivered a successful data governance framework if that infrastructure can successfully support a system of data accountability across all relevant lines of business. It is more likely to achieve this if, as part of a business-focussed approach that emphasises asset management, it actively promotes and supports staff behaviours grounded in good data management practice, while it cultivates a comprehensive knowledge of its data assets, particularly in regards to data flow.

Bottom-Up and Business-Centric

While contributing value to the way an organisation administers its data assets, political data governance frameworks often fail to acknowledge or provide a means of mitigating negative perceptions that adversely influence staff engagement. These perceptions reflect the long-held tenets of a traditional governance model including the idea that it sits across, and by extension, above the organisation. Decisions rendered by governance boards populated by senior management consistently come down from above, in a decidedly top-down fashion.

A re-thinking of data governance, including in particular an acknowledgement of its purpose as enabler and its role as core infrastructure, suggests rather that it is best articulated as something deeply rooted in organisational identity. Its outcomes then have the opportunity to serve as foundations to build upon and surface within the enterprise in a distinctly bottom-up and more operationally-relevant fashion. This encourages an organic alignment between those governance outcomes and the familiar operating environments of staff, since the outcomes are manifest right at that level to begin with. That business scenario expands data governance relevance throughout the organisation, which supports improved engagement amongst line staff and increases the likelihood that well-considered governance outcomes achieve their goals.

Within public sector contexts particularly, there are additional advantages to embracing a more deliberately business-centric stance when developing the elements of a data governance model. The pressing need for organisations across all sectors to properly manage the significant escalation in volume and potential of data has highlighted the benefits of treating these resources as curated business assets. The increasing investment moreover that both public and private organisations are placing in the management of these assets to unleash and expand their potential as sources of significant value, lends further support to this position.

While there are challenges inherent in the wholesale idea that governments would operate more effectively if run like private businesses (Harvey, 2012), the likelihood of outcomes including the formal acknowledgement and treatment of data as a key operational asset are increased within public sector agencies assuming a more intentionally business-oriented view of their data holdings. From this perspective, data is the fuel that enables productivity and is therefore deserving of formal and thoughtful administration. This style of asset management approach supports the premise that data generates, accumulates and furnishes value as it manoeuvres (or likewise rests) along its lifecycle within the organisation's operating model, and as such should be carefully governed.

Data Flow

Effective interaction and communication between the lines of business within an organisation is a particularly important element in the realisation of a more highly responsive and agile operating model. Siloed operating frameworks, while potentially offering value for the delivery of certain project-specific outcomes, do little to enable a coordinated, enterprise-level response to changes in a highly dynamic business environment. And considering the increasing significance and reach of data as an enterprise commodity, they offer as common assets a particularly effective proxy for uncovering, improving, and monitoring the linkages between different parts of the organisation.

The characteristic of data flow provides especially meaningful insights into the role and significance of data assets as enablers of organisational goals and outcomes. Generating a clear and comprehensive picture of how data moves over the course of its lifecycle – how it enters the sphere of organisational influence, moves within lines of business and across business unit boundaries, and how it exits the organisation's ambit – is paramount for an organisation seeking to mature its data governance thinking beyond traditional approaches. It is only with this understanding of data movement that accountability can be appropriately mapped and a governance framework properly designed and successfully implemented within a particular organisational context.

Data assets in a flow model are envisioned as the fluid that moves along a system of channels corresponding to the network of organisational business processes. Much like the water in a stream, data assets are subject to a host of forces and influences, moving at different rates and with different volumes, exhibiting variable levels of quality, sometimes turning back on itself in eddies, and at times directed out of the main flow channel into storage reservoirs. And just as the measured condition of water can serve as an indicator of stream health, so too can the assessed quality condition of data assets indicate the effectiveness of the underlying business process model.

The broad, landscape-scale view resulting from a data flow model corresponds in the business sense to an enterprise perspective and encourages holistic thinking that extends across different parts of the organisation. This is important on two levels: 1) it facilitates a whole of lifecycle assessment of data assets, which is critical if they are to be legitimately managed as organisational resources, and 2) it extends data asset management out of the situational or projcct domain to the holistic and enterprise, thereby increasing opportunities for data assets in support of strategic outcomes.

Practical Components

The practical execution of the approach to data governance proposed in this chapter manifests itself as an operational framework designed to reflect new thinking. The success of that framework rests ultimately with the extent that staff, particularly line staff, consider it germane and of value to their work. If staff cannot readily interact with the framework, assume a certain level of ownership in it, and comprehend clearly how it benefits them in their roles, they will most certainly circumvent it, choosing the familiarity of status quo over a change agenda that offers no obvious return on their investment. The framework in that case risks irrelevance and the fate of a solution offering little more than what might already be available from a political data governance model.

Emphasising practicality, the implementation of a new data governance framework should be designed in a manner that allows for its components to embed easily within existing workflow. This will help situate the concept of governance and related data accountability directly into the familiar and process-oriented context of individual line staff. Beyond assisting with staff engagement, this also helps establish a clear line of sight between daily routine and broader organisational goals concerned with data management good practice.

Good Data Management Behaviour

A data governance framework is given life by the actions of people and, as a means of instilling data accountability across the enterprise, specifically through the proper behaviours of those individuals in respect to data management. A framework established to deliver accountability outcomes in the face of poorly managed data makes little sense. It is also of limited strategic use to the organisation as it cannot contribute legitimate value to other business outcomes. Rather, a data governance framework should unambiguously acknowledge its basis in good data management practice, and through its function as an enabling infrastructure, provide a viable means of embedding that practice throughout the enterprise.

Data Governance Capabilities

To instil good data management practice across the enterprise, there needs to be an agreed understanding of the underlying set of data governance capabilities that, when put into practice, will facilitate consistent and persistent data accountability.

Encompassing the full set of structural elements – or business architecture "building blocks" – that make up and enable a functioning organisation, capabilities represent a viable means of organising operating models. In this regard, they represent the full suite of resources that contribute to organisational business capacity including people, process, information, and technology. The business value of a capability-based approach lies in the resultant clarity about what resources an organisation has at its disposal (or might be lacking) to deliver outcomes or goals within a given business context (Deleu & Clendon, 2015).

More than just a summary of skills, people capabilities capture how an organisation does its work and what it is good at; they can in that sense express the very identity of the organisation. An organisation operating with a well-defined and thoroughly integrated set of people capabilities can enjoy a host of beneficial outcomes, including positive performance assessments, higher market valuations and a competitive operating advantage (Smallwood & Ulrich, 2004).

As an example of what these might comprise, the data governance framework being implemented in New Zealand employs the following set of data governance people capabilities, to foster data accountability (Sweeney, 2017):

- Data point of contact
- Subject matter expertise
- Access control
- Risk management
- Internal relationship management
- External relationship management
- Quality Assurance (QA)/Quality Control (QC) management
- Data management
- Data champion
- Data innovation

A brief description of each of these capabilities can be found in *Appendix 2*.

The capabilities should comprise a list that accommodates all of the dimensions of good data management practice that are relevant to the organisation. These dimensions might include: technical and subject matter expertise, risk and data management, communications and engagement, and design and improvement. When used to organise the list of capabilities, these dimensions provide potential areas of development for staff with a direct line of sight to the organisation's strategic goals for data.

As is the case with the New Zealand examples, the capabilities themselves are best delineated to a degree of specificity that draws out any nuanced characteristics of each. This provides two levels of benefits: each capability is detailed enough to inform appropriately targeted discussions with staff regarding their current job responsibilities and growth areas, while considered as a collection, the capabilities provide a comprehensive view of data governance expectations across the organisation as a whole.

Human Resource System Integration

An inventory of capabilities in and of itself provides no measurable data governance benefit without a viable option to implement them amongst staff with data responsibilities. Indeed, it is this focus on the operationalisation of conceptual governance outcomes that distinguishes the proposed data governance framework from its traditional counterparts.

If the capabilities are successfully adopted, it paves the way for good data practice to become standard and accepted behaviour, and assuming accountability for data assets under their care a matter of course for all staff. In this scenario, good data management practice becomes integrated within a familiar workflow environment and is well positioned to foster a sense of ownership and improved engagement with the organisation's data assets. For line staff, it is just another element of their normal duties.

The corporate Human Resource department is well equipped to facilitate this embedding of data governance capabilities. As data governance stakeholders, Human Resource staff are likely to intrinsically understand how a well-crafted set of people capabilities can exert wide-reaching influence, inform external engagement, and positively impact the delivery of strategic outcomes. People capabilities themselves are a particularly familiar concept from a human resources perspective, meaning that data governance characterised in this fashion can leverage that inherent level of comfort to resonate with a corporate function offering extensive reach throughout the enterprise.

Drawing from a capability framework (People Measures, n.d.), Human Resource departments can provide numerous mechanisms for guiding the adoption of data governance capabilities throughout the organisation's systems and culture. They will have at their disposal established structures that enable them to adopt these capabilities and promote their value, which can itself represent a positive selling point for the organisation. In this way data governance capability documentation can be absorbed into recruitment tools and materials, learning and development approaches, and succession planning and performance management systems, thereby insuring the capabilities exert a much stronger and persistent influence on staff behaviours than they might otherwise.

Cultivated Data Knowledge

In addition to enabling an environment of good data management practice, a re-imagined data governance framework will promote the development and cultivation of a thorough knowledge base, applicable at all scales across the enterprise, for organisational data assets. Without a comprehensive understanding of relevant data assets, staff with data responsibilities are disadvantaged in their ability to help realise the full potential of those assets. Lacking a complete picture, they will in some cases certainly not know what they don't know, and this gap in knowledge will influence how effectively their lines of business operate internally and in conjunction with one another to support organisational strategic outcomes.

Steady States

An important element of a data asset knowledge base is a comprehensive model of organisational data flow, including the mapping of data assets within and across lines of business. As noted earlier, data flow provides an effective means of facilitating a strategic view, where the roles of various business units are properly situated within the broader landscape of the organisation as a whole. This then encourages a decidedly holistic perspective which serves not only better management of organisational data assets but also improved data engagement with entities external to the organisation. A modelling approach that offers particular promise in this regard is that of steady states.

The concept of a steady state has been applied across a wide range of fields including chemistry, engineering, and economics, but has a particular relevance as an analysis tool in the manufacturing industry. In a general sense and as the name suggests, a steady states references a point within a process that is unchanging over time. In the manufacturing context, steady states have been employed to delineate and map production systems as a means of improving productivity (Ajeeli, 2016).

This idea of capturing a detailed, steady state view of manufacturing process flow was subsequently adapted for use within statistical data environments by Statistics Netherlands (Braaksma & Zeelenberg, 2014). In the Dutch case, a steady states model was applied to characterise organisational data flow and improve levels of understanding about statistical production process models (Struijs, Camstra, Renssen,

& Braaksma, 2013). The significance of this seminal work by Statistics Netherlands lies in its publication of an effective method for mapping macro patterns of data flow within a process network, and a means of establishing a set of points along that network to enable targeted monitoring of data lifecycle milestones.

Data Value Chain

Steady state models make use of basic value chains, where production consists of a series of inputs subjected to value-adding transformations that result in new output states, themselves available to serve as inputs, until an end state is achieved.

Within a value chain view, data begins its journey in something of a raw state and through a series of defined processes involving amongst other things cleaning, formatting, transformation, and analysis – all of which require investment by the organisation – transitions and evolves during the course of its lifecycle, until it contributes to a product or some other form of final output.

If data is managed as a business asset, each process transformation should result in the addition of value, or in this context, in an improvement of quality, which can be monitored and which accumulates across the data lifecycle. Steady states as a flow model delineates the most significant steps along the value chain where data (and associated metadata) achieves a predefined quality level and is maintained (Braaksma & Zeelenberg, 2014). This last point is important as it provides the link between an asset management approach based in data – where use of a value chain is expressed through steady states with criteria based on measures of quality – and traditional uses of value chain models, based in process and incorporating measures that capture changes in product value.

A straightforward implementation of a steady states model, and one developed successfully in the data context by the Australian Bureau of Statistics, is that of quality gates. Quality gates represent a "systematic approach for assessing...quality...at specific points in the process, such that the overall quality of outputs are fit for their intended purposes" (Pink, 2010, p. vi). The value proposition of quality gates suggests that through quality monitoring of data at numerous junctures along its lifecycle, production process errors can be detected and mitigated close to their source. This offers an easier, less expensive management pathway involving reduced exposure to reputational risk than error discovery and resolution that happens after product release.

Quality Criteria

Since a steady states model provides points along the data lifecycle where a predefined level of quality has been achieved, it necessitates a set of criteria and associated measures or tolerances to characterise and test quality at each of those lifecycle points. Organisations are free to employ whatever set of steady state quality criteria best serves their needs, though they must be agreed and employed consistently across the enterprise. This speaks to the inherent scalability and portability of this approach. Because steady states criteria can be as simple or as complex as required, the model offers a valid approach for organisations exhibiting a wide range of data governance maturity.

Once established as practice, the use of steady states quality criteria provides advantages both internally, in terms of encouraging an enterprise view and facilitating staff buy-in, and externally, as a means of system-level engagement. The key to realising this range of benefits lies in the proper structuring and delineation of quality criteria to accommodate their relevance at multiple scales.

At their most generalised, and serving purely as an engagement mechanism to encourage a consistent approach to data flow modelling at the system level, steady states criteria would consist of easily consumed quality dimensions. The use of broadly defined and relatively generic criteria – like timeliness, accuracy, and accessibility – supports uptake across a spectrum of organisations operating in different contexts while providing them a means of communicating across boundaries that might otherwise hinder such transactions.

Positioned below these engagement-oriented quality dimensions and functioning at the organisational level would be a set of enterprise quality criteria. Exhibiting more granularity than the system engagement criteria, but applicable across all business units within a given organisation, these criteria would be designed to promote and measure good practice in areas like data management, processing or methodology. Data management criteria might cover proper data storage and preservation, efficient discovery and access, persistence of supporting documentation, and design for re-use. Various measures are available for such criteria, but most certainly would include things like verification of metadata maintenance and the use of accepted data standards.

Lastly at an operational level, situated below the enterprise criteria, would be those quality measures of relevance and potentially unique to a particular line of business. These are likely to technical in nature, requiring a certain level of subject matter expertise, and exhibiting the greatest variability, both in terms of the criteria themselves and the measures associated with them. Each business unit is free to establish however many criteria and of whatever type it wants, to support its needs. A key advantage of including business unit specific criteria is that they facilitate a sense of ownership. While enterprise criteria might be construed by line staff as an external imposition into their part of the operation, the line of business criteria are their own and will exhibit a unique and meaningful applicability to their jobs.

Data Flow Mapping

When employed as part of a re-imagined data governance framework, a primary output of a steady states model is a set of organisational data flow maps. The library of maps would include one for each line of business that handles data assets and an aggregated enterprise map, based on the intersections of line of business maps. This documentation offers the potential for a host of valuable data lifecycle insights into how and at what entry points data assets arrive at the organisation, operate within it, and ultimately exit an organisation's sphere of influence. The resultant comprehensive view of data flow, available for presentation in a highly intuitive manner at both line of business and enterprise scales, is indispensable from a governance perspective.

It is important to recognise that the framework proposed here emphasises an integral connection between a data flow map and the organisational business process model or process map. While there is merit in analysing data assets for their own sake, as is the case with information supply chain or value chain analysis applications, that view is ultimately limiting. The role of data assets as the fuel for processes suggests there is more meaningful benefit in considering them within a broader business context as well.

And in that regard the two perspectives – data and process – are intertwined and highly interdependent. Without a network of defined processes to properly direct it to where it is needed and can generate value, data cannot deliver anywhere near to its potential, and without data as content to leverage, a process network is stuck in a conceptual space, an empty shell also likely to deliver little to the organisation.

In the proposed data governance approach, the mapping of data flow involves the placement of steady state markers directly onto a business process map. The business process model therefore forms the foundation onto which a view of the data lifecycle is superimposed. This not only supports an authentic view of the relationship between data and process, but offers a relatively straightforward and intuitive method for developing a data flow map.

The reasoning that dictates the placement of data flow steady states will likely be influenced by the corresponding positioning of process milestones. So for instance if data is cleaned as part of the process to move it into an enterprise data store, it will have achieved a new measure of quality and a steady state therefore is called for at the data store exit point. But beyond these obvious locations, steady states can also be positioned at points where they provide additional business value, including closer monitoring of data quality or the verification of good practice at processing stages where it is not currently scrutinised. As such the steady states model helps promote a level of data asset mindfulness while illustrating the inherent and complimentary value of a data perspective to staff who are predominantly process-oriented.

For administrative purposes it is recommended that steady states in the line of business or enterprise flow map be sequentially numbered from the point at which data first enters the relevant sphere of influence – referenced as steady state zero (SS_0) – through to the final steady state before it exists outside that business unit's or the organisation's influence. The number of steady states designated in total (SS_n) will vary, effected by amongst other factors, the relative complexity of the underlying process model.

The level of granularity to which steady states are mapped is a decision to be made as part of a value proposition analysis. The ideal level will be specific enough to enable a sufficiently detailed level of insight into data behaviours across the line of business or enterprise lifecycle, but not too detailed to the point where the information it provides is overwhelming and of little practical value. For the purposes of manageability, it is suggested that steady states correspond to major process milestones and not reflect all of the specific sub-processes that fall between them (Braaksma & Zeelenberg, 2014), but that decision is ultimately based on a business unit's or the organisation's agreed governance needs.

Beyond providing a logical starting point for a sequential numbering of steady states, the use of a zero steady state also offers a mechanism for extending the view of data flow outside of the organisation's sphere of influence. Points on the flow map upstream of the SS_0 entry point, representing for instance assets existing within the influence of external data suppliers, can be mapped and designated with increasingly negative numbers (SS_{-1}, SS_{-2}, … SS_{-n}) as distance from SS_0 increases. This provides an opportunity to conceptually continue the data flow map beyond the physical boundaries of the organisation and into the operational environment of a different organisation.

Considering trends that suggest continued potential for the use of administrative data, particularly in census and other statistical contexts (Statistics New Zealand, 2014; Nordbotten, 2010), this capacity of the steady state model represents a particularly valuable benefit. While providing numerous advantages as a means of data collection (Connelly, Playford, Gayle, & Dibben, 2016; Statistics Canada, 2009), the persistent challenge with administrative data involves its efficient use in operating environments potentially very different from those in which it was originally collected. This reliance on data not inherently fit for purpose often translates into a significant data preparation burden – up to 80% of an analyst's time, per DalleMule and Davenport (2017) – before it can be used to generate value.

Since the form and quality of data as it arrives at an organisation's SS_0 entry point directly influences the level of work required to prepare it for subsequent use, the ability to shape the characteristics of that data prior to arrival is especially beneficial. In lieu of a consistent data flow model, the engagement required to influence data suppliers to reassess their data provision regime can represent a challenging and time-consuming prospect. But with the use of steady states, particularly if the supplier organisation is employing a similar mapping of their data lifecycles, a communication mechanism is available to facilitate productive discussions. In that case decisions about where in its business process model a supplier should release data, not only for its own benefit but for that of a downstream consumer as well, can be considered and communicated in terms of a mutually understood frame of reference.

This suggests that the view of data assets resulting from steady states flow mapping is quite naturally extensible across a broader ecosystem landscape, enabling a unified perspective on data and how it interacts throughout various macro-scale environments. It is here that the idea of flow demonstrates its unique potential as a means of managing and leveraging data asset value. The joining up of data perspectives in this way is a critical component of successful cross-organisational and cross-sector integration and offers significant potential to support holistic data approaches and to inform thinking on a global scale.

A Business View of Data Accountability

Steady states as a data flow modelling solution has its genesis in addressing the needs of a manufacturing production environment, and as such maintain a close association with basic value chain analysis. As the examples in the Netherlands and Australia demonstrate, the resultant emphasis on the tracking of accumulating value, when applied to data asset quality monitoring, is a worthwhile exercise, contributing to the perpetuation of good data management practice (Struijs, Camstra, Renssen, & Braaksma, 2013; Pink, 2010). But as noted previously, that style of analysis also runs the risk of perpetuating an isolated view of data assets, where they are not inherently linked to a business perspective as they should be. This dissociation of data assets, even if subtlety expressed, weakens the benefit proposition of considering data flow as something intricately linked with the organisational business process model.

Steady States as Business Decisions

The mapping of steady states directly onto a business process map effectively communicates the inherently close relationship between data and process, but there is the opportunity to further evolve the idea of a steady state to emphasise this close affiliation even more. Within the data governance approach proposed in this chapter, steady states are re-cast as business decisions. More than a simple representation of the data asset itself exhibiting the results of value transformations, steady states in this new rendition reflects staff with responsibilities for data assets determining if a new data lifecycle state has been achieved.

This re-characterisation of steady states represents a maturation in thinking about an important organisational asset, moving it from within a purely data-centric perspective to one where it is actively participating in and influenced by the operational realities of the organisation. Data in that sense becomes a resource situated firmly within business practice and its administration therefore more clearly positioned within the realm of asset management.

The evolution in thinking about a steady states model reveals additional means of characterising the value proposition, opens new avenues of benefit realisation, and provides for a meaningful consideration of asset management behaviours as a critical component of a data governance framework. When thought of as a business decision, a steady state becomes a nexus for a host of operational elements – including published guidance, reference structures, computer applications, and tools – that support and otherwise facilitate a business outcome.

Linking Data Behaviours and Data Knowledge

To progress the decision event associated with a steady state, staff will draw on some combination of the data governance capabilities delineated as part of the proposed data governance framework. It might require for instance tapping into a combination of subject matter expertise, risk management and external relationship management skills to deliver a successful outcome for an external client or stakeholder. This seemingly minor occurrence, repeated numerous times during the course of a business day, represents the point of connection between the two foundational outcomes – staff demonstrating improved data behaviours and an increased level of data knowledge – that shape this new approach to data governance.

Decisions of any type are made based on the consideration of criteria and it is no different in the case of a steady state. In this instance, staff reference an agreed set of quality criteria, published for their use as a combination of enterprise and line of business specific quality measures. As they test the measures associated with the relevant set of criteria and act upon the results of that analysis, they are conducting good data management practice while supporting the goals of their particular business unit.

Moreover, in their ownership of this decision process, staff are also taking accountability for the data assets under their care and thereby delivering a data governance outcome. If the testing of steady state criteria is properly documented, these staff are furthermore contributing to organisational assurance and risk mitigation by perpetuating operational transparency.

When designed properly and incorporated into established workflow, these significant governance results can be facilitated as a business-as-usual activity. From the perspective of staff, they are simply performing their standard duties. Their added responsibility as good stewards of data assets under their care happens as a matter of course.

Providing Data Assurance and Inspiring Trust

Data accountability as covered thus far in this chapter has focussed on the actions of those staff with responsibilities for managing data assets under their care. But accountability in this regard also involves an external dimension, where it serves as an important contributor to customer or constituent assurance.

A user of data or of a product or service based on the data managed by a trusted source can reasonably expect to have their inquiries about that data addressed to their satisfaction. In the proposed governance framework, this type of assurance arises from the embedding of capabilities that promote good data management practice across all staff positions with direct or indirect interests in organisational data assets. It is also supported by the transparency built into the steady states decision process and through the use of a set of informed and unambiguous guidance materials by staff responsible for those decisions.

In contrast, it is unrealistic to expect that those occupying a designated governance role typical of a political data governance model will possess the proper level of insight to provide a comprehensive understanding of data assets and their complex, highly dynamic and increasingly ad hoc patterns of flow across the enterprise.

The desired perspective can, however, emerge from a data governance model designed to facilitate the installation of proper data accountability across all relevant staff positions, in effect seeding an assurance mechanism broadly throughout the enterprise. While still delivered by people, the various capabilities required of good data governance and accountability are now linked more directly with the organisation's data assets themselves as they move and interact in complex ways during their lifecycles. In that regard good data management behaviours can legitimately be touted as part of the organisational "DNA," a condition that can be leveraged successfully to engender high levels of customer or constituent trust.

Line of Business Data Accountability

Though data accountabilities are situated at the level of individual staff, proper access to data knowledge is best initiated at the business unit level and with reference to the enterprise data flow map. While it is possible in some cases that this mapping could be generated from a single and decidedly top-down exercise, taking into account all steady states at once, the associated complexity for most organisations would likely be prohibitive. A more realistic option, which leverages native process knowledge at the line of business level, is to develop a library of business unit flow maps which can then be overlain and merged to create an enterprise view.

The properly aligned layering of business unit flow maps will support the creation of a separate enterprise data flow map, providing an organisational view of data flow while maintaining views within the constituent lines of business. One method posits enterprise steady states positioned wherever there is at least one instance of a business unit steady state below. An alternative approach, designed to limit the number of enterprise steady states, would involve the aggregation of multiple underlying business unit steady states. Regardless, because all business unit steady states are used to form an enterprise map, there should be no gaps – that is, no orphan steady states and process pathways between them that fall outside the responsibility of at least one line of business.

The integration of line of business flow maps will almost certainly present steady states that when considered from the enterprise perspective are associated with or fall under the responsibility of multiple lines of business. This is a reflection of actual practice where data is used simultaneously by different parts of the enterprise. When these shared steady states are viewed from the perspective of the constituent lines of business, they will likely assume different relative positions along their respective flow maps.

So for instance SS_{A1}, representing an early lifecycle steady state of business unit A data flow, might align from an enterprise perspective with SS_{C7}, a relatively late lifecycle position within business unit C data flow. This view of relative steady state positioning is valuable knowledge that can support a meaningful investigative opportunity into how business units interact from a data perspective and how they engage generally across the enterprise. This understanding becomes increasingly important as the complexity of the business operating environment increases.

The line of business perspective built into an organisation's data flow maps provides a means of using inherent data complexity as a path towards improved business insights. It is quite possible for instance that prior to data flow mapping an organisation would not be able to claim widespread or readily available understanding of the full contingent of business units responsible for and interested in data assets at any given point in their lifecycle. And once those responsibilities in all of their complexity are properly mapped and documented, the resultant knowledge base only strengthens the organisation's ability to respond efficiently and confidently to customer inquiries, contributing positively over time to strengthened levels of assurance.

Steady States as Monitoring Stations

If data is the water flowing through a stream network of an organisational business process model, steady states are the monitoring stations established throughout that network. While such stations are primarily put in place as output nodes, employing sensors to collect and transmit various types of stream condition data over time, they can also serve as input points, providing external intervention access to the network.

Quality gates represent a simple manifestation of a steady states model with a function in this sense as network output nodes, providing a means of collecting and reviewing regular measures of quality as data makes its journey through its lifecycle (Pink, 2010). Leveraging these gate nodes to test measures at various points throughout the process network, an organisation can keep an eye on data health over time. Based on the inherently close relationship between data and the business process model, the results of these data quality tests can also be used to inform an assessment of existing processes and workflow and support targeted and timely issue mitigation.

While it represents a conceptually unassuming model, the capacity of steady states to monitor the health of both data assets and the underlying process network makes it a powerful one. Steady states in this regard provide a level of infrastructure established strategically and comprehensively across the enterprise and which can be called upon at any time to help inform thinking and decision-making. As an enabling mechanism data flow mapping serves a vital role, insuring an organisation is well equipped to respond to changing operating conditions.

Steady states as nodes on the network, however, can also be used to inject good practice into the organisation. This would primarily be achieved through the design of quality criteria, which are available to help the organisation consider data variables its feels are worth measuring. The use of enterprise criteria could certainly serve this purpose, representing measures of relevance to business units across the organisation that can be "hard-coded" into the criteria list visible to all staff. The particular value of steady states in this regard is linked with the ability, via pre-established and well-distributed quality criteria, to establish good practice triggers simultaneously across the enterprise and directly into staff workflows.

These opportunities also speak to the portability of a steady states model and its value to an organisation as a future-proofed implementation of the proposed data governance framework. Once work is done to establish steady states and map them onto the business process model, they become components of an easily accessed enabling infrastructure, providing a means of extracting new insights or inserting new thinking or guidance. This flexible and readily available means of curating data knowledge is of particular value in a highly dynamic business environment.

The need to implement a new set of inputs or extract a new type of output might arise from a host of common circumstances including a change in leadership, a structural reorganisation, a refresh of strategy, or the advent of a new set of compliance parameters. A steady states implementation positions the organisation to more easily absorb the change that results and quickly distribute a managed response to it across the enterprise.

CONCLUSION

The conditions that characterise contemporary operating environments present a new set of circumstances for organisations operating across all sectors and include a much more prominent role for data. This has resulted in an increasing level of understanding that data represents a mission-critical business asset and the subsequent spread of that awareness to parts of the organisation where previously such things would have enjoyed little visibility.

To support this broadened appreciation of data in a way that translates to increased value realisation, its consideration and treatment also needs to move from the exclusive control of those operating in information management environments and beyond analysis practices where it is treated as an isolated entity. More than ever data is the business and as such it needs to be treated appropriately as a business asset. An organisation's data management practice should align closely with its business process models and staff behaviours in regard to data should likewise transition to those more common to asset managers. Data governance frameworks, as a particularly foundational and inherently enabling infrastructure, represent a good place to start.

Unfortunately, frameworks commonly employed for data governance are hindered in this regard by an adherence to traditional thinking and approaches established in a time of very different operating conditions. Significant amongst these approaches is the reliance on a top-down, hierarchical form, drawing heavily from the structure of the staff organisational chart. While easy to implement, the reach and influence of governance outcomes within such a politically-oriented framework do not readily extend into the operational contexts of line staff, an area of the business where arguably it is needed most. The reliance moreover by these traditional frameworks on a small set of designated roles like Data Custodian or Data Steward also tends to concentrate data accountability within a limited business context rather than thoroughly embedding it as a standard in the form of good practice data management amongst all staff.

The data governance framework proposed in this chapter, drawing from a model being developed for New Zealand government, reflects a significant change in thinking about the role of governance generally, so that it can better respond to current conditions, address the shortcomings of traditional approaches and deliver improved outcomes. It demonstrates how a realignment of the data business paradigm can help establish basic infrastructure that is better positioned to influence behaviours and enable a deeper level of knowledge about data assets within contemporary contexts. Its adoption offers the opportunity for a refreshed view of governance, establishes the foundation for a maturation of thinking about data generally, and can help organisations evolve beyond data management practices that require regular investment but are not delivering to their potential.

While the adoption of the proposed framework offers an organisation numerous benefits, its potential extends more widely to a system context as well. A consistent approach to data flow based on a steady states model for instance, if expanded appropriately across organisational boundaries, can contribute to a congruent data system, where communication and integration is well facilitated and there is increased potential to achieve the evidence-based and collaborative policy goals of projects like Actionable Intelligence for Social Policy (AISP, n.d.).

Recognising the inevitability and potential of increasingly global operating environments, the Actionable Intelligence for Social Policy initiative relies upon an Integrated Data Systems (IDS) model (Fantuzzo & Culhane, 2015), which itself requires an infrastructure that readily enables the acquisition and integration of different types of data from a host of relevant if disparate sources. Understanding how data flows, at both the organisation and system level, and having access to a consistent and easily adopted model for charting that flow across engagement scales is paramount, and represents an important contribution of the proposed data governance framework to this broader vision.

In light of the conditions that characterise current operating environments, there is a growing realisation that the challenges we face are increasingly global in scale and the implications of how we address them something that we must all own. The solutions we choose to enact therefore necessitate thinking across boundaries, be they political, organisational, or otherwise, and require data likewise free from unnecessary constraints, easily assimilated, and readily integrated to inform our decisions. An important step in this direction is agreement on a common organising or governance model for our collective data resources. Once established, this type of data governance framework is available to help enable the other infrastructures required to deliver the harmonious global data system to which we aspire.

REFERENCES

Actionable Intelligence for Social Policy (AISP). (n.d.). *Integrated Data Systems (IDS)*. Retrieved from http://www.aisp.upenn.edu/integrated-data-systems/

Ajeeli, A. T. A. (2016). Steady state analysis for improving manufacturing productivity. *International Journal of Development Research*, *06*(07), 8729–8738.

Allenby, B. (2015, March 4). Choose at your own risk: How technology is changing our choices and the values that help us make them. *Slate*. Retrieved from http://www.slate.com/articles/technology/future_tense/2015/03/how_technology_is_changing_our_choices_and_values.html

Bevir, M. (2012). *Governance: A very short introduction*. Oxford, UK: Oxford University Press. doi:10.1093/actrade/9780199606412.001.0001

Braaksma, B., & Zeelenberg, K. (2014). *Information management as a tool for standardization in statistics, Discussion Paper 2014-02*. The Hague: Statistics Netherlands.

Callahan, K. (2006). *Elements of effective governance: Measurement, accountability and participation*. Boca Raton, FL: CRC Press. doi:10.1201/9781420013429

Chen, W. (2010, June 25). A brief history of data governance. *Magnitude*. Retrieved from http://magnitude.com/blog/a-brief-history-of-data-governance/

Clarke, G. (2017, March 2). How data governance is now a strategic boardroom consideration in a data-driven world. *Microsoft Asia News Center*. Retrieved from http://news.microsoft.com/apac/2017/03/02/how-data-governance-is-now-a-strategic-boardroom-consideration-in-a-data-driven-world/

Connelly, R., Playford, C. J., Gayle, V., & Dibben, C. (2016). The role of administrative data in the big data revolution in social science research. *Social Science Research*, *59*, 1–12. doi:10.1016/j.ssresearch.2016.04.015 PMID:27480367

Cukier, K. (2010, February 25). Data, data everywhere. *The Economist*. Retrieved from http://www.economist.com/node/15557443

DalleMule, L., & Davenport, T. (2017, May-June). What's your data strategy? *Harvard Business Review*. Retrieved from http://hbr.org/2017/05/whats-your-data-strategy

Dataversity. (2012, January 19). *Data governance demystified - Lessons from the trenches*. Retrieved from http://www.dataversity.net/data-governance-demystified-lessons-from-the-trenches/

Deleu, R., & Clendon, J. (2015). *Government capability model*. Wellington: New Zealand Department of Internal Affairs - Office of the Government Chief Information Officer.

Fantuzzo, J., & Culhane, D. P. (Eds.). (2015). *Actionable intelligence: Using integrated data systems to achieve a more effective, efficient, and ethical government*. New York: Springer. doi:10.1057/9781137475114

Gandomi, A., & Haider, M. (2015, April). Beyond the hype: Big data concepts, methods, and analytics. *International Journal of Information Management, 35*(2), 137–144. doi:10.1016/j.ijinfomgt.2014.10.007

Gotkin, Z. (2012, October 17). America's innovative companies are going flat [Blog post]. Retrieved from http://www.huffingtonpost.com/zev-gotkin/corporate-hierarchy-work_b_1962345.html

Harper, J. (2017, March 1). Disrupting the data landscape again with linked open data. *KMWorld, 26*(3). Retrieved from http://www.kmworld.com/Articles/Editorial/Features/Disrupting-the-data-landscape-again-with-linked-open-data-116493.aspx

Harvey, J. T. (2012, October 5). Why government should not be run like a business. *Forbes*. Retrieved from http://www.forbes.com/sites/johntharvey/2012/10/05/government-vs-business/#187a72732a54

Higson, C., & Waltho, D. (2009). *Valuing information as an asset, White paper.* London: SAS.

Hutchins, G. (2011, July 28). Transformational times call for transformational change. *The Guardian*. Retrieved from http://www.theguardian.com/sustainable-business/blog/transformational-change-firms-future-ecosystems-communities

Institute of Directors in New Zealand. (n.d.). *What is governance?* Retrieved from http://www.iod.org.nz/FirstBoards/What-is-governance

Kemp, S. (2013, July 18). Big Data in the boardroom. *Dataversity*. Retrieved from http://www.dataversity.net/big-data-in-the-boardroom/

Lämmerhirt, D. (2017, February 16). Mapping open data governance models: Who makes decisions about government data and how? [Blog post]. Retrieved from http://blog.okfn.org/2017/02/16/mapping-open-data-governance-models-who-decides-and-how/

Lohr, S. (2012, February 12). The age of big data. *The New York Times*. Retrieved from http://www.nytimes.com/2012/02/12/sunday-review/big-datas-impact-in-the-world.html

Morgan, L. (2017, March 21). 3 data governance challenges today's companies face. *InformationWeek*. Retrieved from http://www.informationweek.com/big-data/3-data-governance-challenges-todays-companies-face/a/d-id/1328449

Nordbotten, S. (2010). The use of administrative data in official statistics – past, present and future – with special reference to the Nordic countries. In *Official Statistics – Methodology and Applications in Honour of Daniel Thorburn*. Stockholm: Stockholm University. Retrieved from http://www.nordbotten.com

People Measures. (n.d.). *Capability frameworks: A source of competitive advantage*. Retrieved from http://static1.squarespace.com/static/5248dad5e4b0dcb066334568/t/528021 1be4b03df6782bb316/1384128795517/People+Measures+-+Capability+Frameworks.pdf

Pink, B. (2010). *Quality management of statistical processes using quality gates, Information Paper 1540.0*. Canberra: Australian Bureau of Statistics.

Rick, T. (2014, August 16). Constant change is the new normal [Blog post]. Retrieved from http://www.torbenrick.eu/blog/business-improvement/is-constant-change-the-new-normal/

Smallwood, N., & Ulrich, D. (2004, June). Capitalizing on capabilities. *Harvard Business Review*. Retrieved from http://hbr.org/2004/06/capitalizing-on-capabilities

Statistics Canada. (2009, December). *Use of administrative data*. Ottawa, Canada: Statistics Canada. Retrieved from http://www.statcan.gc.ca/pub/12-539-x/2009001/administrative-administratives-eng.htm

Statistics New Zealand. (2014, July). *An overview of progress on the potential use of administrative data for census information in New Zealand*. Wellington, New Zealand: Statistics New Zealand.

Struijs, P., Camstra, A., Renssen, R., & Braaksma, B. (2013). Redesign of statistics production within an architectural framework: The Dutch experience. *Journal of Official Statistics*, *29*(1), 49–71. doi:10.2478/jos-2013-0004

Sweden, E. (2008). *Data governance - Managing information as an enterprise asset part I - An introduction*. Lexington, KY: National Association of State Chief Information Officers.

Sweden, E. (2009). *Data governance part III: Frameworks – Structure for organizing complexity*. Lexington, KY: National Association of State Chief Information Officers.

Sweeney, K. (2017). A behavioural capability-based data governance framework for New Zealand government. Wellington, New Zealand: Stats NZ. Retrieved from http://cdm20045.contentdm.oclc.org/digital/collection/p20045coll1/id/2657/rec/15

The Wharton School. (2003, August 27). The move from tall to flat: How corporate hierarchies are changing. *Knowledge @ Wharton*. Retrieved from http://knowledge.wharton.upenn.edu/article/the-move-from-tall-to-flat-how-corporate-hierarchies-are-changing/

Wessel, M. (2016, January 27). How big data is changing disruptive innovation. *Harvard Business Review*. Retrieved from http://hbr.org/2016/01/how-big-data-is-changing-disruptive-innovation

KEY TERMS AND DEFINITIONS

Accountability: Assuming a transparent and appropriate level of responsibility for data assets that are under one's care, which includes honoring obligations associated with good practice.

Administrative Data: Data collected as a matter of course by an organization for the purposes of supporting the normal business operations for which it is responsible. It contrasts with survey or research data which is gathered to answer a particular question or need.

Asset: A business resource with strategic, economic, or intrinsic value that an organization manages with the expectation that it will provide future benefit.

Capability: A measurable capacity to use resources that an organization needs to deliver to its strategy and achieve its agreed outcomes. It includes elements of people, process, information, and technology.

Data Flow: The lifecycle movement and storage of data assets along business process networks, including creation and collection from external sources, movement within and between internal business units, and departure through disposal, archiving, or as products or other outputs.

Data Lifecycle: The complete set of development stages from creation to disposal, each with its own characteristics and management responsibilities, through which organizational data assets pass.

Data Management: The full lifecycle care of organizational data assets, through the implementation of accepted good practice, to develop and maintain their value.

Governance: The framework of rules, norms, and accepted practice established as an organizational infrastructure to enable strategic outcomes, accountability, transparency, oversight, and the management of data, risk, and relationships.

Steady States: Those stages in the value chain where the output of a process satisfies a set of pre-agreed quality indicators. In a business context, data asset decision points where an agreed set of quality criteria are satisfied.

Value Chain: A business management concept or analytical model where production is viewed as a sequence of inputs, transformation processes, and outputs. Each transformation process adds value, which accumulates to the final product.

APPENDIX 1

Data governance principles from the data governance framework developed for New Zealand government (Sweeney, 2017).

- **Transparency:** A well-established data governance framework will enhance existing levels of transparency or help instil transparency where it is lacking. It does this by promoting and facilitating good practice data management behaviours which themselves result in increased levels of standardised documentation, encourage openness and improve communication in regards to data assets, across the enterprise. The results provide levels of assurance that strengthen trust amongst customers or constituents.
- **Business Process Alignment:** If organisations are to leverage meaningful insights from the plethora of data at their disposal, respond appropriately to the sea-change in the relative significance of data as a resource, a deliberate shift to a more intrinsically business-oriented consideration of data as asset is of value. This serves to expand the purview of data beyond purely technical considerations, which amongst other benefits, facilitates an alignment of data management approaches with business process models, inciting improved outcomes from both.
- **Holistic/Enterprise:** Data as an asset can be managed at many different scales and has the potential to deliver value across all of them, right down to its role as a component of a specific piece of work situated deep within a particular business unit. But leveraging data assets to their full strategic potential requires a holistic view distributed across the enterprise. It is only at this scale that a complete view of how data operates in the organisational context, including significantly how it flows through and between lines of business, is possible. A view developed at this scale is then positioned to provide valuable guidance in both directions, internally within the organisation and more widely across the contextual system.
- **Pragmatism:** A key shortcoming of traditional data governance models has been their failure to deliver meaningful value and relevancy throughout the organisation, and in particular to line staff. In contrast and considering the potential of an effective data governance framework, a practical execution based on a deliberately bottom-up implementation stands to deliver significant benefits throughout the enterprise, and directly into its operational environments. When incorporated within workflow and functioning as a matter of course, operational data governance is positioned to improve efficiency, while equipping line staff to deliver to strategic data imperatives like good practice data management.

APPENDIX 2

Data governance people capabilities from the data governance framework developed for New Zealand government (Sweeney, 2017).

1. **Data Point of Contact:** Delivery of this data governance capability on a practical level involves acting as the primary point of contact for those data assets within one's particular area of responsibility. This includes serving as the designated "go-to" person for internally and externally sourced questions, issues, or information requests about the data, and providing resolution or alternatively, coordinating escalation or delegation of matters appropriately.
2. **Subject Matter Expertise:** The proper management and fully realised business use of a data asset requires a level of expertise in either the data itself, the processes used to manipulate it, the part(s) of the business where that data is critically utilised, or a combination of all of these. If not providing a level of de facto expertise themselves, the individual delivering this capability would know how to secure such knowledge and the most efficient means of drawing from such resources when required.
3. **Access Control:** Aligned with the responsibilities of a data point of contact, this capability further involves the administration of and accountability for proper access to relevant data assets, thereby promoting good practice data security. Drawing on the proper level of implicit or delegated authority to make decisions in this regard, the person delivering this capability ensures that data assets designated as sensitive are only accessed by individuals with the proper authority, clearance and permissions to do so.
4. **Risk Management:** Those responsible for delivering to this capability will be well positioned to provide oversight for data assets under their responsibility such that potential risk to the organisation is identified, managed, and mitigated. In coordination with other parts of the business and drawing from organisational risk registers, provision of this capability would ideally involve the publication and maintenance of data asset risk profiles. This promotes good practice data management within the source line of business and helps inform other parts of the enterprise operating with data dependencies or concerned with risk management generally.
5. **Internal Relationship Management:** Properly managing the linkages between and across the parts of the enterprise where data exchanges hands is paramount to ensuring that data consistently contributes value as an operational asset. Drawing on point of contact and subject matter expertise capabilities, delivery of this capability includes the management of internal relationships to make sure a particular portion of the data asset lifecycle is connected to and aligned with those preceding and those following it, helping to maintain data flows and data asset positioning to deliver value.
6. **External Relationship Management:** If an enterprise is organised around a simple linear business process model, the ability to manage productive relationships with outside agents will be of particular significance at either end of the data lifecycle, where data is sourced from outside the organisation and again where fully processed data or derived products are disseminated to customers or stakeholders. If the organisation operates an open model, where data assets can be called upon to provide value at any point in their lifecycle, external relationship management is a capability requirement throughout the lifecycle and the charge of all staff with organisational data asset responsibilities.

7. **Quality Assurance/Quality Control Management:** A properly implemented data governance framework will supply an organisational infrastructure that provides a set of administrative entry points to enterprise data assets, representing opportunities to influence how those assets contribute to and themselves satisfy organisational quality requirements. Depending on the needs of the organisation, the manifestation of this data governance capability might fall at different points along a quality management spectrum, from providing a hands on, quality control focus, to maintaining oversight with more of an assurance-based perspective. In either case successful delivery of this data governance capability provides the enterprise with an acceptable level of confidence that the data assets and derivative products within a particular area of the business satisfy organisational quality requirements.
8. **Data Management:** Working closely and regularly with data assets means that in order to satisfy the responsibilities of their role, those tasked with a data management capability retain a sufficient familiarity with relevant data and information management policy, legislation, and guidance, and are confident in their ability to apply this knowledge. In those cases where they do not have or are not able to secure sufficient knowledge themselves, they will know how to readily access it or escalate issues to an enterprise governance body for resolution. In this capacity they serve as data management representatives throughout the enterprise, promoting good practice, and helping embed it within business activities like the negotiation of data agreements and the delivery of change management programmes.
9. **Data Champion:** Those with this data governance responsibility will actively promote the proper management and use of the data assets under their care, to realise value from those assets. Value realisation may be defined differently in different situations, but at its core it is generated through the successful use of those assets or derived outputs, by customers. There exists an associated championing capability therefore to serve as a consistent voice promoting this perspective across the organisation and ensuring it remains top of mind amongst staff performing their duties. This capability involves coordinating and delivering communications and providing education in good data and information management practice.
10. **Data Innovation:** The implementation of a data governance framework supports a culture of continuous improvement in regards to the oversight and management of enterprise data assets, expressed through a capability for innovative thinking. With a view across both the day to day operational and long-term strategic management of those assets, those delivering this capability can help stimulate innovation through an inherent openness to and recognition of better ways of doing things. They will also exercise a penchant for nurturing new ideas and presenting them in a meaningful way to the organisation for consideration. As a line of business contact for an enterprise data governance body, those delivering this capability are positioned to escalate innovative thinking to senior leadership for consideration and further action.

Chapter 15
Efficient Clustering Algorithms in Educational Data Mining

Anupama Chadha
Manav Rachna International Institute of Research and Studies, India

ABSTRACT

Higher education institutions are competing for excellence, and in this process, they are utilizing information technologies to gather relevant information for achieving academic excellence. The institutes are putting greater emphasis on meeting students' academic needs, enhancing the quality of service provided to students, providing better placements, course excellence, etc. The use of modern information technologies helps in storing huge data but requires the use of data mining technologies to extract useful information and knowledge from this data. Some of the knowledge achievable for higher education institutes through implementing several data mining techniques (classification, association learning, clustering, etc.) is the correlation between specialization and the chosen employment path, determining the subjects, courses, labs with high degree of difficulty, interesting subjects, courses, labs, facilities that might attract new students, etc. This chapter explores efficient clustering algorithms in educational data mining.

INTRODUCTION

Clustering is a technique of segregating the objects into partitions such that the objects in a group are more similar to each other than the objects in the other group. Clustering has its applications in variety of domains like health sector (Kaur, Harleen & Wasan, Krishan, Siri, 2006; Sharma, A. & Mansotra, V., 2014), E Commerce (Cheng, Yu & Ying, Xiong, 2009; Li, Mei & Feng, Cheng, 2010; Li, Yong-hong & Liu, Xiao-liang, 2010) etc. One of the areas where clustering is gaining boom is education (Hung, Jui-Long & Gao, Qingcheng, 2011; Hung, Jui-Long, Hsu, Yu-Chang & Rice, Kerry, 2012; Jin, Hanjun, Wu, Tianzhen, Liu, Zhiliang & Yan, Jianlin, 2009; Jing-miao, Zhang & Wei-xiao, Gao, 2008; Ma, Yiming, Liu, Bing, Wong, Kian, Ching, Yu, S., Philip & Lee, Ming, Shuik, 2000; Mei-lan, Chen, 2010; Ogor, 2007; Pal, 2012)

DOI: 10.4018/978-1-5225-3725-0.ch015

Many clustering algorithms have been proposed in the literature (Gan, Guojun, Ma, Chaoqun, & Wu, Jianhong, 2007; Jain, K., Anil & Dubes C. Richard, 1988; Wu, Xindong, Kumar, Vipin, Quinlan, Ross, J.,...Dan, 2007; Xu, Rui, & Wunsch, Donald, 2005). The clustering algorithms are broadly classified into two categories, Hierarchical and Partitional. K-Means is a famous partitonal clustering algorithm. Simplicity and speed in classification of massive data are two features which have made K-Means a very popular algorithm. However, K-Means has a major limitation -- the number of clusters, 'K', need to be pre-specified as an input to the algorithm. In absence of thorough domain knowledge, or for a new and unknown dataset, this advance estimation and specification of cluster number typically leads to "forced" clustering of data, and proper classification does not emerge. As K-Modes and K-prototype algorithms are variants of K-Means, they carry this demerit of K-Means.

In this chapter, new algorithms based on the K-Means, K-Modes and K-Prototype are presented which have advance features of intelligent data analysis and automatic generation of appropriate number of clusters. The clusters generated by the new algorithm are compared against results obtained with the original K-Means, K-Modes and K-Prototype. The practical application of these algorithms is discussed in the field of education to cluster the similar students based on their academic performance using datasets of different types and dimensions.

BACKGROUND

The work of some researchers to remove the limitation of giving the number of clusters required as an input in the K-Means for numerical data is discussed below:

Pelleg et al. (2000) presented XMeans algorithm as an extension of K Means which overcomes the limitation of inputting the value of K and performs faster than the original K Means. The algorithm starts with K as the lower bound of the given range and continues adding centroids until the upper bound is reached. During this process the centroid set that scores the best is recorded using the data structure kd-tree and is produced as output. The user has to input a range suggesting the lower and upper bound of K.

Tibshirani et al. (2000) used the technique of Gap Statistic that utilizes the output generated by any clustering algorithm to compare the change within cluster dispersion to that expected under an appropriate reference null distribution. This Gap method works well when the clusters are well separated.

Wagstaff, et al. (2001) utilized information about the problem domain in performing clustering. This information about the problem domain is used in specifying the constraints on the data set. While assigning the data points to a cluster it is ensured that none of the constraint is violated.

Cheung (2003) presented a new clustering technique named STep-wise Automatic Rival penalized (STAR) K-Means algorithm. This new algorithm is a generalization of the conventional K-Means algorithm but overcoming its two major limitations discussed earlier in this paper. The algorithm consists of two separate steps. The first step provides each cluster a center. The next step then adjust the units adaptively by a learning rule. This algorithm is computationally complex.

Leela et al. (2013) presented Y-Means algorithm based on K-Means algorithm. Initially, it runs K-Means algorithm on the data set and then follows the sequence of splitting, deleting and merging the clusters. The algorithm depends on K-Means algorithm to find the clusters initially.

Shafeeq et al. (2012) introduced an algorithm to problem of inputting the required number of clusters by finding the optimal number of clusters on the run. The main drawback of the proposed approach is that it takes more computational time than the K-Means for larger data sets. Also the user has to input the number of clusters 'K' as 2 in the first run.

Abubaker et al. (2013) presented a new approach to overcome two of the major limitations of K-means algorithm: Firstly, to select efficiently the initial centroids and second to remove the need of giving the number of clusters required as input to the algorithm. The proposed algorithm is based on the k-nearest neighbor method. They have suggested two versions of the algorithm. The first version takes k_n (the number of nearest neighbors), and the number of clusters k in the data set as input parameters. Then the sorted list of data points is investigated until the number of obtained prototypes reached the specified k and the algorithm is aborted. The second version takes k_n as the only input parameter and obtains both the number of clusters and the prototypes in parallel. The user has to input the number of nearest neighbors k_n.

This section discusses the research work dealing with the limitation of inputting the value of K in K-Modes and K-Prototype algorithm.

Liao et al. (2009) introduced an algorithm which used a regularization parameter to control the number of clusters in the clustering process of categorical data. A suitable value of regularization parameter was chosen to find the most stable clustering results. The algorithm requires an input parameter representing the initial cluster centers.

Cheung et al. (2013) presented a general clustering framework based on the concept of object-cluster similarity. Also a unified similarity metric which can be simply applied to the data with categorical, numerical, and mixed attributes is introduced. Moreover, to circumvent the difficult selection problem of cluster number, a penalized competitive learning algorithm within the proposed clustering framework is presented. The embedded competition and penalization mechanisms enable this improved algorithm to determine the number of clusters automatically by gradually eliminating the redundant clusters. The algorithm requires as input some initial value of k which should not be less than the original value of k.

Liang et al. (2012) extended K-Prototype algorithm by proposing a new dissimilarity measure for mixed data set. A mechanism was developed to make use of within-cluster entropy and between-cluster entropy to identify the worst cluster in a mixed dataset. The algorithm requires input parameters representing the minimum and maximum number of clusters that can be generated from the dataset.

MAIN FOCUS OF THE CHAPTER

A lot of work has been done on the K-Means algorithm and its extensions to overcome the limitation of providing the value of K as an input but all the suggested algorithms require some parameter to be input to perform clustering for the given dataset. This motivated the author to propose new algorithms based on the K-Means, K-Modes and K-Prototype algorithms for numerical, categorical and mixed datasets to make them more efficient by making them work without taking any parameter as input. The practical application of the algorithms is discussed in the education sector to categorize the students according to their academic performance. The other areas where these algorithms can be applied are Agriculture, Healthcare and Banking sector.

INTRODUCTION TO K-MEANS ALGORITHM

The K-Means is a partition based iterative algorithm. This algorithm divides the given dataset into required number of clusters (K). The procedure starts with the random selection of K centroids one for each cluster. The objects are moved from one cluster to another and centroids are recomputed until all the objects in each cluster are at their minimum distance from their centroids. In this technique Euclidean distance is taken as the distance measure given in Equation 1.

$$d(x,c) = \sum_{i=i}^{n} \sqrt{(x_i - c_i)^2} \,, \tag{1}$$

where x= (x1, x2,……xn) is an object in a cluster and c=(c1, c2,…..cn) is the centroid of a cluster.
The basic algorithm works as follows:

Algorithm: Basic K-Means
Input: Numerical dataset (D), Number of clusters (K)
Output: Elements of dataset classified into K clusters

1. Select K random points as initial centroids.
2. Repeat.
3. Create K clusters by assigning all data points to the closest centroid.
4. Recompute centroids (mean value of the objects in the cluster) for each cluster to improve accuracy.
5. Until the cluster centroids don't change.

The K-Means algorithm has the following advantages:

- The K-Means algorithm is inexpensive in terms of time.
- Highly cohesive clusters are produced by the algorithm.

The algorithm has some limitations also:

- The final clusters produced are highly sensitive to initial centroids because the initial centroids are chosen randomly.
- The algorithm is sensitive to outliers because centroids are calculated as mean of the values lying in that cluster.
- The algorithm requires an initial input of K. Providing this value becomes difficult sometimes because the person using the algorithm may not be the domain expert.

Various extensions of K-Means have been discussed in literature to overcome the above mentioned limitations (Huang, J., Z., Ng, M., K., Rong, H. & Li, Z., 2005; Jain, Anwiti, Rajavat, Anand & Bhartiya, Rupali, 2012; Li, Wei, 2008; Panda, Sandeep, Sahu, Sanat, Jena, Pradeep & Chattopadhyay, Subhagata, 2012; Singh, Vijay, Ran & Bhatia, M., P., S., 2011; Visalakshi, Karthikeyani, N. & Suguna, J., 2009; Yuepeng, Sun, Wu, Cheng & Liu, Min, 2011).

THE PROPOSED K-MEANS ALGORITHM

The proposed K-Means algorithm which does not require an initial estimation and specification of number of clusters (K) as input, and hence can generate much more meaningful clusters is proposed below. This algorithm works best with datasets in which all the attributes have numeric values measured on the same scale.

In comparison to other methods discussed above, no additional input except the dataset itself is needed. This algorithm starts by initially partitioning the dataset into two clusters by choosing two objects as initial centroids. The sum of attribute values of the chosen objects represent the minimum and maximum values. This is done so that in the initial step itself, the dataset can be broken into two clusters with high degree of inter cluster dissimilarity. The algorithm proceeds further by breaking these two initial clusters if the objects in the clusters do not satisfy the objective function representing the intra cluster similarity. This objective function is based on Euclidean distance. The pseudo code of the proposed algorithm is discussed below (Chadha, Anupama, Kumar, & Suresh, 2016).

- **Input:** D: The set of n objects with attributes A_1, A_2, . . ., A_m where m = Number of attributes and all the attributes are numeric.
- **Output:** Clusters or groups distributing the objects in the given dataset.

Method

1. Compute sum of the attribute values of each object.
2. Take objects with minimum and maximum values of the sum as initial centroids.
3. Create two initial partitions (clusters) based on the Euclidean distance between every object and the initial centroids.
4. Find the average of Euclidean distances of the objects from their centroid in each cluster. Calculate the average of euclidean distances for every cluster as:

$$d_a vg(C_j) = 1 / n ?^{n}_{(i=1)} ? d_i \tag{2}$$

where d_i=distance of ith object from its centroid in cluster j, n=number of objects in cluster j.

The minimum of the two average distances (other than 0) is taken as d_m.

5. Compute new means (centroids) for the partitions created in step 3.
6. Compute Euclidean distance of every object from the new centroids and find the outliers depending on the following objective function:

$$\text{If } d(x, c) < d_m \text{ then not an Outlier.} \tag{3}$$

Obtain the transformed clusters.

7. Compute centroids of the transformed clusters.

8. Calculate Euclidean distance of every outlier from the cluster centroids and find the outliers not satisfying the objective function mentioned in step 6. Put back the outliers satisfying the objective function and obtain transformed clusters. This step is performed to check whether any of the outliers can be adjusted in the existing clusters. Remaining outliers are added to set B.
9. Let B={Y_1,Y_2,.....Y_p} be the set of outliers obtained in step 8.
10. If set B contains one object then:
    a. Create a new cluster containing that object
    b. Else
    c. Repeat
        i. Assume this set B as a new dataset (D)
        ii. Perform steps 1 to 10
    iii.until (B==Φ)

ILLUSTRATIVE EXAMPLE

The proposed algorithm is explained using a small datasets representing the marks of the students in three subjects. The algorithm divides the students into different clusters based on their academic performance.

As per proposed algorithm:

Step 1: Find the sum of the attribute values of each object as shown in the Sum column in Table 3.5.

Table 1. Dataset Showing Marks of Students

Roll No.	Subject 1	Subject 2	Subject 3	Sum
1.	22	40	30	92
2.	60	60	58	178
3.	65	60	63	188
4.	98	88	90	276
5.	98	88	90	276
6.	58	60	55	173
7.	60	58	62	180
8.	62	64	66	192
9.	59	60	62	181
10.	60	65	66	191
11.	60	59	58	177
12.	57	58	59	174
13.	60	60	58	178
14.	75	80	72	227
15.	80	88	89	257
16.	85	75	70	230
17.	98	98	92	288
18.	98	98	92	288

Step 2: The shaded objects are chosen as initial centroids (minimum and maximum values).
Step 3: After calculating the distance of all the objects from the two initial centroids following clusters were formed:

Cluster 1: {(**22, 40, 30**), (60, 60, 58), (65, 60, 63), (58, 60, 55), (60, 58, 62), (59, 60, 62), (60, 59, 58), (57, 58, 59), (60, 60, 58)}
Cluster 2: {(**98, 98, 92**), (98, 88, 90), (98, 88, 90), (62, 64, 66), (60, 65, 66), (75, 80, 72), (80, 88, 89), (85, 75, 70), (98, 98, 92)}

Step 4: Calculate Euclidean distance of every object in Cluster 1 from its centroid (22, 40, 30) and find the average distance which comes out to be 51.77.

Similarly, the average of all the object distances in Cluster 2 from its centroid (98, 98, 92) is 28.03. The minimum of the two is taken as d_m. d_m=28.03.

Step 5: Compute new centroid for Cluster 1 as:

Centroid Cluster1: (55.67, 57.22, 56.11)
Similarly, compute new centroid for Cluster 2:
Centroid Cluster2: (83.77, 82.66, 80.78)

Step 6: In Cluster1 outliers are: (22, 40, 30)

So Cluster 1 transforms into: {(60, 60, 58), (65, 60, 63), (58, 60, 55), (60, 58, 62), (59, 60, 62), (60, 59, 58), (57, 58, 59), (60, 60, 58)}
In Cluster 2 outliers are: (62, 64, 66), (60, 65, 66)
So Cluster 2 transforms into: {(98, 98, 92), (98, 88, 90), (98, 88, 90), (75, 80, 72), (80, 88, 89), (85, 75, 70), (98, 98, 92)}

Step 7: Calculate centroid of transformed cluster1 and cluster2 after removing the outliers:

Centroid Cluster 1: (59.87, 59.38, 59.38)
Centroid Cluster 2: (90.28, 87.85, 85)

Step 8: Calculate distance of the outliers from the centroids of Cluster 1 and Cluster 2. The outliers (62, 64, 66), (60, 65, 66) fit in Cluster 1. The outliers (22, 40, 30) does not fit in any of the cluster.
Step 9: Take B= {(22, 40, 30)} as a new dataset.
Step 10: As B contains only one object so create a new cluster containing this object. Finally three clusters are obtained as shown below:

Cluster 1: {(60, 60, 58), (65, 60, 63), (58, 60, 55), (60, 58, 62), (59, 60, 62), (60, 59, 58), (57, 58, 59), (60, 60, 58), (62, 64, 66), (60, 65, 66)}
Cluster 2: {(98, 98, 92), (98, 88, 90), (98, 88, 90), (75, 80, 72), (80, 88, 89), (85, 75, 70), (98, 98, 92)}
Cluster 3: {(22, 40, 30)}

These three clusters represent the Weak, Average, and Bright students respectively. Those students who have scored somewhat similar marks are placed in the same cluster. These results are compared with the original K-Means algorithm with K=3 using RapidMiner and the results are shown in in Table 2. Both the algorithms have generated the same results.

K-MODES ALGORITHM

The K-Modes extends the K-Means algorithm to cluster categorical data in the following manners (Khan et al. 2013):

- A Simple matching dissimilarity function suitable for categorical data is used instead of Euclidean distance.
- Modes are used to represent centroids instead of Mean values.
- A frequency based method is used to find centroids in each iteration of the algorithm.

Basic K-Modes works as follows:

Algorithm: Basic K-Modes

Input: Categorical dataset (D), Number of clusters (K)
Output: Elements of dataset classified into K clusters

1. Select arbitrarily K objects as initial centroids.
2. Allocate an object to the cluster whose mode is the nearest to it according to:

$$d(x,c) = \sum_{i=1}^{n} \delta(x_i c_i), \quad (4)$$

where $x=(x_1, x_2, \ldots x_n)$ is an object in a cluster, $c=(c_1, c_2, \ldots c_n)$ is the centroid of a cluster and δ is Kronker delta defined by

$$\delta(i,j) = \begin{cases} 0 \text{ if } i=j \\ 1 \text{ if } i \neq j \end{cases} \quad (5)$$

Table 2. Results of Marks Dataset

	K-Means Algorithm	Proposed Algorithm
Cluster1	{(60, 60, 58), (65, 60, 63), (58, 60, 55), (60, 58, 62), (59, 60, 62), (60, 59, 58), (57, 58, 59), (60, 60, 58), (62, 64, 66), (60, 65, 66)}	{(60, 60, 58), (65, 60, 63), (58, 60, 55), (60, 58, 62), (59, 60, 62), (60, 59, 58), (57, 58, 59), (60, 60, 58), (62, 64, 66), (60, 65, 66)}
Cluster2	{(98, 98, 92), (98, 88, 90), (98, 88, 90), (75, 80, 72), (80, 88, 89), (85, 75, 70), (98, 98, 92)}	{(98, 98, 92), (98, 88, 90), (98, 88, 90), (75, 80, 72), (80, 88, 89), (85, 75, 70), (98, 98, 92)}
Cluster3	{(22, 40, 30)}	{(22, 40, 30)}

Update the centroids (modes of the objects in the cluster) after each allocation.

3. After all objects have been allocated to clusters, retest the dissimilarity of objects against the current modes. If an object is found such that its nearest mode belongs to another cluster rather than its current one, reallocate the object to that cluster and update the modes of both clusters.
4. Repeat (3) until no object has changed clusters after a full cycle test of the whole dataset.

The K-Modes algorithm carries in itself the benefits and limitations of the K-Means because it follows the same iterative process as that of K-Means. To overcome these limitations various extensions of K-Modes have been presented in literature (Bai, L., Liang, J., Dang, C. & Cao, F., 2012; Cao, Fuyuan, Liang, Jiye, Li, Deyu & Zhao, Xingwang, 2013; Gan, Guojun, Ma, Chaoqun, & Wu, Jianhong, 2009; Huang, Z., 1997, Won, K., D., Lee, K., Lee, K., D. & Lee, K., H., 2005).

THE PROPOSED K-MODES ALGORITHM

The proposed algorithm starts by dividing the given dataset into some initial clusters. The objects in the clusters which do not satisfy the objective function are taken as outliers. This objective function is discussed in subsection 6.1. The outliers obtained are then checked for whether any of them can be put back in the clusters based on a condition which is discussed later in this chapter. This step is performed so that any object which was not able to satisfy the objective function because of the presence of some indifferent object can now be put back in the cluster. The outliers after this step are then taken as a new dataset and this process is repeated until all the objects are assigned to some clusters satisfying the objective function.

In the proposed algorithm, the concept of significance of attribute presented by Ahmad et al. (2007) is used to create initial clusters. The attributes which display a good separation of co-occurrence of values into different groups, play a more significant role in clustering of data elements. In other words, an attribute plays a significant role in clustering, provided any pair of its attribute values are well separated against all attributes i.e. have an overall high value of d(x, y), for all pairs of x and y (Ahmad, A. & Dey, L., 2007). The frequency based method introduced by Huang (1998) is used to find centroids of the clusters and the distance between an object and the centroid is calculated using the distance measure introduced by San et al. (2004). The author has got this work published (Chadha, Anupama, Kumar, & Suresh, 2016).

To deal with high dimension datasets, a dimensionality reduction step is included in the second version of the algorithm so that only the relevant attributes (having high significance value) participate in the process of clustering.

The Proposed Objective Function

In order to check for outlier in each cluster, the following objective function is used:

If $d(X_i, C_j) <= d_m$, then not an outlier, (6)

where $d(X_i, C_j)$ is the distance between object X_i and centroid C_j,

$X_i=x_{i1}, x_{i2}, \ldots x_{im}, C_j=c_{j1}, c_{j2}, \ldots c_{jm},$

d_m= The minimum of all the distance values.

The distance of every object from its centroid is calculated. The minimum of these distance values (other than 0) is represented as d_m.

Generation of Initial Clusters

To Generate Initial Clusters Following Steps are Performed:

Step 1: Find the most significant attribute.
Step 2: Generate initial clusters with attribute values with maximum distance in most significant attribute in different clusters.

These steps are explained using a small dataset as shown in Table 3.

Step 1: In order to find the most significant attribute, calculate the distance between every pair of values for each attribute in Table 3. The distance between the pair of values x and y of A_j with respect to the attribute A_i is defined as follows:

$$\delta^{ij}(\mathrm{x}, \mathrm{y}) = P_i(\omega / x) + P_i(\sim \omega / y) - 1 \tag{7}$$

Where ω is the subset w of values of A_i that maximizes the quantity $P_i(\omega/x) + P_i(\sim\omega/y)$, $P_i(\omega/x)$ denote the conditional probability that an element having value x for A_j, has a value belonging to ω. for A_i, $P_i(\sim\omega/y)$ denotes the conditional probability that an element having value y for A_j has a value belonging to $\sim\omega$ for A_i.

Calculate the conditional probabilities for all the attributes in Table 3 as given in Table 4, 5 and 6.

Table 4 shows the conditional probability values of attribute Subject1 with respect to Subject2 and Subject3.

Table 5 shows the conditional probability values of attribute Subject2 with respect to Subject1 and Subject3.

Table 3. Academic Record of Students

Roll No.	Subject 1	Subject 2	Subject 3
1.	A	B	A
2.	B	D	D
3.	C	A	C
4.	C	A	A
5.	C	A	B
6.	A	D	A

Table 4. Probability Table for Subject 1

Subject 2	Subject 3
P(A|A)=0 P(B|A)=1/2 P(D|A)=1/2 P(A|B)=0 P(B|B)=0 P(D|B)=1 P(A|C)=1 P(B|C)=0 P(D|C)=0	P(A|A)=1 P(B|A)=0 P(C|A)=0 P(D|A)=0 P(A|B)=0 P(B|B)=0 P(C|B)=0 P(D|B)=1 P(A|C)=1/3 P(B|C)=1/3 P(C|C)=1/3 P(D|C)=0

Table 5. Probability Table for Subject 2

Subject 1	Subject 3
P(A|A)=0 P(B|A)=0 P(C|A)=1 P(A|B)=1 P(B|B)=0 P(C|B)=0 P(A|D)=1/2 P(B|D)=1/2 P(C|D)=0	P(A|A)=1/3 P(B|A)=1/3 P(C|A)=1/3 P(D|A)=0 P(A|B)=1 P(B|B)=0 P(C|B)=0 P(D|B)=0 P(A|D)=1/2 P(B|D)=0 P(C|D)=0 P(D|D)=1/2

Table 6 shows the conditional probability values of attribute Subject 3 with respect to Subject 1 and Subject 2.

Calculate the distance between various values of the attributes of Table 3 to obtain Table 7.

The significance of an attribute is calculated by taking the average of all the distance values to get Table 8.

The attributes Subject 2 has maximum significance value as shown in Table 8, so it is chosen as the most significant attribute.

Step 2: As can be seen from Table 7, the distance between the values 'A' and 'B' and the distance between the values 'A' and 'D' is maximum, so initial clusters are formed by keeping the objects with values 'A' and 'B' of attribute Subject2 into separate clusters. Also the objects with value 'D' are kept in the cluster containing the objects with value 'B' as the distance of 'D' from 'B' is less as compared to distance from 'A'.

The initial clusters are shown in Table 9.

Table 6. Probability Table for Subject 3

Subject 1	Subject 2
P(A|A)=2/3 P(B|A)=0 P(C|A)=1/3 P(A|B)=0 P(B|B)=0 P(C|B)=1 P(A|C)=0 P(B|C)=0 P(C|C)=1 P(A|D)=0 P(B|D)=1 P(C|D)=0	P(A|A)=1/3 P(B|A)=1/3 P(D|A)=1/3 P(A|B)=1 P(B|B)=0 P(D|B)=0 P(A|C)=1 P(B|C)=0 P(D|C)=0 P(A|D)=0 P(B|D)=0 P(D|D)=1

Table 7. Distance between Various Values of Attributes of Table 3

Subject 1	Subject 2	Subject 3
δ (A, B)=3/4 δ (A, C)=5/6 δ (B, C)=1/2	δ (A, B)=5/6 δ (A, D)=5/6 δ (B, D)=1/2	δ (A, B)=2/3 δ (A, C)=2/3 δ (A, D)=5/6 δ (B, C)=0 δ (B, D)=1 δ (C, D)=1

Table 8. The Significance of the Attributes of Table 3

Significance of Subject1=0.69
Significance of Subject2=0.72
Significance of Subject3=0.69

Table 9. Initial Clusters

Cluster 1	Cluster 2
{(A, B, A), (B, D, D), (A, D, A)}	{(C, A, C), (C, A, A), (C, A, B)}

Finding Centroids of the Clusters

Find the centroid of a cluster as stated below:

1. Calculate the frequencies of all categories for all attributes and store them in a category array in descending order of frequency for every cluster as shown below in Category Array.

$$\begin{matrix} c_{1,1} & c_{1,2} & c_{1,3} \\ c_{2,1} & c_{2,2} & c_{2,3} \\ c_{3,1} & & c_{3,3} \end{matrix} \textit{Category Array}$$

Here, $c_{i,j}$ denotes category i of attribute j and $f(c_{i,j}) \geq f(c_{i+1,j})$ where $f(c_{i,j})$ is the frequency of category $c_{i,j}$.

2. Assign the most frequent categories in the category array as centroid.

Step 3: This way the centroid of Cluster 1 is: (A, D, A)

Similarly, centroid of Cluster 2: (C, A, C)

Computation of Distance of an Object From Its Centroid

The distance of an object from its centroid is calculated as:

d (x, c) is the distance between object x and centroid c and is calculated as:

$$\sum_{\substack{j=1 \\ c_{j \neq x_j}}}^{m} f_{c_j} \delta\left(x_j, c_j\right), \quad (8)$$

where $x=(x_1,x_2,\ldots\ldots x_m)$, $c=(c_1,c_2,\ldots.c_m)$,

Here, is the relative frequency of c_j within a cluster of categorical objects C and is Kronker delta defined by;

$$\delta(i,j) = \begin{cases} 0 if\, i = j \\ 1 if\, i \neq j \end{cases}$$

The distance values of objects from their respective centroids in Cluster 1 and Cluster 2 are shown in Table 10.

The Pseudocode of the Proposed K-Modes Algorithm

```
Input: Dataset (D) of N objects with m categorical attributes
Output: Clusters or groups distributing the objects in the given dataset
Steps:
1. Find the most significant attribute from the given 'm' attributes.
2. Create initial clusters.
3. Find the centroids of the clusters.
4. Find the distance of every object from its centroid. The minimum of these
distance values (other than 0) is represented as d_m.
5. Find the outliers in the initial clusters according to the objective func-
```

Table 10. Distance of Objects from their Respective Centroids

Distances in Cluster1	Distances in Cluster 2
d(A, B, A)=2/3=0.67	d(C, A, C)=0
d(B, D, D)=4/3=1.33	d(C, A, A)=1/3=0.33
d(A, D, A)=0	d(C, A, B))=1/3=0.33

```
tion. Obtain transformed clusters.
6. For each cluster find the number of attributes in which objects have match-
ing values. Maximum of these values is represented as n. Take only those ob-
jects from the outliers obtained in step 5 which have values matching in n-1
attributes with the objects of the transformed clusters obtained in step 5.
Add these outliers to set A. The remaining outliers are added to set B.
7. Repeat
      For each cluster:
          a. Find the number of outliers in set A having matching values in
n-1 attributes and put it in k.
          b. If k > 1 then
                     If outliers have matching values at different positions
then
                               Put those outliers back in cluster whose dis-
tance from the centroid is least. Add other outliers to set B.
                     Else if k=1
                               Put the outlier back in the cluster.
   Until (A== Φ)
8. Let B={Y1,Y2,.....Yp} be the set of outliers.
9. If set B contains one object then,
           Create a new cluster containing that object
      Else
           Repeat
           a. Assume this set B as a new dataset (D)
           b. Perform steps 1 to 9
           until (B==Φ)
```

ILLUSTRATIVE EXAMPLE

The first three steps of the algorithm in have already been explained in previous sections, continuing with the same dataset the rest of the steps are explained below:

Step 4: The minimum distance value is 0.33 and is of the objects (C, A, A) and (C, A, B) from their centroid as shown in Table 10.

Step 5: Taking d_m=0.33, obtain transformed cluster1 after removing the outliers according to the objective function mentioned in step 5 of the algorithm. Cluster 2 has no outlier.

The outliers in Cluster1 are: {(A, B, A), (B, D, D)}
Transformed Cluster 1: {(A, D, A)}

Step 6: Take n=2, as Cluster 2 has objects with matching values in two attributes. The outlier (A, B, A) can be put back in Cluster 1. (A, B, A) has matching value with other records in cluster1 at attribute Subject 1 and Subject 3. The remaining outlier (B, D, D) is added to set B.
Step 7: Object (A, B, A) is put back in Cluster 1. Transformed cluster1 is: {(A, D, A), (A, B, A)}
Step 8: Take B={(B, D, D)}
Step 9: Since only one record is left in set B, create a new cluster and put this record.

Finally, three clusters are obtained. These results are compared with the results obtained using K-Modes algorithm with K=3 using software RapidMiner as shown in Table 11.

The results in Table 11 show that both the algorithms have generated similar clusters.

K-PROTOTYPE ALGORITHM

Earlier the clustering algorithms focused on single type of dataset either all attributes numerical or all attributes categorical. As mixed datasets are becoming common in real life, so clustering algorithms are being developed to cluster these datasets.

K-Prototype is a variant of K-Means that can be used with mixed datasets. K-Prototype uses the basic idea of the K-Means by applying Euclidean distance to numeric attributes and Binary distance to categorical attributes. The K-Prototype algorithm works as follows:

Algorithm: Basic K-Prototype
Input: Mixed dataset (D), Number of Clusters (K)
Output: Elements of Dataset classified into K clusters

1. Select arbitrarily K objects as initial centroids.
2. Allocate each object in D to a cluster whose centroid is nearest to it according to the following distance measure:

Table 11. Results of Academic Dataset

	K-Modes with K=3	Proposed Algorithm
Cluster1	{(A, B, A), (A, D, A)}	{(A, B, A), (A, D, A)}
Cluster2	{(C, A, C), (C, A, A), (C, A, B)}	{(C, A, C), (C, A, A), (C, A, B)}
Cluster3	{(B, D, D)}	{(B, D, D)}

$$d\left(X_i,Q_l\right)=\sum_{j=1}^{m_r}(x_{ij}^{\ r}-q_{lj}^{\ r})^2+\gamma_l\sum_{j=1}^{m_c}\delta(x_{ij}^{\ c},q_{lj}^{\ c}),\tag{9}$$

where X_i =(x_{i1}, x_{i2},……x_{in}) is ith object in a cluster, Q_l =(q_{l1}, q_{l2},……q_{ln}) is centroid of cluster l and δ is Kronker delta defined by

$$\delta(i,j)=\begin{cases}0\,if\,i=j\\1\,if\,i\neq j\end{cases}$$

$x_{ij}^{\ r}$ and $q_{lj}^{\ r}$ are values of numeric attributes for object i and the centroid of cluster l, $x_{ij}^{\ c}$ and $q_{lj}^{\ c}$ are values of categorical attributes for object i and the centroid of cluster l, m_r and m_c are the numbers of numeric and categorical attributes, γ_l is a weight for categorical attributes for cluster l.

Update the centroid (mean for numerical attributes and mode for categorical attributes) of the cluster after each allocation.

3. After all objects have been allocated to a cluster, retest the similarity of objects against the current centroid. If an object is found such that its nearest centroid belongs to another cluster rather than its current one, reallocate the object to that cluster and update the centroids of both clusters.
4. Repeat (3) until no object has changed clusters after a full cycle test of the whole dataset.

However, taking the Binary distance for categorical attributes does not give accurate results because in many real life situations the categorical values may have some other degree of difference rather than just 0 or 1. To overcome this limitation various extensions of the K-Prototype algorithms have been presented in the literature (Hunt, L. & Jorgensen, M., 2011; Lui, H., He, H., Dai, B. & Yan, Y., 2006; Luo, H., Kong, F. & Li, Y., 2006; Naija, Yosr, Chakhar, Salem, Blibech, Kaouther & Robbana, Riadh, 2008; Reddy, M., V., Jagannatha & Kavitha, B., 2012; Roy, K., Dharmendra & Sharma, K., Lokesh, 2010; Sen, Wu, Hong, Chen, Xiaodong, Feng, 2013; Shih, Ming-Yi, Jheng, Jar-Wen & Lai, Lien-Fu, 2010; Wang, Can, Chi, Chi-Hung, Zhou, Wei & Wong, Raymond, 2015; Yang, Yang, Liu, Qian, Gao, Zhipeng, Qiu, Xuesong, Rui, & Lanlan, 2015; Yin, Jian, Tan, Zhi-Fang, Ren, Jiang-Tao & Chen, Yi-Qun, 2005).

THE PROPOSED K-PROTOTYPE ALGORITHM

The proposed algorithm starts by dividing the given dataset into some initial clusters. These initial clusters are then checked for outliers based on the objective function discussed in subsection 8.1. The set of outliers obtained are then taken as a new dataset and this process is repeated until all the objects are assigned to some clusters satisfying the objective function. In the proposed algorithm, the methods suggested by Ahmad et al. (2007) to find the most significant attribute, to find the centroid in a mixed dataset and to find the distance of an object from centroid are used. The author has got this work published. (Chadha, Anupama, Kumar, & Suresh, 2015).

The Proposed Objective Function

In order to check for outlier in each cluster, the following objective function is used:

$d(X_i, C_j) <= d_m$ not an outlier, (10)

where $d(X_i, C_j)$ is the distance between object X_i and centroid C_j,

$X_i=x_{i1}, x_{i2}, \ldots .x_{im}, C_j=c_{j1}, c_{j2}, \ldots\ldots c_{jm},$

d_m= The minimum of all the average distances.

The distance of every object is calculated from its centroid in every cluster. The average distance is calculated for each cluster.

Generation of Initial Clusters

To generate initial clusters following steps are performed:

Step 1: Discretize all numerical attributes. Find the most significant attribute using the method presented by Ahmad et al. (2007).
Step 2: Generate initial clusters with attribute values with maximum distance in most significant attribute in different clusters.

These steps are explained using a small dataset as shown in Table 12.
Discretize attribute Gamma and represent the values as 'a' and 'b'. Discretization is done as:

$$interval\,width = \left(Max\,value - Min\,value\right) / \,N \quad (11)$$

The first categorical attribute contains values 'A' and 'B' and the second attribute contains values 'C' and 'D'. The numeric attribute will be discretized into two values 'a' and 'b' because the maximum

Table 12. Dataset1 with Mixed Attributes

S.No.	Alpha	Beta	Gamma
1.	A	C	1.2
2.	A	C	3.0
3.	A	D	3.2
4.	B	D	5.0
5.	B	C	4.2
6.	B	D	3.5
7.	A	D	4.8

number of values contained by both categorical attributes in the dataset is two. Taking N=2, Max value=5.0, Min value=1.2 interval width=(5.0-1.2)/2= 1.9

After discretizing the Table 12 turns into Table 13.

Step 1: In order to find the most significant attribute, calculate the distance between every pair of values for each attribute in Table 13 as discussed.

The conditional probabilities for all the attributes in Table 12 are given in Table 14, 15 and 16. Table 14 shows the conditional probability values of attribute Alpha with respect to Beta and Gamma. Table 15 shows the conditional probability values of attribute Beta with respect to Alpha and Gamma. Table 16 shows the conditional probability values of attribute Gamma with respect to Alpha and Beta. Calculate the distance between various values of the attributes of Table 13 to obtain Table 17.

Table 13. Dataset after Discretizing Table 12

S.No.	Alpha	Beta	Gamma
1.	A	C	A
2.	A	C	A
3.	A	D	B
4.	B	D	B
5.	B	C	B
6.	B	D	B
7.	A	D	B

Table 14. Probability Table for Attribute Alpha

Beta	Gamma
P(C|A)=1/2	P(a|A)=1/2
P(D|A)=1/2	P(b|A)=1/2
P(C|B)=1/3	P(a|B)=0
P(D|B)=2/3	P(b|B)=1

Table 15. Probability Table for Attribute Beta

Alpha	Gamma
P(A|C)=2/3	P(a|C)=2/3
P(B|C)=1/3	P(b|C)=1/3
P(A|D)=1/2	P(a|D)=0
P(B|D)=1/2	P(b|D)=1

Table 16. Probability Table for Attribute Gamma

Alpha	Beta
P(A|a)=1	P(C|a)=1
P(B|a)=0	P(D|a)=0
P(A|b)=2/5	P(C|b)=1/5
P(B|b)=3/5	P(D|b)=4/5

Table 17. Distance between Various Values of Attributes of Table 13

Alpha	Beta	Gamma
δ (A, B)=1/3	δ(C, D)=5/12	δ(a, b)=7/10

The significance of an attribute is calculated by taking the average of all the distance values to get Table 18. Since only one value is there for each attribute in the distance table as shown in Table 17, so significance values remain same as the distance values.

Table 18 shows that attribute Gamma is having the maximum significance value, so it is chosen as the most significant attribute.

Step 2: Initial clusters are formed by keeping the objects with values 'a' and 'b' of attribute Gamma into separate clusters.

Cluster 1: {(A, C, a), (A, C, a)}
Cluster 2: {(A, D, b), (B, D, b), (B, C, b), (B, D, b), (A, D, b)}

Finding Centroids of the Clusters

The numeric attributes were discretized to create initial clusters but in the further steps of the algorithm, their numerical values are considered. In order to find the centroids, normalize the numerical attributes. The normalized value d_{ik} of x_{ik} is given by:

$$d_{ik} = \left(x_{ik} - x_{i,min}\right) / \left(x_{i,max} - x_{i,min}\right) \tag{12}$$

Table 18. Significance of Attributes of Table 13

Alpha	Beta	Gamma
1/3=0.33	5/12=0.412	7/10=0.7

Step 3: After normalizing the attribute Gamma the records in Cluster1 and Cluster 2 appear as shown in Table 19.

The central value for categorical attributes for a cluster C is represented as:

$$1 / N_c \left(\left(N_{1,1,c}, N_{1,2,c}, \ldots . N_{1,p1,c} \right), \ldots \left(N_{m,1,c}, N_{m,2,c}, \ldots . N_{m,pm,c} \right) \right) \tag{13}$$

where N_c is the number of data objects in cluster C, $N_{i,k,c}$ denotes the number of elements in cluster C which has the kth attribute value for the ith attribute, assuming that ith attribute has pi different values.

Attribute Gamma is numeric attribute so center can be defined as normalized mean. The mean of the values of attribute Gamma in Table 19 for cluster1 is 0.5 and cluster2 is 0.52.

In this way, centroid of cluster1 is:

(1/2(2A), 1/2(2C), 0.5), that is, (A, C, 0.5)

Similarly, centroid of cluster2 is:

(1/5(2A,3B), 1/5(C,4D), 0.52)

Computation of Distance of an Object From Its Centroid

The distance between an object and its centroid is given by:

$$d\left(d_i, C_j\right) = \sum_{t=1}^{m_r} \left(w_t \left(d_{it}^r - C_{jt}^r \right) \right)^2 + \sum_{t=1}^{m_c} (\Omega \left(d_{it}^c , C_{jt}^c \right))^2 \tag{14}$$

where m_r and m_c represent the number of numeric and categorical attributes respectively,

Table 19. Objects in Cluster1 and Cluster2 after Normalizing Attribute Gamma

Cluster 1			Cluster 2		
Alpha	**Beta**	**Gamma**	**Alpha**	**Beta**	**Gamma**
A	C	0	A	D	0
A	C	1	B	D	1
			B	C	0.56
			B	D	0.17
			A	D	0.89

$$\sum_{t=1}^{m_r}\left(w_t\left(d_{it}^r - C_{jt}^r\right)\right)^2$$

denotes the distance of object d_i from its closest cluster center C_j for numeric attributes only, w_t denotes the significance of the *t*th numeric attribute which is to be computed from the dataset,

$$\sum_{t=1}^{m_c}(\Omega\left(d_{it}^c\ ,\ C_{jt}^c\right))^2$$

denotes the distance between data object d_i and its closest cluster center C_j in terms of categorical attributes only.

In order to calculate these distance values, the distance between various values of the attributes in cluster1 and cluster2 has to be calculated. For numeric attribute Gamma, the significance is also calculated. The Table 20 and Table 21 show the distance between various values of attributes of Cluster1 and Cluster 2 respectively.

The significance of attribute Gamma in cluster1 and cluster2 is calculated by taking the average of all the distance values under attribute Gamma in Table 20 and Table 21. As there is only one value under attribute Gamma in Table 20 and Table 21, so the significance of Gamma is 0 in both the clusters.

The various components of distance of record (A, C, 0) in cluster1 from the centroid (A, C, 0.5) is calculated as:

$$\Omega\left(d_{11}^c, C_{11}^c\right) = \left(\delta\left(A, A\right)\right)^2 = 0 as \delta\left(A, A\right) = 0$$

$$\Omega\left(d_{12,}^c\ C_{12}^c\right) = \left(\delta\left(C, C\right)\right)^2 = 0$$

Table 20. Distance between Various Values of the Attributes of Cluster 1

Alpha	Beta	Gamma
δ (A, A)=0	δ (C, C)=0	δ (a, a)=0

Table 21. Distance between Various Values of the Attributes of Cluster 2

Alpha	Beta	Gamma
δ (A, B)=0.166	δ (C, D)=0.25	δ (b, b)=0

$$(w_1(d_{11}^r - C_{11}^r))^2 = (0(0-0.5))^2 = 0$$

The distance of the records from their respective centroids for Cluster 1 and Cluster 2 is shown in Table 22.

The Pseudocode of the Proposed K-Prototype Algorithm

```
Input: Dataset (D) of n objects with m mixed attributes
Output: Clusters or groups distributing the objects in the given dataset
1. Find the most significant attribute.
2. Create initial clusters.
3. Find the centroids of all the clusters.
4. Find the distance of every object from the respective centroids. Find the
average of all the distance values for every cluster. The minimum of these av-
erage distance values (other than zero) is taken as d_m.
5. Find the outliers in the initial clusters according to the objective func-
tion as given in Eq.(1).
6. Let B={Y_1, Y_2,.....Yp} be the set of outliers obtained in step 5.
7. If set B contains one object then
            Create a new cluster containing that object
   Else
      Repeat
   a. Assume this set B as a new dataset (D)
   b. Perform steps 1 to 7
      until (B==Φ)
```

ILLUSTRATIVE EXAMPLE

The first three steps of the algorithm are explained in section 8.2, 8.3 and 8.4, continuing with the same dataset the rest of the steps are explained below:

Table 22. Distance of Objects from their Respective Centroids

Distances in Cluster 1	Distances in Cluster 2
d(A, C, 0)=0	d(A, D, 0)=0.012
d(A, C, 1)=0	d(B, D, 1)=0.007
	d(B, C, 0.56)=0.044
	d(B, D, 0.17)=0.007
	d(A, D, 0.89)=0.012

Step 4: From Table 22, the average of all the distances in cluster1 is 0 and that in cluster2 is 0.02. So the minimum distance d_m=0.02. (0 is not considered).
Step 5: The only outlier in Cluster 2 is (B, C, 4.2).

Therefore the cluster2 transforms into
{(A, D, 3.2), (B, D, 5.0), (B, D, 3.5), (A, D, 4.8)}

Step 6: B={(B, C, 4.2)}
Step 7: As set B contains one object, create a new cluster containing this object.

Finally three clusters are obtained:

Cluster 1: {(A, C, 1.2), (A, C, 3.0)}
Cluster 2: {(A, D, 3.2), (B, D, 5.0), (B, D, 3.5), (A, D, 4.8)}
Cluster 3: {(B, C, 4.2)}

The clusters obtained are compared with the clusters obtained using K-Prototype algorithm with K=3 using software RapidMiner. The observations are recorded in Table 23.

It can be seen from Table 23, both the algorithms have tried to categorize the dataset with objects having similarity in two of the attributes out of three, though the results are slightly different. The proposed algorithm creates clusters by putting maximum number of similar objects together which is better than K-Prototype approach.

Dataset 2

This dataset is similar to Dataset1 discussed above with one difference that the attribute 'Alpha' contains three values 'A', 'B' and C'. The numeric attribute will be discretized into three values 'a', 'b' and 'c' because the maximum number of values contained by a categorical attribute in the dataset is three as shown in Table 24.

As per proposed algorithm we have:

Step 1: Discretize attribute Gamma and represent the values as 'a', 'b' and 'c'. After discretizing the Table 24 transforms into Table 25.

In order to find the most significant attribute, calculate the conditional probabilities as given in Table 26, 27 and 28.

Table 23. Results of Dataset1

	K-Prototype	Proposed Algorithm
Cluster1	{(A, C, 1.2), (A, C, 3.0)}	{(A, C, 1.2), (A, C, 3.0)}
Cluster2	{(B, D, 5.0), (B, C, 4.2)}	{(A, D, 3.2), (B, D, 5.0), (B, D, 3.5), (A, D, 4.8)}
Cluster3	{(A, D, 3.2), (B, D, 3.5), (A, D, 4.8)}	{(B, C, 4.2)}

Table 24. Dataset2 with Mixed Attributes

S.No.	Alpha	Beta	Gamma
1.	A	C	3.2
2.	A	C	3.0
3.	A	D	3.2
4.	B	D	5.0
5.	B	C	4.2
6.	B	D	3.5
7.	C	D	4.8

Table 25. Dataset after Discretizing Table 24

S.No.	Alpha	Beta	Gamma
1.	A	C	C
2.	A	C	C
3.	A	D	C
4.	B	D	A
5.	B	C	B
6.	B	D	C
7.	C	D	A

Table 26. Probability Table for attribute Alpha

Beta	Gamma
$P(C \mid A)=2/3$	$P(a \mid A)=0$
$P(D \mid A)=1/3$	$P(b \mid A)=0$
$P(C \mid B)=1/3$	$P(c \mid A)=1$
$P(D \mid B)=2/3$	$P(a \mid B)=1/3$
$P(C \mid C)=0$	$P(b \mid B)=1/3$
$P(D \mid C)=1$	$P(c \mid B)=1/3$
	$P(a \mid C)=1$
	$P(b \mid C)=0$
	$P(c \mid C)=0$

Table 26 shows the conditional probability values of attribute Alpha with respect to Beta and Gamma.
Table 26 shows the conditional probability values of attribute Alpha with respect to Beta and Gamma.
Table 27 shows the conditional probability values of attribute Beta with respect to Alpha and Gamma.
Table 28 shows the conditional probability values of attribute Gamma with respect to Alpha and Beta.
Calculate the distance between various values of the attributes of Table 25. Table 29 shows all the distance values.

Table 27. Probability Table for attribute Beta

Alpha	Gamma
P(A|C)=2/3	P(a|C)=0
P(B|C)=1/3	P(b|C)=1/3
P(C|C)=0	P(c|C)=2/3
P(A|D)=1/4	P(a|D)=1/2
P(B|D)=1/2	P(b|D)=0
P(C|D)=1/4	P(c|D)=1/2

Table 28. Probability Table for attribute Gamma

Alpha	Beta
P(A|a)=0	P(C|a)=0
P(B|a)=1/2	P(D|a)=1
P(C|a)=1/2	P(C|b)=1
P(A|b)=0	P(D|b)=0
P(B|b)=1	P(C|c)=1/2
P(C|b)=0	P(D|c)=1/2
P(A|c)=3/4	
P(B|c)=1/4	
P(C|c)=0	

Table 29. Distance between Various Values of Attributes of Table 25

Alpha	Beta	Gamma
d(A, B)=1/2 d(A, C)=5/6 d(B, C)=1/3	d(C,D)=11/24	d(a, b)=3/4 d(a, c)=5/8 d(b, c)=5/8

The significance of an attribute is calculated by taking the average of all the distance values to get Table 30.

The attribute Gamma is the most significant attribute.

Step 2: Generate initial clusters by keeping the values ‘a’ and ‘b’ of attribute Gamma into separate clusters as the distance between them is more than the distance between ‘a’, ‘c’ and the distance between ‘b’, ‘c’. The objects with value ‘c’ for attribute Gamma can be kept in the cluster with value ‘a’ or value ‘b’ because the distance between value ‘a’ and ‘c’ is same as the distance between value ‘b’ and ‘c’.

Cluster 1: {(A, C, c), (A, C, c), (A, D, c), (B, D, a), (B, D, c), (C, D, a)}
Cluster 2: {(B, C, b)}

Table 30. Significance of Attributes of Table 25

Alpha	Beta	Gamma
0.61	0.46	0.67

Step 3: After normalizing the attribute Gamma, the objects in Cluster1 and Cluster2 are shown in Table 31.

Now centroid of cluster1 is:
(1/6(3A, 2B, C), 1/6(2C, 4D), 0.39)
As cluser2 contains one object, so it is its centroid.

Step 4: Table 32 shows the distance of the objects from their centroid for Cluster 1.

The average of all the distances in Cluster 1 is 0.28. As Cluster 2 contains one object, so the minimum distance d_m=0.28.

Step 5: There are four outliers in Cluster 1:

Table 31. Objects in Cluster1 and Cluster2 after Normalizing Attribute Gamma

Cluster 1			Cluster 2		
Alpha	Beta	Gamma	Alpha	Beta	Gamma
A	C	0.1	B	C	0.45
A	C	0			
A	D	0.1			
B	D	1			
B	D	0.25			
C	D	0.9			

Table 32. Distance of Objects of Cluster1 from their Centroid

Distances in Cluster 1
d(A, C, 1.2)=0.31
d(A, C, 3.0)=0.34
d(A, D, 3.2)=0.18
d(B, D, 5.0)=0.29
d(B, D, 3.5)=0.16
d(C, D, 4.8)=0.39

(A, C, 3.2), (A, C, 3.0), (B, D, 5.0), (C, D, 4.8)

Therefore, the transformed cluster1 is: {(A, D, 3.2), (B, D, 3.5)}

Step 6: Take B={(A, C, 3.2), (A, C, 3.0), (B, D, 5.0), (C, D, 4.8)}
Step 7: Repeat steps 1-7 on the above dataset. Finally the following four clusters are obtained.

Cluster 1: {(A, D, 3.2), (B, D, 3.5)}
Cluster 2: {(B, C, 4.2)}
Cluster 3: {(A, C, 3.2), (A, C, 3.0)}
Cluster 4: {(B, D, 5.0), (C, D, 4.8)}

The clusters obtained above are compared with the clusters obtained using K-Prototype algorithm, with K=4, using software RapidMiner as shown in Table 33.

Table 33 shows that the proposed algorithm has generated clusters and has put the most similar objects together. The maximum attributes in which the objects match is three in cluster3. Whereas, in K-Prototype the maximum attributes in which the values match is two.

Dataset 3

The algorithm is further explained using a dataset with two numerical and one categorical attribute.

As per proposed algorithm:

Step 1: Discretize attributes Subject 2 and Subject 3. After discretizing Table 34 transforms into Table 35.

Table 33. Results of Dataset2

	K-Prototype	Proposed Algorithm
Cluster 1	{(B, D, 3.5)}	{(A, D, 3.2), (B, D, 3.5)}
Cluster 2	{(B, C, 4.2)}	{(B, C, 4.2)}
Cluster 3	{(A, C, 3.2), (A, C, 3.0), (A, D, 3.2)}	{(A, C, 3.2), (A, C, 3.0)}
Cluster 4	{(B, D, 5.0), (C, D, 4.8)}	{(B, D, 5.0), (C, D, 4.8)}

Table 34. Dataset3 with Mixed Attributes

Roll No.	Subject 1	Subject 2	Subject 3
1.	A	80	90
2.	B	60	68
3.	C	40	38
4.	B	65	67
5.	B	62	65
6.	C	35	36

Table 35. Dataset after Discretizing Table 34

Roll No.	Subject 1	Subject 2	Subject 3
1.	A	A	A
2.	B	B	B
3.	C	C	C
4.	B	A	B
5.	B	B	B
6.	C	C	C

The significance value of Subject 1 and Subject 3 come out to same, so choose any of the two as the most significant attribute.

Step 2: Choosing Subject1 as the most significant attribute, initial clusters are obtained as:

Cluster 1: {(A, A, A), (B, B, B), (B, A, B), (B, B, B)}
Cluster 2: {(C, C, C), (C, C, C)}

Step 3: After normalizing the attributes Subject 2 and Subject 3, the objects in Cluster 1 and Cluster 2 transform as shown in Table 36.

Now centroid of Cluster 1:

(1/4(A, 3B), 0.34, 0.3)

centroid of Cluster 2:

(1/2(2C), 0.5, 0.5), that is, (C, 0.5, 0.5)

Step 4: The distance of the objects from their respective centroids is shown in Table 37.

Table 36. Objects in Cluster1 and Cluster2 after normalizing Attributes Subject 2 and Subject 3

Cluster1			Cluster 2		
Subject 1	**Subject 2**	**Subject 3**	**Subject 1**	**Subject 2**	**Subject 3**
A	1	1	C	1	1
B	0	0.12	C	0	0
B	0.25	0.08			
B	0.1	0			

Table 37. Distance of the Objects from their Respective Centroids

Distances in Cluster 1	Distances in Cluster 2
d(A, 80, 90)=0.838	d(C, 40, 38)=0
d(B, 60, 68)=0.094	d(C, 35, 36)=0
d(B, 65, 67)=0.078	
d(B, 62, 65)=0.12	

The average of all the distances in Cluster1 is 0.28 and cluster2 is 0. So the minimum distance is d_m=0.28.

Step 5: Outlier in Cluster 1 is (A, 80, 90).

Cluster 1 transforms into: {(B, 60, 68), (B, 65, 67), (B, 62, 65)}
Cluster 2: {(C, 40, 38), (C, 35, 36)}

Step 6: Take B={(A, 80, 90)}
Step 7: As there is only one object in set B, create a new cluster containing the object.

Cluster 1: {(B, 60, 68), (B, 65, 67), (B, 62, 65)}
Cluster 2: {(C, 40, 38), (C, 35, 36)}
Cluster 3: {(A, 80, 90)}

Table 38 compares the results of the proposed algorithm with the K-Prototype algorithm for Dataset3. As can be seen from Table 38, the results of both the algorithms are same.

CONCLUSION

In this chapter we have presented efficient clustering algorithms based on the partitional algorithm K-Means and its extensions K-Modes and K-Prototype. These algorithms create appropriate number of clusters without need of prior input of number of clusters, K. The application of these algorithms has been shown to group students according to their academic performance. This will help the educational institutes to filter out the weak students and provide them more academic assistance. This way the institute can achieve academic excellence and have competitive edge over their counterparts.

Table 38. Results of Dataset 3

	K-Prototype	Proposed Algorithm
Cluster 1	{(B, 60, 68), (B, 65, 67), (B, 62, 65)}	{(B, 60, 68), (B, 65, 67), (B, 62, 65)}
Cluster 2	{(C, 40, 38), (C, 35, 36)}	{(C, 40, 38), (C, 35, 36)}
Cluster 3	{(A, 80, 90)}	{(A, 80, 90)}

REFERENCES

Abubaker, M., & Ashour, W. (2013). Efficient Data Clustering Algorithms: Improvements over Kmeans. *International Journal of Intelligent Systems and Applications*, *5*(3), 37–49. doi:10.5815/ijisa.2013.03.04

Ahmad, A., & Dey, L. (2007). A K-Mean Clustering Algorithm for Mixed Numeric and Categorical Data. *Data & Knowledge Engineering*, *63*(2), 503–527. doi:10.1016/j.datak.2007.03.016

Ahmad, A., & Dey, L. (2007). A Method to Compute Distance between Two Categorical Values of Same Attribute in Unsupervised Learning for Categorical Data Set. *Pattern Recognition Letters*, *28*(1), 110–118. doi:10.1016/j.patrec.2006.06.006

Bai, L., Liang, J., Dang, C., & Cao, F. (2012). A cluster centers initialization method for clustering categorical data. *Expert Systems with Applications*, *39*(9), 8022–8029. doi:10.1016/j.eswa.2012.01.131

Bresfelean, P., Vasile, G., & Nicolae, L. (2009). Towards the development of decision support in academic environments. In *Proceedings of the 31st International Conference on Information Technology Interfaces* (pp. 343-348). Cavtat, Croatia: Academic Press. 10.1109/ITI.2009.5196106

Cao, F., Liang, J., Li, D., & Zhao, X. (2013). A weighting k-modes algorithm for subspace clustering of categorical data. *Journal of Neurocomputing*, *108*, 23–30. doi:10.1016/j.neucom.2012.11.009

Chadha, A., & Kumar, S. (2015). Extension to the K-Means Algorithm for Automatic Generation of Clusters for Mixed Datasets. *International Conference on Advances on Computers, Communication and Electronic Engineering* (pp. 480-485). University of Kashmir.

Chadha, A., & Kumar, S. (2016). An Efficient K-Means Algorithm and its Benchmarking against other Algorithms. *International Journal of Grid and Distributed Computing*, *9*(11), 119–132. doi:10.14257/ijgdc.2016.9.11.10

Chadha, A., & Kumar, S. (2016). Extension of K-Modes Algorithm for Generating Clusters Automatically'. *International Journal of Information Technology and Computer Science.*, *8*(3), 51–57. doi:10.5815/ijitcs.2016.03.06

Cheng, Y., & Ying, X. (2009). Application of Data Mining Technology in E-Commerce. In *International Forum on Computer Science-Technology and Applications* (pp. 291-293). IEEE.

Cheung, Y., & Jia, H. (2013). Categorical-and-Numerical-Attribute Data Clustering based on a Unified Similarity Metric without Knowing Cluster Number. *Pattern Recognition*, *46*(8), 2228–2238. doi:10.1016/j.patcog.2013.01.027

Cheung, Y.-M. (2003). K*-Means: A New Generalized K-Means Clustering Algorithm. *Pattern Recognition Letters*, *24*(15), 2883–2893. doi:10.1016/S0167-8655(03)00146-6

Dharmendra & Lokesh. (2010). Genetic k-Means clustering algorithm for Mixed Numerical and Categorical Datasets. *International Journal of artificial Intelligence and Applications*, *1*(2), 23-28.

Emmanuel, O. N. (2007). Student Academic Performance Monitoring and Evaluation Using Data Mining Techniques. In *Fourth Congress of Electronics, Robotics and Automotive Mechanics* (pp. 354-359). IEEE.

Gan, G., Ma, C., & Wu, J. (2007). *Data clustering: Theory, Algorithms and Applications*. SIAM: Society for Industrial and Applied Mathematics. doi:10.1137/1.9780898718348

Gan, G., Wu, J., & Yang, Z. (2009). A genetic fuzzy k-Modes algorithm for clustering categorical data. *Expert Systems with Applications: An International Journal*, *36*(2), 1615–1620. doi:10.1016/j.eswa.2007.11.045

Huang, J. Z., Ng, M. K., Rong, H., & Li, Z. (2005). Automated variable weighting in k-mean type clustering. *IEEE Transactions on Pattern Analysis and Machine Intelligence*, *27*(5), 657–668. doi:10.1109/TPAMI.2005.95 PMID:15875789

Huang, Z. (1997). A Fast Clustering Algorithm to Cluster Very Large Categorical Data Sets in Data Mining. In *Proceeding SIGMOD workshop research issues on data mining and knowledge discovery* (pp. 1–8). Canberra, Australia: ACM.

Huang, Z. (1998). Extensions to the k-Means Algorithm for Clustering Large Data Sets with Categorical Value. *Data Mining and Knowledge Discovery*, *2*(3), 283–304. doi:10.1023/A:1009769707641

Hung, J.-L., & Gao, Q. (2011). Incorporating Data Mining into Course Evaluation: A Case Study of K-12 Virtual School. *The 11th International DSI and the 16th APDSI Joint Meeting.*

Hung, J.-L., Hsu, Y.-C., & Rice, K. (2012). Integrating Data Mining in Program Evaluation of K-12 Online Education. *Journal of Educational Technology & Society*, *15*(3), 27–41.

Hunt, L., & Jorgensen, M. (2011). Clustering mixed data. *Wiley Interdisciplinary Reviews. Data Mining and Knowledge Discovery*, *1*(4), 352–361. doi:10.1002/widm.33

Jain, A., Rajavat, A., & Bhartiya, R. (2012). Design, Analysis and Implementation of Modified K- Mean Algorithm for Large Data-set to Increase Scalability and Efficiency. In *Fourth International Conference on Computational Intelligence and Communication Networks* (pp. 627-631). IEEE. 10.1109/CICN.2012.95

Jain, K. A., & Dubes, C. R. (1988). Algorithms for clustering data. Upper Saddle River, NJ: Prentice-Hall Inc.

Jin, H., Wu, T., Liu, Z., & Yan, J. (2009). Application of Visual Data Mining in Higher-education Evaluation System. *First International Workshop on Education Technology and Computer Science*, 101-104. 10.1109/ETCS.2009.285

Jing-miao, Z., & Wei-xiao, G. (2008). Application of Association Rules Mining in the System of University Teaching Appraisal. *International Workshop on Education Technology and Training & International Workshop on Geoscience and Remote Sensing*, 26-28.

Kaur, H., & Wasan, K. (2006). Empirical Study on Applications of Data Mining Techniques in Healthcare. *Journal of Computational Science*, *2*(2), 194–200. doi:10.3844/jcssp.2006.194.200

Leela, V., Sakthipriya, K., & Manikandan, R. (2013). A Comparative Analysis between K-Mean and Y-Means Algorithms in Fisher's Iris Data Sets. *IACSIT International Journal of Engineering and Technology*, *5*(1), 245–249.

Li, M., & Feng, C. (2010). Overview of Web Mining Technology and its Applications in E Commerce. In 2nd *International Conference on Computer Engineering and Technology* (pp. 277-280), Beijing, China: Academic Press.

Li, T., & Chen, Y. (2008). An Improved k-means Algorithm for Clustering Using Entropy Weighting Measures. In *Proceedings of the 7th World Congress on Intelligent Control and Automation* (pp.149-153). IEEE.

Li, W. (2008). Modified K-means clustering algorithm. In IEEE Computer Society Congress on Image and Signal Processing (pp. 618-621). IEEE.

Li, Y-H., & Liu, X-L. (2010). Research of data mining based on e-commerce. In *International Conference on Computer Science and Information Technology* (pp. 719-722). IEEE.

Liang, J., Zhao, X., Li, D., Cao, F., & Dang, C. (2012). Determining the Number of Clusters using Information Entropy for Mixed Data. *Pattern Recognition*, *45*(6), 2251–2265. doi:10.1016/j.patcog.2011.12.017

Liao, H., & Ng, M. K. (2009). Categorical Data Clustering with Automatic Selection of Cluster Number. *Fuzzy Information and Engineering*, *1*(1), 5–25. doi:10.100712543-009-0001-5

Lui, H., He, H., Dai, B., & Yan, Y. (2006). The K-Prototype Algorithm Of Clustering High Dimensional And Large Scale Mixed Data. *Proceedings of the International Computer Conference on Wavelet Active Media Technology and Information Processing*, 738-743.

Luo, H., Kong, F., & Li, Y. (2006). Clustering mixed data based on evidence accumulation. *Lecture Notes in Computer Science*, *4093*, 348–355. doi:10.1007/11811305_38

Ma, Y., Liu, B., Wong, K., & Ching, Y. (2000). Targeting the right students using data mining. In *Proceedings of the sixth ACM SIGKDD international conference on Knowledge discovery and data mining* (pp. 457-464). Boston: ACM. 10.1145/347090.347184

Mei-lan, C. (2010). Cluster Analysis and its Application in Student Grants. *Second International Workshop on Education Technology and Computer Science*, 631-634.

Naija, Y., Chakhar, S., Blibech, K., & Robbana, R. (2008). Extension of Partitional Clustering Methods for Handling Mixed Data. In *International Conference on Data Mining Workshops* (pp. 257-266). IEEE. 10.1109/ICDMW.2008.85

Pal, S. (2012). Mining Educational Data Using Classification to Decrease Dropout Rate of Students. *International Journal of Multidisciplinary Sciences and Engineering*, *3*(5), 35–39.

Panda, S., Sahu, S., Jena, P., & Chattopadhyay, S. (2012). Comparing Fuzzy-C Means and K-Means Clustering Techniques: A Comprehensive Study. *Advances in Intelligent and Soft Computing*, *166*, 451–460. doi:10.1007/978-3-642-30157-5_45

Pelleg, D., & Moore, A. (1999). Accelerating Exact K-Means Algorithms with Geometric Reasoning. In *Proceedings of the fifth ACM SIGKDD International Conference on Knowledge Discovery and Data Mining* (pp. 277-281). Pittsburgh, PA: ACM. 10.1145/312129.312248

Reddy, M., Jagannatha, V., & Kavitha, B. (2012). Clustering the Mixed Numerical and Categorical Dataset using Similarity Weight and Filter Method. *International Journal of Database Theory and Application*, *5*(1), 121–133.

San, O. M., Huynh, V., & Nakamori, V. (2004). An Alternative Extension of the *k*-Means Algorithm for Clustering Categorical Data. *International Journal of Applied Mathematics and Computer Science*, *14*(2), 241–247.

Sen, W., Hong, C., & Xiaodong, F. (2013). Clustering Algorithm for Incomplete Data Sets with Mixed Numeric and Categorical Attributes. *International Journal of Database Theory and Application*, *6*(5), 95–104. doi:10.14257/ijdta.2013.6.5.09

Shafeeq, A. B. M., & Hareesha, K. S. (2012). Dynamic Clustering of Data with Modified K-Means Algorithm. In *International Conference on Information and Computer Networks* (pp. 221-225). Singapore: Academic Press.

Sharma, A., & Mansotra, V. (2014). Emerging applications of data mining for healthcare management - A critical review. In *International Conference on Computing for Sustainable Global Development* (pp. 377-382). IEEE. 10.1109/IndiaCom.2014.6828163

Shih, M.-Y., Jheng, J.-W., & Lai, L.-F. (2010). A Two-Step Method for Clustering Mixed Categroical and Numeric Data. *Tamkang Journal of Science and Engineering*, *13*(1), 11–19.

Singh & Bhatia. (2011). Data Clustering with Modified K-means Algorithm. In *International Conference on Recent Trends in Information Technology* (pp. 717-721). IEEE.

Tibshirani, R., Walther, G., & Hastie, T. (2000). *Estimating the Number of Clusters in a Dataset via the Gap Statistic.* Technical Report 208, Department of Statistics, Stanford University.

Visalakshi, K. N., & Suguna, J. (2009). K-Means Clustering using Max-min Distance Measure. *The 28th North American Fuzzy Information Processing Society Annual Conference*, 14-17.

Wagstaff, K., Cardie, C., Rogers, S., & Schroedl, S. (2001). Constrained K-Means Clustering with Background Knowledge. *Proceedings of the Eighteenth International Conference on Machine Learning*, 577-584.

Wang, C., Chi, C.-H., Zhou, W., & Wong, R. (2015). Coupled Interdependent Attribute Analysis on Mixed Data. *Proceedings of the Twenty-Ninth AAAI Conference on Artificial Intelligence*, 1861-1867.

Won, K. D., Lee, K., Lee, K. D., & Lee, K. H. (2005). A k-populations algorithm for clustering categorical data'. *Pattern Recognition Letters*, *38*(7), 1131–1134. doi:10.1016/j.patcog.2004.11.017

Wu, X., Kumar, V., & Quinlan, R. (2007). Top 10 Algorithms in Data Mining. *Journal of Knowledge and Information Systems*, *14*(1), 1–37. doi:10.100710115-007-0114-2

Xu, R., & Wunsch, D. II. (2005). Survey of Clustering Algorithms. *IEEE Transactions on Neural Networks*, *16*(3), 645–678. doi:10.1109/TNN.2005.845141 PMID:15940994

Yang, Y., Liu, Q., Gao, Z., Qiu, X., & Rui, L. (2015). A Similarity-based K-prototypes Algorithm for Mixed Attributes. *Journal of Computer Information Systems*, *11*(14), 5013–5021.

Yin, J., Tan, Z.-F., Ren, J.-T., & Chen, Y.-Q. (2005). An efficient clustering algorithm for mixed type attributes in large dataset. In *Proceedings of 2005 International Conference on Machine Learning and Cybernetics* (pp. 1611-1614). IEEE.

Yuepeng, S., Wu, C., & Liu, M. (2011). A Modified k-means Algorithm for Clustering Problem with Balancing Constraints. In *Third International Conference on Measuring Technology and Mechatronics Automation*, (pp. 127-130). IEEE. 10.1109/ICMTMA.2011.37

Chapter 16
Information Systems for the Management of the Organizations:
Conceptual Model for Its Application in Organizations

Antonio Juan Briones Penalver
Polytechnic University of Cartagena, Spain

ABSTRACT

This chapter investigates the main concepts and activities of information in strategic decision-making systems. Since information became the global economy value source for organizations, information assumes a key role in contributing to the development of the performance of organizations through the selection of relevant information for businesses. The relationship of the strategic management of information with business activities contributes to the process of strategic decision making for more effective and efficient decisions. The understanding of the importance of information as a strategic resource in the management of organizations is becoming more important to strategists than the formulation of strategy models of industrial society. In the twenty-first century, no manager will be able to set and implement the strategy successfully without a basic understanding of information for strategic decision making.

INTRODUCTION

The title of this chapter *Information Systems for the Management of the Organizations* can seem surprising insofar as information systems are seen in computer science, as one of the essential components of technology and not as an end in itself, since the technicians speak in information systems, but confuse the technology with the information (information sciences).

Virtually all the manuals of the information and communications technologies talk about technological perspective information systems (computer science) and not from the perspective of management (business sciences), for which there has been a lot of confusion between these subject, what are the

DOI: 10.4018/978-1-5225-3725-0.ch016

product (software) technology, process technology (hardware) and the product (information), a time that was ever done in a clear and accurate separation between what supports (the technology) and what is supported (the information).

OBJECTIVES

The purpose of this chapter is to discuss with managers, technicians and all those who are interested in this topic, and get them to think about what are the key variables and indicators (information) that may support the managers in making the decision, in order to reduce the risk of failure in this global world and turbulent. This means that new variables and indicators to support in decision-making are appear and diffuse. But nothing in this matter happens from one day to the next.

The term variable and key indicator (quantified information) which measure the efficiency of the whole or part of a standard of a plan or of an objective that was given and accepted as part of the overall management of the organization. A variable or an indicator can be expressed in quantity and or value, although sometimes be hard to express themselves in the form of a financial amount or because it may not be very significant.

The variables and or key indicators measure the effectiveness of all or part of the various systems (financial, productive, commercial, logistical, human, informational, etc.) and processes in relation to a norm, a plan or a goal previously set and accepted. It is necessary to ensure the coherence and completeness of the set of variables and their indicators used by the various managers of the organization. This consistency can only be guaranteed through the looking for the information of the organizations as a whole and not in isolation.

It presents a conceptual model with the main variables and key indicators to support in decision-making that are emerging with enough strength to become critical in the information and knowledge society and shows in more detail what the key variables and their indicators for each level of management (top, middle or coordination and operational), in order to generate the maximum added value at the very least, to a reader who does not need to waste a lot of time to apply the template to your organization.

METHODOLOGY OF APPROACH

This is an exploratory study, developed through literature search and my professional experience as management consultant. The work seeks to systematize the terms and concepts on information systems for the management of organizations, presented in the literature of business sciences and Information Sciences. This type of study is recommended for the research that proposes to clarify concepts, establish priorities that may guide future research etc. (Selltiz, C., Wrightsman, L.S., & Cook, S.W., 1981).

Proposes a conceptual model of new terms and concepts for the information systems for the management of organizations, from the attributes of information, so that makes it possible to your identity, use and relevance in the context in which the terms are applied. Is a qualitative character with the intention to promote a reflection on the different variables and management indicators (information) for managers of different levels of responsibility in organizations (top managers, business unit managers or area of responsibility and operational managers).

THEORETICAL APPROACH: IMPORTANCE OF INFORMATION IN DECISION-MAKING

The information is recognized as a phenomenon of extreme relevance in society in General, since it is the vehicle of content that establishes the social conviviality and feeds the knowledge. The information, regardless of your importance, even for being a phenomenon crucial to the process of human communication and decision making, *is not even a concept elucidated and instructive* (Morin, 2002).

Thus, it is possible to observe in the literature several definitions-not exclusive to each other-for information, both in the search for a conceptual consensus but also looking to differentiate it from other terms whose definitions are similar, such as messages, data, etc. The information different clothes flow wins a communication. In this context, the terms ares identified and applied with different meanings, as illustrates the classification presented by Buckland: information, process information as knowledge and information as thing. (Buckland, 1991).

As a process, information is the act of informing and is identified in the flow of communication. While knowledge the information is identified, as the content of the message. And finally, while the information is identified by its informative role, however represented through documents, data etc.

The classification concerning the use/application organizes information from the context of managers/users, that is, for whom it is intended. The classification as to formatting includes the structured information, defined as information encoded and systematized within a pre-established framework, and the unstructured information, understood as the not contextualized or not documented, according to the structure established in the information systems for the management of organizations, computerized or not.

The same information is interpreted and analyzed differently by managers with various profiles, since they include knowledge and previous experience, about the fact or event. For taking decision to understand, interpret and analyze the information and it is therefore necessary that the same is:

- **Relevant:** It is important for decision-makers;
- **Timely:** The right information, at the right time;
- **Available:** Information is easily accessible, at the right time;
- **Reliable:** Be credible for the decision maker;
- **Frequency:** Depending on the purpose and the context in which it will be used;
- **Clear and Understandable:** Not all managers, for example have economic and financial training;
- **Only the Essential:** Too much information can be detrimental to performance and generate many problems at the moment of decision-making; can be a cost in terms of opportunity and time spent in the selection and analysis of the same; too much can cause disorientation in decision-making; as normal, is that there is little information relevant and hard to find.
- **Management Information:** Concerning key variables (information), that is, which should pay greater attention, making it essential to characterize the information required for each officer, in support of decision-making, the three levels of responsibilities in terms of reliability:
- **Unbiased:** That allows managers to play the role without interference of your personal brand;
- **Objective:** That there is no kind of conditioning or restriction on information;
- **The Need:** To differentiate various similar aspects;
- **Verifiable:** There is the possibility to prove the veracity of the information obtained, the criteria used for the collection, selection and the methods and techniques applied in your treatment.

Decision-Making

In possession of the information, is essential to the development of the Organization Manager to make a decision about your use because, only with the effective selection of information, organization can get some benefit.

The decision is based on the information available about a considered problem, in order to provide to the Manager a reasonable number of alternatives, one of which is chosen as the best or better (Vaitsman, 2001).

It is common for the decision maker to be bombarded by a high amount of information. In this environment, it is essential that the decision makers are able to identify the relevant information and to develop the ability to discard what is irrelevant. The decision-making process involves a cycle of control, decision and execution. In this sense, second Gorry and Morton (1989), the decision-making process can occur within individual or collective and, commonly, assume-if five steps: initial recognition of the problem or opportunity, when it raises the problem as a need or possibility for reaching a new position; search for alternatives, when it establishes the various possibilities and possible solutions; alternative analysis phase that determines an evaluation criterion within the context determined by the first step; choosing the best alternative, and must order the solutions by selecting the more acceptable or grouping the best for a subsequent evaluation; and implementation of the chosen alternative, which is the use of the information chosen to implement an organizational action.

Decision-making, involving multiple interests, can cause tensions between the participants in that process. Soon, requires that decision-makers to develop the ability to deal with political issues and often confronting personal interests with interests of third parties. Therefore, it is important to stress the importance of systematically seeking common points, collaboration and team cooperation in all stages of the decision-making process.

Relationship Between the Decision Models

The information is differentiated according to the decision-making process and are separated in operational information, for the coordination and management of organizational resources and for strategic decision making. Operating information aims to ensure the supervision and control of the day-to-day operations within the operating cycle of the organization.

At this level, the decision-making process is repeatable, once you're back to daily problems, that is, operational decisions are related to the day that is the normal functioning of the organization. These decisions affect the Organization in a very short period of time, in a specific location and are taken by lower-level managers, namely operational managers.

The next level of decision are tactical decisions, which are those involving the implementation of policies in the Organization, such as the commercial policy of the company. These decisions are taken by the managers of intermediate level (coordination), refers to an area of responsibility specifies (financial, production, commercial, etc.) and affect the Organization during a longer period of time than operational decisions, but never more than one year.

The highest level of decision are strategic decisions are taken by the top managers of the hierarchy, i.e. by administrators. These decisions involve the entire organization and include the medium and long term and refer to the definition of the company's strategy, namely about the evolution of the Organization's development in the coming years.

The quality of information is another important factor for effective decision-making, it must be reliable and accurate, according to each level of management within the Organization and rose in a timely manner. Otherwise, the value of information is lost; not contributing to what was intended. The value that information provides managers is directly related to the way that assists managers in decision making to achieve the goals and objectives of the organization.

The flow of information available is another factor for the effectiveness of decision making. A large volume of information can consume time and cause difficulties for to distinguish what information relevant to the decision-making process. Operational decisions have an immediate impact. Tactical decisions or coordination has impact in the short-medium term and strategic decisions impact the medium-long term.

The second characteristic of decisions in management is the frequency of repetition of the same decision. Operational decisions are taken frequently (daily). For example, to satisfy the customers ' requests. Intermediate level decisions (coordination) are taken less frequently. For example, to revise the prices is a monthly, quarterly, semiannual or yearly, depending on the commercial policy of the organization or to do a promotional campaign about a particular product or service. The third features of decisions are the degree of structure of the information in the decision-making process.

Tableau de Bord for the Management of the Organizations

Concept

The French concept of Bord for pilotage – Tableau or control of company – has been practiced successfully in France for over 40 years, and is generally accepted as a best practice. The Tableau de Bord has a number of similarities with the Balanced Scorecard concept much more recent, as well as some differences.

A main difference is the much stronger focus on the concept of Bord control Tableau operating system process. In addition, standard procedures for implementing systems of Tableau de Bord in companies were formulated explicitly. To introduce the concept of Tableau de Bord and the context of design, explain its philosophy, and demonstrate its features and usage is based on specific examples.

Tableau French word can mean table, Panel or chalkboard — that is, something that provides an overview. Tableau de Bord, in the technical sense is a dashboard or control panel of a complex piece of machinery-specifically, a vehicle or aircraft – as the suffix indicates to bord.

The Tableau de Bord in a car or plane — that is, the Panel or the flight deck-is used by the driver or pilot to "steer" forward-looking and advanced target – control – with the aim to reach a certain destination, on schedule. To do this, the driver or pilots just focus on the main variables (information) that he or she has to handle in order to achieve the goal.

The question is not to determine deviations from the plan after landing to arrival (or at the end of the accounting period) in order to make corrections for the next flight or trip, but instead, to allow direct intervention in transit. Nor it is the goal to constantly monitor every single process equipment (machinery of the vehicle or aircraft). Instead, the aim is to concentrate on the decisive factors for success, thus enabling the active direction, reaction and decision making, despite the complexity of the overall system.

The Tableau de Bord has the following features:

- It is simple and therefore can be "implemented" quickly. It focuses on just a few key variables (only the information really relevant to the decision), which focus on specific area of responsibility, and does not attempt to give answer to all possible questions. It provides information about the status of the processes in the operational areas (such as sales or production), and less about the purely financial aspects that are considered the results of operating activities.
- The information is immediately available to the decision maker and, outside the frequency and periodicity of accounting. Another newer definition focuses on the character of tableau de bord model, broadening, its scopes to include not only the information system itself, but also the process of definition of its content.
- The Tableau de Bord is a management tool that is composed of a set of indicators that are related to each other (not by algebraic operations and deterministic) causal relations, selection process, documentation and interpretation of these indicators.

Each of these indicators is chosen to measure the status of a part of the business to be managed, so that all the indicators, taken together, offer a model of the general functioning of the undertaking (System) to achieve their goals.

Each Tableau de Bord is designed and implemented to each business unit manager / area of responsibility or decision-maker. Within a company, the Tableaux de Bord is defined in a cascade along the hierarchy of decision-making.

How Does the Tableau de Bord

Its objectives are to reduce the complexity and focus the attention of managers in the variables (information) that are relevant (key) for action and decision-making and that allow the piloting and the control of the organization. To your approach is based on the premise that to run a business (or business unit / area of responsibility) with success, managers need to manage some key variables (information) that change over time.

In other words, provides managers with a concentrated and consistent set of information in the form of indicators they need to control their areas of responsibility or business units. In addition, through the creation of a coherent system of tableaux de bord, the concept allows any organization to achieve the overall objectives and implement successfully the strategy.

The Tableau de Bord is an explicit model, describes how the underlying factors critical success settings can help to create the desired effects in terms of the overall result. In this sense, means that the information displayed in the Tableau de Bord focus more in the future and less on examining the past.

The implementation process of the Tableaux de Bord begins with the definition of the company's control framework: strategy and goals – as well as the individual management units (business units and or areas of responsibility). The first step includes an analysis of the hierarchy of the structure/management responsibility of the Organization and identifying the main activities of each management unit, as well as the plans and initiatives to achieve the goals, as well as determine which key indicators (information) that will be used to monitor the performance of the implementation of the strategy.

In addition to the top-down process be consistent and uniform, focuses on objectives, strategies and indicators, which supports bottom-up communication, with supervision of managers – who, after all, have to know how their subordinate managers are making progress in the implementation of its delegated tasks and objectives.

This principle supports (horizontal) coordination with peer managers, whose performance depends on the pursuit of their own objectives. This support simultaneous separates the content of Tableau de Bord of a management unit in clusters of different information for each target group and channel of information and derives from these contents or feed them in other Tableaux de Bord, through a cascading scheme clearly defined. Figure 1 shows how to operationalize this model.

Generic Model of Tableau de Bord

The objective of the model is to systematize the concept of Tableau de Bord through a systemic approach, whose representation is the way the theories and methods can be applied to solve practical problems in any organization.

Figure 1 shows the basic processes of information cycle, in three levels. Each level represents an overview of the areas of expertise of managers. In practice, the Tableau de Bord can be seen as a set of methods and techniques for the design of management information systems is applicable to any organization. The model explains that is designed at global level (level 1), are developed in practical terms in the level 2 and level 3 which are implemented with the support of information and communication technologies.

According to Khazanchi and Munkvold (2000) the management information systems have a comprehensive sense and the following interrelated components: information; Equipment, programs (software) and networks (information and communication technology); Procedures (Organization); People (make decisions).

Information and communication technologies are the mechanism of data collection and processing, generating outputs and disseminating information for managers/users.

Levels of Tableau de Bord

The model is intended to represent the basic processes of information cycle, superimposed on three or more levels. These can be seen from the perspective of top management-responsible for global strategy and objectives, intermediate management or coordination (tactical)-responsible for the management and control of resources and operational management-supervision and control of everyday life. It is also possible to make a parallel with the ontology of Popper, being the 3 level, the practical level analogous to the world 1 (physical objects or states), theoretical level equivalent to world 3 (objective knowledge) and similar to epistemological level 2 world (consciousness or mental state).

To design the Tableau de Bord: Determine what information and management indicators at each level; Apply the theories to guide the development of the model; Integrate/variables and management indicators at each level and validate them; Disseminate the model whose variables are based on theories and models of information science as a way to illustrate possible applications without claiming the complexity.

Figure 1. Generic Model of Tableau of Bord
Source: Adapted Lima-Marques, Macedo, F. L. O., (2005), Arquitectura da Informação: aspectos epistemológicos, científicos e práticos

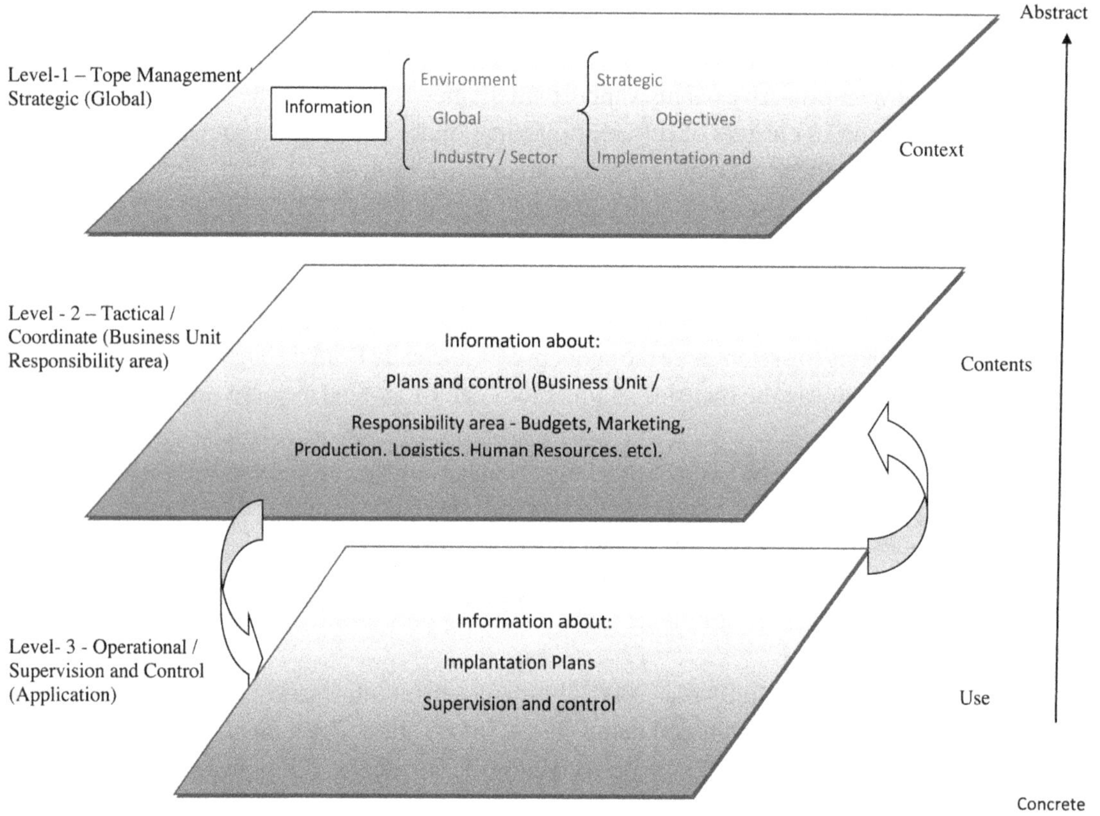

Source: Adapted Lima-Marques, **Macedo, F. L. O., (2005), Arquitectura da Informação: aspectos epistemológicos, científicos e práticos**

PRACTICAL APPROACH

Contents of the Tableau de Bord

Don't lose sight of the fundamental objectives to be achieved with the *Tableau de Bord*, since without these; it is difficult to understand the usefulness of it. Thus, a *Tableau de Bord* has as main objectives:

- To be a distinct source of information, in order to eliminate the bureaucracy in the collection, processing, analysis and production of results;
- To be a diagnostic tool, to show what works well or less well, IE is a warning instrument, highlighting and variables or indicators that do not evolve as expected. The key variables and indicators can move within the following limits (minimum and maximum):
  - **Green Zone:** Predicted values;
  - **Yellow Zone:** Zone of tolerance and to which we must be alert;
  - **The Red Zone:** Values that are not in accordance with the provisions and that are necessary to take decisions in order to correct them.

The structure of the *Tableau de Bord* for different managers of organizations does not vary a lot in terms of presentation format and contains the common elements, among which stand out: use data quantitative in nature; Have a fixed time horizon (day or week for operational managers, month or quarter for intermediate managers and quarter or year to top managers); Compare the forecasted data with those made with deviations (in the period and accumulated); Use explanatory graphics, especially for top managers.

Examples

Caption:

- V-means that the product is in accordance with the foreseen or better (light green);
- T-means that the product is in a delicate situation-(yellow light zone-alert)
- R-means that the product is in a dangerous level and it is necessary to take the decision to correct the situation (red zone)

OPERATIONAL MANAGERS

Caption:

- V-means that the product is in accordance with the foreseen or better (light green);
- T-means that the product is in a delicate situation-(yellow light zone-alert)
- R-means that the product is in a dangerous level and it is necessary to take the decision to correct the situation (red zone)

Table 1. Practical model for the Tableau de Bord

	In	Period			Accumulated	to Date				Proposal for a	Solution
Country/Geographic Area/Product/Market	Weather Forecast	Real	Detour	Provided for	Real	Detour	R	T	V	Price	Sales

Table 2. Example-Map sales analysis by Seller

	In	Period			Accumulated	to Date			
Country/ Geographic Area/ Product/Market	**Weather Forecast**	**Real**	**Detour**	**Provided for**	**Real**	**Detour**	**R**	**T**	**V**
1 Seller									
-The Product	100	75	-25	2,000	2,100	100			√
-Product B	120	150	30	1,450	1,200	-250	√		
Sub-Total	220	225	5	3,450	3,300	-150	√		
Seller 2									
-The Product	75	80	5	1,300	1,450	150			√
-Product B	50	60	10	1,200	1,000	-200	√		
Sub-Total	125	140	15	2,500	2,600	-50		√	
Seller 3									
-The Product	75	80	5	1,300	1,600	300			√
-Product B	50	60	10	1,200	1,000	-200	√		
Sub-Total	125	140	15	2,500	2,600	100			√
Total	470	505	35	8,450	8,500	-100			√

Interim Managers

Caption:

- V-means that the product is in accordance with the foreseen or better (light green);
- T-means that the product is in a delicate situation-(yellow light zone-alert)
- R-means that the product is in a dangerous level and it is necessary to take the decision to correct the situation (red zone)

Senior Management

Caption:

- V-means that the product is in accordance with the foreseen or better (light green);
- T-means that the product is in a delicate situation-(yellow light zone-alert)
- R-means that the product is in a dangerous level and it is necessary to take the decision to correct the situation (red zone)

Caption:

- V-means that the product is in accordance with the foreseen or better (light green);
- T-means that the product is in a delicate situation-(yellow light zone-alert)

Table 3. Example-Map sales analysis by geographical area

	In	Period			Accumulated	To Date	If	Ma	Foro		
Country/Geographic Area/Product/Market	**Weather forecast**	**Real**	**Detour**	**Provided for**	**Real**	**Detour**	**R**	**T**	**V**	**Price**	**Sales**
North Zone											
-The Product	100	75	-25	2,000	2,100	100			√		
-Product B	120	150	30	1,450	1,200	-250	√				
Total Area	220	225	5	3,450	3,300	-150	√				
Zone Center											
-The Product	75	80	5	1,300	1,450	150			√		
-Product B	50	60	10	1,200	1,000	-200	√				
Total Area	125	140	15	2,500	2,600	-50		√			
South Zone											
-The Product	75	80	5	1,300	1,600	300			√		√
-Product B	50	60	10	1,200	1,000	-200	√				
Total Area	125	140	15	2,500	2,600	100			√		√
Grand Total	470	505	5	8,450	8,500	-100		√			

Table 4. Example-Map sales analysis

	In	Period			Accumulated	to Date	If	Ma	Foro	Proposals for	Solution
Country/Geographic Area/Product/Market	**Weather Forecast**	**Real**	**Detour**	**Provided for**	**Real**	**Detour**	**R**	**T**	**V**	**Price**	**Sales**
North Zone	220	225	5	3,450	3,300	-150	√			200	150
Zone Center	125	140	15	2,500	2,600	-50		√			50
South Zone	125	140	15	2,500	2,600	100			√		
Total	470	505	35	8,450	8,500	-100		√			200

Table 5. Example-Map sales analysis of products and or services

	Volume	of Sales		Phase	the	Cycle of	Life	If	Ma	Foro	Suggested solution
Products	**Year-2**	**Year-1**	**Year**	**L**	**C**	**M**	**(D)**	**R**	**T**	**V**	
-The Product	2,000	2,200	2,500		√					√	
-Product B	0	0	1,200	√						√	
-C Product	1,500	1,450	1,475			√			√		Attention to the Margin
-D Product	3,000	2,000	1,000				√	√			Replace Product

- R-means that the product is in a dangerous level and it is necessary to take the decision to correct the situation (red zone)

The Pyramidal Structure of the Tableau de Bord

The structure of the *Tableau de Bord* is built through a *top-down* approach, i.e. from the General to the particular, as well as at each level of responsibility, namely the level of top management, middle management (business unit / areas of responsibility-financial, production, human resources, commercial, etc.), as well as at the level of operational management (each location or team).

The setting takes into account the nature of the decisions as well as the main key indicators (KPI's) control. It alludes to the coordination between the different levels of responsibility, in the process of decision making, focusing, on the one hand, in the more or less decentralized management, and on the other, to the hierarchical nature of the *Tableau de Bord.*

It should be recalled that the information that communicates in *reporting* to higher levels responsibility has to be clear, precise, so as to ensure consistency and integrity of information transmitted, i.e. the operating level is accurate, the level of coordination is summarized and the level of top managers is synthesized.

Tableau de Bord for Top Managers

Competitiveness requires that companies have a management information system oriented to identify opportunities. Given the relevance of these variables the management information system is designed, so that the information reaches the managers time and format useful to support in decision-making.

Top managers need, inside information, to synthesize the essential aspects. So, the information synthesized a *Tableau de Bord* includes among others the following aspects:

- The most significant results of the key variables of each of the different business units and or areas of responsibility;
- The critical success factors are key variables and indicators that give an overview of the situation;
- The variances of the main and / or key indicators, in order to allow conclusions on the causes and the consequences of decisions, as well as identifying who's responsible;
- The most relevant aspects are key variables on the evolution of global and immediate surroundings (macroeconomic, technological developments, socio-cultural, environmental, legal, and political developments in the industry and your structure, etc.);
- Graphical presentation of the main and or key indicators to get a more global appreciation;
- Proposals for action in order to be able to correct the deviations with the greatest impact on competitiveness.

The *Tableau de Bord* obeys a pyramidal structure, in order to have information about each of the variables and or key indicators from the highest level to the lowest level. Is a tool that shows, at the time the evolution of the variables and indicators. In some industries / sectors, there are typically three to six critical factors for the success of organizations.

Table 6. Example of critical success factors

Automotive Industry	Distribution	Banca
Design	Quality of products	Distribution network (branches)
Technology	Sales force	Range of products
Quality	Communication policy	Quality of service
Delivery time	Price	Cost of financing
Price		

It is important to note that not all managers of the organizations in the sector or industry attribute the same importance to the critical success factors. It may even happen that certain critical success factor may have the greatest importance to an organization's managers and little, or no importance, to other managers. You can define two types of critical success factors:

- **Cyclical Factors:** Are accepted as key during a limited period of time and will losing relevance gradually (e.g. the business cycle);
- **Structural Factors:** Are factors that meet the criterion of temporality and that can be broken down into: factors the company itself - the way to compete; Factors and sector or industry - the nature of the industry itself and / or industry; Environment factors-factors difficult to control by the company.

Performance Indicators (KPI's) for the Overall Management

It is necessary for top managers to define what are the main variables and key indicators for the overall management of the organization, a system of alerts that allow them to accompany their evolution, every moment. For each of the key variables, you can define one or several indicators to control. Remember that there are internal variables which the organization has control, and can influence them directly, and that there are external variables and indicators on which the organization has no control, but which eventually, will be able to influence.

Once defined the key variables for the overall management is necessary to define what are the key indicators that allown you to follow the evolution of those. According to j. m. Amat[1] (1992) the definition of the key variables and their indicators allows: a) define the management information system, it makes the process of decision making and control, a task easier and feasible; b) Quantify the objectives correctly; c) Measure the contribution of each business unit or centre of responsibility, in the final result; d) Evaluate the performance of each responsible.

In summary it is necessary to define the information system for the management of the organization in an integrated manner, eliminating any redundancy of information, so that there is only one global and detailed vision about the same subject and / or event. The indicators have a vital importance for the top management, not only the economic and financial (profitability, solvency and liquidity), but also the indicators related to the critical success factors, i.e. indicators that measure the reality of the company, the evolution and tendency of variables not controllable by the company, such as GDP, inflation rate, legislation, etc.

Table 7. Example-areas of responsibility vs. Main Key Indicators

Area	Key Variables
Strategic Management	• Evolution of the global environment • Evolution of immediate surroundings • Attractiveness and industry or sector • Structure and industry or sector • Critical success factors
Financial Management	• Economic and financial profitability • Margins and rotation • Financial structure • Financial costs
Commercial Management	• Market share • Sales volume • Competitiveness • Price • Delivery time • Distribution network • Quality of products and or services • Degree of satisfaction of customers
Production Management	• Quality • Occupancy capacity • Technology • Stock • Production costs • Productivity (man and machine) • Research and development
Management of Human Resources	• Social climate • Motivation • Wage level • Training • Competence • Productivity
Information Management	• Opportunity • Relevance • Relevance • Accessibility

Performance Indicators (KPI's) for Strategic Management

Ansoff (1965)[2] summarized the problem of formal strategy to meet the needs of organizations, the overall level of direction and management through the classic "Corporate Strategy" which is still considered as a reference of excellence.

Part of the function of the Manager-make decisions to guide actions (decision) of the organization, in relation to the surroundings, i.e. position the set of current and future products and markets, and which will serve as guidance for the business management and allowing their economic potential wanted to perceive both the characteristics and competitive profiles, view of the surroundings.

The main variables and their respective key indicators for the development of strategic analysis depend on the model adopted by the company.

Table 8. Example of indicators on the Global Environment

Key Variables	Indicators
Environment: Economy	• GDP • Interest rates • Rate of inflation • Exchange rate • Unemployment rate • Balance Of Trade • Household saving rate
Technological Surroundings	• Technological evolution • Incentives for research
Socio-Cultural Surroundings	• Lifestyles • Change of social values • Birth rate • Age structure • Geographical distribution • Educational level
Legal-Political Surroundings	• Political stability • Economic policies • Legal framework (fiscal, financial, environmental, etc.) • Labour and social policy • Environmental policy • Antitrust legislation • Lobbying
Environmental Surroundings	• Environmental policy • Degree of population information • Environmental protection associations • Social climate

Table 9. Example of indicators on the Immediate Surroundings

Key variables	Indicators
Customers	• Private individuals o Income level o Family structure o Attitudes and behaviors • Companies o Sector of activity o Dimension o Management capacity o Technological level o Economic and financial situation
Suppliers	• Products and services o Type of products and services o Dimension o Prices o Technology o Financial resources o Labor market dynamics
Competitors	• Capabilities • Objectives • Strategy • Level of economic performance • Substitutes
Community	• General trends of the town and country • Interest groups (associations, Government, etc.)

Table 10. Example of productivity indicators

Key Variables	Indicators
Global Productivity	• Benefits/features ratio applied
The Company's Productivity	• Gross Value Added (GVA) • RAND/administrative expenses
Labor Productivity	• Gross margin/wages and social charges • Units produced per unit of time • Units produced per employee

Table 11. Example of non-financial Indicators

Quantitative	Quality
• Market share	• Customer loyalty
• Delivery time	• Motivation
• Number of returned products	• Training
• Number of complaints	• Company image

Performance Indicators (KPI's) for the Production Management

See Table 12.

Performance Indicators (KPI's) Commercial Management

See Table 13.

Performance Indicators (KPI's) for Financial Management

See Table 14

Table 12. Example of indicators on the production

Key Variables	Indicators
Quality	• Number of defective products • Number of products that are recoverable • Number of complaints to suppliers
Production	• Total capacity • Busy capacity • Number of units produced per unit of time • Number of units produced the first time
Stocks	• Quantity in stock • Quantity in process of manufacture
Production Costs	• Cost of each production process • Total cost for each product

Table 13. Example of indicators for the commercial management

Key Variables	Indicators
Sales	• Global sales volume • Market share • Number of units sold per unit of time • Market growth • Banks
Distribution	• Number of routes • Sales volume by route • Number of sellers • Margin • Average delivery period
Promotion and Advertising	• Promotion and advertising expenses • Results of each campaign
Competitiveness	• *Benchmarking* analysis • Sector ranking (comparison)
Degree of Satisfaction of Customers	• Number of customers that repeat purchase • Average time spent with each customer • Number of complaints
Product Quality	• Sales volume by product/number of customers who buy • Number of complaints • Number of products they buy for the first time

Table 14. Example of indicators of financial Performance

Key Variables	Indicators
Profitability	• Economic profitability • Financial profitability
Financial Structure	• Liquidity • Solvency • Debt capacity • Financial autonomy
Investment and Long-Term Financing Capacity	• Coefficient of financing • Asset aging
Financial Costs	• Financial expenses coverage ratio • Process costs and activities • Average cost of the foreign capital

Performance Indicators (KPI's) for the Management of People

To follow the evolution of these variables and management indicators refers to the trend analysis and or deviations, as it provides a clear idea about the level of achievement, or not, of the objectives pursued. The presentation can be done in a simple way, showing the difference between the predicted value and the actual, in relative terms, or as a percentage, in the case of deviations and the trend of past and future evolution. This information provides better guidance on the degree of suitability of the management model adopted.

Table 15. Example-main variables and global Indicators on the management of People

Key Variables	Indicators
Establishment Plan	• Number of employees for each area/total number of employees • Qualified personnel/total number of employees • Middle ages • Average qualification
Wage Policy	• Number of levels • Salary range (lower and higher) • Number of promotions/total number of employees • The stability level of the responsible
Social Environment	• Level of absenteeism • Number of casualties • Level of motivation
Training	• Ratio of expenses spent on training/total expenditure • Number of hours of training
Health at Work	• Number of serious accidents per unit of time • Number of minor accidents per unit of time • Number of casualties

The main purpose of practice of the control focuses on the possibility of carrying out corrective actions, whenever they consider it appropriate managers. In any case it is important to note that any indicator and or key variable should have a range of fluctuation (green, yellow and red zone), as described previously.

The information on the monitoring of the evolution of the organization can be presented in map and or graphic, and highlight the face that are provided for, so that the decision can be taken. And values or quantities that present meet the following aspects:

- **Accuracy:** Is a basic aspect of all data and communications and should not depend on the arbitrariness of who prepares, but being obtained through the information system for the management, preferably automatically;
- **News:** Time is crucial in any information, since when current decreases the risk and help the decision maker;
- **Efficiency:** Covers the economic aspect, that is, the opportunity and speed, access to information is fundamental to the decision maker, and the use of information and communication technologies is very important;
- **Relevance:** Is related to the relevance and usefulness of information (map or chart).

The pyramid structure of information allows the managers of top synthetic information for decision making, but if you need greater detail can get it browsing the tree of information up to the desired level.

Tableau de Bord for Intermediate Managers or Coordination

The Tableau de Bord for Intermediate managers is set for each business unit for each area of responsibility. The model structure of Tableau de Bord of a commercial enterprise is similar to that of a company to provide services, but it is certainly similar to that of an industrial company.

Table 16. Example of an array of comprehensive analysis of the company

Key Variables	Indicators	Year N-1	Year N	Year N + 1	Trend	Objective
Quality	Number of complaints	200	180	150		100
Profitability						
Market Share						
Delivery Time						
Productivity						

The choice of variables and key indicators depends on the model of management and education of managers. For example, a manager whose academic training is the engineering will have more difficulty in understanding and interpreting the economic and financial information, than a Manager and vice versa.

Performance Indicators (KPI's): Commercial Management- Intermediate Level

Given the diversity of business activities, it is only possible to give examples in order to select some key variables and indicators, among others. It should be however there are other enterprises and key indicators, depending on variables in any case of objectives to be achieved and of the priorities of the company.

Performance Indicators (KPI's) for the Production Management: Intermediate Level

At the time when the products were rare, but indispensable production dominated the other functions. The development of goods, your range, innovations of all kinds and the increase of the offer allowed customers to make a choice, either on the basis of the own products, either on the basis of price.

The companies ' strategy has changed and the production had to adapt by making to marketing confining itself to purely technical tasks, requiring today that produce quality products at low cost and to reduce delivery times, with productivity gains.

The Quality

The products are manufactured according to the specifications and in accordance with the needs of customers. The quality can be assessed by reference to external or internal standards. The first are defined by public or private bodies, fixing the minimum quality. The internal rules are established by standards setters' managers or tolerances.

The quality is evaluated by comparison with the quality of competing products, or through organizations, such as the Portuguese Institute of Quality, or by examination of compliance with the specifications. The improvement he goes through training, investment in technology and improves the organization.

Table 17. Example of Performance indicators (KPI's) Commercial Management

Key Variables	Key Indicators
Customers	• Degree of satisfaction • Degree of customer loyalty • Structure of customer • Rotation and or renewal of customers
Distribution	• Adequacy of the sales network • Quality of service • Sales efficiency • Seasonality of sales
Products and or Services	• Development of new products and services • Life cycle analysis • Rotation
Market	• Market share • Sector ranking • Market analysis • Market trend
Sales	• Volume of sales (global, geographical region, vendor, product, etc.) • Analysis of deviations to various levels
Price and Margins	• Price developments • Evolution of banks • Price trend • Ranking of prices and margins
Promotion and Advertising	• Expenditure on promotion and advertising • Result of promotions and advertising • Ranking promotion and advertising
Commercial Quality	• Commercial service quality (ante and post sale) • Fitness clients • Quality in accordance with the specifications
Commercial Planning	• Sales planning • Sales objectives and control • Prices and trade discounts • Investments in promotion and advertising
Business Productivity	• Productivity for each salesperson • Overall productivity
Staff	• Productivity • Motivation • Efficiency and effectiveness

Delivery Times

Manufacturing times are related to the nature of the products and markets, as well as the technology used. The importance is greater the higher the competition. Deadlines are a variable of marketing, such as the price. The production capability to maintain the deadlines can be measured by the low level of disruption and the percentage of compliance with delivery dates.

Costs

The calculation of production costs raises some problems that depend on at the same time, the microeconomic theory and analytical accounting. Analytical Accounting shall conform to the structure, which assumes of course, a good knowledge of the organization of production. The costs can be classified according to two criteria: allocation and variability, i.e., join or not the costs, indirect costs not attributable directly to the products.

The method of direct cost equates the problem, considering only the cost variables, understanding the variability in function and proportional to the activity, which is not always the case, so, the holding shall develop a so called "raw" likely to cover fixed costs, often assimilated as structural costs.

Flexibility

Flexibility means for production, the ability to adapt rapidly to changes in activity and the introduction of new products and / or services. It can be ensured by technology or by personnel. There are three very important concepts: versatility, training and learning.

Another way to ensure flexibility is conserving capacity reservations can be expressed from the point of view of production technology (production capacity higher than demand) and of the organization.

Production Types

The production can be classified into three types: continuous, discontinuous and per project. Continuous production is defined as the production in large amounts of one or more products, using production lines. It is necessary to take into consideration the capacity of equipment in order to avoid bottlenecks.

In discontinuous production, products are manufactured in small quantities (lots) and equipment are grouped by function; manufacturing orders are numerous and behave normally to many instructions; the stock of raw materials and products in the process of manufacture is high; the flexibility is paramount, but it's an expensive production.

The production per project is related only to a single product, such as a film, a work of art, a building, etc. The production process is represented by a sequence of operations that only happen once, generating numerous transformations during the period of implementation, and should be managed in terms of deadlines and costs.

Production Scheduling

The operation poses programming problems, production monitoring and control. The production schedule is related to the company's management estimates. The prediction of demand is essential to a good stock management and the planning of resource requirements (raw materials or components, personal, etc.).

Nomenclature

The nomenclature is a list of the components that make up a product and that indicate: composition: assemblies, sub-assemblies and components; the IDs; the quantities of composition. The nomenclature is more than a list, since it shows the structure of the product and its different levels, thus constituting the bones, the skeleton of the production.

Range of Operations

The range of operations is the list of the different production operations necessary to manufacture or assemble a piece, a subset or a set, compiling the following information: nature of matter used; quantities of raw material to be used (the difference is the waste); economic amount (amount resulting from the optimization of the release and storage costs); rational amount (minimum quantity manufacturing); release amount (amount reserved for the launch in manufacture-multiple amount reasonable and close to the economic quantity); procedure (all operations listed in chronological order of production); of time granted to the machine; number of operators (for each operation).

To achieve these goals using variables and key indicators, such as:

- **ABC Analysis:** Classification of product references in descending order of values (cost and or quantity) that usually leads to the creation of three classes A, B and C. Class A, consists of a small percentage of references and is associated with a high percentage of cost or amount. The goods in class approximately 20%, represent 80% of the total value of stocks of such material;
- **Stock Rotation:** Is the ratio between the total volume of annual outputs and the average value of stock ownership. The increase of rotation of stocks (which lets you improve the profitability) can be achieved by increasing output, or by reduction of stocks;
- **Stocks Break-Index:** Is the quotient between the requests and the requests made, inverse of the level of service. Is in function of this index that is defined the safety stock, since this indicator is connected to the supply risk and the service to be provided to the client.

To manage the stocks it is essential to bear in mind two key variables: the safety stock and the economic quantity to purchase. The safety stock is stock that protects the company against any fluctuations in demand and avoids breakages. The function of the safety stock is to ensure protection against the variation of the terms of delivery and consumption, through the creation of a stock level which should download in exceptional cases, thereby minimizing the risk of rupture.

Another key variable is the amount the economic to buy and which is determined by the costs involved in the management of stocks: the acquisition cost price paid to the supplier plus the transport costs and customs; The gross cost of all purchase orders placed throughout the year (prospecting, consultation, negotiation, etc.); The cost of ownership of stock is the sum of the costs (storage, stock management, financial cost of stock-interest of capital assets, obsolescence, etc.)

In addition to the register of quantities manufactured, factory control also includes the summary and the analysis of time man and machine, namely: Meet each day, week, month, the number of production hours; Control the rate of utilization of labor and machinery, to adjust permanently the charges and production capacity; Improve productivity, control of unproductive time; Collect the information about the time of production, absence overtime, overtime work, individual and group performances that serve to compute any production awards.

The efficiency of man and machine is calculated by load Center and by reference, with the following formula:

$$\text{Efficiency} = \frac{\text{Time allocated}}{\text{Real time declared}}$$

The Time Allocated = (good quantities and defective) x (operating time of the range).

The most relevant priority in the past is the cost. However, new synergies tend to be established and customers are becoming more demanding as regards the quality and delivery time, which can allow lower costs and more flexibility, if the company has ability to reply.

To compete with the cost as a priority, is crucial to know your components, differentiating value added cost. In this context the key components and cost that matters to aggregate and analyze are the following: cost of inputs purchased: (raw materials; Materials; Energy); Cost of workmanship; (Manufacturing, administrative); Costs of distribution and sales; Financial charges; Depreciation.

Table 18. Performance indicators (KPI's) for the production management

Key Variables	Key Indicators
Planning	• Production planning • Planning of the Needs • Capacity planning • Investments in new technologies
Ability	• Installed capacity • Busy capacity
Productivity	• Technical productivity • Economic productivity
Quality	• Number of defective parts • Number of recovered pieces • Quality of suppliers
Technology	• Research and development of new products • Technological sector ranking
Stocks	• Stock level • Rotation
Production	• Production volume • Level of productivity
Staff	• Productivity • Desktop • Structure and effectiveness • Motivation
Production Costs	• Cost structure (global and per unit) • Cost of production process • Cost of labor • Cost of manufacturing overheads • Cost of raw materials

The indicators have a quantitative in nature and primarily revolve around the quality, productivity and cost, which are the basis of the production management. Among the indicators are the capacity occupied, which is calculated by the ratio between the actual capacity and total capacity; economic rate of defective products defined as the relationship between the values of faulty production and total production.

As an indicator of productivity, production can be used daily or average duration of the process obtained by the ratio between the quantity of products in the process of manufacture and the daily production. Capacity, costs and planning require greater attention, due to variations in production. The staff also needs supervision, since the change in behavior and attitude towards work is frequent.

To avoid disruption of stocks of materials and raw materials it is necessary to do the shopping in a timely manner, in order to avoid turbulence in production, so the aim of the person responsible for the purchases is to synchronize business needs and suppliers, minimizing the costs of supply and storage of materials and raw materials.

Performance Indicators (KPI's) for Financial Management: Intermediate Level

According to r. Brealey and Myers[3] (1988) the financial manager faces two fundamental problems. The first is how much the company should invest, and the second how to obtain the necessary funds to ensure the investments, namely the responsibility comes down to a matter of getting the financing for

Table 19. Performance indicators (KPI's) for the management of purchases

Key Variables	Key Indicators
Management of Suppliers	• Level of cooperation and future stability • JIT Control • Level of dependency • Rotation of suppliers • Marketing policies • Market analysis
Purchase Orders and Deadlines	• Frequency of purchase • Safety stock • Meeting the deadlines
Commercial Situation	• Commercial profitability • Commercial developments
Quality	• Quality of production • Distribution and reception • Quality of suppliers
Production and Productivity	• Production rate • Stability • Levels of productivity • Analysis of the consumption of materials and raw materials • Stock rotation • Procurement and storage costs
Planning of Purchases	• Planning of purchases • Level of control • Analysis of suppliers (evolution of prices, delivery time, product quality, etc.)
Staff	• Productivity • Motivation • Structure and effectiveness

the investments. So they can identify themselves as main key variables financial function the following: financial costs; Financial structure; Investments and long-term financing; Profitability; Rotation and margins; Financial planning; Personal.

Results and Monetary Surplus

The profit and loss account shows the net balance of income and costs incurred by the company throughout the year. The profit or loss explains clearly what was won or lost in the optical sheet which is the shareholders. However the financial manager can only be based on net income as a measure of performance, but in other additional indicators, such as:

1. **Commercial Margin** = Value of the sale of goods - purchase Cost of goods sold
2. **Value Added** = Turnover-exercise Consumption to
3. **Gross Operating Surplus** = Value added + exploration subsidies-taxes (related to)-personal expenses
4. **Operating Result** = Gross operating surplus + use of provisions and depreciation-depreciation and provisions
5. **Current Result before Tax** = Net operating result before financial charges and income + Financial Income financial charges
6. **Extraordinary Results** = Extraordinary gains extraordinary losses
7. **Net Profit** = Current Results before tax + extraordinary results-Reimbursement for employees - taxes on profits

The monetary surplus or *cash flow* corresponds to the cash flow released by the activity of the company over the period, for which numerous obligations result for monetary disbursements, such as: remuneration of capital used-interest and dividends; Compulsory surveys-taxes and holdings; Stay in the company-depreciation and profit not distributed.

The concept of *cash flow* can be considered in terms of:

- **Investment Cash Flow:** Records the cash payments associated with the investment project expenditure, net of cash receipts associated with the extinction of the project;
  - **Investment Cash Flow** = Investment in capital assets + working capital-residual value of investment
- **Operating Cash-Flow:** Register receipts net of cash payments associated with the operation.
  - **Operating Cash-Flow** = Net operating Result + depreciation and amortization for the year + provisions + exercise financial charges

Self-financing is the global monetary surplus produced by the company over the course of a financial year. The origin of the cash flow is the depreciation and provisions and net profit. So you could say that the self-financing capacity of an undertaking is given by the following expression:

Gross Cash Flow = Net profit + depreciation and provisions

Self-Financing = Gross margin of Self-financing-dividends distributed

Analysis of Profitability

A key element in assessing the profitability of a company is the consideration of the risk that weighs about the same. A distinction is made between two types of risk, the economic and financial risk. In both cases, a relationship with profitability can be evidenced through:

- Effect of operating lever for economic risk;
  - **Effect of Operating Lever** = Gross margin of contribution/extraordinary operating results
- The Financial leverage effect for the financial risk.
  - **Financial Leverage Effect** = Current Results/operational results x (times) Economic Asset/ equity > 1

Among others the following indicators or ratios for assessing the profitability of a company: **Economic Profitability** = Operating Result/total assets;

Financial profitability = NET Result for the year/shareholders ' equity

The economic risk depends on the nature of the relationship between the volume of production and costs. The interest of cost-volume analysis result is put clearly highlighted the importance of the allocation of costs of production. It is from the cost structure that appreciates the company's ability to adapt to changes in business volume.

The cost structure defines a point at which the company has no losses or profits, i.e. is the *neutral of the holding*. The financial leverage effect means the favorable effect that recourse to indebtedness can exert on the return on equity. This effect depends only on the financial structure and is independent of the economic risk.

Financial Balance

The financial balance is the expression of the solvency requirement, i.e. the balance between revenue and expenditure. The financial balance results from the adjustment of all the cash flows of the company and for this to happen, the financial situation must be structured in your set, so as to generate sufficient liquidity to ensure solvency. A distinction is usually two determinants of financial stability:

1. **The Revolving Fund** (permanent capital-net fixed assets);
2. **The Financing Needs.**

The financing needs of the Exploration involve the arrest of physical assets (stocks, etc.) and financial services (credits/customers). The existence of a need for funding is due primarily to the existence of time lags between the flows of income and operating costs, on the one hand and the cash flow, on the other.

Treasury

The Treasury is fundamentally financial equilibrium, being the combination of the two determining factors: working capital and revolving fund necessary. The Treasury of a company sets: Treasury = working capital-financing needs.

The analysis of the financial situation of the company leads us to observe how the financial stability was ensured and how it evolved over time. Several methods are available to assess the financial and balance among them emphasizes the map of origin and application of funds, since it is used currently and is based around components of financial equilibrium and more particularly of the Revolving Fund on which it relies to explain the variations. The map of origin and application of funds is drawn from the variance between two balances-the balance of home and the bottom line of the period under analysis, in order to understand the reasons (s) increases and reductions (applications) of the Revolving Fund in the period.

The analysis of the operating cycle of the firm is very facilitated by knowledge of the retention times of the different assets and current liabilities. The quantification and the regular monitoring of these values appear as a necessity in day-to-day management. The measuring instruments used to obtain relevant information are the three medium term ratios of operating elements, namely:

Average stocks

Average Stock Rotation = x 360

Turnover tax free

- **Average Rotation of Stocks** Average Stocks of raw materials

Raw Materials = x 360

Tax-free purchases of raw materials

Current account customers + account letters to receive discounted + effects + effects sent to the Bank but not yet discounted

• Average **Receipts** = x 360 turnover including all taxes

Current account providers + suppliers account letters to pay

- **Average Payment Period** = x 360

Purchases including all taxes

The financial envelope is essentially the external funding; self-financing, although, by definition, a built-in feature, suffers from abroad influences The different financial partners with which the companies maintain a relationship are: investors, financial institutions and the State (taxation, subsidies, loans, etc.)

The investment decision is the basis of the development options of the company, once that guides this activity in the long run by making the future profitability. The decision must be made with the utmost rigor and information, whereas the economic profitability of the same depends on three key factors:

1. **Time:** The different cash flows are not directly comparable between themselves, intervening in different periods;
2. **Uncertainty:** The value of the future cash flows can only be expected;
3. **Financing of the Project:** Is to make a judgment about the non-financial and economic profitability.

The evaluation criteria based on the cash flow are the criteria for the evaluation of the profitability of investment projects. There are several alternative criteria, such as: recovery period (Payback); Net present value (VLA); Internal rate of return (IRR); Integrated internal rate of return (TIRI); Cost-benefit ratio and index of profitability; Discretion of the annuity.

Other information that may be considered:

- **Investment Budget:** Allows the inclusion of the priorities as regards the investments to be made; the analysis of the availability of financial resources, allows contrast the viability of investments, being for such necessary to resort to techniques of analysis of investment projects, such as the internal rate of return, net present value, the period of recovery, etc.
- **Treasury Budget:** Assumes the estimated cash flows of the period considered. It is to quantify, from a financial point of view, the operations actually provided for an annual time horizon, sorted by collections and payments, chronological manner emphasizing the flow amount of balances at the end of each period. By this instrument can verify which periods (month or quarter) with liquidity difficulties with anticipation enough to allow decision-making financial imbalances at the same time makes it possible to determine what should be the optimal structure of financial resources, to maintain balance and minimize cost, according to the financial alternatives possible.

Table 20. Performance indicators (KPI's) for financial management

Key Variables	Key Indicators
Financial Costs	• Level of coverage • Costs of processes and activities
Financial Structure	• Level of liquidity • Level of solvency • Level of indebtedness • Analysis of suspension of payments and breaks
Investments and Long-Term Financing	• Level of funding • Aging assets • Return on assets
Profitability	• Economic profitability • Financial profitability
Rotation and Margins	• Rotations • Analysis of banks • Analysis of deviations
Financial Planning	• Planning of investments • Finance planning • Objectives of profitability • Other financial objectives
Staff	• Productivity • Motivation • Structure and effectiveness

- **Forecast Balance Sheet:** Constitutes a summary of the main estimates of the assets and liabilities of the company. Is useful because through it if they can establish predictions about some of the most significant ratios to control by the managers, in addition to providing an overview of the assets of the company at any given time.

Performance Indicators (KPI's): People Management- Intermediate Level

Human resources have a very large weight on the cost structure of the companies. The proper management of this resource depends on the remaining resources, since the motivation and training are vital to the functioning of companies. Thus, the main management key variables are the following: working environment; Training and promotions; Wage level; Productivity; Establishment plan; Safety and hygiene.

The evaluation of the performance of individuals is based primarily on non-financial variables, such as the rate of absenteeism, staff rotation, motivation, functional or geographical mobility, etc. This function is crucial in implementing the strategy of organizations, being to point out the degree of relevance that has variables, the identification with the objectives of the Organization, motivation and training.

Tableau de Bord for Operational Managers

The information to the operational management follows the definition of the objectives to be achieved by each of the operational managers, in order to identify the information needs in each situation and have the information available at the right time for decision making.

Table 21. Performance indicators (KPI's) for the management of people

Key Variables	Key Indicators
Desktop	• Level of absenteeism • Degree of motivation • Number of levels of intermediate leaders • Level of internal conflicts
Staff Composition	• Average level of qualifications • Level of expertise • Degree of employment stability • Average rate of staff rotation • Geographic mobility • Punctuality rate
Training and Promotions	• Value of investment in training • Average level of training • Number of training courses • Average number of training frequency
Wage Level	• Number of salary levels • Average inflation rate • Average rate of salary increase
Safety and Hygiene	• Number of accidents • Degree of hazardousness of the company
Productivity	• Productivity for professional categories • Productivity per area of responsibility • Shift productivity

Performance Indicators (KPI's): Commercial Management- Operational Level

The creation of the necessary indicators and homogeneous groups for the operational management is a complicated task, since there are a wide variety of organizations with much differentiated activities. With regard to the sales information is the sales budget, wich is, for top level managers one of the most important information. Main information on the planning and control of sales, are the main suggestions:

- **Planning and Sales Control:**
  - Sales budget by type of seller, seller and / or product, geographical area, distribution channels, etc. comparative analysis between the forecast and the actual clearance of deviations; Daily Distribution planning.
- **Information about Customers:**
  - Order products and or services; Distribution; Invoicing; Discharge of VAT; Control of debts; Volume of returns; Complaints; Distribution costs; Delivery time.

May establish another kind of operational indicators that provide relevant and timely information for solving everyday problems and less frequent, depending on however the activities of each organization and each team manager and or location.

Performance Indicators (KPI's): Production Management- Operational Level

The main problems facing the operational managers of production refers to the obtaining of better product quality, as the production process, such as the management of raw materials and the management of the workforce. In this sense, according to J. Batty[4] (1984) the objectives of this sub-area are linked to three basic functions: production planning and control; manufacturing; support services.

According to J. M. Roehl-Anderson and S. M. Bragg[5] (1996) production officials use correctly the information always applying certain fundamental rules, information, such as basic to be clear and precise; Be available sufficiently in advance so that serve the purpose for which it was drawn up; The form and the content of the information to be in harmony with the responsibility of the performer.

Performance Indicators (KPI's): Financial Management- Operational Level

Financial operating managers are responsible for developing financial studies so important as the balance sheet and the profit and loss account, from which conceive of numerous maps of information such as basic information of control of accounting entries, the financial budget and the Treasury budget, etc. The information to draw up a financial plan in the short term is formed from the previous year's information and estimated as expected that will take place year round, such as:

- **Provisional Results Account:** Sales and selling price of each product; Predicted consumption of raw materials and costs of acquisition of the same; The forecast of production of each product; Indirect costs, manufacturing times, hours available, depreciation, financial expenses, taxes, etc.
- **Cash Budget:** Billing and payment Policies; Purchases of raw materials; Minimum balance of Treasury; Increase and decrease of credits, etc.

Table 22. Performance indicators (KPI's) for operational management

Sub-Areas	Main Key Variables
Production:	• Planning and control of production-daily, weekly, monthly; • Planning and control of material and human resources needs; • Control of the production process;
Quality	• Quality control: o of raw materials, o developing products manufacture o of the finished products.
Maintenance	• Planning and Control of the interventions of lubrication and o inspection of equipment; • Planning and control of intervention teams; • Management of repair works
Research and Development	• Research and testing of new products and processes.
Stocks	• Day-to-day movement of inputs and outputs of warehouse • Stock Ruptures
Purchases	• Planning and control of purchases; • Monitoring of purchases • Portfolio management of suppliers • Vendor analysis

Table 23. Performance indicators (KPI's)

Main Key Variables	Description
Balance	• Assessment of the initial situation
Sales	• Estimate of the volume of sales (growth, market share, price, etc.)
Investments	• Investment projects
Profit and Loss Account	• Cost of sales • Structure costs • Annual depreciation rate of fixed assets • Capital cost of other • Financial interests of Treasury surpluses • Tax Rate
Financial Policy	• Revolving Fund • Financing • Change in cash and cash equivalents • Change in share capital • Dividends • Payments

Performance Indicators (KPI's): People Management- Operational Level

The cost of people are of great concern to managers, so it is essential to prepare timely and pertinent information for the management of this resource, such as absenteeism, productivity, temporal planning of shifts, etc. For your setting are important lines of action, such as the level of accountability, an indication of the levels of efficiency to be achieved, the hiring needs of people, etc., as well as the costs of training, in the definition of the profile of the job to consider and the qualification required. It is essential to control the rate of absenteeism, since it has a direct impact on productivity and wages of each employee.

Compile maps with individualized information about personal and group performance, to check whether the objectives were achieved or not, in order to take corrective action, when necessary. An inadequate planning of the work to be carried out by each person makes subsequent reorientation of global planning of the organization.

CONCLUSION

We live in a complex and turbulent society and organizations to live a moment of profound change imposed by the information and knowledge society. That change the new paradigm is the information and knowledge that enable a new business vision, facilitating decision-making and enabling the repositioning of the organizations strategy.

The management and performance of organizations need to be evaluated for economic reasons. The management models of organizations will have to change. The "Tools" of evaluation have remained stable for a long time. Today it is no longer possible to expect financial results. First because they are not usually historical information are available at the time of making the decision and it is therefore necessary to find new variables and indicators that can assist managers in making the decision.

The key variables and their indicators must cover two aspects: one associated with the results and another associated with the processes, which can define two types of variables and key indicators:

- **Of Results:** Indicate the result you can achieve (example: the quantity produced or sold, the number of customers visited, the volume of sales, etc.);
- **Of Process:** Express the way of obtaining a result (example: the number of requests satisfied, not the number of rejected products, the number of defective product, etc.).

Kaisen, M. Imai (1992) shows the Western companies favor the variables and indicators of results, while Japanese companies make in relation to the process.

Table 24. Performance indicators (KPI's)- Operational management of people

Sub-Areas	Main Variables
Training	• Planning of training • List of employees for training
Management Staff	List of collaborators • State and evolution of the workforce • List of promotions • Personal transfers • Wage increases • Relationship of skills by Developer • Skills analysis
Personnel Structure	• Objectives to be achieved by each employee • List of collaborators by areas of responsibility • Rotation
Time Management	Temporal Planning of tasks

ACKWNOLEDGMENT

Writing for managers, for students and for those interested in this subject, is a huge challenge, since managers are flooded with large amounts of information, but to identify what is the information, while system, which leads them to make a coherent decision to the detriment of other alternatives.

The Profº Juan Antionio-Briones Peñalver asked for my help in the study and participation in the drafting of this chapter. We start by gathering the literature related to management models and evaluate the information that leads managers to make the decision. The task proved easy since with regard to management models there is a lot of literature. Already with regard to information systems for the management of organizations, on the one hand, the literature is scarce and on the other computer scientists write much about technology and very little about the product (the information).

Most computer scientists does not make separation between information and technology that collects, stores, processes and allows easy access to information and therefore much confusion reigns and a misuse of this theme, having as a consequence the existence of many works about technology and very little about the information, while system.

What I wanted was to answer this question: what is the information, while system, which helps managers to make the decision? As such it was necessary to extract articles and works, key variables (information) of each model and then merge them into a single post. In other words, what we wanted was to define a model of the information system for decision making in a precise way, resulting from the synthesis of the literature that describes precisely what managers do.

In hindsight we have the impression of having worked in a "*puzzle*" giant to which there are still many variables. Some of the available seemed to have a clear place and when they reached a sufficient number, an image of the model began to emerge in our spirit.

When we were done, we had the impression of having found a logical model that encompassed all the key variables (information) that we had identified as important for decision-making at various levels of management.

REFERENCES

Amat, J. M. (2000). *El Control de Gestión: una dirección perspective*. Barcelona: Gestión.

Ansoff. (1965). *Corporate Strategy*. McGraw-Hill.

Batty, J. (1984). *How to write economic Reports y. Foundations, structure display, y*. Bilbao: Deusto.

Brealey, R., & Myers, N. (1988). *Fundamentals of business Financiación*. Madrid: McGraw-Hill.

Buckland, M. K. (1991). Information as thing. *Journal of the American Society for Information Science*, *42*(5), 351–360. doi:

Gorry, G. A., & Monton, H. S. S. (1989). A Framework for Management Information System. *MIT*, *30*, 49–61.

Imai & Kaisen. (1992). *La Clefde la competivité japonaise*. Eyrolles.

Lima-marques, M., & Macedo, F. (2005). Arquitetura da informação: base para a gestão do conhecimento. In Gestão da informação e do conhecimento em organizações (pp. 177-192). Academic Press.

Morin, E., & Le Moigne, J.-L. (2000). *A Inteligência da complexidade*. São Paulo: Peirópolis.

Roehl-Anderson, J. M. Y., & Bragg, S. M. (1996). Del Manual Controller. Functions, procedures y responsibilities. Deusto.

Selltiz, C., Wrightsman, L. S., & Cook, S. W. (1981). *Métodos de Pesquisa nas Relações Sociais.Delineamentos de Pesquisa*. São Paulo: EPU – Editora Pedagógica e Universitária.

Waitsman, H. S. (2001). *Inteligência Empresarial*. Rio de Janeiro: Interciência.

Chapter 17
The Information and the Strategy Business

George Leal Jamil
Fumec University, Brazil

ABSTRACT

In recent years we have witnessed a major transformation in society. We went from a society based on industry and transport to another based on information and knowledge. A major challenge for managers is to understand what the information is for formulation, definition, implementation, and control the strategy. The strategy for any organization can be set from the outside in. According to the schools of positioning, the offer of products will have to adapt to changes in the environment. Or from the inside out. According to the movement's schools, the organization influences the middle engaging with your innovative product offerings, since it has skills and capabilities that competitors don't have and that are difficult to imitate or buy. This chapter explores information and business strategies.

INTRODUCTION

Managers are people who occupy a large part of their time to make decisions of various nature and dimension. The requirements in relation to the time available for the decision-making always seem to be greater than the total time available. Decisions of great importance mingle with trivial decisions. This diversity of decisions tends to increase with the level of responsibility and becomes particularly pronounced in the case of the highest hierarchical level managers.

The function of Manager involves a very broad set of activities, including analysis, decisions (including the strategic), communication, leadership, motivation, evaluation and control. Of all these activities, we isolated the strategic decision-making process, as it is the "foundation stone" of a Manager. Peter Ducker (1958), States that "decisions and actions are the final product of managers' work".

Strategic decisions made explicitly or implicitly by managers precede any action, regardless the organizational process, by which they are taken, either through the formal hierarchy or through the broad participation of middle managers (managers) or by omission. The strategic decision-making process is complex, so put some problems to managers, in terms of methodology of approach, to choose the preferred strategy among the various alternatives.

DOI: 10.4018/978-1-5225-3725-0.ch017

Strategic decisions involve aspects of external and internal problems, that is, involve the choice of the set of products and/or services that companies can offer to their customers, looking to develop and take advantage of their position, vis-à-vis application of resources among possible alternatives, so that they can achieve their objectives.

The companies' employees are concerned with the operational problems, the hierarchies are concerned with finding ways to increase efficiency, reduce costs and sell more. The problems are automatically generated at all levels of the hierarchy and are in addition to the lower levels of this, they become cause for attention of top managers (administrators) and have to do with the future.

The issue relating to the strategy is one of the tasks of the functions of the directors of the companies. This idea is in line with one of the premises on which the *Design* school is based (Andrews et al., 1965), which considers that the responsibility for the definition of the strategy is the Manager (the leader).

The problems are very complex, and it is very difficult for an administrator to resolve the problems of the strategy alone. Consequently, the responsibility for strategic management tasks disperses through the organizational structure. Some companies create very specialized structures to support strategic decision making, such as departments and or agencies of *staff* to draw up strategic analysis.

These support structures are in accordance with the Carnegie school (Ansoff, et al. 1965) when considering that the role of managers is to make decisions, but that they are not responsible for their formulation, but they are the planners. The positioning school (Porter et al., 1980) follows a similar approach methodology, in which analysts formulate the strategy and managers approve it.

The Strategy

The strategy in companies is typically set: at the economic group level; managers and investors are involved in defining / revising the strategy and some of them rely on the support of external consultants;

The fact that the strategy is defined / reviewed at the economic group level means that the objectives and the strategy are defined globally by top managers of the Group and that each business unit (company) is limited to implement the strategy to achieve their objectives. These describe what the Group wants to achieve in the long run, in terms of some specific performance indicators, such as market share and return on investment.

The objectives of each business unit (company) translate the medium-and short-term objectives, as a way of measuring the progress to achieve the overall objectives. Each business unit (company) is an element of the *portfolio* of the Group's businesses. There is a hierarchy of objectives, strategies, budgets and plans. This assumes that the "trick" is to take relevant information up to the managers, "at the top", can be informed about the consequences of the details, "down there", without having to engage in them.

The operationalization of the strategy gives rise to a set of hierarchies, at different levels and with different temporal perspectives. At the top are the "strategic plans" and include the long term (economic group), followed by the medium-term plans which in its time give rise to short-term operational plans (companies). The group chooses a market positioning and strategies coming out of this process to be articulated and implemented. The strategy is divided into sub-strategies (companies) for success in implementation, giving rise to a whole set of hierarchies with different levels of duties and responsibilities and with different temporal perspectives.

In Portuguese companies there is a clear separation between the formulation of the strategy and its implementation. The formulation of the strategy (design) is a divergent and open process; some companies involve administrators, the middle managers (managers) and shareholders, in which the imagination can flourish, while the implementation is closed and convergent, to subject the new strategy to the problems of operationalization.

The objectives drive the formulation of the strategy, which in turn evokes the programs, the results of which influence the budgets for control purposes. Top managers remain as the architects of the strategy, but they are not who conceive the strategic plans, but rather who approve them. Strategic plans often are reduced to a "game of numbers" of performance control that has little to do with strategy.

A metaphor can be defined for the multiple businesses: "there are different roles within the family, the father (Group) and the children (companies-business units). The father needs to recognize that the children (business) change and mature with time and that a relationship in the early years works fine, but it probably need to be changed, as they grow. The children (business) like to know, as they are in relation to parents and what will be a good or bad behavior. The father has an important behavior in the creation of the family environment, "(Goold, Campbell and Alexander, 1994).

The fact that some of the managers participate in the definition of the strategy means that the process of formulation of the strategy is seen as an analytical and planning process, in which analysts (internal and/or consultants) play an important role in the process, passing the result of the analysis for top managers to formally make the decisions. This concept conforms to the Carnegie schools (Ansoff et al., 1965) and positioning (Porter, et al 1980) in which the planners or analysts are those that formulate the strategic alternatives (design) and top managers take the decision (approve them).

Some companies also tend to consider the strategic, as a collective learning process over time, through the involvement of the top managers manage men in addition to other resources, so collective action goes through the human brain of factors definition, as there are in the collective system many potential contributions. These initiatives aim to develop and exploit existing skills difficult to imitate. This concept is in line with the school of resources in which the role of the leader (s) is to manage learning (Prahalad and Hamel, 1990).

Top managers manage men in addition to other resources, so collective action goes through the human brain of actors (top managers, intermediate and shareholders). This action is subject to the filter of the cognitive capacities and to the "game" of influences, alliances and maneuvers, and the process of strategy formulation can also be seen as a process of negotiation and concession between managers, and investors. The strategy emerges from the "wars", negotiations and maneuvering in pursuit of power, between the parties concerned. The middle managers and managers conceive the strategy and shareholders approve it. This concept conforms to the power school that emphasizes the use of power and politics to negotiate strategies in favor of certain interest groups (Pettigrew, 1977 and Bower and Davis, 1979).

Enterprises are organizations with a set of representations, symbols, values, beliefs and rules lived in common by the members of the group that enable the convergence of interests of the various parties and to facilitate the harmonious evolution of social group to achieve their objectives, we can call the company's culture. The definition of the strategy can also be seen as a process that takes the form of a perspective rooted in the collective intentions and reflecting the patterns of use of resources and capacities as a competitive advantage, such as the school of culture (perspective Prahalad and Betis, 1986).

Some companies adopt two types of strategies: the deliberate that takes the form of plans or patterns, positions or perspectives as a way of adaptation to the surroundings and the emerging answer to the surroundings at the time and appropriate context. This concept is identified with the school of model configuration (Mintzberg et al, 1985, 1994).

The fact that the strategy in some companies be defined based on regular intervals and with annual reviews means that the process of strategy formulation is scheduled, with a schedule by which all process steps are performed. The strategy is deliberate and follows a planning that every year is repeated (Steiner, 1979).

Information Surveillance for Strategic Decision-Making

The process of "surveillance" of information is essentially a process of observing the behavior of the market and competitors and is intended to monitor the development of the surroundings and of the private sector. That "surveillance" is ensured in most cases, by an organic unit (organ of *Staff*- the "analysts" or the planners) that conforms to the model of the Carnegie schools (Ansoff, 1965 et al), and positioning (Porter, 1980 et al).

The process of "surveillance" on economic activity of many Portuguese companies focuses essentially on the monitoring of the evolution and economic predictions about the European Union and Portugal, in particular the countries with highest expression in the European economy (Germany, France and United Kingdom), as well as on the countries with which there is a greater affinity, such as Italy, Ireland and Greece, and their evolution is accompanied by the internal structures of the companies (the "analysts").

This information is collected, selected, processed and analyzed by the "analysts". These in their treatment use techniques of forecasting by extrapolation and analysis of problems, as a way to understand the structure of domestic, European and international economy as well as the interdependence between the various sectors of the economy as a way to identify possible future scenarios. Information about the foreseeable development of the European economy and of Portugal thus becomes critical in defining the strategy of each economic group or of the company.

The process of "surveillance " about socio-cultural and demographic changes in some companies is an irregular process of, temporary and periodic evaluation, mainly on social and demographic changes in Portugal and includes the demographic patterns, lifestyles, the social structure, social trends and is intended to determine the changes in this time interval, such as the birth rate, the level of education, debt capacity, being assured by the "analysts" of each company (internal and/or consultants).

However, the importance given to this information is less when compared with the information on the economic aspects, but it is important in the implementation of the strategy of each company, as a way to identify which customers to target for each product and or service, to the extent that allows them to understand local needs, available resources, legal requirements and funding adjustments. For the treatment of this information, the "analysts" use simple techniques of analysis.

The process of "surveillance" related to policy issues is a permanent process that is intended to "continuously "monitor, the Government's policy decisions with an impact on the sector, such as the unemployment policy, employment policy, taxation policy, so as the Community directives which may have impact on the sector and society in General (e.g. Basel II agreement), is ensured by the "analysts" and or consultants.

The information collected, selection, processing and analysis is the legislation on various aspects, such as economic, fiscal policy, education, employment, health, tourism, as a way of identifying potential opportunities and threats to the sector. In the treatment of this information the companies resort to simple techniques of analysis to understand the political influence in the business.

Information in Support of Strategic Decision-Making

There is a significant difference between the quality and quantity of information in which managers rely on strategic decision making. The fact that the value of qualitative information is recognized, is however the quantitative information that has more meaning to the "analysts" and to the managers of the companies. It is easier to get and allows them to make comparisons of performance and also because the "analysts" and managers want to know to what extent their organization is performing well, as this will help them decide more easily what to do about the future.

Information in support for strategic decision-making by the managers of the companies is a very important subject in this globalised world, to the extent that strategic decisions are taken based on that information. The quantified information is collected, selected, treated and analyzed by internal and / or external "analysts" (consultants) and presented in the most favorable way to managers, since they make the decisions according to the numbers presented in each alternative. Business managers want to know how their organization is likely to have a superior performance, as this will help them better understand the current situation and to decide the future, namely to define the positioning.

There are various dimensions of quantitative information that are collected, selection, processing and analysis. Managers are much more satisfied with the amount of information about the economic and financial context than with the information about the other contexts, as this is qualitative information and that is quantitative information that determines the current performance in the scope of objectives such as customer satisfaction with greater or lesser efficiency and effectiveness than their competitors

The managers believe they can be informed of a formal way by the "analysts" internal (*Staff* or agencies of planning) and or by consultants. They believe that the turbulence of the environment needs to be reduced to quantified and firm information, aggregated in such a manner that they can be provided regularly and in a digestible format (Mintzberg, 1995, pp. 257-266). However, the factual information (quantitative) has some shortcomings:

- Are mainly historical, lacking in wealth and often do not cover important non-economic information;
- Are concrete and accurate however.
- Are used in the formulation of deliberate strategies;

Some qualitative information is worthy of little credibility and confidence. Intangible (qualitative) information is subject to all kinds of interpretations and emphasizes the individual perspective of the "analyst and / or decision maker" in the "reading" of the environment and the sector as well as its the trends.

The intangible information analyzed by the "analysts" and companies or by internal consultants is speculative and may be distorted. The informal (qualitative) information, for example about the dissatisfaction of one or more customers, can be worth a lot more, because it can suggest a solution, against for example, information about a market survey (quantitative) that just might identify a problem. The factual information (quantitative) informs the intellect, but is the intangible information that builds the wisdom (Mintzberg, 1998).

The "analysts" internal companies, in extreme case, may in about 1 hour, assessing the environment, identify distinctive skills, generate alternative strategies and discuss which of them should be selected on the basis of the information collected on the day before or on the same day, through a formal and analytical exercise that focuses attention on the selection of factual information (quantitative) considered most relevant and sorted according to its degree of importance. This concept is approaching the case studies in the classroom (Christensen et al., 1982). This process conforms to *Design* schools (Andrews et al., 1982) (the leader), Carnegie (Ansoff et al., 1965) (planners) and positioning (analysts) (Porter et al., 1980).

The consultants (external analysts) that some companies resort to, come to a company without any knowledge of the business, conduct a SWOT analysis in several ways, which allows them in a few days of work (discussion), formulate the strategy, over a period of two or three months (analysis and design), ie two or three days are sufficient for the review and annual update of the strategy (Tregoe and Zimmerman, 1980).

This means that gathers, select, treat and analyze factual information (quantitative), "play" with a set of generic strategies from participation and growth matrices of experience, write the report, send the invoice and leave (BCG, 1974-79, ADL, 1974-79, Mckinsey, 1976-79, PIMS, 1972).

There are a number of variables on which the managers of the companies have special attention in the process of formulating the strategy, such as the position on the market, the quality of products and services, the intensity of the investment, the return of investment and profit. This set of strategic variables is according to the PIMS model (1972), in: (Schoeffer et al., 1974, 1980, Buzzell et al., 1975). "All situations of the companies are basically similar, in obedience to the same market laws, so that a quarterback trained can operate profitably, in any business" (Schoeffer, 1980, pp. 2-5).

The strategic plan adopted by some firms requires not only the predictability to formulate the strategy, but also stability, during its formulation. Although certain repetitive patterns can be predictable (e.g. seasonality), the estimate of the discontinuities are virtually impossible to predict (Spiro Makridakis, 1990, p. 115). Strategic planning adopted by some companies is the extrapolation of the past, based on the recent past or historical information (quantitative) as a way to anticipate future trends and hope for the best. Long-term forecasts (two or more years) are notoriously inaccurate (Hogarth and Makridakis, 1981, p. 122).

In military strategy, this approach is also very common, "we need to determine what will be our foreign policy, formulating a *strategy* to implement this policy and then form the military forces to conduct successfully the strategy" (Robert McNamara, in: Smalter and Ruggles, 1966, p. 70).

The traditional military art emphasizes the importance of being informed of the enemy and the location of the battle and identifies a set of relevant information such as the location of the army against the mountains and rivers, fight downhill and occupy horizontal or tall lands, anticipating the advantage of the first man who moves and who occupies the battlefield and who awaits his enemy, is an advantage, for whoever arrives after the scene and hastens to fight is tired (Sun Tzu, 1971).

Information on the art of warfare are firstly the measurement of space, secondly the estimation of quantities, thirdly the calculations, fourth comparisons and fifth the odds. With many calculations can win; with a few do not. There's much less likelihood of victory that it doesn't make any calculation (Sun Tzu, 1971). Comparatively few companies also measure their position by market share, and make performance simulation exercises (calculations) to determine the most favorable scenario. This concept is in line with the positioning school (Porter et al., 1980) which makes emphasis on the study of industry in which the company operates.

The Importance of Strategic Surveillance Process

The idea of the existence of a surveillance process in companies is in accordance with *Design* schools, Carnegie and Positioning. At the school of *Design* the surveillance process is ensured by the leader, once the strategy is the result of a *design* process for the identification of threats and opportunities, externally and the strengths and weaknesses in internal terms, through the preparation of tables/matrices with the concept of SWOT analysis (Learned, Cristensen, Andrews and Guth, 1965).

The managers are the architects of the strategy, but in practice they do not conceive the strategy, but they approve it. The design of alternative strategies is the responsibility of the planning team or "analysts" (internal and or consultants). The strategy is the result of a controlled process and conscious (deliberate), formal, broken down into distinct steps and supported by a comprehensive list of variables (information) and quantitative forecasting techniques. This concept conforms to the Carnegie school (Ansoff et al., 1965).

The study of competition is done by the "analysts" (internal and or consultants) to determine a set of competitive forces that influence or may influence the sector and identify the competitive advantages and thus be possible to determine the generic strategies: cost leadership, differentiation and the niche or focus. This concept is in line with the school's positioning, (Porter et al., 1980).

Some companies, especially the most recent are resulting from the entrepreneurship (s) their (s) leader (s), by which the process of formulation of the strategy focuses on the leader (s), by which the process of "surveillance" is ensured by the mind of the leader (s) and is associated with his intuition, to his knowledge (the information feeds the knowledge) and his experience in the construction of strategic vision, which will guide them in future terms (Schumpeter, 1947, Drucker, 1970).

The Change in the Face of Turbulence and the Complexity of the Environment

The continuity of change happens at the level of science, to the extent that innovation depends on the existing accumulated knowledge about that fact. The speed of innovation is more common at the level of the particular technologies of information and communication technologies, to the extent that today practically it is possible to have access to some information about facts or events that occur anywhere in the world. The speed of the changes at the level of political and economic market is a result of policy decisions of the Governments of the developed countries and is related to the ongoing globalization process.

For managers, changes that are easier to predict are demographic, economic, and policy changes. This "predictability" is associated with the government policies of the different countries that are driving economic development, as demographic movements are the result of labor shortages in certain regions and the economic, social and defense policies of the governments of these countries.

The fact that consider themselves as predictable economic changes, those are associated to the Government economic policies of the countries of market economy boosters, such as the United States and the European Union and the econometric models (provisional) of industrial economy, which no longer correspond to the current situation, since such models are no longer able to predict how once the global economic development and the respective countries, since its predictability has become unreliable, so it will be necessary to take into account other variables (information) in the current models.

The predictability of change depends on the magnitude of the impact and the time required for a company affected answer the change. If the impact is small and the response is fast, predictability is of no importance. An enterprise can react after having felt the full impact. However, a company well in advance can prepare for change when it is sequential. Response time is a function of the knowledge in which the company initiates the response of change.

This concept is in accordance with the models of *Design* schools (Andrews et al., 1965), Carnegie (Ansoff, et al., 1978) and Positioning (Porter et al., 1980), through the definition of deliberate strategies in which the focus is the control of the implementation of the strategy that is, making sure that their intentions are carried out in action. This is contrary to the emerging strategies of the school of learning, in which the focus is on learning, i.e. come to understand the changes through the implementation of actions governed by the intent (Mintzberg, 1972, 1978).

The predictability of the changes in the surroundings in perspective by managers is contradicted by the schools and learning resources in the "early signs for strategic change rarely provide formal information systems of horizon scanning or reports of companies (quantitative information) "(Quinn, 1982). Instead, the initial signs of the need for major strategic changes are "something that people do not feel well", "inconsistencies" or "anomalies" (Normann, 1977).

There is a strong relationship between the concept of organizational culture and strategy of organizations. That culture acts as a perceptive filter, which sets forth the assumptions of decision-making. Culture gives life to the interpretative wing of the collective world that is an organization. As a result organizations develop a "dominant logic" that acts as a filter of information, leading to a focus on certain information (the economic and technological in nature) for the creation of the strategy, to the detriment of other information (Prahalad and Betis, 1986).

The characterization of the policy changes as unpredictable and discontinuous by managers is in accordance with the school of power in the formulation of the strategy depends on individual or group interests, sometimes antagonistic and decisions emerge from "wars", negotiations and maneuvers in search of positions between the different interested (Zald and Berger, 1978). This characterization distances us from the idea that the formulation of the strategy is the product of a single "architect" of the school of *Design,* or a team of "homogeneous" Carnegie school strategy and positioning.

Companies are partially dependent on the behavior of their competitors, so the selection of the correct competitive movement involves the discovery of a result that is rapidly "inclined" to the interests of the same, overcoming and surviving retaliation (Porter, 1980).

With the rapid rise of the cooperative relationships, the formation of the strategy leaves the exclusive limits of businesses and becomes a joint process, to be developed with partners. Companies do business through a network of relationships and they formulate a collective strategy. There are clearly part of planning and positioning in this formulation, but the power, negotiated aspects of the strategy are many (e.g., alliances, partnerships) as defined by the school of power (Elfring and Volberda, 1998).

It can be said that the process of formulation of the strategy of companies is based on models of schools whose strategy is based on concept suitability/adaptation of the internal capabilities of organizations with external possibilities (outside to inside), as described by the schools of *Design*, Carnegie and positioning. The "rational strategy (economic)" is seen as the Union between the skills and opportunities to position companies in the surroundings.

The process of formulation of the strategy in some companies is a process of designing, not learning. The organizational structure follows the strategy and is determined for her (Chandler, 1962). The key variables (exhaustive list) most influential in the process of formulation of the strategy of the companies are mainly external macroeconomic and financial variables as opposed to socio-cultural variables, not political and economic quantifiable. The objectives to be achieved are quantitative in nature, so the formal information (quantitative) is privileged to respond to the organization structure and their relationships, that is, companies use as approach methodology, models in which the strategy is deliberate, as described by the schools of *Design,* Carnegie and of positioning.

Models of Strategic Adjustment vs. Models of Strategic Intent

Some managers in the definition of the strategy chosen by the models of strategic adjustment to the detriment of strategic intent, that is, the function of which is to approve one of the deliberate alternative strategies that "analysts" (internal and or consultants) formulate, in the expense of the emerging strategies. Managers continue to remain as the architects of the strategy and they orchestrate the resources at their disposal and have an overview.

The process of strategy formulation follows a sequence of steps that are repeated periodically, although with different periodicity and the definition of new strategies, or for the annual review of the same and is associated with the principles of adaptation and the positioning, this is the strategy assumes an adaptation to surroundings that allow acquiring a dominant position and then to their defense. There is a clear tendency to be based on the place of supply over demand, in the definition of the strategy.

Some managers, in addition to the "analysts", tend to involve also the intermediate managers (middle managers or executives), in the process of formulation, thus approaching the model of the resource and learning schools (models of strategic intention) that assume that the process of formulating the strategy is a moment of transformation and renewal (rupture with the past) and aim essentially at the permanent transformation of competition and organization.

Some managers develop or acquire premium features or a combination thereof to obtain competitive advantages, once a feature is "any jealousy that can be thought of as strength or a weakness of a given company," (1985, Wernerfelt in., Antonio, Nelson, 2003). The "specific assets of a company are difficult to acquire and to imitate, if not impossible. Such assets are difficult to transfer from one company to another, due to transaction costs and transfer these assets contain some tacit knowledge ", (Teece, Pisano and Shuen, 1997 in: Antonio, Nelson, 2003).

The fact that some companies involved the managers (intermediate managers) in the definition of the strategy seek to create a "nuclear competence" through collective learning, especially on how to coordinate different competences (knowledge) and integrate multiple chains of opinion (Prahalad and Hamel, 1990, Antonio, Nelson, 2003).

Some managers regard the information as a "*substance*" which can be acquired, stored and possessed by an "analyst" or jointly by a group of "analysts" and that can be transmitted from person to person or from group to group, having for such created formal structures of *Staff* or planning to take the process of strategy formulation. The information gives them a certain stability and comfort. The "analysts" to internalize the information to the point that they can use in new situations acquire knowledge about the industry and about the surroundings (Davenport and Prusak, 1998).

The "*warehouses*" of knowledge of the "analysts" are the information that was selected and structured. The information that the "analysts" have is not knowledge, but there is no knowledge without information. Knowledge is the mix of information, experience and understanding which provide a structure that can be applied in the evaluation of new information or new situations (William Zikmund, 2000).

The most relevant information currently used by the "analysts" of the companies are mainly the financial and economic. The information is historical, but allows them to compare the level of performance (e.g., growth rate, results, market share) and serve as well as a basis for the definition of future positioning (products/markets), through supply rather than demand. The macroeconomic forecasts are the prime source of the "analysts" to the formal construction of the alternative strategies (deliberate), through the use of simulation techniques, in order to serve as a basis for defining the overall objectives and specific to each business or organizational unit. We can thus conclude that the non-quantifiable information of the surroundings (e.g., weak and / or strong signals) are not yet considered in the strategy formulation process. We can also conclude that this information shall not be regarded as a strategic resource for managers, as defined by Wernerfelt (1985).

The formal forecast of alternative scenarios of the banks is subject to the limitations of prediction filter of the "analysts", i.e. the methodology, techniques and technologies adopted. If the "analysts" have an attitude and a conservative behavior relies on experience and probably do not realize any formal forecasting. If the attitude is reactive extrapolate the future on the basis of information about the past, even if booked. If the attitude is characterized by the anticipation, then incorporate the extrapolation of past performance to predict the future.

"Analysts" adopt increasingly elaborate methodologies and are based on the assumption that the future tends to be a natural extension of the past and not to incorporate significant changes in trends as well as possible discontinuities, which is in line with the models of schools of strategic adequacy (*Design,* Carnegie and positioning) to use in the process of strategy formulation.

There are other limitations beyond forecasts and lagging awareness of bank managers regarding to major changes that occur in cycles (economic, technological, etc.), such as the limitation of non-quantifiable information, the "signs" of the changes that develop quickly in the environment. The "analysts" and managers are used to analyze only the results of past performance and have some difficulties in understanding and interpreting the new information (ex: weak and strong signals of the surroundings) and therefore their challenges. So, as a result of a change in turbulence and on the complexity of the environment, the expectations of managers change suddenly, and the perception of expectations suffers a gap (Ansoff, 1980).

Some "analysts" in the process of strategy formulation tend to give greater emphasis to the analysis and insufficient emphasis to the real strategic criteria, since even the strategic thinking to strategic planning that is; the process focuses on the Middle engaging in detriment of competences and of the internal capabilities, what becomes critical to the implementation of the strategy.

In the process of formulating the strategy, some managers give little emphasis to social and cognitive processes, since they use all kinds of informational inputs, many of which are not quantifiable and accessible only to the strategists who have their feet on the ground, since they do not follow predetermined schedules, or fixed routes. The process requires *insigth,* creativity and synthesis, exactly what the formalization of planning discourages.

Some of the managers are not happy with the quality of information to support strategic decision making, reflecting the contradictions in the process alternative strategies formulation, in which the information about the economic and financial aspects is quantified and can be compared and serve as a basis for simulations about the future scenarios, while the social and cognitive information (qualitative) is difficult to quantify, as such cannot be compared or object of simulation, and so managers are satisfied with the quantity and dissatisfied with the quality.

To improve the quality of information to support strategic decision-making is fundamental the existence of a strategic information monitoring process that includes not only the factual information, but also the qualitative information (cognitive and social), which assumes the need to include some variables (information) not covered in the formulation of the current strategy used by some of the managers.

About the characterization of the environment change profile related to the speed, predictability and continuity there is a tendency to consider economic issues first and political issues secondly, once the sector traditionally has been driven more by supply than by demand. For such economic forecasts (quantitative information) has been instrumental in defining the strategy, over the inclusion of qualitative information in its models.

So the "analysts" resort to the techniques of analysis and simulation to predict the alternative scenarios, based on the most credible economic forecasts in world terms, such as the World Bank, the European Union, the OECD and the Bank of Portugal. Yet some companies use the "analysts" (consultants) their national and / or global experience.

Strategic decisions of some enterprises have a sequential nature, namely decisions are influenced by business opportunities identified by the "analysts". These opportunities are identified in the context of uncertainty and are a function of knowledge (the information feeds the knowledge) of the "analysts" to formulate the strategic alternatives after present managers. Through this information managers may agree or not with the alternatives.

STRATEGIC INFORMATION

In economic theory taking account of perception by the managers of the surroundings was successively ruled by the function of the information leading to corresponding anticipations and underlying beliefs. On the theory of managing these same concepts were gradually introduced and acquired around the strategy, because the environment is composed of other "actors" acting similarly.

The belief of managers is increasingly formalized on help from cognitive science, as well as on epistemic logic (hierarchical beliefs) and in cognitive psychology (review of beliefs). The exchanges of information between the managers are also studied in conjunction with the cognitive sciences, regarding the coordination that allow (distributed cognition) and how the dynamics that they induce (learning process).

After having recalled the relevant typologies of information in management theory, some issues linked to the believers are progressively discussed and illustrated. The structure of individual believers which translates a uniform probabilistic uncertainty finds its explanation on the information value.

The Imperfections of Information

Although there are types of market imperfections (Yao, 1988), the strategic information theory focuses only on the competition of the imperfections of information. The theory focuses and elaborates the principles of basic features of neoclassical assumption of complete and perfect information. These imperfections of information create opportunities for the called return of information that companies can explore and take advantage of the meaning of strategic information. The theory immediately gives emphasis to the information resource and the capabilities to:

- Identify the imperfections of information on product and market factors;
- Maintain or change the perceived information imperfections.

In order to be possible to identify the imperfections of information and its origins it is necessary to first understand them. The imperfections of information are derived from the behavior of the assumptions of rationality and opportunism and two types are distinguished: the incomplete information and asymmetric information.

Incomplete Information

Incomplete information is associated with the bounds of rationality that explain the limits of rationality of human behavior information. Asked to complete the survey to all relevant information, the only decision-maker tries to reach the subjectivity of incomplete information level satisfaction (Wigand, *et al.,* 1997, p. 75).

This type of behavior is known as satisfactory. Satisfactory behavior and incomplete information are part of strategic decision making in both product and market factors. About market factors, for example about the incomplete information from suppliers that offer private resources, whose search for the competitors is, what price they are willing to practice and that there are quality differences between the capabilities of different suppliers.

About products for example, incomplete information about what customers should be interested to buy the products, what competitors are competing for, what is the demand for a particular product, what price are customers willing to pay and how do they differ from the competitors' products. Not only companies, but also all or part of the market, including competitors, customers and suppliers face imperfections of incomplete information.

The Asymmetric Information

Due to incomplete information and fragmentation of knowledge in society as described by (Hayek, 1945), information can be asymmetrically distributed through parts of the market. Asymmetries of information have been reviewed extensively in all the risks of economic transactions (Nobel Foundation, 2001); however, according to Nayyar (1990), rarely information asymmetries have been looked at as a strategic opportunity. This assumes that the asymmetries of information provide opportunities under two conditions:

- High costs to obtain equality of information;
- The trend for opportunistic behavior (Williamson, 1975, p. 31).

Asymmetries of information may result from a situation favorable to the supplier or to the client, depending on the one that has the advantage of the information and which explores this advantage opportunistically.

Keep or Change the Imperfections of Information

Strategic information focuses attention on the way the companies do business with incomplete information and or with asymmetric information. Companies that identify the moments of incomplete information and market factors or product, decide what their strategic information is and what is desirable:

- Right now there is incomplete information;
- At this point develops information asymmetries, meaning both, advantages or disadvantages vis-à-vis competitors, suppliers or customers. Companies decide on dedicated resources and informational capabilities for:
    - Keep or change the incomplete information in product and market factors, influencing the positive or negative transparency;
    - Keep or change information asymmetries and create advantages or disadvantages of information or of information equality.

Having taken the decision to change a particular asymmetry of information in relation to competitors, suppliers or customers, managers must understand that these economic actors are also characterized by having rational and opportunistic behaviors. That is why organizations must use their resources and their capacity to identify the imperfections of information, creating equal information and should take advantage of their expertise in the information asymmetry and the differences of interpretation (Williamson, 1975, pp. 32).

The theoretical contribution of this study is to be based on the empirical basis of the recent development of the concepts of strategic information and information profitability. The theory was available to examine and analyze the contribution of strategic information.

The concept developed in this research is based on current economic theory and based on contemporary theories about the functioning of the market. The capabilities of organizations appear to provide a basic approach to examine how organizations expect realize the economic return based on the market imperfections. By adding the informational perspective, the role of information and information imperfections in business strategy can be explained through the base capabilities of organizations according to Barney (1986) and Itami (1987).

Identification of Information Imperfections

To understand how the economic profitability can be identified and suitable for strategic intelligence is through the knowledge of the origin of information imperfections. The costs of economic transactions (CTE) describe these origins and three types of information imperfections result of them (Williamson, 1975).

The transaction costs theory assigns two behavioral appropriations to the man: the limits of rationality and opportunism. We assume that men are intentionally rational, but are limited by this. The limits of rationality are out of the inability of the human brain. "This involves neuron-psychological boundaries of a skill, on the one hand, and on the other, the limits of language. Physical limits take the form of value and the storage limits of the power of individuals to receive, store and process the information without errors "(Williamson 1975, p. 21).

"The human cognitive capacities are as a rule insufficient, to understand particularly complex tasks, to recognize the need for relevant information and to render completely all relevant information" (Wigand, Picot et al., 1997, p. 75). It explains the limited rationality of rational information behavior (Simon 1955). "Its Instead of a full search of relevant information the only decision-maker attempts to get a subjective satisfaction, incomplete level of information" (Wigand, Picot et al., 1997, p. 75). This type of behavior is known as "satisfactory": looking for a solution which meets the aspirations of the decider level and therefore the acceptable.

Humans are not only rational; they also assume some opportunistic behavior. Williamson (1975) describes how opportunism "for own interests shrewdly" involving "disbelief of the threats and opportunities", in order to perform the individual advantages (Williamson, 1975, p. 26). These advantages are also suitable for "select and distort the information discovery or discredit the opportunities that lead to future" (Williamson 1975, p. 26). The claim is that, although not all humans to behave opportunistically, is difficult to predict in advance whether they will behave as such.

These two types of behaviors reflect the relationship between suppliers and customers in the market. The combination of opportunistic and rational behavior is the main cause for the three types of information imperfections in the market of transactions:

- **Asymmetric Information:** An asymmetric distribution of information from the parties involved in a transaction causes a strategic opportunity. "The critical impact of information on optimal allocation of risk, it is not merely its presence or absence, but its inappropriateness between economic operators" (Arrow 1969, p. 55). Williamson (1975) joins two conditions under which the asymmetry of information provides a strategic opportunity for transactions:
    - High costs to obtain equality of information;
    - Propensity to opportunistic behavior (Williamson 1975, p. 31). In other words, the asymmetric information occurs when one of the parties has information that is unknown by the other and difficult to obtain by the other party and an opportunity to exploit this information advantage through strategic alternatives.

The asymmetric information may result in a favorable situation for suppliers or customers depending on the one that has that information. The opportunity is caused by hidden information for the current transaction. One of the parties in a commercial transaction is better informed about a relevant variable than the other. Is the invisibility of this private information which constitutes the essence of the imperfections of information and introduces the risk for the other party (Douma and Schreuder 1992, p. 54).

Considering the possibility of opportunistic behavior, the part that has the hidden information, has no incentive to reveal information if it is detrimental to her. As a result, some vendor who enters the market with a product or service that is particularly suitable for a specific market segment, with the major benefits of competitors who benefit from this hidden information. The imperfections of information are known as enemies of the selection (Arrow 1984).

- **Ambiguity of the Information:** The ambiguity of the information in a commercial transaction could cause a strategic opportunity. Although in the case of complete information, different interpretations on the same information may occur. As a result of opportunism, these representations can be opportunistic in the sense that they can lead to a single advantage to any supplier or customer.

- The strategic opportunity for one of them is discovered, when such an opportunistic interpretation is not recognized by the other and results in:
  - Customer will pay a high price for a product;
  - The willingness of the supplier to offer a product at a low price.

As a result of this opportunistic behavior, the part with the opportunistic interpretation has no incentive to share this information, if it becomes a disadvantage to it.

- **Incomplete Information:** The strategic opportunity of incomplete information is tightly related to the assumption of rationality. "The limits of rationality are interested certainly in the extension of the limits of rationality are achieved-I mean under conditions of uncertainty and complexity. In the absence of any of these conditions of appropriation of contingent actions can be completely specific of this principle. (Williamson 1975, p. 22).

In an environment characterized by a high degree of complexity and uncertainty, the possibility of certain events occurs quickly, become numerous. Under these circumstances, it is impossible for humans to acquire and analyze complete information relevant to the strategic decision-making. As explained before, this inability leads to "satisfactory" behavior. The opportunity of incomplete information occurs when a client is not fully informed about the range of possibilities of the transaction and the products offered and vice versa.

Therefore, a client that allows an incomplete comparison of suppliers and their mutual differences can start a transaction with the worst supplier. For the supplier this opportunity could be exploited by the establishment of a brand and advertising, in order to become part of the subset of suppliers in incomplete comparison of clients.

Appropriation of the Profitability of Information

After have been identified the imperfections of information in two relevant factors products and markets, organizations decide how to manage your strategic information. Organizations choose to keep or take advantage of these imperfections of information, with the purpose to take ownership of their profitability or to anticipate other forms of ownership. Strategic information helps keep information imperfections in unknown markets on the one hand and on the other, to undo information imperfections and increases the transparency of the market.

The theoretical work of strategic information results in 12 basic choices to maintain or alter the choices. Briefly, these choices are related to three types of information imperfections both to the Organization and to the suppliers in the market factors and to the Organization and to customers in the products/market. The choice for any of them to maintain or alter the existence and identification of information imperfections depends on the volume of the profitability of information which may be held by any of them.

Transaction Costs and the Imperfections of Market Information

The transaction costs theory does not allow information problems to exist. So is the theory that last the objectives to ensure that the most efficient way to coordinate financial transactions, information problems will be solved, because they cause an increase in transaction costs, that is, a lower efficiency (Williamson, 1999).

However, in practice the problems of information are the basis for the competitive advantages for many organizations and form the basis for their strategy and business model. However, the resolution of the problems of the information may result in a decrease of competitiveness.

On the other hand, if the transaction costs theory allows the existence of problems of information as the basis for the strategy, will be needs to work the concept of strategy. This reveals a critique, which according to Williamson, (1999) the theory of transaction costs need to understands the concept of strategy. The concept of strategic information can fill this gap and bridge the gap between the theory of transaction costs and the thought of strategic management.

Considering criticism rose above, the theory of the base organizations resources allows information problems that exists and contributes to the concept of strategy. The theory of basic resources is an attempt to explain and predict that some companies are able to establish sustainable competitive advantages position and therefore obtain higher return.

The view base resources understands the companies as a single set of idiosyncratic resources and capabilities where the first task of management is to maximize the value through the great development of existing resources and capacities (Grant, 1996, p. 110). Developing existing resources and capacities are believed to be the rationale of the strategy in the medium and long term, because the built-in features and capabilities provide the basic direction for the company's strategy and are the first source of competitive advantage (Grant, 1991, p. 5).

With respect to the problems of information, that implies you don't solve the problems of information definition of low transaction costs. Instead, the path of the behavior with the problems of information can be inspected as the source of competitive advantage, and so the theme of the formulation of the strategy. The problems of information provide strategic information resource-based opportunities and capabilities of specific organizations.

Strategic Information

Organizations when formulating the strategy of outside to inside tend to be more aggressive and restless. The wording from the inside out is based on the strategic move (sociological) and that is why organizations are less dynamic, that is, they tend to be more passive and inclined to react to events (Mintzberg, 1998). These models represent the two extremes between which there is a range of behaviors. Based on the concept of opening the organizational systems theory, this is determined by the (Ansoff, 1978):

- Perception of strategic information that describes the Futurity (trends);
- Perspective of action that describes the familiarity of an organization, about their past experiences.
- The opening feature and the prospect of action correspond generally to information perspective:
- The retrograde nature managers prefer the successful alternatives in the past and rely on known historical information;
- Managers whose attention is focused on the present are willing to shut down the past, as long as it's not too different from the present, that is, seeking support on information relevant to the environment;

- Managers who seek to predict the threats and opportunities tend to be active in nature, so the search for new paths, based on past information and using forward-looking models, bearing in mind that the future will be an extrapolation of the past;
- The managers Beyond extrapolation of the past, in order to realize new worlds and discontinuities, seek opportunities that are new and unusual, that is, assume that the future is not an extrapolation of the past;
- Entrepreneurs are also the creators of deliberate actions. Looking for markets that have never been explored, human needs that were never met, and their motto is: "inventing in the future".

The range of possible answers and behavior are determined by the skills and abilities of organizations. There are two factors that determine the capacity of managers:

- The competence (knowledge leading to strategic behavior);
- Capacity (volume of strategic work).

One of the main attributes is the strategic problem solution approach comprising the individual skills, personal knowledge along with group dynamics. The reactive method of solution the problem demands through strategic systematic analysis of the causes, with the use of analytical procedures to identify all the possible alternatives and to establish explicit and quantified relationships between variables, and select the best alternative ("great") (Ansoff, 1978).

Another attribute of the empowerment of managers is the leadership in the definition and implementation of the strategy, requiring dexterity to capture and direct social energy. A fourth element of the competence of the Manager is to support in decision-making, which assumes the existence of a surveillance process of future-oriented strategic information and we can call the *informational skills* of Manager

The information about the future possibilities comes from the surroundings and the company's performance capabilities, and industry or in the field, which means that the company has access to information about your performance and that of its competitors. It also has access to information about the events and forces that determined the performance, as well as what the capabilities and skills that has developed within a specific period of time.

Strategic information this is relevant information that enables organizations to have a better *performance* through active exploration of *information imperfections* of the market and product factors (Truijens, 2001).

Strategic Information Research

The behavior is influenced by external factors, such as the turbulence of the surroundings, the addiction resources, organizational factors, such as the nature of the business and the strategy adopted, informational factors (availability and quality of information) and personal factors, such as knowledge or cognitive style. The study of situational dimensions organizational strategies, information needs and personal characteristics of the behavior.

The situational dimensions are studied for the measurement of perception of uncertainty about the environment, a concept that is strictly related to the perception of the environment analysis of the search template-interpretation. The organizational strategy refers to the positioning or to the attitude of the organization before the surroundings (Ansoff, 1965, Porter, 1980, Andrews, 1965, Grant, 1996,

Prahalad and Hamel, 1990, Pfeffer and Salancik, 1978, Miles and Snow, 1978, Mintzberg et al., 1976, Grant, 1996, Daft and Weick, 1984).

The characteristics of managers include the specialties, the level of the hierarchy and the cognitive style. The note as a behavioral form comprises the information needs, information and use of information. In the context of the observation of the surroundings, the information needs are often restricted to the focus and scope of the research, particularly the sectors of the environment where research is more intensive. The research of information is examined in terms of the sources that are used for observing the surroundings, as well as the organizational methods and systems adopted for the note. Finally, the use of information is seen in support of strategic decision making.

What can be determined from a survey that was completed through observation of the surroundings, as a learning model of organizational strategy? A summary can include the following observations (Choo, 2002):

- **Situational Dimensions:** *The effect of perception of uncertainty of the surroundings.* The managers who understand the uncertainties of the surroundings will tend to search better. The uncertainties are indicated by the complexity, dynamics and importance of the sectors that comprise the surroundings.
- **Strategy:** *The effect of perception of the uncertainties of the surroundings.* The organizational strategy is related to the sophistication and scope of activities. This should provide the information that allows defining the strategic alternatives and the choice of the optimal strategy.
- **Characteristics of Managers:** *Effects of managers' work and the cognitive characteristics of observation.* Top managers seem to observe more than lower level managers. Functional managers observe beyond the limits of their expertise.
- **Information Needs:** *The focus of the observation of the surroundings.* Many studies observe various contexts of the surroundings: customers, competitors, suppliers, technology, social, political and economic conditions. The focus of the note related to the strategy is industry-related markets.
- **Sources of Information:** *Usual and preferred sources.* Although managers use many sources, they prefer the formal personal sources, impersonal sources especially when researching information about the development of potential markets in this sector.
- **Information Search:** *Methods of observation.* Organizations use a variety of methods, depending on their size, dependency and perception of surroundings, observation and experience in the industry in which they are competing.
- **Use of Information:** *Strategy and organizational learning.* The information under observation is used increasingly in the definition of the strategy. The effective observation is related to the improvement of organizational learning and performance.

The Analysis of the Surroundings and the Organizational Intervention

Each change in surroundings passes through a natural evolution that progressively increases the knowledge. In the initial stage, it is possible to identify weak signals of the General State of the changes and the consequences of these signs are still subject to uncertainty, since the signs are based on conjecture and not on performance.

This means, that as the escalation of change and the complexity of the surrounding environment develops, knowledge increases (or decreases the ignorance), associated with all the changes, if explicit through one or more information and whose content is taken into consideration in the elaboration of alternatives to evolution.

Another factor that characterizes the new phenomena related to changes in the environment are the successive States of knowledge whose speed of evolution differs, becoming one of the useful measures of speed, the time that elapses until the full impact on organization, in each successive State of knowledge.

Changes are increasingly coming from sources of information that are outside the historical boundaries of industry and becomes more and more difficult to recognize them and their implications. The predictability of change of surroundings has been decreasing steadily. The importance of predictability depends on the magnitude of the impact and the time required for the affected organization respond to change. If the impact is small and the response quick predictability is of no importance.

However, the detection of a signal of change with enough anticipation, allowing time for strategic decision making, can be important when the change is sequential. If the change is completely new requires additional time to assemble the appropriate resources to change. In any case the response time is always a function of knowledge that organizations have to start their answer.

In the case of change be known all the information is available and the various components of the response can be planned and executed in an efficient sequence. If the answer is initiated in advance, the strategies possible alternatives will be limited by the available information. More and more managers are pressured to shorten response time, by analyzing and interpreting the information available and or of the signs (weak or strong).

By extrapolation forecast techniques and the related decision-making methods used become inadequate, the fact that only work when the results of the responses can be quantified. Non-extrapolation prediction techniques (opportunities and threats analysis) uses new information (signals), but less complete (qualitative).

For changes that occur today, a timely response is only possible if the change is perceived before formulating the strategy, namely, enabling organizations to respond to weak signals (information) produced by a change in the initial state of their development. The appropriate methods for the collection, selection, analysis and interpretation of information (signs) about the evolution of the environment, as well as the necessary skills to deal with this information reveal the State of knowledge that the Organization has to start the reply, the in order to respond effectively to changes in the environment- *awareness* of the need for strategic decision-making or the identification of opportunities (the discovery phase).

Learning in advance enables organizations to prepare to face the changing processes, through the adjustment of its capabilities and competencies to the turbulence and the complexity of the environment, in order to lessen the impact.

One of the key points for effective strategy formulation process is, on the one hand, the use of a filtering process of strategic information about the surroundings and on the other, the establishment of a prospective vision of the set of challenges with which the Organization will be faced in the future, in order to enable the Organization to anticipate the opportunities and threats in new opportunities (Prahalad and Hamel, 1994).

The signs (information) early warning turn into competitive advantages for the organization that earlier can "detect", so it is important to adopt methods that help detect signs of change (weak or strong signs) and to react to the first signs in order to improve their competitiveness.

Strategic information filtration focuses on the set of economic changes, technological, socio-cultural, legal, environmental, political and other affecting global and immediate surroundings of the Organization (competitors, customers, suppliers, products surrogates and other).

The sources of information are two: the surroundings characterized by the level of turbulence and complexity and their own organizations. Companies that do not record the information about their performance (past), nor are they aware of the evolution of the surroundings, there are typically a point of satisfaction, whose threshold is a crisis. They are facing the problems of everyday life and the managers do not have any shared expectations about the future.

The companies that record the historical information, but who are not attentive to the evolution of the environment, have a sense of history, thanks to the records of historical information about the past performance or memory shared by managers. There is a third set of companies that are aware of both the history and the future environment and record information about the various events and transactions from the past. Information can be obtained through informal contact with the surroundings, to the sophisticated systems that seek to identify the significant signs, in addition to the immediate perceptions of managers.

Typically, only a part of the available information is collected, analyzed and treated by the companies, since they are filtered through the filters of thorough analysis (research). Organizations that have no formal system for information support in strategic decision making, the filters are personal limitations of dexterity of the "analysts" and or of the managers, in order to observe, analyze and interpret the information. If there are formal systems, filter characteristics are determined by the system support technology.

If the observation capacity of managers or "analysts" is more limited or narrower than the target of turbulence and the complexity of the environment, the research filter deletes important opportunities. As a result the vision of external reality is incomplete and inaccurate. If the organization does not have a strategic information monitoring process, it will go directly to the decision maker, who will interpret and analyze it in detail.

The decision-maker will use the information to form his own personal expectations about the possible future of the company. In doing so, he judges the validity and reliability of the information being researched and thus subjects it to the perception filter. The limits of this filter are established by the personal strategic culture, by personality and previous experience of managers. The cultural filter determines the richness of the information used by managers in making strategic decision.

The perception of changes in the surrounding environment uses both historical information and the conversion of detected signals into information and knowledge of potential future demand. This provides a more reliable basis for predictable performance than a direct extrapolation of the past (Prahalad and Hamel, 1994). If the filtering process of strategic information is not sufficiently adequate to address the full extent of the changes would not be able to realize all the wealth (potential) (Ansoff, 1978, pp. 140-144).

The Quality of Strategic Information

The strategy is concerned with attuning, on the one hand, to what is within the organizations and on the other hand what is outside the organizations. The quality of this tuning is limited by the *quality of strategic information* that is fed, the main function of the strategic is a "*survey*" of the surroundings in order to detect the changes, analyze them and interpret them in terms of performance potential of the Organization (opportunities). This is a complex process, based on information and or signs (weak and strong) both objectives as subjective. The result is the objective perception of the reality of the environment, a set of beliefs (performance expectations) about what is going to happen, that is, the performance that managers believe to be possible (Ansoff, 1990).

There are two sources of *strategic information* that contribute to expectations. One source is the inside information about the abilities and skills (often called strengths and weaknesses) to deal with the aspects not characterized by the perception of the future environment that is, allows:

- The transformation of industry and / or sector;
- Increase the results through new niches beyond market share;
- Provide a *Strategic Architecture* – dreaming about what you can do with the knowledge and with the known resources;
- Designing the strategy as an override, any more than an adaptation of ambitions to the surroundings;
- Make progress on the competitors, in the diffusion and commercialization of the products;
- Striving for leadership on key skills for business,

The second source is the environment that provides the information (weak and strong signals) about the changes and the complexity. When the changes are significant is "important to be informed about the enemy and the battle, allowing the first advantages that moves, that is, one who occupies first the battlefield and awaits your enemy is at ease; who comes to the scene and rushes to fight are tired "(Sun Tzu, 1971). This information allows the Organization to search for shaping the future; however, the intentions may be frustrated by chance and by ignorance (Clausewitz, c., 1989).

In small organizations, the process is informal, the manager says, and at the same time does not clarify the sequence and interaction between the various elements. The main element is the *strategic culture* of the Manager, which determines both the temporal perspective in which he realizes the surroundings, as the alternatives he accepts as credible. The culture acts as a lens or filter perceptive, which, in its turn, establishes the assumptions of decisions of managers (Snodgrass, 1984).

If the temporal perspective coincides with the time horizon required by the speed of change and the complexity of the environment, the perspective of the Manager is in tune with the turbulence of the surroundings. If the time perspective of the Manager is lower than the speed of change have a myopic perspective, otherwise we have a thoughtful perspective. A myopic perspective is caused by poor quality of strategic information and the Manager will have inaccurate performance expectations. The advantage of a prescient perception allows the Manager to understand the trends of the turbulence of the surroundings and avoid surprises, predict and respond to threats and opportunities (Ansoff, 1990).

There are other factors besides the culture that contributes to the vagueness of the expectations formulated informally, such as the limited power of observation of the surroundings, the limitations of the Organization, of the knowledge and experience of managers. Immersive media stable and reactive intuition and experience are useful, but they become inadequate in environments characterized by anticipation and exploration/creation.

The surveillance of strategic information (collection, sorting, processing and analysis) can be carried out by specialized teams who then submit the alternative decision-makers for strategic decision making and or by their own managers. The formal process is explicit and sequential. The insights are drawn up by the technical teams and or by the managers, being then converted in visions by the managers.

The formal forecast is subject to the same limitations inherent in the informal process, IE is limited by the filter forecasting methodology used to make predictions. Stable competence relies on experience and does not perform any "poll" or formal forecast. Reactive competence goes beyond past performance formally. The competence characterized by anticipation incorporates the extrapolation of formal performance (Ansoff, 1978).

These approaches are based on the assumption that the future will tend to be a natural extension of the past and are unable to understand the significant changes, as well as the possible discontinuities. The skills characterized by inquiry and creation using techniques that make the prediction of likely deviations from the past. However collect some information about the potential future.

So the technology used for the prevention interposes a filter between the decision-makers and the surroundings. A myopic filter that is narrower than the turbulence and the complexity of the environment, will present inaccurate information to the Manager. A filter tuned to reflect adequately the surroundings, since the turbulence level is stable. A thoughtful filter will make a forecast of changes in turbulence (Ansoff, 1978).

The tuning filter with the surroundings is used through the cultural perspective of the decision-makers. If the cultural perception filter is narrower than the prediction, the Manager will restrict further the perception of surroundings future, rejecting as inaccurate or irrelevant information that are inconsistent with your experience.

The accuracy of the performance expectations of an organization is limited or for prediction filter or the filter of perception, depending on which of the two is narrower. When the narrower filter deletes environment important trends and probable events, performance expectations are inaccurate, regardless of the computational and refinement of forecasting methodology.

Knowledge and awareness of expectations whatever their quality, are limited to a small number of participants who are the most knowledgeable about the environment or about the capabilities and distinctive competences of organizations. Usually the most numerous group of managers dealing with internal operations, have little concern about what will happen with the Organization, for which they have little knowledge of what will be its future.

The communication opportunities of important strategic information managers are considerably higher in large organizations than in small and medium-sized. However there are some limitations. One is the limitation of prediction systems, which slows down the organizational awareness with regard to major changes in the environment. Another is the limitation of information to "strong signals", which deprives the Organization of an appropriate notice of changes (weak signals) that develop quickly.

The Problems of Strategic Decision Making

The fact that all organizations are a more or less coherent whole and whose dynamism depends on the people who work in it, that is, make decisions to solve problems, shows clearly the relationship between the concepts of decision and of system. This means that the science of organizations is based on two theoretical foundations: theory and systems theory. However, most of the theorizing in the field of strategic management has evolved from the concept of the Act or decision from open system.

The model of decision of economic theory of the firm, with the linear concept of input-processing-output, always used a mechanical model in which entries are the inputs and the outputs are the products and or services. This template is very far from what might be called a model of open system. This is rather a model of circular nature. Linearity combined with efficiency, that is, profit maximization goal will be the limit.

The model of decision making is too rational and cognitive, insofar as a person or at best a group of homogenous decision can make strategic decisions. The decision model is strongly linked to the rational

Manager (s) (s) who know (m) all even when the Act of deciding is considered sophisticated and bad structured. The decision-making model points to the Manager (s) who takes (m) decisions, but at the cost of excessive simplification of the organizational model.

The market structure or in other words, the global environment (affects all or almost all organizations of any industry) and immediately (only affects the industry or sector in which the organization is inserted) is too important to survival and to the autonomy of the organizations, that is, so that they do not lose the relative freedom and flexibility to react appropriately to the needs of society.

The clear separation between the Organization and its surroundings, which fits this half or top placement, maintains through its capacities and skills, give us clues about the role and the place that organizations should occupy in society and on how they should be managed in order to carry out your function properly. However, there is another dilemma that is the exercise of power, that is, the generation of changes and acceptance of the influence, i.e. the absorption of change. It is an approach to strategic decision-making in type-out or outside-in.

There are some models of strategic analysis from the analysis of the environment for the adaptation of the Organization to that same media that is, from the outside in, that is, the chosen strategic alternative adapts to the changing and tendencies of the surrounding environment (ex: Andrews, 1965, Ansoff, 1965, Porter, 1980). These models assume that the "*organizational structure follows the strategy*", who means that the internal structure of an organization is dictated mainly by strategy and those priorities, are reoriented in the sense that strategy formulation is the most important task of management, which allows the organization:

- Leave from the situation of the environment as it is for decisions that in fact are based on subjective interpretation and analysis of the situation;
- Keep alive the institutionalization of values, in order to generate certain consensus about what to do;
- Select in advance the portion of the surroundings (segmentation that is important at the moment) (Porter, 1980);
- Differentiate the internal system in order to approach the stability by building different types of boundaries between subsystems;
- Flexibility in changing from one strategy to another.

Other models from the analysis of the capacities and skills of internal resources for the definition of the most appropriate strategic alternative to existing resources, i.e., from the inside to the outside, so as to influence the structure of the industry, namely, seek to build their own future (ex: Barney, 1987, Robert Grant, 1987, Gary Hamel and Prahalad, 1995, Mintzberg, 1976).

Managers need relevant information, but often are victims of abundance of irrelevant information, generated by the macro-economic system and by organizations and the inadequacy and inappropriateness of the necessary information for decision making strategic (Ackoff, 1967, Smith, 1978). The more information the human brain attempts to receive less information gets in reality (Streufert, Driver and 1969).

In this context, the managers are currently with very serious problems relating to information, since it is scattered by the Organization and requires great effort to locate and integrate. The important information, sometimes, are retained exclusively by other managers and usually arrive late and sometimes unreliable.

The power to make decisions does not give anyone, neither the information nor the cognitive capacity necessary for decision-making. The decision-making process consists of a series of steps: the selective collection of information to pass to the decision maker, the treatment of information to advise the decision-maker, the exercise of choice (strategic alternatives), that is, determining what to do (take the strategic decision), the permission to do what you chose and finally the implementation of what has been decided and authorized (implementation of the strategy).

The power related to the decision-making process tends to stay at the level at which the necessary information can be accumulated in an effective way, to various levels of management. Regardless of the model of internal configuration top managers always retain the power of decision related to the strategic management.

Are multiple factors, both internal and external organizations that influence in a way important decision-making. This situation is forcing top managers to a constant analysis of these factors, in order to achieve the objectives. To achieve the desired balance, one of the stocks that the managers practice with appropriate diligence is the strategic decision making.

This action requires a process of reasoning by which, from the detection of changes in the environment, collecting information in a selective way that allows to clarify its characteristics, both as exogenous and endogenous impact in your organization and that allows take the strategic decision. The collection of information and the treatment your present no great difficulty. About the internal situation the organizations have today-management information systems, whose usefulness to the operational management and coordination has been widely demonstrated, although to the level of top management is only applicable in some cases.

The final product of strategic decisions is simply misleading, insofar as they choose a combination of products and markets is obtained by the addition of new products and markets, abandonment of old products and markets and the expansion of the current position. The change requires a redistribution of resources of the company – a pattern of disinvestment and investment in acquisition activities of other companies, in the development of new products, distribution channels, advertising, etc.

The solution of any problem of decision making requires an awareness of the need for a decision or opportunity (discovery), the formulation of alternative actions, the evaluation of these alternatives in terms of their respective contributions and the choice of one or more alternatives for the purposes of execution. The perception of needs is an important aspect of strategic decision making, since it is a method that allows conditions to choose between a continued concern with the operational problem and some attention to the strategic problem, leaving a key part to intuition and subjective judgments. A method is needed that creates conditions for a permanent research activity and a diagnosis of the need for strategic decision making.

The search for alternatives is an iterative process which covers the products and the traditional markets of the company, the research and development projects already running, and a list of the companies interested in a merger. Other alternatives may include market opportunities and joint ventures with other organizations.

Partial ignorance conditions pose two problems: a leading the company in an active search of attractive opportunities and the other is the allocation of the limited resources of the company between the opportunities that have been identified and those that are to arise. The evaluation uses the long-term profitability as evaluation standard. However, there are some difficulties to make projections regarding the company's position in terms of products and markets.

CONCLUSION

Although it is recognized for long time, many strategic decisions are made with incomplete information, the tendency is to give more weight to internal information and over competitors, than to information about the environment (surrounding), which can often lead managers ' preferences in making strategic decision.

Decision-making of managers considers only the variables that are less susceptible to influence, by lack of information. The decision on the lack of information can have immediate impact and or in the medium and long term. In decision making, and managers or customers rarely have all the information.

However, when complete information is available for all the alternatives, it is possible to make comparisons between variables and it is much easier to make the decision. The most widespread problem is that managers do not have complete information of all variables. Although the importance of this problem has been recognized for a long time, we know very little about the decision-making under incomplete information.

Strategic decision-making under incomplete information has important practical implications. Managers today have greater control over the information they provide or not to customers and how this information is presented. For example, comparing the traditional distribution channels, with those who use the *Internet* or catalog, administrators have more control over the information made available on the *Website* (complete or incomplete).

Given the abundance of information available, the managers can "draw" the information they consider as the most attractive to strategic decision making. Incomplete information can often lead to inadequate alternatives preference, although the effect may not be easily observed, since the managers choose, at the time, one of several alternatives. The lack of information may have systemic effect comparative trials.

The strategic decision is based on scientific principles and lies between the right and the uncertain commitment. The strategic add a hyphen process absorbs the time decision-makers. The effectiveness of the strategic decision is intrinsically based on the use of the highest level of conceptual knowledge, the actions that are deduced fall within the limited scope of the capacity of those who have the responsibility to implement them, ie decision making has its own systematic process and its clearly defined elements.

In a historical perspective, the relationship between the ecosystem of the company its strategy and the organizational structure gave rise to the development of the theory of the company from the point of view of the decision-maker (Chandler, 1962, Sloan, 1964, Cyert and March, 1970). Regardless of differences in point of view and of the concepts, these complement each other because each one is concerned with a different aspect of the general problem of *making decision.*

Rational decision making requires the acquisition of information and the processing thereof, in addition to the capacity of organizations. In practice, organizational add a hiffen part of a rational idea and depends on:

- Clarity of objectives of the organization which run counter to the preferences and choices (objectives ambiguity or conflict).
- Uncertainty or quantity of information about methods and processes by which the objectives are defined (technical or procedural uncertainty).

We can consider four modes: rational decision-making, political, procedural and anarchic. Rational mode, when the objectives and the procedures are clear, the choice is guided by the performance of programs. Makers simplify their representations of the strategic problem, satisfy more than maximize information search and follow routinized procedures or actions programmer.

Procedural mode, when the strategic objectives are clear, but the methods to achieve them are not, policy-makers are divided the process into three phases: the ID that recognizes the needs of information for decision making and develop an understanding of issues of decision. The active development of information research and develops one or more strategic alternatives. The selection it is the phase evaluates the alternatives and chooses the alternative best suited to be implemented. This process is highly dynamic with many internal and external factors stopping and changing the time and the direction of the decision-making process.

Political objectives mode are contested by individual or group interests, but the procedural sequence leaves between the groups: each group believes that your preferred alternative is best for the organization. Decision-making and actions are the result of negotiating power between the groups, in pursuit of its interests and in handling the evaluation of instruments of influence.

In the anarchic way, when the objectives and procedures are highly uncertain, decision-making consists of very varied forms, number of participants in decision-making, choice of identified and abandoned opportunities. Decision making happens when the choice and the participants coincide, have the interest, time and energy to do so.

ACKNOWLEDGEMENT

The strategic management and the information is a little science developed, in which the information (in broad sense) is treated as a potential strategic resource. Obviously, you're not thinking in cases where the information is a commodity asset, e.g.. in companies that sell information.

The Prof° George Leal Jamil asked for my help in the study and participation in the drafting of this chapter. If we consider realistically that the operation in perfect competition is a utopia so the opacity or asymmetry of information can be sources of competitive advantage. For that market imperfections are managed, the Organization has to provide specific capabilities for the collection and processing of data, selective dissemination of information, and creation of specific knowledge that will have to be carefully managed. After all, the secret is the soul of business.

The emergence of "competitive intelligence", always distinguished by the military and diplomats, must not only enable understand others, including rivals, as the abilities and motivations permitting to anticipate future behaviors, but also regarding the ignorance and the idiosyncrasies of their myopia underlying visions.

Instead of the theme of the chapter is consideration of standardized information management support. In this context, information is the raw material of the decision-making process, whether strategic, operating either. To your collection and treatment procedure are target of numerous scientific disciplines associated with decision theory, information systems, etc. The strategic management encompasses both the strategic decision, concerning the relationship between the Organization and the surroundings, whether the operational decision.

REFERENCES

Andrews, K. R. (1980, November). Directors Responsibility for Corporate Strategy. *Harvard Business Review*, 28–43.

Andrews, K. R. (1981, May). Replacing the Board's Role in Formulating Stratcgy. *Harvard Business Review*, 18–27.

Andrews, K. R. (1982). Corporate Strategy as a Vital Function of the Board. *Harvard Business Review, 59*(6), 174-184.

Andrews, K. R. (1971). The Concept of Corporate Strategy. Irwin.

Andrews, Learned, Christensen, & Guth. (1965). *Business Policy*. Irwin.

Ansoff, H. I. (1965). *Corporate Strategy*. New York: McGraw-Hill.

Ansoff, H. I. (1975). Managing Strategic Surprise by Response to Weak Signals. *California Management Review*, *18*(2), 21–33. doi:10.2307/41164635

Ansoff, H. I. (1978). *Strategic Management*. Macmillan.

Ansoff, H. I. (1984). *Implanting Strategic Management*. Prentice Hall International.

Ansoff, H. I. (1985). Conceptual Underpinnings of Systematic Strategic Management. *European Journal of Operational Research*, *19*(1), 2–19. doi:10.1016/0377-2217(85)90303-0

Ansoff, H. I., & Mc Donnell, E. (1990). *Implanting strategic Management* (2nd ed.). New York: Prentice Hall.

Blanck, M., & Janissek-Muniz, R. (2014). Inteligência estratégica antecipativa coletiva e crowdfunding: Aplicação do método L.E.SCAnning em empresa social de economia peer-to-peer (P2P). *RAUSP*, *49*(1), 1–17. doi:10.5700/rausp1140

Blanco, S. (1998). *Gestion de l'information et intelligence stratégique: cas de la selection des signes d'alerte précoce* (PhD thesis). Univ. de Grenoble 2.

Boyd, B., & Fulk, J. (1996). Executive Scanning and Perceived Uncertainty: A Multidimensional Model. *Journal of Management*, *22*(1), 1–22. doi:10.1177/014920639602200101

Buzzell, R. D., Bradley, T. G., & Sultan, R. G. M. (1975, January). Market Share: A Key to Profitability. *Harvard Business Review*, 97–111.

Chandler, A. D. Jr. (1962). *Strategy and Structure: Chapters in the History of the Industrial Enterprise*. Cambridge: MIT Press.

Choo & Auster. (1993). Environment Scanning: Acquisition and Use of Information by Managers. Annual Review of Information Science and Technology.

Choo, C. W. (1997). *Organizations as Information-use Systems: A process model of information management*. PrimaVera Working Paper 1997-17, University van Amsterdam.

Choo, C. W. (1998), The Knowing Organization: How Organizations Use Information to Construct Meaning, Create Knowledge and Make decisions. Oxford University Press.

Choo, C. W. (2002). *Environment Scanning as Information Seeking and Organizational Knowing*. PrimaVera Working Paper 2002-01, University van Amsterdam.

Choo, C. W. (2002). *Information Management for the Intelligent Organization: The Art of Scanning the Environment (3rd ed.)*. Medford, NJ: Information Today, Inc.

Choo, C. W. (2008). *The knowing organization*. Oxford University Press.

Choo, C. W. (2009). Information use and early warnings effectiveness: Perspectives and prospects. *Journal of the American Society for Information Science and Technology*, *60*(5), 1071–1082. doi:10.1002/asi.21038

Christensen, C. R. (1997). *The Innovator's Dilema: When New Technologies Cause Great Firms to Fail*. Boston: Harvard Business School Press.

Christensen, C. R., Andrews, K. R., Bower, J. L., Hamermesh, G., & Porter, M. E. (1982). *Business Policy: Text and Cases (5th ed.)*. Homewood, IL: Irwin.

Cyert, J. J., & March, J. G. (1963). *A Behavioral Theory of Firm*. Prentice Hall.

Cyert, J. J., & March, J. G. (1970). *Processus de Décision dans L'entreprise, Dunod, d'alerte précoce*. Colloque VSST 2001, Paris, France.

Cyert, J. J., Richard, M., & March, J. G. (1992). *A Behavioral Theory of the Firm (2nd ed.)*. Oxford, UK: Blackwell.

Daft, R. L., Sormunen, J., & Parks, D. (1984). Chief Executive Scanning Environmenal Caracteristics and Company Performance: An Empirical Study. *Strategic Management Journal*, *9*(2), 123–139. doi:10.1002mj.4250090204

Daft, R. L., Sormunen, J., & Parks, D. (1988). Chief Executive Scannning, Environment Characteristics and Company Performance: An Empirical Study. *Strategic Management Journal*, *9*(2), 123–139. doi:10.1002mj.4250090204

Daft, R. L., & Weick, K. E. (1984). Toward a Model of Organization as Interpretation Systems. *Academy of Management Review*, *9*(2), 284–295.

Drucker, P. (1970). Entrepreneurship in Business Enterprise. *Journal of Business Policy*, (1), 3-12.

Duncan, R. B. (1972). Characteristics of Organizational environments and Perceived Environment Uncertaint. *Administrative Science Quarterly*, *17*(3), 313–327. doi:10.2307/2392145

Elfring, T., & Volberda, H. W. (1998). New Directions in Strategy: Beyond Fragmentation. Sage.

Freitas, H., & Janissek-Muniz, R. (2006). Uma proposta de plataforma para Inteligência Estratégica. Texto indicado ao II Prêmio de Inovação em Inteligência Competitiva da ABRAIC, e recebeu Menção Honrosa. III ENA – Encontro Nacional da ABRAIC. *Anais. Congresso Ibero Americano de Gestão do Conhecimento e Inteligência Competitiva*.

Grant, R. (1998). A Resource-Based Approach to Strategy Analysis – A Practical Framework (3rd ed.). Blackwell Business.

Hogart & Makridakis. (1981). Forecasting and Planning: An Evaluation. *Management Science, 27*(2), 115-138.

Holopainen, M., & Toivonen, M. (2012). Weak signals: Ansoff today. *Futures, 44*(3), 198–205. doi:10.1016/j.futures.2011.10.002

Janissek-Muniz, R., & Blanck, M. R. M. (2014). *Gestão de sinais fracos, empreendedorismo e incerteza: um ensaio teórico relacional sob a ótica da inteligência.* Paper presented at CONTECSI, 11, São Paulo, Brasil.

Janissek-Muniz, R, Freitas, H., & Lesca, H. (2007). *A Inteligência Estratégica Antecipativa e Coletiva como apoio ao desenvolvimento da capacidade de adaptação das organizações.* Paper presented at CONTECSI, 4, São Paulo, Brasil.

Janissek-Muniz, R., Lesca, H., & Freitas, H. (2006). Inteligência Estratégica Antecipativa e Coletiva para Tomada de Decisão. *3rd CONTECSI - International Conference on Information Systems and Technology Management and 11th WCA - World Continuous Auditing Conference.*

Kärkkäinen, H., Piippo, P., Puumalainen, K., & Tuominen, M. (2001). Assessment of hidden and future customer needs in Finnish business-to-business companies. *R & D Management, 31*(4), 391–406. doi:10.1111/1467-9310.00227

Lesca, H. (1986). *Systèmes d'Information pour le Management Stratégique de l'Enterprise.* Paris: McGraw-Hill.

Lesca, H. (1995). The crucial problem of the strategic probe: The construction of the puzzle. *CERAG, ESA, série Recherche, 95*(2), 24.

Lesca, H. (2001). Veille stratégique: passage de la notion de signal faible à la notion de signe d'alerte précoce. *Actes du colloque VSST,* 1, 98-105.

Lesca, H. (2003). *Veille stratégique: la méthode.* L:E:SCAnning®, Editions EMS.

Lesca, H., & Almeida, F. C. (1994). Administração Estratégica da Informação. *Revista ADM, 29*(3), 66–75.

Lesca, H., & Blanco, S. (2002). *Contribution à la capacite d'anticipation des entreprises par la sensibilisation aux signaux faibles.* Paper presented at Congrès International Francophone Sur La Pme, Montreal, Canada.

Lesca, H., & Lesca, N. (2011). *Weak signals for strategic intelligence anticipation tool for managers.* Hoboken, NJ: Wiley. doi:10.1002/9781118602775

Leszczynska, D., & Lesca, H. (2004). *Veille Stratégique: utilité des « informations de terrain » pour la PME-PMI à la recherche de nouveaux débouchés produit/marché.* Etude d'un cas. Cahier de Recherche CERAG (Grenoble) – IAE (Nice), CERAG UMR 5820 CNRS.

Mahoney, J., & Pandian, J. R. (1992). The Resource-Based View Within The Conservation of Strategic Management. *Strategic Management Journal, 13*(5), 363–380. doi:10.1002mj.4250130505

Makridakis, S. (1990). *Forecasting, Planning, and Strategy for the 21st Century.* Free Press.

March & Simon. (1958). *Organizations.* John Wiley.

March & Simon. (1993). *Organizations (2nd ed.).* Cambridge: Blackwell.

Mayer, J. H., Steinecke, N., Quick, R., & Weitzel, T. (2013). More applicable environmental scanning systems leveraging "modern" information systems. *Information Systems and e-Business Management, 11*(4), 507–540. doi:10.100710257-012-0207-7

Mendonça, S., Cardoso, G., & Caraça, J. (2012). The strategic strength of weak signal analysis. *Futures, 44*(3), 218–228. doi:10.1016/j.futures.2011.10.004

Miles & Snow. (1978). *Organizational Strategy, Structure and Process.* McGraw-Hill.

Mintzberg, H. (1946). *The Rise and Fall of Strategic Planning.* Free Press.

Mintzberg, H. (1972). Research on Strategy-Making. *Proceedings of the 32nd Annual Meeting of the Academy of Management.*

Mintzberg, H. (1977). *Planifier à gauche et gérer à droite.* Harvard-l'Expansion.

Mintzberg, H. (1978). Patterns in Strategy Formation. *Management Science, 24*(9), 934–948. doi:10.1287/mnsc.24.9.934

Mintzberg, H. (1978). Strategy-making in Three Modes. *California Management Review, 16*(2), 44–53. doi:10.2307/41164491

Mintzberg, H. (1979). *The Structuring of Organizations: A Synthesis of the Research.* Englewood Cliffs, NJ: Prentice Hall.

Mintzberg, H. (1980). Structure in 5's: A Synthesis of the Research on Organizational Design. *Management Science, 26*(3), 322–341. doi:10.1287/mnsc.26.3.322

Mintzberg, H. (1981). *Organiser l'entreprise: prêt-à-porter ou sur mesure?* Harvard L'Expansion.

Mintzberg, H. (1982). Structure & Dynamique des Organisations. Les éditions d'Organisations.

Mintzberg, H. (1987a). The Strategy Concept: Five Ps for Strategy. *California Management Review, 30*(1), 11-24.

Mintzberg, H. (1987b, July). *Crafting Strategy. Harvard Business Review.*

Mintzberg, H. (1988). *Generic Strategies: Toward a Comprehensive Framework. In Advances in Strategic Management* (Vol. 5, pp. 1–67). Greenwich, CT: Jai Press.

Mintzberg, H. (1989). *Mintzberg on Management: Inside Our Strange World of Organizations.* New York: Free Press.

Mintzberg, H. (1990). Strategy Formation: Schools of Thought. In J. Frederickson (Ed.), *Perspectives on Strategic Management.* Boston: Ballinger.

Mintzberg, H. (1990). The Design School: Reconsidering the Basic Premises of Strategic Management. *Strategic Management Journal*, *11*(3), 171–195. doi:10.1002mj.4250110302

Mintzberg, H. (1991). Strategic Thinking as Seeing. In J. Nasi (Ed.), *Arenas of Strategic Thinking*. Helsinki, Finland: Foundation for Economic Education.

Mintzberg, H. (1994). *The Rise and Fall of Strategic Planning*. New York: Free Press.

Mintzberg, H., & Lampel, J. (1999). Reflexion about the Strategic Process. *Sloan Management Review*, *40*(3).

Mintzberg, H., & McHugh, A. (1985). Strategies Formation in Adhocracy. *Administrative Science Quarterly*, *30*(2), 160–197. doi:10.2307/2393104

Mintzberg, H., Quinn, J. B., & Ghoshal, S. (1999). *The Strategy Process: Concepts, Contexts e Cases* (2nd ed.). Prentice Hall Europe.

Mintzberg, H., Raisinghani, D., & Thêorét, A. (1976). The Structure of Unstructured Decision Processes. *Administrative Science Quarterly*, *21*(2), 246–275. doi:10.2307/2392045

Mintzberg, H., & Waters, J. A. (1982). Tracking Strategy in an Entrepreneurial Firm. *Academy of Management Journal*, *25*(3), 465–499. doi:10.2307/256075

Mintzberg, H., & Waters, J. A. (1983). The Mind of the Strategist. In The Executive Mind. Jossey Bass.

Mintzberg, H., & Waters, J. A. (1984). *Researching the Formation of Strategies: The History of Canadian Lady 1939-1976*. Englewood Cliffs, NJ: Prentice-Hall.

Mintzberg, H., & Waters, J. A. (1999). Of Strategies, Deliberate and Emergent. *Strategic Management Journal*, *6*(257), 252–272.

Mintzberg & Quinn. (1991). *The Strategy Process: Concepts, Contexts & Cases*. Prentice Hall.

Mintzberg, H., Ahlstre, B., & Lampel, J. (1998). *Strategic Safary: A Guide Tour Througth the Wilds of Strategic Management.* Prentice-Hall.

Nonaka & Takeuchi. (1995). The Knowledge-creating Company: How Japanese Companies Create the Dynamics of Innovation. New York: Oxford University Press.

Normann, R. (1977). *Management for Growth.* Wiley.

Pfeffer, J., & Salancik, G. R. (1978). *The External Control of Organizations: A resource Dependence Perspective*. Harper & Row, Nova Iorque.

Porter, M. (1979, March). *How Competitive Forces Shape Strategy. Harvard Business Review*.

Porter, M. (1980). *Competitive Strategy: Techniques for Analysing Industries and Competitors*. Free Press.

Porter, M. (1981). The Contributions of Industrial Organizations to Strategic Management. *Academy of Management Review*, *6*(4), 609–620.

Porter, M. (1982). *Choix stratégique et concurrence*. Paris: Economica.

Porter, M. (1984). *Vantagem Competitiva (5th ed.)*. Editora Campos.

Porter, M. (1985). *Competitive Advantage: Creating and Sustaining Superior Performance*. New York: The Free Press.

Porter, M. (1986). Changing Patterns of International Competition. *California Management Review*.

Porter, M. (1987). *From Competitive Advantage to Corporate Strategy*. Harvard Business Review, Maio-Junho.

Porter, M. (1990). *The Competitive Advantage of Nations*. New York: Free Press. doi:10.1007/978-1-349-11336-1

Porter, M. (1996, November). What Is Strategy? *Harvard Business Review*, 61–64. PMID:10158475

Porter, M. (1999). *Competição: Estratégias Competitivas Essenciais (2nd ed.)*. Editora Campos.

Porter, M., & Millar, V. (1985, July). How Information Gives You Competitive Advantage. *Harvard Business Review*, 149–160.

Prahalad & Hamel. (1990). The Core Competence of the Corporation. *Harvard Business Review*, *68*(3), 79–91.

Prahalad & Hamel. (1994). *Competing for the Future, Breakthrough Strategies for Seizing Control of Yor Industry and Creating the Markets of Tomorrow*. Harvard Business School.

Prahalad, Barlett, Hamel, Stalk Jr., Mintzberg, Ohmae … Levit. (1999). *Estratégia - A Busca da Vantagem Competitiva* (6th ed.). Harvard Business Review.

Prahalad, C., & Betis, R. A. (1986). The Dominant Logic: A New Linkage Between Diver sity and Performance. *Strategic Management Journal*, *7*(6), 485–501. doi:10.1002mj.4250070602

Quinn, J. B. (1982). Managing Strategic Incrementally. *Omega, The International Journal of Management Science, 10*(6), 613-627.

Rossel, P. (2011). Beyond the obvious: Examining ways of consolidating early detection schemes. *Technological Forecasting and Social Change*, *78*(3), 375–385. doi:10.1016/j.techfore.2010.06.016

Rossel, P. (2012). Early detection, warnings, weak signals and seeds of change: A turbulent domain of futures studies. *Futures*, *44*(3), 229–239. doi:10.1016/j.futures.2011.10.005

Schoeffler, S. (1980). *Nine Basic Findings on Business Strategy*. Cambridge: The Strategic Planning Institute.

Schoeffler, S., Buzzell, R. D., & Heany, D. E. (1974, March). Impact of Strategic Planning on Profit Performance. *Harvard Business Review*, 137–145.

Schoemaker, P. J. H., & Day, G. S. (2009). How to make sense of weak signals. *MIT Sloan Management Review*, *50*(30), 81–89.

Schumpeter, J. (1934). *The Theory of Economic Performance*. Cambridge, MA: Harvard University Press.

Schumpeter, J. (1942), *Capitalisme, Socialisme et Démocratie*. Reedição, Payot.

Schumpeter, J. (1947). The Creative Response in Economic History. *The Journal of Economic History, 7*, 149–159. doi:10.1017/S0022050700054279

Schumpeter, J. (1950). *Capitalisme, Socialisme et Démocratie* (3rd ed.). Harper & Row.

Schumpeter, J. (1959). History of Economic Analysis. Oxford University Press.

Schumpeter, J. (1963). *Teoria del desenvolvimiento económico*. Academic Press.

Shannaon, C. E., & Weaver, W. (1948). The Mathematical Theory of Communication. *Bell System Technical Journal, 27*, 379-423, 623-656.

Shannaon, C. E., & Weaver, W. (1949). *The Mathematical Theory of Communication*. Chicago: University of Illinois Press.

Shannaon, C. E., & Weaver, W. (1972). *The Mathematical Theory of Communication*. Urbana, IL: University of Illinois Press.

Smalter, D. J., & Ruggles, R. L. (1966, March). Six Business Lessons from the Pentagon. *Harvard Business Review*, 64–75.

Snodgrass, C. R. (1984). *Cultural Influences on Strategic Control System Requirements* (Ph.D. dissertation). University of Pittsburg.

Strauss, J. D., & Radnor, M. (2004). Roadmapping for Dynamic and Uncertain Environments. *Research Technology Management, 47*(2), 51–58. doi:10.1080/08956308.2004.11671620

Tregoe & Zimmerman. (1980). *Top Management Survey*. Simon & Schuster.

Truijens, O. (2001). *Aspects of Information Strategy Formulation for Customer Orientationt*. PrimaVera Working Paper 2001-06, University van Amsterdam.

Truijens, O. (2001). *Information Strategy at TravelCom: searching for InfoRent in the Dutch travel industry*. PrimaVera Working Paper 2001-12, University van Amsterdam.

Truijens, O. (2001). Aspects of Information Strategy Formulation for Customer Orientation. *Proceedings Resource Management Association International Conference*.

Truijens, O. (2002). *Towards* a Resource-based Theory of Information Strategy. British Academy of Management Annual Conference 2002, Hammersmith, UK.

Tzu, S. (1978). *L'Art de la Guerre*. Paris: L'Impensé Radical.

Tzu, S. (1971). The Art of War. Oxford University Press.

Von Clausewitz, C. (1989). *On War*. Princeton, NJ: Princeton University Press.

Weick & Daft. (1983). The Effectiviness of Interpretation Systems. In Organizational Effectiviness: A Comparison of Multiple Models. Academic Press.

Weick, K. E. (1979). *The Social Psychology of Organizing* (2nd ed.). Random House.

Weick, K. E. (1990). Cartographic Myths in Organizations. In A. S. Huff (Ed.), Mapping Strategic Thought. New York: Academic Press.

Weick, K. E. (1995). *Sensemaking in Organizations*. Thousand Oaks, CA: Sage Publications.

Weick, K. E. (2000). *Making Sense of the Organizations*. Blackwell Publishers.

Wilensky, H. (1967). *Organisational Intelligence: Knowledge and Policy in Government and Industry*. New York: Basic Books.

Zald, M. N., & Berger. (1978). Social Movements in Organizations: Coup d' Etat, Insurgency and Mass Movements. *American Journal of Sociology, 83*(4), 823-861.

Compilation of References

Abbês, C., & Massaro, A. (2004). Acolhimento com avaliação e classificação de risco: um paradigma ético estético no fazer em saúde. *Ministério da Saúde. Núcleo Técnico da Política Nacional de Humanização. Brasília-dF. Série B. Textos Básicos em Saúde*. Retrived from: http://bvsms.saude.gov.br/bvs/publicacoes/acolhimento.pdf

Abdullah, H. S., Hassim, A. A., & Chik, R. (2009). Knowledge Sharing in a Knowledge Intensive Organisation: Identifying the Enablers. *International Journal of Business and Management*, *4*(4), 115–123. doi:10.5539/ijbm.v4n4p115

Abubaker, M., & Ashour, W. (2013). Efficient Data Clustering Algorithms: Improvements over Kmeans. *International Journal of Intelligent Systems and Applications*, *5*(3), 37–49. doi:10.5815/ijisa.2013.03.04

Ackerman, L. D. (2000). *Identity is Destiny: Leadership and the Roots of Value Creation*. San Francisco: Berrett-Koehler Publishers, Inc.

Acosta, H. (2014). *Burnout y su relación con variables sociodemográficas, socio laborales y organizacionales en profesores universitarios chilenos*. Universitat Jaume I Departamento de Psicología Evolutiva, Educativa, Social y Metodología Castellón de la Plana, España.

Acosta, M., & Burguillos, A. I. (2014). Stress and burnout in teachers of primary and secondary education of Huelva: Coping like protection factor. *International Journal of Developmental and Educational Psychology*, *1*(4), 303–331.

Actionable Intelligence for Social Policy (AISP). (n.d.). *Integrated Data Systems (IDS)*. Retrieved from http://www.aisp.upenn.edu/integrated-data-systems/

Aguayo, C. V., la Fuente, E. D., & Lozano, L. M. (2011). A meta-analytic reliability generalization study of the Maslach Burnout Inventory. *International Journal of Clinical and Health Psychology*, *11*, 343–361.

Aguirre, N. H., Medellín, J., Vázquez, L., Gutiérrez, G., & Fernández, M. C. (2014). Síndrome de quemarse por el trabajo y su relación con el puesto de trabajo en empleados de la industria maquiladora. *Revista PsicologiaCientifica.com*, *16*(1). Retrieved from http://www.psicologiacientifica.com/sindromequemarse-trabajo-relacion-puesto-trabajo-empleados

Ahmad, A., & Dey, L. (2007). A K-Mean Clustering Algorithm for Mixed Numeric and Categorical Data. *Data & Knowledge Engineering*, *63*(2), 503–527. doi:10.1016/j.datak.2007.03.016

Ahmad, A., & Dey, L. (2007). A Method to Compute Distance between Two Categorical Values of Same Attribute in Unsupervised Learning for Categorical Data Set. *Pattern Recognition Letters*, *28*(1), 110–118. doi:10.1016/j.patrec.2006.06.006

Ahola, K., Honkonen, T., Isometsä, E., Kalimo, R., Nykyri, E., Aromaa, A., & Lönnqvist, J. (2005). The relationship between job-related burnout and depressive disorders — results from the Finnish Health 2000 Study. *Journal of Affective Disorders*, *88*(1), 55–62. doi:10.1016/j.jad.2005.06.004 PMID:16038984

Ahola, K., Pulkki-Råback, L., Kouvonen, A., Rossi, H., Aromaa, A., & Lönnqvist, J. (2012). Burnout and Behavior-Related Health Risk Factors: Results From the PopulationBased Finnish Health 2000 Study. *Journal of Occupational and Environmental Medicine*, *54*(1), 17–22. doi:10.1097/JOM.0b013e31823ea9d9 PMID:22157806

Ahola, K., Vaananen, A., Koskinen, A., Kouvonen, A., & Shirom, A. (2010). Burnout as a predictor of all-cause mortality among industrial employees: A 10-year prospective register-linkage study. *Journal of Psychosomatic Research*, *69*(1), 51–57. doi:10.1016/j.jpsychores.2010.01.002 PMID:20630263

Ajeeli, A. T. A. (2016). Steady state analysis for improving manufacturing productivity. *International Journal of Development Research*, *06*(07), 8729–8738.

Akturan, A., & Çekmecelioğlu, H. G. (2016). The effects of knowledge sharing and organizational citizenship behaviors on creative behaviors in educational institutions. *Procedia: Social and Behavioral Sciences*, *235*, 342–350. doi:10.1016/j.sbspro.2016.11.042

Aktürk, B. K., & Kurt, M. (2016). An empirical study of the relationship between knowledge management practices and strategy formulation capabilities. *Procedia: Social and Behavioral Sciences*, *235*, 739–745. doi:10.1016/j.sbspro.2016.11.075

Al Saifi, S., Dillon, S., & McQueen, R. (2016). The relationship between management support and knowledge sharing: An exploratory study of manufacturing firms. *Knowledge and Process Management*, *23*(2), 124–135. doi:10.1002/kpm.1506

Alberta Heritage Foundation for Medical Research. (2003). *Emergency department fast-track system*. Alberta Heritage Foundation for Medical Research.

Alexander, A. T., Neyer, A. K., & Huizingh, K. R. E. (2016). Introduction to the special issue: Transferring knowledge for innovation. *R & D Management*, *46*(2), 305–311. doi:10.1111/radm.12195

Allenby, B. (2015, March 4). Choose at your own risk: How technology is changing our choices and the values that help us make them. *Slate*. Retrieved from http://www.slate.com/articles/technology/future_tense/2015/03/how_technology_is_changing_our_choices_and_values.html

Alsina, M. R. (1992). La construcción de la noticia. In Ed. Rev. Ampl. Barcelona: Paidós.

Alvarez, I., Cilleruelo, E., & Zamanillo, I. (2016). Is formality in knowledge management practices related to the size of organizations? The Basque case. *Human Factors and Ergonomics in Manufacturing & Service Industries*, *26*(1), 127–144. doi:10.1002/hfm.20618

Amat, J. M. (2000). *El Control de Gestión: una dirección perspective*. Barcelona: Gestión.

Andreeva, T. (2009). Tensions between knowledge creation and knowledge sharing: Individual preferences of employees in knowledge-intensive organizations. In D. Jemielniak & J. Kociatkiewicz (Eds.), *Handbook of research on knowledge-intensive organizations* (pp. 459–477). Hershey, PA: IGI Global. doi:10.4018/978-1-60566-176-6.ch028

Andrews, K. R. (1971). The Concept of Corporate Strategy. Irwin.

Andrews, K. R. (1982). Corporate Strategy as a Vital Function of the Board. *Harvard Business Review*, *59*(6), 174-184.

Andrews, Learned, Christensen, & Guth. (1965). *Business Policy*. Irwin.

Andrews, K. M., & Delahaye, B. L. (2000). Influences On Knowledge processes In Organizational Learning: The Psychosocial Filter. *Journal of Management Studies*, *37*(6), 797–810. doi:10.1111/1467-6486.00204

Andrews, K. R. (1980, November). Directors Responsibility for Corporate Strategy. *Harvard Business Review*, 28–43.

Andrews, K. R. (1981, May). Replacing the Board's Role in Formulating Strategy. *Harvard Business Review*, 18–27.

Andrioni, F., & Popp, L. E. (2012). Organizational communication in social care organizations from Hunedoara county, Romania. *Procedia: Social and Behavioral Sciences*, *62*, 590–594. doi:10.1016/j.sbspro.2012.09.099

Ansoff. (1965). *Corporate Strategy*. McGraw-Hill.

Ansoff, H. I. (1965). *Corporate Strategy*. New York: McGraw-Hill.

Ansoff, H. I. (1975). Managing Strategic Surprise by Response to Weak Signals. *California Management Review*, *18*(2), 21–33. doi:10.2307/41164635

Ansoff, H. I. (1978). *Strategic Management*. Macmillan.

Ansoff, H. I. (1984). *Implanting Strategic Management*. Prentice Hall International.

Ansoff, H. I. (1985). Conceptual Underpinnings of Systematic Strategic Management. *European Journal of Operational Research*, *19*(1), 2–19. doi:10.1016/0377-2217(85)90303-0

Ansoff, H. I., & Mc Donnell, E. (1990). *Implanting strategic Management* (2nd ed.). New York: Prentice Hall.

Antoine, A., & Blum, G. (2014). La gestion des connaissances ou le Knowledge Management (KM). *Revue Internationale de Psychosociologie et de Gestion des Comportements Organisationnels. ESKA*, *49*, 23–31. doi:10.3917/rips.049.0021

Aranda, I. (2014). Factores psicosociales y trastornos psíquicos en trabajadores de una empresa maquiladora de electrónica, Guadalajara, México. Revista Costarricense de Salud Pública, 23(1).

Arazy, O., Gellatly, I., Brainin, E., & Nov, O. (2016). Motivation to share knowledge using wiki technology and the moderating effect of role perceptions. *Journal of the Association for Information Science and Technology*, *67*(10), 2362–2378. doi:10.1002/asi.23579

Arduin, P. E., Grundstein, M., & Rosenthal-Sabroux, C. (2015). *Système d'information et de connaissance*. London, UK: ISTE Editions.

Arenas, L., & Cantú, O. (2013). Factores de riesgo de trastornos musculo-esqueléticos crónicos laborales. *Medicina Interna de México*, *29*(4), 370–379.

Armenta. (2015). *Determinación de la presencia de Burnout y el índice de estrés del trabajo en mandos medios y superiores de la industria maquiladora de ciudad Juárez*. Tesis.

Arnhold, U. (2010). *User Generated Branding: Integrating User Generated Content into Brand Management*. Wiesbaden, Germany: GWV Fachverlage GmbH. doi:10.1007/978-3-8349-8857-7

Arpaci, I., & Baloğlu, M. (2016). The impact of cultural collectivism on knowledge sharing among information technology majoring undergraduates. *Computers in Human Behavior*, *56*, 65–71. doi:10.1016/j.chb.2015.11.031

Arroyo, S., & Castillo, V. M. (2017). Innovacion y Gestion del conocimiento en las organizaciones. Inceptum, 7(12).

Asociación-de-Maquiladoras-A, C. (2013). *Panorama general 2013*. Retrieved from http://www.indexjuarez.org/INICIO/2013/Maquila%20Overview%202013/MAQUIL A%20OVERVIEW%202013.pdf

Asterhan, C. S. C., & Bouton, E. (2017). Teenage peer-to-peer knowledge sharing through social network sites in secondary schools. *Computers & Education*, *110*, 16–34. doi:10.1016/j.compedu.2017.03.007

Attour, A., & Ayerbe, C. (2012). Connaissances et innovation au sein des écosystèmes d'affaires, le cas des services mobiles. *Revue Française de Gestion*, *221*, 78–94. doi:10.3166/rfg.221.77-94

Aurand, T. W., Gorchels, L., & Bishop, T. R. (2005). Human resource management's role in internal branding: An opportunity for cross-functional brand message synergy. *Journal of Product and Brand Management*, *14*(3), 163–169. doi:10.1108/10610420510601030

Babe, R. E. (1994). The Place of Information in Economics. In R. E. Babe (Ed.), *Information and Communication in Economics* (pp. 41–67). Boston: Kluwer Academic Publishers. doi:10.1007/978-94-011-2204-7_2

Babita Gupta, L. S. (2000). Knowledge Management Practices and Challenges. *Industrial Management & Data Systems*, *100*(1), 17–21. doi:10.1108/02635570010273018

Badea, M. (2014). Social media and organizational communication. *Procedia: Social and Behavioral Sciences*, *149*, 70–75. doi:10.1016/j.sbspro.2014.08.192

Baets, W. (1996). Some Empirical Evidence on IS strategy Alignment in Banking. *Information & Management*, *30*(4), 155–177. doi:10.1016/0378-7206(95)00056-9

Bai, L., Liang, J., Dang, C., & Cao, F. (2012). A cluster centers initialization method for clustering categorical data. *Expert Systems with Applications*, *39*(9), 8022–8029. doi:10.1016/j.eswa.2012.01.131

Ballay, J. F. (1999). Les processus clés de la gestion des savoirs. *L'Expansion Management Review*, *95*, 111–119.

Ballou, D. P., & Pazer, H. L. (1985). Modeling data and process quality in multi-input, multioutput information systems. *Management Science*, *31*(2), 530–545. doi:10.1287/mnsc.31.2.150

Balmer, J. M. T., & Greyser, S. A. (2002). Managing the Multiple Identities of the Corporation. *California Management Review*, *44*(3), 72–86. doi:10.2307/41166133

Barab, S. A., Makinster, J. G., Moore, J. A., & Cunningham, D. J. (2001). Designing and Building an On-line Community: The Struggle to Support Sociability in the Inquiry Learning Forum. *Educational Technology Research and Development*, *49*(4), 71–96. doi:10.1007/BF02504948

Barattucci, Y. (2011). *Estrés y Alimentación. (Licenciatura en Nutrición)*. Universidad Fasta.

Barbarroux, P. (2014a). Innovation disruptive et naissance d'un écosystème: Voyage aux origines de l'internet? *Revue d'Économie Industrielle, Ecosystèmes et Modèles d'Affaires, 146*(2), 27-59. Retrieved from www.cairn.info/article_p.php?ID_ARTICLE=REI_146_0027

Barbarroux, P. (2012). Identifying collaborative innovation capabilities within knowledge-intensive environments: Insights from the ARPANET project. *European Journal of Innovation Management*, *15*(2), 232–258. doi:10.1108/14601061211220995

Barbosa, R. R. (2007). O uso de fontes de informação por consultores empresariais: Um estudo junto ao mercado de consultoria de Belo Horizonte. *Perspectivas em Ciência da Informação, Belo Horizonte*, *13*(1), 95–101.

Bardin, L. (2002). *Análise de Conteúdo*. Lisboa: Edições 70.

Barney, J. (1991). Firm resources and sustained competitive advantage. *Journal of Management*, *17*(1), 99–120. doi:10.1177/014920639101700108

Barreto, A. A. (2011). A eficiência Técnica e Econômica e a viabilidade de produtos e serviços de informação. *Ciência da Informação, 25*(3), 1-18. Retrieved from http://revista.ibict.br/ciinf/index.php

Barreto, A. A. (1997). As tecnologias intensivas de informação e comunicação e o reposicionamento dos atores do setor. *Info*, 97.

Bartholy & Grandpierre. (1978). *La Science*. Epistemologie general.

Bartol, K. M., & Srivastava, A. (2002). Encouraging Knowledge Sharing: The Role of Organizational Reward Systems. *Journal of Leadership & Organizational Studies Organizational Studies*, *9*(1), 64–76. doi:10.1177/107179190200900105

Bateson, G. (1972). *Steps to Ecology of Mind: Collected Essays in Anthropology, Psychiatry, Evolution, and Epistemology*. University Of Chicago Press.

Bateson, G. (1987). Steps to Ecology of Mind. London: Ballantine.

Batista, E. (2004). *O. Sistema de Informação: o uso consciente da tecnologia para o gerenciamento*. São Paulo: Saraiva.

Batty, J. (1984). *How to write economic Reports y. Foundations, structure display, y*. Bilbao: Deusto.

Becerra-Fernandez, I., & Sabherwal, R. (2015). *Knowledge Management Systems and Processes*. New York: Taylor & Francis.

Beck, U. (1992). *Risk Society*. London: Sage Publications.

Benevides-Pereira, A., Moreno-Jiménez, B., Garrosa Hernández, E., & González, J.L. (2006). *Un estudio transcultural acerca de los procesos de estrés y burnout en profesores*. Interpsiquis.

Bergeron, F., Poulin, D., & Ellouz, S. (2000). Les technologies de l'information: Un synonyme d'alliance réussie. *Proceedings of the 9th Conférence de Management Stratégique*. Montpellier: AIMS. Retrieved from http://jepelet.free.fr/studies/MBA/strategie/doc/chap5/bergeron.pdf

Berger, P. L., & Luckmann, T. (1966). *The Social Construction of Reality: A Treatise in the Sociology of Knowledge*. New York: Anchor Books.

Berger, P., & Luckmann, T. (1985). *A construção social da realidade: tratado de sociologia do conhecimento*. Petrópolis: Vozes.

Bernal, J. D. (1967). *The Social function of science*. Cambridge, MA: MIT Press.

Berthon, P., Pitt, L. F., & Campbell, C. (2009). Does brand meaning exist in similarity or singularity? *Journal of Business Research*, *62*(3), 356–361. doi:10.1016/j.jbusres.2008.05.015

Bettiol, M., Di Maria, E., & Grandinetti, R. (2012). Codification and creativity: Knowledge management strategies in KIBS. *Journal of Knowledge Management*, *16*(4), 550–562. doi:10.1108/13673271211246130

Bevir, M. (2012). *Governance: A very short introduction*. Oxford, UK: Oxford University Press. doi:10.1093/actrade/9780199606412.001.0001

Bhatti, W. A., Larimo, J., & Carrasco, I. (2016). Strategy's effect on knowledge sharing in host country networks. *Journal of Business Research*, *69*(11), 4769–4774. doi:10.1016/j.jbusres.2016.04.028

Bijker, W. E., Hughes, T. P., & Pinch, T. (Eds.). (1987). *The Social Construction of Technological Systems: New Directions in the Sociology and History of Technology*. Cambridge, MA: MIT Press.

Bio, S. R. (1996). *Sistemas de Informação: um enfoque gerencial*. São Paulo: Atlas.

Blanck, M., & Janissek-Muniz, R. (2014). Inteligência estratégica antecipativa coletiva e crowdfunding: Aplicação do método L.E.SCAnning em empresa social de economia peer-to-peer (P2P). *RAUSP*, *49*(1), 1–17. doi:10.5700/rausp1140

Blanco, S. (1998). *Gestion de l'information et intelligence stratégique: cas de la selection des signes d'alerte précoce* (PhD thesis). Univ. de Grenoble 2.

Boblin, N., & Brenner, P. (1996). L'art de mesurer l'apprentissage organisationnel. *L'Expansion Management Review*, 17-23.

Bobrowski, M., Marre, M., & Yankelevich, D. (1999). A Homogeneous framework to measure data quality. In *International Conference on Information Quality*. Cambridge, MA: MIT.

Boisot, M. H. (1998). *Knowledge Assets – Securing Competitive Advantage in the Information Age*. Oxford, UK: Oxford University Press.

Boisot, M. H. (1998). *Knowledge Assets: Securing Competitive Advantage in the Information Economy*. Oxford University Press.

Boland, R. J. (1987). The In-formation of Information Systems. Academic Press.

Boland, R. J. (1987). The In-Formation of Information Systems. In *Critical Issues in Information Systems Research*. Boland.

Bonifacio, M., Camussone, P., & Zini, C. (2004). Managing the KM Trade-Off: Knowledge Centralization versus Distribution. *Journal of Universal Computer Science*, *10*(3), 162–175.

Bontis, N., Dragonetti, N. C., Jacobsen, K., & Roos, G. (1999). Les indicateurs de l'immatériel. *L'Expansion Management Review*, *95*, 37–46.

Borda, N., & Aun, B. (2007). Síndrome de Burnout en estudiantes de internado del Hospital Universidad del Norte. *Salud Uninorte. Barranquilla (Col.)*, *23*(1), 43–51.

Borko, H. (1968). Information science: What is this? *American Documentation*, *19*(1), 3–5. doi:10.1002/asi.5090190103

Bounfour, A. (1998). *Le management des ressources immatérielles. Maîtriser les Nouveaux Leviers de l'Avantage Compétitif*. Paris, France: Dunod.

Bourdieu, P. (1979). *A distinção: uma crítica social da faculdade do juízo. História e Sociedade* (Vol. 2). Lisboa: Edições 70.

Bourdieu, P. (1977). *Outline of a Theory of Practice*. Cambridge, UK: Cambridge University Press. doi:10.1017/CBO9780511812507

Bourdieu, P. (1983). Esboço de uma teoria da prática. In R. Ortiz (Ed.), *Pierre Bourdieu: sociologia* (pp. 46–81). São Paulo: Ática.

Boyd, B., & Fulk, J. (1996). Executive Scanning and Perceived Uncertainty: A Multidimensional Model. *Journal of Management*, *22*(1), 1–22. doi:10.1177/014920639602200101

Braaksma, B., & Zeelenberg, K. (2014). *Information management as a tool for standardization in statistics, Discussion Paper 2014-02*. The Hague: Statistics Netherlands.

Bradbury, S., & Middlemiss, L. (2015). The role of learning in sustainable communities of practice. *Local Environment*, *20*(7), 796–810. doi:10.1080/13549839.2013.872091

Brasil, C. C. (1990). Lei nº 8.080, de 19 de setembro de 1990: Dispõe sobre as condições para a promoção, proteção e recuperação da saúde, a organização eo funcionamento dos serviços correspondentes e dá outras providências. *Diário Oficial da união*, *128*(182). Retrived from: http://www.planalto.gov.br/ccivil_03/leis/l8080.htm

Brealey, R., & Myers, N. (1988). *Fundamentals of business Financiación*. Madrid: McGraw-Hill.

Brelade & Harman. (2000). Using Human Resource Management to put Knowledge to Work. *Knowledge Management Review*, *3*(1), 26–29.

Bresfelean, P., Vasile, G., & Nicolae, L. (2009). Towards the development of decision support in academic environments. In *Proceedings of the 31st International Conference on Information Technology Interfaces* (pp. 343-348). Cavtat, Croatia: Academic Press. 10.1109/ITI.2009.5196106

Bronowski, J. (1977). O senso comum da ciência. In *Belo Horizonte*. São Paulo: Editora da USP.

Brown, A. (1998). *Organizational Culture*. London: Financial Times Pitman.

Bruneau, J. M., & Pujos, J. F. (1992). *Le management des connaissances dans l'entreprise*. Paris, France: Les Éditions d'Organisation.

Bryant, A., & Maes, R. (2005). *The role of the information architect: Conquering cognitive parochialism*. Retrieved from www.imresearch.org

Bryson, J. M., Crosby, B. C., & Stone, M. M. (2006). The Design and Implementation of Cross-Sector Collaborations: Propositions from the Literature. *Public Administration Review, 66*(1), 44–55. doi:10.1111/j.1540-6210.2006.00665.x

Buckland, M. (1991). Information as a thing. *JASIS, 42*(5), 351–360. doi:

Burgess, M. S. E., Gray, W. A., & Fiddian, N. J. (2004). Quality measures and the information consumer. In *International Conference on Information Quality*. Cambridge, MA: MIT.

Burmann, C., & Zeplin, S. (2005). Building brand commitment: A behavioural approach to internal brand management. *Journal of Brand Management, 12*(4), 279–300. doi:10.1057/palgrave.bm.2540223

Buzzell, R. D., Bradley, T. G., & Sultan, R. G. M. (1975, January). Market Share: A Key to Profitability. *Harvard Business Review*, 97–111.

Caballero, I., Gómez, Ó., & Piattini, M. (2004). Getting better information quality by assessing and improving information quality management. In *International Conference on Information Quality*. Cambridge, MA: MIT.

Calabrese, G. (2010). Impacto del estrés laboral crónico en la salud del anestesiólogo. *Revista mexicana de anestesiología, 33*(1), S183-S185.

Calabrese, G. (2006). Impacto del estrés laboral en el anestesiólogo. *Revista Colombiana de Anestesiología, 34*(4), 233–240.

Calazans, A. T. S. (2006). Conceitos e uso da informação organizacional e informação estratégica. *Pesquisa Brasileira em Ciência da Informação e Biblioteconomia, 1*(2).

Callahan, K. (2006). *Elements of effective governance: Measurement, accountability and participation*. Boca Raton, FL: CRC Press. doi:10.1201/9781420013429

Callon, M. (1986). Some elements of a sociology of translation: domestication of the scallops and the fishermen of St Brieuc Bay. In *Power, action and belief: a new sociology of knowledge?* (pp. 196–223). London: Routledge.

Calvo-Porral, C., Martínez-Fernández, V. A., & Juanatey-Boga, O. (2011). Análisis de dos modelos de ecuaciones estructurales alternativos para medir la intencion de compra. *Revista Investigación Operacional, 34*(3), 230–243.

Camacho, R., Maldonado, A., García, J.L., Palacios, J. & Valenzuela, J. Camacho, Maldonado, García, Palacios, & Valenzuela. (2015). Modelo estructural del síndrome de Burnout y obesidad en mandos medios y superiores de la industria maquiladora en Ciudad Juárez. *Culcyt, 55*, 78-85.

Camacho-Alamilla, R., Maldonado-Macias, A., García-Alcaraz, J. L., & Hernández-Arellano, J. L. (2014). Determination of Burnout Syndrome among Middle and Senior Managment Personnel in Autootive Industry in Juarez City México. In C. EspejoGuasco, E. De la Vega Bustillos, & E. Chacón Martínez (Eds.), Ergonomía Ocupacional. Investigaciones y aplicaciones (Vol. 7, pp. 306-317). Sociedad de Ergonomistas de México, A.C.

Campos, V. F. (1992). TQC: controle de qualidade total (no estilo japonês). Belo Horizonte: Fundação Christiano Ottoni: UFMG.

Cao, F., Liang, J., Li, D., & Zhao, X. (2013). A weighting k-modes algorithm for subspace clustering of categorical data. *Journal of Neurocomputing*, *108*, 23–30. doi:10.1016/j.neucom.2012.11.009

Capriotti, P. (2009). E-communication in the information society and the impact of new technologies on employee communication. In T. Torres-Coronas & M. Arias-Oliva (Eds.), *Encyclopedia of human resources information systems: Challenges in e-HRM* (pp. 248–255). Hershey, PA: IGI Global. doi:10.4018/978-1-59904-883-3.ch038

Capurro, R. (1996). *On the genealogy of information. First published in: Information. New questions to a multidisciplinary concept.* Akademie V. Retrieved from http://www.capurro.de/cottinf.htm

Capurro, R., & Hjorland, B. (2003). The concept of information. In B. Cronin (Ed.), Annual Review of Information Science and Technology (Vol. 37, pp. 343–411). Academic Press.

Capurro, R., & Hjorland, B. (2007). O conceito de informação, Perspectivas em Ciência da Informação. *Belo Horizonte, 12*(1). Retrieved from http://www. eci.ufmg.br/pcionline/index.php/pci/article/ viewFile/54/47

Capurro, R., & Hjorland, B. (2003). The concept of information. *Annual Review of Information Science and Technology*, 37, 343–411.

Cardoso, A. M. P. (1996). Pós-Modernidade e informação: Conceitos complementares? *Perspectivas em Ciência da Informação, Belo Horizonte*, *1*(1), 63–79.

Carey, J. W. (1989). *Communication As Culture: Essays on Media and Society.* Winchester, MA: Unwind Hyman.

Caridi-Zahavi, O., Carmeli, A., & Arazy, O. (2016). The influence of CEOs' visionary innovation leadership on the performance of high-technology ventures: The mediating roles of connectivity and knowledge integration. *Journal of Product Innovation Management*, *33*(3), 356–376. doi:10.1111/jpim.12275

Carlotto, M., & De Santos Palazzo, L. (2006). Síndrome de burnout factores asociados: un estodo epidemiológico com profesores. *Cadernos Saude Pública, 22*(5).

Carlson, R. (2014). *Fisiología de la conducta (8th ed.).* Pearson-Educación.

Carpenter, M., Bauer, T., & Erdogan, B. (2016, March 11). *Organizational Structure.* Retrieved from http://catalog.flatworldknowledge.com/bookhub/5?e=carpenter-ch07_s01

Casanova, M. B. (1990). Information: the major element for change. In I. Wormell (Ed.), *Information quality: definitions and dimentions* (pp. 42–53). London: Taylor Graham.

Cecan, S., & Marian, L. (2015). Theoretical and practical considerations regarding the risk factors in organizational communication. *Procedia Technology*, *19*, 1053–1058. doi:10.1016/j.protcy.2015.02.150

Cervo, A. L., & Bervian, P. A. (2002). *Metodologia científica. 5.* São Paulo: Pearson Prentice Hall.

Cesario, E., Lackovic, M., Talia, D., & Trunfio, P. (2013). Programming knowledge discovery workflows in service-oriented distributed systems. *Concurrency and Computation*, *25*(10), 1482–1504. doi:10.1002/cpe.2936

Cevik, A. A., Aksel, G., Akoglu, H., Eroglu, S. E., Dogan, N. O., & Altunci, Y. A. (2016). Social media, FOAMed in medical education and knowledge sharing: Local experiences with international perspective. *Turkish Journal of Emergency Medicine*, *16*(3), 112–117. doi:10.1016/j.tjem.2016.07.001 PMID:27857988

Chadha, A., & Kumar, S. (2015). Extension to the K-Means Algorithm for Automatic Generation of Clusters for Mixed Datasets. *International Conference on Advances on Computers, Communication and Electronic Engineering* (pp. 480-485). University of Kashmir.

Chadha, A., & Kumar, S. (2016). An Efficient K-Means Algorithm and its Benchmarking against other Algorithms. *International Journal of Grid and Distributed Computing*, *9*(11), 119–132. doi:10.14257/ijgdc.2016.9.11.10

Chadha, A., & Kumar, S. (2016). Extension of K-Modes Algorithm for Generating Clusters Automatically'. *International Journal of Information Technology and Computer Science.*, *8*(3), 51–57. doi:10.5815/ijitcs.2016.03.06

Chaiklin, S., Hedegaard, M., & Jensen, U. (Eds.), *Activity Theory and Social Practice: Cultural-Historical Approaches*. Aarhus, Denmark: Aarhus University Press.

Chandler, A. D. Jr. (1962). *Strategy and Structure: Chapters in the History of the Industrial Enterprise*. Cambridge: MIT Press.

Chan, S. H. J., & Lai, H. Y. I. (2017). Understanding the link between communication satisfaction, perceived justice and organizational citizenship behavior. *Journal of Business Research*, *70*, 214–223. doi:10.1016/j.jbusres.2016.08.017

Charreire, S., & Durieux, F. (2003). Explorer et tester: Deux voies pour la recherche. In *Méthodes de Recherche en Management*. Paris, France: Dunod.

Chatterjee. (2014). Managing Constraints and Removing obstacles to Knowledge Management. *The IUP Journal of Knowledge Management*, *12*(4), 24–39.

Chen, W. (2010, June 25). A brief history of data governance. *Magnitude*. Retrieved from http://magnitude.com/blog/a-brief-history-of-data-governance/

Chen, C.-J., Huang, J.-W., & Hsiao, Y.-C. (2010). Knowledge management and Innovativeness: The Role of Organizational Climate and Structure. *International Journal of Manpower*, *31*(8), 848–870. doi:10.1108/01437721011088548

Cheng, Y., & Ying, X. (2009). Application of Data Mining Technology in E-Commerce. In *International Forum on Computer Science-Technology and Applications* (pp. 291-293). IEEE.

Chen, L., Gable, G. G., & Hu, H. (2013). Communication and organizational social networks: A simulation model. *Computational & Mathematical Organization Theory*, *19*(4), 460–479. doi:10.100710588-012-9131-0

Chen, L., Holsapple, C. W., Hsiao, S. H., Ke, Z., Oh, J. Y., & Yang, Z. (2017). Knowledge-dissemination channels: Analytics of stature evaluation. *Journal of the Association for Information Science and Technology*, *68*(4), 911–930. doi:10.1002/asi.23725

Chen, P. T., & Kuo, S. C. (2017). Innovation resistance and strategic implications of enterprise social media websites in Taiwan through knowledge sharing perspective. *Technological Forecasting and Social Change*, *118*, 55–69. doi:10.1016/j.techfore.2017.02.002

Chen, Y., Vanhaverbeke, W., & Du, J. (2016). The interaction between internal R&D and different types of external knowledge sourcing: An empirical study of Chinese innovative firms. *R & D Management*, *46*(S3), 1006–1023. doi:10.1111/radm.12162

Cheung, Y., & Jia, H. (2013). Categorical-and-Numerical-Attribute Data Clustering based on a Unified Similarity Metric without Knowing Cluster Number. *Pattern Recognition*, *46*(8), 2228–2238. doi:10.1016/j.patcog.2013.01.027

Cheung, Y.-M. (2003). K*-Means: A New Generalized K-Means Clustering Algorithm. *Pattern Recognition Letters*, *24*(15), 2883–2893. doi:10.1016/S0167-8655(03)00146-6

Chiang, H. H., Han, T.-S., & Chuang, J.-S. (2011). The Rellationship between High Commitment HRM and Knowledge Sharing Behaviour and its Mediators. *International Journal Of Manpower(Emerald)*, *32*(5/6), 604–622. doi:10.1108/01437721111158224

Chong, M. (2007). The Role of Internal Communication and Training in Infusing Corporate Values and Delivering Brand Promise: Singapore Airlines' Experience. *Corporate Reputation Review*, *10*(3), 201–212. doi:10.1057/palgrave.crr.1550051

Choo & Auster. (1993). Environment Scanning: Acquisition and Use of Information by Managers. Annual Review of Information Science and Technology.

Choo, C. W. (1997). *Organizations as Information-use Systems: A process model of information management.* PrimaVera Working Paper 1997-17, University van Amsterdam.

Choo, C. W. (1998), The Knowing Organization: How Organizations Use Information to Construct Meaning, Create Knowledge and Make decisions. Oxford University Press.

Choo, C. W. (2002). *Environment Scanning as Information Seeking and Organizational Knowing.* PrimaVera Working Paper 2002-01, University van Amsterdam.

Choo, C. W. (1998). *The Knowing Organization: How Organizations Use Information for Construct Meaning, Create Knowledge and Make Decisions.* Oxford Press.

Choo, C. W. (2002). *Information Management for the Intelligent Organization: The Art of Scanning the Environment (3rd ed.).* Medford, NJ: Information Today, Inc.

Choo, C. W. (2003). *A organização do conhecimento: como as organizações usam a informação para criar conhecimento, construir conhecimento e tomar decisões.* São Paulo: SENAC.

Choo, C. W. (2006). *The knowing organization; how organizations use information to construct meaning, create knowledge, and make decisions.* Oxford, UK: Oxford University Press.

Choo, C. W. (2007). Social Use of Information. In *Information Management: Setting the Scene.* Oxford, UK: Elsevier.

Choo, C. W. (2008). *The knowing organization.* Oxford University Press.

Choo, C. W. (2009). Information use and early warnings effectiveness: Perspectives and prospects. *Journal of the American Society for Information Science and Technology*, *60*(5), 1071–1082. doi:10.1002/asi.21038

Chory, R. M., Vela, L. E., & Avtgis, T. A. (2016). Organizational surveillance of computer-mediated workplace communication: Employee privacy concerns and responses. *Employee Responsibilities and Rights Journal*, *28*(1), 23–43. doi:10.100710672-015-9267-4

Chow, W. S., & Lui, K. H. (2003). A Structural Analysis of the Significance of a Set of the Original TQM Measurement Items in Information Systems Function. *Journal of Computer Information Systems.*

Christensen, C. R. (1997). *The Innovator's Dilema: When New Technologies Cause Great Firms to Fail.* Boston: Harvard Business School Press.

Christensen, C. R., Andrews, K. R., Bower, J. L., Hamermesh, G., & Porter, M. E. (1982). *Business Policy: Text and Cases (5th ed.)*. Homewood, IL: Irwin.

Chung, T. R., Liang, T., Peng, C., & Chen, D. (2014). How knowledge creation capabilities lead to competitive advantage. In M. Chilton & J. Bloodgood (Eds.), *Knowledge management and competitive advantage: Issues and potential solutions* (pp. 36–52). Hershey, PA: IGI Global. doi:10.4018/978-1-4666-4679-7.ch003

Ciborra, C. U. (2004). *The Labyrinths of Information: Challenging the Wisdom of Systems*. Oxford, UK: Oxford University Press. doi:10.1093/acprof:oso/9780199275267.001.0001

Clarke, G. (2017, March 2). How data governance is now a strategic boardroom consideration in a data-driven world. *Microsoft Asia News Center*. Retrieved from http://news.microsoft.com/apac/2017/03/02/how-data-governance-is-now-a-strategic-boardroom-consideration-in-a-data-driven-world/

Classificação Decimal Universal. (1997). Edição padrão internacional em língua portuguesa. Brasília: IBICT.

Coadic, L. (1994). *La Science de l'Information*. Paris: Presses Universitaires de France.

Cole, M. (2003). *Cultural psychology: a once and future discipline (6th ed.)*. Cambridge, MA: Harvard University Press.

Congiusta, A., Talia, D., & Trunfio, P. (2008). Using grids for distributed knowledge discovery. In G. Felici & C. Vercellis (Eds.), *Mathematical methods for knowledge discovery and data mining* (pp. 284–298). Hershey, PA: IGI Global. doi:10.4018/978-1-59904-528-3.ch017

Connelly, R., Playford, C. J., Gayle, V., & Dibben, C. (2016). The role of administrative data in the big data revolution in social science research. *Social Science Research*, *59*, 1–12. doi:10.1016/j.ssresearch.2016.04.015 PMID:27480367

Cooney, J. P. (1991). Qual o real valor da informação? *Revista Escola de Biblioteconomia/UFMG, Belo Horizonte*, *20*(2), 176-190.

Corporate Branding. (2007). Sage Publications. Retrieved 6 May 2010 from http://www.sage-ereference.com/organization/Article_n97.html

Correia, M. (1995). O léxico na economia da língua. *Ciência da Informação, Brasília*, *24*(3), 299–307.

Costa, V., & Monteiro, S. (2016). Knowledge processes, absorptive capacity and innovation: A mediation analysis. *Knowledge and Process Management*, *23*(3), 207–218. doi:10.1002/kpm.1507

Cronbach, L. (1951). Coefficient alpha and the internal structure of tests. *Psychometrika*, *16*(3), 297–334. doi:10.1007/BF02310555

Crosby, P. B. (1979). *Quality is free*. New York: McGraw-Hill.

Crossan, M. M., Lane, R. E., & White, R. E. (1999). An Organizational Learning Framework: From Intuition to Institution. *Academy of Management Review*, *24*(3), 522–537.

Crumlish, C., & Malone, E. (2009). *Designing Social Interfaces*. O'Reilly Media.

Cruz-Cunha, M. M., Gonçalves, P., Lopes, N., Miranda, E. M., & Putnik, G. D. (2012). *Handbook of research on business social networking: Organizational, managerial, and technological dimensions* (Vols. 1–2). Hershey, PA: IGI Global. doi:10.4018/978-1-61350-168-9

Cukier, K. (2010, February 25). Data, data everywhere. *The Economist*. Retrieved from http://www.economist.com/node/15557443

Cummings, T. G., & Whorley, C. G. (2009). *Organizational Development and change. Cengage learning.*

Cunningham, J., Seaman, C., & McGuire, D. (2016). Knowledge sharing in small family firms: A leadership perspective. *Journal of Family Business Strategy*, *7*(1), 34–46. doi:10.1016/j.jfbs.2015.10.002

Cyert, J. J., & March, J. G. (1970). *Processus de Décision dans L'entreprise, Dunod, d'alerte précoce*. Colloque VSST 2001, Paris, France.

Cyert, J. J., & March, J. G. (1963). *A Behavioral Theory of Firm*. Prentice Hall.

Cyert, J. J., Richard, M., & March, J. G. (1992). *A Behavioral Theory of the Firm (2nd ed.)*. Oxford, UK: Blackwell.

Daft, R. L., & Huber, G. P. (1987). How Organizations Learn: A Communication Framework. *Research in the Sociology of Organizations*, *5*, 1–36.

Daft, R. L., Sormunen, J., & Parks, D. (1984). Chief Executive Scanning Environmenal Caracteristics and Company Performance: An Empirical Study. *Strategic Management Journal*, *9*(2), 123–139. doi:10.1002mj.4250090204

Daft, R. L., & Weick, K. E. (1984). Toward a Model of Organization as Interpretation Systems. *Academy of Management Review*, *9*(2), 284–295.

Dahlberg, I. (1978). Teoria do conceito. *Ciência da Informação, 7*(2), 101-107.

Dai, Y. S., Gao, Q., Fan, Z., & Kang, R. G. (2007). User perceived quality of online social information services: from the perspective of knowledge management. *Proceedings of the 2007 IEEE IEEM*, 482-486. 10.1109/IEEM.2007.4419236

DalleMule, L., & Davenport, T. (2017, May-June). What's your data strategy? *Harvard Business Review*. Retrieved from http://hbr.org/2017/05/whats-your-data-strategy

Dallman, M. F. (2010). Stress-induced obesity and the emotional nervous system. *Trends in Endocrinology and Metabolism*, *21*(3), 159–165. doi:10.1016/j.tem.2009.10.004 PMID:19926299

Dasí, A., Pedersen, T., Gooderham, P. N., Elter, F., & Hildrum, J. (2017). The effect of organizational separation on individuals' knowledge sharing in MNCs. *Journal of World Business*, *52*(3), 431–446. doi:10.1016/j.jwb.2017.01.008

Dataversity. (2012, January 19). *Data governance demystified - Lessons from the trenches*. Retrieved from http://www.dataversity.net/data-governance-demystified-lessons-from-the-trenches/

Davenport, D. W. (1998). Successful Knowledge Management Projects. *Sloan Management Review*, *39*(2), 43–57.

Davenport, T. H., & Markus, M. L. (1999). Rigor versus Relevance Revisited: Response to Benbasat and Zmud. *MIS Quarterly, 23*(1), 19-23.

Davenport, T. H., & Prusak, L. (1997). *Information Ecology*. Oxford University Press.

Davenport, T. H., & Prusak, L. (1997). *Information Ecology: Mastering the Information and Knowledge Environment*. Oxford University Press.

Davenport, T. H., & Prusak, L. (1998). *Working Knowledge*. Boston: Harvard Business School Press.

Davenport, T. H. (1998). *Ecologia da Informação: por que só a tecnologia não basta para o sucesso na era da informação. 6*. São Paulo: Futura.

Davenport, T. H., & Prusak, L. (1998). *Conhecimento empresarial: como as organizações gerenciam o seu capital intelectual*. Rio de Janeiro: Campus.

Davenport, T. H., & Prusak, L. (1998). *Working Knowledge*. Boston: Harvard Business School Press.

Davenport, T. H., & Prusak, L. (2001). *Ecologia da informação*. São Paulo: Futura.

Davidson, B., Lee, Y. W., & Wang, R. (2004). Developing Data Production Maps: Meeting patient discharge data submission requirements. *International Journal of Healthcare Technology and Management*, *6*(2), 223–240. doi:10.1504/IJHTM.2004.004978

Dávila-Torres, J., González-Izquierdo, J. J., & Barrera-Cruz, A. (2015). Panorama de la obesidad en México. *Obesity in Mexico, 53*(2), 240. Retrieved from http://search.ebscohost.com/login.aspx?direct=true&db=edb&AN=101483297&lang=es&site=eds-live

de Almeida, P. P. (2012). *Variações Sobre o Trabalho Moderno. Coleção Questões de Partida*. Lisboa: Editora Mundos Sociais.

de Chernatony, L., & Riley, F. (1998). Modelling the components of the brand. *European Journal of Marketing*, *32*(11/12), 1074–1090. doi:10.1108/03090569810243721

De Kermadec, Y. (2001). *Innover grâce au brevet: Une révolution déclenchée par internet*. Paris, France: INSEP Consulting Éditions.

de Long, D. W., & Fahey, L. (2000). Diagnosing cultural barriers to knowledge management. *The Academy of Management Perspectives*, *14*(4), 113–127. doi:10.5465/AME.2000.3979820

De Pablo, C. (2007). *Estrés y hostigamiento laboral* (2nd ed.). Jaén: Formación Alcalá.

Dees, J. G. (1998). The Meaning of 'Social Entrepreneurship'. *Innovation*, 1–5.

Deleu, R., & Clendon, J. (2015). *Government capability model*. Wellington: New Zealand Department of Internal Affairs - Office of the Government Chief Information Officer.

Delone, W. H., & Mclean, E. R. (1992). Information systems success: The quest for the dependent variable. *Information Systems Research*, *3*(1), 60–95. doi:10.1287/isre.3.1.60

Deltour, F., & Roussel, C. S. (2010). L'intégration des connaissances par les équipes projets ERP: deux études de cas en PME. *Système d'information et management, 15*(1), 98-34.

Deming, W. E. (1990). Qualidade: a revolução da administração. Marques Saraiva.

Denervaud, I., & Chatin, O. (2009). *L'ADN de l'entreprise innovante, comment accroître les capacités créatives des entreprises*. Paris, France: Pearson Education.

Dervin, B., & Nilan, M. (1986). Information needs and uses. *Annual Review of Information Science & Technology*, *21*, 3–32.

Dhamdhere, S. N. (2015). Knowledge Management Model for Higher Educational Institutes. *Journal of Commerce and Management Thought*, *6*(1), 130–161. doi:10.5958/0976-478x.2015.00010.5

Dharmendra & Lokesh. (2010). Genetic k-Means clustering algorithm for Mixed Numerical and Categorical Datasets. *International Journal of artificial Intelligence and Applications*, *1*(2), 23-28.

Dias, E. J. W. (2002). O específico da ciência da informação. In *O campo da ciência da informação: gênese, conexões e especificidades* (pp. 87–99). João Pessoa: Editora Universitária.

Dicle, Ü., & Okan, R. Y. (2015). The Relationship between Organizational Structure and Organizational Learning in Turkish Automotive R&D Companies. *International Journal of Managerial Studies and Research*, 62-71.

Djeflat, A. (2007). Les nouvelles exigences de la PME dans une économie fondée sur la connaissance, cas des entreprises maghrébines, TIC & développement. *La Revue Électronique*. Retrieved from http://www.tic.ird.fr

Douglas, M. (1986). *How Institutions Think*. London: Routledge.

Dowbor, L. (2010). *Informação para a cidadania e o desenvolvimento sustentável*. Retrieved from http://dowbor.org/09propriedadeintelectual7out.doc

Downes, S. (2012). *Connectivism and Connective Knowledge. Essays on meaning and learning networks*. National Research Council Canada.

Drucker, P. (1969). The Pratice of Management. Pan Books, Ltd.

Drucker, P. (1970). Entrepreneurship in Business Enterprise. *Journal of Business Policy*, (1), 3-12.

Drucker, P. (2000). Management Challenges for the 21 st Century. Edição Portuguesa da Livraria Civilização Editora.

Drucker, P. (1985). *Innovation and entrepreneurship: practice and principles*. New York: Harper & Row.

Dube, L., & Pare, G. (1999). Les technologies de l'information et l'organisation à l'ère du virtuel. *Gestion*, *24*(2), 14–22.

Dubois, J. (1973). *Dicionário de lingüistica*. São Paulo: Cultrix.

Dudezert, A., Dugage, M. R., Chauvin, F., Martin, F., Lemieux, E., Boisserpe, P., ... Bruillon, E. (2012). Le knowledge management au cœur de la stratégie d'entreprise. *Documentaliste - Sciences de l'Information*, *49*(2), 26–43. doi:10.3917/docsi.492.0026

Duffy, J. (2000). Knowledge Management: To be or not to be? *Information Management Journal*, *34*(1), 64–67.

Duncan, R. B. (1972). Characteristics of Organizational environments and Perceived Environment Uncertaint. *Administrative Science Quarterly*, *17*(3), 313–327. doi:10.2307/2392145

Dunford, R. (2000). Key Challenges in the search for the effective management of knowledge in management consulting firms. *Journal of Knowledge Management, 4*(4), 295-302.

Dupuich-Rabasse, F. (2008). *Management et gestion des compétences*. Paris, France: L'Harmattan.

Durand, T. (2000). L'alchimie de la compétence. *Revue Française de Gestion*, *127*(1), 84–102.

Dutton, J. E., Fahey, L., & Narayana, V. K. (1983). Toward understanding strategic Issue Diagnosis. *Strategic Management Journal*, *4*(4), 307–323. doi:10.1002mj.4250040403

Edelwich, J., & Brodsky, A. (1980). *Burnout: Stages of disillusionment in the helping professions. Nueva York*. Human Sciences Press.

Elfring, T., & Volberda, H. W. (1998). New Directions in Strategy: Beyond Fragmentation. Sage.

Elkjaer, B. (1999). In Search of a Social Learning Theory. In M. Easterby-Smith, J. Burgoyne, & L. Araujo (Eds.), *Organizational learning and the learning organization* (pp. 75–91). London: Sage. Retrieved from http://citeseerx.ist.psu.edu/viewdoc/download?doi=10.1.1.474.1667&rep=rep1&type=pdf

Emmanuel, O. N. (2007). Student Academic Performance Monitoring and Evaluation Using Data Mining Techniques. In *Fourth Congress of Electronics, Robotics and Automotive Mechanics* (pp. 354-359). IEEE.

Empson, L. (2001). Fear of exploitation and fear of contamination: Impediments to knowledge transfer in mergers between professional service firms. *Human Relations*, *54*(7), 839–862. doi:10.1177/0018726701547003

Engeström, Y. (1999). Activity theory and individual and social transformation. In Y. Engeström, R. Miettinen, & R. L. Punamaki (Eds.), *Perspectives on Activity Theory* (pp. 19–38). Cambridge, UK: Cambridge University Press. doi:10.1017/CBO9780511812774.003

English, L. P. (2001), Information quality management: The next frontier. *ASQ's Annual Quality Congress Proceedings*, 529-533.

English, L. P. (2005). Information Quality: Critical ingredient for national security. *Journal of Database Management*, *16*(1), 18–32. doi:10.4018/jdm.2005010102

Epinard, P. (1999). *L'investissement immatériel, cœur d'une économie fondée sur le savoir*. Paris, France: CNRS Éditions.

Erceau, J. (1997). Subir l'information ou partager la connaissance. *L'Expansion Management Review*, 104-110.

Ercilia, S.M. (2000). Artigo aceito para publicação em 24-10-2000. *Ci. Inf.*, *29*(3), 50-70.

Ermine, J. L., Moradi, M., & Brunel, S. (2012). Une chaîne de valeur de la connaissance. International Management, 16, 29-40. doi:10.7202/1012391ar

Ermine, J. L. (2003). *La gestion des connaissances*. Paris, France: Lavoisier.

Evrad, Y., Pras, B., & Roux, E. (2003). *Market, études et recherches en marketing* (3rd ed.). Paris, France: Dunod.

Fantuzzo, J., & Culhane, D. P. (Eds.). (2015). *Actionable intelligence: Using integrated data systems to achieve a more effective, efficient, and ethical government*. New York: Springer. doi:10.1057/9781137475114

Fehr, D. (2017). Costly communication and learning from failure in organizational coordination. *European Economic Review*, *93*, 106–122. doi:10.1016/j.euroecorev.2017.01.006

Fei Gao, M. L. (2008). Knowledge, Management, and Knowledge Management in Business Operations. *Journal of Knowledge Management (Emerald)*, *12*(2), 3–17. doi:10.1108/13673270810859479

Feldman, M. (1989). *Order without Design: Information Production and Policy Making*. Stanford, CA: Stanford University Press.

Feldman, M. S., & March, J. G. (1981). Information in Organizations as Signal and Symbol. *Administrative Science Quarterly*, *26*(2), 171–186. doi:10.2307/2392467

Fernandes, S., Mozzicafreddo, J., & Cardoso, G. (2010). *Contributo da Web 2.0 para a inovação nos processos de trabalho nas organizações públicas - Ambiente de trabalho 2.0. Departamento de Ciência Política e Políticas Públicas*. Lisboa: Instituto Universitário de Lisboa.

Ferraresi, A. A., Quandt, C. O., dos Santos, S. A., & Frega, J. R. (2012). Knowledge management and strategic orientation: Leveraging innovativeness and performance. *Journal of Knowledge Management*, *16*(5), 688–701. doi:10.1108/13673271211262754

Ferray, M., & Presque, Y. V. A. (2011). *Management de la connaissance, knowledge management, apprentissage organisationnel et la société de la connaissance* (2nd ed.). Paris, France: Economica.

Ferreira. (1975). *Novo dicionário da língua portuguesa*. Rio de Janeiro: Nova Fronteira.

Ferreira, F., Faria, J., Azevedo, A., & Marques, A. L. (2017). Product lifecycle management in knowledge intensive collaborative environments: An application to automotive industry. *International Journal of Information Management*, *37*(1), 1474–1487. doi:10.1016/j.ijinfomgt.2016.05.006

Ferreira, M. P., Santos, J. C., & Serra, F. A. R. (2010). *The International Entrepreneurial Firms Social Networks. Cadernos Abape, 8*(1), 134–145.

Figueiredo, L.M. (1977). O conceito de relevância e suas implicações. *Ciência da Informação, 6*(2), 75-78.

Figueiredo, N. M. (1994). *Estudos de uso e usuários da informação*. Brasília: IBICT.

Filieri, R., & Willison, R. (2016). Antecedents of knowledge sourcing and reuse from a knowledge repository in the virtual product prototyping: The role of knowledge and system quality dimensions. *Knowledge and Process Management, 23*(2), 147–160. doi:10.1002/kpm.1512

Fiol, C. M., & Lyles, M. A. (1985). Organizational Learning. *Academy of Management Review, 10*(4), 803–813.

Fischer, G. (2002). Beyond 'Couch Potatoes': From Consumers to Designers and Active Contributors. *Firstmonday*. Available at http://firstmonday.org/issu

Fischer, G. (2007). Designing Socio-Technical Environments in Support of Meta-Design and Social Creativity. *Computer Supported Collaborative Learning (CSCL '2007)*. Rutgers University. Retrieved 14/03/2011 from http://l3d.cs.colorado.edu/~gerhard/papers/CSCL-2007.pdf

Fiske, J. (1991). *Introduction to Communication Studies* (2nd ed.). London: Rutledge.

Fong, P. S. (2011). Multidisciplinary project teams. In D. Schwartz & D. Te'eni (Eds.), Encyclopedia of knowledge management (2nd ed.; pp. 1183–1191). Hershey, PA: IGI Global. doi:10.4018/978-1-59904-931-1.ch113

Fonseca, E. N. (1987). Ciência da Informação e prática bibliotecária. *Ciência da Informação, Brasília, 16*(2), 25–127.

Fontcuberta, M. (1993). *La noticia*. Barcelona: Paidós.

Foray, D. (2000). *L'économie de la connaissance (Collection Repères)*. Paris, France: La Découverte.

Foray, D., & Lundvall, B. A. (1996). The knowledge-based economy: From the economics of knowledge to the learning economy. In *Employment and growth in the knowledge-based economy*. Paris, France: The Organisation for Economic Co-operation and Development.

Forbes, R. (2011). El síndrome de burnout: síntomas, causas y medidas de atención en la empresa. *Éxito empresarial, 160*.

Foucault, M. (1997). *A arqueologia do saber*. Rio de Janeiro: Forense.

Foucault, M. (1997). *As palavras e as coisas*. São Paulo: Martins Fontes.

Freitas, H., & Janissek-Muniz, R. (2006). Uma proposta de plataforma para Inteligência Estratégica. Texto indicado ao II Prêmio de Inovação em Inteligência Competitiva da ABRAIC, e recebeu Menção Honrosa. III ENA – Encontro Nacional da ABRAIC. *Anais. Congresso Ibero Americano de Gestão do Conhecimento e Inteligência Competitiva*.

Freitas, A. L. P., Manhães, N. R. C., & Cozendey, M. I. (2006). Emprego do Servqual na avaliação da qualidade de serviços de tecnologia da informação: uma análise experimental. In *ENEGEP, 26., 2006. Fortaleza. Anais....* Fortaleza: ENEGEP.

Freudenberger. (1998). *Desgaste profesional: burnout personalidad y salud percibida*. Empleo, estrés y salud.

Furquim, T. (2004). Fatores motivadores de uso de site web: Um estudo de caso. *Ciência da Informação, 33*(1), 48–54. doi:10.1590/S0100-19652004000100006

Gackowski, Z. J. (2005), Operations quality of data and information: teleological operations research-bases approach, call for discussion. In *International Conference on Information Quality*. Cambridge, MA: MIT.

Gaimon, C., Hora, M., & Ramachandran, K. (2017). Towards building multidisciplinary knowledge on management of technology: An introduction to the special issue. *Production and Operations Management*, *26*(4), 567–578. doi:10.1111/poms.12668

Galbraith, B., Cleland, B., Martin, S., Wallace, J., Mulvenna, M., & McAdam, R. (2013). Engaging user communities with eParticipation technology: Findings from a European project. *Technology Analysis and Strategic Management*, *25*(3), 281–294. doi:10.1080/09537325.2013.764986

Gandomi, A., & Haider, M. (2015, April). Beyond the hype: Big data concepts, methods, and analytics. *International Journal of Information Management*, *35*(2), 137–144. doi:10.1016/j.ijinfomgt.2014.10.007

Gan, G., Ma, C., & Wu, J. (2007). *Data clustering: Theory, Algorithms and Applications*. SIAM: Society for Industrial and Applied Mathematics. doi:10.1137/1.9780898718348

Gan, G., Wu, J., & Yang, Z. (2009). A genetic fuzzy k-Modes algorithm for clustering categorical data. *Expert Systems with Applications: An International Journal*, *36*(2), 1615–1620. doi:10.1016/j.eswa.2007.11.045

Garvey, W. D. (1979). *Communication: the essence of science*. Oxford, UK: Pergamon Press.

Gelle, E., & Karhu, K. (2003). Information Quality for Strategic Technology Planning. *Industrial Management & Data Systems*, *103*(8), 633–643. doi:10.1108/02635570310497675

George, D., & Mallery, P. (2003). SPSS for Windows step by step: A Simple Guide and Reference. 11.0 Update (4th ed.). Boston: Allyn & Bacon.

Gestal, J. (2003). *Riesgos laborales del personal sanitario (3rd ed.)*. Madrid: McGraw Hill Interamericana.

Giddens, A. (1984). *The Constitution of Society*. Cambridge, UK: Polity Press.

Gil Monte, P. R., & Peiro, J. M. (1997). *Desgaste psíquico en el trabajo: El síndrome de Quemarse*. Madrid: Síntesis Psicológica.

Gil, A. C. (2002). *Como elaborar projetos de pesquisa. 4*. São Paulo: Atlas.

Gilchrist, A. (2009). *The well-connected community. A networking approach to community development*. Bristol, UK: The Policy Press. doi:10.1332/policypress/9781847420565.001.0001

Gill, J. S. (2003). *The Managers Organizational Learning*. Mumbai: Jaico Publishing Hse.

Gil-Monte, P. (2008). El síndrome de quemarse por el trabajo (*burnout*) como fenómeno transcultural. *Información psicológica*, 91-92. Retrieved from http://www.uv.es/unipsico/pdf/Publicaciones/Articulos/01_SQT/2007_08_Gil_Monte.pdf

Gil-Monte, P. R. (2002). Validez Factorial de la adaptación al español de Maslach Burnout Inventory Genereal Survey. *Salud Pública de México*, *44*(1), 33–40. doi:10.1590/S0036-36342002000100005 PMID:11910717

Ginman, M. (1989), Quality information, and information for quality. In *Information quality definitions and dimensions: Proceedings of a NORDINFO Seminar*. Royal School of Librarianship.

Giri, V. N., & Kumar, B. P. (2010). Assessing the impact of organizational communication on job satisfaction and job performance. *Psychological Studies*, *55*(2), 137–143. doi:10.100712646-010-0013-6

Goh, S. C. (2002). Managing Effective Knowledge Transfer: An Integrative Framework and Some Practice Implications. *Journal of Knowledge Management, 6*(1), 23-30.

Gold, A., Malhotra, A., & Segars, A. (2001). Knowledge management: An organizational capabilities perspective. *Journal of Management Information Systems*, *18*(1), 185–214. doi:10.1080/07421222.2001.11045669

Gómez, M. N. G. (2000). Metodología de pesquisa no campo da Ciencia da informação. *DataGramaZero, 1*(6).

Goodhue, D. L. (1995). Understanding user evaluations of information systems. *Management Science*, *4*(12), 1827–1844. doi:10.1287/mnsc.41.12.1827

Gorini, A., & Pravettoni, G. (2011). An overview on cognitive aspects implicated in medical decisions. *European Journal of Internal Medicine*, *22*(6), 547–553. doi:10.1016/j.ejim.2011.06.008 PMID:22075278

Gorry, G. A., & Monton, H. S. S. (1989). A Framework for Management Information System. *MIT*, *30*, 49–61.

Gotkin, Z. (2012, October 17). America's innovative companies are going flat [Blog post]. Retrieved from http://www.huffingtonpost.com/zev-gotkin/corporate-hierarchy-work_b_1962345.html

Granovetter, M. (1973). The strength of weak ties. *American Journal of Sociology*, *78*(6), 1360–1380. doi:10.1086/225469

Grant, R. (1998). A Resource-Based Approach to Strategy Analysis – A Practical Framework (3rd ed.). Blackwell Business.

Grant, R. M. (1996). Prospering in dynamically-competitive environments: Organizational capability as knowledge integration. *Organization Science*, *7*(4), 375–387. doi:10.1287/orsc.7.4.375

Grant, R. M. (2003). Strategic Planning in a Turbulent Environment: Evidence from the Oil Majors. *Strategic Management Journal*, *24*(6), 49–517. doi:10.1002mj.314

Grigoriou, K., & Rothaermel, F. T. (2017). Organizing for knowledge generation: Internal knowledge networks and the contingent effect of external knowledge sourcing. *Strategic Management Journal*, *38*(2), 395–414. doi:10.1002mj.2489

Gruber, T.R. (1995). Towards principles for the design of ontologies used for knowledge sharing. *Int. J. Human-Computer Studies*, *43*(5-6).

Guerrero, E., & Vicente, F. (2001). *Síndrome de "Burnout" o desgaste profesional y afrontamiento del estrés en el profesorado*. Cáceres: Universidad de Extremadura.

Guimarães, C. G. (1996). Problematização do conceito "qualidade" da informação. *Perspectivas em Ciência da Informação, Belo Horizonte*, *1*(1), 111–119.

Gurbaxani, V., & Whang, S. (1991). The Impact of Information Systems on Organizations and Markets. *Communications of the ACM*, *34*(1), 59–73. doi:10.1145/99977.99990

Gurteen, D. (1999). Creating a Knowledge Sharing Culture. Knowledge Management Magazine, 2(5).

Haag, M., Duan, Y., & Mathews, B. (2010). The impact of culture on the application of the SECI model. In D. Harorimana (Ed.), *Cultural implications of knowledge sharing, management and transfer: Identifying competitive advantage* (pp. 26–47). Hershey, PA: IGI Global. doi:10.4018/978-1-60566-790-4.ch002

Habib, J. (2010). La dynamique de création de connaissances dans le processus d'innovation: Analyse comparée de quatre études de cas dans le secteur de la santé electronique. *Système d'Information et Management, 15*(4), 93-133. Retrieved from http://aisel.aisnet.org/sim/vol15/iss4/4

Hair, J. F., Black, W. C., Babin, B., Anderson, R. E., & Tatham, R. L. (2006). *Multivariate data analysis* (Vol. 6). Pearson Prentice Hall.

Hambrick, D. C., & Mason, P. A. (1984). Upper Echelons: The Organization as a Reflection of its Top Managers. *Academy of Management Review*, *9*(2), 193–206.

Hansen, M. T. (1999). The search-transfer problem: The role of weak ties in sharing knowledge across organization subunits. *Administrative Science Quarterly*, *44*(1), 82–111. doi:10.2307/2667032

Harkema, S. J., & Browayes, M. J. (2003). Managing innovation successfully: A complex process, *Proceedings of the European Academy of Management (EURAM)*.

Harper, J. (2017, March 1). Disrupting the data landscape again with linked open data. *KMWorld, 26*(3). Retrieved from http://www.kmworld.com/Articles/Editorial/Features/Disrupting-the-data-landscape-again-with-linked-open-data-116493.aspx

Harris, F., & Chernatony, L. D. (2001). Corporate branding and corporate brand performance. *European Journal of Marketing*, *35*(3/4), 441–456. doi:10.1108/03090560110382101

Harris, P. (2007). We the people: The importance of employees in the process of building customer experience. *Journal of Brand Management*, *15*(2), 102–114. doi:10.1057/palgrave.bm.2550123

Harvey, J. T. (2012, October 5). Why government should not be run like a business. *Forbes*. Retrieved from http://www.forbes.com/sites/johntharvey/2012/10/05/government-vs-business/#187a72732a54

Harvey, J. F. (2011). Comment favoriser le partage des connaissances? Le cas des communautés de pratique pilotées. *Revue Internationale de Gestion*, *35*(4), 73–80. doi:10.3917/riges.354.0073

Hatch, M. J. (2000). *Théories des organisations, de l'intérêt des perspectives multiples*. Paris, France: De Boeck Université.

Hatchuel, A., Le Masson, P., & Benoit, W. (2002). De la gestion des connaissances aux organisation orientées conception. *Revue Internationale des Sciences Sociales*, *171*(1), 29–42. doi:10.3917/riss.171.0029

Hau, Y. S., & Kang, M. (2016). Extending lead user theory to users' innovation-related knowledge sharing in the online user community: The mediating roles of social capital and perceived behavioral control. *International Journal of Information Management*, *36*(4), 520–530. doi:10.1016/j.ijinfomgt.2016.02.008

Hayek, F. A. (1945). The Use of Knowledge in Society. *The American Economic Review*, *35*, 519–530.

Hayes, N., & Walsham, G. (1999). Safe Enclaves, Political Enclaves and Knowledge Working. *First International Critical Management Studies Conference*.

Hayes, R. H., Upton, D., & Pisano, G. (2008). Produção, estratégia e tecnologia: Em busca da vantagem competitiva. *The Bookman*.

Higson, C., & Waltho, D. (2009). *Valuing information as an asset, White paper.* London: SAS.

Hislop D. (2013). *Knowledge Management in Organization: A Critical Introduction* (3rd ed.). Oxford University Press.

Hjelmslev, L. (1961). *Prolegômenos a uma teoria da linguagem*. São Paulo: Perspectiva.

Hodgkinson, G. P. (2003). The interface of cognitive and industrial, work and organizational psychology. *Journal of Occupational and Organizational Psychology*, *76*(1), 1–25. doi:10.1348/096317903321208862

Hogart & Makridakis. (1981). Forecasting and Planning: An Evaluation. *Management Science, 27*(2), 115-138.

Holopainen, M., & Toivonen, M. (2012). Weak signals: Ansoff today. *Futures*, *44*(3), 198–205. doi:10.1016/j.futures.2011.10.002

Hong, J. (1999). Structuring for Organizational Learning. *The Learning Organization*, *6*(4), 173–186. doi:10.1108/09696479910280631

Hong, J.-C., & Kuo, C.-L. (1999). Knowledge Management in the Learning Organization. *Leadership and Organization Development Journal*, *20*(4), 207–215. doi:10.1108/01437739910277019

Hooff, B. V. D., & Ridder, J. A. (2004). Knowledge sharing in context: The influence of organizational commitment, communication climate and CMC use on knowledge sharing. *Journal of Knowledge Management*, *8*(6), 117–130. doi:10.1108/13673270410567675

Hopp, W. J., & Lovejoy, W. S. (2013). *Hospital operations: Principles of high efficiency health care*. FT Press.

Hori, M., & Ohashi, M. (2007). Knowledge creation and adaptive collaboration based on XML web services. In G. Putnik & M. Cruz-Cunha (Eds.), *Knowledge and technology management in virtual organizations: Issues, trends, opportunities and solutions* (pp. 292–305). Hershey, PA: IGI Global. doi:10.4018/978-1-59904-165-0.ch014

Hossain, L., Murshed, S. T., & Uddin, S. (2013). Communication network dynamics during organizational crisis. *Journal of Informetrics*, *7*(1), 16–35. doi:10.1016/j.joi.2012.07.006

Hsu, C., & Cai, L. (2009). Brand Knowledge, Trust and Loyalty-A Conceptual Model of Destination Branding. *International CHRIE Conference*, 1-8. doi: 10.1111/1468-5884.00177

Hu, J., & Peyton, L. (2012). A framework for privacy assurance and ubiquitous knowledge discovery in health 2.0 data mashups. In I. Management Association (Ed.), Cyber crime: Concepts, methodologies, tools and applications (pp. 263–283). Hershey, PA: IGI Global. doi:10.4018/978-1-61350-323-2.ch204

Huang, K. T., Lee, Y.W., & Wang, R.Y. (1999). Quality information and Knowledge. Prentice-Hall.

Huang, J. Z., Ng, M. K., Rong, H., & Li, Z. (2005). Automated variable weighting in k-mean type clustering. *IEEE Transactions on Pattern Analysis and Machine Intelligence*, *27*(5), 657–668. doi:10.1109/TPAMI.2005.95 PMID:15875789

Huang, Q., Davison, R. M., Liu, H., & Gu, J. (2008). The impact of leadership style on knowledge-sharing intentions in China. *Journal of Global Information Management*, *16*(4), 67–91. doi:10.4018/jgim.2008100104

Huang, Z. (1997). A Fast Clustering Algorithm to Cluster Very Large Categorical Data Sets in Data Mining. In *Proceeding SIGMOD workshop research issues on data mining and knowledge discovery* (pp. 1–8). Canberra, Australia: ACM.

Huang, Z. (1998). Extensions to the k-Means Algorithm for Clustering Large Data Sets with Categorical Value. *Data Mining and Knowledge Discovery*, *2*(3), 283–304. doi:10.1023/A:1009769707641

Huber, G. P. (1982). Organizational Information Systems: Determinants of their Performance and Behavior. *Management Science*, *28*(2), 135–155. doi:10.1287/mnsc.28.2.138

Huber, G. P. (1991). Organizational learning: The contributing processes and the literatures. *Organization Science*, *2*(1), 88–115. doi:10.1287/orsc.2.1.88

Hung, J.-L., & Gao, Q. (2011). Incorporating Data Mining into Course Evaluation: A Case Study of K-12 Virtual School. *The 11th International DSI and the 16th APDSI Joint Meeting*.

Hung, J.-L., Hsu, Y.-C., & Rice, K. (2012). Integrating Data Mining in Program Evaluation of K-12 Online Education. *Journal of Educational Technology & Society*, *15*(3), 27–41.

Hunt, L., & Jorgensen, M. (2011). Clustering mixed data. *Wiley Interdisciplinary Reviews. Data Mining and Knowledge Discovery*, *1*(4), 352–361. doi:10.1002/widm.33

Hutchins, G. (2011, July 28). Transformational times call for transformational change. *The Guardian*. Retrieved from http://www.theguardian.com/sustainable-business/blog/transformational-change-firms-future-ecosystems-communities

Ikujiro Nonaka, H. T. (1995). *The Knowledge Creating Company: How Japanese Companies Create the Dynamics of Innovation*. New York: Oxford University Press.

Illich, L. (1982). *Le genre vernaculaire*. Editions du Seuil.

Imai & Kaisen. (1992). *La Clefde la competivité japonaise*. Eyrolles.

Ind, N. (2007). *Living the Brand: How to Transform Every Member of Your Organization Into a Brand Champion* (3rd ed.). London: Kogan Page.

Ind, N., & Bjerke, R. (2007). *Branding governance: a participatory approach to the brand building process*. West Sussex, UK: John Wiley & Sons Ltd.

Ingwersen, P. (1992). Information and information science in context. *Libri*, *42*(2), 99–135. doi:10.1515/libr.1992.42.2.99

Institute of Directors in New Zealand. (n.d.). *What is governance?* Retrieved from http://www.iod.org.nz/FirstBoards/What-is-governance

International Labour Organization (ILO). (2016). *Mental Health in the workplace*. Retrieved from http://www.newunionism.net/library/working%20life/ILO%20%20Mental%20Health%20in%20the%20Workplace%20-%202000.pdf

Introna, L. D. (1997). *Management, Information and Power*. MacMillan Press Ltd.

Ipe, M. (2003). Knowledge Sharing on Organizations: A Conceptual Framework. *Human Resource Development Review*, *2*(4), 3370358. doi:10.1177/1534484303257985

Jackson, S., Chuang, C.-H., Harden, E. E., Jiang, Y., & Joseph, J. M. (2006). Toward Developing Human Resource Management Systems for Knowledge Intensive Teamwork. *Research in Personnel and Human Management*, *25*(6), 27–70.

Jacob, R., & Pariat, R. (2002). Savez-vous vraiment ce que vous savez. *Réseau CEFRIO*, *3*(2), 3-7. Retrieved from http://www.cefrio.qc.ca/media/uploader/Reseau_Cefrio-final_2002.pdf

Jain, K. A., & Dubes, C. R. (1988). Algorithms for clustering data. Upper Saddle River, NJ: Prentice-Hall Inc.

Jain, A., Rajavat, A., & Bhartiya, R. (2012). Design, Analysis and Implementation of Modified K- Mean Algorithm for Large Data-set to Increase Scalability and Efficiency. In *Fourth International Conference on Computational Intelligence and Communication Networks* (pp. 627-631). IEEE. 10.1109/CICN.2012.95

Jakobsone, A., Cakula, S., & Florea, M. (2017). Modelling of knowledge sharing for the provision of sustainable cooperation between adult educational institutions and enterprises. *Procedia Computer Science*, *104*, 160–165. doi:10.1016/j.procs.2017.01.095

Jamil & Armando Malheiro. (2013). *Rethinking the Conceptual Base for New Practical Applications in Information Value and Quality*. IGI Global.

Jamil, G., & Armando Malheiro. (2013). *Rethinking the Conceptual Base for New Practical Applications in Information Value and Quality*. IGI Global.

Janissek-Muniz, R, Freitas, H., & Lesca, H. (2007). *A Inteligência Estratégica Antecipativa e Coletiva como apoio ao desenvolvimento da capacidade de adaptação das organizações*. Paper presented at CONTECSI, 4, São Paulo, Brasil.

Janissek-Muniz, R., & Blanck, M. R. M. (2014). *Gestão de sinais fracos, empreendedorismo e incerteza: um ensaio teórico relacional sob a ótica da inteligência*. Paper presented at CONTECSI, 11, São Paulo, Brasil.

Janissek-Muniz, R., Lesca, H., & Freitas, H. (2006). Inteligência Estratégica Antecipativa e Coletiva para Tomada de Decisão. *3rd CONTECSI - International Conference on Information Systems and Technology Management and 11th WCA - World Continuous Auditing Conference.*

Järvenpää, S., & Staples, D. (2000). The use of collaborative electronic media for information sharing: An exploratory study of determinants. *The Journal of Strategic Information Systems*, *9*(2-3), 129–154. doi:10.1016/S0963-8687(00)00042-1

Jennex, M. E. (2013). *Dynamic models for knowledge-driven organizations*. Hershey, PA: IGI Global. doi:10.4018/978-1-4666-2485-6

Jensen, M. D., Ryan, D. H., & Apvian, C. M. (2014). 2013 AHA/ACC/TOS guideline for the management of overweight and obesity in adults: A report of the American College of Cardiology/American Heart Association Task Force on Practice Guidelines and The Obesity Society. *Circulation*, *129*(25), S102–S138. doi:10.1161/01.cir.0000437739.71477.ee PMID:24222017

Jiang, J. J., Klein, G., Tesch, D., & Chen, H. (2003). Closing the user and provider service quality gap: A method for measuring service quality that includes both the user and IS service provider perspectives. *Communications of the ACM*, *46*(2), 72–76. doi:10.1145/606272.606276

Jin-Feng, W., Ming-Yan, C., Li-Jie, F., & Jun-Ju, Y. (2017). The construction of enterprise tacit knowledge sharing stimulation system oriented to employee individual. *Procedia Engineering*, *174*, 289–300. doi:10.1016/j.proeng.2017.01.139

Jing-miao, Z., & Wei-xiao, G. (2008). Application of Association Rules Mining in the System of University Teaching Appraisal. *International Workshop on Education Technology and Training & International Workshop on Geoscience and Remote Sensing*, 26-28.

Jin, H., Wu, T., Liu, Z., & Yan, J. (2009). Application of Visual Data Mining in Higher-education Evaluation System. *First International Workshop on Education Technology and Computer Science*, 101-104. 10.1109/ETCS.2009.285

Juani Swart, N. K. (2003). Sharing Knowledge in Knowledge Intensive Firms. *Human Resource Management Journal*, *13*(2), 60–75. doi:10.1111/j.1748-8583.2003.tb00091.x

Juárez-García, A., Idrovo, A. J., Camacho-Ávila, A., & Placencia-Reyes, O. (2014). Síndorme de burnout en población mexicana: Una revisión sistemática. *Salud Mental*, *37*(2), 159–176. doi:10.17711/SM.0185-3325.2014.020

Juno, J., & Noriega, M. (2004). Los Trastornos Musculoesqueléticos y la Fatiga como Indicadores de Deficiencias Ergonómicas y en la Organización del Trabajo. *Salud de los Trabajadores*, *12*(2), 27-41

Juran, J. M. (1990). *Planejando para a qualidade*. São Paulo: Pioneira.

Kakihara, M., & Sørensen, C. (2002). Exploring Knowledge Emergence: From Chaos to Organizational Knowledge. *Journal of Global Information Technology Management*, *5*(33), 48–66. doi:10.1080/1097198X.2002.10856331

Kalika, M. (2006). *Management et TIC*. Éditions Liaisons.

Kang, K. W., & Rosen, D. E. (2006). Knowledge creation in online communities. In M. Khosrow-Pour (Ed.), *Encyclopedia of e-commerce, e-government, and mobile commerce* (pp. 691–697). Hershey, PA: IGI Global. doi:10.4018/978-1-59140-799-7.ch111

Kärkkäinen, H., Piippo, P., Puumalainen, K., & Tuominen, M. (2001). Assessment of hidden and future customer needs in Finnish business-to-business companies. *R & D Management*, *31*(4), 391–406. doi:10.1111/1467-9310.00227

Kaschig, A., Maier, R., & Sandow, A. (2016). The effects of collecting and connecting activities on knowledge creation in organizations. *The Journal of Strategic Information Systems*, *25*(4), 243–258. doi:10.1016/j.jsis.2016.08.002

Kasemsap, K. (2013a). Innovative human resource practice: A synthesized framework and causal model of leader-member exchange, organizational justice, job satisfaction, and organizational citizenship behavior. *International Journal of e-Education, e-Business, e-Management and e-Learning*, *3*(1), 13–18. doi:10.7763/IJEEEE.2013.V3.185

Kasemsap, K. (2013b). Conceptual framework: Factors affecting performance of pulp and paper mill employees in Thailand. *International Proceedings of Economics Development and Research*, *57*, 133–137. doi:10.7763/IPEDR. 2012. V57. 25

Kasemsap, K. (2013c). Strategic human resource practice: A functional framework and causal model of leadership behavior, job satisfaction, organizational commitment, and job performance. *Journal of Social and Development Sciences*, *4*(5), 198–204.

Kasemsap, K. (2014). The role of social capital in higher education institutions. In N. Baporikar (Ed.), *Handbook of research on higher education in the MENA region: Policy and practice* (pp. 119–147). Hershey, PA: IGI Global. doi:10.4018/978-1-4666-6198-1.ch007

Kasemsap, K. (2016). Applying Lean Production and Six Sigma in global operations. In U. Akkucuk (Ed.), *Handbook of research on waste management techniques for sustainability* (pp. 44–74). Hershey, PA: IGI Global. doi:10.4018/978-1-4666-9723-2.ch003

Kasemsap, K. (2016). The roles of e-learning, organizational learning, and knowledge management in the learning organizations. In E. Railean, G. Walker, A. Elçi, & L. Jackson (Eds.), *Handbook of research on applied learning theory and design in modern education* (pp. 786–816). Hershey, PA: IGI Global. doi:10.4018/978-1-4666-9634-1.ch039

Kasemsap, K. (2017a). Investigating the roles of neuroscience and knowledge management in higher education. In S. Mukerji & P. Tripathi (Eds.), *Handbook of research on administration, policy, and leadership in higher education* (pp. 112–140). Hershey, PA: IGI Global. doi:10.4018/978-1-5225-0672-0.ch006

Kasemsap, K. (2017b). Mastering knowledge management in academic libraries. In B. Gunjal (Ed.), *Managing knowledge and scholarly assets in academic libraries* (pp. 27–55). Hershey, PA: IGI Global. doi:10.4018/978-1-5225-1741-2.ch002

Kasemsap, K. (2017b). The fundamentals of organizational citizenship behavior. In B. Christiansen & H. Chandan (Eds.), *Handbook of research on human factors in contemporary workforce development* (pp. 1–23). Hershey, PA: IGI Global. doi:10.4018/978-1-5225-2568-4.ch001

Kasemsap, K. (2017c). The fundamentals of social capital. In G. Koç, M. Claes, & B. Christiansen (Eds.), *Cultural influences on architecture* (pp. 259–292). Hershey, PA: IGI Global. doi:10.4018/978-1-5225-1744-3.ch010

Kasemsap, K. (2017c). The significance of job satisfaction in modern organizations. In B. Christiansen & H. Chandan (Eds.), *Handbook of research on human factors in contemporary workforce development* (pp. 181–200). Hershey, PA: IGI Global. doi:10.4018/978-1-5225-2568-4.ch008

Kasemsap, K. (2017d). Examining the roles of job satisfaction and organizational commitment in the global workplace. In P. Ordoñez de Pablos & R. Tennyson (Eds.), *Handbook of research on human resources strategies for the new millennial workforce* (pp. 148–176). Hershey, PA: IGI Global. doi:10.4018/978-1-5225-0948-6.ch008

Kasemsap, K. (2017d). Knowledge discovery and data visualization: Theories and perspectives. *International Journal of Organizational and Collective Intelligence*, *7*(3), 56–69. doi:10.4018/IJOCI.2017070105

Kasemsap, K. (2017e). Management education and leadership styles: Current issues and approaches. In N. Baporikar (Ed.), *Innovation and shifting perspectives in management education* (pp. 166–193). Hershey, PA: IGI Global. doi:10.4018/978-1-5225-1019-2.ch008

Kasemsap, K. (2017e). Organizational learning: Advanced issues and trends. In A. Bencsik (Ed.), *Knowledge management initiatives and strategies in small and medium enterprises* (pp. 42–66). Hershey, PA: IGI Global. doi:10.4018/978-1-5225-1642-2.ch003

Kasemsap, K. (2017f). Advocating information system, information integration, and information sharing in global supply chain. In G. Jamil, A. Soares, & C. Pessoa (Eds.), *Handbook of research on information management for effective logistics and supply chains* (pp. 107–130). Hershey, PA: IGI Global. doi:10.4018/978-1-5225-0973-8.ch006

Kasemsap, K. (2018a). Knowledge management: Applications and implications. In A. Gyamfi & I. Williams (Eds.), *Evaluating media richness in organizational learning* (pp. 232–261). Hershey, PA: IGI Global. doi:10.4018/978-1-5225-2956-9.ch012

Kasemsap, K. (2018b). Promoting strategic human resource management, organizational learning, and knowledge management in modern organizations. In M. Khosrow-Pour (Ed.), *Encyclopedia of information science and technology* (4th ed.; pp. 4347–4357). Hershey, PA: IGI Global. doi:10.4018/978-1-5225-2255-3.ch377

Kattan, M. W. (2009). *Encyclopedia of medical decision making* (Vol. 1). Sage. doi:10.4135/9781412971980

Kaur, H., & Wasan, K. (2006). Empirical Study on Applications of Data Mining Techniques in Healthcare. *Journal of Computational Science*, *2*(2), 194–200. doi:10.3844/jcssp.2006.194.200

Keller, K. L. (2003). *Strategic Brand Management: building, measuring and managing brand equity*. Upper Saddle River, NJ: Pearson Education.

Kelloway, E. K., & Barling, J. (2000). Knowledge work as organizational behavior. *International Journal of Management Reviews*, *2*(3), 287–304. doi:10.1111/1468-2370.00042

Kemp, S. (2013, July 18). Big Data in the boardroom. *Dataversity*. Retrieved from http://www.dataversity.net/big-data-in-the-boardroom/

Khan, B. K., Strong, D. M., & Wang, R. Y. (2002). Information quality benckmarks: Product and service performance. *Communications of the ACM*, *45*(4).

Kim, H. (2014). Job conditions, unmet expectations, and burnout in public child welfare workers: How different from other social workers? *Children and Youth Services Review*, *33*(2), 358–367. doi:10.1016/j.childyouth.2010.10.001

Kim, W. C., & Mauborgne, R. A. (1993). Procedural Justice, Attitudes, and Subsidiary Top Management Compliance With Multinationals' Corporate Strategic Decisions. *Academy of Management Journal*, *36*(3), 502–526. doi:10.2307/256590

King, C., & Grace, D. (2008). Internal branding: Exploring the employee's perspective. *Journal of Brand Management*, *15*(5), 358–372. doi:10.1057/palgrave.bm.2550136

King, C., & Grace, D. (2010). Building and measuring employee-based brand equity. *European Journal of Marketing*, *44*(7/8), 938–971. doi:10.1108/03090561011047472

King, D. B. (2005). *Max Wertheimer & Gestalt Theory*. New Brunswick, NJ: Transaction Publisher.

Klein, S., Fabbrini, E., & Romijn, J. A. (2011). Obesity. In Williams Textbook of Endocrinology (12th ed.). Philadelphia, PA: Saunders Elsevier.

Knauf, A. (2010). *Les dispositifs d'intelligence économique, compétences et fonctions utiles à leur pilotage*. Paris, France: L'Harmattan.

Knorr-cetina, K. (1997). Sociality with objects: Social relations in postsocial knowledge societies. *Theory, Culture & Society*, *14*(4), 1–30. doi:10.1177/026327697014004001

Kock, N. (2013). *WarpPLS©4.0 User Manual*. Laredo, TX: ScriptWarp Systems.

Kock, N. (2014). *A note on how to conduct a factor-based PLS-SEM analysis*. Laredo, TX: ScriptWarp Systems.

Kontonasios, K. N., Spyropoulou, E., & De Bie, T. (2012). Knowledge discovery interestingness measures based on unexpectedness. *Wiley Interdisciplinary Reviews: Data Mining and Knowledge Discovery*, *2*(5), 386–399. doi:10.1002/widm.1063

Kwahk, K. Y., & Park, D. H. (2016). The effects of network sharing on knowledge-sharing activities and job performance in enterprise social media environments. *Computers in Human Behavior*, *55*, 826–839. doi:10.1016/j.chb.2015.09.044

Lage, N. (1999). *Linguagem Jornalística*. São Paulo: Ática.

Lage, N. (2005). *A Reportagem: teoria e técnica de entrevista e pesquisa jornalística*. Rio de Janeiro: Record.

Lakoff, G., & Johnson, M. (1980). *Metaphors We Live By*. Chicago: The University of Chicago Press.

Lalic, D., Marjanovic, U., & Lalic, B. (2012). The influence of social networks on communication satisfaction within the organizations. In M. Cruz-Cunha, P. Gonçalves, N. Lopes, E. Miranda, & G. Putnik (Eds.), *Handbook of research on business social networking: Organizational, managerial, and technological dimensions* (pp. 545–566). Hershey, PA: IGI Global. doi:10.4018/978-1-61350-168-9.ch029

Lämmerhirt, D. (2017, February 16). Mapping open data governance models: Who makes decisions about government data and how? [Blog post]. Retrieved from http://blog.okfn.org/2017/02/16/mapping-open-data-governance-models-who-decides-and-how/

Landowski, E. (1992). *A sociedade refl etida*. São Paulo: EDUC/Pontes.

Langdon, M. (1998). La chaîne de la connaissance, stratégie d'entreprise pour Internet (Village ed.). Paris, France: Mondial.

Latour, B. (2010). Networks, Societies, Spheres: Reflections of an Actor-network Theorist. In *International Seminar on Network Theory: Network Multidimensionality in the Digital Age* (pp. 1–18). Los Angeles, CA: Annenberg School for Communication and Journalism.

Latour, B. (2005). *Reassembling the Social – An Introduction to Actor-Network-Theory*. Oxford, UK: Oxford University Press.

Latour, B. (2005). *Reassembling the Social: An Introduction to Actor-Network Theory*. Oxford, UK: Oxford University Press.

Lau, H. C. W., Choy, K. L., Wong, C. W. Y., & Fung, R. Y. K. (2003). A Generic Management Information System for Small and Medium Enterprises. *International Journal Manufacturing Technology and Management*, *5*(1), 162–176. doi:10.1504/IJMTM.2003.002539

Law, K. S., Wong, C.-S., & Mobley, W. H. (1998). Toward a Taxonomy of Multidimensional Constructs. *Academy of Management Review*, *23*(4), 741–755.

Law, W. K., & Woo, M. T. (2003). Quality Control Information Representation Using Object-oriented Data Models. *International Journal of Computer Integrated Manufacturing*, *16*(3), 192–209. doi:10.1080/0951192021000036849

Le Boterf, G. (2002). Mise en place d'une démarche compétence. *Revue de l'Entreprise*, *60*, 41–50.

Le Coadic, Y.-F. (1997), La science de l'information (2nd ed.). Paris: Universitaires de France.

Le Coadic, Y. (2004). *A Ciência da Informação*. Brasília: Briquet de Lemos.

Le Coadic, Y. F. (1998). *Le besoin d'information*. Paris: ADBS Editions.

Le Coadic, Y.-F. (1996). *A ciência da informação*. Brasília: Briquet de Lemos Livros.

Leela, V., Sakthipriya, K., & Manikandan, R. (2013). A Comparative Analysis between K-Mean and Y-Means Algorithms in Fisher's Iris Data Sets. *IACSIT International Journal of Engineering and Technology*, *5*(1), 245–249.

Lee, Y. W., Strong, D. M., Kahn, B., & Wang, R. Y. (2002). Aimq: A methodology for information quality assessment. *Information & Management*, *40*(2), 133–146. doi:10.1016/S0378-7206(02)00043-5

Leibowitz, J. (1999). Key Ingredients to the Success of an Organization's Knowledge Management Strategy. *Knowledge and Process Management*, *6*(1), 37–40. doi:

Leidner, M. A. (1999). *KMS-Emerging views and practices from the field*. Academic Press.

Leidner, D. L., Alavi, M., & Kayworth, T. (2006). The Role of Culture in Knowledge Management: A Case Study of Two Global Firms. *International Journal of e-Collaboration*, *2*(1), 17–40. doi:10.4018/jec.2006010102

Lelis, C., & Mealha, O. (2014). BEODE — Brand Experience Oriented Design Environments. *BrandTrends: Journal of Strategic Communication and Branding*, *6*, 6-18.

Lelis, C., & Mealha, O. (2015). Heuristic for brand artefacts co-design: A computer-mediated proposal. *CoDesign*, *11*(2), 83–98. doi:10.1080/15710882.2015.1054840

Leonardi, P. M. (2017). The social media revolution: Sharing and learning in the age of leaky knowledge. *Information and Organization*, *27*(1), 47–59. doi:10.1016/j.infoandorg.2017.01.004

Lesca, H. (1995). The crucial problem of the strategic probe: The construction of the puzzle. *CERAG, ESA, série Recherche*, *95*(2), 24.

Lesca, H. (2003). *Veille stratégique: la méthode*. L:E:SCAnning®, Editions EMS.

Lesca, H., & Blanco, S. (2002). *Contribution à la capacite d'anticipation des entreprises par la sensibilisation aux signaux faibles*. Paper presented at Congrès International Francophone Sur La Pme, Montreal, Canada.

Lesca, H. (1986). *Systèmes d'Information pour le Management Stratégique de l'Enterprise*. Paris: McGraw-Hill.

Lesca, H. (2001). Veille stratégique: passage de la notion de signal faible à la notion de signe d'alerte précoce. *Actes du colloque VSST*, 1, 98-105.

Lesca, H., & Almeida, F. C. (1994). Administração Estratégica da Informação. *Revista ADM*, *29*(3), 66–75.

Lesca, H., & Lesca, N. (2011). *Weak signals for strategic intelligence anticipation tool for managers*. Hoboken, NJ: Wiley. doi:10.1002/9781118602775

Leszczynska, D., & Lesca, H. (2004). *Veille Stratégique: utilité des « informations de terrain » pour la PME-PMI à la recherche de nouveaux débouchés produit/marché*. Etude d'un cas. Cahier de Recherche CERAG (Grenoble) – IAE (Nice), CERAG UMR 5820 CNRS.

Li, M., & Feng, C. (2010). Overview of Web Mining Technology and its Applications in E Commerce. In *2nd International Conference on Computer Engineering and Technology* (pp. 277-280), Beijing, China: Academic Press.

Li, W. (2008). Modified K-means clustering algorithm. In IEEE Computer Society Congress on Image and Signal Processing (pp. 618-621). IEEE.

Li, Y-H., & Liu, X-L. (2010). Research of data mining based on e-commerce. In *International Conference on Computer Science and Information Technology* (pp. 719-722). IEEE.

Liang, J., Zhao, X., Li, D., Cao, F., & Dang, C. (2012). Determining the Number of Clusters using Information Entropy for Mixed Data. *Pattern Recognition*, *45*(6), 2251–2265. doi:10.1016/j.patcog.2011.12.017

Liao, H., & Ng, M. K. (2009). Categorical Data Clustering with Automatic Selection of Cluster Number. *Fuzzy Information and Engineering*, *1*(1), 5–25. doi:10.100712543-009-0001-5

Lichtenstein, S., Parker, C. M., & Cybulski, M. (2005). Email and knowledge creation: Supporting inquiring systems. In J. Courtney, J. Haynes, & D. Paradice (Eds.), *Inquiring organizations: Moving from knowledge management to wisdom* (pp. 89–108). Hershey, PA: IGI Global. doi:10.4018/978-1-59140-309-8.ch005

Lillrank, P. (2003). The quality of information. *International Journal of Quality & Reliability Management*, *20*(6), 691–703. doi:10.1108/02656710310482131

Lima, L. F. R., Maçada, A. C. G., & Vargas, L. M. (2006). Research into information Quality: a study of the state of the art in IQ and its consolidation. In *International Conference on Information Quality*. Cambridge, MA: MIT.

Lima-marques, M., & Macedo, F. (2005). Arquitetura da informação: base para a gestão do conhecimento. In Gestão da informação e do conhecimento em organizações (pp. 177-192). Academic Press.

Lin, S., Gao, J., & Koronios, A. (2006). The need for a data quality framework in asset management. *Australian Workshop on Information Quality Proceedings*.

Linda Argote, P. I. (2000). Knowledge Transfer: A basis for competitive advantage in firms. *Organizational Behavior and Human Decision Processes*, *82*(1), 150–169. doi:10.1006/obhd.2000.2893

Lin, Y., Wang, Y., & Kung, L. A. (2015). Influences of cross-functional collaboration and knowledge creation on technology commercialization: Evidence from high-tech industries. *Industrial Marketing Management*, *49*, 128–138. doi:10.1016/j.indmarman.2015.04.002

Li, S., & Lin, B. (2006). Accessing information sharing and information quality in supply chain management. *Decision Support Systems*, *42*(3), 1641–1656. doi:10.1016/j.dss.2006.02.011

Li, T., & Chen, Y. (2008). An Improved k-means Algorithm for Clustering Using Entropy Weighting Measures. In *Proceedings of the 7th World Congress on Intelligent Control and Automation* (pp.149-153). IEEE.

Liu, L., & Chi, L. N. (2004). Evolutional data quality: a theory specific view. In *International Conference on Information Quality*. Cambridge, MA: MIT.

Li, X., & Fawcett, T. N. (2014). Clinical decision making on the use of physical restraint in intensive care units. *International Journal of Nursing Sciences*, *1*(4), 446–450. doi:10.1016/j.ijnss.2014.09.003

Li, X., Zhang, J., Zhang, S., & Zhou, M. (2017). A multilevel analysis of the role of interactional justice in promoting knowledge-sharing behavior: The mediated role of organizational commitment. *Industrial Marketing Management*, *62*, 226–233. doi:10.1016/j.indmarman.2016.09.006

Li, Z., Yang, F., & Zhang, D. (2016). The virtual alliance knowledge sharing model and selection strategy. *Procedia Computer Science*, *91*, 276–283. doi:10.1016/j.procs.2016.07.075

Llaneza, J. (2002). *Ergonomía y psicología aplicada: Manual para la formación del especialista*. España: Lex Nova.

Lobach, D., Sanders, G. D., & Bright, T. J. (2012). *Enabling Health Care Decisionmaking Through Clinical Decision Support and Knowledge Management*. Rockville, MD: Agency for Healthcare Research and Quality (US). Available from: https://www.ncbi.nlm.nih.gov/books/NBK97318/

Lohr, S. (2012, February 12). The age of big data. *The New York Times*. Retrieved from http://www.nytimes.com/2012/02/12/sunday-review/big-datas-impact-in-the-world.html

Lopes, I. L. A. S. (2004). Novos paradigmas para avaliação da qualidade da informação em saúde recuperada na web. *Ciência da Informação, 33*(1), 81–90. doi:10.1590/S0100-19652004000100010

Lubit, R. (2001). Tacit Knowledge and Knowledge Management: The keys to Sustainable Competitive Advantage". *Organizational Dynamics, 29*(4), 164–178. doi:10.1016/S0090-2616(01)00026-2

Lui, H., He, H., Dai, B., & Yan, Y. (2006). The K-Prototype Algorithm Of Clustering High Dimensional And Large Scale Mixed Data. *Proceedings of the International Computer Conference on Wavelet Active Media Technology and Information Processing*, 738-743.

Luo, H., Kong, F., & Li, Y. (2006). Clustering mixed data based on evidence accumulation. *Lecture Notes in Computer Science, 4093*, 348–355. doi:10.1007/11811305_38

Lyle, E. R. (2012). Learning organization. *International Journal of Business and Social Science, 3*(6).

Mabey, C., & Zhao, S. (2017). Managing five paradoxes of knowledge exchange in networked organizations: New priorities for HRM? *Human Resource Management Journal, 27*(1), 39–57. doi:10.1111/1748-8583.12106

Mack, M. (1995, September-October). L'organisation apprenante comme système de transformation de la connaissance en valeur. *Revue Française de Gestion, 105*, 43–48.

Madanchian, M., & Taherdoost, H. (2016). Perusing of organizational culture effects on e-mail communication. *Procedia Technology, 22*, 1076–1083. doi:10.1016/j.protcy.2016.01.152

Madnick, S., Wang, R., & Xian, X. (2004). The Desing and Implementation of a Corporate Householding Knowledge Processor to Improve Data Quality. *Journal of Management Systems, 20*(3), 41–69.

Maes, R. (2007). Information management: an integrative perspective. In A. Huizing & E. de Vries (Eds.), *Information Management: Setting the Scene*. London: Elsevier.

Mahoney, J., & Pandian, J. R. (1992). The Resource-Based View Within The Conservation of Strategic Management. *Strategic Management Journal, 13*(5), 363–380. doi:10.1002mj.4250130505

Mair, J., & Martí, I. (2004). *Social Entrepreneurship Research: a Source of Explanation, Prediction, and Delight (No. 546)*. Navarra.

Maisiri, E. (2017). Utilization of indigenous knowledge for competitiveness among curio makers of Matobo National Park, Zimbabwe. In P. Ngulube (Ed.), *Handbook of research on social, cultural, and educational considerations of indigenous knowledge in developing countries* (pp. 202–225). Hershey, PA: IGI Global. doi:10.4018/978-1-5225-0838-0.ch011

Majid, S., & Wey, S. M. (2009). Perceptions and knowledge sharing practices of graduate students in Singapore. *International Journal of Knowledge Management, 5*(2), 21–32. doi:10.4018/jkm.2009040102

Mäkäräinen-Suni, I., & Hong, J. (2011). Ba and communities of practice in research and strategic communities as a way forward. In O. Hernáez & E. Bueno Campos (Eds.), *Handbook of research on communities of practice for organizational management and networking: Methodologies for competitive advantage* (pp. 46–69). Hershey, PA: IGI Global. doi:10.4018/978-1-60566-802-4.ch004

Makridakis, S. (1990). *Forecasting, Planning, and Strategy for the 21st Century.* Free Press.

Maldonado-Macías, A., Camacho-Alamilla, R., Torres, S. G. V., Alcaraz, J. L. G., & Limón, J. (2015). Determination of Burnout Syndrome among Middle and Senior Managers in Manufacturing Industry in Ciudad Juarez. *Procedia Manufacturing, 3*, 6459–6466. doi:10.1016/j.promfg.2015.07.927

Mandke, V. V., & Nayar, M. K. (2004). Quality: The information integrity imperative. *Total Quality Management*, *15*(5), 645–654. doi:10.1080/14783360410001680134

Mangold, W. G., & Miles, S. J. (2007). The employee brand: Is yours an all-star? *Business Horizons*, *50*(5), 423–433. doi:10.1016/j.bushor.2007.06.001

Ma, R., & Huang, Y. C. (2016). Opportunity-based strategic orientation, knowledge acquisition, and entrepreneurial alertness: The perspective of the global sourcing suppliers in China. *Journal of Small Business Management*, *54*(3), 953–972. doi:10.1111/jsbm.12222

March & Simon. (1993). *Organizations (2nd ed.)*. Cambridge: Blackwell.

Marchand, D. (1989), Managing information quality. In *Information quality definitions and dimensions proceedings*. Royal School of Librarianship.

Marchand, D. (1990). Managing Information quality. In I. Wormell (Ed.), *Information quality: definitions and dimensions* (pp. 7–17). London: Taylor Graham.

March, J. G., & Simon, H. A. (1958). *Organizations*. New York, NY: Wiley.

Marewski, J. N., & Gigerenzer, G. (2012). Heuristic decision making in medicine. *Dialogues in Clinical Neuroscience*, *14*(1), 77–89. PMID:22577307

Margit Osterloh, B. S. (2002). Motivation Knowledge Transfer and Organizatinal Forms. *Organization Science*, *11*(5), 538–550. doi:10.1287/orsc.11.5.538.15204

Mariano, S., & Casey, A. (2016, March 11). *The process of knowledge retrieval: A case study of an American High-Technology Research, Engineering and Consulting Company*. Retrieved from http://www2.warwick.ac.uk/fac/soc/wbs/conf/olkc/archive/olkc1/papers/298_mariano.pdf

Marques, G. Q., & Da Silva Lima, M. A. D. (2007). Demandas de usuários a um serviço de pronto atendimento e seu acolhimento ao sistema de saúde. *Revista Latino-americana de enfermagem, 15*(1), 13-19. Retrived from: http://www.scielo.br/pdf/rlae/v15n1/pt_v15n1a03.pdf

Marrau, M. (2009). El síndrome de quemarse por el trabajo (burnout), en el marco contextualizador del estrés laboral. *Fundamentos en humanidades, 19*(1), 167-177.

Martín-Barbero, J. (2009). La educación desde la comunicación. *Eduteka*. Retrieved from http://www.eduteka.org/pdfdir/SaberNarrar.pdf

Martínez-León, M., & Martínez-García, J. A. (2011). The Influence of Organizational Structure on Organizational Learning. *International Journal of Manpower*, *32*(5), 537–566. doi:10.1108/01437721111158198

Martin, R. L., & Osberg, S. (2007). Social Entrepreneurship: The Case for Definition. *Stanford Social Innovation Review*, 28–39. Retrieved from https://www.law.berkeley.edu/php-programs/courses/fileDL.php?fID=7288

Martins, A. T. (2015). *How Personal Mastery can increase Organizational Performance*. Retrieved on 19th march 2017, from http://www.strategicbusinessteam.com/self-improvement-advice/how-personal-mastery-can-increase-organizational-performance/

Martinsons, M. G., Davison, R. M., & Huang, Q. (2017). Strategic knowledge management failures in small professional service firms in China. *International Journal of Information Management*, *37*(4), 327–338. doi:10.1016/j.ijinfomgt.2017.04.003

Masino, G., & Zamarian, M. (2003). Information technology artefacts as structuring devices in organizations: Design, appropriation and use issues. *Interacting with Computers, 15*(5), 693–707. doi:10.1016/S0953-5438(03)00059-6

Maslach, C., & Jackson, S. E. (1981). *MBI: Maslach Burnout Inventory. Manual.* Palo Alto, CA: University of California, Consulting Psychologist Press.

Maslach, C., & Leiter, M. P. (2008). Early predictors of job burnout and engagement. *The Journal of Applied Psychology, 93*(3), 498–512. doi:10.1037/0021-9010.93.3.498 PMID:18457483

Massingham, O., & Al Holaibi, M. (2017). Embedding knowledge management into business processes. *Knowledge and Process Management, 24*(1), 53–71. doi:10.1002/kpm.1534

Matsudaira, Y. (2013). Ethos as enablers of organisational knowledge creation. In I. Management Association (Ed.), Industrial engineering: Concepts, methodologies, tools, and applications (pp. 1749–1765). Hershey, PA: IGI Global. doi:10.4018/978-1-4666-1945-6.ch093

Ma, Y., Liu, B., Wong, K., & Ching, Y. (2000). Targeting the right students using data mining. In *Proceedings of the sixth ACM SIGKDD international conference on Knowledge discovery and data mining* (pp. 457-464). Boston: ACM. 10.1145/347090.347184

Mayer, J. H., Steinecke, N., Quick, R., & Weitzel, T. (2013). More applicable environmental scanning systems leveraging "modern" information systems. *Information Systems and e-Business Management, 11*(4), 507–540. doi:10.100710257-012-0207-7

Mazita, A., & Kamsidi, Z. (2016). A critical review on the effect of knowledge management on the organization performance. Journal of Technical and Vocational Education, 1(2), 20-25.

Mc Kenna, S. D. (1992). A Culture Instrument: Driving Organisational Learning. *Leadership and Organization Development Journal, 13*(6), 24–29. doi:10.1108/EUM0000000001174

McEnally, M., & de Chernatony, L. (1999). The Evolving Nature of Branding: Consumer and Managerial Considerations. *Academy of Marketing Science Review, 2.* Available http://www.amsreview.org/articles/mcena

McGee, J., & Prusak, L. (1994). *Gerenciamento estratégico da informação: aumente a competitividade e a eficiência de sua empresa utilizando a informação como uma ferramenta estratégica. 12.* Rio de Janeiro: Campos.

McHugh, D., Groves, D., & Alker, A. (1998). Managing learning: What do we learn from a learning organization? *The Learning Organization, 5*(5), 209–220. doi:10.1108/09696479810238215

McLaughlin, J. (2016). *Understanding Organizational Culture.* Retrieved from study.com: http://study.com/academy/lesson/what-is-organizational-culture-definition-characteristics.html

McLoughlin, C., & Lee, M. (2007). Social software and participatory learning: Pedagogical choices with technology affordances in the Web 2.0 era. *ASCILITE Singapore 2007.* Retrieved 30/09/2011 from www.ascilite.org.au/conferences/singapore07

Meadows, J. (1990). Science de l'information. *Brises, 16.*

Meadows, J. (1991). Science de l'information. *Brises, 16*(1), 9-13.

Mei-lan, C. (2010). Cluster Analysis and its Application in Student Grants. *Second International Workshop on Education Technology and Computer Science*, 631-634.

Melgosa, J. (1999). Sin Estrés. Editorial Safeliz, S.L.

Mendonça, S., Cardoso, G., & Caraça, J. (2012). The strategic strength of weak signal analysis. *Futures*, *44*(3), 218–228. doi:10.1016/j.futures.2011.10.004

Men, L. R. (2014). Internal reputation management: The impact of authentic leadership and transparent communication. *Corporate Reputation Review*, *17*(4), 254–272. doi:10.1057/crr.2014.14

Mercier, P. A., & Plassard, V. S. (1984). Société digital les nouvelles technologies au future quotidien. Editions du Seuil.

Merz, M., He, Y., & Vargo, S. L. (2009). The evolving brand logic: A service-dominant logic perspective. *Journal of the Academy of Marketing Science*, *37*(3), 328–344. doi:10.100711747-009-0143-3

Michel, J. (2001). Le knowledge management, entre effet de mode et (ré) invention de la roue. *Documentaliste - Sciences de l'Information*, *38*(3-4), 176–186. doi:10.3917/docsi.383.0176

Mick, C. K., Lindsey, G. N., & Callahan, D. (1980). Toward usable user studies. *Journal of the American Society for Information Science*, *31*(5), 347–356. doi:10.1002/asi.4630310506

Miguel, P. A. C. (2007). Estudo de caso na engenharia de produção: Estruturação e recomendações para sua condução. *Revista Produção*, *17*(1), 216–229. doi:10.1590/S0103-65132007000100015

Mikhailov, A. I. (1980). Estrutura e principais propriedades da informação científica. In Ciência da informação ou informática? Rio de Janeiro: Calunga.

Miles & Snow. (1978). *Organizational Strategy, Structure and Process.* McGraw-Hill.

Miles, S. J., & Mangold, W. G. (2004). A conceptualization of the employee branding process. *Journal of Relationship Marketing*, *3*(2-3), 65–87. doi:10.1300/J366v03n02_05

Miles, S. J., Mangold, W. G., Asree, S., & Revell, J. (2011). Assessing the Employee Brand: A Census of One Company. *Journal of Managerial Issues*, *23*(4), 491–507.

Miller, W., & Morris, L. (1999). Fourth generation R&D: Managing knowledge. *Technology and Innovation*. Innovation Labs. Accessed from https:// journals.sagepub.com/doi/abs/10.1177/2394964315627259

Miller, B., Malloy, M. A., Masek, E., & Wild, C. (2001). Towards a framework for managing the information environment. *Information, Knowledge, Systems Management*, *2*(4), 359–384.

Ministério Da Saúde. (2007). *Pesquisa para Saúde Por que pesquisa em Saúde? Textos para tomada de decisão.* Council on Health Research for Development and Global Forum for Health Research. Secretaria de Ciência, Tecnologia e Insumos Estratégicos Departamento de Ciência e Tecnologia, Brasília.

Mintzberg & Quinn. (1991). *The Strategy Process: Concepts, Contexts & Cases.* Prentice Hall.

Mintzberg, H. (1946). *The Rise and Fall of Strategic Planning.* Free Press.

Mintzberg, H. (1977). *Planifier à gauche et gérer à droite.* Harvard-l'Expansion.

Mintzberg, H. (1981). *Organiser l'entreprise: prêt-à-porter ou sur mesure?* Harvard L'Expansion.

Mintzberg, H. (1982). Structure & Dynamique des Organisations. Les éditions d'Organisations.

Mintzberg, H. (1987a). The Strategy Concept: Five Ps for Strategy. *California Management Review, 30*(1), 11-24.

Mintzberg, H., & Waters, J. A. (1983). The Mind of the Strategist. In The Executive Mind. Jossey Bass.

Mintzberg, H., Ahlstre, B., & Lampel, J. (1998). *Strategic Safary: A Guide Tour Througth the Wilds of Strategic Management.* Prentice-Hall.

Mintzberg, H. (1972). Research on Strategy-Making. *Proceedings of the 32nd Annual Meeting of the Academy of Management.*

Mintzberg, H. (1975). The Manager's Job: Folklore and Fact. *Harvard Business Review, 53*, 49–61.

Mintzberg, H. (1978). Patterns in Strategy Formation. *Management Science, 24*(9), 934–948. doi:10.1287/mnsc.24.9.934

Mintzberg, H. (1978). Strategy-making in Three Modes. *California Management Review, 16*(2), 44–53. doi:10.2307/41164491

Mintzberg, H. (1979). *The Structuring of Organizations: A Synthesis of the Research.* Englewood Cliffs, NJ: Prentice Hall.

Mintzberg, H. (1980). Structure in 5's: A Synthesis of the Research on Organizational Design. *Management Science, 26*(3), 322–341. doi:10.1287/mnsc.26.3.322

Mintzberg, H. (1987b, July). *Crafting Strategy. Harvard Business Review.*

Mintzberg, H. (1988). *Generic Strategies: Toward a Comprehensive Framework. In Advances in Strategic Management* (Vol. 5, pp. 1–67). Greenwich, CT: Jai Press.

Mintzberg, H. (1989). *Mintzberg on Management: Inside Our Strange World of Organizations.* New York: Free Press.

Mintzberg, H. (1990). Strategy Formation: Schools of Thought. In J. Frederickson (Ed.), *Perspectives on Strategic Management.* Boston: Ballinger.

Mintzberg, H. (1990). The design school: Reconsidering the basic premises of strategic management. *Strategic Management Journal, 11*(3), 171–195. doi:10.1002mj.4250110302

Mintzberg, H. (1991). Learning 1, planning 0 reply to Igor Ansoff. Research notes and communications. *Strategic Management Journal, 12*(6), 463–466. doi:10.1002mj.4250120606

Mintzberg, H. (1991). Strategic Thinking as Seeing. In J. Nasi (Ed.), *Arenas of Strategic Thinking.* Helsinki, Finland: Foundation for Economic Education.

Mintzberg, H. (1994). *The Rise and Fall of Strategic Planning.* New York: Free Press.

Mintzberg, H., & Lampel, J. (1999). Reflexion about the Strategic Process. *Sloan Management Review, 40*(3).

Mintzberg, H., & McHugh, A. (1985). Strategies Formation in Adhocracy. *Administrative Science Quarterly, 30*(2), 160–197. doi:10.2307/2393104

Mintzberg, H., Quinn, J. B., & Ghoshal, S. (1999). *The Strategy Process: Concepts, Contexts e Cases* (2nd ed.). Prentice Hall Europe.

Mintzberg, H., Raisinghani, D., & Thêorét, A. (1976). The Structure of Unstructured Decision Processes. *Administrative Science Quarterly, 21*(2), 246–275. doi:10.2307/2392045

Mintzberg, H., & Waters, J. A. (1982). Tracking Strategy in an Entrepreneurial Firm. *Academy of Management Journal, 25*(3), 465–499. doi:10.2307/256075

Mintzberg, H., & Waters, J. A. (1984). R*esearching the Formation of Strategies: The History of Canadian Lady 1939-1976*. Englewood Cliffs, NJ: Prentice-Hall.

Mintzberg, H., & Waters, J. A. (1999). Of Strategies, Deliberate and Emergent. *Strategic Management Journal*, *6*(257), 252–272.

Mitrofan, N., & Bulborea, A. (2013). The role of organizational communication in structuring interpersonal relationships. *Procedia: Social and Behavioral Sciences*, *76*, 511–515. doi:10.1016/j.sbspro.2013.04.155

Moghavvemi, S., Sharabati, M., Paramanathan, T., & Rahin, N. M. (2017). The impact of perceived enjoyment, perceived reciprocal benefits and knowledge power on students' knowledge sharing through Facebook. *International Journal of Management Education*, *15*(1), 1–12. doi:10.1016/j.ijme.2016.11.002

Mohamad, B., Bakar, H. A., Halim, H., & Ismail, A. R. (2014). Corporate communication management (CCM) and organisational performance: A review of the current literature, conceptual model and research propositions. *Procedia: Social and Behavioral Sciences*, *155*, 115–122. doi:10.1016/j.sbspro.2014.10.266

Moles, A. A. (1974). *Sociodinâmica da cultura*. São Paulo: Perspectiva.

Montiel, O., Ramírez, A., Esparza, V. M., & Guerrero, A. (2014). Relatos de vida de gerentes de producción en la industria maquiladora de Cd. Juárez, México. *Global Conference on Business & Finance Proceedings*, *9*(1), 1700-1709. Retrieved from http://ezproxy.uacj.mx/login?url=http://search.ebscohost.com/login.aspx?direct=true&db=bth&AN=94260555&lang=es&site=eds-live Moreno

Moore, L. (2007). Brands. In *Encyclopedia of Business Ethics and Society*. Thousand Oaks, CA: Sage Publications. Retrieved 6 May 2010 from http://www.sage-ereference.com/ethics/Article_n88.html

Moran, P., & Ghoshal, S. (1999). Markets, Firms, and the Process of Economic Development. *Academy of Management Review*, *24*(3), 390–412.

Moreira, J. A., Costa, P. M., & Vieira, C. P. (2016). Navegar na web: as redes sociais como espaços de comunicação, partilha de conhecimento e de promoção de competências de aprendizagem. In P. Dias, D. Moreira, & A. Quintas-Mendes (Eds.), *Práticas e Cenários de Inovação em Educação Online* (pp. 99–126). Lisbon: Universidade Aberta.

Moreno, B., Rodríguez, R., & Escobar, E. (2001). La evaluación del burnout profesional factorialización del MBI-GS. Un análisis preliminar. *Ansiedad y Estrés*, *7*, 69–78.

Moresi, E. A. D. (2011). Delineando o valor do sistema de informação de uma organização. *Ciência da Informação*, *29*(1), 14-24. Retrieved from http://www.scielo.br/pdf/ci/v29n1/v29n1a2.pdf

Morgan, L. (2017, March 21). 3 data governance challenges today's companies face. *InformationWeek*. Retrieved from http://www.informationweek.com/big-data/3-data-governance-challenges-todays-companies-face/a/d-id/1328449

Morgan, G. (1996). *Imagens da Organização*. São Paulo: Atlas.

Morgan, G., Bergamini, C. W., & Coda, R. (2010). *Imagens da organização*. São Paulo: Atlas.

Morin, E., & Le Moigne, J.-L. (2000). *A Inteligência da complexidade*. São Paulo: Peirópolis.

Morris, T., & Empson, L. (1998). Organization and Expertise: An Exploration of Knowledge Bases and the Management of Accounting and Consulting Firms. *Accounting, Organizations and Society*, *23*(5-6), 609–624. doi:10.1016/S0361-3682(98)00032-4

Mort, G. S., Weerawardena, J., & Carnegie, K. (2003). Social entrepreneurship: Towards conceptualization. *International Journal of Nonprofit and Voluntary Sector Marketing*, *8*(1), 76–88. doi:10.1002/nvsm.202

Mostafa, S.P. (1996). Ciência da informação: uma ciência, uma revista. *Ciência da Informação*, *25*(3).

Motta, P. (2012). *Formulação de políticas e definição de objetivos: Imposições do contexto administrativo. In Gestão em Saúde*. Rio de Janeiro: Guanabara Koogan.

Mott, J. (2010). Envisioning the Post-LMS Era: The Open Learning Network. *EDUCAUSE Quarterly*, *33*(1), 1–8. Retrieved from http://er.educause.edu/articles/2010/3/envisioning-the-postlms-era-the-open-learning-network

Mowday, R. T., Steers, R. M., & Porter, L. W. (1979). The measurement of organizational commitment. *Journal of Vocational Behavior*, *14*(2), 224–247. doi:10.1016/0001-8791(79)90072-1

Mruthyunjaya, H. C. (2011). *Knowledge Management*. New Delhi: PHI.

Müeller, S. P. M. (1985). O ensino de biblioteconomia no Brasil. *Ciência da Informação, 14*(1), 3–15.

Muhammed, S., Doll, W. J., & Deng, X. (2013). Impact of knowledge management practices on task knowledge: An individual level study. In M. Jennex (Ed.), *Dynamic models for knowledge-driven organizations* (pp. 282–301). Hershey, PA: IGI Global. doi:10.4018/978-1-4666-2485-6.ch017

Mulgan, G., Tucker, S., Ali, R., & Sanders, B. (2007). Social Innovation: what is it, why it matters and how can be accelerated. London: Academic Press.

Mulgan, G. (2006). The Process of Social Innovation. *Innovations: Technology, Governance, Globalization, 1*(2), 145–162. doi:10.1162/itgg.2006.1.2.145

Muñoz Torres, J. R. (1997). Aproximación al concepto de Información Periodística Especializada. In *Estudios sobre información periodística especializada*. Valencia: Fundación Universitaria San Pablo C.E.U.

Murteira, Mendes, & Martins. (2001). *Serviços Informacionais e transição para a economia do conhecimento em Portugal*. IDEG/ISCTE, estudo realizado para o GEPE do Ministério da Economia.

Naija, Y., Chakhar, S., Blibech, K., & Robbana, R. (2008). Extension of Partitional Clustering Methods for Handling Mixed Data. In *International Conference on Data Mining Workshops* (pp. 257-266). IEEE. 10.1109/ICDMW.2008.85

Nakayama, H. (1986). Tradução e adaptação de tesauros. *Ciência daInformação, 15*(1), 5-25.

Narang, S. K., Kumar, S., & Verma, V. (2017). Knowledge discovery from massive data streams. In A. Singh, N. Dey, A. Ashour, & V. Santhi (Eds.), *Web semantics for textual and visual information retrieval* (pp. 109–143). Hershey, PA: IGI Global. doi:10.4018/978-1-5225-2483-0.ch006

Nardi, B. A., Whittaker, S., & Schwarz, H. (2002). Networkers and their activity in intentional networks. *Computer Supported Cooperative Work, 11*(1/2), 205–242. doi:10.1023/A:1015241914483

Nassim, B. (2011). Investigating the impact of knowledge management factors on new product development performance. In M. Jennex (Ed.), *Global aspects and cultural perspectives on knowledge management: Emerging dimensions* (pp. 210–226). Hershey, PA: IGI Global. doi:10.4018/978-1-60960-555-1.ch014

Natarajan, T., Balasubramaniam, S. A., & Srinivasan, T. (2017). Relationship between Internal Branding. *Employee Brand and Brand Endorsement., 12*, 95–110. doi:10.5539/ijbm.v12n1p95

Naumann, F., & Rolker, C. (1996). *Assessment methods for information quality criteria*. German Research Society. Retrieved from http://www.hiqiq.com/quality.html

Navimipour, N. J., & Charband, Y. (2016). Knowledge sharing mechanisms and techniques in project teams: Literature review, classification, and current trends. *Computers in Human Behavior, 62*, 730–742. doi:10.1016/j.chb.2016.05.003

Nbr ISO 8402. (1994). Gestão da qualidade e garantia da qualidade.

Nehmy, R. M. Q. (1996). *Leitura epistemológico-social da qualidade da informação. 1996. Dissertação (Mestrado em Ciências da Informação)*. Belo Horizonte: Escola de Ciência da Informação, Universidade Federal de Minas Gerais.

Nehmy, R. M. Q., & Paim, I. (1998). A desconstrução do conceito de qualidade da informação. *Ciência da Informação, 27*(1), 36–45. doi:10.1590/S0100-19651998000100005

Neto, R. D. C. A. (2002). *Gestão do conhecimento em organizações*. Curitiba: Saraiva.

Neumann, G. (2011). The Changing Role of Knowledge in Companies: How to Improve Business Performance Through Knowledge. *The Electronic Journal of Knowledge Management, 9(1)*, 73–84.

Neumeier, M. (2006). *The brand gap*. Berkeley, CA: New Riders.

Neus, A. (2001). Managing information quality in virtual communities of practice. In *International Conference on Information Quality*. Cambridge, MA: MIT.

Nevanpera, N. J., Hopsu, L., Kuosma, E., Ukkola, O., Uitti, J., & Laitinen, J. H. (2012). Occupational burnout, eating behavior, and weight among working women. *The American Journal of Clinical Nutrition, 95*(4), 934–943. doi:10.3945/ajcn.111.014191 PMID:22378728

Newman, M. (1985). Managerial Access to Information: Strategies for Prevention and Promotion. *Journal of Management Studies, 22*(2), 193–212. doi:10.1111/j.1467-6486.1985.tb00072.x

Ngah, R., & Ibrahim, A. R. (2016, March 11). *The Effect of Knowledge Sharing on Organizational Performance in Small and Medium Enterprises*. Retrieved from kmice.cms: http://www.kmice.cms.net.my/ProcKMICe/KMICe2010/Paper/PG467_472.pdf

Ngah, R., Tai, T., & Bontis, N. (2016). Knowledge management capabilities and organizational performance in roads and transport authority of Dubai: The mediating role of learning organization. *Knowledge and Process Management, 23*(3), 184–193. doi:10.1002/kpm.1504

Nikoi, E., & Boateng, K. (2014). *Collaborative communication processes and decision making in organizations*. Hershey, PA: IGI Global. doi:10.4018/978-1-4666-4478-6

Nonaka & Takeuchi. (1995). The Knowledge-creating Company: How Japanese Companies Create the Dynamics of Innovation. New York: Oxford University Press.

Nonaka, I. (1994, February). A dynamic theory of organizational knowledge creation. Organization Science, 5(1), 14-37. doi:1047-7039/94/0501/0014

Nonaka, I., & Takeuchi, H. (1995). *The Knowledge Creating Company*. Oxford, UK: Oxford University Press.

Nonaka, I., & Takeuchi, H. (1995). *The knowledge-creating company - how japanese companies create the dynamics of innovation*. New York: Oxford University Press.

Nonaka, I., & Takeuchi, H. (1995). *The Knowledge-creating Company*. New York: Oxford University Press.

Nonaka, I., & Takeuchi, H. (1997). *Criação de conhecimento na empresa: como as empresas japonesas geram a dinâmica da inovação*. Rio de Janeiro: Campus.

Nordbotten, S. (2010). The use of administrative data in official statistics – past, present and future – with special reference to the Nordic countries. In *Official Statistics – Methodology and Applications in Honour of Daniel Thorburn*. Stockholm: Stockholm University. Retrieved from http://www.nordbotten.com

Normann, R. (1977). *Management for Growth*. Wiley.

O'Brien, J. A. (2004). *Sistemas de informação e as decisões gerenciais na era da internet. 2*. São Paulo: Saraiva.

OECD. (2015). *Fiscal Sustainability of Health Systems: Bridging Health and Finance Perspectives*. Paris: OECD Publishing.

Olaisen, J. (1989). Information quality factors and the cognitive authority of electronic information. In I. Wormell (Ed.), *Information quality definitions and dimensions: Proceedings of a Nordinfo Seminar, Royal School of Librarianship* (pp. 91–121). Copenhagen: Taylor Graham.

Olaisen, J., & Revang, O. (2017). Working smarter and greener: Collaborative knowledge sharing in virtual global project teams. *International Journal of Information Management*, *37*(1), 1441–1448. doi:10.1016/j.ijinfomgt.2016.10.002

Oleto, R. R. (2003). *A qualidade da informação na percepção do usuário em diferentes contextos informacionais. Tese (Doutorado)*. Universidade Federal de Minas Gerais, Escola de Ciência.

Oleto, R. R. (2006). Percepção da qualidade da informação. *Ciência da Informação*, *35*(1), 57–62. doi:10.1590/S0100-19652006000100007

Oliveira, D. P. R. (1992). *Sistemas de Informações Gerenciais: Estratégias e táticas operacionais. 8*. São Paulo: Atlas.

Oliveira, D. P. R. (2002). *Sistemas, organização e métodos: uma abordagem gerencial* (13th ed.). São Paulo: Editora Atlas.

Oltra, V. (2005). Knowledge management effectiveness factors: The role of HRM. *Journal of Knowledge Management*, *9*(4), 70–86. doi:10.1108/13673270510610341

Omar, M. K., Dahalan, N. A., & Yusoff, Y. H. M. (2016). Social media usage, perceived team-efficacy and knowledge sharing behaviour among employees of an oil and gas organisation in Malaysia. *Procedia Economics and Finance*, *37*, 309–316. doi:10.1016/S2212-5671(16)30130-7

Organización Mundial de la Salud – OMS Europa. (2015). *Mental health and well-being at the workplace- protection and inclusion in challenging times*. Retrieved from http://www.euro.who.int/__data/assets/pdf_file/0018/124047/e94345.pdf

Organización Mundial de la Salud – OMS. (2010). *Health impact of psychosocial, hazards at work: an overview*. Retrieved from http://whqlibdoc.who.int/publications/2010/9789241500272_eng.pdf

Osmo, A. A. (2012). *Processo gerencial. In Gestão em saúde* (pp. 127–137). Rio de Janeiro: Guanabara Koogan.

Ou, C. X. J., Davison, R. M., & Wong, L. H. M. (2016). Using interactive systems for knowledge sharing: The impact of individual contextual preferences in China. *Information & Management*, *53*(2), 145–156. doi:10.1016/j.im.2015.09.007

Owrang, O. M. M. (2009). Discovering quality knowledge from relational databases. In J. Erickson (Ed.), *Database technologies: Concepts, methodologies, tools, and applications* (pp. 238–256). Hershey, PA: IGI Global. doi:10.4018/978-1-60566-058-5.ch018

Oyateru, D. (2011). *The Learning Organization and Competitive Advantage: A study of The service sector*. Retrieved from http://trap.ncirl.ie/567/1/Dupe's_ThesisEditied_version_

Oyemomi, O., Liu, S., Neaga, I., & Alkhuraiji, A. (2016). How knowledge sharing and business process contribute to organizational performance: Using the fsQCA approach. *Journal of Business Research*, *69*(11), 5222–5227. doi:10.1016/j.jbusres.2016.04.116

Paillard, S. (Ed.). (2002). Les indicateurs de l'économie de la connaissance. Commissariat général du plan: Service du Developpement Technologique et Industrie. La documentation française.

Paim, I. (1998). A desconstrução do conceito de "qualidade da informação". *Ciência da Informação, Brasília*, *27*(1), 36–45.

Paim, I., & Nehmy, R.M.Q. (1998). Questões sobre a avaliação da informação: Uma abordagem inspirada em Giddens. *Perspectivas em Ciência da Informação, Belo Horizonte*, *3*(1), 81–95.

Paim, I., & Nehmy, R. M. Q. (1996). Problematização do conceito "Qualidade" da Informação. *Perspectivas em Ciência da Informação, Belo Horizonte*, *1*(1), 111–119.

Pal, S. (2012). Mining Educational Data Using Classification to Decrease Dropout Rate of Students. *International Journal of Multidisciplinary Sciences and Engineering*, *3*(5), 35–39.

Panda, S., Sahu, S., Jena, P., & Chattopadhyay, S. (2012). Comparing Fuzzy-C Means and K-Means Clustering Techniques: A Comprehensive Study. *Advances in Intelligent and Soft Computing*, *166*, 451–460. doi:10.1007/978-3-642-30157-5_45

Pankaj Madan, S. K. (2010). Contribution of Knowledge Management Practices in Creating Sustainable Competitive Advantage for Business Schools in India. *Journal of Information and Knowledge Management*, *9*(4), 387–397. doi:10.1142/S0219649210002760

Parasuraman, A., Zeithaml, V. A., & Berry, L. L. (1985). A conceptual model of services quality and its implication for future research. *Journal of Marketing*, *49*(4), 41–50. doi:10.2307/1251430

Parasuraman, A., Zeithaml, V. A., & Berry, L. L. (1988). Servqual: A multiple-item scale for measuring consumer perceptions of service quality. *Journal of Retailing*, *64*(1), 12–40.

Park, R. E. (2008a). A história natural do jornal. In A era glacial do jornalismo: teorias sociais da imprensa (vol. 2). Porto Alegre: Sulina.

Park, R. E. (2008b). A notícia como forma de conhecimento: um capítulo dentro da sociologia do conhecimento. In *A era glacial do jornalismo: teorias sociais da imprensa* (Vol. 2, pp. 51–70). Porto Alegre: Sulina.

Pedler, M., Burgoyne, J., & Boydell, T. (1991). The Learning Company. A Strategy for Sustainable Development. McGraw-Hill.

Pelleg, D., & Moore, A. (1999). Accelerating Exact K-Means Algorithms with Geometric Reasoning. In *Proceedings of the fifth ACM SIGKDD International Conference on Knowledge Discovery and Data Mining* (pp. 277-281). Pittsburgh, PA: ACM. 10.1145/312129.312248

Penrose, E. (1959). Les principes du management des ressources fondées sur le savoir. *Revue Française de Gestion*, *105*, 70–75.

People Measures. (n.d.). *Capability frameworks: A source of competitive advantage*. Retrieved from http://static1.squarespace.com/static/5248dad5e4b0dcb066334568/t/528021 1be4b03df6782bb316/1384128795517/People+Measures+-+Capability+Frameworks.pdf

Pfeffer, J., & Salancik, G. R. (1978). *The External Control of Organizations: A resource Dependence Perspective*. Harper & Row, Nova Iorque.

Phillips, W., Lee, H., Ghobadian, A., O'Regan, N., & James, P. (2015). Social Innovation and Social Entrepreneurship: A Systematic Review. *Group & Organization Management*, *40*(3), 428–461. doi:10.1177/1059601114560063

Phills, J. A., Deiglmeier, K., & Miller, D. T. (2008). Social Innovation. *Stanford Social Innovation Review*, 34–43.

Pinheiro, L., & Loureiro, J. (1995). Traçados e limites da ciência da informação. *Ciência da informação*, *24*(1).

Pink, B. (2010). *Quality management of statistical processes using quality gates, Information Paper 1540.0*. Canberra: Australian Bureau of Statistics.

Pipino, L. L., Yang, W., & Wang, R. Y. (2002). Data quality assessment. *Communications of the ACM*, *45*(4), 211–218. doi:10.1145/505248.506010

Pires, M. G., & Marcondes, R. C. (2004). Conhecimento, Inovação e Competência em Organizações Financeiras: Uma análise sob o ponto de vista de Gestores de Bancos. RAC, Edição especial, 61-78.

Pitta, A. (1994). *Hospital: dor e morte como ofício*. Hucitec.

Pitt, L. F., Watson, R., Berthon, P., Wynn, D., & Zinkhan, G. (2006). The Penguin's Window: Corporate Brands From an Open-Source Perspective. *Journal of the Academy of Marketing Science*, *34*(2), 115–127. doi:10.1177/0092070305284972

Porter, M. (1980). *Competitive Strategy: Techniques for Analysing Industries and Competitors*. Free Press.

Porter, M. (1986). Changing Patterns of International Competition. *California Management Review*.

Porter, M. (1979, March). *How Competitive Forces Shape Strategy. Harvard Business Review*.

Porter, M. (1981). The Contributions of Industrial Organizations to Strategic Management. *Academy of Management Review*, *6*(4), 609–620.

Porter, M. (1982). *Choix stratégique et concurrence*. Paris: Economica.

Porter, M. (1984). *Vantagem Competitiva (5th ed.)*. Editora Campos.

Porter, M. (1985). *Competitive Advantage: Creating and Sustaining Superior Performance*. New York: The Free Press.

Porter, M. (1987). *From Competitive Advantage to Corporate Strategy*. Harvard Business Review, Maio-Junho.

Porter, M. (1990). *The Competitive Advantage of Nations*. New York: Free Press. doi:10.1007/978-1-349-11336-1

Porter, M. (1996, November). What Is Strategy? *Harvard Business Review*, 61–64. PMID:10158475

Porter, M. (1999). *Competição: Estratégias Competitivas Essenciais (2nd ed.)*. Editora Campos.

Porter, M., & Millar, V. (1985, July). How Information Gives You Competitive Advantage. *Harvard Business Review*, 149–160.

Powell, W. W. (1990). Neither markets nor hierarchy: Network forms of organisation. *Research in Organizational Behavior*, *12*, 295–336.

Prahalad & Hamel. (1990). The Core Competence of the Corporation. *Harvard Business Review*, *68*(3), 79–91.

Prahalad & Hamel. (1994). *Competing for the Future, Breakthrough Strategies for Seizing Control of Yor Industry and Creating the Markets of Tomorrow*. Harvard Business School.

Prahalad, Barlett, Hamel, Stalk Jr., Mintzberg, Ohmae … Levit. (1999). *Estratégia - A Busca da Vantagem Competitiva* (6th ed.). Harvard Business Review.

Prahalad, C. K., & Ramaswamy, V. (2004). The co-creation experiences: The next practice in value creation. *Journal of Interactive Marketing*, *18*(3), 5–14. doi:10.1002/dir.20015

Prahalad, C., & Betis, R. A. (1986). The Dominant Logic: A New Linkage Between Diver sity and Performance. *Strategic Management Journal*, *7*(6), 485–501. doi:10.1002mj.4250070602

Prax, J. Y. (2012). *Manuel du knowledge management, mettre en réseau les hommes et les savoirs pour créer de la valeur* (3rd ed.). Paris, France: Dunod.

Preece, J. (2000). *Online Communities: designing usability, supporting sociability*. West Sussex, UK: John Wiley & Sons.

Proper, K. I., Koppes, L. J., Meijer, S., & Bemelmans, J. E. (2013). The Association Between Body Mass Index Status and Sick Leave and the Role of Emotional Exhaustion—A Mediation Analysis Among a Representative Sample of Dutch Employees. *Journal of Occupational and Environmental Medicine*, *55*(10), 1213–1218. doi:10.1097/JOM.0b013e31829f2f5c PMID:24064779

Prusak, L. (1998). *Conhecimento Empresarial: como as organizações gerenciam o seu capital intelectual*. Rio de Janeiro: Campus.

Prusak, L., & McGee, J. (1994). *Gerenciamento estratégico da informação*. Rio de Janeiro: Campus.

Pugh, D. S., Hickson, D. J., & Turner, C. (1968). Dimensions of Organization Structure. *Administrative Science Quarterly*, *13*(1), 65–105. doi:10.2307/2391262

Punjaisri, K., & Wilson, A. (2007). The role of internal branding in the delivery of employee brand promise. *Journal of Brand Management*, *15*(1), 57–70. doi:10.1057/palgrave.bm.2550110

Punjaisri, K., & Wilson, A. (2011). Internal branding process: Key mechanisms, outcomes and moderating factors. *European Journal of Marketing*, *45*(9/10), 1521–1537. doi:10.1108/03090561111151871

Putnam, L. L. (1983). The Interpretative Perspective: An Alternative to Functionalism. In L. L. Putnam & M. E. Pacanowsky (Eds.), Communication and Organizations: An Interpretative Approach. Sage Publications.

Putz, P., & Arnold, P. (2001). Communities of Practice: Guidelines for the design of online seminars in higher education. *Education Communication and Information*, *1*(2), 181–195. doi:10.1080/14636310120091922

Quesada Pérez, M. (1998). *Periodismo Especializado*. Madrid: Ediciones Internacionales Universitárias.

Quinn, J. B. (1982). Managing Strategic Incrementally. *Omega, The International Journal of Management Science, 10*(6), 613-627.

Quinn, R. E., & Cameron, K. S. (2005). *Diagnosing and Changing Organizational Culture: Based on the Competing Values Framework*. John Wiley and Sons.

Racheline, P. (1999). Les hébreux et l'entreprise apprenante. *L'Expansion Management Review*, 120-126.

Rahimli. (2012). Knowledge Management and Competitive advantage. Information and Knowledge Management, 2(7).

Rajagopal, K., Brinke, D. J., Van Bruggen, J., & Sloep, P. B. (2012). Understanding personal learning networks: Their structure, content and the networking skills needed to optimally use them. *First Monday*, *17*(1). doi:10.5210/fm.v17i1.3559

Ramirez, R. (1999). *Pour une nouvelle conception de la création de valeur: L'art de l'entreprise globale. In Guide de la mondialisation* (pp. 108–113). Paris, France: Les Echos.

Rascão, J. (2012). Novas Realidades na Gestão e na Gestão da Informação. Editora, Sílabo, Lda.

Rascão, J. (2012). Novas Realidades na Gestão e na Gestão da Informação. Sílabo, Lda.

Rasula, J., Vuksic, B. V., & Stemberger, I. M. (2012). The Impact of Knowledge Management on Organizational *Performance. Economic and Business Review*, *14*(2), 147–168.

Razak, N. A., Pangil, F., Zin, M. L. M., Yunus, N. A. M., & Asnawi, N. H. (2016). Theories of knowledge sharing behavior in business strategy. *Procedia Economics and Finance*, *37*, 545–553. doi:10.1016/S2212-5671(16)30163-0

Reddy, M., Jagannatha, V., & Kavitha, B. (2012). Clustering the Mixed Numerical and Categorical Dataset using Similarity Weight and Filter Method. *International Journal of Database Theory and Application*, *5*(1), 121–133.

Rehder, B. (2003). Categorization as causal reasoning. *Cognitive Science*, *27*(5), 709–748. doi:10.120715516709cog2705_2

Reichwald, R., Möslein, K., & Piller, F. (2008). Creating Value Interactively — Challenges for Company Management. Bloomington, IN: iUniverse, Inc.

Reige, A. (2005). Three-dozen knowledge -sharing barriers managers must consider. *Journal of Knowledge Management, 9*(3), 18-35.

Reix, R. (1990). L'impact organisationnel des nouvelles technologies de l'information. *Revue Française de Gestion*, *77*, 100–106.

Reix, R. (1995). Savoir tacite et savoir formalisé dans l'entreprise. *Revue Française de Gestion*, *105*, 17–28.

Richards, I., Foster, D., & Morgan, R. (1998). Brand Knowledge Management: Growing Brand Equity. *Journal of Knowledge Management*, *2*(1), 47–54. doi:10.1108/13673279810800762

Richet, J. (2016). Internal communication failure in times of change. In A. Goksoy (Ed.), *Organizational change management strategies in modern business* (pp. 289–300). Hershey, PA: IGI Global. doi:10.4018/978-1-4666-9533-7.ch014

Rick, T. (2014, August 16). Constant change is the new normal [Blog post]. Retrieved from http://www.torbenrick.eu/blog/business-improvement/is-constant-change-the-new-normal/

Rivera, J. (2013). Estrés laboral y sus repercusiones. *Revista Mexicana de Anestesiología*, *36*(3), 173–175.

Robins, S. P. (1989). *Organization Behaviour, Concepts, Controversies and Applications*. New Delhi: Prentice-Hall.

Rodrigues, P. P., Gama, J., & Lopes, L. (2010). Knowledge discovery for sensor network comprehension. In A. Cuzzocrea (Ed.), *Intelligent techniques for warehousing and mining sensor network data* (pp. 118–135). Hershey, PA: IGI Global. doi:10.4018/978-1-60566-328-9.ch006

Roehl-Anderson, J. M. Y., & Bragg, S. M. (1996). Del Manual Controller. Functions, procedures y responsibilities. Deusto.

Rossel, P. (2011). Beyond the obvious: Examining ways of consolidating early detection schemes. *Technological Forecasting and Social Change*, *78*(3), 375–385. doi:10.1016/j.techfore.2010.06.016

Rossel, P. (2012). Early detection, warnings, weak signals and seeds of change: A turbulent domain of futures studies. *Futures*, *44*(3), 229–239. doi:10.1016/j.futures.2011.10.005

Russel, B. (2012). *Human Knowledge- Its scope and limits*. London: George Allen & Unwin Ltd.

Sabaté, F. T. (1989). *Fundamentos de Economia de la Empresa (2nd ed.)*. Barcelona: Librería Hispano Americana.

Sacchetti, S., & Campbell, C. (2014). Creating Space for Communities: Social Enterprise and the Bright Side of Social Capital. *Journal of Entrepreneurial and Organizational Diversity*, 32–48.

Safa, N. S., & Solms, R. V. (2016). An information security knowledge sharing model in organizations. *Computers in Human Behavior*, *57*, 442–451. doi:10.1016/j.chb.2015.12.037

Salazar, A., & Vergara, L. (2008). Knowledge discovery from e-learning activities. In F. García-Peñalvo (Ed.), *Advances in e-learning: Experiences and methodologies* (pp. 173–198). Hershey, PA: IGI Global. doi:10.4018/978-1-59904-756-0.ch010

Salomi, G. G. E., Miguel, P. A. C., & Abackerli, A. J. (2005). Servqual x Servperf: Comparação entre instrumentos de avaliação da qualidade de serviços internos. Gestão & Produção, 12(2), 279-293.

Sandhawalia, B. S., & Dalcher, D. (2011). Developing knowledge management capabilities: A structured approach. *Journal of Knowledge Management*, *2*(15), 313–328. doi:10.1108/13673271111119718

San, O. M., Huynh, V., & Nakamori, V. (2004). An Alternative Extension of the *k*-Means Algorithm for Clustering Categorical Data. *International Journal of Applied Mathematics and Computer Science*, *14*(2), 241–247.

Santos, F. M. (2012). A Positive Theory of Social Entrepreneurship. *Journal of Business Ethics*, *111*(3), 335–351. doi:10.100710551-012-1413-4

Saracevic, T. (1992). Information Science: origin, evolution and relations. In *Conceptions of library and information science. Proceedings of the international conference for the celebration of 20th anniversary of the Departament os Information Studies*. University of Tampere.

Saracevic, T. (1992). Information Science: origin, evolution and relations. In *Conceptions of library and information science. Proceedings of the international conference for the celebration of 20th anniversary of the Department of Information Studies*. University of Tampere.

Saracevic, T. (1996). Ciência da informação: Origem, evolução e relações. *Perspectivas em Ciência da Informação, Belo Horizonte*, *1*(1), 41–62.

Say, J.-B. (1841). *Traité D'Économie Politique ou Simple exposition de la manière dont se forment, se distribuent et se consomment les richesses*. Paris: Institut Coppet.

Scarbrough, H. (2003). Knowledge management, HRM and the innovation process. *International Journal of Manpower*, *24*(5), 501–516. doi:10.1108/01437720310491053

Scarbrought, H., Swan, J., Newell, S., & Hislop, D. (2000). *Innovation processes and the management of knowledge, knowledge management: Concepts and controversies*. Coventry, UK: University of Warwick.

Schaffers, H., Brodt, T., Pallot, M., Prinz, W., & Instituut, T. (2006). *The Future Workspace. Perspectives on Mobile and Collaborative Working*. Holanda: MOSAIC.

Schaufeli, W. B., & Enzmann, D. (1998). *The burnout companion to study and practice: A critical analisys*. Padstow, UK: Taylor & Francis.

Schaufeli, W. B., Leiter, M. P., Maslach, C., & Jackson, S. E. (1996). The Maslach Burnout Inventory-General Survey. In C. Maslach, S. E. Jackson, & M. P. Leiter (Eds.), *Maslach Burnout Inventory*. Palo Alto, CA: Consulting Psychologis Press.

Schiuma, G. (2012). Managing knowledge for business performance improvement. *Journal of Knowledge Management*, *4*(16), 515–522. doi:10.1108/13673271211246103

Schoeffler, S. (1980). *Nine Basic Findings on Business Strategy*. Cambridge: The Strategic Planning Institute.

Schoeffler, S., Buzzell, R. D., & Heany, D. E. (1974, March). Impact of Strategic Planning on Profit Performance. *Harvard Business Review*, 137–145.

Schoemaker, P. J. H., & Day, G. S. (2009). How to make sense of weak signals. *MIT Sloan Management Review*, *50*(30), 81–89.

Schultz, M., & Hatch, M. J. (2003). The Cycles of Corporate Branding: The case the LEGO company. *California Management Review*, *46*(1), 6–26. doi:10.2307/41166229

Schultz, M., & Hatch, M. J. (2006). *A cultural perspective on corporate branding - The case of LEGO Group*. Oxon, UK: Routledge.

Schultz, M., Hatch, M. J., & Ciccolella, F. (2006). *Brand Life in Symbols and Artifacts: the LEGO Company*. Mahwah, NJ: Lawrence Erlbaum.

Schumpeter, J. (1950). *Capitalisme, Socialisme et Démocratie* (3rd ed.). Harper & Row.

Schumpeter, J. (1959). History of Economic Analysis. Oxford University Press.

Schumpeter, J. (1934). *The Theory of Economic Performance*. Cambridge, MA: Harvard University Press.

Schumpeter, J. (1942), *Capitalisme, Socialisme et Démocratie*. Reedição, Payot.

Schumpeter, J. (1947). The Creative Response in Economic History. *The Journal of Economic History*, *7*, 149–159. doi:10.1017/S0022050700054279

Schumpeter, J. (1963). *Teoria del desenvolvimiento económico*. Academic Press.

Schumpeter, J. A. (1934). *The Theory of Economic Development*. Cambridge, MA: Harvard University Press.

Schumpeter, J. A. (1949). *Theory of Economic Development*. Cambridge, MA: Harvard University Press.

Schware, R. (2005). *E-Development: From excitement to effectiveness*. Washington, DC: Banque Mondiale. doi:10.1596/0-8213-6442-1

Seleim, A., & Khalil, O. (2009). Knowledge management and organizational performance in the Egyptian software firms. In P. Tiako (Ed.), *Software applications: Concepts, methodologies, tools, and applications* (pp. 2614–2644). Hershey, PA: IGI Global. doi:10.4018/978-1-60566-060-8.ch153

Selltiz, C., Wrightsman, L. S., & Cook, S. W. (1981). *Métodos de Pesquisa nas Relações Sociais.Delineamentos de Pesquisa*. São Paulo: EPU – Editora Pedagógica e Universitária.

Sennett, R. (2007). *The Culture of the New Capitalism*. New Haven, CT: Yale University Press.

Sen, W., Hong, C., & Xiaodong, F. (2013). Clustering Algorithm for Incomplete Data Sets with Mixed Numeric and Categorical Attributes. *International Journal of Database Theory and Application*, *6*(5), 95–104. doi:10.14257/ijdta.2013.6.5.09

Serrano, M. A., Moya, L., & Salvador, A. ((2009). Estrés laboral y salud: Indicadores cardiovasculares y endocrinos. *Anales de Psicología*, *25*, 150-159.

Sève, L. (1969). *Marxisme et théorie de la personalité*. Paris: Editions Sociales.

Shafeeq, A. B. M., & Hareesha, K. S. (2012). Dynamic Clustering of Data with Modified K-Means Algorithm. In *International Conference on Information and Computer Networks* (pp. 221-225). Singapore: Academic Press.

Shahmansouri, S., Esfahan, M. D., & Niki, N. (2013). Explain the Theory of Competitive Advantage and Comparison with Industries based on Advanced Technology. *International Journal of Economy. Management and Social Sciences*, *2*, 841–848.

Shannaon, C. E., & Weaver, W. (1948). The Mathematical Theory of Communication. *Bell System Technical Journal*, *27*, 379-423, 623-656.

Shannaon, C. E., & Weaver, W. (1949). *The Mathematical Theory of Communication*. Chicago: University of Illinois Press.

Shannon, C.E. (1948). A mathematical theory of communication. *Bell System Technical Journal*, *27*, 379-423, 623-656.

Shannon, C. E., & Weaver, W. (1949). *A mathematical theory of communication*. Chicago: University of Illinois Press.

Shapiro, C., & Varian, H. R. (1999). *Information Rules – A Strategic Guide to the Network Economy*. Boston: Harvard Business School Press.

Shapiro, C., & Varian, H. R. (1999). *Information Rules – A Strategic Guide to the Network Economy*. Boston: Harvard Business School Press.

Sharma, A., & Mansotra, V. (2014). Emerging applications of data mining for healthcare management - A critical review. In *International Conference on Computing for Sustainable Global Development* (pp. 377-382). IEEE. 10.1109/IndiaCom.2014.6828163

Sharp, D. (2003). Knowledge Management Today: Challenges and Opportunities. *Information Systems*, 32–37.

Shen, L., & Austin, L. (2017). Communication and job satisfaction. In B. Christiansen & H. Chandan (Eds.), *Handbook of research on human factors in contemporary workforce development* (pp. 201–225). Hershey, PA: IGI Global. doi:10.4018/978-1-5225-2568-4.ch009

Shera, J. (1997). Epistemologia social, semântica geral e biblioteconomia. *Ciência da Informação, 6*(1), 9-12.

Shih, M.-Y., Jheng, J.-W., & Lai, L.-F. (2010). A Two-Step Method for Clustering Mixed Categroical and Numeric Data. *Tamkang Journal of Science and Engineering*, *13*(1), 11–19.

Shukla, R. (2012). Knowledge Management in Higher Education. *International Journal of Reviews, Surveys and Research, 1*(1).

Silva, A. P., & Favaretto, F. (2007). *Sistemas de Informação: um fator competitivopara empresas de pequeno porte*. XIV SIMPEP.

Silveira, I., & Silva, G. G. (2008). A capacidade do branding na criação do conhecimento da marca. 1° Seminário de Branding e Design Gráfico.

Simon, H. A. (1957). *Models of man: Social and rational; mathematical essays on rational human behavior in society setting*. Wiley.

Simon, H. A. (1976). *Administrative Behaviour* (3rd ed.). New York: Free Press.

Sin, A. B., Zailani, S., Iranmanesh, M., & Ramayah, T. (2015). Structural equation modelling on knowledge creation in Six Sigma DMAIC project and its impact on organizational performance. *International Journal of Production Economics*, *168*, 105–117. doi:10.1016/j.ijpe.2015.06.007

Singh & Bhatia. (2011). Data Clustering with Modified K-means Algorithm. In *International Conference on Recent Trends in Information Technology* (pp. 717-721). IEEE.

Sinha, A. (2014). KM in Academic Libraries. *Journal of Indian Research*, *2*(1), 123–125.

Skinnarland, K. I., Asa, I., Oslo, & Sharp, P. (2016, March 11). *Knowledge Sharing (KS), Organizational Learning and Competitive Advantage in a Scandinavian Hotel Company*. Retrieved from http://www2.warwick.ac.uk/fac/soc/wbs/conf/olkc/archive/olkc6/papers/id_110_sharp_p_skinnarland_k.pdf

Small, C. T., & Sage, A. P. (2008). A complex adaptive systems-based enterprise knowledge sharing model. *International Journal of Information Technologies and Systems Approach*, *1*(2), 38–56. doi:10.4018/jitsa.2008070103

Smallwood, N., & Ulrich, D. (2004, June). Capitalizing on capabilities. *Harvard Business Review*. Retrieved from http://hbr.org/2004/06/capitalizing-on-capabilities

Smalter, D. J., & Ruggles, R. L. (1966, March). Six Business Lessons from the Pentagon. *Harvard Business Review*, 64–75.

Snodgrass, C. R. (1984). *Cultural Influences on Strategic Control System Requirements* (Ph.D. dissertation). University of Pittsburg.

Somoza, M. L., Prado, J. A., & Rivera, C. M. (2011). Knowledge creation, Ba and CoP: The experience at IADE-UAM. In O. Hernáez & E. Bueno Campos (Eds.), *Handbook of research on communities of practice for organizational management and networking: Methodologies for competitive advantage* (pp. 145–161). Hershey, PA: IGI Global. doi:10.4018/978-1-60566-802-4.ch009

Sousa, J. P. (2002). Teorias da notícia e do jornalismo. Chapecó. *Argos.*

Spender, J. (1993). Competitive Advantage from Tacit Knowledge? Unpacking the Concept and Its Strategic Implications. *ACAD Manage Proc*, 37-41.

Spender, J. C., & Grant, R. M. (1996). Knowledge and the firm: Overview. *Strategic Management Journal, 17*(SI). doi:10.1002mj.4250171103

Spender, J. C., & Scherer, A. G. (2007). The Philosophical Foundations of Knowledge Management. *Editor's Introduction. Organization, 14*(1), 5–28.

Spiegel, T. (2014) An Overview of Cognition Roles in Decision-Making. In Encyclopedia of Business Analytics and Optimization. IGI Global. doi:10.4018/978-1-4666-5202-6.ch008

Spiegel, T. (2017). Influences of Personal Experience in Decision-Making. In Exploring the Influence of Personal Values and Cultures in the Workplace. IGI Global. doi:10.4018/978-1-5225-2480-9.ch005

Spiegel, T., & Assad, D. B. N. (2016). Operations Project and Management in Trauma Centers: The Case of Brazilian Units. In Handbook of Research on Healthcare Administration and Management. IGI Global. doi:10.4018/978-1-5225-0920-2.ch007

Spiegel, T. (2013). *Cognitive sciences contributions to operations management: analysis of experience impact in operations manager.* Federal University of Rio de Janeiro.

Sponaugle, B. (2016, March 11). *Types of Organizational Culture: Which One Are You.* Retrieved from udemy.com: https://blog.udemy.com/types-of-organizational-culture/

SPSS. (2007). *Manual del Usuario de SPSS Statistics Base 17.0.* Chicago, IL: SPSS Inc.

Stair, R. M., & Reynolds, G. W. (2011). *Princípios de sistemas de informação. 9.* São Paulo: Cengage Learning.

Starbucks, W. H., & Whalen, P. S. (2008). *Learning by Organizations: Organizational Learning and Knowledge Management* (Vol. 2). Northamptone: Edward and Elgar Publishing Inc. doi:10.4337/9781785366970

Statistics Canada. (2009, December). *Use of administrative data.* Ottawa, Canada: Statistics Canada. Retrieved from http://www.statcan.gc.ca/pub/12-539-x/2009001/administrative-administratives-eng.htm

Statistics New Zealand. (2014, July). *An overview of progress on the potential use of administrative data for census information in New Zealand.* Wellington, New Zealand: Statistics New Zealand.

Stenmark, D. (2000). Turning Tacit Knowledge Tangible. *33rd Hawaii International Conference on System Sciences.*

Stevenson, H. H., & Sahlman, W. A. (1991). *Introduction to the Entrepreneurial Venture.* Boston, MA: Harvard Business School Press.

Stewart, T. A. (1988). *Intellectual Capital: The New Wealth of Organizations, Currency. Stigler, Memoirs of an Unregulated Economist.* New York: Basic Books.

Stigler. (1988). *Memoirs of an Unregulated Economist.* New York: Basic Books.

Storey, J., & Barnett, E. (2000). Knowledge management initiatives: Learning from failure. *Journal of Knowledge Management, 4*(2), 145–156. doi:10.1108/13673270010372279

Strauss, J. D., & Radnor, M. (2004). Roadmapping for Dynamic and Uncertain Environments. *Research Technology Management, 47*(2), 51–58. doi:10.1080/08956308.2004.11671620

Streader, T., & Whitehouse, D. (2008). Not another logo! Designing corporate identity systems that drive change within institutional culture: A case study in participatory design. *International DMI Education Conference.*

Strong, D. M., Lee, Y. W., & Wang, R. Y. (1997). 10 Potholes in the road to information quality. *IEEE Computer, 18*(162), 38–46. doi:10.1109/2.607057

Strong, D. M., Lee, Y. W., & Wang, R. Y. (1997). Data quality in context. *Communications of the ACM, 40*(5), 103–109. doi:10.1145/253769.253804

Struijs, P., Camstra, A., Renssen, R., & Braaksma, B. (2013). Redesign of statistics production within an architectural framework: The Dutch experience. *Journal of Official Statistics, 29*(1), 49–71. doi:10.2478/jos-2013-0004

Suchman, L. (2005). Affiliative Objects. *Organization, 12*(3), 379–399. doi:10.1177/1350508405051276

Suganuma, S. (2005). *Qualidade da Informação uma construção metodológica de definição de conceito. 2005. Dissertação (Mestrado em Ciência da Informação).* Brasília: Faculdade de Economia, Administração, Contabilidade e Ciência da Informação e Documentação, Universidade de Brasília.

Sulistiyani, R., & Harwiki, W. (2016). How SMEs build innovation capability based on knowledge sharing behavior? Phenomenological approach. *Procedia: Social and Behavioral Sciences, 219*, 741–747. doi:10.1016/j.sbspro.2016.05.070

Sung Jung Jo, B.-K. J. (2011). Knowledge Sharing: The nflurnces of learning organization culture, organizational commitment and organizational citizenship behaviour. *Journal of Leadership & Organizational Studies, 18*(3), 353–364. doi:10.1177/1548051811405208

Sveiby, K. E. (1996, March 1). Retrieved March 28, 2016, from www.seviby.com: http://www.sveiby.com/articles/KnowledgeManagement.html

Svetlana Sajeva, R. J. (2010). Determination of essential knowledge Management System Componeents and their Parameters. *Social Sciences, 1*(67), 80–90.

Sweden, E. (2008). *Data governance - Managing information as an enterprise asset part I - An introduction.* Lexington, KY: National Association of State Chief Information Officers.

Sweden, E. (2009). *Data governance part III: Frameworks – Structure for organizing complexity.* Lexington, KY: National Association of State Chief Information Officers.

Sweeney, K. (2017). A behavioural capability-based data governance framework for New Zealand government. Wellington, New Zealand: Stats NZ. Retrieved from http://cdm20045.contentdm.oclc.org/digital/collection/p20045coll1/id/2657/rec/15

Tapia, C. (1980). *Colloques et sociétés.* Paris: Publications de la Sorbonne.

Tarondeau, J. C. (1998). *Le management des savoirs.* Paris, France: Presses Universitaires de France.

Tarondeau, J. C., & Wright, R. W. (1995). La transversalité dans les organisations ou le contrôle par les processus. *Revue Française de Gestion*, *104*, 112–121.

Taton, R. (1981). *Histoire general des Sciences*. Paris: PUF.

Te'eni, D. (2008). Organizational communication. In M. Jennex (Ed.), *Knowledge management: Concepts, methodologies, tools, and applications* (pp. 3004–3012). Hershey, PA: IGI Global. doi:10.4018/978-1-59904-933-5.ch245

Tharpe, B. M. (2009). *Organizational Culture White Paper*. Haworth.

The Wharton School. (2003, August 27). The move from tall to flat: How corporate hierarchies are changing. *Knowledge @ Wharton*. Retrieved from http://knowledge.wharton.upenn.edu/article/the-move-from-tall-to-flat-how-corporate-hierarchies-are-changing/

Thomas, H., & Davenport, L. P. (2000). *Working Knowledge-How Organizations Manage What they Know*. Boston: Harvard Business School Press.

Tibshirani, R., Walther, G., & Hastie, T. (2000). *Estimating the Number of Clusters in a Dataset via the Gap Statistic*. Technical Report 208, Department of Statistics, Stanford University.

Tisseyre, R. C. (1999). *Knowledge management: Théorie et pratique de la gestion des connaissances*. Paris, France: Hermes Sciences Publications.

Toften, K., & Olsen, S. O. (2004). The Relationships Among Quality, Cost, Value, and Use of Export Market Information: An empirical study. *Journal of International Marketing*, *12*(2), 104–131. doi:10.1509/jimk.12.2.104.32899

Toivonen, T. (2013). *The Emergence of the Social Innovation Community: Towards Collaborative Changemaking?* Retrieved from https://ssrn.com/abstract=2369540

Toivonen, T. (2016). What is the Social Innovation Community? Conceptualizing an Emergent Collaborative Organization. *Journal of Social Entrepreneurship*, *7*(1), 49–73. doi:10.1080/19420676.2014.997779

Torquato, F. G. (1986). *Comunicação Empresarial/Comunicação Institucional: Conceitos, estratégias, sistemas, estrutura, planejamento e técnicas. 5*. São Paulo: Summus.

Townsend, P., & Gebhardt, J. (2002). Simple Quality for Smaller Organizations. *Quality Progress*, *35*(10), 76–80.

Traquina, N. (1993). As Notícias. Jornalismo: Questões, Teorias e "Estórias", 167-176.

Tregoe & Zimmerman. (1980). *Top Management Survey*. Simon & Schuster.

Tress, B., Tress, G., & Fry, G. (2005). Defining concepts and the process of knowledge production in integrative research. *From landscape research to landscape planning: Aspects of integration, education and application*, 13-26.

Trevino, L. K., Daft, R. L., & Lengel, R. H. (1990). Understanding Managers Media Choices: A Symbolic Interactionist Perspective. In J. Fulk & C. Steinfield (Eds.), *Organizations and Communication Technology*. Newbury Park, CA: Sage. doi:10.4135/9781483325385.n4

Truijens, O. (2001). *Aspects of Information Strategy Formulation for Customer Orientationt*. PrimaVera Working Paper 2001-06, University van Amsterdam.

Truijens, O. (2001). *Information Strategy at TravelCom: searching for InfoRent in the Dutch travel industry*. PrimaVera Working Paper 2001-12, University van Amsterdam.

Truijens, O. (2002). *Towards* a Resource-based Theory of Information Strategy. British Academy of Management Annual Conference 2002, Hammersmith, UK.

Truijens, O. (2001). Aspects of Information Strategy Formulation for Customer Orientation. *Proceedings Resource Management Association International Conference.*

Tsoukas, H. (2005). *Complex Knowledge.* Oxford, UK: Oxford University Press.

Tzu, S. (1971). The Art of War. Oxford University Press.

Tzu, S. (1978). *L'Art de la Guerre.* Paris: L'Impensé Radical.

Vähätalo, M., & Kallio, T. J. (2015). Organising health services through modularity. *International Journal of Operations & Production Management, 35*(6), 925–945. doi:10.1108/IJOPM-12-2013-0523

Valecillo, M., Quevedo, A.L., Lubo, A., Dos Santos, A., Montiel, M., Camejo, & Sánchez, M. (2009). Síntomas musculoesqueléticos y estrés laboral en el personal de enfermería de un hospital militar. *Salud trab, 17*(2), 85-95.

Valentim, L., Lisboa, J. V., & Franco, M. (2016). Knowledge management practices and absorptive capacity in small and medium-sized enterprises: Is there really a linkage? *R & D Management, 46*(4), 711–725. doi:10.1111/radm.12108

Valls, V. M. V., & Waldomiro, C. S. (1998). A gestão da qualidade em serviços de informação no Brasil: Uma revisão da literatura. *Perspectivas em Ciência da Informação, Belo Horizonte, 3*(1), 47–59.

Van Grembergen, W., & Haes, D. E. S. (2007). Implementing IT governance: Models, practices and cases. Hershey, PA: IGI Global.

Värlander, S. (2010). The role of situated embodied interaction in the banking customer knowledge creation process. In M. Jennex (Ed.), *Ubiquitous developments in knowledge management: Integrations and trends* (pp. 236–251). Hershey, PA: IGI Global. doi:10.4018/978-1-60566-954-0.ch015

Vasilcovschi, N. (2013). Organizational communication-strategies at international level. *Transition Studies Review, 19*(4), 493–502. doi:10.100711300-013-0259-5

Vergara, S. C. (2002). *Projetos e Relatório de Pesquisa em Administração. 3.* São Paulo: Atlas.

Vicente, A., Diaz, C., Zimmermann, M., & Galiana, L. (2012). *El trastorno musculoesquelético en el ámbito laboral en cifras. Departamento de información e investigación del Instituto Nacional de Seguridad e Higiene en el Trabajo. MEISS.* Gobierno de España.

Visalakshi, K. N., & Suguna, J. (2009). K-Means Clustering using Max-min Distance Measure. *The 28th North American Fuzzy Information Processing Society Annual Conference*, 14-17.

Vlaisavljevic, V., Cabello-Medina, C., & Pérez-Luño, A. (2016). Coping with diversity in alliances for innovation: The role of relational social capital and knowledge codifiability. *British Journal of Management, 27*(2), 304–322. doi:10.1111/1467-8551.12155

Von Clausewitz, C. (1989). *On War.* Princeton, NJ: Princeton University Press.

Vygotski, L. (2007). *Pensamento e Linguagem.* Lisboa: Relógio d'Água.

Wagstaff, K., Cardie, C., Rogers, S., & Schroedl, S. (2001). Constrained K-Means Clustering with Background Knowledge. *Proceedings of the Eighteenth International Conference on Machine Learning*, 577-584.

Waitsman, H. S. (2001). *Inteligência Empresarial.* Rio de Janeiro: Interciência.

Wand, Y., & Wang, R. Y. (1996). Data quality dimensions in ontological foundations. *Communications of the ACM, 39*(11), 86–95. doi:10.1145/240455.240479

Wang, R. Y., Ziad, M., & Lee, Y. W. (2000). Data Quality. Kluwer Academic Publishers.

Wang, C., Chi, C.-H., Zhou, W., & Wong, R. (2015). Coupled Interdependent Attribute Analysis on Mixed Data. *Proceedings of the Twenty-Ninth AAAI Conference on Artificial Intelligence*, 1861-1867.

Wang, D., Zhongfeng, S. U., & Yang, D. (2011). Organizational culture and knowledge creation capability. *Journal of Knowledge Management*, *15*(3), 363–373. doi:10.1108/13673271111137385

Wang, R. W., Storey, V., & Firth, C. P. (1995). A framework of analysis for data quality research. *IEEE Transactions on Knowledge and Data Engineering*, *7*(4), 623–640. doi:10.1109/69.404034

Wang, R. Y., & Strong, D. M. (1996). Beyond Accuracy: What data quality means to data consumers. *Journal of Management Information Systems*, *12*(4), 5–33. doi:10.1080/07421222.1996.11518099

Wang, T., & Libaers, D. (2016). Nonmimetic knowledge and innovation performance: Empirical evidence from developing countries. *Journal of Product Innovation Management*, *33*(5), 570–588. doi:10.1111/jpim.12306

Ward, A. (2000). Getting Strategic Value from Constellations of Communities. *Strategy and Leadership*, *28*(2), 4–9. doi:10.1108/10878570010341537

Weeks, M. R., & Veltri, N. F. (2013). Virtual communities as narrative networks: Developing a model of knowledge creation for crowdsourced environments. *International Journal of Knowledge Management*, *9*(1), 21–41. doi:10.4018/jkm.2013010102

Wegwarth, O., Gaissmaier, W., & Gigerenzer, G. (2009). Smart strategies for doctors and doctors-in-training: Heuristics in medicine. *Medical Education*, *43*(8), 721–728. doi:10.1111/j.1365-2923.2009.03359.x PMID:19573016

Weick & Daft. (1983). The Effectiviness of Interpretation Systems. In Organizational Effectiviness: A Comparison of Multiple Models. Academic Press.

Weick, K. C. (1999). Theory Construction as Disciplined Imagination. *Academy of Management Review*, *14*(4), 516-531.

Weick, K. E. (1979). *The Social Psychology of Organizing* (2nd ed.). Random House.

Weick, K. E. (1990). Cartographic Myths in Organizations. In A. S. Huff (Ed.), Mapping Strategic Thought. New York: Academic Press.

Weick, K. E. (1995). *Sensemaking in Organizations*. Thousand Oaks, CA: Sage.

Weick, K. E. (2000). *Making Sense of the Organizations*. Blackwell Publishers.

Wenger, E. (1998). *Communicaties of practice: learning, meaning, and identity*. Cambridge, UK: Cambridge University Press. doi:10.1017/CBO9780511803932

Wenger-Trayner, E., & Wenger-Trayner, B. (2015). *Communities of practice a brief introduction*. Retrieved from http://wenger-trayner.com/wp-content/uploads/2015/04/07-Brief-introduction-to-communities-of-practice.pdf

Wen, Q., & Qiang, M. (2016). Coordination and knowledge sharing in construction project-based organization: A longitudinal structural equation model analysis. *Automation in Construction*, *72*, 309–320. doi:10.1016/j.autcon.2016.06.002

Wersig, G. (1993). Information science: The study of postmodern knowledge usage. *Information Processing & Management*, *29*(2), 229–239. doi:10.1016/0306-4573(93)90006-Y

Wessel, M. (2016, January 27). How big data is changing disruptive innovation. *Harvard Business Review*. Retrieved from http://hbr.org/2016/01/how-big-data-is-changing-disruptive-innovation

Wickramasinghe, N. (2011). Knowledge creation. In D. Schwartz & D. Te'eni (Eds.), Encyclopedia of knowledge management (2nd ed.; pp. 527–538). Hershey, PA: IGI Global. doi:10.4018/978-1-59904-931-1.ch051

Widén-Wulff, G., & Suomi, R. (2007). Utilization of information resources for business success: The knowledge sharing model. *Information Resources Management Journal*, *20*(1), 46–67. doi:10.4018/irmj.2007010104

Wilensky, H. (1967). *Organisational Intelligence: Knowledge and Policy in Government and Industry*. New York: Basic Books.

Willem, A., Scarbrough, H., & Buelens, M. (2008). Impact of coherent versus multiple identities on knowledge integration. *Journal of Information Science*, *34*(3), 370–386. doi:10.1177/0165551507086259

Williamson, O. E. (1975). *Markets and Hierarchies: Analysis and Antitrust Implications*. New York: Free Press.

Wilson, T. D. (2002). The Nonsense of Knowledge Management. Information Research, 8(1).

Wilson, T. D. (1997). *Information management: International Encyclopedia of Information and Library Science*. London: Routledge.

Wise, R., & Zednickova, J. (2009). The rise and rise of the B2B brand. *The Journal of Business Strategy*, *30*(1), 4–13. doi:10.1108/02756660910926911

Wittel, A. (2001). Toward a Network Sociality. *Theory, Culture & Society*, *18*(6), 51–76. doi:10.1177/026327601018006003

Won, K. D., Lee, K., Lee, K. D., & Lee, K. H. (2005). A k-populations algorithm for clustering categorical data'. *Pattern Recognition Letters*, *38*(7), 1131–1134. doi:10.1016/j.patcog.2004.11.017

Woodfield, P., & Husted, K. (2017). Intergenerational knowledge sharing in family firms: Case-based evidence from the New Zealand wine industry. *Journal of Family Business Strategy*, *8*(1), 57–69. doi:10.1016/j.jfbs.2017.01.001

Woolsey Biggart, N., & Delbridge, R. (2004). Systems of exchange. *Academy of Management Review*, *29*(1), 28–49.

Wu, Q., McGinnity, M., Prasad, G., & Bell, D. (2009). Knowledge discovery in databases with diversity of data types. In J. Wang (Ed.), *Encyclopedia of data warehousing and mining* (2nd ed.; pp. 1117–1123). Hershey, PA: IGI Global. doi:10.4018/978-1-60566-010-3.ch173

Wurman, R. S. (1989). Information Anxiety. *The New York Times,* p. 32.

Wu, X., Kumar, V., & Quinlan, R. (2007). Top 10 Algorithms in Data Mining. *Journal of Knowledge and Information Systems*, *14*(1), 1–37. doi:10.100710115-007-0114-2

Xia, Y., & Mao, Y. (2016). Mobile phone usage in organizational communication and decision-making: Experience of employees in a multinational company's China branch. In I. Management Association (Ed.), Leadership and personnel management: Concepts, methodologies, tools, and applications (pp. 1673–1689). Hershey, PA: IGI Global. doi:10.4018/978-1-4666-9624-2.ch074

Xia, H., & Gupta, A. (2008). Common knowledge sharing model of 24-hour knowledge factory of grid computing based on case based reasoning. *International Journal of Knowledge Management*, *4*(3), 1–18. doi:10.4018/jkm.2008070101

Xu, R., & Wunsch, D. II. (2005). Survey of Clustering Algorithms. *IEEE Transactions on Neural Networks*, *16*(3), 645–678. doi:10.1109/TNN.2005.845141 PMID:15940994

Yada, K. (2004). Knowledge discovery process and introduction of domain knowledge. In B. Montano (Ed.), *Innovations of knowledge management* (pp. 86–98). Hershey, PA: IGI Global. doi:10.4018/978-1-59140-281-7.ch005

Yang, J., Yu, G., Liu, M., & Rui, M. (2016). Improving learning alliance performance for manufacturers: Does knowledge sharing matter? *International Journal of Production Economics, 171*, 301–308. doi:10.1016/j.ijpe.2015.09.022

Yang, Y., Liu, Q., Gao, Z., Qiu, X., & Rui, L. (2015). A Similarity-based K-prototypes Algorithm for Mixed Attributes. *Journal of Computer Information Systems, 11*(14), 5013–5021.

Yin, J., Tan, Z.-F., Ren, J.-T., & Chen, Y.-Q. (2005). An efficient clustering algorithm for mixed type attributes in large dataset. In *Proceedings of 2005 International Conference on Machine Learning and Cybernetics* (pp. 1611-1614). IEEE.

Yuan, D., Lin, Z., & Zhuo, R. (2016). What drives consumer knowledge sharing in online travel communities?: Personal attributes or e-service factors? *Computers in Human Behavior, 63*, 68–74. doi:10.1016/j.chb.2016.05.019

Yue Wah, C., Menkhoff, T., Loh, B., & Evers, H. (2007). Social capital and knowledge sharing in knowledge-based organizations: An empirical study. *International Journal of Knowledge Management, 3*(1), 29–48. doi:10.4018/jkm.2007010103

Yuepeng, S., Wu, C., & Liu, M. (2011). A Modified k-means Algorithm for Clustering Problem with Balancing Constraints. In *Third International Conference on Measuring Technology and Mechatronics Automation*, (pp. 127-130). IEEE. 10.1109/ICMTMA.2011.37

Yu, L. (2009). Knowledge discovery from genomics microarrays. In M. Khosrow-Pour (Ed.), *Encyclopedia of information science and technology* (2nd ed.; pp. 2332–2336). Hershey, PA: IGI Global. doi:10.4018/978-1-60566-026-4.ch369

Yusof, N., & Shafiei, M. W. (2011). Knowledge creation and sharing in the Malaysian housebuilding industry: Improving the housing delivery system. In M. Al-Shammari (Ed.), *Knowledge management in emerging economies: Social, organizational and cultural implementation* (pp. 141–156). Hershey, PA: IGI Global. doi:10.4018/978-1-61692-886-5.ch008

Zald, M. N., & Berger. (1978). Social Movements in Organizations: Coup d' Etat, Insurgency and Mass Movements. *American Journal of Sociology, 83*(4), 823-861.

Zhang, J. (2016). Facilitating exploration alliances in multiple dimensions: The influences of firm technological knowledge breadth. *R & D Management, 46*(S1), 159–173. doi:10.1111/radm.12127

Zikmund, W. G. (2000). *"Bussiness" Research Methods* (6th ed.). Dryden Press Harcourt College Publishers.

Ziman, J. (1974). *Public Knowledge*. Cambridge University Press.

Zorrinho. (2004). *Aula aberta*. Escola Superior de Ciências Empresariais do Instituto Politécnico de Setúbal.

Zucchi, P., Del Nero, C., & Malik, A. M. (2000). Gastos em saúde: Os fatores que agem na demanda e na oferta dos serviços de saúde. *Saúde e Sociedade, 9*(1-2), 127–150. doi:10.1590/S0104-12902000000100010

About the Contributors

Armando Barreiros Malheiro da Silva is Associated Professor of the Faculty of Arts of the University of Porto and member of the coordinating committee of the Information Science degree taught by the Arts and Engineering Faculties of the University of Porto. Born in Braga, PdD in Contemporary History in the University of Minho, graduated in Philosophy by Philosophy Faculty of the Catholic University of Braga and in History by the Faculty of Arts of the University of Porto. He obtained the diploma of the course of Librarian-Archivist of the Faculty of Arts of the University of Coimbra. Is member of the Center for Studies in Technology, Arts and Communication Sciences (CETAC.Media) and shares his researches in areas such as the archivist and information science; the metanalysis; political and ideological history in Portugal in the nineteenth-twentieth century; family history and local studies.

Fernanda Ribeiro has been Professor at the Faculty of Arts and Humanities of University of Porto (Portugal) since 1989. Graduation in History from the University of Porto in 1980 and post-graduation in Library and Archival Studies from the University of Coimbra in 1982. PhD at the University of Porto (1999) with a dissertation entitled *The Access to Information in Archives*, under the supervision of Michael Cook. Currently Full Professor of the Department of Communication and Information Sciences, she has been president of the same department between feb. 2010 and sept. 2014. She has been also director of the bachelor in Information Science (2003-2014) and director of the Doctoral Program in Information and Communication in Digital Platforms (2013-2014). She still was scientific coordinator of the research centre CETAC.MEDIA (Centre of Studies in Techonologies and Communication Sciences). Develops academic research focused on organization and representation of information, access and retrieval of information, mainly in archives, subject indexing and theory and methodology of Information Science as well as professional training in the same area. Since 6th october 2014 she is Dean and President of the Scientific Board of the Faculty of Arts and Humanities of University of Porto.

George Leal Jamil is a professor of several post-graduation courses from Minas Gerais, Brazil. He has a PhD in Information Science from the Federal University of Minas Gerais (UFMG), master degree in Computer Science (UFMG) and his graduate area was Electric Engineering (UFMG) and a pos-doctorate certificate at FLUP – Communication School at University of Porto, Portugal. He wrote more than thirty books in the information technology and strategic management areas, with more than ten works in books as co-author and Editor. Yearly, he manages the doctoral consortium of the International Conference on Information Systems and Technology Management at the University of Sao Paulo (USP) as one of his main activities. His main research interests are information systems management, strategy, knowledge management, software engineering, marketing and IT adoption in business contexts.

Jose Poças Rascão (PhD, ISCTE/ULI) is a Professor of Management Information Systems at the Polytechnic Institute of Setúbal, Portugal. From 2010 to 2015 was Director of course management of distribution and logistics. It is research in the Research Unit in the development of enterprise (UNIDE) at the Lisbon University Institute (ISCTE/ULI). Since 2000 has published 8 books and 8 chapters of books on strategy management and management of information and more than 36 publications on strategy and information management. Under his supervision, 17 Masters Theses have been successfully from 2007 to 2016, with 3 more coming up for defense in next 2 years. He also works the private management consultant for large and medium-sized enterprises. He worked the management consult at Price Waterhouse and Coopers & Lybrand between 1989 and 1995.

Óscar Mealha is Associate Professor at the Department of Communication and Art, University of Aveiro, Portugal. He develops his research in the area of "Information and Communication in Digital Platforms" in the context of "Knowledge Media and Connected Communities" with several projects, masters and doctoral supervisions and publications on methods and usability evaluation techniques and visualization of interaction/infocommunication activity. He is now involved in infocommunication mediation projects such as "Visualization of Open Data Dashboards for Citizen Engagement and Learning" in intelligent territories, e.g. Àgueda Smart City, Murtosa cyclable, ASLERD - aslerd.com ORCID URL: https://orcid.org/0000-0002-4564-0496.

* * *

Oziely Armenta-Hernández has a Bachelor and Master Degree in Industrial Engineering by the Autonomous University of Ciudad Juárez. She is actually a full time student for the Doctorate in Science of Advanced Engineering by the same institution. She has participated in the international congress of Ergonomics and the International Work Organization and Psychosocial Factors Congress. She has published book chapters of IGI Global Editorial.

Daniel Assad is a Researcher for LEGOS laboratory (health operations management laboratory).

Liliana Avelar-Sosa has a bachelor degree in Electronic Engineering, a master degree in Industrial Sciences, a Pd. D. in Engineering Sciences. She is a National Researcher from the National Council for Science and Technology in Mexico, expert in logistics and supply chain aspects applied to manufacturing companies. She has experience in maquiladora industry and, currently she has published papers in JCR journals as a first author, she has attended some international and national congress and conferences and book chapters.

Antonio-Juan Briones-Peñalver is an Assistant Professor of Management at Technical University of Cartagena (Spain) and researcher for the Portugal International Centre (CIEO), mention of European Doctorate (Doctorate with European accreditation). His research interest is focused on the study of entrepreneurs, start-up business projects, firms´ cooperation & strategic alliances, and, in general, business collaboration relationships along the European Union. In the last years he has been leading several Projects of International Cooperation for Development issues between the European Union and Central America, sponsored by the Spanish Ministry of Foreign Affairs. He is currently the Director of the Postgraduate and Permanent Formation at Technical University of Cartagena. As well as Deputy

Director at the "Young Entrepreneurs Chair". Before joining the University, he occupied positions as Economist and Executive Director in several Agribusiness companies.

Anupama Chadha is working as an Associate Professor in the Department of Computer Applications, Manav Rachna International University, Faridabad, India. She has done her PhD in Data Mining and her research areas include Big Data and Software Engineering.

Jorge Luis Garcia-Alcaraz is a full time researcher of the Department of Industrial Engineering at the Autonomous University of Ciudad Juarez. He received a MSc in Industrial Engineering from the Colima Technology Institute (Mexico), a PhD in Industrial Engineering from Ciudad Juarez Technology Institute (Mexico) and a Postdoc from University of La Rioja (Spain). His main research areas are related to Multicriteria decision making applied to manufacturing, production process modeling and statistical inference. He is founding member of the Mexican Society of Operation Research and active member in the Mexican Academy of Industrial Engineering. Currently, Dr. Garcia is a National Researcher recognized by the National Council of Science & Technology of Mexico (CONACYT) as level II and is working with group research from Colombia, Spain and Dominican Republic. Actually. Dr. Garcia is author/coauthor in around 120 journals, international conferences and congress. ORCID number: orcid.org/0000-0002-7092-6963, Scopus Author ID: 55616966800.

Kijpokin Kasemsap received his BEng degree in Mechanical Engineering from King Mongkut's University of Technology, Thonburi, his MBA degree from Ramkhamhaeng University, and his DBA degree in Human Resource Management from Suan Sunandha Rajabhat University. Dr. Kasemsap is a Special Lecturer in the Faculty of Management Sciences, Suan Sunandha Rajabhat University, based in Bangkok, Thailand. Dr. Kasemsap is a Member of the International Economics Development and Research Center (IEDRC), the International Foundation for Research and Development (IFRD), and the International Innovative Scientific and Research Organization (IISRO). Dr. Kasemsap also serves on the International Advisory Committee (IAC) for the International Association of Academicians and Researchers (INAAR). Dr. Kasemsap is the sole author of over 250 peer-reviewed international publications and book chapters on business, education, and information technology. Dr. Kasemsap is included in the TOP 100 Professionals–2016 and in the 10th edition of 2000 Outstanding Intellectuals of the 21st Century by the International Biographical Centre, Cambridge, England.

Ayesha Khatun is a Senior Research Fellow, Department of Business Administration, Assam University, Silchar (India).

Catarina Lelis began her professional experience back in 1997 as graphic and software interface designer. In 2006 she co-founded both a publishing start-up and the Portuguese Association for Innovation and Creativity in Organisations. She was the creative director and content manager of the first Portuguese mass distribution magazine specialised in innovation issues. She started her teaching experience in 2007, at the Polytechnic Institute of Viseu, and she was an Invited Lecturer in the University of Aveiro. Her research and entrepreneurial ideas were recognised and funded by FCT, the Portuguese national funding agency for science, research and technology. She was the winner of the first edition of IdeaPuzzle Prize, which aims to award the best Portuguese PhD research design created with IdeaPuzzle® software, in 2012. In 2013 she won a national entrepreneurship contest which prize consisted of an immersion program in Silicon Valley. She was also the team leader of one of the winning teams of the Iberian CEBT, with the best business plan and elevator pitch presentation, in 2014. Her research interests include Participatory Brand Design, Brand-Oriented Ecologies, Dynamic/Mutant Brands, Creative Skills Development, Visual-Digital Literacy, Technology-Mediated Communication and User Experience. Currently, she is a Senior Lecturer in Branding and Innovation at the University of West London, UK.

Faten Louati has a Ph.D. in Management Sciences and Teaching Researcher at the Higher Institute of Accounting and Business Administration. His area of research is knowledge management, innovation, organization and human resource management. She is a member of the Tunisian Academy of Management Sciences, member of the Tunisian Association of Intelligence and Competitive Intelligence and also a member of the RIGUEUR laboratory at the University of Manouba, Tunisia.

Aide Maldonado-Macías works as a professor-Investigator for the Autonomous University of Juarez Mexico. Dr. Maldonado has published several papers in various international journals and conference proceedings. She has been a member of the programme committee and scientific committee of several national and international conferences, in most cases also serving as referee. She is a certified professional in ergonomics in Mexico and she serves as Member of the Mexican Society on Ergonomics and the Society of Industrial Engineers. She is a member of the National Investigators System in Mexico. She also serves as Associate Editor of the AcademiaJournals.com journals and the Occupational Ergonomics Advances and Applications. She serves as referee for the International Journal of Advanced Manufacturing Technology and the World Conference of Industrial Engineering. She has also been evaluator and reviewer for research projects in Mexico. She has obtained the recognition with her research the best investigation in Industrial Engineering in Mexico for the Tecnological Institute of Juarez México and has participated in the most prestigious International Conferences and Congresses on Ergonomics and Computers and Industrial Engineering. She has publications on indexed journals in her country and the International Journal of Advanced Manufacturing Technology and the International Journal of Industrial Engineering. Also has contributions in book chapters for prestigious editorials. ORCID Number: orcid.org/0000-0002-4959-161X and SCOPUS AUTHOR ID:551819988000.

Ana Melro has a Ph.D. in Information and Communication in Digital Platforms, from University of Aveiro and University of Porto (2013). A master degree in Sociology and a degree in Sociology (2004), from University of Minho. Ana Melro was a post-doctoral researcher funded by FCT (2015-2017) at DigiMedia, University of Aveiro. Her research interests are: Cyberculture; New Media; Social Entrepreneurship and Innovation; Territorial Development; Smart Territories.

Juliana M. Namada is an Assistant Professor of Strategic Management at United States International University- Africa, School of Business. She holds a PhD in Business Administration specializing in Strategic Management from the University of Nairobi, School of Business. She teaches and supervises students in Business Administration at undergraduate, Masters and Doctoral levels. Her research interests are in strategic management with a bias in strategic planning. In terms of service to the profession, Dr. Juliana serves as a reviewer for the Academy of Management, Africa Academy of Management, American Journal of Industrial and Business Management and many others. Dr. Juliana is the current Global Representative for Africa 2016-2019 in Strategic Management Division (STR) in the Academy of Management. She is also an expert in Student Centered Learning, Strategic Planning, Program Assessment and Reviews for Institutions of Higher Learning.

Lídia J. L. Oliveira Silva has a degree in Philosophy from the University of Coimbra (1990), a Master's degree in Educational Technology from the University of Aveiro, in partnership with the University of Valenciennes (France) and Mons (Belgium) (1995), and a PhD in Sciences and Technologies of Communication from the University of Aveiro (2002). She did her post-doctorate (2009-2010) at CES - Centre for Social Studies - Associate Laboratory of the University of Coimbra. In 2010 she did her Aggregation Examination at the University of Aveiro, in the scientific area of Sciences and Technologies of Communication.

Miguel Serrano is a full-time professor and researcher by the Universidad de Valencia, Spain.

Ana Carolina Silva has a Master's Degree in Production Engineering, in the Production Management area, by the Industrial Engineering Department of the Pontifical Catholic University of Rio de Janeiro (DEI / PUC-Rio). Graduated in Production Engineering from the Industrial Engineering Department of the State University of Rio de Janeiro (DEIN / FEN / UERJ). Currently, she participates as a researcher at LEGOS (Laboratory of Engineering and Health Management), a laboratory of DEIN / UERJ. She participated as researcher at Lab HANDs (Humanitarian Assistance and Needs for Disasters), a laboratory of the DEI PUC-Rio focused on Disaster Operations Management and Humanitarian Logistics researchs. She also acted as researcher of the Integrated Production Group (GPI - Poli & COPPE / UFRJ), in the Hospital Operations Management area. She was Assistant lecturer of Business Logistics and Planning and Production Control disciplines at the Industrial Engineering Department of UERJ (DEIN / FEN / UERJ). She has experience in Production Engineering, with emphasis on Operations Management, Healthcare Operations Management, Disaster Operations Management, Business Process Engineering and Project Management. She participated in extension projects applying these bodies of knowledge in several organizations, such as: Pedro Ernesto University Hospital, Sindicom, Cancer Foundation, Hospital de Clínicas de Niterói, Hospital São Lucas and RioSaúde.

Thais Spiegel is an Associate Professor in the Industrial Engineering Department of Rio de Janeiro State University. Coordinator and researcher for LEGOS laboratory (health operations management laboratory) Her research interests include healthcare operations management and design, process modeling, decision making, logistic and supply chain management in health care settings.

Kevin J. Sweeney is the Principal Advisor – Information Management at Stats NZ, New Zealand's national statistical agency. In this role he provides advice and advocacy for best practice management of data and information assets and served as chair of the Data Governance Framework Working Group. Kevin has also held a role as New Zealand's senior geospatial official, administering the NZ Geospatial Office, chairing the national Geospatial Steering Committee, and providing oversight for the national Geospatial Strategy. He has worked in numerous capacities in New Zealand and the US as a strategic and management consultant, advising senior government officials and business executives to help scope and implement data and information strategies and systems. A certified GIS professional (GISP), Kevin received his MA in Geography & Regional Development from the University of Arizona and graduated summa cum laude with a BS in Geography from Northern Arizona University.

Index

A

B

C

D

E

F

G

H

I

K

L

M

N

O

P

Q

R

S

T

V

W

www.ingramcontent.com/pod-product-compliance
Lightning Source LLC
LaVergne TN
LVHW062109300926
849161LV00010B/2414